SpringerBriefs in Computer Science

SpringerBriefs present concise summaries of cutting-edge research and practical applications across a wide spectrum of fields. Featuring compact volumes of 50 to 125 pages, the series covers a range of content from professional to academic.

Typical topics might include:

- A timely report of state-of-the art analytical techniques
- A bridge between new research results, as published in journal articles, and a contextual literature review
- A snapshot of a hot or emerging topic
- An in-depth case study or clinical example
- A presentation of core concepts that students must understand in order to make independent contributions

Briefs allow authors to present their ideas and readers to absorb them with minimal time investment. Briefs will be published as part of Springer's eBook collection, with millions of users worldwide. In addition, Briefs will be available for individual print and electronic purchase. Briefs are characterized by fast, global electronic dissemination, standard publishing contracts, easy-to-use manuscript preparation and formatting guidelines, and expedited production schedules. We aim for publication 8–12 weeks after acceptance. Both solicited and unsolicited manuscripts are considered for publication in this series.

More information about this series at http://www.springer.com/series/10028

Branka Stojanović • Oge Marques
Aleksandar Nešković

Segmentation and Separation of Overlapped Latent Fingerprints

Algorithms, Techniques, and Datasets

 Springer

Branka Stojanović
Vlatacom Research and
Development Institute Ltd Belgrade
Belgrade, Serbia

Aleksandar Nešković
School of Electrical Engineering
University of Belgrade
Belgrade, Serbia

Oge Marques
College of Engineering
and Computer Science
Florida Atlantic University
Boca Raton, FL, USA

ISSN 2191-5768   ISSN 2191-5776   (electronic)
SpringerBriefs in Computer Science
ISBN 978-3-030-23363-1   ISBN 978-3-030-23364-8   (eBook)
https://doi.org/10.1007/978-3-030-23364-8

This Springer imprint is published by the registered company Springer Nature Switzerland AG.
The registered company address is: Gewerbestrasse 11, 6330 Cham, Switzerland

B.S.: To the memory of my father.
O.M.: For Ingrid, with love and appreciation.
A.N.: For George and Milan—my lovely kids.

Preface

The field of biometrics is well situated in the research community and has intrigued researchers for many years. Although there are numerous biometric modalities in use today, fingerprints remain the dominant one, because of its noninvasive nature and ease of applicability. This is especially important when it comes to security and forensic applications. A very challenging task in fingerprint recognition is overlapped latent fingerprint processing, which includes segmentation and separation processes prior to (individual) fingerprints matching.

This book presents an overview of problems and technologies behind segmentation and separation of overlapped latent fingerprints. Written from a technical perspective, and yet using language and terminology accessible to non-experts, it describes the technologies, introduces relevant datasets, highlights the most important research results in each area, and outlines the most challenging open research questions.

It is targeted at a scientific audience and enthusiasts interested in the field of fingerprints matching, in particular, and biometrics, in general. By offering a structured overview of the most important approaches currently available, putting them in perspective, and suggesting numerous resources for further exploration, the book gives its readers a clear path for learning new topics and engaging in related research.

We expect that the book will fulfill its goal of serving as a preliminary reference on the subject. Readers who want to deepen their understanding of specific topics will find more than 100 references to additional sources of related information.

We want to express our gratitude to the Vlatacom Research and Development Institute, Belgrade, Serbia—management, scientific council, and personnel—for their encouragement and support during overlapped latent fingerprint research process and writing this book.

This book represents a part of the doctoral dissertation of Dr. Branka Stojanović at the School of Electrical Engineering, University of Belgrade. It is also one of the results of a joint research project between Florida Atlantic University and Vlatacom Research and Development Institute.

We owe special gratitude to Dr. Borko Furht—Professor of Computer Science and Engineering and Director of the NSF Industry/University Cooperative Research Center (CAKE) at Florida Atlantic University, Boca Raton, FL—for his help and support.

We would also like to thank Susan Lagerstrom-Fife and her team at Springer for their support throughout this project.

Belgrade, Serbia   Branka Stojanović
Boca Raton, FL, USA   Oge Marques
Belgrade, Serbia   Aleksandar Nešković
January 2019

Contents

Chapter 1
Latent Fingerprints Matching Systems

Abstract This chapter presents fundamental concepts and terminology associated with latent fingerprint processing, with particular reference to overlapped latent fingerprints. It introduces the matching process itself, including classical manual latent fingerprints matching procedures. It also presents the design of a modern automated latent fingerprints matching system and describes its main components and steps.

1.1 Introduction

Fingerprints have been widely used for personal identification and criminal investigations for more than a century. The popularization of computer-based biometric authentication in recent years has driven a significant body of research associated with fingerprint processing and verification [16].

When used as a biometric modality, such as passport control at immigration booths and official ID cards or badges, fingerprints can be captured using offline (inked) or live-scan methods, following well-established protocols that ensure that the resulting fingerprints are of good quality for future use in fingerprint verification (matching) operations. In the context of crime scene investigation, however, the lifted fingerprints (called *latent fingerprints*, or simply *latents*) are usually of poor quality and contain large overlap between the foreground area (containing the friction ridge pattern) and a noisy background. These aspects make latent fingerprints segmentation and enhancement (for subsequent matching) a difficult problem [17].

These challenges become even more significant when two or more fingerprints overlap, which happens quite often in fingerprints lifted from crime scenes (the same surface was touched by two or more fingers at different times), but might also occur in live-scan fingerprint images when the surface of fingerprint sensors contains residues of fingerprints of previous users [17]. Overlapped latent fingerprints separation is an open research challenge for which there have been several recently proposed solutions in the literature (see Chaps. 5 and 6).

B. Stojanović et al., *Segmentation and Separation of Overlapped Latent Fingerprints*, SpringerBriefs in Computer Science, https://doi.org/10.1007/978-3-030-23364-8_1

1.2   Latent Fingerprints

Latent fingerprints (or simply *latents*) are partial fingerprints lifted from a crime scene. They are usually produced by the transfer of sweat and/or grease accumulated in the ridges of a person's fingers when they come in contact with an object. In forensic applications, they are collected using chemical development and enhancement methods, such as powder dusting and iodine fuming. The resulting fingerprint images are then matched against a database in order to arrest suspects and bring them to justice [13].

The quality of the resulting latent fingerprint images can vary significantly among different exemplars (Fig. 1.1).

1.3   Manual Latent Fingerprints Matching: The ACE-V Method

Manual examination of latent fingerprints follows the ACE-V (Analysis, Comparison, Evaluation, Verification) method, which consists of four sequential phases [1, 15]:

1. Analysis: where the latent print examiner analyzes the latent impression(s) in order to determine the sufficiency of a latent impression. This stage has two major outcomes: (1) the fingerprint is labeled to convey a sense of its quality for performing following steps, (2) the matching features are marked.
2. Comparison: where a manual comparative measurement (*matching*) is made between the latent and the available exemplar fingerprints (i.e., fingerprints of known subjects), based on previously marked matching features. The result of this stage is the list of similarities and differences between the latent and available exemplar fingerprints.

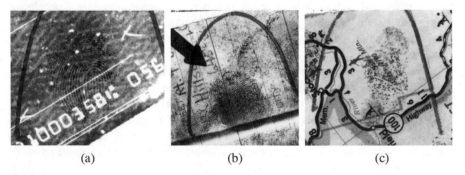

(a)   (b)   (c)

Fig. 1.1 Examples of latent fingerprint images of varying quality from NIST Special Database 27 (SD-27A): (**a**) good, (**b**) bad, and (**c**) ugly [9]

3. Evaluation: where the examiner derives a conclusion of: (1) *Identification* (or *Individualization*)—when there is evidence to conclude that the latent and the exemplar record have come from the same source; (2) *Exclusion*—when the latent print cannot be assigned to any known exemplar labels; or (3) *Inconclusive*—when the examiner is unable to make a decision regarding the unknown latent prints. The conclusion is made based on the previously created list of similarities and differences.
4. Verification: where a second examiner reviews all findings in order to verify the original conclusions.

The scientific accuracy, reliability, and consistency of manual latent fingerprints matching have been the subject of many studies and debates. The results of multiple studies on the consequences and implications of human performance in matching latent fingerprints [3–6, 8, 10, 12, 19] are rather inconsistent, and sometimes even contradictory.

1.4 Automated Latent Fingerprints Matching System

An automated latent fingerprint recognition system is designed with three main goals in mind: (1) there should be minimal human intervention; (2) the decisions should be deterministic, thereby eliminating subjective inconsistency; and (3) the time required for comparison should be substantially shorter than the time taken by the human counterpart [14].

As shown in Fig. 1.2, an automated latent fingerprint recognition system consists of four main tasks, which are performed in a predetermined sequence, as follows [17]:

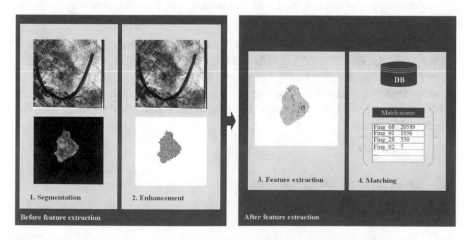

Fig. 1.2 Schematic view of a typical automated latent fingerprint recognition system

1. Latent fingerprint *segmentation*, also known as *region of interest (ROI) extraction*: The goal of the segmentation stage is to separate the foreground latent fingerprint from its background. In addition to the usual challenges of automatic image segmentation, latent fingerprints segmentation is particularly hard because it should not only be capable of marking out the outline boundary of a latent, but also—ideally—leave out any smudges and structured noises inside the boundary, producing a region of interest (ROI) that labels all the foreground regions accurately, while including as minimum background information as possible.

2. Latent fingerprint *enhancement*: Once a latent fingerprint has been segmented, it is usually post-processed to remove noise and enhance the ridge structure. The goal of the enhancement stage is to produce at its output a fingerprint image that is more suitable for feature extraction than the original segmented image. This process is usually accompanied by a quality assessment step, where *quality*, in this case, is a prediction of the "matchability" of the fingerprint image [13]: if the segmented impression does not contain the minimally required information to make a valid confident match, it should be discarded as FTE (Failure To Enroll) or FTR (Failure To Register) fingerprints.

3. *Feature extraction*: The feature extraction stage encodes the contents of a (segmented and enhanced) fingerprint into a compact and robust representation, which should ensure fast matching while maintaining the fingerprint's uniqueness. Fingerprint features can be broadly classified into three categories: overall ridge flow pattern (Level 1), minutiae points (Level 2), and extended features (Level 3) such as dots, pores, and incipient ridges.

4. *Matching*: A fingerprints matching algorithm compares two fingerprint images and returns either a degree of similarity between the two fingerprints or a binary decision (match/no match) [13]. Fingerprints matching process is a challenging problem, mainly due to the large *intra-class* variations involved, i.e., the large variability in different impressions of the same finger [13]. The two most prominent problems associated with automated latent fingerprints matching are: the limited amount of available information and the presence of noise.

A comparative study of research results in each of the individual stages described earlier—namely: segmentation, quality assessment, enhancement, automatic feature extraction, and feature matching—has shown that, even with manual annotation of minutiae features, a maximum accuracy of about 75% can be achieved in the NIST SD-27 database [14], which supports the argument for additional research in every aspect of the system [17].

1.5   Overlapped Fingerprints

Overlapped fingerprints are typically found in latent fingerprints lifted from crime scenes as well as in live-scan fingerprint images, when the surface of fingerprint sensors contains residues of fingerprints of previous users [17]. Figure 1.3 shows examples of overlapped latent fingerprint images from different datasets.

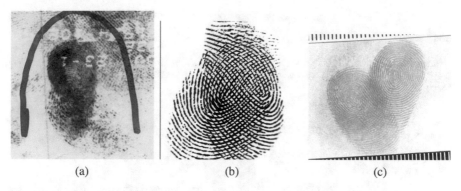

(a)   (b)   (c)

Fig. 1.3 Examples of overlapped latent fingerprint images from different databases: (**a**) NIST Special Database 27 (SD-27A) [9], (**b**) Tsinghua SOF [7], and (**c**) Tsinghua OLF [7]

An overlapped fingerprint image might contain two or more component fingerprints; however, due to the complexity of the problem, all recent studies deal with overlapped fingerprints containing only two component fingerprints. Processing such overlapped fingerprints presents a challenge, which begins at the segmentation stage: when overlapped fingerprints are present in the image, the segmentation algorithm must—in addition to separating foreground from background—segment and distinguish the individual component fingerprints as well [17] (see Chaps. 3 and 4).

An automated overlapped latent fingerprints matching system contains the same basic building blocks as the automated latent fingerprints matching system described in Sect. 1.4, with additional challenges in the two steps that take place before feature extraction, namely: latent fingerprints segmentation (or ROI extraction) and latent fingerprint enhancement.

A typical solution consists of the following steps (Fig. 1.4) [17]:

- **Segmentation**—This step involves latent fingerprints segmentation (also known as *ROI extraction*), which consists of manual[1] segmentation of component fingerprints' region masks.
- **Initial orientation field estimation and enhancement**—The initial orientation field (which consists of a matrix containing information about ridge angle in every pixel/block on fingerprint image) for the overlapped fingerprint image is usually estimated and enhanced using a block-based approach. This step

---

[1]Manual segmentation is still the norm in the current state of the art. In Chap. 4 we present experimental results for an algorithm capable of performing automatic ROI extraction of component fingerprint regions—background (B), single fingerprint (S), and overlapped fingerprints (O)—from the overlapped fingerprint image.

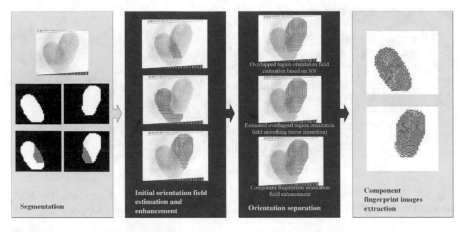

Fig. 1.4 Example of an automated overlapped fingerprint separation solution (Neural Network (NN) based solution, adapted from [18])

produces a labeled image containing three different regions: (1) *background* region without orientation values, (2) *single* region with one orientation value per block, and (3) *overlapped* region with two orientation values, randomly distributed, per block.

- **Orientation separation**—Mixed orientation fields of overlapped regions for two component fingerprints are separated, smoothed, and enhanced in order to correct remaining errors. The output of this step are component fingerprints' orientation fields.
- **Component fingerprint images extraction**—Two component fingerprints are extracted from the overlapped fingerprints image by filtering the overlapped image with the appropriate filters—usually two different Gabor filters [2, 11], tuned to the corresponding component fingerprints' orientation fields.

1.6   Concluding Remarks

In this chapter we discussed the process of latent fingerprints matching, its applications, and associated problems. We have shown that latent fingerprint recognition is a very challenging problem from the point of view of image analysis and pattern recognition, which becomes even more complex in cases where two or more fingerprints overlap. Overlapped latent fingerprint recognition introduces another step in the matching workflow, namely the separation of individual component fingerprints, which is still an open research question.

Takeaways from this chapter:

- Fingerprints matching has numerous applications, both in the civil sphere (where fingerprints are a popular biometric identifier) and in investigations of crimes based on fingerprints left at the crime scene.
- The problem of latent fingerprints matching is particularly challenging, due to the fact that the fingerprints are often noisy and incomplete.
- Overlapped latent fingerprints matching represents an even more complex problem—compared to single latent fingerprints matching—since it requires fingerprint separation as an additional (and the most complex) step in the fingerprint processing pipeline.
- The process of overlapped latent fingerprints matching is still semi-automated, because fingerprints segmentation in most approaches is performed manually.
- Latent fingerprints matching remains an open and very active research area.

References

1. D. Ashbaugh, *Quantitative-Qualitative Friction Ridge Analysis: An Introduction to Basic and Advanced Ridgeology* (CRC Press, Boca Raton, 1999)
2. J.G. Daugman, Uncertainty relation for resolution in space, spatial frequency, and orientation optimized by two-dimensional visual cortical filters. J. Opt. Soc. Am. A **2**(7), 1160–1169 (1985)
3. I.E. Dror, D. Charlton, Why experts make errors. J. Forensic Identif. **56**(4), 600 (2006)
4. I.E. Dror, A.E. Peron, S.-L. Hind, D. Charlton, When emotions get the better of us: the effect of contextual top-down processing on matching fingerprints. Appl. Cogn. Psychol. **19**(6), 799–809 (2005)
5. I.E. Dror, D. Charlton, A.E. Péron, Contextual information renders experts vulnerable to making erroneous identifications. Forensic Sci. Int. **156**(1), 74–78 (2006)
6. I.E. Dror, C. Champod, G. Langenburg, D. Charlton, H. Hunt, R. Rosenthal, Cognitive issues in fingerprint analysis: inter-and intra-expert consistency and the effect of a 'target' comparison. Forensic Sci. Int. **208**(1), 10–17 (2011)
7. J. Feng, Y. Shi, J. Zhou, Robust and efficient algorithms for separating latent overlapped fingerprints. IEEE Trans. Inf. Forensics Secur. **7**(5), 1498–1510 (2012)
8. P.A. Fraser-Mackenzie, I.E. Dror, K. Wertheim, Cognitive and contextual influences in determination of latent fingerprint suitability for identification judgments. Sci. Justice **53**(2), 144–153 (2013)
9. M.D. Garris, R.M. McCabe, Fingerprint minutiae from latent and matching tenprint images, in *Tenprint Images*, (National Institute of Standards and Technology, 2000)
10. L.J. Hall, E. Player, Will the introduction of an emotional context affect fingerprint analysis and decision-making? Forensic Sci. Int. **181**(1), 36–39 (2008)
11. L. Hong, Y. Wan, A. Jain, Fingerprint image enhancement: algorithm and performance evaluation. IEEE Trans. Pattern Anal. Mach. Intell. **20**(8), 777–789 (1998)
12. G. Langenberg, Precision, reproducibility, repeatability, and biasability of conclusions resulting from the ACE-V process. J. Forensic Identif. **59**(2), 219 (2009)

13. D. Maltoni, D. Maio, A. Jain, S. Prabhakar, *Handbook of Fingerprint Recognition* (Springer Science and Business Media, London, 2009)
14. A. Sankaran, M. Vatsa, R. Singh, Latent fingerprint matching: a survey. IEEE Access **2**, 982–1004 (2014)
15. Document #9 Standard for the Documentation of Analysis, Comparison, Evaluation, and Verification (ACE-V) in Tenprint Operations, Ver. 2.0, Scientific Working Group on Friction Ridge Analysis, Study and Technology (SWGFAST), National Institute of Standards and Technology
16. B. Stojanović, A. Nešković, O. Marques, Fingerprint ROI segmentation using Fourier coefficients and neural networks, in *23rd Telecommunications Forum Telfor (TELFOR), 2015* (IEEE, Piscataway, 2015), pp. 484–487
17. B. Stojanović, O. Marques, A. Nešković, Latent overlapped fingerprint separation: A review. Multimed. Tools Appl. **76**(15), 16263–16290 (2017)
18. B. Stojanović, A. Nešković, O. Marques, A novel neural network based approach to latent overlapped fingerprints separation. Multimed. Tools Appl. **76**(10), 1–25 (2016)
19. K. Wertheim, G. Langenburg, A. Moenssens, A report of latent print examiner accuracy during comparison training exercises. J. Forensic Identif. **56**(1), 55 (2006)

Chapter 2
Latent Fingerprint Datasets

Abstract This chapter presents an overview of existing image datasets that can be used for evaluating approaches for overlapped fingerprint separation. It gives special attention to the Vlatacom dataset, created by the authors and publicly available, which consists of 120,000 synthetically overlapped test images (and the associated masks), with and without noise, processed with three different rotation angles, and in two variations of overall brightness.

2.1 Introduction

Every field of scientific research requires datasets that can be used to evaluate new approaches to a problem, benchmark solutions, and ensure research reproducibility. The fields of fingerprints segmentation, enhancement, verification (matching), and overlapped fingerprint separation are no exception to this rule. The systematic evaluation of fingerprint processing and analysis algorithms usually requires a large number of sample images, which ideally should be made freely and publicly available to the research community at large.

Collecting a sufficiently large number of fingerprints of suitable quality is, however, an expensive, tedious, and delicate process. To circumvent those limitations, competitions for collecting large number of fingerprints, such as FVC 2000 [5] and 2002 [6], have been organized in the past. Collecting overlapped fingerprints is an even more challenging task, since, in addition to the need to find volunteers willing to participate in fingerprint acquisition, the process also involves using forensic techniques which require experienced examiners [10].

Until recently, there were two main datasets of overlapped fingerprints in use: Tsinghua OLF and Tsinghua SOF, which are described in more detail in Sect. 2.2. More recently, a new dataset, called the Vlatacom dataset (*VLD*) was proposed [12] to overcome several limitations of the Tsinghua SOF dataset. The Vlatacom

B. Stojanović et al., *Segmentation and Separation of Overlapped*
Latent Fingerprints, SpringerBriefs in Computer Science,
https://doi.org/10.1007/978-3-030-23364-8_2

dataset, freely and publicly available,[1] consists of 120,000 synthetically overlapped test images (and the associated masks), with and without noise, processed with three different rotation angles, and in two variations of overall brightness. It will be described in detail throughout this chapter.

2.2 Latent Fingerprint Datasets

Research in the field of latent fingerprints requires large publicly available datasets, preferably acquired in real environments. Producing such latent fingerprint datasets is a very challenging process for several reasons, summarized in [9], including:

- The need for professional expertise in collecting and lifting latent fingerprints.
- The time required to lift and collect latent fingerprints.
- The appropriate equipment and scarcity of trained practitioners associated with several latent fingerprint lifting techniques.
- Difficulty in agreeing on the meaning of "simulating real-time environments", since latent fingerprints collected from crime scenes may vary widely in terms of quality and possible backgrounds.
- The challenge of creating datasets with large enough number of samples and enough variability (e.g., multiple sensors, multiple backgrounds, multiple sessions, and varying quality).

2.2.1 Publicly Available Latent Fingerprint Datasets

There are three publicly available latent fingerprint datasets: NIST SD-27A[2] [3], IIIT-D Latent Fingerprint[3] [7], and IIIT-D Simultaneous Latent Fingerprint (SLF)[4] [8]. The fingerprints in these datasets have been acquired at different times, in different environments, and have significantly different characteristics, summarized in Table 2.1.

---

[1]If you are interested in obtaining the Vlatacom dataset, please send your request by email to branka.stojanovic@vlatacom.com. The archive includes all the image files (organized into folders as described in Sect. 2.3.3), the masks for all component images, the CSV files with x and y coordinates (and type) of singular points within the overlapped region, and a README file that explains how to use the dataset.

[2]http://www.nist.gov/itl/iad/ig/sd27a.cfm.

[3]http://www.iab-rubric.org/resources.html.

[4]http://www.iab-rubric.org/resources.html.

Table 2.1 Latent fingerprint datasets

Dataset	NIST SD-27A	IIIT-D latent fingerprint	IIIT-D simultaneous latent fingerprint (SLF)
Size	291	1046	1080
Description	Consists of grayscale fingerprint images, corresponding minutiae and selected latent fingerprints corresponding to fingerprint images in the data set. Contains images of 500 and 1000 ppi resolutions	Consists of latent fingerprints of 15 subjects and their mated optical slap fingerprints. Contains multiple instances for every fingerprint, enabling latent to latent fingerprint comparison. Contains images of 500 and 1000 ppi resolutions	Consists of latent fingerprints of 15 subjects and their mated optical slap fingerprints. Contains images of 500 and 1000 ppi resolutions

Table 2.2 Overlapped latent fingerprint datasets

Dataset	Tsinghua OLF	Tsinghua SOF
Size	100	100
Description	Consists of: (1) grayscale overlapped fingerprint images obtained by pressing two of twelve different fingers on a white paper, enhanced with forensic dust and scanned; (2) corresponding component fingerprint masks; and (3) corresponding template fingerprints. Contains images of 500 ppi resolution	Consists of: (1) grayscale simulated overlapped fingerprint images synthesized from the Db1_b (impressions no. 3 and no. 4) [2] subset of the Db1 fingerprint dataset from FVC2002[a] [6]; (2) corresponding component fingerprint masks; and (3) corresponding template fingerprints. Contains images of 500 ppi resolution

[a] The FVC 2002 dataset is publicly available (http://bias.csr.unibo.it/fvc2002/). The Db1 subset of FVC 2002 is divided into two parts, Db1_a and Db1_b: Db1_a contains 800 samples (8 impressions of 100 different fingerprints), while Db1_b contains 80 samples (8 impressions of 10 different fingerprints); it contains grayscale single fingerprint images of size 388 × 374 pixels (500 ppi), taken from the subjects in organized sessions [6]

2.2.2 Specialized Overlapped Latent Fingerprint Datasets

For overlapped fingerprint verification, until recently, there were only two publicly available datasets: the Tsinghua Overlapped Latent Fingerprint dataset (Tsinghua OLF)[5] [2] and Tsinghua Simulated Overlapped Fingerprint dataset (Tsinghua SOF)[6] [2]. Their main characteristics are summarized in Table 2.2.

The main differences between the Tsinghua OLF and Tsinghua SOF datasets are [12]: (1) the overlapped fingerprints in OLF are obtained by forensic means, while the fingerprints in SOF are artificially overlapped; (2) the samples in the

---

[5]http://ivg.au.tsinghua.edu.cn/.

[6]http://ivg.au.tsinghua.edu.cn/.

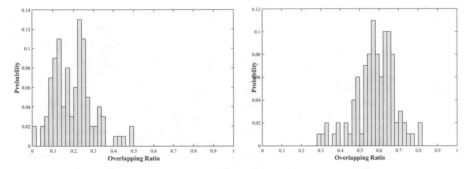

Fig. 2.1 Overlapping ratios histogram for the Tsinghua OLF (left) and Tsinghua SOF (right) datasets (adapted from [12])

OLF dataset are of lower quality than their SOF counterpart, since the former contains background noise; and (3) the size of the overlapped region (expressed as *overlapping ratios*—defined as the ratio between the size of the overlapped region and the size of the whole fingerprint region) varies significantly between the two, as indicated by the corresponding histograms (Fig. 2.1).

2.3   The Vlatacom Dataset

This section describes in detail the processes followed by the authors for the creation and organization of the Vlatacom dataset (*VLD*) [12].

2.3.1   Motivation

The decision to create the *VLD* stemmed in great part from the realization that existing datasets for research on overlapped fingerprints have shown some limitations, among them [12]:

- Both Tsinghua SOF and Tsinghua OLF datasets contain a small number of samples: only 100 overlapped fingerprints each.
- The Tsinghua SOF dataset consists of synthetically overlapped images of good quality whereas real latents contain noise caused by forensic dust.
- The Tsinghua SOF dataset does not include variations in component fingerprints' rotation angles.
- Both datasets lack information about the samples' complexity factors, such as the number of singular points (and their location) and the image's overall brightness.

The creation of the Vlatacom dataset was motivated by the overlapped fingerprint separation research community's need for large and comprehensive overlapped fingerprint dataset, which has enough samples to be used for training, validation, and testing purposes, and overcomes the aforementioned limitations.

2.3.2   Requirements

The Vlatacom dataset was created with the following requirements in mind [12]:

- **Size**: 10,000 or more images, to enable a broad range of combinations for training, cross-validation, and test partitions.
- **Variability**: images should contain a diverse range of variation in parameters such as amount of noise, angle of rotation of individual fingerprints, and overall brightness.
- **Access**: the dataset should be made free and publicly available for academic research.
- **Additional features**: besides the images themselves, the dataset should provide supplemental information about the number and the position of the *singular points* contained within the overlapped region, as a metric for distinguishing between "easy" and "hard" samples—in general, the more singular points are present in the overlapped area, the harder the separation problem.[7]

2.3.3   Dataset Structure and Organization

The process of building the Vlatacom dataset started from 200 fingerprint images from a subset of the Db1 fingerprint dataset from FVC2002 [6]. Each image is 388×374 pixels (500 ppi[8]), grayscale, and contains single fingerprints. We chose to use impressions no. 3 and no. 4 of the Db1_a dataset (200 images) because these impressions contain differences in fingerprint rotation.

We implemented the following transformations on the images[9] [12]:

- **Rotation** (3 variations): each individual fingerprint image is rotated by one of the following angles: $0°$, $45°$, or $90°$.

---

[7]Singular points are points where fingerprint ridges show discontinuity. Since overlapped fingerprint separation approaches usually rely, at least partially, on the continuity of ridges, they are more prone to errors when singular points appear in the overlapped area [11].

[8]500 ppi is a standard resolution for all latent fingerprint datasets.

[9]The MATLAB code for producing such variations is available upon request.

Fig. 2.2 Examples of
overlapped fingerprint images
from the Vlatacom dataset: (l)
without noise, (r) with added
Gaussian noise that resembles
the noise from forensic dust,
usually present in latent
images

- **Noise** (2 variations): each overlapped fingerprint image is available in two
  variations: (1) noiseless; and (2) with added Gaussian noise that resembles the
  noise from forensic dust, usually present in latent images (Fig. 2.2).
- **Overall brightness** (2 variations): each overlapped fingerprint image is available
  in brighter and darker versions. Since we have no control over the original
  brightness of each original component image, we use the histogram matching
  technique as follows: before overlapping, we compute the average brightness of
  each component image, and use the brighter (cf. darker) image histogram as a
  reference against which the histogram of the other component image must be
  matched.

The Vlatacom dataset is organized in four main folders, as follows [12]:

- **overlap_nn**: This folder contains 60,000 overlapped fingerprints *without* background noise. It is organized into three subdirectories (overlap_00, overlap_45,
  and overlap_90), corresponding to three different rotation angles between component images (0°, 45°, and 90°, respectively). Each of these folders is further
  divided in two subfolders (simply named '1', and '2'), corresponding to the
  brighter or darker version of each overlapped image, respectively.
- **overlap_wn**: This folder contains 60,000 overlapped fingerprints *with* background (Gaussian noise) noise. Its subdirectories follow the same convention as
  the overlap_nn folder, namely three angles of rotation and—for each of them—
  two levels of average brightness.
- **mask**: This folder contains 60,000 manually marked binary mask images
  (Fig. 2.3) for the overlapped fingerprints (two masks per image).[10] It is organized into three subfolders (overlap_m_00, overlap_m_45, and overlap_m_90)
  according to the rotation angle between component images (0°, 45°, and 90°,
  respectively).
- **template**: The first impressions of 100 fingers (used for creating the overlapped
  fingerprints) in FVC2002 `Db1_a` (Fig. 2.4).

---

[10]Note that average brightness and presence or absence of noise have no impact on the masks.

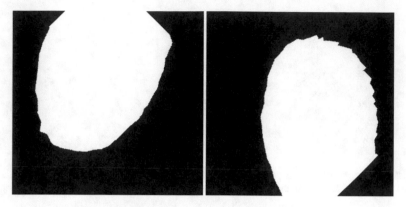

Fig. 2.3 Examples of mask images for the overlapped fingerprint images from Fig. 2.2

Fig. 2.4 Examples of templates for the overlapped fingerprint images from Fig. 2.2

The main motivation behind the naming convention adopted in the Vlatacom dataset was to assign to each sample a name that uniquely identifies it and encapsulates as much data about the included variations as possible. Hence, the filename convention concatenates the title of the first and the second component fingerprints, information about noise, amount of rotation, and brightness, and—as a bonus, for the convenience of quick reference—the number of singular points within the overlapped region.[11] For example, a file whose name is image_3_image_4_nn_90_2_06 is a combination of image_3 and image_4 from the Db1 fingerprint dataset from FVC2002 [6], without noise, with a total of 90° rotation (i.e., image_3 was rotated by −45° and image_4 was rotated by 45°). It is the darker of the two variants, and it contains six singular points within the overlapped area.

Singular points are points where fingerprint ridges show discontinuity. Fingerprint separation approaches based on the continuity of ridges can show poor

---

[11]Please refer to the README file for more details about the naming convention used in the dataset, including the naming convention for the mask images.

Fig. 2.5 Examples of singular points locations on the overlapped fingerprint images from (left to right) Vlatacom dataset, SOF dataset and OLF dataset

performance when singular points appear within the overlapped area—especially at the very edge of the overlapped area—because it is quite possible for some error propagation to occur, causing unreliable separation results. Figure 2.5 shows typical overlapped fingerprints examples, with marked singular points.

2.3.4   Additional Aspects

These are some additional aspects behind the creation of the Vlatacom dataset that are worth mentioning [12]:

- The Vlatacom dataset was designed to provide a broad range of overlapping ratios, thereby circumventing a limitation of both Tsinghua SOF and OLF datasets, mentioned in Sect. 2.2. In contrast to the histograms shown in Fig. 2.1, the proposed dataset shows a Gaussian-like distribution—see, for example, the histogram of the size of the overlapped region (overlapping ratios) for the subset with 90° rotation between component images, presented in Fig. 2.6.
- In response to a requirement listed in Sect. 2.3.2, the images in the Vlatacom dataset contain information about the number of the singular points in the overlapped region (encoded as the last two digits in the name of each sample). The vast majority of the images in the dataset contain between 2 and 3 singular points in the overlapped region.
- The Vlatacom dataset also includes three CSV files with information about the *position* (*x* and *y* coordinates) and *type* of singular points (delta or core) contained in the overlapped region: SP_00.csv, SP_45.csv, SP_90.csv, for the subsets with 0°, 45°, and 90° rotation between component images, respectively.

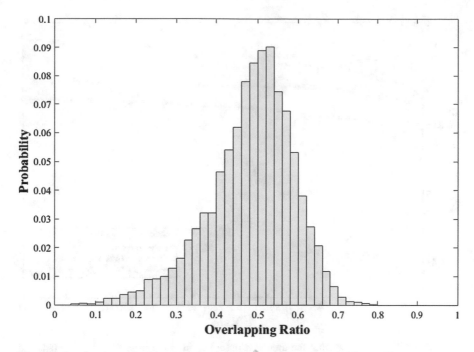

Fig. 2.6 Overlapping ratios histogram for the Vlatacom dataset (adapted from [12])

2.3.5 *Experiments and Results*

Preliminary experiments, originally reported in [12], have demonstrated the feasibility of the proposed dataset for scientific research in the field of overlapped fingerprint separation. The performance of the algorithm described in [11] was evaluated for the following four datasets: (1) Tsinghua SOF dataset; (2) Tsinghua OLF dataset; (3) Vlatacom dataset *variant A*: 90° rotation, lighter brightness, *without* noise; and (4) Vlatacom dataset *variant B*: 90° rotation, lighter brightness, *with* noise.

These experiments include matching of separated component fingerprints with the corresponding template fingerprints using a commercial fingerprint matcher (VeriFinger 6.7 SDK) and plotting of the corresponding receiver operating characteristic (ROC) and cumulative match characteristic (CMC) curves. The ROC curve plots the true acceptance rate (TAR) against the false acceptance rate (FAR) for different possible FAR values. It is a widely used measure of verification performance, based on aggregate statistics of match scores corresponding to all biometric samples [1]. The CMC curve measures identification performance based on the relative ordering of match scores corresponding to each biometric sample [1]. We followed the same approach as [13] to plot the CMC curves.

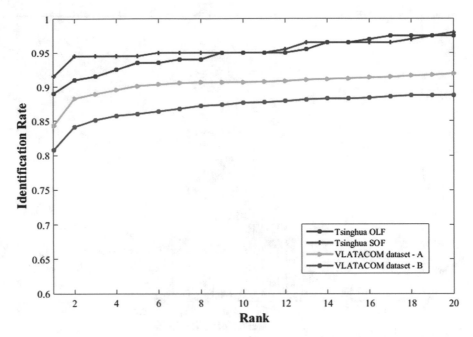

Fig. 2.7 CMC curve comparing the approach described in [11] across four datasets (adapted from [12])

The comparative CMC and ROC curves are shown in Figs. 2.7 and 2.8, respectively. They demonstrate that the two variants of the proposed dataset offer "harder" test cases for existing algorithms, which is a welcome change,[12] especially in the case of the CMC curves, whose values for the Tsinghua OLF and SOF datasets were approaching the (illusory) perfect 100% identification rate. Moreover, as intuitively expected, the case labeled as *variant B* (*with* noise) leads to lower performance than *variant A* (*without* noise) [12].

In summary, the Vlatacom dataset has several distinctly unique and useful properties, among them: larger number of images than its predecessors, meaningful variants (with or without noise, different brightness levels, different rotation angles), and a Gaussian-shaped distribution of overlapped ratios among its images. It offers an easy way to use subsets of the proposed dataset for specific needs (such as brightness/contrast correction or noise removal, for instance) and/or "levels of difficulty" (e.g., based on the amount of overlap and/or the number of singular points within the overlapped region). We expect that it will be widely used by the fingerprint processing research community.

---

[12]The transition from Tsinghua datasets to the proposed Vlatacom dataset mirrors, somehow, the creation of the Caltech 256 object category dataset (to replace its predecessor, Caltech 101) in the field of object recognition [4].

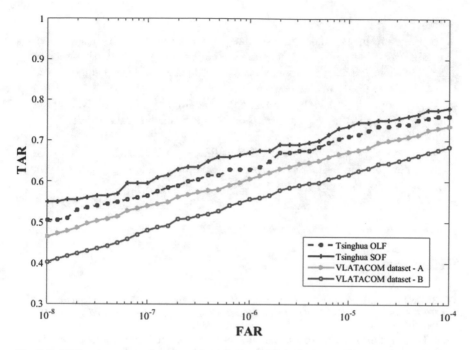

Fig. 2.8 ROC curve comparing the approach described in [11] across four datasets (adapted from [12])

2.4 Concluding Remarks

In this chapter we introduced publicly available datasets in the field of overlapped latent fingerprints and discussed their essential role in benchmarking and evaluating algorithms in the field of fingerprint processing and matching. Until recently, there were two main datasets of overlapped fingerprints in use: Tsinghua OLF and Tsinghua SOF. We have highlighted some of their limitations and have shown that a new dataset, called the Vlatacom dataset (*VLD*), was recently created to overcome them.

Takeaways from this chapter:

- Every field of scientific research requires datasets that can be used to evaluate new approaches to a problem, benchmark solutions, and ensure research reproducibility.
- The field of overlapped latent fingerprints research still lacks large publicly available databases collected in real-life conditions.

(continued)

- There are many challenges associated with the creation of a large latent fingerprint dataset, among them: the need for professional expertise, large amounts of time, proper equipment, trained personnel, and a standardized procedure for data collection, annotation, and organization.
- A newly released, publicly available, and more comprehensive dataset for overlapped fingerprint processing—the Vlatacom dataset (VLD)—is described.
- It has been experimentally confirmed that the VLD dataset can be used to develop and evaluate fingerprinting methods including segmentation, separation, and other related processes.

References

1. B. DeCann, A. Ross, Relating ROC and CMC curves via the biometric menagerie, in *2013 IEEE Sixth International Conference on Biometrics: Theory, Applications and Systems (BTAS)* (2013), pp. 1–8
2. J. Feng, Y. Shi, J. Zhou, Robust and efficient algorithms for separating latent overlapped fingerprints. IEEE Trans. Inf. Forensics Secur. **7**(5), 1498–1510 (2012)
3. M.D. Garris, R.M. McCabe, Fingerprint minutiae from latent and matching tenprint images, in *Tenprint Images*, (National Institute of Standards and Technology, 2000)
4. G. Griffin, A. Holub, P. Perona, Caltech-256 Object Category Dataset (2007)
5. D. Maio, D. Maltoni, R. Cappelli, J.L. Wayman, A.K. Jain, FVC2000: fingerprint verification competition. IEEE Trans. Pattern Anal. Mach. Intell. **24**(3), 402–412 (2002)
6. D. Maio, D. Maltoni, R. Cappelli, J.L. Wayman, A.K. Jain, FVC2002: Second fingerprint verification competition, in *Proceedings of the 16th International Conference on Pattern Recognition, 2002*, vol. 3 (IEEE, Piscataway, 2002), pp. 811–814
7. A. Sankaran, T.I. Dhamecha, M. Vatsa, R. Singh, On matching latent to latent fingerprints, in *International Joint Conference on Biometrics (IJCB), 2011* (IEEE, Piscataway, 2011), pp. 1–6
8. A. Sankaran, M. Vatsa, R. Singh, Hierarchical fusion for matching simultaneous latent fingerprint, in *IEEE Fifth International Conference on Biometrics: Theory, Applications and Systems (BTAS), 2012* (IEEE, Piscataway, 2012), pp. 377–382
9. A. Sankaran, M. Vatsa, R. Singh, Latent fingerprint matching: a survey. IEEE Access **2**, 982–1004 (2014)
10. B. Stojanović, O. Marques, A. Nešković, Latent overlapped fingerprint separation: A review. Multimed. Tools Appl. **76**(15), 16263–16290 (2017)
11. B. Stojanović, A. Nešković, O. Marques, A novel neural network based approach to latent overlapped fingerprints separation. Multimed. Tools Appl. **76**(10), 1–25 (2016)
12. B. Stojanovic, O. Marques, A. Neskovic, A novel synthetic dataset for research in overlapped fingerprint separation, in *Proceedings of the IPTA, Seventh International Conference on Image Processing Theory, Tools and Applications (IPTA2017)* (2017)
13. N. Zhang, Y. Zang, X. Yang, X. Jia, J. Tian, Adaptive orientation model fitting for latent overlapped fingerprints separation. IEEE Trans. Inf. Forensics Secur. **9**(10), 1547–1556 (2014)

Chapter 3
Overlapped Latent Fingerprints Segmentation: Problem Definition

Abstract This chapter describes the problem of segmentation of overlapped fingerprints, which is a required prerequisite step in the fingerprint processing pipeline, performed before the processes of fingerprint separation and subsequent verification. Overlapped fingerprints segmentation is usually performed manually, and only recently there have been (semi-)automatic approaches proposed in the literature. The evaluation procedure to assess the quality of such approaches is also discussed.

3.1 Introduction

Overlapped fingerprints can be found in latent fingerprints lifted from crime scenes as well as in live-scan fingerprint images, when the surface of fingerprint sensors contains residues of fingerprints of previous users. Overlapped fingerprints must be extracted out of the image (i.e., segmented from the background) and separated from one another before they can be processed by contemporary commercial fingerprint matchers (Fig. 3.1).

The overlapped fingerprints matching procedure typically consists of two steps [14]:

1. *Segmentation* of component fingerprints regions, in order to distinguish the region of the image that belongs to both component fingerprints (*overlapped* region, i.e. the region of the image where component fingerprints are overlapped) from the regions of the image belong to separate component fingerprints (*single* regions, i.e. regions where only one fingerprint is present).
2. *Separation* of the resulting overlapped region into component fingerprint images, a process by which individual pixels can be labeled as belonging to the ridges of either overlapped fingerprint, which will be described in Chap. 5.

After these steps, each of the separated component fingerprints can be processed by a typical automated fingerprints matching system.

© The Author(s), under exclusive license to Springer Nature Switzerland AG 2019   21
B. Stojanović et al., *Segmentation and Separation of Overlapped
Latent Fingerprints*, SpringerBriefs in Computer Science,
https://doi.org/10.1007/978-3-030-23364-8_3

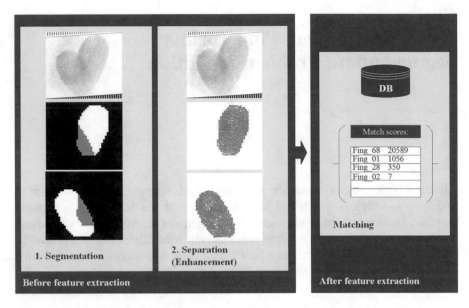

Fig. 3.1 Typical overlapped latent fingerprints matching procedure. See text for explanation

Figure 3.2 presents an overview of the overlapped latent fingerprints segmentation process, where the input is an image containing overlapped fingerprints and the outputs are *region masks* corresponding to pixels that belong to each individual fingerprint (M_{1S}, M_{2S}) or the overlapped region between them (M_O).

The topic of single latent fingerprints segmentation has received a lot of attention in recent years, and many successful approaches have emerged as a result of these efforts [3, 4, 9, 10, 12, 15, 18–21]. The segmentation of *overlapped* fingerprints, however, remains a technically challenging problem, usually performed manually using a drawing tool (such as Photoshop or Gimp) to create ("paint") region masks. The resulting region masks, along with the overlapped fingerprint images, are then used as inputs to overlapped fingerprint separation algorithms. Region masks are an integral part of all existing overlapped fingerprints datasets (see Chap. 2), since those masks are necessary to ensure reproducibility of results and meaningful comparisons among competing fingerprint separation methods. The creation of such masks is, therefore, a manual process, with only few recent attempts to develop fully automated segmentation of overlapped fingerprints (see Chap. 4).

3.2   The Mask Segmentation Problem

The original problem of (*individual*) latent fingerprints segmentation comprises two steps: (1) segmentation of the region of interest (ROI), i.e. the fingerprint area and (2) removal of background noise from the fingerprint area.

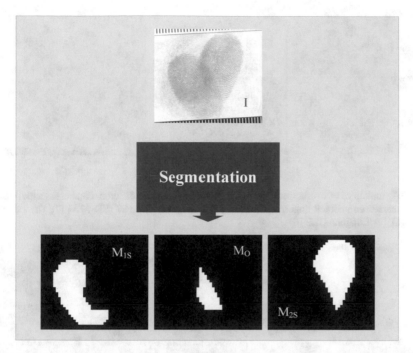

Fig. 3.2 Overlapped latent fingerprints segmentation process: the input is an image containing two overlapping fingerprints and the outputs are region masks corresponding to pixels that belong to each individual fingerprint (M_{1S}, M_{2S}) or the overlapped region between them (M_O)

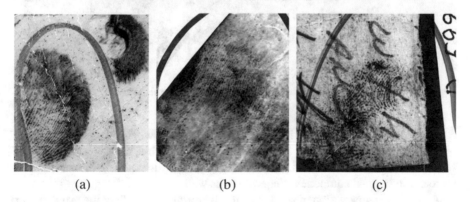

(a)   (b)   (c)

Fig. 3.3 Examples of latent fingerprint images of varying quality from NIST Special Database 27 (SD-27A) [7]. (**a**) good, (**b**) bad, (**c**) ugly

The examples in Fig. 3.3—classified as *good*, *bad*, and *ugly* by the creators of the NIST Special Database 27 (SD-27A) [7]—provide compelling examples of some of the challenges in individual latent fingerprints segmentation.

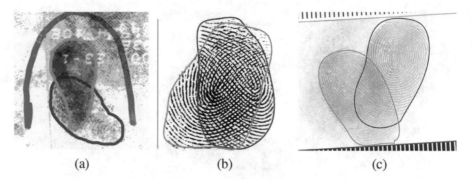

Fig. 3.4 Examples of overlapped latent fingerprint images from different databases, with illustratively marked component fingerprints. (**a**) NIST Special Database 27 (SD-27A) [7], (**b**) Tsinghua SOF [6], (**c**) Tsinghua OLF [6]

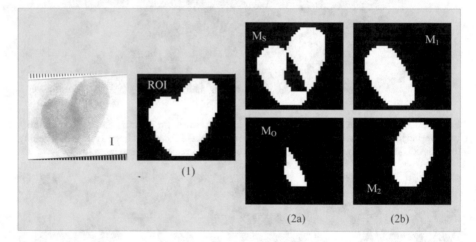

Fig. 3.5 Overlapped fingerprints mask segmentation. See text for details

The segmentation problem is even more challenging when two or more latents overlap (Fig. 3.4), since now the segmentation algorithm must—in addition to separating ROI from the background—segment and distinguish the overlapped region or individual component fingerprints as well.

Automatic segmentation of single latent fingerprints is a challenging problem, for which several solutions have been proposed in recent years [1, 3, 4, 8–12, 15, 18–21], some of which dealing with difficult databases, but none of them addressing the segmentation of *overlapped* latent fingerprints, the special case where the overlapping fingerprint area should distinct from single fingerprint area, in addition to distinguishing between fingerprint area and background.

Segmentation of *overlapped* fingerprints involves the following tasks (Fig. 3.5): (1) segmentation of fingerprint area (ROI) from the background, regardless of which component fingerprint that area belongs to; (2a) segmentation of single (S)

and overlapped (O) regions (blocks), regardless of which component fingerprint single area the blocks belongs to; (2b) segmentation of the individual component fingerprints ROIs; and (3) removal of unstructured background noise, caused by forensic dust.

Both segmentation options (Fig. 3.5, (2a) and (2b)) can be used as input for the subsequent separation tasks, depending on the separation algorithm. The core difficulty of overlapped fingerprints segmentation includes the fact that fingerprints are not opaque objects (with consistent—and easily distinguishable—color/texture patterns), for example. This is in contrast with the usual case of (natural scene) semantic segmentation [16, 17].

Algorithms capable of performing automatic ROI extraction of component fingerprint regions—background, single region, and overlapped region—from the overlapped fingerprint image have just recently started to appear in the literature [13, 14] and will be described in Chap. 4.

3.3 Evaluation Methodology

The performance evaluation of single fingerprints segmentation methods is usually done indirectly, by computing metrics related to fingerprints matching performance, under the following rationale: the better the performance of the fingerprints matching algorithm, the better (presumably) the segmentation method. There are several problems associated with relying on indirect indicators of segmentation quality, among them the fact that the performance of the segmentation algorithm can be masked by the quality of the fingerprint matcher [13].

In order to evaluate the quality of the segmentation approach directly, one can treat the segmentation problems as binary classification problems, and adopt commonly used figures of merit for the performance evaluation of binary classifiers, such as confusion matrix (Fig. 3.6) and ROC (receiver operating characteristic) curve, which is a widely used measure of performance of supervised classification rules [2, 13].

The metrics used to compare the automatically segmented fingerprint regions against manually created masks, considered as the ground truth, are [14]:

- TPR—True Positive Rate, also known as TAR (True Acceptance Rate), sensitivity, hit rate, or recall, depending on the context (ideal value = 1);
- FPR—False Positive Rate, equivalent to FAR (False Acceptance Rate) or fall-out (ideal value = 0);
- ACC—Accuracy (ideal value = 1).
- PPV—Positive Predictive Value, equivalent to precision (ideal value = 1).
- $F1$ score—The harmonic mean of precision and recall (ideal value = 1).
- AUC—Area Under the ROC Curve (ideal value = 1).

They are mathematically defined as follows:

Fig. 3.6 Typical confusion matrix

Confusion Matrix	PCP *Predicted Condition Positive*	PCN *Predicted Condition Negative*
TCP *True Condition Positive*	**TP** *True Positive*	**FN** ***Type II error*** *False Negative*
TCN *True Condition Negative*	**FP** ***Type I error*** *False Positive*	**TN** *True Negative*

$$TPR = \frac{TP}{TP + FN} \tag{3.1}$$

$$FPR = \frac{FP}{FP + TN} \tag{3.2}$$

$$ACC = \frac{TP + TN}{TP + FP + FN + TN} \tag{3.3}$$

$$PPV = \frac{TP}{TP + FP} \tag{3.4}$$

$$F1 = \frac{2TP}{2TP + FP + FN} \tag{3.5}$$

where: TP, TN, FP, and FN stand for true positives, true negatives, false positives, and false negatives, respectively.

The ROC curve plots TPR against FPR and provides a graphical representation of the relative tradeoffs between true positives and false positives [5]. The area under the ROC curve (AUC) represents the probability that a randomly chosen positive example is correctly ranked with greater suspicion than a randomly chosen negative example [2].

The special case of overlapped fingerprints can be represented as a multi-class classification problem. Image blocks/pixels should be classified in one of three classes—background (B), single (S), and overlapped (O). The evaluation of such a

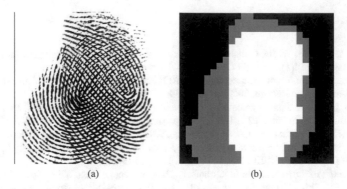

Fig. 3.7 Evaluation cases. (**a**) Overlapped fingerprints sample, (**b**) Segmentation

system can be performed in two evaluation cases, which are essentially two separate binary classification problems [14]:

- *Region of Interest segmentation*, in which we measure the algorithm's ability to segment both fingerprints (painted white and gray in Fig. 3.7b) from the background (painted black in Fig. 3.7b);
- *Overlapped region segmentation*, in which the area of overlap (painted white in Fig. 3.7b) is segmented from the remaining of the ROI (painted gray in Fig. 3.7b).

3.4 Concluding Remarks

In this chapter we discussed the problem of latent fingerprints segmentation, with particular reference to overlapped latent fingerprints, since this step is performed manually in the most of the published approaches. We also introduced and explained the typical evaluation methodology and associated figures of merit.

Takeaways from this chapter:

- The process of individual latent fingerprints segmentation consists of outlining the region of interest and removing any kind of background noise.
- Segmentation of overlapped latent fingerprints requires an additional step, namely the segmentation of different component fingerprints regions.
- Overlapped latent fingerprints segmentation is still performed manually in most of the published overlapped fingerprint separation and matching approaches, which is a way such techniques are referred to as *semi-automated*.
- Overlapped latent fingerprints segmentation remains an open, challenging, and active research area.

References

1. W. Bian, S. Ding, W. Jia, Collaborative filtering model for enhancing fingerprint image. IET Image Process. **12**(1), 149–157 (2017)
2. A.P. Bradley, The use of the area under the ROC curve in the evaluation of machine learning algorithms. Pattern Recogn. **30**(7), 1145–1159 (1997)
3. K. Cao, E. Liu, A. Jain, Segmentation and enhancement of latent fingerprints: a coarse to fine ridgestructure dictionary. IEEE Trans. Pattern Anal. Mach. Intell. **36**(9), 1847–1859 (2014)
4. H. Choi, M. Boaventura, I.A. Boaventura, A.K. Jain, Automatic segmentation of latent fingerprints, in *IEEE Fifth International Conference on Biometrics: Theory, Applications and Systems (BTAS) 2012* (IEEE, Piscataway, 2012), pp. 303–310
5. T. Fawcett, An introduction to ROC analysis. Pattern Recogn. Lett. **27**(8), 861–874 (2006)
6. J. Feng, Y. Shi, J. Zhou, Robust and efficient algorithms for separating latent overlapped fingerprints. IEEE Trans. Inf. Forensics Secur. **7**(5), 1498–1510 (2012)
7. M.D. Garris, R.M. McCabe, Fingerprint minutiae from latent and matching tenprint images, in *Tenprint Images*, (National Institute of Standards and Technology, 2000)
8. M. Ghafoor, I.A. Taj, W. Ahmad, N.M. Jafri, Efficient 2-fold contextual filtering approach for fingerprint enhancement. IET Image Process. **8**(7), 417–425 (2014)
9. S. Karimi-Ashtiani, C.-C.J. Kuo, A robust technique for latent fingerprint image segmentation and enhancement, in *15th IEEE International Conference on Image Processing, 2008. ICIP 2008* (IEEE, Piscataway, 2008), pp. 1492–1495
10. A. Sankaran, A. Jain, T. Vashisth, M. Vatsa, R. Singh, Adaptive latent fingerprint segmentation using feature selection and random decision forest classification. Inf. Fusion **34**, 1–15 (2017)
11. P. Schuch, S. Schulz, C. Busch, Survey on the impact of fingerprint image enhancement. IET Biom. **7**(2), 102–115 (2017)
12. N.J. Short, M.S. Hsiao, A.L. Abbott, E.A. Fox, Latent fingerprint segmentation using ridge template correlation, in *4th International Conference on Imaging for Crime Detection and Prevention 2011 (ICDP 2011)* (IET, Stevenage, 2011), pp. 1–6
13. B. Stojanović, O. Marques, A. Nešković, Latent overlapped fingerprint separation: a review. Multimed. Tools Appl. **76**(15), 1–28 (2016)
14. B. Stojanović, O. Marques, A. Nešković, Deep learning-based approach to latent overlapped fingerprints mask segmentation. IET Image Process. **12**(11), 1934–1942 (2018)
15. D.H. Thai, C. Gottschlich, Global variational method for fingerprint segmentation by three-part decomposition. IET Biom. **5**(2), 120–130 (2016)
16. Q. Wang, J. Gao, Y. Yuan, Embedding structured contour and location prior in Siamesed fully convolutional networks for road detection. IEEE Trans. Intell. Transp. Syst. **19**(1), 230–241 (2017)
17. Q. Wang, J. Gao, Y. Yuan, A joint convolutional neural networks and context transfer for street scenes labeling. IEEE Trans. Intell. Transp. Syst. **19**(5), 1457–1470 (2017)
18. X. Yang, J. Feng, J. Zhou, S. Xia, Detection and segmentation of latent fingerprints, in *2015 IEEE International Workshop on Information Forensics and Security (WIFS)* (IEEE, Piscataway, 2015), pp. 1–6
19. J. Zhang, R. Lai, C.-C.J. Kuo, Latent fingerprint segmentation with adaptive total variation model, in *2012 5th IAPR International Conference on Biometrics (ICB)* (IEEE, Piscataway, 2012), pp. 189–195
20. J. Zhang, R. Lai, C.-J. Kuo, Latent fingerprint detection and segmentation with a directional total variation model, in *2012 19th IEEE International Conference on Image Processing (ICIP)* (IEEE, Piscataway, 2012), pp. 1145–1148
21. J. Zhang, R. Lai, C.-C.J. Kuo, Adaptive directional total-variation model for latent fingerprint segmentation. IEEE Trans. Inf. Forensics Secur. **8**(8), 1261–1273 (2013)

Chapter 4
Machine Learning Based Segmentation of Overlapped Latent Fingerprints

Abstract This chapter describes a convolutional neural network (CNN)-based approach for overlapped fingerprint mask segmentation. The CNN classifies each image block within the overlapped fingerprint image into three classes—background (B), single fingerprint (S), and overlapped fingerprint (O). The proposed segmentation method has been successfully tested on three different datasets.

4.1 Introduction

This chapter presents a machine learning based approach for overlapped fingerprint mask segmentation. As discussed in Chap. 3, the segmentation of overlapped fingerprints (and creation of associated masks) is usually performed manually, with only few recent attempts to develop fully automated segmentation of overlapped fingerprints.

The method presented in this chapter (and described in greater detail in [7]) is based on previously developed neural network-based methods for single fingerprint image ROI segmentation [4, 5], which were trained and tested on fingerprint images of good quality (i.e., *not* latents).

The proposed method is based on convolutional neural networks (CNNs) [2, 3], which—in addition to an ever-growing number of applications in computer vision— have also shown good performance in single fingerprints processing, for different applications [1, 6, 8].

4.2 Description of the Algorithm

The CNN-based method for overlapped fingerprints segmentation—represented schematically in Fig. 4.1—consists of the following steps [7]:

1. The fingerprint image is divided into overlapping blocks.
2. The blocks are sequentially presented to the input layer of the CNN.

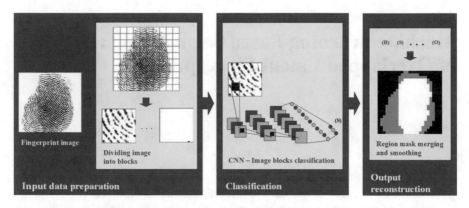

Fig. 4.1 Overlapped fingerprints mask segmentation based on convolutional neural networks

3. The CNN classifies each block in one of three classes—*background (B)*, *single (S)*, or *overlapped (O)* region.
4. Results for each block are finally merged into a *region mask*.

The proposed method uses a simplified AlexNet (SAlNet) CNN architecture, designed to determine the orientation field of latent fingerprints [1]. The optimal block size (40 × 40 pixels) was determined experimentally (see [7] for details).

The VLD dataset (described in Chap. 2) was chosen for algorithm training purposes. Additionally, the Tsinghua SOF and OLF datasets (also described in Chap. 2) were used for algorithm verification purposes.

4.2.1   CNN Architecture

The SAlNet CNN architecture (Fig. 4.2) consists of three convolutional layers (conv1–3) and one fully connected layer (fc4). The input of the CNN is a fingerprint patch of size 40 × 40 pixels. The first layer (conv1) contains convolutional sub-layer with 96 filters of size 11 × 11 and stride of 4. The output of the neurons are modeled by the ramp activation function (ReLU), $f(x) = max(0, x)$. This layer also contains max-pooling sub-layer, which takes the maximum over 3 × 3 spatial neighborhoods with a stride of 2. The third sub-layer of conv1 is a local response normalization. Similar definitions are used for layers conv2 and conv3. The fully connected layer (fc4) is applied after the last convolutional layer (conv3). A dropout regularization (with probability of 0.5) is performed after fc4 layer, in order to avoid overfitting [7].

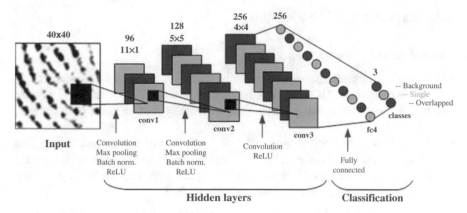

Fig. 4.2 SAlNet architecture. See text for details

4.2.2 CNN Training

Two separate CNNs are involved: (1) CNN-SO: a network designed for segmentation of synthetically overlapped fingerprints (Tsinghua SOF dataset) and (2) CNN-OL: a network designed for segmentation of latent overlapped fingerprints (Tsinghua OLF dataset).

For CNN-SO training purposes, 30,000 overlapped fingerprint images' blocks were randomly chosen from synthetically overlapped fingerprints (500 ppi) contained in the VLD dataset. As described in Chap. 2, the VLD dataset contains significantly larger amount of fingerprints and provides additional variations compared to the Tsinghua SOF dataset in terms of overlapping parameters, as well as the availability of samples containing Gaussian noise. Training blocks were selected such that half of the samples contain Gaussian noise, and all three classes (background, single, and overlapped region) were equally presented [7].

For CNN-OL training purposes, 30,000 overlapped fingerprint images' blocks were randomly chosen from the 60 latent overlapped fingerprints, created for this purpose in a similar manner as the prints from Tsinghua OLF dataset, using forensic methods and using different component fingerprints. Training blocks were also selected in a manner that all three classes (background, single, and overlapped region) are equally presented [7].

The 30,000 blocks from the training dataset were randomly divided into two subsets according to the following percentages: (1) 60% of a dataset was used for training and (2) 40% of the dataset was used for validation. In order to avoid any correlation between training and testing datasets, testing of the CNN-SO and CNN-OL was performed on the Tsinghua OLF and SOF datasets, created from different component fingerprints comparing to VLD dataset, and without any correlation between them [7].

4.3   Experimental Evaluation

Two different CNNs were trained [7]:

- CNN-OL, designed for segmentation of latent overlapped fingerprints (with noisy background). This CNN can be used in investigative applications without additional network training, where samples usually contain noise from forensic dust residues.
- CNN-SO, designed for segmentation of synthetically overlapped fingerprints (without background noise). This CNN can be used in civil applications, where the source of overlapped images is a fingerprint scanner with residues of the previous subject fingerprints on its scanning surface.

Figures 4.3 and 4.4 show examples of the CNN-OL and the CNN-SO in action, respectively.

Both networks, CNN-OL and CNN-SO, were tested extensively and demonstrated convincing numerical results, substantially better than previously published methods (see [7] for details). For an example of the occasionally produced incorrect results, see Figs. 4.5 and 4.6. The CNN-OL failure case (Fig. 4.5) shows how segmentation becomes more difficult when the input image's fingerprint ridges are not clear, and both single and overlapped area contains smudges. The smudgy area is incorrectly detected by the network as overlapped area. The CNN-SO failure case (Fig. 4.6) shows how segmentation can be problematic when the input image contains one or more areas of poor quality, in this case, that fingerprint ridges are not continuous lines but more dot-like. The area with dots is incorrectly detected by the network as the overlapped area [7].

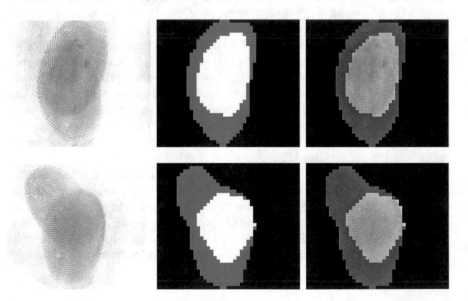

Fig. 4.3 CNN-OL segmentation results examples 1 (top) and 2 (bottom): input image (left), generated mask (center), and masked image (right)

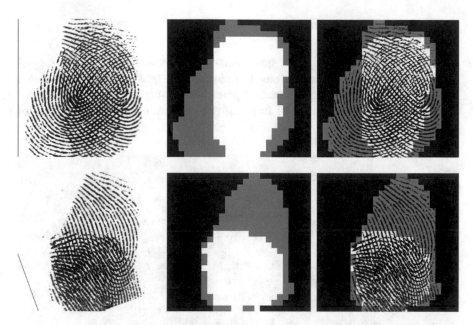

Fig. 4.4 CNN-SO segmentation results examples 1 (top) and 2 (bottom): input image (left), generated mask (center), and masked image (right)

Fig. 4.5 Typical segmentation failure cases. CNN-OL exemplar (left), corresponding mask (center), and masked fingerprints (right)

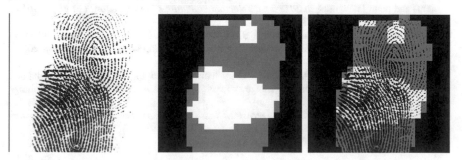

Fig. 4.6 Typical segmentation failure cases. CNN-SO exemplar (left), corresponding mask (center), and masked fingerprints (right)

4.4 Concluding Remarks

In this chapter we discussed a new method for segmentation of overlapped fingerprints based on machine learning techniques, specifically convolutional neural networks (CNNs). The proposed method gives good results and opens the field for new research and development of fully automated methods for the separation of overlapped fingerprints.

Takeaways from this chapter:

- The recent popularity of machine learning and deep learning methods for image analysis tasks has opened new avenues for the development of a fully automated algorithm for separating overlapped fingerprints.
- The overlapped fingerprints separation algorithms published so far include manual segmentation of the component fingerprints region.
- The proposed CNN-based method represents a significant advance towards the development of a fully automated system for overlapped fingerprints separation.

References

1. K. Cao, A. Jain, Latent orientation field estimation via convolutional neural network, in *2015 International Conference on Biometrics (ICB)* (2015), pp. 349–356. https://doi.org/10.1109/ICB.2015.7139060
2. I. Goodfellow, Y. Bengio, A. Courville, *Deep Learning* (MIT Press, Cambridge, 2016)
3. Y. LeCun, Y. Bengio, G. Hinton, Deep learning. Nature **521**(7553), 436–444 (2015)
4. B. Stojanovic, A. Neskovic, Z. Popovic, V. Lukic, ANN based fingerprint image ROI segmentation, in *2014 22nd Telecommunications Forum Telfor (TELFOR)* (IEEE, Piscataway, 2014), pp. 505–508
5. B. Stojanović, A. Nešković, O. Marques, Fingerprint ROI segmentation using Fourier coefficients and neural networks, in *2015 23rd Telecommunications Forum Telfor (TELFOR)* (IEEE, Piscataway, 2015), pp. 484–487
6. B. Stojanović, O. Marques, A. Nešković, S. Puzović, Fingerprint ROI segmentation based on deep learning, in *2016 24th Telecommunications Forum (TELFOR)* (IEEE, Piscataway, 2016), pp. 1–4
7. B. Stojanović, O. Marques, A. Nešković, Deep learning-based approach to latent overlapped fingerprints mask segmentation. IET Image Process. **12**(11), 1934–1942 (2018). https://doi.org/10.1049/iet-ipr.2017.1227
8. R. Wang, C. Han, Y. Wu, T. Guo, *Fingerprint Classification Based on Depth Neural Network* (2014). ArXiv:1409.5188

Chapter 5
Overlapped Latent Fingerprints Separation: Problem Definition

Abstract Overlapped fingerprints are often found in latent fingerprints lifted from crime scenes and in live-scan fingerprint images when the surface of fingerprint sensors contains residues of fingerprints of previous users. Such overlapped fingerprints must be separated before they can be processed by a fingerprint matcher, which has led to the creation of several different methods designed to separate the overlapped fingerprints. This chapter describes the problem of latent overlapped fingerprint separation and presents a brief overview of selected contemporary techniques for overlapped fingerprint separation in the context of latent overlapped fingerprints matching.

5.1 Introduction

The problem of overlapped latent fingerprint separation consists in separating and enhancing component fingerprints in order to make them suitable candidates for later feature extraction and matching procedures. This process usually includes four major steps [3, 8, 27, 30, 35] (Fig. 5.1):

- **Segmentation**—This step involves latent fingerprints segmentation (also known as *ROI extraction*), whose output produces the component fingerprints' region masks. See Chaps. 3 and 4 for details.
- **Initial orientation field estimation and enhancement**—The initial orientation field (which consists of a matrix containing information about ridge angle in every pixel/block on fingerprint image) for the overlapped fingerprint image is usually estimated and enhanced using a block-based approach. This step produces a labeled image containing three different regions: (1) *background* region without orientation values, (2) *single* region with one orientation value per block, and (3) *overlapped* region with two orientation values, randomly distributed, per block.
- **Orientation separation**—Mixed orientation fields of overlapped regions for two component fingerprints are separated, smoothed, and enhanced in order to correct

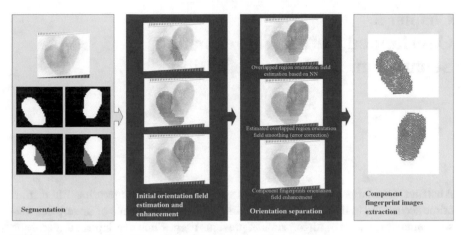

Fig. 5.1 Overlapped latent fingerprint enhancement: a block diagram

remaining errors. The output of this step are component fingerprints' orientation fields.

- **Component fingerprint images extraction**—Two component fingerprints are extracted from the overlapped fingerprints image by filtering the overlapped image with the appropriate filters—usually two different Gabor filters [6, 13], tuned to the corresponding component fingerprints' orientation fields.

In some approaches (for example, [36]), the second and third steps are combined, i.e. there is no initial orientation field estimation and separation, but orientation fields of separate component fingerprints are estimated in one step.

5.2 Orientation Field Estimation

A fingerprint orientation field is a matrix, whose value at (x, y) denotes the dominant ridge orientation at point (x, y) [20]. The main difference between the orientation field of an overlapped fingerprint image and the orientation field of a single fingerprint image is that the former contains one dominant orientation in the nonoverlapped regions and two dominant orientations in the overlapped region. The state of the art in overlapped fingerprint separation relies on manually marked region masks outlining the component fingerprints; hence, the overlapped region can be obtained by finding the intersection of two fingerprint region masks [3].

The problem of initial orientation field estimation consists of estimating one dominant ridge orientation in the nonoverlapped fingerprint regions and two dominant ridge orientations in the overlapped region. The initial orientation field, together with region masks, will then be used as input by the subsequent orientation field separating algorithm [3].

Traditional orientation field estimation algorithms consist of two steps: (1) initial estimation (i.e., using a gradient-based method) and (2) orientation field regularization. Regularization may be done by a simple averaging filter or global model-based methods. However, for overlapped fingerprints containing ridges of two different orientations in the overlapped area, the initial orientation field obtained by gradient-based methods may be a random mix of the orientation fields of the two component fingerprints which cannot be resolved by existing regularization algorithms [3].

5.2.1 Orientation Field Estimation Algorithms for Single Fingerprint

Orientation field estimation algorithms can be classified into three categories [9].

1. Local Estimation

    Local estimation approaches compute a local ridge orientation at pixel $\mathbf{x} = (x, y)$ using only the neighborhood around $\mathbf{x}$, which is typically 32×32 pixels for 500 ppi fingerprints.

    Widely used local estimation approaches include:

- Gradient-based approaches [1, 2, 17, 25], which use classical gradient operators, such as Prewitt or Sobel, to compute the dominant orientation in the local neighborhood.
- Slit-based approach [23], which explicitly exploits the fact that the variation of intensity is the smallest along the ridge orientation and largest along the orthogonal orientation. By testing such a hypothesis along a number of different orientations, the best orientation is chosen [9].
- Fourier transform-based approach, which approximates the ridge pattern in a local area of a fingerprint by a 2D sine wave, whose Fourier transform's magnitude spectrum will contain a pair of peaks whose location corresponds to the parameters of the sine wave. The magnitude spectrum can then be mapped to the polar coordinate system and normalized; the resulting normalized magnitude spectrum can be viewed as a probability distribution [4]. The best orientation can then be estimated as the most probable orientation according to the resulting distribution [9].

    These approaches perform very well for fingerprint images of good quality, but their performance is quite poor for latent images that contain structural background noise [29].

2. Smoothing

    Orientation fields obtained by local estimation approaches for poor quality fingerprints are usually very noisy and need to be regularized, which can be achieved using an image smoothing algorithm, such as the well-known low-pass filtering [1]. Low-pass filtering results depend critically on the size of the filtering window: larger windows are better at reducing noise whereas smaller windows are capable of preserving the true orientation in a high curvature region [9].

Many alternatives to the standard low-pass filter have been proposed in the literature, such as the implementation of orientation field smoothing by using the Markov random field (MRF) model [5, 16, 24] and the use of multiresolution orientation fields [18, 19, 22, 23]. Fingerprints of very poor quality still offer a significant challenge to any of these approaches [9].

3. Global Parametric Models

Global parametric model fitting methods constitute another category of regularization algorithms that use mathematical models to represent the whole fingerprint orientation field. The models can be general (e.g., polynomials [12] and Fourier series [31], or specific to fingerprints [14, 26, 37]. General models may be prone to overfitting or underfitting problems, especially when the initial orientation field is very noisy [9].

There are models which explicitly consider singular points [14, 26, 37], which cannot be easily extracted from latents. Consequently, certain orientation field estimation approaches in the literature (e.g., [32] and [33]) require manually marked singular points as input [9].

5.2.2 Orientation Field Estimation Algorithms for Overlapped Fingerprints

Orientation field estimation for the overlapped region is a very challenging problem for traditional fingerprint orientation estimation methods [8]. In overlapped latent fingerprint processing approaches most authors [3, 7, 27, 30] have adopted the local Fourier analysis method proposed in [15] for initial orientation field estimation.

The process of orientation field estimation for the overlapped region consists of the following steps (Fig. 5.2) [29]:

1. The fingerprint image is divided into non-overlapping image segments (blocks), typically of size 16×16 pixels.
2. Fourier coefficients are calculated for these segments, as follows [15]:

   (a) The local window of size 64×64 pixels, centered at each block, is multiplied by a bivariate isotropic Gaussian function;
   (b) For the resulting image, the discrete Fourier transform (DFT) is calculated;
   (c) The amplitude of low-frequency components (points within three pixels from the center in the frequency domain) is set to zero.

Local maxima points in the frequency domain correspond to 2D sine waves (stripes) on the image block. For single region blocks (S blocks) one estimates orientation as the orientation (direction) of the 2D sine wave that corresponds to the brightest local maxima. For overlapped region blocks (O blocks) one estimates two orientations as the orientations of the 2D sine waves that correspond to the two brightest local maxima.

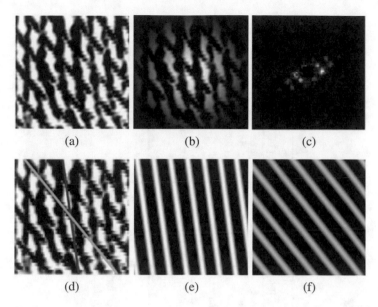

Fig. 5.2 Initial orientation estimation for one overlapped region block. (**a**) Overlapped (O) block; (**b**) O block multiplied by Gaussian function; (**c**) two local maxima points in the frequency domain; (**d**) two dominant orientations; (**e, f**) corresponding 2D sine waves (Adapted from [30])

Besides the local Fourier analysis method, there are other noteworthy approaches in literature. Zhao and Jain in [36] proposed reconstruction of the orientation fields of component fingerprints via modeling orientation fields and then predicting unknown orientation fields based on a certain number of manually marked orientation cues in fingerprints. Zhang et al. in [35] proposed block-based orientation field estimation from the overlapped fingerprint image by Gabor filters approach. In this approach K Gabor filters corresponding to K different orientations are applied to filter the image, and the orientations are obtained according to the filters' responses [29].

5.3   Overlapped Latent Fingerprint Separation: Representative Approaches

Table 5.1 presents a summary of some of the most significant latent overlapped fingerprint separation approaches proposed during the past few years. The table contains information on the separation method, the initial orientation field estimation method, the level of manual work, and whether the approach was tested on real overlapped latents (Tsinghua OLF database) or not.[1]

---

[1]For additional information on each method listed in Table 5.1, please see [29] or refer to the original publications.

Table 5.1 Overlapped latent fingerprint separation approaches (adapted from [30])

Approach	Singh et al. [28]	Chen et al. [3]	Shi et al. [27]	Feng et al. [8]	Zhao and Jain [36]	Zhang et al. [34, 35]	Stojanović et al. [30]
Separation method	Independent Component Analysis (ICA)	Relaxation labeling	Constrained relaxation labeling	Constrained relaxation labeling	Model-based separation	Adaptive orientation model fitting	Neural networks
Initial orientation estimation method	n/a	Local Fourier analysis	Local Fourier analysis	Local Fourier analysis	Other	Other	Local Fourier analysis
Level of manual work	n/a	Region masks and singular points	Region masks	Region masks	Region masks and orientation cues	Region masks	Region masks
Tested on real overlapped latents (OLF)	No	No	No	Yes	No	Yes	Yes
Impact	First published approach	Additional manual work required	–	State-of-art for SOF dataset	The highest level of manual work required	–	State-of-art for OLF database

5.4 Evaluation Methodology

The performance of overlapped (latent) fingerprint separation approaches is usually evaluated indirectly, based on the performance evaluation of the matching process. Matching experiments consist of matching separated component fingerprints with the corresponding template fingerprints and plotting of the receiver operating characteristic (ROC) curves and the cumulative match characteristic (CMC) curves, as typical biometric systems matching accuracy indicators. For matching experiments, typically a commercial fingerprint matcher, such as the popular VeriFinger [21], is often used [29].

The ROC curve is a widely used measure of verification performance, based on aggregate statistics of match scores corresponding to all biometric samples [7]. It plots the true acceptance rate (TAR) against the false acceptance rate (FAR) for different possible FAR values. To plot the ROC curves, only genuine matches are executed because the output scores of the VeriFinger matcher are linked to the FAR. For each database, 200 genuine matches are executed [29].

The CMC curve measures identification performance based on the relative ordering of match scores corresponding to each biometric sample [7]. To plot the CMC curves, the approach used in [35] consists of 2000 rolled fingerprints in the NIST SD4 database combined with the 12 template fingerprints in the OLF database (10 template fingerprints in the case of the SOF database), which are used as the background database [29].

The NIST SD4 database contains 2000 gray scale fingerprint images, of resolution 512×512 pixels, and is widely used for evaluating fingerprint systems on a statistical sample of fingerprints because it is evenly distributed over the five major classifications (Arch, Left and Right Loops, Tented Arch, Whirl) [29].

Since both the ROC (aggregate-based) and CMC (rank-based) curves are estimated from the same set of match scores, they are, not surprisingly, correlated to some degree. Recently, the notion that the ROC and CMC are directly related has been challenged by the work of Gorodnichy who first presented an argument stating that aggregate based metrics such as the ROC fail to appropriately evaluate operational systems characterized by large sample size and non-static populations[10, 11]. Furthermore, Gorodnichy argues that verification systems should be evaluated (and developed) as 1:N identification systems [11], and states that "measures for identification (i.e., ranked statistics) reveal more information regarding the relationships between users involved in a biometric system [7]". These arguments suggest that CMC curves are more meaningful representations of performance measures for biometric systems than ROC curves [29].

Figure 5.3 shows examples of ROC and CMC curves. The curves in red are from a representative approach in the literature [30], whereas the dashed curves in blue represent ideal values.

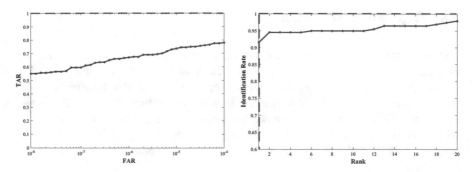

Fig. 5.3 Examples of ROC (left) and CMC (right) curves

5.5   Concluding Remarks

In this chapter we discussed the problem of overlapped latent fingerprints separation, as the most challenging task in overlapped latent fingerprints matching process. We paid special attention to approaches published so far and their limitations. We also introduced and explained the typical evaluation methodology and associated figures of merit.

> Takeaways from this chapter:
>
> - Overlapped latent fingerprints separation is the most challenging task in the overlapped latent fingerprints matching pipeline.
> - Overlapped latent fingerprints separation is still a semi-automated process due to the adoption of manual overlapped fingerprints segmentation.
> - Comparative evaluation of competing approaches is still limited by the lack of datasets with real-life samples.
> - This is an active research area, with many open problems, such as separation of more than two overlapped fingerprints and handling other types of (structured) background noise.

References

1. A.M. Bazen, S.H. Gerez, Systematic methods for the computation of the directional fields and singular points of fingerprints. IEEE Trans. Pattern Anal. Mach. Intell. **24**(7), 905–919 (2002)
2. J. Bigun, Optimal orientation detection of linear symmetry, in *Proceedings of the IEEE First International Conference on Computer Vision*, London, June 8–11 (1987), pp. 433–438
3. F. Chen, J. Feng, A. Jain, J. Zhou, J. Zhang, Separating overlapped fingerprints. IEEE Trans. Inf. Forensics Secur. **6**(2), 346–359 (2011). ISSN 1556-6013. https://doi.org/10.1109/TIFS.2011.2114345

4. S. Chikkerur, A.N. Cartwright, V. Govindaraju, Fingerprint enhancement using STFT analysis. Pattern Recogn. **40**(1), 198–211 (2007)
5. S.C. Dass, Markov random field models for directional field and singularity extraction in fingerprint images. IEEE Trans. Image Process. **13**(10), 1358–1367 (2004)
6. J.G. Daugman, Uncertainty relation for resolution in space, spatial frequency, and orientation optimized by two-dimensional visual cortical filters. J. Opt. Soc. Am. A **2**(7), 1160–1169 (1985)
7. B. DeCann, A. Ross, Relating ROC and CMC curves via the biometric menagerie, in *2013 IEEE Sixth International Conference on Biometrics: Theory, Applications and Systems (BTAS)* (2013), pp. 1–8. https://doi.org/10.1109/BTAS.2013.6712705
8. J. Feng, Y. Shi, J. Zhou, Robust and efficient algorithms for separating latent overlapped fingerprints. IEEE Trans. Inf. Forensics Secur. **7**(5), 1498–1510 (2012). ISSN 1556-6013. https://doi.org/10.1109/TIFS.2012.2204254
9. J. Feng, J. Zhou, A. Jain, Orientation field estimation for latent fingerprint enhancement. IEEE Trans. Pattern Anal. Mach. Intell. **35**(4), 925–940 (2013). ISSN 0162-8828. https://doi.org/10.1109/TPAMI.2012.155
10. D.O. Gorodnichy, Multi-order analysis framework for comprehensive biometric performance evaluation, in *SPIE Defense, Security, and Sensing* (International Society for Optics and Photonics, Bellingham, 2010), p. 76670G
11. D. Gorodnichy, Multi-order biometric score analysis framework and its application to designing and evaluating biometric systems for access and border control, in *2011 IEEE Workshop on Computational Intelligence in Biometrics and Identity Management (CIBIM)* (2011), pp. 44–53. https://doi.org/10.1109/CIBIM.2011.5949204
12. J. Gu, J. Zhou, C. Yang, Fingerprint recognition by combining global structure and local cues. IEEE Trans. Image Process. **15**(7), 1952–1964 (2006)
13. L. Hong, Y. Wan, A. Jain, Fingerprint image enhancement: algorithm and performance evaluation. IEEE Trans. Pattern Anal. Mach. Intell. **20**(8), 777–789 (1998)
14. S. Huckemann, T. Hotz, A. Munk, Global models for the orientation field of fingerprints: an approach based on quadratic differentials. IEEE Trans. Pattern Anal. Mach. Intell. **30**(9), 1507–1519 (2008)
15. A. Jain, J. Feng, Latent palmprint matching. IEEE Trans. Pattern Anal. Mach. Intell. **31**(6), 1032–1047 (2009). ISSN 0162-8828. https://doi.org/10.1109/TPAMI.2008.242
16. T. Kamei, Image filter design for fingerprint enhancement, in *Automatic Fingerprint Recognition Systems* (Springer, New York, 2004), pp. 113–126
17. M. Kass, A. Witkin, Analyzing oriented patterns. Comput. Vis. Graph. Image Process. **37**(3), 362–385 (1987)
18. M. Liu, X. Jiang, A.C. Kot, Fingerprint reference-point detection. EURASIP J. Adv. Sig. Process. **2005**(4), 1–12 (2005)
19. P.Z. Lo, Y. Luo, Method and apparatus for adaptive hierarchical processing of print images (2006). US Patent App. 11/456,622
20. D. Maltoni, D. Maio, A. Jain, S. Prabhakar, *Handbook of Fingerprint Recognition* (Springer Science & Business Media, New York, 2009)
21. Neurotechnology, *VeriFinger SDK: Fingerprint Identification for Stand-Alone or Web Solutions* (2016). http://www.neurotechnology.com/verifinger.html
22. L. O'Gorman, J.V. Nickerson, An approach to fingerprint filter design. Pattern Recogn. **22**(1), 29–38 (1989)
23. M. Oliveira, N.J. Leite, A multiscale directional operator and morphological tools for reconnecting broken ridges in fingerprint images. Pattern Recogn. **41**(1), 367–377 (2008)
24. S. Prabhakar et al., Probabilistic orientation field estimation for fingerprint enhancement and verification, in *BSYM'08 Biometrics Symposium, 2008* (IEEE, Piscataway, 2008), pp. 41–46
25. N.K. Ratha, S. Chen, A.K. Jain, Adaptive flow orientation-based feature extraction in fingerprint images. Pattern Recogn. **28**(11), 1657–1672 (1995)
26. B.G. Sherlock, D.M. Monro, A model for interpreting fingerprint topology. Pattern Recogn. **26**(7), 1047–1055 (1993)

27. Y. Shi, J. Feng, J. Zhou, Separating overlapped fingerprints using constrained relaxation labeling, in *Proceedings of the International Joint Conference on Biometrics* (2011)
28. M. Singh, D.K. Singh, P.K. Kalra, *Fingerprint Separation: An Application of ICA*, vol. 6982 (2008), pp. 69820L–69820L-11. https://doi.org/10.1117/12.777541
29. B. Stojanović, O. Marques, A. Nešković, Latent overlapped fingerprint separation: a review, in *Multimedia Tools and Applications* (2016), pp. 1–28. https://doi.org/10.1007/s11042-016-3908-y
30. B. Stojanović, A. Nešković, O. Marques, A novel neural network based approach to latent overlapped fingerprints separation. Multimed. Tools Appl. 1–25 (2016). https://doi.org/10.1007/s11042-016-3696-4
31. Y. Wang, J. Hu, D. Phillips, A fingerprint orientation model based on 2D Fourier expansion (FOMFE) and its application to singular-point detection and fingerprint indexing. IEEE Trans. Pattern Anal. Mach. Intell. **29**(4), 573–585 (2007)
32. S. Yoon, J. Feng, A.K. Jain, On latent fingerprint enhancement, in *SPIE Defense, Security, and Sensing* (International Society for Optics and Photonics, Bellingham, 2010), p. 766707
33. S. Yoon, J. Feng, A. Jain, Latent fingerprint enhancement via robust orientation field estimation, in *2011 International Joint Conference on Biometrics (IJCB)* (2011), pp. 1–8. https://doi.org/10.1109/IJCB.2011.6117482.
34. N. Zhang, X. Yang, Y. Zang, X. Jia, J. Tian, Overlapped fingerprints separation based on adaptive orientation model fitting, in *2014 22nd International Conference on Pattern Recognition (ICPR)* (2014), pp. 678–683. https://doi.org/10.1109/ICPR.2014.127
35. N. Zhang, Y. Zang, X. Yang, X. Jia, J. Tian, Adaptive orientation model fitting for latent overlapped fingerprints separation. IEEE Trans. Inf. Forensics Secur. **9**(10), 1547–1556 (2014). ISSN 1556-6013. https://doi.org/10.1109/TIFS.2014.2340573
36. Q. Zhao, A. Jain, Model based separation of overlapping latent fingerprints. IEEE Trans. Inf. Forensics Secur. **7**(3), 904–918 (2012). ISSN 1556-6013. https://doi.org/10.1109/TIFS.2012.2187281
37. J. Zhou, J. Gu, A model-based method for the computation of fingerprints' orientation field. IEEE Trans. Image Process. **13**(6), 821–835 (2004)

Chapter 6
Machine Learning Based Separation of Overlapped Latent Fingerprints

Abstract This chapter describes a machine learning based approach for overlapped fingerprint separation. The algorithm works in a block-based fashion: after producing an initial estimation of the orientation fields present in the overlapped fingerprint image, it uses a neural network to separate the mixed orientation fields, which are then post-processed to correct remaining errors and enhanced using the global orientation field enhancement model. The proposed separation method has been successfully tested on two different datasets.

6.1 Introduction

This chapter presents a neural network based approach for overlapped fingerprint mask separation. As discussed in Chap. 5, the problem of overlapped latent fingerprint separation consists in separating and enhancing component fingerprints in order to make them suitable candidates for later feature extraction and matching procedures. This process usually includes four steps [1, 3, 9–11] (Fig. 6.1):

1. **Segmentation**—This step involves latent fingerprints segmentation (also known as *ROI extraction*), whose output produces the component fingerprints' region masks. See Chaps. 3 and 4 for details.
2. **Initial orientation field (OF) estimation and enhancement**—The initial orientation field (which consists of a matrix containing information about ridge angle in every pixel/block on fingerprint image) for the overlapped fingerprint image is usually estimated and enhanced using a block-based approach. This step produces a labeled image containing three different regions: (1) *background* region without orientation values, (2) *single* region with one orientation value per block, and (3) *overlapped* region with two orientation values, randomly distributed, per block.
3. **Orientation separation**—Mixed orientation fields of overlapped regions for two component fingerprints are: (1) separated using a neural network-based approach, (2) smoothed in order to correct remaining errors, and (3) additionally

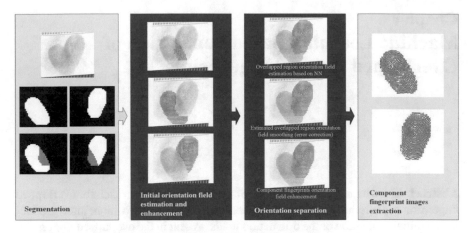

Fig. 6.1 Overlapped latent fingerprint separation: a block diagram

enhanced using the global orientation field enhancement model. The output of this step are component fingerprints' orientation fields.

4. **Component fingerprint images extraction**—Two component fingerprints are extracted from the overlapped fingerprints image by filtering the overlapped image with the appropriate filters—usually two different Gabor filters [2, 6], tuned to the corresponding component fingerprints' orientation fields.

The approach described in this chapter (and described in greater detail in [10]) focuses on step 3—Orientation separation—where we propose a neural network based method for separating overlapped orientations. A secondary contribution of the proposed method relates to step 2—Initial orientation field (OF) estimation and enhancement—due to the fact that our method was the first method to utilize a global-based orientation field enhancement model of initially estimated single region orientation field *prior* to separating overlapped region orientations. This was done in order to minimize influence of local-based orientation estimation model and to produce a more lifelike orientation field as an input for subsequent processing steps [10].

6.2 Segmentation

In this stage, segmentation masks are manually created from pre-processed and size-normalized input images (Fig. 6.2).

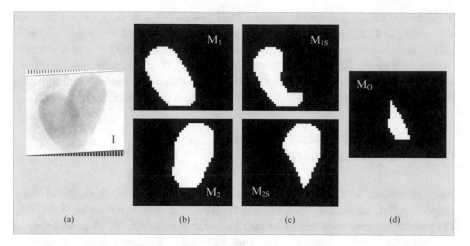

Fig. 6.2 Segmentation of an exemplar overlapped fingerprint image: (**a**) Overlapped fingerprint image exemplar (I); (**b**) component fingerprints' region masks (M_1, M_2); (**c**) single region masks (M_{1S}, M_{2S}); (**d**) overlapped region mask (M_O)

6.3 Initial Orientation Field Estimation and Enhancement

The initial orientation field for the overlapped fingerprint image is estimated and enhanced using a block-based approach, which consists of two steps: (1) a Fourier analysis-based estimation of orientation field for the whole overlapped fingerprint image and (2) enhancement of single region orientation field using a global dictionary-based orientation field enhancement approach [4].

6.3.1 Initial Orientation Field Estimation

The initial orientation field consists of three different regions: (1) *background* region without orientation values, (2) *single* region with one orientation value per block, and (3) *overlapped* region with two orientation values, randomly distributed, per block.

We adopted the local Fourier analysis method proposed in [7] and used by several other authors in their work on similar problems [1, 3, 9]. See Sect. 5.2.2 for details.

6.3.2 Single Region Orientation Field Enhancement

The method used for initial orientation field estimation (Fourier analysis) is block-based and does not take into account information from the rest of the fingerprint image. In order to correct occasional orientation estimation errors caused by the local nature of the estimation process (and ensure more accurate input data for the subsequent stages of our algorithm) we applied Feng et al.'s publicly available global dictionary based orientation field enhancement method [4] to the single region orientation field of component fingerprints. This enhancement step minimizes the influence of the local-based orientation estimation model. Consequently, the resulting single region orientation field becomes more realistic and accurate [10].

6.4 Orientation Separation

The orientation separation process consists of three stages (Fig. 6.3): (1) overlapped region orientation field estimation based on neural networks (Sect. 6.5); (2) estimated overlapped region orientation field smoothing, which provides error correction to results from the previous step; and (3) component fingerprints' orientation field enhancement (see [10] for details).

6.5 Neural Network: Architecture and Training

The method described in this chapter uses two neural networks, one for each type of segment (square or T segment), trained with single blocks' orientation values in order to calculate one overlapped block orientation value. For this type of problem, multilayer feed-forward neural networks with error back-propagation as a learning rule, sigmoid hidden neurons and linear output neurons, are an appropriate choice [5]. The chosen neural network structure consists of the input layer, two hidden

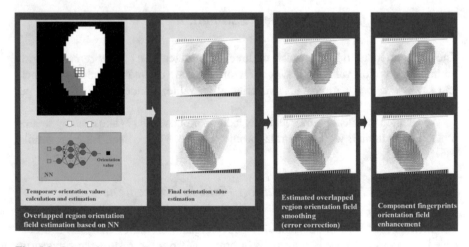

Fig. 6.3 Orientation separation process

layers, and the output layer. The number of perceptrons in the two hidden layers was determined experimentally to be 50 and 20 perceptrons, respectively (see [10] for details).

A subset of the Db1 fingerprint database from FVC2002 [8] was used for training purposes. The Db1 database is divided into two parts, Db1_a and Db1_b: Db1_a contains 800 samples (8 impressions of 100 different fingerprints), while Db1_b contains 80 samples (8 impressions of 10 different fingerprints). Each image is 388×374 pixels (500 ppi), grayscale, and contains single fingerprints taken from the subjects in organized sessions [8].

We used impressions no. 3 and no. 4 of the Db1_a database (200 fingerprint images), from which 10,000 suitable image segments of outer size of 3×3 blocks were randomly chosen. In order to be suitable for training, the selected image segments must belong to the fingerprint area (Region of Interest-ROI) of that fingerprint image. There are four possible variants for each type of image segment patterns used in the proposed algorithm. We ensure that the 10,000 training samples contain 2500 samples of each of the four variations [10].

The proposed method was implemented in MATLAB. To ensure reproducibility of results, the critical parameters related to the orientation separation process—and more specifically to neural network training—have also been published (see [10] for details).

6.6 Experimental Evaluation

The performance of the algorithm was evaluated and compared against the equivalent curves from the most prominent approaches from the literature as well as two baseline cases: (1) experiments of direct matching of overlapped fingerprint images with the template fingerprints and (2) experiments of matching of overlapped fingerprint images segmented with component fingerprints masks with the template fingerprints (see [10] for details).

Experimental results demonstrate that the proposed method shows better or comparable performance to the most prominent approaches in the literature for both (Tsinghua OLF and Tsinghua SOF) datasets and both figures of merit (ROC and CMC curves) (see [10] for details).

Figure 6.4 presents some typical failure cases. The first failure case (Fig. 6.4a) is mostly caused by poor manual mask segmentation—the segmented mask contains only part of the fingerprint area, and the resulting fingerprint image contains too little useful data to perform the matching procedure successfully. This problem is related to any overlapped fingerprint separation approach and highlights the need for a fully automated mask generation system. The second failure case (Fig. 6.4b) is caused by singular points placed at the very edge of the overlapped area. Singular points are points where fingerprint ridges show discontinuity. Since our approach separates orientations partially based on the continuity of ridges, when singular points appear at the very edge of the overlapped area it is very possible for some error to occur

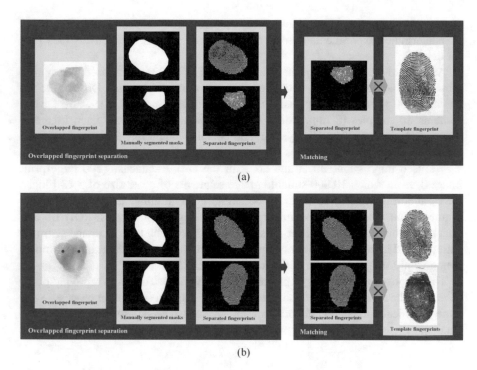

Fig. 6.4 Failure cases, caused by: (**a**) poor manual mask segmentation; (**b**) singular points (marked with red dots) placed at the edge of overlapped area

in the first iterations of orientation separation process. The error propagates to the whole overlapped area, causing unreliable separation results (see [10] for details).

6.7   Concluding Remarks

In this chapter we discussed a new method for separation of overlapped fingerprints based on machine learning techniques, specifically neural networks. This method was the first to use neural networks to address the overlapped fingerprint separation problem. It was also the first method in the literature that utilizes a global-based orientation field enhancement model of single region orientation field prior to separating overlapped region orientations in order to minimize influence of local-based orientation estimation model. As a result, the orientation field becomes more lifelike and produces a more accurate input data for the subsequent processing steps. Similarly to all previous approaches in this field, the proposed method does not use additional manual intervention except for component fingerprint masks markup [10].

Takeaways from this chapter:

- The overlapped fingerprint orientation separation method described in this chapter consists of three stages: (1) overlapped region orientation field estimation based on neural networks; (2) estimated overlapped region orientation field smoothing; and (3) component fingerprints' orientation field enhancement.
- Experimental results show that the described method is competitive with the most prominent approaches to the same problem in the literature.
- The proposed neural network based method represents a significant advance towards the development of a fully automated system for overlapped fingerprints separation.

References

1. F. Chen, J. Feng, A. Jain, J. Zhou, J. Zhang, Separating overlapped fingerprints. IEEE Trans. Inf. Forensics Secur. **6**(2), 346–359 (2011). ISSN 1556-6013. https://doi.org/10.1109/TIFS.2011.2114345
2. J.G. Daugman, Uncertainty relation for resolution in space, spatial frequency, and orientation optimized by two-dimensional visual cortical filters. J. Opt. Soc. Am. A **2**(7), 1160–1169 (1985)
3. J. Feng, Y. Shi, J. Zhou, Robust and efficient algorithms for separating latent overlapped fingerprints. IEEE Trans. Inf. Forensics Secur. **7**(5), 1498–1510 (2012). ISSN 1556-6013. https://doi.org/10.1109/TIFS.2012.2204254
4. J. Feng, J. Zhou, A. Jain, Orientation field estimation for latent fingerprint enhancement. IEEE Trans. Pattern Anal. Mach. Intell. **35**(4), 925–940 (2013). ISSN 0162-8828. https://doi.org/10.1109/TPAMI.2012.155
5. M.H. Hassoun, *Fundamentals of Artificial Neural Networks* (MIT Press, Cambridge, 1995)
6. L. Hong, Y. Wan, A. Jain, Fingerprint image enhancement: algorithm and performance evaluation. IEEE Trans. Pattern Anal. Mach. Intell. **20**(8), 777–789 (1998)
7. A. Jain, J. Feng, Latent palmprint matching. IEEE Trans. Pattern Anal. Mach. Intell. **31**(6), 1032–1047 (2009). ISSN 0162-8828. https://doi.org/10.1109/TPAMI.2008.242
8. D. Maio, D. Maltoni, R. Cappelli, J.L. Wayman, A.K. Jain, FVC2002: second fingerprint verification competition, in *Proceedings of the 16th International Conference on Pattern Recognition, 2002*, vol. 3 (IEEE, Piscataway, 2002), pp. 811–814
9. Y. Shi, J. Zhou, Separating overlapped fingerprints using constrained relaxation labeling, in *Proceedings of the International Joint Conference on Biometrics* (2011)
10. B. Stojanović, A. Nešković, O. Marques, A novel neural network based approach to latent overlapped fingerprints separation. Multimed. Tools Appl. 1–25 (2016). https://doi.org/10.1007/s11042-016-3696-4
11. N. Zhang, Y. Zang, X. Yang, X. Jia, J. Tian, Adaptive orientation model fitting for latent overlapped fingerprints separation. IEEE Trans. Inf. Forensics Secur. **9**(10), 1547–1556 (2014). ISSN 1556-6013. https://doi.org/10.1109/TIFS.2014.2340573

Printed in the United States
By Bookmasters

Herbs and Healers from the Ancient Mediterranean through the Medieval West

Essays in Honor of John M. Riddle

Edited by

ANNE VAN ARSDALL
University of New Mexico, USA

TIMOTHY GRAHAM
University of New Mexico, USA

Routledge
Taylor & Francis Group

LONDON AND NEW YORK

First published 2012 by Ashgate Publishing

2 Park Square, Milton Park, Abingdon, Oxon OX14 4RN
711 Third Avenue, New York, NY 10017, USA

Routledge is an imprint of the Taylor & Francis Group, an informa business

First issued in paperback 2017

British Library Cataloguing in Publication Data
Herbs and healers from the ancient Mediterranean through
  the medieval West : essays in honor of John M. Riddle. --
  (Medicine in the medieval Mediterranean)
  1. Medicine, Ancient. 2. Medicine, Medieval. 3. Pharmacy--History--To 1500.
  4. Materia medica, Vegetable--History--To 1500. 5. Healers--History--To 1500.
  I. Series II. Riddle, John M. III. Van Arsdall, Anne, 1939-
  IV. Graham, Timothy.
  615.3'21'09-dc23

Library of Congress Cataloging-in-Publication Data
Herbs and healers from the Ancient Mediterranean through the Medieval West :
essays in honor of John M. Riddle / edited by Anne Van Arsdall and Timothy Graham.
    p. cm. -- (Medicine in the medieval Mediterranean)
  Includes index.
  ISBN 978-1-4094-0038-7 (hardcover)
  1. Medicine, Ancient. 2. Medicine, Medieval. 3. Materia medica, Vegetable--Great Britain--Early
works to 1500. 4. Pharmacy--History--To 1500. 5. Healers--History--To 1500. I. Riddle, John M. II.
Van Arsdall, Anne, 1939- III. Graham, Timothy.
  R135.H47 2012
  610.938--dc23

                                                                              2011047281

  ISBN 978-1-4094-0038-7 (hbk)
  ISBN 978-1-138-11595-8 (pbk)

Contents

List of Figures

List of Tables and Boxes

Note on Font

We would like to thank Alec McAllister for permission to use the LeedsUni font in this book.

List of Contributors

Winston Black received his Ph.D. from the Centre for Medieval Studies at the University of Toronto and is the Haslam Postdoctoral Fellow in the Marco Institute for Medieval and Renaissance Studies at the University of Tennessee, Knoxville. His research and publications are dedicated to the intersections of religion and medicine in the High Middle Ages, particularly in the realms of canon law and pastoral care. He has edited and translated the verse herbal *Anglicanus ortus* by Henry, Archdeacon of Huntingdon, published by the Pontifical Institute of Mediaeval Studies and the Bodleian Library (2012). He is the recipient of the 2012 Jerry Stannard Memorial Prize for his contribution to the present volume.

John K. Crellin holds British qualifications in medicine and in pharmacy and a M.Sc. and Ph.D. in the History of Science. His career spans three countries, at the Wellcome Institute for the History of Medicine in the U.K., at Southern Illinois and Duke Universities in the U.S.A., and at Memorial University of Newfoundland, Canada, where he was John Clinch Professor of Medical History until 2002. He is now Honorary Research Professor at Memorial. His papers and books span a variety of topics, but with a sustained interest in the history of therapy.

Maria Amalia D'Aronco taught Germanic philology at the University of Udine from 1969 until her retirement in 2008. She held the rank of Professor from 1990 and was Deputy Rector of the university from 2001 to 2008, with special responsibility for international programs. Her research and publications address Old and Middle English language and literature and their relationship with the Latin language and the late classical tradition. In particular, in the field of Old English medicine and botany, she has studied the diffusion of medical and scientific knowledge in England from the eighth to the twelfth century. Among her many other publications, she is principal editor of *The Old English Illustrated Pharmacopoeia: British Library Cotton Vitellius C III* (1998).

Florence Eliza Glaze earned her Ph.D. from Duke University and is now Associate Professor of History and Department Chair at Coastal Carolina University. Her special interests include the transmission and adaptations of medical literature from late antiquity to around the year 1200, with a particular focus on extant manuscripts showing evidence of medieval readers' efforts to apprehend Greek and Arabic terminologies. She has published a variety of articles and essays on these interests, and most recently co-edited and contributed to *Between Text and Patient: The Medical Enterprise in Medieval and Early Modern Europe* (2011). She is currently completing a critical edition and analysis of Gariopontus of Salerno's *Passionarius*, which survives in more than 70 manuscripts.

Timothy Graham holds an M.Phil. in Renaissance Studies from the Warburg Institute, University of London, and a Ph.D. in Anglo-Saxon, Norse, and Celtic from Cambridge University. He is currently Director of the Institute for Medieval Studies and Professor of History at the University of New Mexico, having previously held positions at the University of Manchester, Corpus Christi College, Cambridge, and Western Michigan University. His research centers on Anglo-Saxon manuscripts and their use by scholars of the early modern period. He is co-author of *The Recovery of the Past in Early Elizabethan England* (1998) and *Introduction to Manuscript Studies* (2007). His previous edited books include *Medieval Art: Recent Perspectives* (1998) and *The Recovery of Old English: Anglo-Saxon Studies in the Sixteenth and Seventeenth Centuries* (2000).

Gundolf Keil is Professor Emeritus at the University of Würzburg, where he was Director of the Institute for the History of Medicine from 1973 until 2004, then Director of the Gerhard-Möbus-Institut für Schlesienforschung until his retirement in 2011. The Silesian University of Opava (Czech Republic) awarded him an honorary doctorate in 2003. He earned his Ph.D. at the University of Heidelberg in 1961 and his M.D. at the University at Bonn in 1969. He has held academic positions at the universities of Göttingen, Bonn, Freiburg, Stockholm, and Marburg. Professor Keil's research on the history of medicine and medical texts extends from ancient Egypt to the Middle Ages and Renaissance and into the era of modern medicine; in recent publications he has dealt especially with technical medical literature of the late medieval period. He is recognized as an international authority on the history of medicine.

Helmut W. Klug holds a Master's degree in German and English from the University of Graz. His thesis was on "Kräuter in der deutschsprachigen Dichtung des Hochmittelalters: Vorkommen, Anwendung und Wirkung in ausgewählten Texten" (Herbs in Middle High German Poetry: Occurrence, Use, and Effects in Selected Texts). He started working for the online Dictionary of Old English Plant Names project at the university in 2005. His studies of medieval plants led to research on the legend of the mandrake plant, the analysis of medieval plant paintings, and an inquiry into the seasonings used in Middle High German cooking recipes. He is interested in the Internet and social media as means for knowledge generation and academic online collaboration, as well as in their use in media didactics. He is currently working as an Assistant Lecturer at the University of Graz and finishing his dissertation.

Karen Reeds, Princeton Research Forum and Visiting Scholar at the University of Pennsylvania, is an independent historian of science and curator. She is a Fellow of the Linnean Society of London. Her books and exhibitions include *Botany in Medieval and Renaissance Universities* (1991), *A State of Health: New Jersey's Medical Heritage* (2001), *Visualizing Medieval Medicine and Natural History, 1200–1550* (2006; co-editor, with Jean A. Givens and Alain Touwaide), "Come into a New World: Linnaeus and America" (American-Swedish Historical Museum, Philadelphia, 2007), and "Botanica Magnifica: Photographs by Jonathan Singer" (New Jersey State Museum, Trenton, 2012).

John Scarborough is Professor in the School of Pharmacy and the Departments of History and Classics at the University of Wisconsin, Madison. Among his books are *Roman Medicine* (1969, 1976; 2nd edn in preparation), *Facets of Hellenic Life* (1976), *Symposium on Byzantine Medicine* (ed., 1985), *Folklore and Folk Medicines* (ed., 1987), and *Medical Terminologies: Classical Origins* (1992; 2nd edn published as *Medical and Biological Terminologies: Classical Origins*, 1998). He is co-editor, with Paul T. Keyser, of *The Oxford Handbook of Science and Medicine in Classical Antiquity*, to appear in 2013.

Alain Touwaide has been investigating ancient, medieval, and Renaissance texts on botany, medical substances (including venoms and poisons), and pharmacy for over three decades. His activity focuses on locating manuscripts, recovering and publishing texts, interpreting them, and making them available for further investigation, be they historical or pharmaceutico-medical. Originally a classicist (Ph.D. from the University of Louvain, Belgium), he crosses the boundaries of—and brings together—traditional disciplines (humanities, sciences, and medicine). Currently a Historian of Sciences at the Smithsonian Institution in Washington, D.C., he is a co-founder and the Scientific Director of the Institute for the Preservation of Medical Traditions.

Anne Van Arsdall is a Research Associate of the Institute for Medieval Studies at the University of New Mexico. From 2003 to 2010, she was editor of the annual *AVISTA Forum Journal*, devoted to medieval science, technology, art, and medicine. In addition to her book, *Medieval Herbal Remedies: The Old English Herbarium and Anglo-Saxon Medicine* (2002), she has published a number of articles and given presentations primarily in the field of early medieval medicine and topics related to it. Those topics include ancient and medieval legends connected to the mandrake plant, and the relationship of texts to the transmission of technical knowledge, particularly as seen in early medieval medical texts.

Linda Ehrsam Voigts is Curators' Professor of English Emerita at the University of Missouri, Kansas City. Her research concentrates on medicine and science of medieval England, especially on texts in the vernacular. With Patricia Deery Kurtz she published on CD *Scientific and Medical Writings in Old and Middle English* (University of Michigan Press, 2001). A second edition (eVK2), along with an electronic edition of Lynn Thorndike and Pearl Kibre, *A Catalogue of Incipits of Mediaeval Scientific Writings in English* (eTK), can be searched via a link at http://www.medievalacademy.org.

Faith Wallis is Associate Professor at McGill University, Montreal, and holds a joint appointment in the Department of History and the Department of Social Studies of Medicine. Her publications include *Bede: The Reckoning of Time* (Liverpool University Press, rev. ed. 2004), *Bede: On the Nature of Things and On Times* (with Calvin Kendall, Liverpool University Press, 2010), and *Medieval Medicine: A Reader* (University of Toronto Press, 2010). With Steven Livesey and Thomas Glick, she edited *Medieval Science, Technology and Medicine: An Encyclopedia* (Routledge, 2005).

Roman Weinberger is a Web and software developer with several years of professional experience. In addition, he has a M.Sc. degree in Psychology/ Cognitive Sciences from the University of Graz. His areas of expertise cover software development (Zemd Framework, WordPress, Ruby on Rails) as well as cognition, e-learning, and knowledge management. At the University of Graz he supervised the development of the PharmXplorer project at the Institute of Pharmaceutical Sciences and the online Dictionary of Old English Plant Names at the Department of English. His research interests are computer security, the Semantic Web, and the Open Source Movement. He is currently working at TAO Software.

Frontispiece   John M. Riddle

Introduction

Alain Touwaide

From Cleopatra and substitution literature in antiquity, to the possible use of ancient therapeutic information as a source for new pharmacological studies, to an Internet project devoted to medieval plant lore, the essays in the present volume walk in the footsteps of John Riddle along his scientific itinerary. At the same time, these new investigations rooted in and capitalizing on Riddle's activity illustrate the many facets and the fertilizing role of his multiple contributions, identify areas that still need to be explored, and propose new approaches for fresh research.

The almost mythical Cleopatra sets the stage. Credited with an expertise in drugs, venoms, poisons, and perfumes illustrated by an abundant apocryphal literature, and believed to have applied such science to herself to commit suicide in a supposedly painless way, she is at the center of an essay by John Scarborough that throws light on physicians in her entourage. With this contribution and the following by Alain Touwaide on a table of substitution drugs that hints at a possible tension between text and practice, we enter directly into the world of ancient materia medica and the practice of pharmacy, with substances from a multitude of places, collections of formulae for medicines and other preparations, and the healers, charlatans, merchants, and others who populated the streets of the capital of the Ptolemaic kingdom and the cities of the late Roman republic and early empire. This world was probably haunted by such figures as—to mention but a few—Mithridates, who took his own life to escape Roman troops, Nicander of Colophon, who composed two poems in Homeric verses on venoms and poisons, and the Roman general Aelius Gallus, who brought formulae for antidotes against venomous snake bites from Arabia to Rome. It was a colorful and intriguing world, frequented by individuals of every provenance, education, and type of activity, manipulating healing herbs, parts of rare animals, and toxic minerals, reading and writing grimoires, pharmacopoeias, and magic incantations alike, and probably also relieving their patients' ailments, although sometimes, instead, taking their lives.

This is the complex world John Riddle entered and tried to decode. It was a world that was not well understood and was even largely unknown when he first engaged with it, following the precursory explorations of Loren MacKinney, Riddle's mentor at the University of North Carolina. Focusing on the Western Middle Ages—without limiting himself to it, however—Riddle came upon the first-century Greek masterwork of Dioscorides, *De materia medica*, which has nourished Western pharmaco-therapeutic practice throughout its history. His research on this masterpiece spanned the period from its origin to its reception during the Renaissance, and this work defined the aim and scope of his own activity. It also established his method: understanding the way ancient and medieval pharmaco-chemical literature worked by getting out of the framework of formal history and exploring the medico-chemical basis of ancient therapeutics, and tracing the path(s) taken by this body of knowledge from its birthplace to the West, following its reception, assimilation, and transformation(s), and also highlighting its foundational role in shaping modern medico-pharmaceutical science.

Each of these components of John Riddle's work is reflected in the present collection in his honor. It constitutes an itinerary in four stages from the eastern Mediterranean to the West, from antiquity to early modern times. After the first two essays on antiquity mentioned above, we cross the Mediterranean from Alexandria to Salerno, the *porta maior* of the road followed by medicine on its way to the West. As Florence Eliza Glaze tells us, Gariopontus was a link between two universes, late antiquity and the new medical world-in-the-making in Salerno 20 or 30 years before Constantine the African. Gariopontus collected existing texts, and reshaped and reorganized them, creating a new medical synthesis. His work, in turn, was further linked with other texts, commented on, explained, and amplified by generations of teacher-commentators until the fifteenth century, and it contributed to creating the Latin medical lexicon in the West. A key element in the reappropriation of the ancient legacy was the theory on drug actions, particularly the Galenic system of degrees. As Faith Wallis's analysis of Constantine's *Liber graduum* and its commentaries shows, the medieval attempts to reassimilate such theory into medicine were not necessarily successful. Her essay shows that, if Constantine's treatise was studied in the early Middle Ages, including by Bartholomeus of Salerno, it did not make its way into the core text of theoretical medieval medicine, the *Articella*. That work was initially focused on diagnosis and prognosis (with some theoretical notions) and slightly expanded later to include therapeutic actions. Nevertheless, the theory of degrees was not simply ignored in the Middle Ages.

As Winston Black explains in his essay, as early as one or two generations after Constantine lived, his work was versified across the Alps as far away as England. Such poems were reproduced for almost 500 years, reaching the age of printing, most probably because they were read and used. Nevertheless, whereas these works and their subsequent tradition attest to the importance and usefulness of theory, they also point to the reason why such theory failed to be included in some textbooks of learned medicine: in Constantine's *Liber graduum* it was problematic and unclear in more than one passage. These difficult parts were simplified or omitted in many of the poems that versified Constantine's treatise. They thus simplified the *Liber graduum* into basic information so as to make it easily assimilable in the practice of therapeutics and gave to the theory of degrees a sort of extracurricular continuity that guaranteed its presence in medieval medicine.

In its third part, the volume moves toward the heart of Northern Europe and goes beyond the Middle Ages to pre-modern botany. It begins, however, with Maria Amalia D'Aronco commenting on the late antique pharmaceutical corpus and its translation from Latin into Old English in the tenth-century Anglo-Saxon world. Translators did not always know the exact equivalent of the plant names mentioned in the texts they were working on and opted for different strategies to render them. Some resulted in namings that are still mysterious. This is the case of *elehtre*, a plant whose identity has puzzled interpreters for years. A plausible identification is proposed here, which sheds new light on the mechanics of medical lore beyond the transmission of ancient data in England and the discovery of the therapeutic properties of plants. Whereas early Anglo-Saxon translators had difficulty with Latin texts, later English writers, including Chaucer, were so much at ease with medicinal plants and their properties that they could use them as a matter for jokes that all audiences could understand, from the learned to the popular, thus witnessing to the assimilation and diffusion of knowledge of plant lore in society, as Linda Ehrsam Voigts demonstrates here.

The mechanisms underpinning the circulation, assimilation, and transformation(s) of earlier texts in Central Europe were probably not much different and require patient textual analysis to bring to light material hidden in apparently well-known works. As Gundolf Keil shows, this is the case for a group of manuscripts containing the Old German translation of a Salernitan text, Roger's *Aphorisms*, into which they introduced material from other works. A close textual scrutiny uncovers a manual of surgery specifically devoted to the treatment of hemorrhages, extraction of projectiles, and wounds due to weapons. This manual may date back to the early fifteenth century and is probably the most ancient in German on the treatment of wounds caused by firearms. Together with three others previously known, this newly discovered treatise attests to a developed knowledge of field surgery that played an important role in the Central European conflicts of that time.

Turning again to plant lore and its transmission through the ages, Karen Reeds demonstrates how the classical tradition was later challenged by new interpretations, using Saint John's Wort as an example. Whereas the 1546 *Kreüter Buoch* by Tragus, actually Hieronymus Bock, reveals an anti-classical trend—it was written in German, for Germans, and was about German plants, also providing readers with a table of diseases in German—it stayed close to Dioscorides and Galen in the description of the effects of the plant. At the same time, however, it reproduced popular traditions, magical practices, and folklore. Bock's contemporary, Paracelsus, departed further from the classical tradition, emptying out Galenic properties and prescribing Saint John's Wort on a magical, apotropaic basis in a way that meant the end of its classical uses. Strangely enough, however, the modern use of Saint John's Wort as an antidepressant is said to be based on Paracelsus.

The study of Saint John's Wort leads us to the fourth stage in our journey with John Riddle from the Mediterranean into the European West and from the past to the present day. John K. Crellin's study echoes Riddle's pharmacological analysis of ancient and medieval pharmaceutical prescriptions and their possible application in contemporary pharmaceutical studies, and also suggests future scientific research in the history of medieval pharmacy. Firmly convinced of the scientific value and therapeutic efficacy of ancient drug lore—perceptible through the "drug affinity" system that he detected in Dioscorides' classification of drugs—John Riddle explored the world of contraceptive and abortifacient agents in ancient and medieval literature. He believed that such substances were the object of widespread common knowledge that was later forgotten. His two books on this topic, *Eve's Herbs: A History of Contraception and Abortion in the West* and *Contraception and Abortion from the Ancient World to the Renaissance*—now followed by *Goddesses, Elixirs, and Witches: Plants and Sexuality throughout Human History*—triggered a polemic that even today invites us to try to perceive the factors that may have guided and still guide practitioners in choices of one therapeutic strategy over another. The accumulation of micro-decisions over a period of time may lead to significant changes, characterized by the emergence of new drugs and methods of treatment and the abandonment of others, however well rooted and widely practiced for a certain period. This type of fundamental, hard-to-ascertain information is exactly what historians, be they of pharmacy or any other aspect of human life, must try to ascertain in the texts they read.

The current unprecedented development of information technologies, with their cutting-edge ideas and shortening of communication time, enable access to information, sharing of resources, and accumulation of data in a way previously impossible. To conclude the volume, Helmut W. Klug and Roman Weinberger describe their newly developed Internet tool, the Medieval Plant Survey, as an effective means for scholars to collaborate and collectively sum up all currently available information on medieval plants. Such a tool can enable new investigations into the realm of medicinal plants, relying on a collective database that includes not only all available data, but also all approaches to the data.

Through this literary itinerary, the present collection of essays not only revisits John Riddle's journey into medieval pharmaceutical literature—which was almost a *terra incognita* when he embarked on his explorations—but also illustrates the validity of his method: from the deciphering of texts to the interpretation of their contents by introducing medicine, pharmacy, and chemistry into historical studies. This is certainly his most original achievement, one that will undoubtedly be his most enduring contribution to scholarship.

Chapter 1

Pharmacology and Toxicology at the Court of Cleopatra VII: Traces of Three Physicians

John Scarborough

In a tattered papyrus, recovered from the charred scrolls in the Villa dei Papiri in Herculaneum, is a scorched remnant in eight columns of a Latin poem, *Carmen de Bello Actiaco* (*The Battle of Actium*). With some difficulty regarding orthography, since its original unrolling in 1805, scholars gradually have deciphered, edited, and translated this priceless bit of almost contemporary history.[1] The full epic most likely focused on the actions and participants in the naval battle at Actium (31 BC), in which Octavian emerged victorious over Antony and Cleopatra, and the poet—who remains anonymous, although Rabirius seems favored among classical scholars—details characteristic behaviors of the protagonists; two of the eight surviving columns describe, with bloodthirsty relish, Cleopatra's "experiments" with methods of murder on living human beings:

> ... and the place assigned, where the crowd of criminals would collect and provide sad
> spectacles of their own deaths. Just as, for an army and fleet on the point of attack,
> weapons, flags, and trumpets are readied this is what the place looked like, as the cruel
> instruments of death were collected, brought together in varying stages of readiness.
> Thus, every kind of ugly death, every kind of ugly fear, was gathered there on the field.
> One man lies cut down by the sword; another is swollen with poison, or with an asp
> hanging on his throat he slips into sleep, led on by his lust for death; another a small
> basilisk strikes with his hisses alone, without a bite; or a tiny bit of poison smeared in
> a small wound does away with him more quickly; others are forced by tight nooses to
> pour forth their last breath through compressed passages; and others had their throats

---

[1]   *P.Herc.* 817. For the text, see Edward Courtney, *The Fragmentary Latin Poets* (Oxford: Clarendon Press, 1993), 334–41 (*Carmen de Bello Actiaco*), esp. cols 5 and 6 (pp. 338–9), with commentary; discussion in David Sider, *The Library of the Villa dei Papiri at Herculaneum* (Los Angeles: J. Paul Getty Museum, 2005), 66–8.

closed when they were immersed in water. In the midst of this slaughter she descended from her throne and in the midst of ...[2]

Similarly, Plutarch gives purported details of Cleopatra's heartless trials on slaves and criminals, seeking means of rapid demise through poisons[3]—probably tales based on Alexandrian traditions, also reflected in Galen's version of the famous suicide.[4] Many scholars have questioned the standard account of that suicide,[5] and it is clear the bite of an Egyptian cobra would not guarantee an instant and painless death.[6] Cleopatra herself had a fairly well-founded expertise in the lore of drugs and poisons,[7] poisonous snakes, and other presumably harmful creatures native to Egypt, even though she bequeathed in her often-quoted works—assumed by authorities in Roman antiquity to be genuine—a respected proficiency in the arts of cosmetics,[8] as contrasted to the more

---

[2]   The translation is by Sider, *Library*, 67–8.

[3]   Plutarch, *Life of Antony*, 71.6–8; ed. C.P.R. Pelling (Cambridge: Cambridge University Press, 1988), 104. Cf. Dio Cassius, *Roman History*, 51.11.2, ed. Earnest Cary and Herbert Baldwin Foster, Loeb Classical Library (9 vols, London: Heinemann, 1914–27), 6:30–32; and Aelian, *On the Characteristics of Animals*, 9.11, ed. A.F. Scholfield, Loeb Classical Library (3 vols, Cambridge, MA: Harvard University Press, 1958–59), 2:230.

[4]   Galen, *Theriac to Piso*, 8, in *Claudii Galeni Opera omnia*, ed. C.G. Kühn (20 vols in 22, Leipzig: C. Cnobloch, 1821–33; repr. Hildesheim: Georg Olms, 1964–65), 14:233–7; Francesco Sbordone, "La morte di Cleopatra nei medici greci," in his *Scritti di varia filologia* (Naples: Giannini, 1971), 1–32; Plutarch, *Antony*, ed. Pelling, 296 (comm. on Antony, 71.6); Gabrielle Marasco, "Cleopatra e gli esperimenti su cavie umane," *Historia* 44 (1995): 317–25.

[5]   Plutarch, *Antony*, ed. Pelling, 296–7; François P. Retief and Louise Cilliers, "The Death of Cleopatra," in François P. Retief and Louise Cilliers, *Health and Healing, Disease and Death in the Graeco-Roman World* (Bloemfontein: University of the Free State, 2005), 79–88 (esp. 85–7); Duane W. Roller, *Cleopatra: A Biography* (Oxford: Oxford University Press, 2010), 148–9.

[6]   John Scarborough, "Nicander's Toxicology, I: Snakes," *Pharmacy in History* 19 (1977): 3–23 (esp. 17–18), reprinted as ch. 5 in John Scarborough, *Pharmacy and Drug Lore in Antiquity: Greece, Rome, Byzantium* (Farnham, UK, and Burlington, VT: Ashgate, 2010).

[7]   Plutarch, *Antony*, 71.6-8 and 86.4 (ed. Pelling, 104 and 113); Ilse Becher, *Das Bild der Kleopatra in der griechischen und lateinischen Literatur* (Berlin: Akademie-Verlag, 1966), esp. 155–6 and 172; P.M. Fraser, *Ptolemaic Alexandria* (3 vols, Oxford: Clarendon Press, 1972), 1:372 and 2:548 with nn. 305–7.

[8]   E.g., Galen, *Compound Drugs According to Place on the Body*, 1.1, in *Opera omnia*, ed. Kühn, 12:403–5: from Cleopatra's books on cosmetics, esp. on hair loss (*alopecias*); ibid., 1.2 (ed. Kühn, 12:432–5): from Cleopatra's books on hair-growers; and ibid., 1.8 (ed. Kühn, 12:492–3): on cures for dandruff from Cleopatra's books on cosmetics. Galen most likely obtained his blocks of quotations from Cleopatra's works in a circulating collection of texts assembled by Criton, chief physician to Trajan (AD 98–117). Cajus Fabricius, *Galens Exzerpte aus älteren Pharmakologen* (Berlin: Walter de Gruyter, 1972), 201–2 ("Kleopatra"); John Scarborough, "Criton, Physician to Trajan: Historian and Pharmacist," in John W. Eadie and Josiah Ober (eds), *The Craft of the*

ominous reputation (in company with Mithridates VI of Pontus and Attalus III of Pergamon) of being a royal toxicologist.[9]

Plutarch mentions that an important source for his account of Cleopatra's death was a physician named Olympus, who apparently was present when the queen committed suicide.[10] If Olympus was the author of any medical writings, he has left us with no actual tracts, nor do later authorities mention any of his works.[11] Jacoby simply records the Greek text in Plutarch, with his blunt commentary that scholars who have attempted connections with Octavian/ Augustus are sadly misled, quoting the renowned line from Plutarch, "nobody

---

Ancient Historian: Essays in Honor of Chester G. Starr (Lanham, MD: University Press of America, 1985), 387–405, reprinted as ch. 11 in Scarborough, *Pharmacy and Drug Lore in Antiquity*; John Scarborough with Alain Touwaide, "Kriton of Herakleia Salbake, T. Statilius," in Paul T. Keyser and Georgia Irby-Massie (eds), *The Encyclopedia of Ancient Natural Scientists: The Greek Tradition and Its Many Heirs* (London: Routledge, 2008), 494–5. As late as the sixth century, Cleopatra was cited as an authority, e.g., Cleopatra's formula for a beauty soap in Aetius of Amida's *Tetrabiblon*, 8.6; see *Aetii Amideni Libri medicinales V–VIII*, ed. Alexander Olivieri, *Corpus Medicorum Graecorum* 8.2 (Berlin: Academiae Litterarum, 1950), 408.

[9] Hellenistic courts all were famed for their employment of "royal" physicians, whose medical skills often focused on foods and the frequent attempts at assassination through a monarchical meal. The Seleucids, Ptolemies, Attalids, etc., have left traces of their physicians in later sources (mostly Galen), and some achieved political notoriety in their own right. Attilio Mastrocinque, "Les médecins des Séleucides," in Ph. J. van der Eijk, H.F.J. Horstmanshoff, and P.H. Schrijvers (eds), *Ancient Medicine in Its Socio-Cultural Context: Papers Read at the Congress Held at Leiden University, 13–15 April 1992* (2 vols, Amsterdam: Rodopi, 1995), 1:143–51; John Scarborough, "Attalus III of Pergamon: Research Toxicologist," in Louise Cilliers (ed.), *Asklepios: Studies on Ancient Medicine*, Acta Classica Supplementum 2 (Bloemfontein: Classical Association of South Africa, 2008), 138–56; Heinrich von Staden, "Andreas," in *Herophilus: The Art of Medicine in Early Alexandria* (Cambridge: Cambridge University Press, 1989), 472–7.

[10] Plutarch, *Antony*, 82.4 (ed. Pelling, 111). Pelling argues that Olympus is behind much of the account in Plutarch's *Life of Antony*, 77.3, and for details throughout 71–87; ibid., 307 and 313. Roller, *Cleopatra*, 148.

[11] Drugs called "The Olympic" or "The Olympus" (e.g., Paul of Aegina, 3.22.22 and 7.16.24, see *Paulus Aegineta*, ed. J.L. Heiberg, Corpus Medicorum Graecorum 9 [2 vols, Leipzig: Teubner, 1921–24], 1:180 and 2:339) are "brand names," not necessarily named for an individual inventor of a compound. The "Olympionicus" at Galen, *Opera omnia*, ed. Kühn, 12:753, is not "Olympus," the physician to Cleopatra, and for the pharmacologist named at Galen, *Opera omnia*, 13:261, Kühn carries an extra iota, viz. "Olympius." Unless a scribal error or corruption in the printed Greek text, this obscure Olympius is not the same man as recorded by Plutarch. Moreover, the pharmaceutical formula attributed to Olympius is for the fashioning of an emollient plaster (*malagma*) made from seeds (*to dia ton spermaton pharmakon*), and includes garden-variety ingredients, certainly not a "royal" compound.

knows the truth."[12] We cannot, therefore, determine if Olympus had any influence on the queen's learning in pharmaceuticals, but he certainly represents the continual presence of a "royal physician" attending to her requirements. It is also probable that Olympus' "journal" had some limited circulation, and it seems reasonable to suppose that Galen's often-expressed disgust at Alexandrian mores (which included the supposedly humane methods of execution by means of cobra bites)[13] may have surfaced, in part, from such eyewitness accounts, perhaps available through the book trade.

Firmer testimony on the circle of physicians who ministered to the medical needs of Antony, Cleopatra, and others of this late Ptolemaic court[14] offers details of the pharmacology involved in the practice of medicine among royalty, as well as some anecdotal evidence on how a doctor functioned in the milieu of one of the most famous imperial entourages in classical antiquity. Connections are secure in the texts for two other physicians, Philotas of Amphissa (*c.* 55 BC–AD 30) and Dioscorides "Phacas" (*fl. c.* 80–45 BC), but links to the Ptolemaic court during the reign of Cleopatra VII of four more doctors then resident in Alexandria (Sostratus, Apollonius "the Mouse" [*Mys*], Ammonius, and Philoxenus)[15] are woolly at best and generally conjectured alone on simple chronology and locale.

Philotas of Amphissa was one of the young medical attendants serving Marcus Antonius Antyllus, Marc Antony's elder son by Fulvia (born probably

---

[12]   Felix Jacoby, *Die Fragmente der griechischen Historiker*, Pt 2B (Leiden: Brill, 1962), no. 198 (pp. 929–30), and *Kommentar zu Nr. 106–261* (Leiden: Brill, 1962), no. 198 (p. 625); Plutarch, *Antony*, 86.4 (ed. Pelling, 113).

[13]   Galen, *Theriac to Piso*, 8, in *Opera omnia*, ed. Kühn, 14:237. Vivian Nutton, "Galen and Egypt," in Jutta Kollesch and Diethard Nickel (eds), *Galen und das hellenistische Erbe: Verhandlungen des IV. Internationalen Galen-Symposiums veranstaltet vom Institut für Geschichte der Medizin am Bereich Medizin (Charité) der Humboldt-Universität zu Berlin 18.–20. September 1989* (Stuttgart: Franz Steiner, 1993), 11–31 (esp. 26). Nutton presents a strong set of arguments for the acceptance of *Theriac to Piso* as "genuine" from Galen's pen in "Galen on Theriac: Problems of Authenticity," in Armelle Debru (ed.), *Galen on Pharmacology: Philosophy, History, and Medicine. Proceedings of the Vth International Galen Colloquium, Lille, 16–18 March 1995* (Leiden: Brill, 1997), 133–51, an opinion shared with Simon Swain, *Hellenism and Empire: Language, Classicism and Power in the Greek World, AD 50–250* (Oxford: Clarendon Press, 1996), 430–32 (Appendix D: "Galen's *On Theriac to Piso*").

[14]   Fraser, *Ptolemaic Alexandria*, 1:371–2 and 2:547–8 with nn. 303–8.

[15]   Max Wellmann in Franz Susemihl, *Geschichte der griechischen Literatur in der Alexandrinerzeit* (2 vols, Leipzig: Teubner, 1891–92), 2:442–5; von Staden, *Herophilus*, 540–54 (Apollonius "the Mouse").

in late 47 or 46 BC).[16] In the early 30s BC, Philotas returned to Amphissa after completing his medical studies at Alexandria. At the age of about 75,[17] Delphi honored Philotas with an inscription for his numerous years of service.[18] Plutarch's grandfather, Lamprias, listened with unbridled fascination to the stories of the then-elderly and quite garrulous Philotas, tales that included the luxurious culinary habits of Antony and Cleopatra: according to the oral narratives, as reported by Plutarch, Antony and Cleopatra insisted that eight boars should be in separate stages of roasting, so that when the royal couple called for their meal, the meat would be done to perfection.[19] Oral sources were quite important to Plutarch,[20] and he provides a valuable characterization of his grandfather's particular style of storytelling, and why a little wine went a long way: Lamprias was "his most eloquent and resourcefully clever self while imbibing, saying that since frankincense becomes vaporous fumes from heat, thus he was made so by wine."[21]

Philotas acquired some of the usual medical theories while he was a student in Alexandria, most likely attending lectures given by noted medical philosophers of the day, who perhaps espoused a common version of "Hippocratic" or Aristotelian notions of opposites as they existed in the wider universe and in the physiologies of animals and humans. Another third-hand report from the mouth of Lamprias suggests a "social application" of medical theory in debates and conversations some time in the 40s and 30s BC. During an evening meal with Marcus Antonius Antyllus and his cronies and attendants, the youthful Philotas challenged an apparently annoying older physician in his cups with a blunt analysis of how a doctor might treat fevers: "To someone who is slightly feverish, one must administer something cold; and anyone who displays a fever is slightly feverish; therefore everyone who is feverish should be given cold [water]."[22]

---

[16]   Eleanor Goltz Huzar, *Mark Antony: A Biography* (Minneapolis: University of Minnesota Press, 1978), 70–71.

[17]   W.A. Oldfather, "A Friend of Plutarch's Grandfather," *Classical Philology* 19 (1924): 177.

[18]   Plutarch, *Antony*, ed. Pelling, 195; *Supplementum epigraphicum graecum* (Leiden: Brill, 1923–), 1:181.

[19]   Plutarch, *Antony*, 28.3 (ed. Pelling, 70).

[20]   C.P. Jones, *Plutarch and Rome* (Oxford: Clarendon Press, 1971), 10; Fergus Millar, "The Mediterranean and the Roman Revolution: Politics, War and the Economy," *Past and Present* 102 (1984): 3–24 (esp. 23–4 with n. 97); Plutarch, *Antony*, ed. Pelling, 29 and 195.

[21]   Plutarch, *Moralia: Table-Talk*, 1.5.622E, ed. F.C. Babbitt et al., Loeb Classical Library (14 vols, London: Heinemann, 1927–76), 8:64; my trans.

[22]   Plutarch, *Antony*, 28.2 (ed. Pelling, 70; my trans.).

Mirrored in the fragments of Philotas' writings, pharmacology was an important aspect of medical instruction in Alexandria, and one can surmise that he applied such knowledge in the context of the Ptolemaic court. Perhaps Philotas' pharmaceutical formulas and recipes were very useful indeed for soldiers and gladiators, since his *kephalikon* among the *rhaptousi* (compound drugs, normally prepared as plasters, which "sewed up" or "sealed" a wound) would have been immediately applicable in instances of skull fractures and broken bones.[23] Philotas' *kephalikon* includes expected ingredients (beeswax, myrrh and frankincense, the agglutinative Eretrian earth combined with vinegar, four kinds of copper flakes as well as copper rust [*verdigris*], the gummy exudates of birthwort [*Aristolochia* spp.], raw alum, oil of roses, and olive oil), but also, most unusually, 25 *drachmai* of *ichthyokolla*, "fish glue" derived from the natural gelatin made from the sounds or swimming bladders of large freshwater fish, usually sturgeons.[24] Galen notes that Philotas' compound, with its large quantity of fish glue, is also good for inveterate wounds, that is those of "long standing" (*ta chronia*), and for those injuries difficult to treat and heal (*kai dysalthē*), especially "promoting the setting of broken bones and the formation of a callus." Once applied, fish glue dries glass-hard and transparent, and its employment for skull fractures and hard-to-seal wounds continued well into the twentieth century.[25] The Ptolemaic pharmacist first pounded the fish glue in a glass vessel, adding slowly the vinegar, then the copper flakes, and the Greek text concludes

---

[23]   Celsus, *De medicina*, 5.19.7, ed. W.G. Spencer, Loeb Classical Library (3 vols, Cambridge, MA: Harvard University Press, 1935–38), 2:34; Asclepiades in Galen, *Compound Drugs According to Kind*, 4.13, in *Opera omnia*, ed. Kühn, 13:745.

[24]   Often called "isinglass" due to its resemblance to naturally occurring mica sheets. Pliny, *Natural History*, 32.73, 84–5, and 119, ed. H. Rackham et al., Loeb Classical Library (10 vols, Cambridge, MA: Harvard University Press, 1938–63), 8:508, 514–16, and 536; Dioscorides, *De materia medica libri quinque*, 3.88, ed. Max Wellmann (3 vols, Berlin: Weidmann, 1958), 2:103, which is not very informative (Dioscorides does not seem to know how fish glue is manufactured, or from which type of fish). On sturgeons: D'Arcy W. Thompson, *A Glossary of Greek Fishes* (London: Oxford University Press, 1947), 7–8, 19–20, and 42. Pliny's main description is about fish glue's use as a wrinkle remover (*Natural History*, 32.84–5; ed. Rackham et al., 8:514–16).

[25]   Horatio C. Wood and Charles H. LaWall (eds), *The Dispensatory of the United States of America*, 21st edn (Philadelphia: Lippincott, 1926), 1338 col. 2 and 1339 col. 1. Fish glue retains its value as a natural adhesive and in the clarifying of wines, beers, and other alcoholic beverages, and there is limited use by librarians in the glazing and coating of paper in the repair of single sheets, as well as in priming, binding paint media, glazing, and coating of easel and encaustic paintings and icons. Lee Young Kyu et al., "The Adhesion Property of Fish Glue," *Mokchae Konghak/Journal of Korean Wood Science and Technology* 32 (2004): 59–65; Tatyana Petukhova, "Potential Application of Isinglass Adhesive for Paper Conservation," *Book and Paper Group Annual* 8 (1989): 58–61.

by saying that one fashions the compound into pastilles (*trochiskoi*), which then could be used as small plasters as required. Given the fairly large amount of fish glue and other ingredients (50 *drachmai* of the copper flakes/scales, 100 *drachmai* of the Eretrian earth, the 25 *drachmai* of the fish glue, 12 *kotylai* of vinegar), it appears that the compound was made in bulk and applied to the wounds and fractures presumably of soldiers and gladiators over a period of time. Philotas' inclusion of *ichthyokolla* as a prominent constituent of his *kephalikon* stands out as not quite unique in Greco-Roman pharmacy, but his apparently innovative application of the hardening gelatin to fractures merited the approval of both Celsus and Galen. It is uncertain if fish glue is an effective wrinkle remover, but women in the Roman aristocracy of Pliny's own time seemed to think so. Philotas, however, does not suggest fish glue as a cosmetic treatment, if our fragments represent his work reasonably well.

Philotas also composed recipes in verse, if the testimony in Galen is to be trusted.[26] According to this extract, Philotas composed the formula of ingredients in poetry "for a close friend," and it is a complex, multistage compound for the treatment of "lichen-like eruptions on the skin" (the ailment was known as *leichēn*, the pharmaceutical compound was a *leichēnikon*), and *leichēn* is equivalent to the Latin *mentagra*, an eruption that frequently occurred on the chin. A number of minerals are prominent ingredients (copper flakes, *misy* [copper ore from Cyprus, the copper sulfide ore chalcopyrite, found above *chalkitis*],[27] the famous Egyptian "salt" of Ammon, the Eretrian earth in small quantities, others), and the pharmacist is to mix these in a mortar with a goodly quantity of vinegar; then, after five days, one adds frankincense, myrrh, and other fragrant medicinals including two kinds of birthwort (*Aristolochia* spp.) to be ground in the open air, sunlit during the day; then one forms the compound into a kind of liquefied plaster, using beeswax, the oil of the terebinth tree (*Pistacia terebinthus* L.),[28] galbanum,[29] and olive oil. The result is an emollient salve, which "will be applied to the outgrowths [and] removes them quickly from the surface [of the skin]." One can assume that Philotas' cosmetic dermatology could be somewhat reflected in Cleopatra's often-quoted salves, ointments, and powders, redolent soaps occasionally stuffed with fragrant ingredients that enhanced the health of the skin, certainly essential for frequent appearances at court.

---

[26]   Criton in Galen, *Compounds According to Place on the Body*, 5.3 (*Opera omnia*, ed. Kühn, 12:83–89).

[27]   So says Dioscorides, *De materia medica*, 5.100; ed. Wellmann, 3:71.

[28]   This is the so-called "Chian turpentine," and the galls are used for tanning. George Usher, *A Dictionary of Plants Used by Man* (London: Constable, 1974), 466.

[29]   Probably *Ferula galbaniflua* Boiss. and Buhse., the Indian Kasnib resin. Usher, *Dictionary*, 253.

One is inclined to place Philotas' multi-ingredient eye-salve (an *aphroditarion*, "darling")[30] in the contexts of Antony and Cleopatra's court. Here are 12 *drachmai* of the opium poppy latex, 24 *drachmai* of zinc oxide (*kadmeia*, sometimes called calamine), 36 *drachmai* of gum Arabic from *Acacia* spp., and a whopping 12 *drachmai* of the saffron crocus, along with pure rainwater, to be spread on with an egg, then washed off; the *kollyrion* was supposed to engender a copious flowing of tears, and the inclusion of the saffron crocus certainly made this "tear jerker" a phenomenally expensive ointment, profligately flaunting the easily wasted wealth at the Ptolemaic court. One can only guess what the *aphroditarion* had as a function: perhaps the flowing of tears enhanced one's sexual attractiveness at the point of love-making, or such a copious production of lacrimal fluids could underline one's anger at the point of open rage. Possibly the *aphroditarion* offers a glimpse into the stormy years when Cleopatra seduced Antony into thinking he—not Octavian—was destined to inherit command over the faltering Roman Republic from an Egyptian base.

The third physician known to have practiced in and around Cleopatra's court is Dioscorides "Phacas," whose epithet translates as "The Warty One," or "The Mole-Faced One," or "Warty-Faced." In contrast to Philotas of Amphissa, Dioscorides has left less of a trace for his medical knowledge, even though he was a leading actor in the dramas that attended the early years of the joint reign of Ptolemy XIII and Cleopatra VII. He had been a court physician and roving ambassador in the earlier reign of Ptolemy XII (80–51 BC), and Julius Caesar indicates Dioscorides continued in that role.[31] Caesar, however, is somewhat ambiguous regarding the fate of Dioscorides, while functioning as an emissary of Ptolemy XIII to Achillas, at that time threatening civil war when Caesar's troops were in the city of Alexandria (48 BC): "[Achillas] commanded that they [Dioscorides and Serapion] should be arrested and killed, but one of them was merely wounded and was quickly rescued by his friends and carried away as if he were dead." If Dioscorides indeed survived, he would have been an elderly and wily court physician to Ptolemy XIII and Cleopatra VII, and the Byzantine *Suda* indicates a near-linkage with the phrase, "associated with Cleopatra in the time of Antony."[32] Caesar furthermore reports that Dioscorides had acted as an envoy to Rome in the reign of Ptolemy XII, and was "of the greatest influence on [the king]," so one can presume an equally powerful, if not greater, sway over

30   Galen, *Compounds According to Place on the Body*, 4.7 (*Opera omnia*, ed. Kühn, 12:752).

31   Caesar, *The Civil Wars*, 3.109.3–6, ed. A.G. Peskett, Loeb Classical Library (London: Heinemann, 1914), 352.

32   *Suda* D, 1206, s.v. "Dioscorides"; *Suidae Lexicon*, ed. Ada Adler (5 vols, Leipzig, 1928–38; repr. Stuttgart: Teubner, 1967–71), 2:113.

Ptolemy XII's "rancorous children."[33] The Pseudo-Galen, *Hippocratic Lexicon*,[34] notes Dioscorides was a late member of the Herophilean sect, still operative in Alexandria two centuries after the death of its founder, and the *Suda* continues its terse account by relating that Dioscorides had written 24 books on medical topics. It is reasonably certain that Dioscorides wrote exegetical commentaries on various aspects of the vocabulary in the Hippocratic writings,[35] and von Staden argues that Dioscorides was a "follower" of Herophilus in terms of both Hippocratic exegesis and clinical medicine.[36] Rufus of Ephesus in his *Strange Diseases* (excerpted by Oribasius)[37] records that a Dioscorides (most likely our "Phacas"), along with a Posidonius, had written a work on a nodular-swelling ("bubonic") plague of uncertain time ravaging Libya; and Paul of Aegina quotes directly from a "Dioscorides of Alexandria" that shows a keen ability in the detailed description of skin diseases,[38] in this instance *terminthos*: "Dioscorides of Alexandria says that *terminthoi* are protuberances formed on the skin, that are round and colored dark green, similar to the fruit of the terebinth tree."[39] Perhaps it is significant that both Philotas of Amphissa and Dioscorides "Phacas" should give such prominence to the "fruits" and oils from the "Chian turpentine" tree, *Pistacia terebinthus* L. Skin diseases seem to have been specialties of both physicians, and dermatology coupled with careful pharmacology overlaps what is contained in the Greek texts presumably written by Cleopatra.

A century ago, Max Wellmann cautioned against contriving the court of Cleopatra to be a "center" for medical learning,[40] and one has to remember that Alexandria "the Great" (as Galen liked to call the city) was home to many skilled practitioners of several of the arts and sciences, a traditional status hearkening back to the reign of the first Ptolemy. As famed as might be the ultimately tragic story of Cleopatra VII and her two Roman lovers (Julius Caesar and Marc Antony), it behooves the student of Hellenistic Alexandria to shed exaggerations that can only be designated as fiction. To be sure, Cleopatra has been—and

---

[33] von Staden, *Herophilus*, 519.

[34] Galen, *Opera omnia*, ed. Kühn, 19:63.

[35] Erotian, preface and F.5, *Erotiani Vocum Hippocraticarum collectio*, ed. Ernst Nachmanson (Göteborg: Eranos, 1918), 5 and 91.

[36] von Staden, *Herophilus*, 521.

[37] Oribasius, *Medical Collection*, 44.14.2; *Oribasii Collectionum medicarum reliquiae*, ed. J. Raeder, Corpus Medicorum Graecorum 6 (4 vols, Leipzig, 1928–33; repr. Amsterdam: A.M. Hakkert, 1964), 3:132.

[38] Paul of Aegina, 4.24 (ed. Heiberg, 1:345).

[39] Cf. Pseudo-Galen, *Commentary on the Hippocratic Humors*, 3.6 (Galen, *Opera omnia*, ed. Kühn, 16:461).

[40] Wellmann in Susemihl, *Geschichte der griechischen Literatur in der Alexandrinerzeit*, 417.

doubtlessly will be—the subject of many novelists' portrayals, and her image in Western literature has a long if checkered history.

Bibliography

Aelian. *On the Characteristics of Animals*. Ed. and trans. A.F. Scholfield. 3 vols. Loeb Classical Library. Cambridge, MA: Harvard University Press, 1958–59.

Aetius of Amida. *Aetii Amideni Libri medicinales V–VIII*. Ed. Alexander Olivieri. Corpus Medicorum Graecorum 8.2. Berlin: Academiae Litterarum, 1950.

Becher, Ilse. *Das Bild der Kleopatra in der griechischen und lateinischen Literatur*. Berlin: Akademie-Verlag, 1966.

Caesar. *The Civil Wars*. Ed. and trans. A.G. Peskett. Loeb Classical Library. London: Heinemann, 1914.

Celsus. *De medicina*. Ed. and trans. W.G. Spencer. 3 vols. Loeb Classical Library. Cambridge, MA: Harvard University Press, 1935–38.

Courtney, Edward. *The Fragmentary Latin Poets*. Oxford: Clarendon Press, 1993.

Dio Cassius. *Dio's Roman History*. Ed. and trans. Earnest Cary and Herbert Baldwin Foster. 9 vols. Loeb Classical Library. London: Heinemann, 1914–27.

Dioscorides. *De materia medica libri quinque*. Ed. Max Wellmann, 3 vols. Berlin: Weidmann, 1906–14. Repr. Berlin: Weidmann, 1958.

Erotian. *Erotiani Vocum Hippocraticarum collectio*. Ed. Ernst Nachmanson. Göteborg: Eranos, 1918.

Fabricius, Cajus. *Galens Exzerpte aus älteren Pharmakologen*. Berlin: Walter de Gruyter, 1972.

Fraser, P.M. *Ptolemaic Alexandria*. 3 vols. Oxford: Clarendon Press, 1972.

Galen. *Claudii Galeni Opera omnia*. Ed. C.G. Kühn. 20 vols in 22. Leipzig: C. Cnobloch, 1821–33. Repr. Hildesheim: Georg Olms, 1964–65.

Huzar, Eleanor Goltz. *Mark Antony: A Biography*. Minneapolis: University of Minnesota Press, 1978.

Jacoby, Felix. *Die Fragmente der griechischen Historiker*. Pt 2B. *Spezialgeschichten, Autobiographien und Memoiren*. Leiden: Brill, 1962.

———. *Die Fragmente der griechischen Historiker*. Pt 2B. *Kommentar zu Nr. 106–261*. Leiden: Brill, 1962.

Jones, C.P. *Plutarch and Rome*. Oxford: Clarendon Press, 1971.

Kyu, Lee Young, et al. "The Adhesion Property of Fish Glue." *Mokchae Konghak/ Journal of Korean Wood Science and Technology* 32 (2004): 59–65.

Marasco, Gabrielle. "Cleopatra e gli esperimenti su cavie umane." *Historia* 44 (1995): 317–25.

Mastrocinque, Attilio. "Les médecins des Séleucides." In Ph. J. van der Eijk, H.F.J. Horstmanshoff, and P.H. Schrijvers (eds), *Ancient Medicine in Its Socio-Cultural Context: Papers Read at the Congress Held at Leiden University, 13–15 April 1992*, 1:143–51. 2 vols. Amsterdam: Rodopi, 1995.

Millar, Fergus. "The Mediterranean and the Roman Revolution: Politics, War and the Economy." *Past and Present* 102 (1984): 3–24.

Nutton, Vivian. "Galen and Egypt." In Jutta Kollesch and Diethard Nickel (eds), *Galen und das hellenistische Erbe: Verhandlungen des IV. Internationalen Galen-Symposiums veranstaltet vom Institut für Geschichte der Medizin am Bereich Medizin (Charité) der Humboldt-Universität zu Berlin 18.–20. September 1989*, 11–31. Stuttgart: Franz Steiner, 1993.

———. "Galen on Theriac: Problems of Authenticity." In Armelle Debru (ed.), *Galen on Pharmacology: Philosophy, History, and Medicine. Proceedings of the Vth International Galen Colloquium, Lille, 16–18 March 1995*, 133–51. Leiden: Brill, 1997.

Oldfather, W.A. "A Friend of Plutarch's Grandfather." *Classical Philology* 19 (1924): 177.

Oribasius. *Oribasii Collectionum medicarum reliquiae*. Ed. J. Raeder. 4 vols. Corpus Medicorum Graecorum 6. Leipzig: Teubner, 1928–33. Repr. Amsterdam: A.M. Hakkert, 1964.

Paul of Aegina. *Paulus Aegineta*. Ed. J.L. Heiberg. 2 vols. Corpus Medicorum Graecorum 9. Leipzig: Teubner, 1921–24.

Petukhova, Tatyana. "Potential Application of Isinglass Adhesive for Paper Conservation." *Book and Paper Group Annual* 8 (1989): 58–61.

Pliny. *Natural History*. Ed. and trans. H. Rackham, W.H.S. Jones, and D.E. Eichholz. 10 vols. Loeb Classical Library. Cambridge, MA: Harvard University Press, 1938–63.

Plutarch. *Moralia*. Ed. and trans. F.C. Babbitt et al. 14 vols. Loeb Classical Library. London: Heinemann, 1927–76.

Plutarch. *Life of Antony*. Ed. C.P.R. Pelling. Cambridge: Cambridge University Press, 1988.

Retief, François P., and Louise Cilliers. "The Death of Cleopatra." In François P. Retief et al., *Health and Healing, Disease and Death in the Graeco-Roman World*, 79–88. Bloemfontein: University of the Free State, 2005.

Roller, Duane W. *Cleopatra: A Biography*. Oxford: Oxford University Press, 2010.

Sbordone, Francesco. "La morte di Cleopatra nei medici greci." In Francesco Sbordone, *Scritti di varia filologia*, 1–32. Naples: Giannini, 1971.

Scarborough, John. "Nicander's Toxicology, I: Snakes." *Pharmacy in History* 19 (1977): 3–23. Repr. as ch. 5 in Scarborough, *Pharmacy and Drug Lore in Antiquity.*

———. "Criton, Physician to Trajan: Historian and Pharmacist." In John W. Eadie and Josiah Ober (eds), *The Craft of the Ancient Historian: Essays in Honor of Chester G. Starr*, 387–405. Lanham, MD: University Press of America, 1985. Repr. as ch. 11 in Scarborough, *Pharmacy and Drug Lore in Antiquity.*

———. "Attalus III of Pergamon: Research Toxicologist." In Louise Cilliers (ed.), *Asklepios: Studies on Ancient Medicine*, 138–56. Acta Classica Supplementum 2. Bloemfontein: Classical Association of South Africa, 2008.

———. *Pharmacy and Drug Lore in Antiquity: Greece, Rome, Byzantium.* Variorum Collected Studies Series CS 904. Farnham, UK, and Burlington, VT: Ashgate, 2010.

——— and Alain Touwaide. "Kriton of Herakleia Salbake, T. Statilius." In Paul T. Keyser and Georgia Irby-Massie (eds), *The Encyclopedia of Ancient Natural Scientists: The Greek Tradition and Its Many Heirs*, 494–5. London: Routledge, 2008.

Sider, David. *The Library of the Villa dei Papiri at Herculaneum.* Los Angeles: J. Paul Getty Museum, 2005.

Suidae Lexicon. Ed. Ada Adler. 5 vols. Leipzig: Teubner, 1928–38. Repr. Stuttgart: Teubner, 1967–71.

Supplementum epigraphicum graecum. Leiden: Brill, 1927–.

Susemihl, Franz. *Geschichte der griechischen Literatur in der Alexandrinerzeit.* 2 vols. Leipzig: Teubner, 1891–92.

Swain, Simon. *Hellenism and Empire: Language, Classicism and Power in the Greek World, AD 50–250.* Oxford: Clarendon Press, 1996.

Thompson, D'Arcy W. *A Glossary of Greek Fishes.* London: Oxford University Press, 1947.

Usher, George. *A Dictionary of Plants Used by Man.* London: Constable, 1974.

von Staden, Heinrich. *Herophilus: The Art of Medicine in Early Alexandria.* Cambridge: Cambridge University Press, 1989.

Wood, Horatio C., and Charles H. LaWall (eds). *The Dispensatory of the United States of America.* 21st edn. Philadelphia: Lippincott, 1926.

Chapter 2
Quid pro Quo:
Revisiting the Practice of
Substitution in Ancient Pharmacy

Alain Touwaide

I shall tell you a story that, I recall, happened to me in Alexandria. Shortly upon my arrival there, a woman on the verge of death came to me, in a serious condition that is not appropriate to describe now. While I was looking for *luchnis* in order to administer to her the medicine she needed, she would have died quickly hadn't I found immediately the seed of *akanthion*. Since *akanthion* was found to be *analogon* to *luchnis*, we used it immediately, and it led to the same result. The next day, several of the physicians who assisted the woman before came to me asking to know the medicine that was needed. They listened and asked to have this treatise on *antemballomena* written for them ...

[Galen,] *De succedaneis*, preface
(ed. C.G. Kühn, *Claudii Galeni Opera omnia*, vol. 19 [1830], 722–3)

This short story of an apparently autobiographical nature opens the treatise on substitution products in the *Corpus Galenicum*. It is followed by a list of 369 items on the model of the substitution above (that is, *anti akanthiou spermatos, luchnidos sperma*) classified in alphabetical order of the first term (*akanthiou* here). Each of the terms of these 369 items is a substance used for the preparation of medicines, and can be a vegetal, animal, or mineral substance, a derivative of such substances, or also a manufactured product. The work is usually considered as the model of a genre in medieval pharmaceutical literature identified by such titles as *peri antemballomenôn* in Byzantium and *quid pro quo* or *de succedaneis* in the Latin West.

The list of substitutions under the name of Galen is of dubious authenticity.[1] It has been little studied, be it in Galenic studies or in pharmaceutical history.

---

[1]   The work does not appear in Galen, *De libris propriis*, in the recent edition by Véronique Boudon-Millet, *Galien*, vol. 1: *Introduction générale: Sur l'ordre de ses propres livres; Sur ses propres livres; Que l'excellent médecin est aussi philosophe* (Paris: Les Belles Lettres, 2007), 128–73, with commentary on 177–234. Particularly for the therapeutic works, see ch. 7, beginning at p. 157 in Boudon's edition. For a commentary on *De libris propriis*, see Johannes Ilberg, *Über*

More generally, the genre of the *antemballomena* has not been much analyzed. After a review of the all-too-rare literature on the topic, I propose here a detailed examination of the Pseudo-Galenic list in order to verify an interpretation suggested by the *mise-en-scène* that opens the work; that is, substitution was a means for a physician not to be without therapeutic resources when the substance required to treat a patient was not available, particularly in an emergency situation; later on, this principle was generalized and became normal in the daily treatment of patients and management of therapy.

1. *Status Quaestionis*

In 1958, Henry Sigerist briefly mentioned the Pseudo-Galenic *De succedaneis*, which he identified as a "quid pro quo, a short alphabetical list of substitute drugs."[2] It was to the credit of John Riddle to approach again the treatises on substitution in his general survey of *Theory and Practice in Medieval Medicine* published in 1974:

> The working pharmacopoeia [of practitioners] must have been much smaller than the
> learned knowledge of pharmacy. This would explain the manuscripts known as quid
> pro quo, which are guides for substituting drugs, the earliest of which appears in the
> thirteenth century.[3]

---

die Schriftstellerei des Klaudios Galenos (Darmstadt: Wissenschaftliche Buchgesellschaft, 1974), a reprint of his classic analysis published in 1889–97 (see particularly pp. 16–17 and 20–22, as well as 84–7). On the authenticity of the list here, see Johannes Chr. Ackermann, *Historia litteraria Claudii Galeni*, in J.A. Fabricius and A.G.C. Harless (eds), *Bibliotheca graeca*, 4th edn, vol. 5 (1793), 397–500, reproduced in *Claudii Galeni Opera omnia*, ed. C.G. Kühn (20 vols in 22, Leipzig: C. Cnobloch, 1821–33; repr. Hildesheim: Georg Olms, 1964–65), 1:xii–cclxv, esp. clxx–clxxi, no. 138. More recently, and on the same topic, see (in chronological order) Konrad Schubring, "Bemerkungen zur Galenausgabe von Karl Gottlob Kühn und zu ihrem Nachdruck," in the reprint of Kühn's edition, 1:v–lxii, at p. lv, *sub titulo*; Vivian Nutton, *Karl Gottlob Kühn and His Edition of the Works of Galen: A Bibliography* (Oxford: Oxford Microform Publications, 1976), *sub titulo*; Gerhard Fichtner, *Corpus Galenicum: Verzeichnis der galenischen und pseudogalenischen Schriften*, expanded edn (Tübingen: Institut für Geschichte der Medizin, 1997), 80, no. 133.

    2   Henry E. Sigerist, "The Latin Medical Literature of the Early Middle Ages," *Journal of the History of Medicine and Allied Sciences* 13 (1958): 127–46, at 144.

    3   John M. Riddle, "Theory and Practice in Medieval Medicine," *Viator* 5 (1974): 157–84, at 175; reprinted in John M. Riddle, *Quid pro Quo: Studies in the History of Drugs*, Collected Studies Series CS 367 (Aldershot, UK, and Brookfield, VT: Variorum, 1992), ch. 6.

In the footnote following this passage, he refers to six manuscripts containing such lists.

In 1992, Riddle returned to the genre of substitution treatises in an original essay in his volume of collected works entitled *Quid pro Quo*, specifically:

> ... If one of these [drugs] was not available, a physician could substitute. He knew to be careful with the amounts and to take into consideration the condition of the patient. This sensitivity derived more from experience than books, just as Galen, Ibn Sīnā, and other authorities indicated. Just to assist, however, there existed in the Middle Ages treatises called "Quid pro quo," or "This for that," which were lists of drug substitutes. A typical "Quid pro quo" assisted memory; it could not replace reliance on empirical observation.[4]

The same year, the publication of the so-called *Lorscher Arzneibuch* from the late eighth century, which had been discovered a few years before, brought to light a fragment of a *quid pro quo* treatise made of 32 items, which bears some similarity to the Pseudo-Galenic list here.[5] Shortly after, the German historian of pharmacy Rudolf Schmitz linked the lists of synonyms of plant names to the *quid pro quo* treatises in his discussion of medieval materia medica literature. As Schmitz notes: "In manchen Fällen erfüllten die Synonymenlisten auch die Funktion der Quidproquo-Listen, das heisst Listen mit Austauschmitteln (Succedanea, Antiballomena, Quidproquo)."[6]

According to Schmitz, then, lists of synonyms could have a function similar to that of the *quid pro quo* and help when a substitution was necessary. Whatever the validity of the function he attributed to substitution lists—and we shall discuss it—Schmitz pursued his analysis and suggested that the technique of substitution may also have been a two-sided phenomenon: (1) salutary as per the process above (that is, the replacement of a substance by another if the first was not available), but also (2) possibly harmful, if not lethal, when the substitution was in fact an adulteration.[7] Hence, according to Schmitz, arose the interdiction

---

[4] John M. Riddle, "Methodology of Historical Drug Research," in Riddle, *Quid pro Quo*, ch. 15, 14.

[5] See Ulrich Stoll, *Das "Lorscher Arzneibuch": Ein medizinisches Kompendium des 8. Jahrhunderts (Codex Bambergensis medicinalis 1). Text, Übersetzung und Fachglossar*, Sudhoffs Archiv Beiheft 28 (Stuttgart: Franz Steiner, 1992), 78.

[6] Rudolf Schmitz, *Geschichte der Pharmazie*, vol. 1: *Von den Anfängen bis zum Ausgang des Mittelalters* (Eschborn: Govi-Verlag, 1998), 394.

[7] Ibid., 562.

of such practice in the medieval legal texts regulating the pharmaceutical profession, when the substitution was made without the patient's knowledge.[8]

2. The Pseudo-Galenic Treatise: An Overview

A close reexamination of the Pseudo-Galenic treatise on the basis of Kühn's edition,[9] reproduced in Table 2.1 in the Appendix below,[10] shows that there are three major types of substitution:

a. a simple substitution on the model of the Alexandrian case in the pseudo-autobiographical story opening the work; that is, *anti akanthiou spermatos, luchnidos sperma*. This substitution can be expressed by the theoretical formula *if not a1, then b1*;

b. a bidirectional substitution, on the model of the following two items: (i) *anti rêtinês peukinês, rêtinê terebinthinê*;[11] (ii) *anti rêtinês terebinthinês, rêtinê peukinê*.[12] This kind of substitution is actually an equivalence of two products. It can be theorized as follows: *if not a2, then b2*; and *if not b2, then a2*;

---

8   Ibid., 530.

9   The edition certainly needs to be revised. For the manuscripts of the work, see Hermann Diels, *Die Handschriften der antiken Ärzte*, pt 1: *Hippokrates und Galenos*, Abhandlungen der königlichen Akademie der Wissenschaften, Jahre 1905, Abh. 3 (Berlin: Königliche Akademie der Wissenschaften, 1905). Also, more recently, Alain Touwaide, "Byzantine Medical Manuscripts: Toward a New Catalogue," *Byzantinische Zeitschrift* 101 (2008): 199–208, and "Byzantine Medical Manuscripts: Towards a New Catalogue, with a Specimen for an Annotated Checklist of Manuscripts Based on an Index of Diels' Catalogue," *Byzantion* 79 (2009): 453–595. For the manuscripts of the work, see Hermann Diels, *Die Handschriften der antiken Ärzte*, pt 1: *Hippokrates und Galenos*, Abhandlungen der königlichen Akademie der Wissenschaften, Jahre 1905, Abh. 3 (Berlin: Königliche Akademie der Wissenschaften, 1905).

10   All items are reproduced in transliteration into the Latin alphabet (transliterations reproduce the orthographic form of Greek names rather than being phonetic). The sequence of items in Table 2.1 does not reproduce that of the original text, but the alphabetical order of the transliterations (thus Latin alphabetical order, and Greek) of the first substance of each item (that is, the substance to be substituted). Each entry in the table includes a reference to the page number and position on the page of each item in vol. 19 of Kühn's 1830 edition; e.g., *abrotonon/origanon* 723.02 refers to page 723, item 2 on the page.

11   Kühn 741.07.

12   Kühn 741.09.

c. a chain of two or more substitutions with a common element such as, for example, (i) *anti dorukniou, uoskuamou sperma*;[13] (ii) *anti alikakabou, dorukniou sperma*;[14] and (iii) *anti mandragorou chulou, doruknion*.[15] This case can be represented by the following formulas: *if not a3, then b3*; and *if not c (d, and even in some cases e), then a3*.

As a result of the substitutions on the model of the three types above, there is a transformation of the materia medica from $(a1 + a2 + b2 + a3 + c + d + e)$ to $(b1 + b2 + a2 + b3 + a3)$. Since there are common elements in the two groups here (actually $a2, b2, a3$, that is, materia medica that substitutes and is substituted), the three theoretical formulas above can be transformed into the following three groups of materia medica:

substituted materia medica	$a1 + c + d + e$
substituted/substitute materia medica	$a2, b2, a3$
substitute materia medica	$b1, b3$

I will not limit my study to a global analysis of the transformation from the substituted materia medica to its substitute, but I will analyze each category above, including the substituted/substitute materia medica, in order to understand the mechanism(s) underpinning such transformation(s). To this end, I shall first survey the three types of substitutions above, starting with bilateral substitution, case (b) above, which is the clearest.

3. Bilateral Substitutions, or Equivalences

The formula *quid pro quo* (which, in Greek, is structured on the model *anti akanthiou spermatos, luchnidos sperma*, that is, "instead of *a*, [administer] *b*") is a substitution on the model suggested by the pseudo-autobiographical story above. In the category of substitutions that I have defined as bidirectional, the formula *if not a, then b* goes with *if not b, then a*. The two items in such pairs do not follow each other in the list of substitutions; each appears where the first item falls in the alphabetical list of names. Here are two examples of such pairs:[16]

---

13   Kühn 728.03.

14   Kühn 724.06.

15   Kühn 736.02.

16   In referring to the items in the Pseudo-Galenic treatise, I use references to Kühn's edition as described above; that is, page and item numbers. For clarity's sake, I reproduce the Greek name of the substances rather than their scientific botanical name.

| *akanthiou sperma* | can be replaced by | *luchnidos sperma* | (723.01); and |
| *luchnis* | can be replaced by | *akanthiou sperma* | (735.09) |

| *lapathou riza* | can be replaced by | *purethrou riza* | (734.04); and |
| *purethrou riza* | can be replaced by | *lapathou riza* | (741.03) |

In such cases, the bidirectional substitution is made clear by the duplication of the item and the inversion of its two terms (*if not a, then b* and *if not b, then a*). All these cases (which total 24) are listed in Table 2.2 in the Appendix. Equivalent materia medica is always of the same nature, vegetal, mineral, or animal, or manufactured products. Whatever the nature of the materia medica and its degree of similarity or difference, the terms of each pair are credited with therapeutic properties supposed to be identical or very similar. As such, these items do not tell much about substitution, but more about therapeutics and pharmacology, in particular the identity of the therapeutic action of all the materia medica in these pairs of equivalences.

Of a total of 369 items, these 24 pairs correspond to 48 items (actually 49, as one group contains three items); that is, 13 percent of the total. Such a percentage invites deepening the analysis, because it is too low to account for the whole treatise.

4. Chains of Substitutions

The group analyzed next is the third above; that is, the chains of two or more substitutions with a common element presented by the formulas *if not a3, then b3* and *if not c (d, and even in some cases e), then a3*. The following examples illustrate well this principle of substitution, which is more complex:

abrotonon	can be replaced by	*origanon*	(723.02)
apsinthion	can be replaced by	*abrotonon*	(726.03)
santonikon	can be replaced by	*abrotonon*	(742.06)

| *elaias dakruon* | can be replaced by | *upokistidos chulos* | (728.07) |
| *mandragoras* | can be replaced by | *elaias dakruon* | (736.01) |

All such groups are summarized in Table 2.3 in the appendix. They are not built on the premise that a particular item of materia medica is unavailable. In the examples here, indeed, the matter to be substituted in the first item is the substitute of the other(s) in the following item(s).

The total number of groups in this category is 78. Most of the groups are made of two items in the Pseudo-Galenic treatise. However, 20 groups are made of three items, and two of four items.

In order to better understand this second category of substitutions, we can start with the first example here. Interestingly, the three plants in the second and third items (*abrotonon, apsinthion, santonikon*) are different species of the same botanical genus in the ancient Greek system. Whereas *abrotonon* and *apsinthion* (= *Artemisia arborescens* L. and *A. absinthium* L., respectively) seem ubiquitous in the general Mediterranean area, *santonikon* (= *Artemisia maritima* L.)[17] may have a different geographical distribution and biota (as it is typical of the coasts of west to north Europe, from southwest France).[18] Such a case seems to point to a slightly different interpretation of the principle of substitution: it was not necessarily needed because an item of materia medica was unavailable (*abrotonon* and *apsinthion* are ubiquitous, indeed), but it might have introduced some flexibility in the preparation of the medicines by using a local species (*santonikon*) with identical or very similar properties.

The second example here is no less interesting, because it suggests that substitution may have been used to allow for some modulation of the therapeutic action to be generated by administering the medicine. *Mandragora* (a member of the Solanaceae family) is indeed a potent agent, which is not the case with *elaias dakruon*.

This explanation for the substitution of *mandragora* hints at another mechanism: substitution may have been used to eliminate substances whose use required caution because they were toxic. This is the case, for example, with *doruknion*, which is among the toxic substances in the treatise on poisons ascribed to Dioscorides; it is replaced here with *uoskuamou sperma* (728.03). Strangely, however, *doruknion* could be used to replace *mandragorou chulos* (736.02) and *alikakabon* (724.06). Though apparently contradictory, these items demonstrate a great level of awareness of the taxonomical and, hence, pharmacological proximity of *doruknion, uoskuamos, mandragoras*, and *alikakabon*, as the four plants are considered to correspond to different genera of the Solanaceae family

---

[17] On its geographical distribution, see Dioscorides, *De materia medica libri quinque*, 3.23, ed. Max Wellmann, 3 vols (Berlin: Weidmann, 1906–14; repr. Berlin: Weidmann, 1958), 2:33. According to Dioscorides, this species is typical of the part of Galatia (Gaul) "along the Alps"; cf. the new translation of the same work, Pedanius Dioscorides of Anazarbus, *De materia medica*, trans. Lily Y. Beck, Altertumswissenschaftliche Texte und Studien 38 (Hildesheim: Olms-Weidmann, 2005), 190.

[18] On the whole genre, see T.J. Tutin (ed.), *Flora Europea*, vol. 4: *Plantaginaceae to Compositae* (Cambridge: Cambridge University Press, 1976), 178–86; for *A. arborescens* and *absinthium* specifically, see p. 180, and for *A. maritima*, p. 181.

of modern botanical taxonomy, even though some of them (*doruknion* and *alikakabon*) are not necessarily identified with great exactness at the species level.

On the basis of this first approach, substitution may have served as an instrument for both the pharmacist (if I can use this term) and the physician (instead of only the former, as usually stated): for the physician, it may have been a tool to modulate a treatment (including to avoid the possible risk of a substance with lethal properties if such substance was not used with due caution) and, for the pharmacist, it made it possible to use local resources in a flexible way.

The total number of chains of items in this type of substitution is much higher than the first one: 79 chains, composing a total of 185 items; that is, half of the total number of items in the whole Pseudo-Galenic treatise (made up of 369 items). This is thus an important category of substitutions, the mechanisms of which will need to be taken into consideration in the global interpretation of the substitution strategy. From now on, however, we can expect that substitution was not only a pharmaceutical practice aimed at supplying a drug in case the required one was not available; instead, it seems also to have been a tool for the physician to compose a medicine with a therapeutic action duly crafted according to the pathology to be treated—a sort of personalization of the therapeutic action.

5. Substituted Materia Medica

To pursue the study, I ought to analyze the first type of substitution above; that is, the simple replacement modeled on the story opening the treatise under consideration here—the formula *if not a1, then b1* in which an item of materia medica (*a1*) is replaced by another (*b1*), without replacing any other in one or more items of the treatise. I will not do so, however, as I shall regroup all the cases of substitutions in the treatise, thus including those in the first and the third types of substitutions I have identified. In the former (the simple substitutions on the model *if not a1, then b1*), an item of materia medica is eliminated (*a1*), and in the latter (the chains of substitutions), some substances are replaced by another without replacing any other(s).

Substituted items of materia medica total 179 (see Table 2.4), while substituting items total 236 (Table 2.5), as more than one substitute is listed for several items. Substituted items of materia medica are of very different types.[19] Some are plants or derivatives of plants that were expensive, such as *krokos* (733.09) and the *opos Kurēnaikos* (739.01). Also, there is the much sought

---

[19]   The items quoted below are examples, and not all cases of each type.

after and, thus, expensive Egyptian perfume called *kufi* (733.16), the exotic tree *ebenos* (728.05), and such exotic plants (or, in some cases, their derivatives) as *amômon* (725.01), *balsamon* (726.05) and *balsamou opos* (726.06 and 738.11), *fou* (746.04), *fullon* (746.06), *kassia* (731.10), *kuminon* (733.12), *malabathron* (735.13), *méon* (736.10), *nardos Suriakê* (737.07), *smurnê Troglôdutis* (743.06), *xulobalsamon* (737.12), and *xulokasia* (738.02). Not exotic or expensive, instead, but dangerous (or considered as such) and, in some cases, even lethal are the *agarikon* (723.04), *akoniton* (724.02), *armala* (725.08), and *psullion* (747.05).

Among the items of animal materia medica, there are some species that are dangerous for human health: *bouprêstis* (726.09), *kantharides* (731.07), *pituokampê* (740.10), and *salamandra* (742.04). Also, there are animal products that were probably difficult to collect, such as viper bile (*cholê echeôs*, 746.13), *cholê galês* (746.12), crocodile fat (*krokodeilou stear*, 733.11), *cholê mugalês* (747.1), and *cholê uainê* (747.03).

An obvious interpretation would be that these items of materia medica were substituted because of their cost, rarity, or possible danger. Such interpretation is immediately contradicted by the nature of many other items that are substituted and do not substitute any other, such as a wide range of simple and ubiquitous species: *aeizôon* (723.07), *argemônê* (725.04), *bruônia* (726.11), *chamaimêlon* (746.11), *diktamnos* (728.01), *ebiskou riza* (728.06), *elelisfakos* (729.04), *erinou fullon* (729.12), *ippouris* (731.01), *knikou sperma* (732.12), *kotulêdôn* (733.07), *napu* (737.05), *ôkimoeides* (747.08), *orminon* (739.11), *ornithogalon* (739.12), *oruza* (739.13), *panakos riza* (739.15), *peukedanon* (740.07), *poliou sperma* (740.11), *pteris* (741.01), *sêsamoeides* (742.12), *sfondulion* (744.12), *sinêpi* (742.13), *skammônia* (743.01), *stafis agria* (723.05), *stafis êmeros* (743.10), *stoichas* (743.16), *teukrion* (745.02), *thapsia* (730.04), *thridax* (730.08), *tribolos* (745.06), and *uperikon* (745.14); the juice of some of these plants or of other common ones: *elatêriou chulos* (729.02), *oinanthês chulos* (738.03), *peukedanou opos* (739.06), *rododafnês opos* (739.08), *sukês opos* (739.09), and *thapsias chulos* (730.05); a common tree (*aigeiros*, 723.08), a not less common tree production, pine cones (*strobiloi*, 743.17), and such ordinary derivatives of trees as *pisselaion* (740.08), *rêtinê* (741.06), and *rêtinê pituinê* (741.08); ordinary fruits such as *balaustion* (726.04) and *mêlokudônia* (736.09); and nuts (*amugdala pikra*, 724.16).

Among the animals, animal products, and derivatives used as items of materia medica that are replaced, one could list here the *skigkos* (743.02); the dung of various animals—*ailourou kopros* (733.01), *gupos kopros* (727.11 and 733.02), and *lukou kopros* (733.03); and animal products and parts such as *alôpekos stear* (724.12 and 743.11), *elafou keras* (732.01), *moscheion stear* (743.13), and *moschou muelon* (736.18).

Many minerals appear among the substituted materia medica, some of which are toxic, and some are in their natural form whereas others required some treatment: *amianton* (724.14), *Armenion* (725.09), *arsenikon* (725.10), *asbestos* (725.13), *Asios lithos* (725.15), *chalkanthê* (746.08), *Chalkêdonion* (735.03), *gê astêr* (727.03), *gê Megara* (727.06), *gê Samia* (727.07), *ios chalkês* (730.11), *ios sidêrou* (730.10), *kinnabari* (732.06), *Kupria skôria* (743.05), *lêmnia sfragis* (734.08), *magnêsia* (735.11), *magnêtos* (735.12), *misudion* (736.13), *nitron* (737.11), *nitron eruthron* (737.10), *onuchitês lithos* (734.14), *puritês lithos* (734.15), *smaragdos lithos* (735.05), *sôri* (744.16), *spodion* (743.08), *stimmi Koptikon* (743.15), *stuptêria schistê* (744.04), and *theion apuron* (730.07).

A specific group of substituted products is that of plants growing in a marine environment, marine plants, and marine animals: *fukos* (746.05), *korallion* (733.05), *lagôos thalattios* (734.01), *sêpias ostrakon* (742.10), *skilla* (743.03), and *spoggou lithos* (735.06).

Some manufactured products are also included in this list: three types of aromatized oil (*chamaimêlinon elaion*, 728.13; *rafaninon elaion*, 729.01 and 741.05; and *sousinon elaion*, 743.07), a wine (*oinos Suriakos*, 738.07), glue (*tauroukolla*, 745.01), and a perfumed wax (*ussôpou kêrôtê*, 745.15).

More surprising, simple and domestic products that were part of daily life such as *amulon* (724.15), *bouturon* (726.10), *elaion palaion* (728.10), *kêron* (732.02), *omfakion* (738.08), *omfax* (738.09), and *ôôn lekitha* (747.10), *ôou leukon* (747.11), and *ôôn purra* (747.12) are substituted.

6. Substituting Materia Medica

The list of the materia medica used to substitute those items above is longer (236 items instead of 179) because more than one item (plants or parts of plants, minerals, or manufactured products) may be listed as a replacement for another. At the same time, certain items replace two others or more. This is the case with *chalkou lepis* (743.15 and 746.08), *chamaidrus* (743.16 and 745.02), *chamaipitus* (729.16 and 731.01), *chamelaia* (740.05 [*chamailea*] and 740.13), *kalamos arômatikos* (725.11 and 743.06), *kardamon* (730.04, 737.05, and 742.13), *kikinon elaion* (741.05 and 742.09), *kinnamômon* (731.10 and 738.02), *kolokunthis* (729.07 and 743.01), *leukografis* (727.07 and 731.15), *litharguros* (730.10, 744.08, and 744.16), *morea* (729.12 and 739.09), *nardostachus* (746.06 and 737.10), *sandarachê* (724.09, 725.10, 730.07, 734.08, 744.11, and 746.03), *saturion* (737.13, 743.02, and 745.06), *sfagnos* (726.07 and 746.04), *sidia* (738.09 and 744.04 [*sidion*]), and *têlis* (731.06 and 735.14).

The list of the materia medica used to replace those items above (Table 2.5) brings several phenomena to light. First of all, some vegetal species (or animal species, minerals, or manufactured products) are replaced by others supposed to have the same or a similar therapeutic action. Here are some examples:

aeizôon	is replaced by	*thridakos fulla ê chulos*	(723.07)
ornithogalon	is replaced by	*anthullis*	(739.12)
polutrichon	is replaced by	*apsinthion*	(740.14)
teukrion	is replaced by	*chamaidrus*	(745.02)
uperikon	is replaced by	*anêthou sperma*	(745.14)

This mechanism of substitution, which does not present any special characteristic, confirms the conclusion reached about bilateral substitution; that is, ancient pharmacology established the identity or similarity of the therapeutic action of these items of materia medica. The case of eggs is instructive from this viewpoint:

ôôn lekitha	are replaced by	*elafou muelos*	(747.10)
ôou leukon	is replaced by	*gala gunaikeion*	(747.11)
ôôn purra	are replaced by	*meli*	(747.12)

More interesting from our point of view here are items of materia medica that were rare, difficult to find, and expensive. They are replaced with more common ones, easily available in the Mediterranean environment and, hence, not excessively expensive, as the following examples suggest:

alôpekos stear	is replaced by	*arneion stear*	(724.12)
amugdala pikra	are replaced by	*apsinthion*	(724.16)
balsamon	is replaced by	*iou leukou riza*	(726.05)
elafou keras	is replaced by	*aigos keras*	(732.01)
kufi	is replaced by	*ischas kekaumenê*	(733.16)
kuminon Aithiopikon	is replaced by	*melanthion*	(733.13)
lukou kopros	is replaced by	*kunos kopros*	(733.03)
xulobalsamon	is replaced by	*leukoiou riza*	(737.12)

Also, items of materia medica that are toxic (or supposed to be so) are substituted with less harmful products:

kantharides	are replaced by	*falaggia*	(731.07)
lagôos thalattios	is replaced by	*kogchos potamios*	(734.01)
salamandra	is replaced by	*saura chlôra*	(742.04)

Remarkably, in some cases, animal or mineral items of materia medica are replaced by vegetal items. For example:

skigkos	is replaced by	*saturion*	(743.02)
stuptêria schistê	is replaced by	*sidion*	(744.04)

All this points to a strategy of adaptation of formulas for medicines from their original context (whether it was a biota, a socioeconomic milieu, or a type of therapeutics and pharmacy) to another. This may be a result of the circulation of texts around the Mediterranean over time, particularly the *Hippocratic Corpus*, *De materia medica* by Dioscorides, or the whole Galenic oeuvre with the many formulas that it contains compiled from earlier authors. In this case, substitution is a sign of possible tension between canonical texts and the daily practice of therapeutics and pharmacy. Whereas, in later periods, texts were modified according to the different contexts in which they were used, here they were probably preserved *ad litteram*, but accompanied by lists of substitutions such as the one attributed to Galen. More than a unified, monolithic operation, this was probably the result of several interventions, made with different motivations and intentions, which resulted in different layers of data accumulated and amalgamated in a treatise like the Pseudo-Galenic one under analysis here.

7. Toward an Origin?

Concerning this subject, it would be interesting to locate more precisely, if possible, in what area and when these "companion lists" of the canonical therapeutic works of antiquity were produced. Some items on the list here seem indicative. For example, marine products are replaced by terrestrial species:

fukos	is replaced by	*agchousa*	(746.05)
korallion	is replaced by	*sumfuton*	(733.05)
skilla	is replaced by	*bolbos*	(743.03)

Also, exotic species are replaced by more ordinary ones, as is the case with *kufi* (733.16), for example.

However, although the substitution of *oinos Suriakos* by *oinos Rodios* (738.07), *stimmi Koptikon* by *chalkou lepis* (743.15), and *Suriakos opos* by *moreas opos* (739.10) may invite locating the origin of our substitution list in an area that is not the Eastern Mediterranean, it does not seem that substitutions alone can be used to reveal a specific geographical location or environment, particularly because information resulting from such an approach is contradictory. If *kuminon Aithiopikon* is replaced by *melanthion* (733.13), *Kupria skôria*, instead, is substituted by *melantêria Aiguptiakê* (743.05). Similarly, while *krokodeilou stear* is replaced by *kunos thalattiou stear* (733.11), *galês cholê* is substituted by *kamêlou cholê* (746.12). Also, *ailourou kopros* and *echeôs cholê* are replaced by *ichneumonos kopros* and *cholê*, respectively (733.01 and 746.13).

What is more significant is the absence of such a fruit as *balaustion* (726.04), of a common tree like *aigeiros* (723.08), of many simple plants of the Mediterranean area (above), with, instead, Near Eastern plants replacing other ordinary species (*ebiskou riza* replaced by *papurou riza*, 728.06) and some plants replaced by manufactured products (*sêsamoeides* replaced by *amarantinon piesma*, 742.12) or by imported drugs (*stafis agria* substituted by *foinikes Suriakoi*, 723.05, and *stafis êmeros* by *foinikos Suriakou sarx*, 743.10); derivatives of wild species of plants are replaced with the same product of the cultivated species (*oinanthês chulos* is replaced by *ampelinou blastou chulos*, 738.03, or even by the wood of the cultivated species, *ampeloxulon*, 738.04); plants with a short flowering period are replaced with more ordinary vegetal species (*anêthou sperma* instead of *uperikon*, 745.14); parts of animals in the wild are replaced by the same part of domestic animals (*elafou keras* is substituted by *aigos keras*, 732.01, and *elafeion stear* is replaced by either *chêneion* or *ueion stear*, 743.12 and 729.03, respectively); oriental, rare, and expensive products are present as substitutes (*kassia sfairitês*, 735.13; *kinnamômon*, 738.02, and *kinnamômon manna*, 731.10; *murobalanos*, 736.10; *Suriakos opos*, 739.01); products of wild animals are present (*arkteion stear* substituting *alôpekos stear*, 743.11); domestic products of animal origin not necessarily easy to keep fresh are replaced by more stable products (see the case of the eggs and butter, 726.10); rare animal products difficult to obtain replace some mineral substances (*ios chalkês* replaced by *gupos cholê*, 730.11), some plants (*aloê* replaced by *ibeôs kopros*, 724.10), or other animal products (*ailourou kopros* substituted with *ichneumonos kopros*, 733.01, or *mugalês cholê* replaced by *pithêkou cholê*, 747.01); delicate plants or parts of plants difficult to keep are replaced by a manufactured product (*krokomagma* replacing *krokos*, 733.09); and several mineral species are replaced by a single mineral product (*litharguros* replacing *ios sidêrou*, 730.10, *sêrikon*, 744.08, and *sôri*, 744.16; also *sandarachê* substituting six other drugs [above]: *alos anthos, arsenikon, feklê, Lêmnia sfragis, sfeklê,* and *theion apuron*).

All these facts point to a context with little direct contact with the natural environment; with some natural products, but from domesticated types rather than from the wild; with manufactured rather than natural products; using— and apparently preferring—exotic and expensive drugs and products that can be kept for a long time; and relying on a limited range of mineral products (some of which are manufactured) rather than on a wide series of specific products, each being collected in specific geographical areas.

Such characteristics point to an environment apart from rather than immersed in nature; to an opulent and affluent rather than a subsistence economy; to a far-ranging rather than a limited system of exchanges; to a widely open rather than a circumscribed world; to a medicine and pharmacy based on long-term preservation rather than freshly gathered products. In one word: to medicine and pharmacy in an urban context.

The adaptation of classical, canonical texts as outlined above resulted not only from the circulation of such texts around the Mediterranean, with, as a consequence, the necessary adaptation to different locales. It also came about when such texts were transformed from their original socioeconomic context— if not of a rural nature, at least with easy, direct contact with nature—to another one, characterized by an urban structure cut off from the natural environment, with such a high density of urbanization that it did not even allow for a piece of land devoted to agriculture and cattle, let alone an orchard, a cow, some chickens, and a beehive.

As for the location of this type of milieu, if Rome seems to be the most plausible, particularly because, according to Pliny, its urban density was such that nature seemed to be far off,[20] Alexandria could also be taken into consideration. Moreover, the two locations are not necessarily mutually exclusive. Indeed, as we have seen, the list of substitutions ascribed to Galen probably resulted from different processes that may have accumulated over time in a layered conglomerate. It may thus be possible that a first form of substitution took place in Alexandria and further developed in Rome, as well as in the other great cities of the Roman Empire, as a response to a change not only in milieu, but also in socioeconomic context.

---

[20] For Pliny's observations on gardens and orchards in Rome at this time, see sections 49–53 of chapter 19 of book 19 of his *Natural History*, ed. and trans. H. Rackham, W.H.S. Jones, and D.E. Eichholz, Loeb Classical Library (10 vols, Cambridge, MA: Harvard University Press, 1938–63), 5:450–54.

The substitutions mirror a shift from an Eastern Mediterranean world of the *poleis*, with its rural, agricultural, and pastoral nature, to the larger *metropoleis* of empires, international and urbanized, with an affluent population and a pressing need for health services. They mirror having, instead, limited natural resources within the walls of cities and, as a consequence, a slightly reduced choice of materia medica, preferring materials that were not susceptible to rapid deterioration but more suited to long-term preservation. In other words, we are seeing an urban pharmacology developed by transforming the use of canonical texts, not by modifying such texts, but by adding lists of substitutions such as in the Pseudo-Galenic *antemballomena* analyzed here, which could be the prototype of the genre.

Appendix 2.1

Tables

Table 2.1   Substitutions in Pseudo-Galen, *De succedaneis* (Kühn's edition, vol. 19)

Page/ item no.	Instead of	Use
723.02	abrotonon	origanon
735.02	achatos lithos	sardonux lithos
723.07	aeizôon	thridakos fulla ê chulos
723.03	agallochon	kentaurion
723.04	agarikon	epithumon ê euforbion
723.06	agchousa	uakinthos
723.08	aigeirou akremones	sampsuchon
733.01	ailourou kopros	ichneumonos kopros
723.09	akakias	schinou chulisma
723.10	akantha	akanthou keratia
723.01	akanthiou sperma	luchnidos sperma
724.01	akanthou keratia	akanthê
724.02	akoniton	iridos agrias ê riza
724.03	akoron	asarou riza
724.04	aktea	glaukion ê kopros uios
724.05	aktê botanê	akantha ê akanthou keratia
724.07	alas ammôniakon	alas Kappadokikon
724.08	alas Kappadokikon	alas ammôniakon
724.06	alikakabon	dorukniou ê stuchnou sperma
724.10	aloê	ibeôs kopros
724.11	aloê Indikê	aloês chloras fulla, glaukion, lukion, kentaurion
724.12	alôpekos stear	arneion stear
743.11	alôpekos stear	arkteion stear
724.09	alos anthos	sandarachê
724.13	ami	anison
724.14	amiantos	afroselinon
724.17	ammoniakou thumiama	propolis
725.01	amômon	akoros
724.16	amugdala pikra	apsinthion
724.15	amulon	guris xêra
725.02	anison	daukos
726.03	apsinthion	abrotonon

Table 2.1   Continued

725.03	arakos	sêsamon
725.04	argemonê	serifion
725.05	aristolochia	klêmatis xêra
725.06	aristolochia stroggulê	aristolochia makra
725.07	arkeuthides	kuperos
725.08	armala	kardamômon Babulônion
725.09	Armenion	melan Indikon
725.11	arômatikê	kalamos arômatikos
725.10	arsenikon	sandarachê
725.12	asaron	ziggiber
725.13	asbestos	akantha eis ta bafia
725.14	asbestos o legetai titanos	adarkês
726.01	asfalton	pissa ugra bruttia ê gê ampelitis
726.02	asfodelou riza	seutlou chulos
725.15	Asios lithos	gagatês lithos ê ales ammôniakoi ê sandarachê
734.12	Asios lithos	gagatês lithos, kopros aigos ê ales ammôniakoi kekaumenoi ê sandarachê
725.16	aspalathos	ereikês karpos ê agnou sperma
726.04	balaustion	upokistis ê roa skutinê
726.05	balsamon	iou leukou riza
726.06	balsamou opos	smurnês staktê
738.11	balsamou opos	dadinon, smurnês staktê, karpasou opos, balsamou karpos
726.07	bdellion	sfagnos arômatikos
726.08	bêsasa	pêganou agriou ê êmerou sperma
726.09	bouprêstis	silfai bdeousai ê bdella
726.10	bouturon	galaktos boeiou epipagos
726.11	bruônia	asarou riza
746.07	chalbanê	sagapênon ê terebinthinê
746.08	chalkanthê	chalkou lepis
735.03	Chalkêdonion	kuaneos lithos
746.09	chamaidrus	lapathou agriou riza
746.10	chamaileontos chulos	iteas chulou
728.13	chamaimêlinon elaion	rodinon elaion
746.11	chamaimêlon	anthemis
747.04	chamelaias chulos	iteas chulos
727.14	dafnides	erpullon xêron
727.12	damassônion	karpêsion, ê kalaminthê ê êruggion
727.13	daukou sperma	siou sperma

Table 2.1   Continued

728.02	difrugês	misu opton ê lithos frugios ê chalkos kekaumenos ê lithos puritês
728.01	diktamnos	glêchôn ê elelisfakos
728.03	doruknion	uoskuamou sperma ê elelisfakou sperma
728.04	drakontion	aron
728.05	ebenos	lôtinon xulon
728.06	ebiskou riza	papurou riza ê moreas fulla
746.13	echeôs cholê	ichneumonos cholê
730.02	êduosmon	kalaminthê
736.17	elafeios muelos	elafeion stear ê moscheios muelos
743.12	elafeion stear	chêneion stear
729.03	elafeion stear	ueion stear
732.01	elafou keras	aigos keras
728.08	elaias Aithiopikês dakruon	akakias merê b
728.07	elaias dakruon	upokistidos chulos
728.10	elaion palaion	sikuônion, elaiou to diploun, choireion stear palaion, elaion to diploun meta uos palaiou steatos
729.02	elatêriou chulos	prasou chulos
729.04	elelisfakos	kalaminthê
729.06	elenion	kostos
730.03	êliotropiou sperma	goggulidos sperma
729.05	elleboros melas	strouthiou riza ê papurou riza
729.07	enneafullon	kolokunthidos sperma ê potamogeitôn
729.08	epithumon	kolokunthidos sperma
729.09	eregmos	strouthion
729.10	erikê	kikis omfakitis
729.11	erikês karpos	kissos omfax
729.12	erinou fulla	moreas fulla ê ibeôs kopros
729.13	erpullon	potamogeitôn ê purethron
729.14	erusimon	eregmon ê strouthion
729.17	euforbion	peristeras agrias kopros ê agarikon
729.16	eupatorion	chamaipitus
729.15	euzômou sperma	erusimou sperma
746.03	feklê	sandarachê
746.04	fou	sfagnos
735.01	Frugios lithos	arguritês lithos ê puritês
746.05	fukos	agchousa
746.06	fullon	nardostachus ê iris Illurikê
746.12	galês cholê	kamêlou cholê
726.13	gentianê	elenion ê petroselinou riza

Table 2.1 Continued

727.01	gentianês riza	selinou arômatikou riza, petroselinon (ê radion) (elenion)
727.02	gê apalê ê ampelititis	molubdaina
727.03	gê astêr	gê kimôlia
727.04	gê Eretrias	titanos Thêbaikos
727.05	gê Krêtikê	gê Eretrias
727.06	gê Megara	aloês achnê
727.07	gê Samia	leukografis Aiguptia
727.08	glêchôn	ussôpon
727.09	glukurrizês chulos	sukaminou chulos ê glukokalamou chulos
727.10	goggulis	êliotropiou karpos
727.11	gupos kopros	peristeras kopros
733.02	gupos kopros	peristeras kopros
730.11	ios chalkês	gupos cholê ê perdikos cholê
730.10	ios sidêrou	litharguros ê sidêrou skôria
731.01	ippouris	chamaipitus
731.02	iris Illurikê	elenion arômatikon
738.13	iteas opos	kissou melanos opos
730.09	ixos druinos	chamaileôn melas
731.03	kadmia	leukografis Aiguptia
731.12	kagchru	dafnês kokkoi ê purethron
731.05	kalaminthê	êduosmon agrion
731.04	kalamos arômatikos	sfagnos
731.06	kallikeras	têlis
746.14	kamêlou cholê	askalabôtou cholê
731.07	kantharides	falaggia
741.10	kappareôs riza	murikês riza
731.08	kappareôs riza	erikês riza ê murikês riza
731.09	kardamômon	xulokarpason ê kuperis ammôniakê
738.14	karpasou opos	mursinês opos
731.10	kassia	kinnamômon manna diploun ê brathu
731.11	kastorion	agallochon ê silfion ê silfôn bdeousôn entera
731.13	kedrea	kedrides
731.14	kedrides	ladànon
731.15	keraunion	leukografis
732.02	kêron	eregmos meta propoleôs
732.03	kêrukes	ostrea
732.04	kiki	gloios apo palaistras
732.05	kiki	murikês karpos

Table 2.1   Continued

728.09	kikinon elaion	dafninon elaion ê elaion palaion
732.06	kinnabari	rodoeides
732.07	kinnamômon	pêganon agrion diploun ê triploun
741.12	kinnaras riza	asfodelou riza
732.08	kissêri	gê Krêtikê
732.09	kissou opos	Persikos opos
732.10	klinopodion	êliotropion
732.11	knidospermon	koniou sperma
732.12	knikou sperma	agnou sperma
732.14	kolofônia	apochuma
732.13	kolokunthis	kikeôs sperma [o esti krotônos]
732.15	komarea	ammôniakon thumiama
733.17	kôneion	koriandrou ê psulliou sperma
733.05	korallion	sumfuton ê molu
733.06	kostos	ammôniakon, kedrides, elenion
733.07	kotulêdôn	onokardion ê anagallis
733.08	krinanthemon	afrodisias
733.11	krokodeilou stear	kunos thalattiou stear
733.10	krokomagma	aloê Indikê ê agallochon Indikon
733.09	krokos	krokomagma
733.16	kufi	ischas kekaumenê
733.12	kuminon	krambês sperma
733.13	kuminon Aithiopikon	melanthion
733.14	kunosbatos	alikakabou sperma
733.15	kuperi	arkeuthis ê megalê, arkeuthidôn mêla ê kardamômon
743.05	Kupria skôria	melanteria Aiguptiakê
743.09	Kuprias spodion	elaias fullôn spodos
739.01	Kurênaikos opos	Suriakos opos, lasaros ê moschou muelos ê silfiou opos
734.02	ladanon	sampsuchon
734.01	lagôos thalattios	kogchos potamios
734.04	lapathou riza	purethrou riza ê kunaras riza
741.11	lapathou riza	kinnaras riza
734.03	lathurides	knidios kokkos
734.08	lêmnia sfragis	sandarachê
734.06	lepidion	eruthrodanon
734.05	lepidiou riza	kappareôs fulla
734.07	leukinon anthos	strouthion
734.09	libanos	gê ampelitis

Table 2.1 Continued

734.10	libanou floion	libanou manna
734.11	libathron	traktulos
735.08	libustikou sperma	lubistikou riza ê stafulinou sperma ê siou sperma
735.07	linospermon	kuamou chulos
735.10	lôtou sperma	seutlou sperma
735.09	luchnis	akanthiou sperma
733.03	lukou kopros	kunos kopros
735.11	magnêsias uelinon	ptuelon Italikon
735.12	magnêtos	Frugios lithos ê aimatitês
734.13	magnêtos lithos	Frugios lithos
735.13	malabathron	kassia sfairitês ê nardostachus ê traktulos ê nardos Indikê
735.14	malachê	têlis
736.01	mandragoras	elaias dakruon
736.02	mandragorou chulos	doruknion
736.03	manna	libanou floios
736.04	mastichê	schoinou kardia ê terebinthinê
736.08	mêkôn	mandragorou chulos
739.02	mêkônos opos	mandragorou chulos
736.06	meli	epsêma
736.05	melilôton	lôtos agrios
736.09	mêlokudônion	melilôton
736.10	mêon	murobalanos
736.13	misudion	ôchra
736.12	misu Kuprion	ôchra Kupria
736.11	misu opton	difruges
736.14	molubdaina	litharguron
736.15	molubdon kekaumenon	psimmithion
743.04	molubdou skôria	elkusma
739.03	moreas opos	kissou opos
736.16	morôn chulos	batôn fulla
743.13	moscheion stear	choirion stear palaion
736.18	moschou muelos	oisupos ê elafeios muelos
747.01	mugalês cholê	pithêkou cholê
737.01	muochoda	muia
737.02	murobalanon	peukinon ê glaukion
737.03	mursinitês	moreas opos ê rodakinou opos
737.04	mursinon elaion	schininon elaion ê mêlinon elaion
737.05	napu	kardamou sperma ê goggulidos sperma

Table 2.1   Continued

737.06	napuos sperma	goggulidos sperma
737.08	nardos agria	nardos Indikê
737.09	nardos Indikê	nardos Keltikê
737.07	nardos Suriakê	schoinos arômatikos ê schoinou anthos
737.11	nitron	afronitron ê alas opon
737.10	nitron eruthron	nardostachus
747.09	ôchra	misu Kuprion
738.04	oinanthês chulos	ampeloxulon
738.03	oinanthês chulos	ampelinou blastou chulos ê ampelinou dendrou chulos ê omfax xêros
738.05	oinos Italikos	oinos Mendêsios
736.07	oinos Mendêsios	oinos Italikos
738.06	oinos Rodios	oinos austêros
738.07	oinos Suriakos	oinos Rodios
747.08	ôkimoeides	êduosmon agrion
747.07	ôkimon	sisumbrion
738.08	omfakion	rou chulos
738.09	omfax	sidia êkikis omfakitis
738.10	onokardion	psucha botanê
734.14	onuchitês lithos	achatês lithos
747.10	ôôn lekithoi optoi	elafou muelos
747.12	ôôn purra	meli ê epsêma
747.11	ôou to leukon	gala gunaikeion
739.04	opopanax	kastorion, sukaminou gala, ugropissa
739.11	orminon	linospermon
739.12	ornithogalon	anthullis
739.13	oruza	krithinon aleuron ê krithaleuron
739.14	ostrea	kurêkes
739.15	panakos rizês go. a	opopanakos < a
739.16	papurou riza	elleboros melas
740.01	peperi	ziggiber
740.02	peperi leukon	peperi melan diplasion
740.03	peperi makron	pepereôs leukou b
740.04	peristeras kopros	trugonos kopros ê gupos kopros
740.05	peristereôn	chamailea ê chamaileukê
740.06	persaias fulla xêra	roda xêra
739.05	Persikos opos	kissos
740.07	peukedanon	glukurrizês chulos
739.06	peukedanou opos	glukurizês chulos

Table 2.1   Continued

741.07	peukinê rêtinê	terebinthinê rêtinê
739.07	peukinou opos	gleukuriza
740.08	pisselaion	ugropisson
726.12	pissê bruttia	pissa koinê epsêtheisa met' oxous
740.09	pissê bruttia ugra	asfaltos, pissê egchôrios perissê
747.02	pithêkou cholê	kamêlou cholê
741.08	pituinê xêra rêtinê	sagapênon
740.10	pituokampê	sfêkes eis kedrian sapentes
740.11	poliou sperma	euzômou sperma
740.12	polugonou chulos	arnoglôssou chulos
740.13	polupodion	chamelaias riza ê chamaileontos
740.14	polutrichon	apsinthion
740.15	pomfolux	kadmia kekaumenê
740.16	potamogeitôn	erpullos
740.17	propolis	ladanon ê ammôniakon
747.06	psimmuthion	molubdos kekaumenos ê molibdou skôria
747.05	psullion	fakos o epi tôn telmatôn
741.01	pteris	kneôrou sperma ê knidês sperma
741.02	purethron	ziggiber
741.03	purethrou riza	lapathou riza
734.15	puritês lithos	purobolos lithos
729.01	rafaninon elaion	kikinon elaion
741.05	rafaninon elaion	kikinon elaion
741.04	reon	kentaurion
741.06	rêtinê	kolofônias apochuma
728.11	rodinon elaion	mêlinon elaion
739.08	rododafnês opos	ixos druinos
741.14	rodoeides	sinôpis
741.13	roda xêra	persaias fulla xêra
741.15	rous Suriakê	lapathou riza
742.02	rous bursodepsikos	kikides
742.01	rous mageirikos xêros	sampsuchos
742.09	safinos	kikinon elaion
742.03	sagapênon	chalbanê ê pituos rêtinê xêra
742.04	salamandra	saura chlôra
742.05	sampsuchon	rous mageirikos xêros
742.06	santonikon	abrotonon
742.07	sarapias	paiônias riza
742.08	saturion	euzômou sperma ê elelisfakou sperma

Table 2.1   Continued

744.13	schinon	terebinthos
744.14	schoinos	polugonou riza
744.15	schoinos arômatikos	kardamômon ê kinnamômon
742.10	sêpias ostrakon	kissêris
744.08	sêrikon	litharguros
742.12	sêsamoeides	amarantinon piesma
742.11	sêsamon	linospermon
744.09	sfagnos	brathu
744.10	sfagnos arômatikos	schoinos eirgasmenos
744.11	sfeklê	sandarachê
744.12	sfondulion	kuprou spodos ê elaias fullôn spodos
742.13	sinêpi	kardamon ê kardamômon
742.14	sion	asparagou riza ê lubistikou riza
744.07	sisôn Suriakos	petroselinon Makedonikon
742.15	sisumbrion	ôkimon
743.01	skammônia	kolokunthis, kikeôs krotônes, enteriônes ê lathuris
743.02	skigkos	saturion
743.03	skilla	bolbos
735.05	smaragdos lithos	iaspis lithos
743.06	smurnê Trôglodutis	kalamos arômatikos
744.16	sôri	litharguros difruges ê melantêria
743.07	sousinon elaion	têlinon elaion
728.12	spanon elaion	thalloi apaloi
743.08	spodion	pomfolux
735.06	spoggou lithos	exemoumenos lithos
723.05	stafis agria	foinikes Suriakoi
743.10	stafis êmeros	foinikos Suriakou sarx
743.15	stimmi Koptikon	chalkou lepis
743.16	stoichas	chamaidrus
743.17	strobiloi	sikuou sperma
744.01	strouthion	euforbion, elleboros leukos
744.02	strouthiou riza	elleborou melanos riza
744.03	stuptêria	alas orukton
744.04	stuptêria schistê	sidion
744.05	sturax	kastorion
739.09	sukês opos	moreas opos
744.06	sumfuton	kentaurion
739.10	Suriakos opos	moreas opos
745.01	taurokolla	ichthuokolla

Table 2.1   Continued

745.03	terebinthinê	mastichê ê rêtinê strobilinê
741.09	terebinthinê rêtinê	peukinê rêtinê
745.02	teukrion	chamaidrus
730.04	thapsia	kardamou sperma ê euzômou sperma
730.05	thapsias chulos	chamaileontos melanos chulos ê eludrion
738.12	Thêbês opos	mêkônos opos
730.07	theion apuron	sandarachê
730.06	thermountias	glukofullon
730.08	thridax	intubon
745.04	titanos	gê Eretria
745.05	tragakantha	kommi, terebinthinê
745.06	tribolos	saturion
745.07	trôximon	maiounion, maioulion
733.04	trugonos kopros	peristeras kopros
746.02	uainê cholê	perdikos cholê
747.03	uainê cholê	perdikos cholê
743.14	uainês stear	chêneion stear ê alôpekos stear
745.08	uakinthos	isateôs anthos
735.04	uakinthos lithos	bêrullios lithos
745.09	ugropissa	opopanax
745.10	uoskuamou sperma	kunosbatou sperma ê karpos
745.14	uperikon	anêthou sperma
745.13	upokustidos chulos	akakia ê akanthê chulos
745.12	upokustidos sperma	tragakantha
745.11	upokustis	akakias chulos
746.01	ussôpon	thumon
745.15	ussôpou kêrôtês	muelos moscheios
737.13	xifiou gleukiou riza	saturiou sperma
737.12	xulobalsamon	leukoiou riza
738.01	xulokarpason	kinnamômon
738.02	xulokasia	kinnamômon
730.01	ziggiber	purethron

Table 2.2   Equivalences of materia medica

Materia medica (in alphabetical order of the first term in the first item)	Page/item no.
akanthiou sperma/luchnidos sperma	723.01/735.09
akanthou keratia/akanthê	724.01/723.10
arkeuthides (arkeuthis megalê)/kuperos	725.07/733.15
asfaltos/pissa ugra bruttia	726.01/740.09
difruges/misu opton	728.02/736.11
êduosmon (agrion)/kalaminthê	730.02/731.05
elleboros melas (elleborou melanos riza)/strouthiou riza	729.05/744.02
erpullos/potamogeitôn	729.13/740.16
gê Eretria/titanos (Thêbaikos)	727.04/745.04
kêrukes/ostrea	732.03/739.14
kikinon elaion/rafaninon elaion	728.09/729.01+741.05
kissou opos (kissos)/Persikos opos	732.09/739.05
lapathou riza/purethrou riza	734.04/741.03
libanou floios/(libanou) manna	734.10/736.03
misu Kuprion/ôchra (Kupria)	736.12/747.09
molubdos kekaumenos/psimmithion	736.15/747.06
oinos Italikos/oinos Mendêsios	738.05/736.07
peristeras kopros/trugonos kopros	740.04/733.04
persaias fulla xêra/roda xêra	740.06/741.13
peukinê rêtinê/terebinthinê rêtinê	741.07/741.09
purethron/ziggiber	741.02/730.01
rous mageirikos xêros/sampsuchos	742.01/742.05
sagapênon/chalbanê	742.03/746.07
sisumbrion/ôkimon	742.15/747.07

Note: Alphabetical list of the second term of the first item (which becomes the first term of the second item in the pair): *akanthê, chalbanê, kalaminthê, kuperos, luchnidos sperma, manna (libanou), misu opton, ôchra (Kupria), oinos Mendêsios, ôkimon, ostrea, Persikos opos, pissa ugra bruttia, potamogeitôn, psimmithion, purethrou riza, rafaninon elaion, roda xêra, sampsuchos, strouthiou riza, terebinthinê rêtinê, titanos (Thêbaikos), trugonos kopros, ziggiber.*

Table 2.3 Substitution chains of three or more items

p./no.	Substance	is replaced by	and replaces (1),	p./no.	replaces (2),	p./no.	and replaces (3)	p./no.
723.02	abrotonon	origanon	apsinthion	726.03	santonikon	742.06		
723.06	agchousa	uakinthos	fukos	746.05				
723.09	akakia	schinou chulisma	upokustidos chulos	745.13	elaias Aithiopikês dakruon			
723.10	akantha	akanthou keratia	akanthou keratia	724.01	akté botanê	724.05		
724.03	akoros	asarou riza	amômon	725.01				
724.06	alikakabos	doruknion	kunosbatos	733.14				
724.11	aloé Indikê	aloés chlôras fulla	krokomagma	733.10				
724.07	(alas) ammôniakon	alas Kappadokikon	kostos	733.06				
724.17	ammôniakon thumiama	propolis	komarea	732.15				
726.03	apsinthion	abrotonon	amugdala pikra	724.16	polutrichon	740.14		
725.12	asaron	ziggiber	akoron	724.03	bruônia	726.11		
726.02	asfodelou riza	seutlou chulos	kinnaras riza	741.12				
746.09	chamaidrus	lapathou agriou riza	stoichas	743.16	teuktrion	745.02		
727.13	daukou sperma	siou sperma	anison	725.02				
728.03	doruknion	uoskuamou sperma	alikakabon	724.06	mandragorou chulos	736.02		
743.12 729.03	elafeion stear	chéneion stear ueion stear	elafeios muelos	736.17				
728.07	elaias dakruon	upokistidos chulos	mandragora	736.01				
729.06	elenion	kostos	gentianê	726.13				
729.05	elleboros melas	strouthion	papurou riza	739.16				
729.08	epithumon	kolokunthidos sperma	agarikon	723.04				
729.09	eregmon	strouthion	erusimon	729.14				

Table 2.3   Continued

729.14	erusimon	eregmon	euzômou sperma	729.15		
729.17	euforbion	peristeras agrias kopros	strouthion	744.01		
729.15	euzômou sperma	erusimou sperma	poliou sperma	740.11	saturion	742.08
735.01	Frugios lithos	argurités lithos	magnêtos	735.12	magnêtos lithos	734.13
727.02	gê ampelis	molubdaina	libanos	734.09		
727.04	gê Eretrias	titanos Thêbaikos	gê Krétikê	727.05		
727.08	glêchôn	ussôpon	diktamnos	728.01		
727.09	glukurrizés chulos	sukaminou chulos	peukedanos	740.07	peukedanou opos	739.06
730.09	ixos druinos	chamaileôn melas	rododafnês opos	739.08		
731.05	kalaminthê	êduosmon agrion	elelisfakos	729.04		
746.14	kamêlou cholê	askalabôtou cholê	pithêkou cholê	747.02		
731.09	kardamômon	xulokarpason	schoinos arômatikos	744.15		
731.11	kastorion	agallochon	opopanax	739.04	sturax	744.05
731.14	kedrides	ladanon	kedrea	731.13		
728.09	kikinon elaion	dafninon elaion	rafaninon elaion	729.01 741.05	safinon	742.09
732.07	kinnamômon	pêganon agrion	xulokarpason	738.01	xulokasia	738.02
741.12	kinnaras riza	asfodelou riza	lapathou riza	741.11		
732.08	kissêri	gê Krétikê	sêpias ostrakon	742.10		
732.13	kolokunthis	kikeôs sperma	skammônia	743.01		
733.06	kostos	ammôniakon	elenion	729.06		
733.10	krokomagma	aloé Indikê	krokos	733.09		
734.02	ladanon	sampsuchon	kekrides	731.14	propolis	740.17

Table 2.3   Continued

741.11	lapathou riza	kinnaras riza	rous Suriakê	741.15				
735.07	linospermon	kuamou chulos	orminon	739.11	sésamon	742.11		
736.02	mandragorou chulos	doruknion	mêkôn	736.08	mêkônos opos	739.02		
736.04	mastichê	schoinou kardia	terebinthinê	745.03				
739.02	mêkônos opos	mandragorou chulos	Thêbês opos	738.12				
736.06	meli	epsêma	ôôn purra	747.12				
736.14	molubdaina	litharguron	gê apalê ê ampelis	727.02				
739.03	moreas opos	kissou opos	mursinités	737.03	sukês opos	739.09	Suriakos opos	739.10
736.18	moschou muelos	elafeios oisupos	ussôpou kêrotês	745.15				
737.02	murobalanon	peukinon	mêon	736.10				
738.06	oinos Rodios	oinos austêros	oinos Suriakos	738.07				
739.04	opopanax	kastorion	ugropissa	745.09				
739.16	papurou riza	elleboros melas	ebiskou riza	728.06				
740.02	peperi leukon	peperi melan	peperi makron	740.03				
747.02	pithêkou cholê	kamêlou cholê	mugalês cholê	747.01				
740.15	pomfolux	kadmia kekaumenê	spodion	743.08				
740.17	propolis	ladanon	ammôniakou thumiama	724.17				
728.11	rodinon elaion	mêlinon elaion	chamaimêlinon elaion	728.13				
741.14	rodoeides	sinôpis	kinnabari	732.06				
742.05	sampsuchon	rous mageirikos xêros	aigeirou akremones	723.08	ladanon	734.02		
742.08	saturion	euzômou sperma	skigkos	743.02	tribolos	745.06		

Table 2.3 Continued

744.15	schoinos arômatikos	kardamômon	nardos Suriakê	737.07		
742.11	sêsamon	linospermon	arakos	725.03		
744.09	sfagnos	brathu	fou	746.04		
744.10	sfagnos arômatikos	schoinos eirgasmenos	bdellion	726.07		
744.01	strouthion	euforbion	eregmon	729.09	leukinou anthos	734.07
744.06	sumfuton	kentaurion	korallion	733.05		
739.10	Suriakos opos	moreas opos	Kurênaikos opos	739.01		
745.05	tragakantha	kommi	upokustidos sperma	745.12		
745.08	uakinthos	isateôs anthos	agchousa	723.06		
745.10	uoskuamou sperma	kunosbatou sperma ê karpos	doruknion	728.03		
745.11	upokustis	akakias chulos	balaustion	726.04		
745.13	upokustidos chulos	akakias akanthês chulos	elaias Aithiopikês dakruon	728.08		
746.01	ussôpon	thumon	glêchôn	727.08		
730.01	ziggiber	purethron	asaron	725.12	peperi	740.01

Table 2.4   Materia medica substituted

Materia medica substituted	Substitute	Page/item no.
aeizôon	thridakos fulla ê chulos	723.07
agarikon	epithumon ê euforbion	723.04
aigeirou akremones	sampsuchon	723.08
ailourou kopros	ichneumonos kopros	733.01
akoniton	iridos agrias ê riza	724.02
aktê botanê	akantha ê akanthou keratia	724.05
aktea	glaukion ê oios kopros	724.04
aloê	ibeôs kopros	724.10
alôpekos stear	arkeion stear + arkteion stear	724.12 + 743.11
alos anthos	sandarachê	724.09
ami	anison	724.13
amianton	afroselinon	724.14
amômon	akoros	725.01
amugdala pikra	apsinthion	724.16
amulon	guris xêra	724.15
arakos	sêsamon	725.03
argemônê	serifion	725.04
armala	kardamômon Babulônion	725.08
Armenion	melan Indikon	725.09
arômatikê	kalamos arômatikos	725.11
arsenikon	sandarachê	725.10
asbestos	akantha eis ta bafia	725.13
Asios lithos	gagatês lithos ê ales ammôniakoi ê sandarachê	725.15 + 734.12
aspalathos	erikês karpos ê agnou sperma	725.16
balaustion	upokistis ê roa skutinê	726.04
balsamon	iou leukou riza	726.05
balsamou opos	smurnê staktê + dadinon, karpasou opos, balsamou karpos	726.06 + 738.11
bdellion	sfagnos arômatikos	726.07
bêsasa	pêganou agriou (ê êmerou) sperma	726.08
bouprêstis	silfai bdeousai ê bdella	726.09
bouturon	galaktos boeiou epipagos	726.10
bruônia	asarou riza	726.11
chalkanthê	chalkou lepis	746.08
Chalkêdonion	kuaneos lithos	735.03

Table 2.4   Continued

chamaimêlinon elaion	rodinon elaion	728.13
chamaimêlon	anthemis	746.11
damassônion	karpêsion ê kalaminthê ê êruggion	727.12
diktamnos	glêchôn ê elelisfakos	728.01
drakontion	aron	728.04
ebenos	lôtinon xulon	728.05
ebiskou riza	papurou riza ê moreas fulla	728.06
echeôs cholê	ichneumonos cholê	746.13
elafou keras	aigos keras	732.01
elaias Aithiopikês dakruon	akakia	728.08
elaion palaion	sikuônion elaion, choireion palaion stear	728.10
elatêriou chulos	prasou chulos ê sukeas chulos	729.02
elelisfakos	kalaminthê	729.04
enneafullon	kolokunthidos sperma ê potamogeitôn	729.07
erinou fulla	moreas fulla ê ibeôs kopros	729.12
eupatorion	chemaipitus	729.16
feklê	sandarachê	746.03
fou	sfagnos	746.04
fukos	agchousa	746.05
fullon	nardostachus ê iris Illurikê	746.06
galês cholê	kamêlou cholê	746.12
gentianê (riza)	elenion ê petroselinou riza + selinou arômatikou riza	726.13 + 727.01
gê astêr	gê kimôlia	727.03
gê Megara	aloês achnê	727.06
gê Samia	leukografis Aiguptia	727.07
gupos kopros	peristeras kopros	727.11 + 733.02
ios chalkês	gupos ê perdikos cholê	730.11
ios sidêrou	litharguros ê sidêrou skôria	730.10
ippouris	chamaipitus	731.01
kagchru	dafnês kokkoi ê purethron	731.12
kallikeras	têlis	731.06
kantharides	falaggia	731.07
kassia	kinnamômou manna ê brathu	731.10
kedrea	kedrides	731.13
keraunion	leukografis	731.15
kêron	eregmos meta propoleôs	732.02
kêrukes	ostrea	732.03
kinnabari	rodoeides	732.06

Table 2.4   Continued

klinopodion	êliotropion	732.10
knikou sperma	agnou sperma	732.12
komarea	ammôniakon thumiama	732.15
korallion	sumfuton ê môlu	733.05
kotulêdôn	onokardion ê anagallis	733.07
krinanthemon	afrodisias	733.08
krokodeilou stear	kunos thalattiou stear	733.11
krokos	krokomagma	733.09
kufi	ischas kekaumenê	733.16
kuminon (Aithiopikon)	krambês sperma + melanthion	733.12 + 733.13
Kupria skôria	melantêria Aiguptikê	743.05
Kurênaikos opos	Suriakos opos, lasaros, ê moschou muelos, ê silfiou opos	739.01
lagôos thalattios	kogchos potamios ê lagôos potamios	734.01
lathurides	knidios kokkos	734.03
lêmnia sfragis	sandarachê	734.08
lepidion (riza)	eruthrodanon + kappareôs fulla	734.06 + 734.05
leukinou anthos	strouthion	734.07
libathron	traktulos	734.11
lukou kopros	kunos kopros	733.03
magnêsias uelinon	ptuelon Italikon	735.11
magnêtos	Frugios ê aimatitês lithos	735.12
malabathron	kassia sfairitês ê nardostachus ê traktulos ê nardos Indikê	735.13
malachê	têlis	735.14
mêlokudônia	melilôton	736.09
mêon	murobalanos	736.10
misudion	ôchra	736.13
moscheion stear	choirion stear palaion	743.13
moschou muelos	elafou oisupos ê muelos	736.18
mugalês cholê	pithêkou cholê	747.01
muochoda	muia	737.01
napu	kardamou ê goggulidos sperma	737.05
nardos Suriakê	schoinos arômatikos ê schoinou anthos	737.07
nitron	afronitron ê alas opon	737.11
nitron eruthron	nardostachus	737.10
oinanthês chulos	ampelinou blastou ê dendrou chulos ê omfax xêros + ampeloxulon	738.03 + 738.04

Table 2.4   Continued

oinos Suriakos	oinos Rodios	738.07
ôkimoeides	êduosmon agrion	747.08
omfakion	rou chulos	738.08
omfax	sidia ê kikis omfakitis	738.09
onuchitos lithos	achatês lithos	734.14
ôôn lekitha	elafou muelos	747.10
ôôn purra	meli ê epsêma	747.12
ôou leukon	gala gunaikeion	747.11
orminon	linospermon	739.11
ornithogala	anthullis	739.12
oruza	krithinon aleuron	739.13
panakos riza	opopanax	739.15
peristereôn	chamailea ê chamaileukê	740.05
peukedanon (+ opos)	glukurrizês chulos	740.07 + 739.06
pisselaion	ugropisson	740.08
pituinê rêtinê	sagapênon	741.08
pituokampê	sfêkes eis kedrian sapentes	740.10
poliou sperma	euzômou sperma	740.11
polupodion	chamelaias ê chamaileontos riza	740.13
polutrichon	apsinthion	740.14
psullion	fakos o epi tôn telmatôn	747.05
pteris	kneôrou ê knidês sperma	741.01
puritês lithos	purobolos lithos	734.15
rafaninon elaion	kikinon elaion	729.01 + 741.05
rêon	kentaurion	741.04
rêtinê	kolofônias apochuma	741.06
rododafnês opos	ixos druinos	739.08
rous Suriakê	lapathou riza	741.15
rous bursodepsikê	kikides	742.02
safinos	kikinon elaion	742.09
salamandra	saura chlôra	742.04
santonikon	abrotonon	742.06
sarapias	paionias riza	742.07
sêpias ostrakon	kissêris	742.10
serikon	litharguros	744.08
sêsamoeides	amarantinon piesma	742.12
sfeklê	sandarachê	744.11
sfondulion	kuprou ê elaias fullôn spodos	744.12

Table 2.4   Continued

sinêpi	kardamon ê kardamômon	742.13
sisôn Suriakos	petroselinon Makedonikon	744.07
skammônia	kolokunthis, kikeôs krotônes, enteriônes, ê lathuris	743.01
skigkos	saturion	743.02
skilla	bolbos	743.03
smaragdos lithos	iaspis lithos	735.05
smurnê Troglodutis	kalamos arômatikos	743.06
sôri	litharguros difruges ê melantêria	744.16
sousinon elaion	têlinon elaion	743.07
spanon elaion	thalloi apaloi	728.12
spodion	pomfolux	743.08
spoggou lithos	exouroumenos lithos	735.06
stafis agria	foinikes Suriakoi	723.05
stafis êmeros	foinikos Suriakou sarx	743.10
stimmi Koptikon	chalkou lepis	743.15
stoichas	chamaidrus	743.16
strobiloi	sikuou sperma	743.17
stuptêria schistê	sidion	744.04
sturax	kastorion	744.05
sukês opos	moreas opos	739.09
taurokolla	ichthuokolla	745.01
teukrion	chamaidrus	745.02
thapsia (+ chulos)	kardamou ê euzômou sperma ê chamaileontos melanos chulos ê eludrion	730.04 + 730.05
Thêbês opos	mêkônos opos	738.12
theion apuron	sandarachê	730.07
thermountias	glukofullon	730.06
thridax	intubon	730.08
tribolos	saturion	745.06
trôximon	maiounion	745.07
uainê cholê	perdikos cholê	746.02 + 747.03
uakinthos lithos	bêrullios lithos	735.04
uperikon	anêthou sperma	745.14
ussôpou kêrôtê	moscheios muelos	745.15
xifiou gleukiou riza	saturiou sperma	737.13
xulobalsamon	leukoiou riza	737.12
xulokasia	kinnamômon	738.02

Table 2.5   Substitute materia medica

Substitute	Materia medica substituted	Page/item no.
abrotonon	santonikon	742.06
achatês lithos	onuchitos lithos	734.14
afrodisias	krinanthemon	733.08
afronitron	nitron	737.11
afroselinon	amianton	724.14
agchousa	fukos	746.05
agnou sperma	knikou sperma	732.12
aigos keras	elafou keras	732.01
aigos kopros	Asios lithos	734.12
aimatitês	magnêtos	735.12
akakia	elaias Aithiopikês dakruon	728.08
akantha	aktê botanê	724.05
akantha eis ta bafia	asbestos	725.13
akanthou keratia	aktê botanê	724.05
akoros	amômon	725.01
ales ammôniakoi	Asios lithos	734.12
aloês achnê	gê Megara	727.06
amarantinon piesma	sêsamoeides	742.12
ammôniakon thumiama	komarea	732.15
ampelinou blastou ê dendrou chulos + ampeloxulon	oinanthês chulos	738.03 + 738.04
anagallis	kotulêdôn	733.07
anêthou sperma	uperikon	745.14
anison	ami	724.13
anthemis	chamaimêlon	746.11
anthullis	ornithogala	739.12
apsinthion	polutrichon	740.14
apsinthion	amugdala pikra	724.16
arkeion stear + arkteion stear	alôpekos stear	724.12 + 743.11
aron	drakontion	728.04
asarou riza	bruônia	726.11
balsamou karpos	balsamou opos	738.11
bdella	bouprêstis	726.09
bêrullios lithos	uakinthos lithos	735.04
bolbos	skilla	743.03
brathu	kassia	731.10
chalkou lepis	chalkanthê	746.08

Table 2.5   Continued

chalkou lepis	stimmi Koptikon	743.15
chamaidrus	stoichas	743.16
chamaidrus	teukrion	745.02
chamailea	peristereôn	740.05
chamaileôn	polupodion	740.13
chamaileontos melanos chulos	thapsias chulos	730.05
chamaileukê	peristereôn	740.05
chamaipitus	eupatorion	729.16
chamaipitus	ippouris	731.01
chamelaias riza	polupodion	740.13
choireion stear palaion	elaion palaion	728.10
choirion stear palaion	moscheion stear	743.13
dadinon	balsamou opos	738.11
dafnês kokkoi	kagchru	731.12
êduosmon agrion	ôkimoeides	747.08
elafou muelos	ôôn lekitha	747.10
elafou oisupos ê muelos	moschou muelos	736.18
elaias fulla	sfondulion	744.12
elaias fullôn spodos	Kuprias spodos	743.09
elaion to diploun	elaion palaion	728.10
elaion (to diploun) meta uos palaiou steatos	elaion palaion	728.10
elelisfakos	diktamnos	728.01
elenion	gentianê	726.13
êliotropion	klinopodion	732.10
enteriônes	skammônia	743.01
epithumon	agarikon	723.04
epsêma	ôôn purra	747.12
eregmos meta propoleôs	kêron	732.02
ereikês karpos	aspalathos	725.16
êruggion	damassônion	727.12
eruthrodanon + kappareôs fulla	lepidion	734.06 + 734.05
euforbion	agarikon	723.04
euzômou sperma	poliou sperma	740.11
euzômou sperma	thapsia	730.04
exouroumenos lithos	spoggou lithos	735.06
fakos o epi tôn telmatôn	psullion	747.05
falaggia	kantharides	731.07
foinikes Suriakoi	stafis agria	723.05

Table 2.5   Continued

foinikos Suriakou sarx	stafis êmeros	743.10
Frugios lithos	magnêtos	735.12
gagatês lithos	Asios lithos	725.15 + 734.12
gala gunaikeion	ôou leukon	747.11
galaktos boeiou epipagos	bouturon	726.10
gê kimôlia	gê astêr	727.03
glaukion	aktea	724.04
glêchôn	diktamnos	728.01
glukofullon	thermountias	730.06
glukurrizês chulos	peukedanon (peukedanou opos)	740.07 + 739.06
goggulidos sperma	napu	737.05
gupos cholê	ios chalkês	730.11
guris xêra	amulon	724.15
iaspis lithos	smaragdos lithos	735.05
ibeôs kopros	aloê	724.10
ibeôs kopros	erinou fulla	729.12
ichneumonos cholê	echeôs cholê	746.13
ichneumonos kopros	ailourou kopros	733.01
ichthuokolla	taurokolla	745.01
intubon	thridax	730.08
iou leukou riza	balsamon	726.05
iridos agrias ê riza	akoniton	724.02
iris Illurikê	fullon	746.06
ischas kekaumenê	kufi	733.16
ixos druinos	rododafnês opos	739.08
kalaminthê	damassônion	727.12
kalaminthê	elelisfakos	729.04
kalamos arômatikos	arômatikê	725.11
kalamos arômatikos	smurnê Troglodutis	743.06
kamêlou cholê	galês cholê	746.12
kardamômon	sinêpi	742.13
kardamômon Babulônion	armala	725.08
kardamon	sinêpi	742.13
kardamou sperma	napu	737.05
kardamou sperma	thapsia	730.04
karpasou opos	balsamou opos	738.11
karpêsion	damassônion	727.12
kassia sfairitês	malabathron	735.13

Table 2.5   Continued

kastorion	sturax	744.05
kedrides	kedrea	731.13
kentaurion	rêon	741.04
kikides	rous bursodepsikê	742.02
kikinon elaion	rafaninon elaion	729.01 + 741.05
kikinon elaion	safinos	742.09
kikis omfakitis	omfax	738.09
kinnamômon	kassia	731.10
kinnamômon	xulokasia	738.02
kissêris	sêpias ostrakon	742.10
kneôrou sperma	pteris	741.01
knidê	pteris	741.01
knidios kokkos	lathurides	734.03
kogchos potamios	lagôos thalattios	734.01
kolofônias apochuma	rêtinê	741.06
kolokunthidos sperma	enneafullon	729.07
kolokunthis	skammônia	743.01
krambês sperma	kuminon	733.12
krithinon aleuron (krithaleuron)	oruza	739.13
krokomagma	krokos	733.09
krotônes kikeôs	skammônia	743.01
kuaneos lithos	Chalkêdonion	735.03
kunos kopros	lukou kopros	733.03
kunos thalattios stear	krokodeilou stear	733.11
kuprou spodos	sfondulion	744.12
lagôos potamios	lagôos thalattios	734.01
lapathou riza	rous Suriakê	741.15
lasaros	Kurênaikos opos	739.01
lathuris	skammônia	743.01
leukografis	keraunion	731.15
leukografis Aiguptia	gê Samia	727.07
leukoiou riza	xulobalsamon	737.12
linospermon	orminon	739.11
litharguros	ios sidêrou	730.10
litharguros	sêrikon	744.08
litharguros difrugês	sôri	744.16
lôtinon xulon	ebenos	728.05
maiounion	trôximon	745.07

Table 2.5   Continued

manna	kassia	731.10
mêkônos opos	Thêbês opos	738.12
melan Indikon	Armenion	725.09
melantêria	sôri	744.16
melantêria Aiguptiakê	Kuprias skôria	743.05
melanthion	kuminon Aithiopikon	733.13
meli	ôôn purra	747.12
melilôton	mêlokudônia	736.09
môlu	korallion	733.05
moreas fulla	ebiskou riza	728.06
moreas fulla	erinou fulla	729.12
moreas opos	sukês opos	739.09
moscheios muelos	ussôpou kêrôtê	745.15
moschou muelos	Kurênaikos opos	739.01
muia	muochoda	737.01
murobalanos	mêon	736.10
nardos Indikê	malabathron	735.13
nardostachus	fullon	746.06
nardostachus	malabathron	735.13
nardostachus	nitron eruthron	737.10
ôchra	misudion	736.13
oinos Rodios	oinos Suriakos	738.07
oios kopros	aktea	724.04
omfax xêros	oinanthês chulos	738.03
onokardion	kotulêdôn	733.07
opopanax	panakos riza	739.15
ostrea	kêrukes	732.03
paiônias riza	sarapiados	742.07
papurou riza	ebiskou riza	728.06
pêganou agriou (ê êmerou) sperma	bêsasa	726.08
perdikos cholê	ios chalkês	730.11
perdikos cholê	uainê cholê	746.02 + 747.03
peristeras kopros	gupos kopros	727.11 + 733.02
petroselinon Makedonikon	sisôn Suriakos	744.07
pithêkou cholê	mugalês cholê	747.01
pomfolux	spodion	743.08
potamogeitôn	enneafullon	729.07
prasou chulos	elatêriou chulos	729.02

Table 2.5   Continued

ptuelon Italikon	magnêsias uelinon	735.11
purethron	kagchru	731.12
purobolos lithos	puritês lithos	734.15
roa skutinê	balaustion	726.04
rodinon elaion	chamaimêlinon elaion	728.13
rodoeides	kinnabari	732.06
rou chulos	omfakion	738.08
sagapênon	rêtinê pituinê xêra	741.08
sampsuchon	aigeirou akremones	723.08
sandarachê	alos anthos	724.09
sandarachê	arsenikon	725.10
sandarachê	Asios lithos	734.12
sandarachê	feklê	746.03
sandarachê	lêmnia sfragis	734.08
sandarachê	sfeklê	744.11
sandarachê	theion apuron	730.07
saturion	skigkos	743.02
saturion	tribolos	745.06
saturiou sperma	xifiou gleukiou riza	737.13
saura chlôra	salamandra	742.04
schoinos arômatikos (ê schoinou anthos)	nardos Suriakê	737.07
selinou arômatikou riza	gentianê	727.02
serifion	argemônê	725.04
sêsamon	arakos	725.03
sfagnos	fou	746.04
sfagnos arômatikos	bdellion	726.07
sfêkes eis kedrian sapentes	pituokampê	740.10
sidêrou skôria	sidêrou ios	730.10
sidia	omfax	738.09
sidion	stuptêria schistê	744.04
sikuônion	elaion palaion	728.10
sikuou sperma	strobiloi	743.17
silfai bdeousai	bouprêstis	726.09
silfiou opos	Kurênaikos opos	739.01
smurnês staktê	balsamou opos	726.06 + 738.11
strouthion	leukinon anthos	734.07
sukeas chulos	elatêriou chulos	729.02
sumfuton	korallion	733.05

Table 2.5   Continued

Suriakos opos	Kurênaikos opos	739.01
têlinon elaion	sousinon elaion	743.07
têlis	kallikeras	731.06
têlis	malachês	735.14
thalloi apalis elaias	spanon elaion	728.12
thridakos fulla ê chulos	aeizôon	723.07
traktulos	libathron	734.11
traktulos	malabathron	735.13
ugropisson	pisselaion	740.08
upokistis	balaustion	726.04

Bibliography

Ackermann, Johannes Chr. *Historia litteraria Claudii Galeni*. In J.A. Fabricius and A.G.C. Harless (eds), *Bibliotheca graeca*, 4th edn, vol. 5 (Hamburg: C.E. Bohn, 1793), 397–500. Repr. in *Claudii Galeni Opera omnia*, ed. Kühn, 1:xii–cclxv.

Boudon-Millet, Véronique (ed.). *Galien*, vol. 1: *Introduction générale: Sur l'ordre de ses propres livres; Sur ses propres livres; Que l'excellent médecin est aussi philosophe*. Paris: Les Belles Lettres, 2007.

Diels, Hermann. *Die Handschriften der antiken Ärzte*, pt 1: *Hippokrates und Galenos*. Abhandlungen der königlichen Akademie der Wissenschaften, Jahre 1905, Abh. 3. Berlin: Königliche Akademie der Wissenschaften, 1905.

Dioscorides. *De materia medica libri quinque*. Ed. Max Wellmann. 3 vols. Berlin: Weidmann, 1906–14. Repr. Berlin: Weidmann, 1958.

———. *De materia medica*. Trans. Lily Y. Beck. Altertumswissenschaftliche Texte und Studien 38. Hildesheim: Olms-Weidmann, 2005.

Fichtner, Gerhard. *Corpus Galenicum: Verzeichnis der galenischen und pseudogalenischen Schriften*. Expanded edn. Tübingen: Institut für Geschichte der Medizin, 1997.

Galen. *Claudii Galeni Opera omnia*. Ed. C.G. Kühn. 20 vols in 22. Leipzig: C. Cnobloch, 1821–33. Repr. Hildesheim: Georg Olms, 1964–65.

Ilberg, Johannes. *Über die Schriftstellerei des Klaudios Galenos*. Darmstadt: Wissenschaftliche Buchgesellschaft, 1974. Originally published in *Rheinisches Museum für Philologie* 44 (1889): 207–39; 47 (1892): 489–514; 51 (1896): 165–96; and 52 (1897): 591–623.

Nutton, Vivian. *Karl Gottlob Kühn and His Edition of the Works of Galen: A Bibliography*. Oxford: Oxford Microform Publications, 1976.

Pliny. *Natural History*. Ed. and trans. H. Rackham, W.H.S. Jones, and D.E. Eichholz. 10 vols. Loeb Classical Library. Cambridge, MA: Harvard University Press, 1938–63.

Riddle, John M. "Theory and Practice in Medieval Medicine." *Viator* 5 (1974): 157–84. Repr. as ch. 6 in Riddle, *Quid pro Quo*.

———. "Methodology of Historical Drug Research." Ch. 15 in Riddle, *Quid pro Quo*.

———. *Quid pro Quo: Studies in the History of Drugs*. Collected Studies Series CS 367. Aldershot, UK: Variorum, 1992.

Schmitz, Rudolf. *Geschichte der Pharmazie*, vol. 1: *Von den Anfängen bis zum Ausgang des Mittelalters*. Eschborn: Govi-Verlag, 1998.

Schubring, Konrad. "Bemerkungen zur Galenausgabe von Karl Gottlob Kühn und zu ihrem Nachdruck." In *Claudii Galeni Opera omnia*, ed. Kühn, reprint edn, 1:v–lxii.

Sigerist, Henry E. "The Latin Medical Literature of the Early Middle Ages." *Journal of the History of Medicine and Allied Sciences* 13 (1958): 127–46.

Stoll, Ulrich. *Das "Lorscher Arzneibuch": Ein medizinisches Kompendium des 8. Jahrhunderts (Codex Bambergensis medicinalis 1). Text, Übersetzung und Fachglossar*. Sudhoffs Archiv Beiheft 28. Stuttgart: Franz Steiner, 1992.

Touwaide, Alain. "Byzantine Medical Manuscripts: Toward a New Catalogue." *Byzantinische Zeitschrift* 101 (2008): 199–208.

———. "Byzantine Medical Manuscripts: Towards a New Catalogue, with a Specimen for an Annotated Checklist of Manuscripts Based on an Index of Diels' Catalogue." *Byzantion* 79 (2009): 453–595.

Tutin, T.J. (ed.). *Flora Europea*, vol. 4: *Plantaginaceae to Compositae*. Cambridge: Cambridge University Press, 1976.

Chapter 3
Speaking in Tongues: Medical Wisdom and Glossing Practices in and around Salerno, c. 1040–1200[1]

Florence Eliza Glaze

The transmission of Latin medical texts carrying important information useful to medical practitioners of the medieval period, and the adaptation of those texts to reflect the interests of users over time and distance, have long fascinated historians of medicine and philologists alike. The very international nature of the transmission process, by which so many texts originated in the Greek world and were adapted in various ways during the translation and transmission processes across Europe, produced a literature filled with esoteric terminologies of a technical nature.[2] The correct apprehension of these often obscure or unfamiliar terms, as well as the medicinal ingredients' accessibility, were perceived as crucial to the practice of learned medicine by those who commissioned the texts' reproduction, and by those who used them.

[1]   An early version of this paper was presented at the 2009 meeting of the American Association for the History of Medicine in Cleveland, OH. The author is grateful for the excellent comments of the audience and of her copresenters, Monica H. Green and Michael R. McVaugh.

[2]   Consider, for instance, the origins, translations, and adaptations of Dioscorides' treatise on materia medica so neatly delineated by John M. Riddle's "Dioscorides" entry in Ferdinand E. Cranz and Paul Oskar Kristeller (eds), *Catalogus Translationum et Commentariorum: Mediaeval and Renaissance Translations and Commentaries*, vol. 4 (Washington, D.C.: Catholic University of America Press, 1980), 1–143. See also his "Byzantine Commentaries on Dioscorides," *Dumbarton Oaks Papers* 38 (1984): 95–102, and "Pseudo-Dioscorides' 'Ex herbis femininis' and Early Medieval Medical Botany," *Journal of the History of Biology* 14 (1981): 43–81, both of which are reproduced in John M. Riddle, *Quid pro Quo: Studies in the History of Drugs*, Collected Studies Series CS 367 (Brookfield, VT: Ashgate, 1992). One can also find in the latter volume Riddle's essay "The Latin Alphabetical Dioscorides."

Consequently, sets of glosses and dictionaries were accumulated in order to meet this need for greater clarity to aid understanding and facilitate practice.[3]

Nowhere was this need more pressing than in southern Italy during the late eleventh and twelfth centuries, where three textual traditions and three populations—Latin, Greek, and Arabic—all converged during the six decades from *c.* 1040 to 1100 in a way that promoted scholarly debate and a search for greater medical certainty. The efflorescence of texts that ensued, many of them new translations into Latin, but some of them intelligent adaptations or new editions of older Latin sources, reflects an environment where the population of those persons interested and involved in the practice of medicine struggled to find a common language of verbal signifiers that would "track" from one text to another, regardless of the respective texts' origins. Over the course of the twelfth century—the era in which Salerno became a venue for collective medical education focused around the teachings of individual masters who produced both scholastic commentaries on core texts as well as therapeutic manuals of their own—the practice of glossing obscure phrases, the names of medicinal ingredients and preparations, and central theoretical concepts became an important occupation for teachers at the front of the medical classroom. This was especially important when Latin texts based upon late ancient sources, texts translated very recently from Arabic to Latin, or pharmacopoeias dense in Greek-named preparations all had to "speak" to the student and the practitioner in one comprehensible language. As such, the decoding and cross-referencing of terms and ideas performed an essential role in the scholastic process.[4]

---

[3]   Medical dictionaries or glossaries served an essential role in helping readers to decode such terms circulated from antiquity forward, of course, as did the provision of synonyms within texts such as herbals; see Loren C. MacKinney, "Medieval Medical Dictionaries and Glossaries," in James Lea Cate and Eugene N. Anderson (eds), *Medieval and Historiographical Essays in Honor of James Westfall Thompson* (Chicago: University of Chicago Press, 1938), 240–68, and more recently, Alejandro García González, "Hermeneumata medicobotanica vetustiora," *Studi medievali* 49 (2008): 119–40. The Greek-Latin *Hermeneumata* of the early medieval period were edited by Georg Goetz; see vol. 3 of his *Corpus glossariorum latinorum* (Leipzig: Teubner, 1892). Other important foundational studies include Jerry Stannard, "Botanical Data in Medieval Medical Recipes," *Studies in the History of Medicine* 1 (1977): 80–87; idem, "The Herbal as a Medical Document," *Bulletin of the History of Medicine* 43 (1969): 212–20; and idem, "Medieval Herbals and Their Development," *Clio Medica* 9 (1974): 23–33.

[4]   Medical knowledge and practices in southern Italy during the pivotal eleventh and twelfth centuries have become the focus of a significantly renewed scholarly interest since the year 2000. The new series "Edizione Nazionale 'La Scuola Medica Salernitana,'" published by SISMEL, Edizioni del Galluzzo, has resulted in two volumes of conference proceedings and three scholarly text editions, with an additional volume of conference proceedings now in preparation. These volumes include Danielle Jacquart and Agostino Paravicini Bagliani (eds), *La scuola medica*

These glosses and comments, added between lines and into the margins of many surviving manuscripts, stand as the cultural residues of the pedagogical process, but have received as yet only limited attention from modern scholars who seek to understand how many texts of the region were utilized by the population of teachers, students, and practitioners.[5]

Manuscript scholars who pause to examine some of the minutiae of medical texts produced in and around the city of Salerno during the late eleventh and twelfth centuries, as well as the consistency of a given glossed text from one surviving copy to another, are able to detect important details that provide essential information about the scholastic enterprise. Such examinations might reveal the evolution of a text as it was expanded or contracted by subsequent users, materials added to texts to clarify them, or even "dialogues" between different texts manifest in marginal cross-references and commentary.[6] It is the

salernitana: gli autori e i testi, Edizione Nazionale "La Scuola Medica Salernitana" 1 (Florence: SISMEL, Edizioni del Galluzzo, 2007); Alejandro García González (ed.), *Alphita*, Edizione Nazionale "La Scuola Medica Salernitana" 2 (Florence: SISMEL, Edizioni del Galluzzo, 2007); Danielle Jacquart and Agostino Paravicini Bagliani (eds), *La "Collectio Salernitana" di Salvatore De Renzi: convegno internazionale, Università degli Studi di Salerno, 18–19 giugno 2007*, Edizione Nazionale "La Scuola Medica Salernitana" 3 (Florence: SISMEL, Edizioni del Galluzzo, 2008); Monica H. Green (ed.), *Trotula: un compendio medievale di medicina delle donne*, trans. Valentina Brancone, Edizione Nazionale "La Scuola Medica Salernitana" 4 (Florence: SISMEL, Edizioni del Galluzzo, 2009); Ps.-Bartholomaeus Mini de Senis, *Tractatus de herbis (Ms London, British Library, Egerton 747)*, ed. Iolanda Ventura, Edizione Nazionale "La Scuola Medica Salernitana" 5 (Florence: SISMEL, Edizioni del Galluzzo, 2009). The proceedings of the "Terapie e Guarigioni" conference are forthcoming in the same series.

5   I accept Gernot Wieland's assertion that glosses added to manuscripts in an educational context stand "in place of the teacher's tongue," though of course there are some cases where an assiduous reader/owner of a text might have introduced his own glosses during private reader-text interaction. See Gernot R. Wieland, "Interpreting the Interpretations: The Polysemy of the Latin Gloss," *Journal of Medieval Latin* 8 (1998): 59–71.

6   On the construction of such glosses and the development of the tradition in the early Middle Ages, see Martin Irvine, *The Making of Textual Culture: "Grammatica" and Literary Theory, 350–1100* (Cambridge: Cambridge University Press, 1994), esp. "Semeiology of the Page" and "Reading like a *Grammaticus*," 371–91 and 437–47, respectively. On the various types of commentary, see James J. O'Donnell's enumeration of several distinct kinds, each functioning differently in the historical context: (1) "transcription (with or without editing) of oral presentation of exposition of a text read aloud to a broad public," (2) "marginal notes and interlineations in an authoritative text (with important transformation that occurs when the marginalia of an authoritative commentator are extracted and made the center of a book and the text reduced to lemmata)," (3) "compilations of marginalia (e.g., the Glossa Ordinaria or the Talmud)," (4) the "deliberate writing of a 'commentary' as a vehicle for the exposition of the commentator's own views," and (5) "the ambitious learned commentary headed by a *recusatio* purporting that the subjoined work is only a humble commentary-for-students." See O'Donnell's review of Glenn

purpose of this essay to consider in this context sets of glosses of Greek technical terminology, medicinal preparations, and materia medica that were added to the earliest known Salernitan text, the *Passionarius/Liber nosematon* of the physician Gariopontus of Salerno, which was produced prior to *c.* 1050.[7] Such glosses reveal that scholastic features added to the text of the *Passionarius* were designed to improve readers' understanding of the terms involved in Gariopontus' narrative and to draw upon pedagogical concerns and methods in order to build a common language connecting his early text with other, later texts. Thus, this older, pre-scholastic text continued to hold value for the Salernitan teachers and practitioners in the region and helped to teach them the pharmacological and other technical terms they needed to master in their drive to professionalize.

It is essential to clarify from the outset that what Gariopontus did in compiling and editing his text, which was clearly meant to serve as a "complete" manual of diseases and the measures to treat them, intended for the learned practitioner, was at the time of its composition an almost entirely unprecedented undertaking. We get a sense of his agenda as a redactive author when we consider the sources he used, how he manipulated them, and how he introduced his own efforts as a medical writer. The interesting thing about the *Passionarius* is that it was neither a text constructed *de novo* nor a translation of a work from Greek or Arabic; it was put together, instead, from preexisting literature originally rendered into Latin in late antiquity. The source texts Gariopontus employed had appeared sequentially as an ensemble in early medieval manuscripts. These included the late ancient/early medieval Galenic *De medendi methodo ad Glauconem* in two books, an anonymous early Byzantine text which circulated with these as *Liber tertius*, two condensed adaptations of Caelius Aurelianus' *Acute Diseases* and *Chronic Diseases* (known in several early Latin manuscripts as the *Aurelius* and *Esculapius*), excerpts from Theodorus Priscianus' *Euporiston*, and a short excerpt from Alexander of Tralles' medical encyclopedia which first appears in the eleventh century as an independently circulating mini-treatise, *De podagra*, on gout.[8] It thus provided a head-to-foot catalogue of conditions,

---

W. Most, *Commentaries—Kommentare* (Göttingen: Vandenhoeck and Ruprecht, 1999), in *Bryn Mawr Classical Review* online, http://bmcr.brynmawr.edu/2000/2000-05-19.html. On ancient medical commentary, see Heinrich von Staden, "'A woman does not become ambidextrous': Galen and the Culture of Scientific Commentary," in Roy K. Gibson and Christina Shuttleworth Kraus (eds), *The Classical Commentary: Histories, Practices and Theory* (Leiden: Brill, 2002), 109–39.

    7   On the author and his composition, see Florence Eliza Glaze, "Gariopontus and the Salernitans: Textual Traditions in the Eleventh and Twelfth Centuries," in Jacquart and Paravicini Bagliani, *La "Collectio Salernitana" di Salvatore De Renzi*, 149–90.

    8   For the ensemble of texts redacted by Gariopontus, which survives in 12 early medieval manuscripts, see the indices for the texts in Augusto Beccaria, *I codici di medicina del periodo*

most of them bearing their original Greek names; the final two books addressed fevers, which were, of course, a very serious and frequent cause of suffering in the region well into the twentieth century.[9]

But the organization of Gariopontus' source materials, this series of discrete early medieval source-treatises, was haphazard and impractical. Each treated a particular category of illness, and each followed its own organizational schema. But, in addition, these texts were filled also with terminology that had suffered serious corruption over the centuries. So what Gariopontus did was "put them together better," clean up the orthography and more than a little of the grammar, and provide detailed tables of chapters at the head of each of his seven books. In the end, his head-to-foot synthetic text offered a very useful practical manual that could guide the physician in his thoughts and his practice. Gariopontus highlights his intentions in his playful prologue, which appears at the head of nearly every surviving copy of the text:

> If anyone desires to know intently the content of this whole book, let him first peruse
> quickly these preceding chapter headings, which he finds listed in brief citation at the
> head of this little book. Once he knows these, he will be able to know the content
> of the whole book. This is the path that shows you the turnings and twistings of the

---

presalernitano (secoli IX, X, e XI) (Rome: Edizioni di Storia e Letteratura, 1956). An edition of the *Aurelius*, based solely upon the single twelfth-century manuscript Brussels, Bibliothèque Royale, MS 1342–50, was published by Charles Daremberg, "Aurelius," *Janus* 2 (1847): 468–99, 690–96, and 705–31. The *Esculapius* was critically edited by Francisco Manzanero Cano, "Liber Esculapii (Anonymus Liber Chroniorum): edición crítica y estudio," unpublished Ph.D. dissertation, Universidad Complutense de Madrid, 1996; I am grateful to the author for sharing it. On the *Liber tertius*, see Klaus-Dietrich Fischer, "Der pseudogalenische *Liber tertius*" and "Galeni qui fertur ad Glauconem Liber tertius ad fidem codicis Vindocinensis 109," in Ivan Garofalo and Amneris Roselli (eds), *Galenismo e medicina tardoantica: fonti greche, latine e arabe. Atti del Seminario internazionale di Siena, Certosa di Pontignano, 9 e 10 settembre 2002* (Naples: Istituto Universitario Orientale, 2003), 101–32 and 283–346. See David Langslow's discussion of Alexander, *De podagra*, in *The Latin Alexander Trallianus: The Text and Transmission of a Late Latin Medical Book*, Journal of Roman Studies Monograph 10 (London: Society for the Promotion of Roman Studies, 2006), 75–83. We look forward to Valerie Knight's critical edition of the *De podagra*, which is currently in progress.

9   On the impact of malarial fevers, see Robert Sallares, *Malaria and Rome: A History of Malaria in Ancient Italy* (New York: Oxford University Press, 2002); David Soren, "Can Archaeologists Excavate Evidence of Malaria?" *World Archaeology* 35.2 (Oct. 2003): *Archaeology of Epidemic and Infectious Disease*, ed. Peter Mitchell, 193–209; Peregrine Horden, "Disease, Dragons and Saints: The Management of Epidemics in the Dark Ages," in T.O. Ranger and Paul Slack (eds), *Epidemics and Ideas: Essays on the Historical Perception of Pestilence* (Cambridge: Cambridge University Press, 1995), 45–76; and Frank M. Snowden, *The Conquest of Malaria: Italy, 1900–1962* (New Haven: Yale University Press, 2006).

following [text]: if you seek it carefully, no error will lead you astray and prevent you from coming straight to the foot [sole/back cover] of the book's content. If you are able to remember this, fame will be yours and you will be able to be aware of each individual disease and its cure, and so in this manner you will find chapter headings briefly noted before each book.[10]

In the twelfth century, Salernitan lecturers added scholastic prologues to the text of the *Passionarius* that endorsed or even amplified the value of the text and the author's intentions. Each of these scholastic prologues varied somewhat in formulation, but virtually all of them applauded Gariopontus' editorial activities as having improved substantially a set of texts that was not ideally designed as an aid to improved medical practice. One of these prefaces included Gariopontus among the "moderns" who had improved upon the deficient works of his ancient predecessors, a compliment usually reserved for highly regarded textual authorities like Constantine the African or Salerno's twelfth-century scholastic commentators. In fact, by listing the early Latinized Byzantine authors Paul (of Aegina), Alexander (of Tralles), and Theodorus Priscianus as Gariopontus' sources, and labeling them "male ordinatus," one twelfth-century Salernitan lecturer self-consciously imitated Constantine the African's own prologue to the *Pantegni Theorica*. There, as "coadunator," Constantine claimed to have put the *Pantegni* together using the same Byzantine authors as his badly organized source texts.[11] In the unknown twelfth-century Salernitan teacher's words:

---

[10]   First translated at Glaze, "Gariopontus and the Salernitans," 161. The Latin runs: "Si quis intente desiderat cognoscere intentionem totius libri prius cursim haec praenotata capitula relegat quae brevi eulogio in fronte huius libelli repperit. Quibus et cognitis intentionem totius libri cognoscere poterit. Haec est via quae tibi monstrat flexus et reflexus sequentis libri, quam si bene quaeris nullus error te seducet quin recte pervenias ad calcem librariae intentionis. Quae si memoria tenere poteris erit tibi gloria et uniuscuiusque passionis et curationis bene poteris esse conscius et ita per singulos libros breviter capitula praenotata repperies."

[11]   On Constantine's *accessus*, see Danielle Jacquart, "Le sens donné par Constantin l'Africain à son œuvre: les chapitres introductifs en arabe et en latin," in Charles Burnett and Danielle Jacquart (eds), *Constantine the African and Alī ibn al-'Abbās al-Maǧūsī: The "Pantegni" and Related Texts* (Leiden: Brill, 1994), 71–89. The various *accessus*-styles in the scholastic twelfth-century prologues added to the *Passionarius* were first analyzed by Florence Eliza Glaze, "Galen Refashioned: Gariopontus of Salerno's *Passionarius* in the Later Middle Ages and Renaissance," in Elizabeth Lane Furdell (ed.), *Textual Healing: Essays in Medieval and Early Modern Medicine* (Leiden: Brill, 2005), 53–77, and in greater detail by Glaze, "Prolegomena: Scholastic Openings to Gariopontus' *Passionarius*," in Florence Eliza Glaze and Brian K. Nance (eds), *Between Text and Patient: The Medical Enterprise in Medieval and Early Modern Europe*, Micrologus' Library 39 (Florence: SISMEL, Edizioni del Galluzzo, 2011), 57–86.

This book [the ensemble of Gariopontus' sources] ... was badly organized among the Latins. For it began with fevers [i.e., Galen's *Ad Glauconem*]; but Gariopontus put it together better, beginning with the head and adding much from Paul, Alexander, and Theodorus Priscianus. The ancients customarily began with universals and proceeded to particulars; the *moderni*, however, have moved from the parts to the whole, and begun from the head, that is, from the more dignified member of the body.[12]

This prologue appears in its earliest, concise form as a marginal addition to Rome, Biblioteca Angelica, MS lat. 1496, which dates from the opening of the twelfth century, with the main text written by a series of scribes, at least one of whom wrote both the Beneventan script of the area around Salerno as well as the Caroline minuscule that was increasingly preferred in the region for "school books."[13] So Gariopontus, in reorganizing a series of early medieval texts, had produced a handy synthesis of medical knowledge that was expressly valued by the subsequent medical teachers who added these variant prologues, with their different styles for the scholastic *accessus ad auctorem*.

But while the prologues vary in some respects, no doubt representing the successive teachers' perspectives, the glosses added to the *Passionarius* from an early date tend to fall into two broad categories. The first I call nosological glosses, by which I mean glosses added to explain the meanings or etymologies of Greek disease names; these also served to make the explicated names more understandable and more memorable. The second category I call pharmacological glosses. These include glosses to explain the ingredients of compound preparations, to delineate the origins of the names of compounds, and to clarify the identity of individual ingredients.[14] In both cases—nosological and pharmacological glosses—the teachers working in and around Salerno who inscribed these explanations employed terms and explanations that corresponded to other scholastic medical texts being employed and studied in the region.

Such a function has never been suspected for a text like Gariopontus' *Book of Diseases* until now. Indeed, the sheer popularity of Gariopontus' text during the twelfth century, the period of "high Salerno," has surprised many historians of

---

[12] For an analysis of the several different prologues added to the *Passionarius*, see Glaze, "Prolegomena."

[13] Virginia Brown, "Where Have All the Grammars Gone?" in Mario de Nonno, Paolo de Paolis, and Louis Holtz (eds), *Manuscripts and Tradition of Grammatical Texts from Antiquity to the Renaissance* (Cassino: Edizioni dell'Università degli Studi di Cassino, 2000), 389–414.

[14] The difficult terminology of the *Ad Glauconem* was problematic even by Carolingian times; a glossary preceding the text in Einsiedeln, Stiftsbibliothek, MS 304, written *c.* 800, began (fol. 1r): "Hec sunt vocabula que in hoc libro obscura esse videntur." Yet the glossary itself is filled with corruptions.

Salernitan medicine who assumed the text was too old-fashioned to have enjoyed a continued popularity after the influx of Arabic and other translations during the late eleventh and twelfth centuries. However, when we survey the surviving manuscripts of Salernitan texts produced during the "long twelfth century," we find that Gariopontus' text is one of the most numerous reproduced in the area of Salerno and that it circulated northward almost immediately. The text survives in more than 67 copies, 48 of which date from the period between 1050 and 1225.[15] This in itself is remarkable, especially for a text that never appears to have entered the Salernitans' core curriculum of pedagogical texts that later became known as the *Articella*.[16]

Yet, in spite of its non-canonical status, features of these late eleventh- and twelfth-century copies of Gariopontus' text show clear signs of having been used for classroom instruction. More than five different scholastic prologues were constructed for the treatise, just as they were in the Salernitan commentaries on the *Articella* that were identified in the 1970s and 1980s by Paul Kristeller and Mark Jordan. These prologues to Gariopontus' text (which neither Kristeller nor Jordan knew of) detail in different variations the "thumbnail" sketch of scholastic categories known as the *accessus ad auctorem*. As Kristeller and Jordan both showed, commentary prologues to the *Articella* texts identified the *materia, intentio, utilitas, pars philosophiae*, and other conceptual features inherited from scholastic traditions of antiquity and represented in important new medical translations from Arabic, especially Constantine the African's *Pantegni/Total Art of Medicine*. Since their early studies, Charles Burnett, Faith Wallis, and others have further examined unstudied component texts in the

---

[15]   For a table of these manuscripts, see Glaze, "Gariopontus and the Salernitans," 185–90; since 2008, I have identified two additional fragments of the *Passionarius*. These are London, British Library, MS Harley 5966, fol. 44rv, and Oxford, Bodleian Library, MS Lawn 18, fol. 6rv. The former is digitized on the British Library's website at http://www.british-library .uk/catalogues/illuminatedmanuscripts/record.asp?MSID=18889&collID8&NStart=5966. An additional twelfth-century witness has also been identified: Worcester, Cathedral Library, MS Q. 40.

[16]   For the now-standard narrative of Salernitan texts and their evolution, see Paul Oskar Kristeller, "The School of Salerno: Its Development and Its Contribution to the History of Learning," *Bulletin of the History of Medicine* 17 (1945): 138–94, augmented as *Studi sulla scuola medica salernitana* (Naples: Istituto Italiano per gli Studi Filosofici, 1986); idem, "Bartholomaeus, Musandinus and Maurus of Salerno and Other Early Commentators on the *Articella*, with a Tentative List of Texts and Manuscripts," *Italia medioevale e humanistica* 19 (1976): 57–87; Mark D. Jordan, "The Construction of a Philosophical Medicine: Exegesis and Argument in Salernitan Teaching on the Soul," *Osiris*, 2nd ser., 6 (1990): *Renaissance Medical Learning: Evolution of a Tradition*, ed. Michael R. McVaugh and Nancy G. Siraisi, 42–61; and idem, "Medicine as Science in the Early Commentaries on 'Johannitius,'" *Traditio* 43 (1987): 121–45.

Articella commentary tradition.[17] But until recently what no one expected to find in surviving manuscripts of Gariopontus' text is that the earliest marginal *accessus*—the first sign of medical pedagogy based on ancient models—added to a Salernitan medical text appears in the margins of the *Passionarius*. The manuscript Rome, Biblioteca Angelica, MS lat. 1496, a South Italian palimpsest of a slightly earlier medical text in the distinctive Lombard Beneventan script, preserves some badly rubbed lecture notes that bespeak the use of this manuscript in the classroom. On the opening folio we find the core of Scholastic Prologue A copied into the margin of the Angelica manuscript in a hand that dates from *c.* 1130.[18] Within a short period, this brief Prologue A appeared at the head of manuscripts as an integral part of the text, in an expanded format that aligned it more closely with prologues to the *Articella* commentaries.[19] Over the course of the "high period" of Salernitan medicine in the twelfth century, it had become essential, it seems, for medical students and readers to grasp the elemental theoretical positioning of the *Passionarius* and to think of it in relation to other components of the Salernitan corpus. The same is true for a dozen other manuscripts, resulting in at least five variant scholastic prologues. In one of them, Rome, Biblioteca Vallicelliana, MS B. 45, pt 3, discovered in 2008,

---

[17] Charles Burnett, "The Contents and Affiliation of the Scientific Manuscripts Written at, or Brought to, Chartres in the Time of John of Salisbury," in Michael Wilks (ed.), *The World of John of Salisbury* (Oxford: Blackwell, 1984), 127–60; Faith Wallis, "Inventing Diagnosis: Theophilus' *De urinis* in the Classroom," *Dynamis* 20 (2000): *Medical Teaching and Classroom Practice in the Medieval Universities*, ed. Roger French and Cornelius O'Boyle, 31–73; Giles E.M. Gaspar and Faith Wallis, "Anselm and the *Articella*," *Traditio* 59 (2004): 129–74; and also, now, the essays on *Isagoge* commentaries and the commentaries of Bartholomaeus by Irene Caiazzo and Faith Wallis in Jacquart and Paravicini Bagliani, *La scuola medica salernitana*, 93–123 and 125–64, respectively. For a sense of one key text that did not appear formally in the *Articella*, but that was clearly read by several different masters, see Faith Wallis's essay in the present volume.

[18] This same hand, which I call "Glossator A," supplies the vast majority of all other glosses in this manuscript. The late Leonard Boyle, after examining a facsimile of the manuscript, judged the glossator to be, without doubt, a teacher/lecturer who prepared the text for classroom reading. In his judgment, the use of the *paragraphus* mark to signify the opening to the *accessus* reveals a classroom environment. On the variants to the prologue type, see Glaze, "Prolegomena."

[19] See the table of manuscripts provided at the end of Glaze, "Gariopontus and the Salernitans," 185–90. In the right-hand column of that table, I indicate the presence of nosological and pharmacological glosses, or other interesting inclusions. I should add now Worcester, Cathedral Library, MS Q. 40, which dates from the first half of the twelfth century and includes both nosological and pharmacological glosses. The catalogue description is provided by Rodney M. Thomson with Michael Gullick, *A Descriptive Catalogue of the Medieval Manuscripts in Worcester Cathedral Library* (Woodbridge, UK: D.S. Brewer, 2001), 142. I am grateful to the Dean and Chapter of the Cathedral for providing digital images of the Worcester manuscript with remarkable speed and efficiency.

the primary copyist added segments of several different scholastic prologues to the blank recto preceding the text, with the core of one of these repeated in the upper margins of the first page of the treatise itself.[20] Such accumulations indicate a succession of teachers, each emphasizing different aspects of the text and its origins. Prefatory characterizations of this sort are unquestionable proof that this text, although never part of the *Articella*, was all the same the focus of some portion of curricular analysis and lecture during the first half of the twelfth century.

While the *Passionarius* was clearly a text that some masters teaching in Salerno lectured upon, no comprehensive narrative or analytical "commentary" as such has so far been identified.[21] Perhaps the nature of the text, which is largely devoid of extended theoretical discussions, made it possible to teach the text from a glossed or annotated master copy without having to construct a full-length analysis based upon extensive explanations of lemmata. All the same, the many glosses to the *Passionarius* text reveal some of the features these masters found most interesting and significant. If glossing theorists like Gernot Wieland are correct in postulating that a gloss "stands in place of the lecturer's tongue," then the glosses added to the *Passionarius* convey Salernitan masters' interests in and concerns for explicating the material to a student audience of future practitioners: they show us what the masters sought to explain as they sat or stood before their classrooms.[22] Among the most striking features of the interlinear

---

[20]   The only full description is still the handwritten Vallicelliana catalogue by Vincenzo Vettori, *Inventarium omnium codicum manuscriptorum graecorum et latinorum Bibliothecae Vallicellianae digestum anno Domini MDCCXLIX*, pt 1, fol. 179r. This is now available online in facsimile at http://cataloghistorici.bdi.sbn.it/code/seq_elenco_gruppi.asp?ResetFilter=Y&Filtra Catalogo=171. See also, on other contents in this compound volume, G.L. Bursill-Hall, *A Census of Medieval Latin Grammatical Manuscripts* (Stuttgart-Bad Cannstatt: Frommann-Holzboog, 1981), 226; Virginia Brown, *The Textual Transmission of Caesar's "Civil War"* (Leiden: Brill, 1972), 46, 78–81; and Goetz, *Corpus glossariorum latinorum*, 1:175, n. 1. The text of Gariopontus is featured, but misdated, in *Quelli che servono gli infermi: assistenza e medicina a Roma nei secoli XVI e XVII. Mostra bibliografica* (Rome: Ministero per i Beni Culturali e Ambientali/Biblioteca Vallicelliana, 1987), 62–3. The anonymous editors of that volume do not note the existence or importance of the scholastic prologues, which are copied in the hand of the primary text scribe.

[21]   The "commentary" from Paris, Bibliothèque nationale de France, MS lat. 544 mentioned by Irene Caiazzo in her Salerno essay on the *Isagoge* commentary of the same manuscript is in fact nothing more than a strung-together series of interlinear glosses as found in other, earlier manuscripts. See Glaze, "Prolegomena." Caiazzo's essay is "Un inedito commento sulla *Isagoge Iohannitii* conservato a Parigi," in Jacquart and Paravicini Bagliani, *La scuola medica salernitana*, 93–124, esp. 103–5, 122–3.

[22]   Wieland, "Interpreting the Interpretations"; see also also W.M. Lindsay, "Gleaning from Glossaries and Scholia," ch. 17 in his collected essays, *Studies in Early Medieval Latin Glossaries*, ed. Michael Lapidge, Collected Studies Series CS 467 (Aldershot, UK: Variorum, 1996).

and marginal glosses that Salernitans added to the *Passionarius* are the two major categories of interest that I have defined above as pharmacological glosses and nosological glosses. The nosological glosses in particular reveal that masters in the twelfth century were acutely concerned to explain the names of diseases, in most cases literally breaking down the technical terms of Greek origin to their root components, to provide the etymologies of these terms, and to define what aspect of each disease these Greek names signified. The glosses appearing in manuscript upon manuscript of the *Passionarius* are neither inconsistent nor inconsiderable. They are, rather, repeated from one manuscript to another with a significant degree of regularity. Of the 45 manuscripts of Gariopontus' text produced in the period between 1050 and 1225, more than 21 contain these largely consistent sets of glosses. It is, not surprisingly, the manuscripts with a southern Italian connection that preserve these sets of glosses most consistently. In Table 3.1, below, I have arranged a sampling of nosological glosses from Books I and II of the *Passionarius* and have compared them to corresponding texts from Campania that manifest similar interests.

In particular, it is notable that although Constantine's *Pantegni* introduced within its chapters a vastly expanded theoretical understanding of the body—and as such, it was indeed a landmark in the transmission of knowledge—it did not provide Europeans with a medical vocabulary contradictory to that of Gariopontus' text. Constantine's was not an ultra-Arabic medical vocabulary. Yes, there was a small handful of anatomical features and terms introduced from the Arabic and hitherto unknown in the West—*siphac*, for instance, or *nucha*—but these were in the minority. Because they were "new" to Western medicine, however, these few Arabic terms have received a disproportionate amount of scholarly attention. For the most part, though, when it came to naming diseases or conditions, Constantine employed the same Greek terminology as had Gariopontus of Salerno 20 to 30 years earlier. This correspondence was due not to the fact that Constantine used the *Passionarius* as a guide to Latinized forms of Greek terminology (though that is not entirely impossible and requires further consideration), but rather to the likely fact that the Arab authors whose texts he rendered into Latin had borrowed Greek nosological terms from classical texts and had simply written them in their own script: such terms stand, in Constantine's sources, as in his own Latin translations, as emprunts or loanwords. As a consequence, the Greek names of medical conditions remain virtually unchanged between the period when Gariopontus produced his text *c.* 1035, through the translations effected by Constantine and his disciples

---

See also, for broader considerations of the way glosses originated and functioned, Nancy Porter Stork, *Through a Gloss Darkly: Aldhelm's Riddles in the British Library MS Royal 12. C. xxiii* (Toronto: Pontifical Institute of Mediaeval Studies, 1990).

(*c.* 1075–*c.* 1115), and down through the late twelfth century when the great Salernitan glossary known as the *Alphita* was constructed.[23]

This tradition of glossing the names of diseases and signifying their meanings carries through not just in Salerno and not for a short period of time, but for centuries. It becomes the common language of Western medicine. Surely, then, this consistent medical vocabulary helps to explain in part why Gariopontus' text continued to be copied, circulated, read, cited, and annotated well into the fifteenth century. It spoke the same "language" as many of the texts introduced later on, though its theories and therapies evoked a simpler age and thus had to be updated with marginal and other additions.[24] If we look at the nosological glosses added to these few chapters of the *Passionarius* in the twelfth century (Table 3.1, below), we can see that it was not Constantine, but Gariopontus, who gave Salerno its "tongue." His terms, with their spellings corrected from early medieval vernacularized corruptions, and with glosses added by Salernitan masters, echo across the century, appearing in unique practical manuals like the so-called *Trattato delle cure/De curis* from the twelfth century, and later inscribed into the famous alphabetical glossary of medical terms known as the *Alphita*. If we focus more closely on the glosses added to manuscripts of the *Passionarius* by the Salernitan masters, here set apart in italics in the left column of Table 3.1, then we can gain a sense of this pedagogical drive to make the names of diseases

---

[23]   The dates of Constantine's activity as a translator are far from secure. Accounts of his life recorded in the *Chronicle* of Monte Cassino, Peter the Deacon's *De viris illustribus*, and an important alternate account included in a gloss by Master Matthaeus F[errarius] provide no secure dates. On the question of when he arrived, one account indicates that the Lombard prince Gisulf II was still in power at Salerno, which puts it prior to 1077, the year of the Norman conquest of the city by Duke Robert Guiscard. It might in fact have been years earlier. On the debate in general, see Francis Newton, "Constantine the African and Monte Cassino: New Elements and the Text of the *Isagoge*," in Burnett and Jacquart, *Constantine the African*, 16–47, esp. 19–25. Johannes Afflacius outlived Constantine by some decades and, according to Stephen of Antioch, was still working to finalize his master's unfinished medical translations as late as the siege of Majorca, which lasted *c.* 1113–14. See Herbert Bloch, *Monte Cassino in the Middle Ages* (3 vols, Cambridge, MA: Harvard University Press, 1986), 1:97–110, at 102. For the *Alphita*, see the edition and discussion of Alejandro García González, cited in n. 4, above.

[24]   In his unpublished paper from the session on "Relocating Salerno: Shifting Geographies in Medical Historiography" at the 2009 meeting of the American Association for the History of Medicine, "The Meaning of 'Salernitan' in Thirteenth-century Medicine," Michael McVaugh established that one of the earliest efforts of medical scholars at Montpellier was to differentiate their opinions and practices from those of the Salernitans, in spite of the fact that it was the Salernitans' curriculum that the scholars of Montpellier had borrowed wholesale. Thus, as early as the 1230s, Henry of Winchester criticized one of Gariopontus' explanations for a particular type of fever, and then critiqued the transverse incision the Salernitans used in phlebotomy. On the continued use of Gariopontus' text into the age of print, see Glaze, "Galen Refashioned."

fundamentally explicable to an audience of students and readers. Gariopontus' "Cephalea," for instance (item 1), is a disease of the head, "dolor capitis," "cefas" in Greek, "caput" in Latin. "Scotomia" (item 5) receives the gloss "scotos grece, latine tenebre" ("in Greek, *scotos*; in Latin, *tenebre*"). For "melancholia" (Table 3.1, item 8), the Salernitan masters add the gloss "melan grece, latine niger; colon, colera nigra humor," indicating that melancholia signified a disease caused by the black choleric humor. To Gariopontus' chapter reading "Ciliaca est passio assidua ventris solutio," the Salernitan lecturers added the gloss "Greci enim ciliam ventrem dicunt" (Table 3.1, item 29). In some cases, Gariopontus himself provided a gloss to help identify a condition: to "Anorexia" he added as part of his chapter the identifier "id est fastidium." To this, the Salernitan glossators added also "quod greci atrophian vocant; sine appetitu, cacexia" (Table 3.1, item 23). This pattern of clarifying and etymologizing the names of Greek conditions and the Latin equivalents by which they could be better identified goes on and on, through more than one hundred folios of Gariopontus' text.

Moreover, the intelligent glossing provided by the masters finds corroboration in other Salernitan texts. In the anonymous text *De curis*, called by Piero Giacosa the *Trattato delle cure*, the sole manuscript of which dates from the middle of the twelfth century, the unknown author's identifications of each disease are entirely dominated by the combined influences of Gariopontus' definitions of diseases and the nosological glosses of the Salernitan teachers who lectured upon and glossed his *Passionarius*.[25] In virtually every case where the author explains the meanings of the Greek names of diseases, and identifies the signs and symptoms of each condition, these explanations correspond almost verbatim to glossed manuscripts of the *Passionarius*. These two texts speak one language, a learned terminology that is connected through the medium of the teachers' spoken words and here recorded as glosses to guide classroom instruction. The author of the *De curis* repeats, for instance, the glosses added to the *Passionarius*: where Gariopontus wrote "Cephalea est dolor capitis qui multum tempus tenens," to which his glossators added "cefas grece, latine caput," the author of the *De curis* provided as one continuous text, "Cephalea est dolor capitis qui multum tempus tenens ... cephas grece, caput latine, lesis, dolor inde affligens."[26] The relative dates of the glossators' activities and the anonymous author's compilation of the *De curis* (which employs also elements from the *Isagoge* of Johannitius, the *Viaticum*, and the *Particular and Universal Diets* originally by Isaac Israeli) are

---

[25]   Rome, Biblioteca Angelica, MS lat. 1408, s. xii; the text was edited rather haphazardly by Piero Giacosa in his *Magistri salernitani nondum editi* (Turin: Bocca, 1901), 177–279. I have consulted both edition and manuscript, and, where Giacosa's transcription errs, have chosen the reading from the manuscript itself.

[26]   For such equivalents, see Table 3.1, items 1, 3, 4, 5, 6, 7, 8, 9, 10, 13, 15, 16, 29, etc.

roughly contemporary, that is, falling somewhere between *c.* 1080 and 1150. It is certainly not unlikely that the author of *De curis* was at one time a student and later a master. As such, he might well have been the originator of at least some of the interlinear glosses added to the *Passionarius*, which he repeated in his own book of cures for Greek-named diseases. Alternately, he might have learned as a student the importance of such nosological definitions and adopted them when he put together his *De curis*. Further examination of such correspondences, and a careful tracing of the anonymous *De curis* author's sources, might well determine the matter.

It is further notable that the glosses added to the *Passionarius* in the twelfth century, and repeated almost verbatim in the *De curis*, also appear in the late twelfth-century Salernitan glossary, the *Alphita*, which was recently (2007) edited by Alejandro García González. Though García González recognized that the *Passionarius* was cited several times as an authority on select diseases like "sclirosis" and strangury (items 26, 27, and 30, the right column in Table 3.1), he did not appreciate just how many of the nosological glosses—the explanations of the Greek disease names—corresponded to those in Gariopontus' text, especially in versions glossed by the Salernitan educators in the decades prior to the *Alphita*'s composition. Indeed, it seems very likely that the "live" experience of spoken glosses in the classroom, which manifest themselves in the masters' glossed manuscripts, were accumulated by the person or persons who put the *Alphita* together into one long glossary text designed to encompass the whole vocabulary that needed explaining in the classroom environment. As such, the *Alphita* accumulated a learned word-list of incalculable value to medical scholars and students alike. The popularity of the *Alphita* in subsequent centuries certainly bespeaks such a scenario.[27] One can only imagine what further "tracking" from one Salernitan text to another might exist in glossed manuscripts as yet only examined for their base texts.

When we turn to the pharmacological glosses added to Gariopontus' text, the chronological picture becomes more interesting. To be sure, correspondences between interlinear glosses added to identify medicinal ingredients and preparations in the *Passionarius* and the *Alphita* glossary are unquestionable.[28] Thus, to Gariopontus' "stafisagria" the masters added the interlinear gloss "erba pedicularis"; in the *Alphita* glossary we find "staphisagria dicitur a staphis, quod est uva, et agria, id est agrestis ... alio nomine dicitur herba pedicularis."[29] To Gariopontus' "lasar" the masters added the interlinear gloss "asa fetida"; in

---

[27]   See the discussion of the question of the authorship and date of the *Alphita* in García González, *Alphita*, 46–54.

[28]   See, for these examples, Table 3.2, items 18, 19, 30, 33, 36, 13, below.

[29]   García González, *Alphita*, 549, 291.

the *Alphita* we find "lasar, asa fetida idem."[30] For Gariopontus' "caricas" the glossators wrote above the line "id est ficus sicca." In the *Alphita* a near-equivalent occurs: "carica, ficus sicca idem."[31] Or to "alice" in the *Passionarius* the gloss "spelte" is added; in *Alphita*, "alica, spelta idem" is repeated.[32] For Gariopontus' "dimifragiorum" the teachers expanded the identification to include the gloss "id est acruminium." In the *Alphita* this becomes "dimifragia, id est, acrumina."[33] Similarly, "oxirodium" is glossed "acetum roseum oleum" in manuscripts of the *Passionarius*; in the *Alphita*, it is "oxirodon, id est, acetum mixtum cum oleo rosato."[34] The parallels are telling: one language and set of identifications for these essential ingredients had to be provided by the widely read glossators in order to communicate one masterful reading of an important medical manual written decades earlier by an esteemed Salernitan authority. Though the *Passionarius* had been written decades before the Salernitan pharmacopoeia was assembled, those teaching medicine in the twelfth-century classroom had to make it "speak the language" of their own day.[35] This tradition of glossing pharmacological agents had begun in the region somewhat sooner than had the compilation of nosological glosses, however. The recently analyzed *Agriocanna* glossary, whose earliest witness dates from the second half of the eleventh century, includes a number of botanical glosses that appear early in the *Passionarius* glosses, too, and then again in the *Alphita*.[36] The many correspondences between the

---

[30] Ibid., 462, 243.

[31] Ibid., 385, 178.

[32] Ibid., 339, 145.

[33] Ibid., 409, 200.

[34] Ibid., 527, 283, under "Rosa."

[35] On pharmacy in Salerno, see the essay by Faith Wallis in the present volume, as well as Iolanda Ventura, "Per una storia del *Circa Instans*. I *Secreta Salernitana* ed il testo del manoscritto London, British Library, Egerton 747: note a margine di un'edizione," *Schola Salernitana: Annali* 7–8 (2002–03): 39–109; eadem, "Un manuale di farmacologia medievale ed i suoi lettori: il *Circa instans*, la sua diffusione, la sua ricezione dal XIII al XV secolo," in Jacquart and Paravicini Bagliani, *La scuola medica salernitana*, 465–533. The early twelfth-century *Antidotarium Nicholai*, which became the Salernitans' official treatise on compound remedies, has been analyzed by Francesco Roberg, "Studium zum *Antidotarium Nicholai* anhand der ältesten Handschriften," *Würzburger medizinhistorische Mitteilungen* 21 (2002): 73–129; idem, "Text- und redaktionskritische Probleme bei der Edition von Texten des Gebrauchsschrifttums am Beispiel des 'Antidotarium Nicolai' (12. Jahrhundert): Einige Beobachtungen, mit einem Editionsanhang," *Mittellateinisches Jahrbuch* 42 (2007): 1–19.

[36] Alejandro García González, "*Agriocanna*, a New Medico-Botanical Glossary of Pre-Salernitan Origin," in David Langslow and Brigitte Maire (eds), *Body, Disease and Treatment in a Changing World: Latin Texts and Contexts in Ancient and Medieval Medicine. Proceedings of the Ninth International Conference "Ancient Latin Medical Texts," Hulme Hall, University of Manchester, 5th–8th September, 2007*, Bibliothèque d'histoire de la médecine et de la santé

glossed *Passionarius*, the early *Agriocanna*, and the *Alphita* are too numerous to list here in full; a brief examination of Table 3.2 below, which lists glossed pharmacological terms from Book I of the *Passionarius* only, will convince the reader of the texts' terminological agreement.[37]

One subcategory of pharmacological glosses includes some mundane, even amusing, glosses added to the *Passionarius* for clarified exposition in the classroom environment. These are the kinds of terms one might expect any medical person or even the most introductory student to know—but they are glossed anyway, and presumably these terms were a topic of discussion in the classroom. Thus "trociscos" is double-glossed "rotellas" and "rotunde confectiones," signifying a round pill- or wafer-shaped preparation. The *Alphita* does not abstain from repeating this explanation: "trocos interpretatur rotudum [*sic*]; inde trocisci, eo quod rotundam habent formam."[38] Simple mixtures like oxymel are glossed, as is the unique verb "sinapizare," which must mean "to mustard," as the gloss adds "ungere." Some of the antidotes from the larger compound tradition appear here as well, including "unguento lympido bono, id est marciaton" and "gera pigra, id est amari sacri galieni." "Embrocis" is defined as "infusiones" by the glossator, while the *Alphita*'s author writes, "Embroca interpretatur infusio, quod est fomentum dicimus." We meet also here the "Antidotum mitriditis," a complex preparation intended to protect the patient from poisons, or the simple preparation "musa," which is simply glossed "antidotum est."[39] Other compound preparations glossed in Book I of Gariopontus' text include "Barbara" as "confectio est," and the amusingly simple "tetrafarmacium," which is "factum ex quattuor rebus."[40] These are hardly the most advanced glosses, but evidently it was considered advisable to distinguish them lest error creep into practice.

Occasionally, the orthography of pharmacological agents changed as Salernitan lecturers and practitioners sought to identify an ingredient, even

---

(Lausanne: Éditions BHMS, 2010), 223–35. Note that the author considers the *Agriocanna* to be "pre-Salernitan" because it antedates Salerno's scholastic age by several decades; Gariopontus of Salerno's text belongs to the same pre-scholastic/"pre-Salernitan" era. For a description of the earliest *Agriocanna* manuscript, Vatican City, Biblioteca Apostolica Vaticana, MS Vat. lat. 4418, see Beccaria, *I codici*, 309–12.

[37]   A more complete set of indices will accompany my edition of the *Passionarius*, which I hope to complete in 2013.

[38]   See Table 3.2, item 4, below.

[39]   For an interesting analysis of the *Antidotum Mithridatis* tradition, see Laurence Totelin, "Mithridates' Antidote: A Pharmacological Ghost," *Early Science and Medicine* 9 (2004): 1–19. Several types of *Musa* are listed in the *Antidotarium magnum* tradition, including *Musa in achea, Musa enea,* and *Musa prosperito*.

[40]   See items 67, 69 in Table 3.2 below; for similar examples, see items 21–3, 29, 31, 38, 39, 46 in Table 3.2.

though the ingredient remained perfectly identifiable in spite of the variant spellings: the gloss "suco caulis agrestis" was used to clarify Gariopontus' term "extrucio." In the *Agriocanna* we find "strucium id est cauliculi agrestis [*sic*]," and in the *Alphita*, "strucium, id est caulis agrestis."[41] In other cases, the equivalents are less straightforward, though still present. Occasionally, they are offered in reverse: to Gariopontus' "olei siccionii" the glossators added "id est cucumeribus agrestibus"; in the *Alphita* the definition is turned around, giving "elacterium, sucus cucumeris agrestis idem ... siccia."[42] Or to Gariopontus' "resine fructe" the glossators added "pix nigra greca id est colofonia." In the *Alphita* we find "colofonia, pix greca ... arbores quarum gumma est colofonia."[43] The identifications are similar, but the variations indicate what seems to be more of a living tradition of shared practical knowledge rather than the merely textual accumulation of a glossary of pharmacological agents. These are ingredients with which Salernitans dealt regularly in practice, and they were surely familiar with multiple appellatives for single agents.[44] One of the most interesting variations occurs when the master/glossator identifies Gariopontus' ingredient "cantaridis" (the blister-beetle or Spanish fly) as "id est animalium g[ ] inveniuntur in foliis fraxini," a small animal found in the leaves of the ash tree. The *Alphita* merely offers "cantarides, musce sunt oblonge et virides."[45] The gloss added to the *Passionarius* text is closer, in fact, to the early medieval medicinal text called *Alfabetum Galieni*, where the reader could find the definition "cantarides animalicula sunt quorum sunt efficacissime que in spicis frumenti adhuc florescentis inveniuntur."[46] Similarly, the trio of preparations derived

---

41   For the *Agriocanna*, Vatican City, Biblioteca Apostolica Vaticana, MS Chig. F. IV. 57, fol. 217r (ink foliation; stamped foliation 222r). This second-oldest manuscript of the truncated *Agriocanna* (A–Y) dates from the twelfth century, and includes 789 entries, compared to the complete A–Z version in the older manuscript, Biblioteca Apostolica Vaticana, MS Vat. lat. 4418, which has only 572 entries. "Strucium" and "extrucium" are lacking in MS Vat. lat. 4418. For the *Alphita*, see García González, *Alphita*, 552, 289.

42   Ibid., 412, 203.

43   Ibid., 399, 175.

44   For a fine articulation of the role of tacit knowledge in medical traditions, see Anne Van Arsdall, "The Transmission of Knowledge in Early Medieval Medical Texts: An Exploration," in Glaze and Nance, *Between Text and Patient*, 201–16.

45   García González, *Alphita*, 383, 181. Interestingly, manuscripts H and A of the *Alphita* have the added "que in fraxinis degunt." The source of this information about the beetle preferring the ash tree remains unidentified; it may well have been common local knowledge.

46   For the *Alfabetum Galieni* I have utilized the printed version from *Galieni opera*, ed. Diomede Bonardi (2 vols, Venice: F. Pinzi, 1490), vol. 2, sigs mM 1r–mM 9v, or fols 86r–94v, in the digitized version provided by the Bibliothèque Interuniversitaire Santé's Medica site at http://web2.bium.univ-paris5.fr/livanc/?cote=extacadinca11&do=livre; the quoted passage occurs on

from balsamum given in the glossed *Passionarius*—carpobalsamum as "fructus balsamum," xilobalsamum as "lignum balsamum," opobalsamum as "succus balsamum"—find only two parallels in the *Alphita*'s glosses, "carpobalsamum dicitur fructus balsami" and "xilobalsamum, id est lignum balsami." The lacking opobalsamum in the *Alphita* is provided elsewhere; the *Alfabetum Galieni* identifies it as "obobalsamum lachrimus est arboris quam balsamum appellamus" but does not provide any description of carpobalsamum. The *Agriocanna* offers the same two as the *Alfabetum Galieni*: "silobalsum id est lignum balsami," "opobalsamum id est sucus [*sic*] balsami."[47] The Salernitan *Circa instans*, which dates from *c.* 1150–70, offers extended descriptions of all three balsam products: "In anno colliguntur libre 9 illius succi qui dicitur opobalsamus ... rami incisi colligantur et desiccantur et dicuntur xilobalsami, fructus qui in frutice reperitur dicitur carpobalsamus."[48] The relative properties of each are then detailed at length.

On the whole, the level of our current understanding of the many pharmaceutical texts listing both simple and compound medicines, arranged according to various criteria—alphabetical, by degrees, or by action—that circulated in the region of Salerno between *c.* 1050 and 1225 leaves a great deal to be desired. In the complete absence of critical editions, it is difficult to chart the relationships between the various texts, in spite of the fact that many correspondences are evident. The very identity of the pharmaceutical texts rendered into Latin by Constantine the African is as yet not entirely clear: he

---

sig. mM 2vb/fol. 87vb. On the text, see Carmélia Opsomer-Halleux, "Un herbier médicinal du haut Moyen Âge: l'*Alfabetum Galieni*," *History and Philosophy of the Life Sciences*, Section II, 4.1 (1982): 65–97. The forthcoming edition and analysis by Nicholas Everett will be a welcome addition to medical history for this important text; it will be particularly interesting to learn whether the manuscripts contain botanical glosses.

⁴⁷   Cited here from Biblioteca Apostolica Vaticana, MS Chig. F. IV. 57, fols 217r (222r stamped), 213v (218v). The oldest manuscript of the *Agriocanna*, MS Vat. lat. 4418, has "xilobalsamum .i. lignum balsamum" and "opobalsamum [gloss lacking]" at fols 148v and 147r. All three are found in Isidore of Seville's *Etymologies*; see Stephen A. Barney, W.J. Lewis, J.A. Beach, and Oliver Berghof (trans.), *The "Etymologies" of Isidore of Seville* (Cambridge: Cambridge University Press, 2006), 349.

⁴⁸   Like most of the Salernitan pharmacological literature, the *Circa instans* is not available in a modern critical edition, leaving scholars to rely upon the 1939 dissertation of Hans Wölfel, which is based on only one manuscript; see his "Das Arzneidrogenbuch *Circa instans* in einer Fassung des XIII. Jahrhunderts aus der Universitätsbibliothek Erlangen: Text und Kommentar als Beitrag zur Pflanzen- und Drogenkunde des Mittelalters," inaugural dissertation, Friedrich-Wilhelms-Universität Berlin (1939), here at 19–20. The work of Iolanda Ventura is now bringing our understanding of this crucially important Salernitan text up to date; see her two articles cited in n. 35 above. She is currently preparing a book with the provisional title *Studi sull'origine, la diffusione manoscritta, e la ricenzione del "Circa instans."*

seems to have produced both the *Liber graduum* and a *Liber simplicis medicine*. But does the *Antidotarium* listed in the biography of Constantine by Peter the Deacon correspond to the *Antidotarium* in the reconstructed *Pantegni Practica*, which follows a nonalphabetical arrangement and survives only in manuscripts produced after 1200?[49] Or is it, perhaps, the *Antidotarium magnum* that he put together, the great alphabetical antidotary of Salerno that seems to have existed by *c.* 1100 and describes more than twelve hundred compound medicines drawing on both Greek and Arabic ingredients? Was the twelfth-century scholar-practitioner Northungus of Hildesheim right, moreover, in asserting that Constantine the African was responsible for the alphabetical *Antidotarium magnum*?[50] How and why was the Salernitan *Antidotarium Nicholai* constructed from the *Antidotarium magnum*, reproducing fewer than 150 recipes from the earlier great antidotary of the region? Simply establishing a chronology of various texts, tracing surviving manuscripts, and determining circulation patterns has proven a significant challenge but it remains an essential step toward undertaking the work of making these texts available in scholarly forms.[51] What

---

[49] The arrangement in the 1515 printed version is not at all clear but seems to follow a scheme organized by the effects and, in some cases, the conditions that each remedy treats. No one has, to my knowledge, produced any detailed studies of the relations between the 1515 printed version and surviving manuscripts of the text. On the incomplete nature of Constantine's *Practica*, and the ways it was reconstructed by his followers, see the essays of Monica Green and Mary Wack in Burnett and Jacquart, *Constantine the African*, 121–60 and 161–202, respectively.

[50] On Northungus, see Mary Wack's essay, "'Alī ibn al-ʿAbbās al-Maǧūsī and Constantine on Love, and the Evolution of the *Practica Pantegni*," in Burnett and Jacquart, *Constantine the African*, 161–202, and the description of the Bamberg manuscript preserving his texts at 329–30.

[51] The *Antidotarium magnum*, which assembles local remedies already known in southern Italy with new remedies apparently derived from both the Byzantine and Arabic traditions, seems to have been available by *c.* 1100 and may have been the work of either Constantine the African, Johannes Afflacius, or some other unknown authors; the *Antidotarium Nicholai* was composed around 1125–30, i.e., roughly the same period as the commentaries on the *Articella* texts and scholastic glossing of Gariopontus' text begin to appear; the *Liber iste*, attributed usually to Platearius, was first put together by about 1150 but survives in two versions, one of which has much in common with the *Circa instans*. This in turn was composed *c.* 1150. All of this activity appears to have been taking place either in or around Salerno, yet there is no clear study of the whole phenomenon or how it relates to medical practice and teaching. On each of these in turn, see Alfons Lutz, "Der verschollene frühsalernitanische *Antidotarius magnus* in einer Basler Handschrift aus dem 12. Jahrhundert und das *Antidotarium Nicolai*," *Die Vorträge der Hauptversammlung der Internationalen Gesellschaft für Geschichte der Pharmazie*, n.s., 40 (1973): 97–133; Andreas Kramer and Korinna Scheidt, "Die Handschriften des *Antidotarius magnus*," *Sudhoffs Archiv* 83 (1999): 109–16; Willem F. Daems and François Ledermann, "Die *opopira magna*, ein pharmazeutisches Präparat aus dem *Antidotarius magnus*," *Gesnerus* 44 (1987): 177–88; Dietlinde Goltz, *Mittelalterliche Pharmazie und Medizin dargestellt an Geschichte und*

correspondences or evidence of "tracking" might we discover between technical terminologies found in texts like the *Liber iste*, the Salernitan *Circa instans*, the *Antidotarium Nicholai*, and others? In many cases, clues to how the texts were used, and were asked to "speak" to one another, will be manifest not in the base texts themselves, but in the scholarly additions jotted into the margins and blank interlinear spaces of manuscripts during the twelfth century. But until editions and close analyses have been produced taking as many manuscripts as possible into consideration, there will remain many more questions than answers for these problems. Clearly, a tremendous amount of work remains to be done here, but, as I hope I have shown, the textual correspondences that speak from between the lines of surviving manuscripts offer us an essential lens for viewing the activities of medical education, personal study, and medical practice in this pivotal period and region. In particular, we are eager to determine with greater certainty the processes by which students were able to attain a tutored understanding of an ever-increasing corpus of medical literature that, in the twelfth century, brought together a complex of multilingual materials. Thus, the "speaking in tongues" that so characterized the learned medical practitioner (and so angered traditional Latin grammarians like John of Salisbury) was one end result of the process suggested here.[52] One feels sure that a great deal of specialized knowledge passed between practitioners, drug merchants, and the

---

Inhalt des "Antidotarium Nicolai," mit einem Nachdruck der Druckfassung von 1471 (Stuttgart: Wissenschaftliche Verlagsgesellschaft, 1976); the two articles on the *Antidotarium Nicholai* by Francisco Roberg (above, n. 35); Mireille Ausécache, "Un *Liber iste*, des *Liber iste*? Un *Platearius*, des *Platearius*? État des lieux d'un projet d'édition," in Jacquart and Paravicini Bagliani, *La scuola medica salernitana*, 1–30; Ventura, "Un manuale di farmacologia medievale ed i suoi lettori" (above, n. 35); eadem, "Salvatore De Renzi e la letteratura farmacologica salernitana," in Jacquart and Paravicini Bagliani, *La "Collectio Salernitana" di Salvatore De Renzi*, 89–126. An essential overview of the corpus is provided by Monica H. Green, "Rethinking the Manuscript Basis of Salvatore De Renzi's *Collectio Salernitana*: The Corpus of Medical Writings in the 'Long' Twelfth Century," in Jacquart and Paravicini Bagliani, *La "Collectio Salernitana" di Salvatore De Renzi*, 15–60. I regret that I have not had time to take into account the opening chapter of Iolanda Ventura's analysis of the pharmacological tradition in her edition of Ps.-Bartholomaeus Mini de Senis, *Tractatus de herbis (Ms London, British Library, Egerton 747)*, Edizione Nazionale "La Scuola Medica Salernitana" 5 (Florence: SISMEL, Edizioni del Galluzzo, 2010).

[52]   In Book I, ch. IV of his *Metalogicon*, written before 1159, John complained about losing grammar students to the lure of medical studies in the south: "Others, becoming cognizant of their inadequate grounding in philosophy, have departed to Salerno or to Montpellier, where they have become medical students. Then suddenly, in the twinkling of an eye, they have blossomed forth as the same kind of physicians that they had previously been philosophers. Stocked with fallacious empirical rules they return after a brief interval to practice with sedulity what they have learned. Ostentatiously they quote Hippocrates and Galen, *pronounce mysterious words*, and have aphorisms ready to apply to all cases" (emphasis added). Daniel D. McGarry (trans.),

intellectually curious without ever leaving a trace in the surviving books from the region. Such intangibles are difficult to measure, however; as long as the textual correspondences are clear and waiting to be examined, they cannot and should not be ignored.

In the end, then, I hope I have been able to suggest a number of ways in which the *Passionarius* of Gariopontus of Salerno, a rather old-fashioned and underappreciated Salernitan treatise from the eleventh-century Renaissance, enjoyed, in the twelfth century, a peculiar and unexpected popularity as a teaching medium for, among other things, the communication of medical items and disease names, descriptions, and treatments. It should be clear, moreover, even from this cursory examination, that Gariopontus' text played a significant role in the accumulation of bilingual signifiers as part of a century-long tradition of medical education and commentary. The definitions of diseases supplied by Gariopontus himself, and the glosses added to his text in the twelfth century, were ultimately compiled to make up part of the great Salernitan glossary, the *Alphita*. This process, I think, reveals how practitioners and teachers in southern Italy made the *Passionarius* "speak" to other important treatises in the language of medical learning and wisdom. Such a cumulative and shared understanding of the meanings of conditions affecting the body, and the means by which to treat them, allowed those privy to medical education to set themselves apart as purveyors of an increasingly intellectualized discipline: the practice of medicine predicated upon linguistic and theoretical mastery.

The Metalogicon of John of Salisbury: A Twelfth-century Defense of the Verbal and Logical Arts of the Trivium (Gloucester, MA: Peter Smith, 1971), 17–18.

Table 3.1   Establishing nosological terminologies

The glosses added to manuscripts of the *Passionarius* in the later eleventh and twelfth centuries are given in italics. These names persist across the body of texts, including Constantine's translations and the major *practicae* of the Salernitan masters, and are recorded in the great glossary known as the *Alphita*. I have selected only the most widely attested glosses to Books I and II of the *Passionarius* to demonstrate correspondences.[1]

	Gariopontus, *Passionarius*; definitions and glosses[2]	Constantine, *Pantegni* and *Viaticum*,[3] names of conditions	*Trattato della cure/De curis*[4]	*Alphita*[5]
1	Cephalea *id est lesio capitis, est dolor capitis qui multum tempus tenens ...: cefas grece, latine caput*	Cephalea (P IX, ch. iii, fol. xliⁱᵛ; V I, ch. x, fols cxlvʳ–cxlviʳ)	Cephalea est dolor capitis qui multum tempus tenens ... cephas grece, caput latine, lesis, dolor inde affligens	Cephalea: lesio capitis
2	Cephaloponia: *cefalon id est caput; ponos id est dolor*			Cephaloponia: pena capitis
3	Monopagia: *monos grece latine unus; monopagia est passio unius partis*		Dolor capitis particularis, alius monopagicus, alius emigranicus. Monos grece latine unus; pagis pars ...	
4	Emicraneum: *emi grece latine semis, cranium, id est rota que superposita est cerebro. Emicraneon id est dimidium capitis, emi enim semis, craneo cerebrum continens*	Hemicranea[6] capitis (P IX, ch. iii, fol. xliʳ: Dolor capitis qui hemicraneus nuncupari solet in media parte capitis est; see also V I, ch. xi, fol. cxlviʳ: Si in capite aliquorum fumorum ascendat fumus, et a natura in dextra parte propellatur, dolor ibi gignitur. Si in sinistra, idem patitur, et hemicranea vocatur)	Emigranicus [est in] mediam partem: emis, semis; craneos, craneum	[Emigranea:] Emi, semis interpretatur vel medietas, inde emigranea passio, quia medietatem cranei occupat

Table 3.1   Continued

5	Scotomia: *scotos grece, latine tenebre; scotosim id est tenebrositatem*	Scothomia[7] (*P* IX, ch. v, fol. xli[v]; *V* I, ch. xiii, fol. cxlvi[r])	Scotomia est luminis obvolutio et tenebrositas ... Scotosin grece, tenebrositas latine	Scotomia: tenebrositas oculorum
6	Epilensia: *epi grece, latine super; lesis grece, lesio latine.* Epilempticorum genera sunt tria, analempsia, catalempsia, epilempsia	Epilepsia[8] (*P* IX, ch. vi, fol. xli[v]; *V* I, ch. xxii, fol. cxlvi[v])	Epilensia: epi id est supra lesis id est lesio inde epilensia id est superiorum lesio. Epilensie III sunt species, analempsia, catalempsia et epilempsia	Epilemsia: captio; inde epilempsia superiorum captio, scilicet, cerebri, et analempsia et catalempsia
7	Phrenesis est mentis alienatio et insania ...: *greci mentem frenes vocant.* Phrenes est humor tegens pars [*sic*] cerebri in quo manet ratio et intellectus, qui facit ibi apostema aut repletionem	Frenesis (*P* IX, ch. iv, fol. xli[v]; *V* I, ch. xviii, fol. cxlvi[r]–cxlvii[r])	Frenesis est alienatio mentis et insania ... est egritudo vicio apostematis in anteriori cellula cerebri facti; et ipsum apostema dicitur frenesis. Frenes cerebri sunt paniculi quibus cerebrum continetur	Frenesis ... due pellicule que obvolvunt cerebrum, scilicet pia mater et dura mater; et inde dicitur frenesis, apostema factum in eis
8	Melancholia: *melan grece, latine niger; colon, colera nigra humor*	Melancholia (*P* IX, ch. vii, fol. xlii[v])	Melancholia: melan enim grece latine nigrum, colon, humor	Melancholia: melan enim nigrum, colon, humor
9	Lethargia: *id est oblivio,* est passio mentis cum febre acuta, cum gravi pulsu et tardo, et veluti inani, quem Greci dyadmon dicunt	Lethargia[9] (*P* IX, ch. v, fol. xli[v]–xlii[r]; *V* I, ch. xiv, fol. cxlvi[r])	Lithargia est passio mentis cum febre acuta ex vicio apostematis in posteriori cerebri cellula facti contingens. Lithes, oblivio, gios operatio	Lethargia: oblivio ... scilicet labor oblivionis, ergas enim labor ... lethes enim dicitur fluvius infernalis

Table 3.1   Continued

10	Catharrus: *id est defluxio capitis*; catarrus dictus est a fluore, greci enim fluere catarron vocaverunt	Catarrus (*V* II, ch. xv, fol. cxlix'; *P* IX, ch. xxii, fol. xlv': Tussis aut ex catarro aut ex mala complexione nascitur. Ex catarro quia cum humores a capite descendunt et ad pectus et pulmonem veniunt, tussim faciunt)	Catarrus est fluxus humoris a cerebro preter naturam ... Dicitur a fluere; cataron enim greci fluere dicunt	Catarrus: fluxus, inde cataricum medicina laxativa
11	Coriza: id est constrictio narium	Coriza[10] (*V* II, ch. xiv, fol. cxliv'; *P* IX, ch. xvii, fol. xliv': Coriza est humor humidus descendens a ventriculis prore cerebri in naribus)	Coriza ... unde sequitur capitis gravedo, narium constrictio	
12	Synanchis: *greci enim sinancis continere, id est restringem* [?], *dicunt.* Synanche dicta est a praefocatione, quia synanchis grece praefocatio dicitur	Squinantia[11] (*P* IX, ch. xix, fol. xliv'; *V* III, ch. i, fol. clir', and ch. vii, fol. clii')	Sinancia est gutturis praefocatio	Synanchis: prefocatio; inde sinancia, quod est acutissima prefocatio [angina]
13	Emoptoicis: *effusio sanguinis.* Emoptoicorum signa sic intelliges: sanguinem reiciunt	(Not found in *P* or *V*; bur see the *Liber aureus* VIII, ch. xvi, p. 174: De haemophthoycis)	Emoptoica est fluxus sanguinis sputo vel vomitu per os emissus. Ema id est fluxus, tois id est sanguis	Emoptoica: sanguineum sputum
14	Phthisis est passio pulmonum periculosa et maligna valde	Phthysis[12] (*V* III, ch. vii, fol. cliii'; *P* IX, ch. xxii, fol. xlv'')	Ptisis est ulceratio pulmonis cum consumptione humiditatis	

Table 3.1   Continued

15	Empima: empici sunt quibus apostema fit in pulmone, sive in hepate sive in thorace, et si crepuerit, saniem per os putridam mittunt, vel rejiciunt mistam sanguine cum febre et tussi et macie. *Empici id est saniosi*		Empimia est sanies per os emissa inde empiti id est saniosi. Fit autem ex epatis apostemate, exmotoicis, periplemonicis, frequentius ex pleureticis	Empimia: sputum saniosum
16	Periplemonia: in multis locis apostema fit, prae omnibus vero periculosum est quod in pulmonibus fit ... quae est acuta passio, quae cito occidit. *Pneumon grece, latine pulmo dicitur*	Periplemonia (*P* IX, ch. xxii, fol. xlv: Passiones pulmonis sunt fortis tussis, anhelitus asma, angustia spiritus, orthomia,[13] periplemonia screatus sanguinis et sanici, et phthysis)	Periplemonia est egritudo ex distemperantia humoris in pelliculis pulmonis ad apostema collectum ... Pneugmon grece, latine pulmo	
17	Orthopnoia, id est rectus flatus; astma ab aliquibus vocatur comuniter dispnia, id est constrictio	Orthomia (*P* IX, ch. xxii, f. xlv: hec passio vocatur orthomia ab orthos grece quod est rectus latine, quia huiusmodi patiens semper vult erectus esse)	Asma est difficultas spiritus	Orthomia, id est, difficilis respiratio ... ab orthos, quod est rectum, et thimos, quod est spiritus
18	Anathimia stomachi: *anathimiasis grece exaltatio evaporatio fumositas*			Anathimiasis: delatio fumi a stomacho sursum ad caput, vel ventositas
19	Anatropa stomachi est sursum eversio cum vomitu		Anatropa est stomaci sursum eversio ... unde sequitur cibi et potus emissio et defectio	Anatropa: conversio stomachi sursum, id est vomitus

Table 3.1   Continued

			Catatropa vero est subversio stomachi	Catatropa: conversio stomachi deorsum, fluxus ventris dum tamen fiat fluxus ille vicio stomachi
20	Catatropa est stomachi subversio, quae est diarrhea, id est ventris solutio		Catatropa vero est subversio stomachi	Catatropa: conversio stomachi deorsum, fluxus ventris dum tamen fiat fluxus ille vicio stomachi
21	Phlegmonis: nos tumorem cum fervore stomachi dicimus	Phlegmones (*VV*, ch. iii, fol. clix^v: Qui [humores] si fuerint sanguinolenti, generantur apostemata que phlegmones appellantur)		Flegmon dicitur quasi flammon, et est apostema sanguineum, ut in Johannicio de apostematibus
22	Pneumatosis, id est inflatio agnoscitur ... qua magis stomachus inclinat, eructatio, et per anum eventatio assidua fit			Pneumatosis, id est, ventositas
23	Anorexia, id est fastidium *quod greci atrophian vocant; sine appetitu. Cacexia*			Anorexia: sine appetitu, id est fastidium
24	Perielcosis, *quod latine vulnus dicitur in stomacho sic agnoscitur*			
25	Bulismos, *id est nimius appetitus.* Greci hanc passionem bulismon vocaverunt	Bolismos (*P* IX, ch. xxvi, fol. xlvi^v: Bolismus est nimia fames; *V* IV, ch. iii, fol. clv^r)	Bulismo est immoderatus stomaci appetitus	
26	Sclirosis, id est duricia fit in icore grandis ... Sclirosis est tumor et duricia hepatis quae enphraxis dicitur, id est, praeclusio			**Interpretatur durum; inde sclirosis et scleria, ut in Passionario

Table 3.1   Continued

27	Scleria est epatis duritia sicut sclirosis, sed differunt, quia scleria a se incipit, nulla causa epatis precedente ... Scleria est cum sensu et dolore, sine quibus est sclirosis		**Interpretatur durum; inde sclirosis et scleria, ut in Passionario
28	Syrexis est eruptio apostematis		Syrexis: eruptio apostematis
29	Ciliaca est passio assidua ventris solutio ... Ciliacorum multae sunt passiones. *Greci enim ciliam ventrem dicant* ... Ciliaca id est nimia ventris solutio, fit frequenter per corruptelam ciborum, vel crapulam, aut frequenti solutione	Ciliaca est solutio ventris nimia. Cilian grece venter latine. Cujus III sunt species, diarria, dissenteria et lienteria	
30	De variis causis vesicae. Omnes causae vesicae ex renum indignatione fiunt, quae multae sunt et variae. Quarum nos oportet singulariter vocabula et signa, et curationes dicere. Fiunt ergo in vesica tumor, duritia, collectio, hemorrosagia, trombosis, vulneratio, pscoriasin, ptyriasis, trichiasin, atoma, samsudis, lithiasis, dissuria, stranguaria, scuria, rheumatismus, diapsne	Stranguiria, etc. (*P* IX, ch. xxxviii, fol. xlix': Passiones in vesica sunt lapis vulnera stranguiria, exire urinam preter voluntatem)	**Stranguiros interpretatur gutta, inde stranguiria, id est, guttatim minctus. Item sansudis, dissuria, suria, sporiasis, et multa similia que sunt passiones vesice, ut in Passionario

Notes to Table 3.1

1.   For tables emphasizing a range of glosses as they appear in different manuscripts of the *Passionarius*, see Glaze, "Prolegomena," 80–86.

2.   Gariopontus himself supplies many definitions, some of them from his source texts, while, in more than 22 manuscripts of the twelfth century, glossators supply additional terms. They are particularly eager to note the Greek > Latin equivalents for the names of diseases, and sometimes to provide further anatomical details.

3.   For the *Pantegni Theorica* I have consulted vol. 2 of the Lyons 1515 edition, *Omnia opera Ysaac*. I have compared also the Helsinki manuscript edited by Outi Kaltio as Constantine the African, *Theorica Pantegni: Facsimile and Transcription of the Helsinki Manuscript (Codex EÖ.II.14)* (Helsinki: National Library of Finland, 2011), available online at http://www.doria .fi/handle/10024/69831, and the glossed manuscript Cambridge, Trinity College, MS R. 14. 34 (James 906), s. xii med., from Bury St Edmunds. This manuscript was carefully corrected by contemporary scribes against two other copies of the same text. For the *Viaticum*, I have used the Lyons 1515 edition. The *Liber aureus*, often attributed to Johannes Afflacius, is printed with the works of Constantine in the 1536 Basel edition of Henricus Petrus, *Opera Constantini*, where it occupies pp. 168–207. Constantine's *De stomacho* appears at pp. 215–74 of the same volume. The Basel printings are available at the Bibliothèque Interuniversitaire Santé's Medica site: http://www.bium.univ-paris5.fr/histmed/medica/cote?00128x01. Foliation given here is to the Lyons printing of the *Pantegni* and *Viaticum* unless otherwise noted.

4.   The *De curis* is preserved in the unique manuscript, Rome, Biblioteca Angelica, MS lat. 1408 (s. xii); the readings offered here follow the edition of Piero Giacosa, *Magistri salernitani nondum editi*, 177–279.

5.   I have employed the new critical edition of Alejandro García González, *Alphita*, Edizione Nazionale "La Scuola Medica Salernitana" 2 (Florence: SISMEL, Edizioni del Galluzzo, 2007). Those definitons attributed to Gariopontus by the compiler of the *Alphita* are marked also with a double asterisk.

6.   Spelled *Emigranea* in the manuscript tradition: see Cambridge, Trinity College, MS R. 14. 34, fol. 98v; Helsinki, National Library of Finland, MS EÖ.II.14, fol. 142v.

7.   Spelled *Scotomia* in Trinity R. 14. 34, fols 100r, 101r; Helsinki EÖ.II.14, fol. 142v.

8.   *Epilempsia* in Trinity R. 14. 34, fols 100v, 101r; Helsinki EÖ.II.14, fols 142v, 146v.

9.   Spelled *Lithargia* in Trinity R. 14. 34, fol. 100r; Helsinki EÖ.II.14, fol. 142v.

10.   Spelled *Corriza* in Trinity R. 14. 34, fol. 107v.

11.   Spelled *Quinantia* in Trinity R. 14. 34, fol. 108v: "Passiones in membris spiritus ... in lacertis, quinantia et suffocatio. Quinantia est calidum apostema"; but consider also, a few lines later, "Si apostema in lacerto est interiore, appellatur sinuchia." In Helsinki EÖ.II.14, fol. 159r, we find both *quinantia* and *quinancia*.

12.   Spelled *ptisis* and *ptisin* in Trinity R. 14. 34, fols 109r, 110v; in Helsinki EÖ.II.14, fol. 160r, *ptisis*.

13.   The Lyons 1515 edition here gives *ophthalmia*, though later in the paragraph it clarifies this category not as *ophthalmia* but as "orthomia, ab orthos grece quod est rectus latine." Trinity R. 14. 34, fol. 109rv, gives *orthomia*; Helsinki EÖ.II.14, fol. 160r, gives *ortomia*.

Table 3.2 Glosses of remedies in Gariopontus and other regional texts of southern Italy

This table represents samples of terms glossed before the year 1150 in manuscripts containing Gariopontus' *Passionarius*, Book I, for which equivalent identifications appear in other texts that circulated in southern Italy during the eleventh and twelfth centuries. I have left the names of materials in the case, usually accusative, in which they appear in the *Passionarius* in order to make them congruent with the glosses added there. The glosses added to manuscripts of the *Passionarius* are given in italics. Many of these are consistent glosses reproduced in multiple copies of the text. The earliest of these dates to the mid-eleventh century, though most surviving manuscripts were produced in the twelfth century.

	Passionarius, text / glosses	*Agriocanna*[1]	*Alphita*[2]	*Circa instans*[3]
1	Oleo yrino / *ab yreos*		Acorus ... citrino, spatula fetida, que habet purpureum florem et yreos que habet album	Yreos que habet album florem
2	Camomillino / *olero de camomilla*		Camomilla, anthemis idem	
3	Nardium / *de spica nardi*	Nardostacium id est spica nardi (*A1, A2*)	Nardostachium, spica nardi idem; nardus indica, nardus vel spica; quando simpliciter ponitur, spica nardi intelligitur	
4	Trociscos / *rotellas / rotunde confectiones*		Trocos interpretatur rotu[n]dum; inde trocisci, eo quod rotundam habent formam	
5	Peucedani / *feniculus cervini* [stag's fennel, a.k.a. hog's fennel]	Peucidanum id est cauda porcina (*A1, A2*)	Peucedanum, feniculus porcinus idem	
6	Squibala / *stercora dura*			
7	Mulsa / *mel et aqua*		Apomel, ydromel, mellicratum [several methods of preparations]	

Table 3.2   Continued

8	Cymolea / creta albe	Cimolea id est creta de sardia (A1) / Cimolea id est creta sarda (A2)	Chimolea	
9	Acacia trita / fructus spine prunelle	Agcacia id est succus [ ] vel prunelle (A1) / Acatia id est atrinie succus (A2)	Succus prunellarum immaturarum [possibly Prunus spinosa]	Acacia frigida est et sicca in tertio gradu. Est autem acacia succus prunellorum immaturorum
10	Oleum anetemum / ab aneto			
11	Aut rutaceum / de ruta			
12	Saccellannis / cum sacculo cataplasmate		Saccus, saccellus idem, inde saccellatio	
13	Oxirodium / acetum roseum oleum		Oxirodon, id est, acetum mixtum cum oleo rosato	
14	Extrucio / suco caulis agrestis	Strucium id est cauliculi agrestis [sic] (A2)	Strucium, id est caulis agrestis	Strucium
15	Absinthii pontici / id est albi		Centonica, quidam dicunt quod sit absinthium ponticum	
16	Oxymel / acetum et mel			
17	Oxypolium diantilon / acetum elatum id est de malis			
18	Stafisagria / erba pedicularis	Stafrisagria id est fisagria (A1)	Staphisagria dicitur a staphis, quod est uva, et agria, id est agrestis ... alio nomine dicitur herba pedicularis	

Table 3.2   Continued

19	*Lasar / asa fetida*	Lasar id est opium (*A1*)	Lasar, asa fetida idem	
20	*Opio miconis / papaveris albi*	Micon sperma id est papaveris semen (*A1, A2*)	Opomiconium, id est opium miconis	
21	*Gera / galieni*		Yera interpretatur sacrum; inde yerapigra, id est, sacrum amarum	
22	*Pigra / id est amari*			
23	*Gera / id est sacra*			
24	*Resine fructe / pix nigra greca id est colofonia*	Colophonia id est resina frixa vel greca pix (*A1*) / Colofonea id est resina frixa (*A2*)	Colofonia, pix greca ... arbores quarum gumma est colofonia	
25	*Olei sicionii / id est cucumeribus agrestibus*	Oleum sicionium id est quod fit de cucumeris [*sic*] (*A2*)	Elacterium, succus cucumeris agrestis idem ... siccia	
26	*Anagallus / sinfita consolidi maior*	Anagallia id est symphitum sine forma (*A1*) / Anagallicus id est simphitum (*A2*)	Anagallis sive anagallicum sive anagalla, consolida maior idem / Consolida maior, anagallicum, anagallis, simphitum idem	
27	*Ciclaminis / mala terranea* [leg. incert.]	Ciclaminus id est mallum terraneum (Ciclamina *A1*, Ciclaminus *A2*)	Ciclamen, panis porcinus, cassamus, malum terre idem	
28	*Codia / papaver*	Codia id est papaveris flos (*A1*) / Codia id est papaveris capita (*A2*)	Comedium, codium, miconium idem	
29	*Sinapizare / ungere*			
30	*Caricas / id est ficus sicca*		Carica, ficus sicca idem	

Table 3.2 Continued

31	Unguento lympido bono / *id est marciaton*			
32	Poligonium / *id est centinodium*	Poligonos id est centinodia id est proserpinacia vel sanguinaria (*A1*) / Poligonia id est sanguinaria; Poligonia id est porcinatia; Poligonos id est preserpinaca [*sic*] (*A2*)	Poligonia, lingua passerina, geniculata, proserpinata, centinodia idem	
33	Alice / *spelte*		Alica, spelta idem	
34	Cantaridis / *id est animalium g[ ] inveniuntur in foliis fraxini*	Cantarides id est genus musce (*A2*)	Cantarides, musce sunt oblonge et virides	
35	Cocognidium / *id est semen laureole*	Cocognidium id est semen laureole (*A1, A2*)	Coconidium, gindium, semen laureole idem, ut in Alexandro	
36	Dimifragiorum / *id est acruminium*		Dimfragia, id est, acrumina	
37	Epithimia / *erba que dicitur super thimum*		Epithimum fila quedam sunt que nascuntur super thimum et super alias herbas et frutices, sed eo magis utimur quod supra thimum nascitur	
38	Embrocis / *infusiones*		Embroca interpretatur infusio, quod nos fomentum dicimus	
39	Antidotum mitriditis / *maceroris* [lect. incert.]			

Table 3.2 Continued

40	Piscibus marinis aspratilibus / squamosis		Aspratiles dicuntur pisces ab asperitate squamarum	
41	Pistacias / amidgalas [sic] minores	Pistatia id est similis nocelle (A2)	Pistacee sunt fructus habentes nucleos et testas	Fructus sunt in ultramarinis nascentes, similes pineis … Contra frigiditatem pectoris valent comeste ut amigdale
42	Sisimbrium / balsamitum	Balsamites id est sisimbrium (A1, sisimbrio A2)	Xisimbrium, id est, balsamita	
43	Glaucinum / id est celidonia	Glaucium id est celidonia alii viola; Glaucius rizi id est celidonia (A1) / Glaucium id est celidonia; Glaucium id est viola (A2)	Glaucium agreste, celidonia idem	
44	Afronitrum / id est spumis nitri		Affronitrum, spuma nitri idem	
45	Strigni succi / id est solatri	Strignum id est solatrum (A1) / Strignus id est solatrus; Strignos id est uva palacina (A2)	Uva lupina, strignum, solatrum, morella idem	
46	Musa / antidotum est			
47	Ocimi / id est basilico	Ozimum id est basilicon (A1) / Ocimum id est basilicon herba (A2)	Ozimum, id est, basilicon, herba est cuius semina magis utuntur apotecarii	Ozimum calidum est et siccum. Alio nomine basilicon appellatur
48	Libanotidos / id est ros marinus	Libanotidos id est est ros marino [sic] (A1, A2)	Libanotidos, ros marinus, dendrolibanum idem	Ros marinus … herba ipsa libanotidos vel dendrolibanum dicitur, in locis marinis crescit

Table 3.2   Continued

49	Lactis celsi / *sicbomori*	Celsi id est mora domestica (*A1,A2*) / Sicamina id est celsa mora (*A1,A2*)	Sicomorus, id est, ficus fatua, arbor est cuius fructus dicitur siccamina	
50	Anthere / *de floribus rosarum*		Antera, semen rose idem	Antera dicitur quidam flos rosarum scilicet qui interius reperitur
51	Palmulas / *dactilos*		Finicon, dactilus palme idem, et finicon balanon idem est quod dactilus, et dicitur balanon eo quod glandi assimilatur in forma	
52	Sapam / *vinum coctum*			
53	Rore syriaco / *flos orniale*	Ros syriacus id est flos orni (*A1*) / Ros syriacus id est ornus (*A2*)	Ros syriacus id est flos orni [< ornix]	
54	Ypoquiride / *fungus que nascitur in pede rose canine*	Ypoquistidos id est rosa canina (*A2*)	Ypoquistidos est succus fungi qui nascitur ad pedem rose canine	Ypoquistidos frigidus est et siccus in secundo gradu, fungus est qui reperitur circa pedem rose canine
55	Acacia / *sucus prunellarum*		Acatia, succus prunellarum immaturarum. Item acatia cirra, id est, dura	Acacia frigida est et sicca in tertio gradu. Est autem acacia succus prunellorum immaturorum
56	Gummi / *arabica*		Gummi, quando simpliciter positur, arabicum intelligitur	
57	Diascilles / *de cepa marina*		Squilla id est cepa marina	

Table 3.2   Continued

58	Diatrion pipereon / ex albo et nigro et longo			
59	Glaucini / celidonia		Glaucium agreste, celidonia idem	
60	Stipteria / aluminosa	Stepteria id est alumen (*A1*, Stipteria *A2*)	Stipterea id est alumen	
61	Bitumine / aspalto	Bitumen id est aspaltum iudaicum (*A1*, *A2*)	Bitumen iudaicum, aspaltum idem	
62	Diaspermaton / de seminibus		Diaspermaton, id est de seminibus	
63	Masticis / gumma		Mastix, gumma est	
64	Evisco / malva	Evisci id est malva visco (*A1*, *A2*)	Altea, eviscis, bismalva, malvaviscus	
65	Asara / baccara	Asaru id est baccara (*A1*, *A2*)	Asara, buccara	
66	Petroselini macedonici / vel maioris			
67	Barbara / confectio est			
68	Mirre trocliten / rotunde		Mirra trocliten, id est rotunda	
69	Tetrafarmacium / factum ex quattuor rebus			Tetrafarmacum, igitur unguentum de quattuor medicinis
70	Carpobalsamum / fructus balsamum		Carpobalsamum dicitur fructus balsami	Balsamus ... fructus qui in frutice reperitur dicitur carpobalsamus

Table 3.2 Continued

	Xilobalsamum / lignum balsamum	Xilobalsamum id est lignum balsamum (A1) / Silobalsamum id est lignum balsami (A2)	Xilobalsamum, id est lignum balsami	Balsamus ... rami ... colligantur et desiccantur et dicuntur xilobalsami
71		Xilobalsamum id est lignum balsamum (A1) / Silobalsamum id est lignum balsami (A2)	Xilobalsamum, id est lignum balsami	Balsamus ... rami ... colligantur et desiccantur et dicuntur xilobalsami
72	Opobalsamum / succus balsamum	Obobalsamum (A1, gloss lacking) / Opobalsamum id est sucus balsami (A2)		Balsamus ... succi qui dicitur opobalsamus

Notes to Table 3.2

1.   For the *Agriocanna* I rely upon the two earliest extant manuscripts, Vatican City, Biblioteca Apostolica Vaticana, MSS Vat. lat. 4418 (here *A1*) and Chig. F. IV. 57 (here *A2*). I believe the dates of both to be *c.* 1070–1100 and *c.* 1090–1140, respectively. Alejandro García González's announced edition of the *Agriocanna*, based on four extant manuscripts, will resolve important issues in the expansion of this glossary and its relation to the slightly later *Alphita*.

2.   García González, *Alphita*.

3.   Hans Wölfel, "Das Arzneidrogenbuch *Circa instans* in einer Fassung des XIII. Jahrhunderts aus der Universitätsbibliothek Erlangen: Text und Kommentar als Beitrag zur Pflanzen- und Drogenkunde des Mittelalters," inaugural dissertation, Friedrich-Wilhelms-Universität Berlin (1939).

Bibliography

Ausécache, Mireille. "Un *Liber iste*, des *Liber iste*? Un *Platearius*, des *Platearius*? État des lieux d'un projet d'édition." In Jacquart and Paravicini Bagliani, *La scuola medica salernitana*, 1–30.

Barney, Stephen A., W.J. Lewis, J.A. Beach, and Oliver Berghof (trans.). *The "Etymologies" of Isidore of Seville*. Cambridge: Cambridge University Press, 2006.

Beccaria, Augusto. *I codici di medicina del periodo presalernitano (secoli IX, X, e XI)*. Rome: Edizioni di Storia e Letteratura, 1956.

Bloch, Herbert. *Monte Cassino in the Middle Ages*. 3 vols. Cambridge, MA: Harvard University Press, 1986.

Bonardi, Diomede (ed.). *Galieni opera*. 2 vols. Venice: F. Pinzi, 1490. Digital facsimile, Bibliothèque Interuniversitaire Santé (Paris): http://web2.bium .univ-paris5.fr/livanc/?cote=extacadinca11&do=livre (accessed February 19, 2012).

Brown, Virginia. *The Textual Transmission of Caesar's "Civil War."* Leiden: Brill, 1972.

———. "Where Have All the Grammars Gone?" In Mario de Nonno, Paolo de Paolis, and Louis Holtz (eds), *Manuscripts and Tradition of Grammatical Texts from Antiquity to the Renaissance*, 389–414. Cassino: Edizioni dell'Università degli Studi di Cassino, 2000.

Burnett, Charles. "The Contents and Affiliation of the Scientific Manuscripts Written at, or Brought to, Chartres in the Time of John of Salisbury." In Michael Wilks (ed.), *The World of John of Salisbury*, 127–60. Oxford: Blackwell, 1984.

————— and Danielle Jacquart (eds). *Constantine the African and 'Alī ibn al-'Abbās al-Maǧūsī: The "Pantegni" and Related Texts*. Leiden: Brill, 1994.

Bursill-Hall, G.L. *A Census of Medieval Latin Grammatical Manuscripts*. Stuttgart-Bad Cannstatt: Frommann-Holzboog, 1981.

Caiazzo, Irene. "Un inedito commento sulla *Isagoge Johannitii* conservato a Parigi." In Jacquart and' Paravicini Bagliani, *La scuola medica salernitana*, 93–123.

Constantine the African. *Theorica Pantegni: Facsimile and Transcription of the Helsinki Manuscript (Codex EÖ.II.14)*. Ed. Outi Kaltio in collaboration with Heikki Solin and Matti Haltia. Helsinki: National Library of Finland, 2011. Available online at http://www.doria.fi/handle/10024/69831 (accessed February 19, 2012).

Constantini Africani post Hippocratem et Galenum, quorum, Græcæ linguæ doctus, sedulus fuit lector, medicorum nulli prorsus, multis doctissimis testibus, posthabendi opera. Basel: Henricus Petrus, 1536. Digital facsimile, Bibliothèque Interuniversitaire Santé (Paris): http://www.bium.univ-paris5 .fr/histmed/medica/cote?00128x01 (accessed February 19, 2012).

Cooke, Miriam, Erdağ Göknar, and Grant Parker (eds). *Mediterranean Passages: Readings from Dido to Derrida*. Chapel Hill: University of North Carolina Press, 2008.

Daems, Willem F., and François Ledermann. "Die *opopira magna*, ein pharmazeutisches Präparat aus dem *Antidotarius magnus*." *Gesnerus* 44 (1987): 177–88.

Daremberg, Charles. "Aurelius." *Janus* 2 (1847): 468–99, 690–96, and 705–31.

Fischer, Klaus-Dietrich. "Der pseudogalenische *Liber tertius*." In Ivan Garofalo and Amneris Roselli (eds), *Galenismo e medicina tardoantica: fonti greche, latine e arabe. Atti del Seminario internazionale di Siena, Certosa di Pontignano, 9 e 10 settembre 2002*, 101–32. Naples: Istituto Universitario Orientale, 2003.

—————. "Galeni qui fertur ad Glauconem Liber tertius ad fidem codicis Vindocinensis 109." In Ivan Garofalo and Amneris Roselli (eds), *Galenismo e medicina tardoantica: fonti greche, latine e arabe. Atti del Seminario internazionale di Siena, Certosa di Pontignano, 9 e 10 settembre 2002*, 283–346. Naples: Istituto Universitario Orientale, 2003.

García González, Alejandro. "Hermeneumata medicobotanica vetustiora." *Studi medievali* 49 (2008): 119–40.

————. "*Agriocanna*, a New Medico-Botanical Glossary of Pre-Salernitan Origin." In David Langslow and Brigitte Maire (eds), *Body, Disease and Treatment in a Changing World: Latin Texts and Contexts in Ancient and Medieval Medicine. Proceedings of the Ninth International Conference "Ancient Latin Medical Texts," Hulme Hall, University of Manchester, 5th–8th September, 2007*, 223–35. Bibliothèque d'histoire de la médecine et de la santé. Lausanne: Éditions BHMS, 2010.

———— (ed.). *Alphita*. Edizione Nazionale "La Scuola Medica Salernitana" 2. Florence: SISMEL, Edizioni del Galluzzo, 2007.

Gaspar, Giles E.M., and Faith Wallis. "Anselm and the *Articella*." *Traditio* 59 (2004): 129–74.

Giacosa, Piero. *Magistri salernitani nondum editi*. Turin: Bocca, 1901.

Glaze, Florence Eliza. "Galen Refashioned: Gariopontus of Salerno's *Passionarius* in the Later Middle Ages and Renaissance." In Elizabeth Lane Furdell (ed.), *Textual Healing: Essays in Medieval and Early Modern Medicine*, 53–77. Leiden: Brill, 2005.

————. "Gariopontus and the Salernitans: Textual Traditions in the Eleventh and Twelfth Centuries." In Jacquart and Paravicini Bagliani, *La "Collectio Salernitana" di Salvatore De Renzi*, 149–90.

————. "Prolegomena: Scholastic Openings to Gariopontus' *Passionarius*." In Glaze and Nance, *Between Text and Patient*, 57–86.

———— and Brian K. Nance (eds). *Between Text and Patient: The Medical Enterprise in Medieval and Early Modern Europe*. Micrologus' Library 39. Florence: SISMEL, Edizioni del Galluzzo, 2011.

Goetz, Georg (ed.). *Corpus glossariorum latinorum*. 7 vols in 8. Leipzig: Teubner, 1888–1923.

Goltz, Dietlinde. *Mittelalterliche Pharmazie und Medizin dargestellt an Geschichte und Inhalt des "Antidotarium Nicolai," mit einem Nachdruck der Druckfassung von 1471*. Stuttgart: Wissenschaftliche Verlagsgesellschaft, 1976.

Green, Monica H. "The Re-creation of *Pantegni, Practica*, Book VIII." In Burnett and Jacquart, *Constantine the African*, 121–60.

————. "Rethinking the Manuscript Basis of Salvatore De Renzi's *Collectio Salernitana*: The Corpus of Medical Writings in the 'Long' Twelfth Century." In Jacquart and Paravicini Bagliani, *La "Collectio Salernitana" di Salvatore De Renzi*, 15–60.

———— (ed.). *Trotula: un compendio medievale di medicina delle donne*. Trans. Valentina Brancone. Edizione Nazionale "La Scuola Medica Salernitana" 4. Florence: SISMEL, Edizioni del Galluzzo, 2009.

Horden, Peregrine. "Disease, Dragons and Saints: The Management of Epidemics in the Dark Ages." In T.O. Ranger and Paul Slack (eds), *Epidemics and Ideas: Essays on the Historical Perception of Pestilence*, 45–76. Cambridge: Cambridge University Press, 1995.

Irvine, Martin. *The Making of Textual Culture: "Grammatica" and Literary Theory, 350–1100*. Cambridge: Cambridge University Press, 1994.

Jacquart, Danielle. "Le sens donné par Constantin l'Africain à son œuvre: les chapitres introductifs en arabe et en latin." In Burnett and Jacquart, *Constantine the African*, 71–89.

——— and Agostino Paravicini Bagliani (eds). *La scuola medica salernitana: gli autori e i testi*. Edizione Nazionale "La Scuola Medica Salernitana" 1. Florence: SISMEL, Edizioni del Galluzzo, 2007.

——— (eds). *La "Collectio Salernitana" di Salvatore De Renzi: convegno internazionale, Università degli Studi di Salerno, 18–19 giugno 2007*. Edizione Nazionale "La Scuola Medica Salernitana" 3. Florence: SISMEL, Edizioni del Galluzzo, 2008.

Jordan, Mark D. "Medicine as Science in the Early Commentaries on 'Johannitius.'" *Traditio* 43 (1987): 121–45.

———. "The Construction of a Philosophical Medicine: Exegesis and Argument in Salernitan Teaching on the Soul." *Osiris*, 2nd ser., 6 (1990): *Renaissance Medical Learning: Evolution of a Tradition*, ed. Michael R. McVaugh and Nancy G. Siraisi, 42–61.

Kramer, Andreas, and Korinna Scheidt. "Die Handschriften des *Antidotarius magnus*." *Sudhoffs Archiv* 83 (1999): 109–16.

Kristeller, Paul Oskar. "The School of Salerno: Its Development and Its Contribution to the History of Learning." *Bulletin of the History of Medicine* 17 (1945): 138–94.

———. "Bartholomaeus, Musandinus and Maurus of Salerno and Other Early Commentators on the *Articella*, with a Tentative List of Texts and Manuscripts." *Italia medioevale e humanistica* 19 (1976): 57–87.

———. *Studi sulla scuola medica salernitana*. Naples: Istituto Italiano per gli Studi Filosofici, 1986.

Langslow, D.R. *The Latin Alexander Trallianus: The Text and Transmission of a Late Latin Medical Book*. Journal of Roman Studies Monograph 10. London: Society for the Promotion of Roman Studies, 2006.

Lindsay, W.M. "Gleaning from Glossaries and Scholia." Ch. 17 in W.M. Lindsay, *Studies in Early Medieval Latin Glossaries*, ed. Michael Lapidge. Collected Studies Series CS 467. Aldershot, UK: Variorum, 1996.

Lutz, Alfons. "Der verschollene frühsalernitanische *Antidotarius magnus* in einer Basler Handschrift aus dem 12. Jahrhundert und das *Antidotarium Nicolai.*" *Die Vorträge der Hauptversammlung der Internationalen Gesellschaft für Geschichte der Pharmazie*, n.s., 40 (1973): 97–133.

MacKinney, Loren C. "Medieval Medical Dictionaries and Glossaries." In James Lea Cate and Eugene N. Anderson (eds), *Medieval and Historiographical Essays in Honor of James Westfall Thompson*, 240–68. Chicago: University of Chicago Press, 1938.

Manzanero Cano, Francisco. "Liber Esculapii (Anonymus Liber Chroniorum): edición crítica y estudio." Unpublished Ph.D. dissertation. Universidad Complutense de Madrid, 1996.

McGarry, Daniel D. (trans.). *The Metalogicon of John of Salisbury: A Twelfth-century Defense of the Verbal and Logical Arts of the Trivium*. Gloucester, MA: Peter Smith, 1971.

Newton, Francis. "Constantine the African and Monte Cassino: New Elements and the Text of the *Isagoge.*" In Burnett and Jacquart, *Constantine the African*, 16–47.

O'Donnell, James J. Review of Glenn W. Most, *Commentaries—Kommentare* (Göttingen: Vandenhoeck & Ruprecht, 1999). *Bryn Mawr Classical Review* online, http://bmcr.brynmawr.edu/2000/2000-05-19.html (accessed February 19, 2012).

Omnia opera Ysaac. 2 vols. Lyons: J. de Platea, 1515. Digital facsimile, Universidad Complutense Madrid, Biblioteca Digital Dioscórides: http://www.ucm.es/BUCM/atencion/24063.php (accessed February 19, 2012).

Opsomer-Halleux, Carmélia. "Un herbier médicinal du haut Moyen Âge: l'*Alfabetum Galieni.*" *History and Philosophy of the Life Sciences*, Section II, 4.1 (1982): 65–97.

Ps.-Bartholomaeus Mini de Senis. *Tractatus de herbis (Ms London, British Library, Egerton 747)*. Ed. Iolanda Ventura. Edizione Nazionale "La Scuola Medica Salernitana" 5. Florence: SISMEL, Edizioni del Galluzzo, 2010.

Quelli che servono gli infermi: assistenza e medicina a Roma nei secoli XVI e XVII. Mostra bibliografica. Rome: Ministero per i Beni Culturali e Ambientali/ Biblioteca Vallicelliana, 1987.

Riddle, John M. "Dioscorides." In Ferdinand E. Cranz and Paul Oskar Kristeller (eds), *Catalogus Translationum et Commentariorum: Mediaeval and Renaissance Translations and Commentaries*, vol. 4, 1–143. Washington, D.C.: Catholic University of America Press, 1980.

———. "Pseudo-Dioscorides' 'Ex herbis femininis' and Early Medieval Medical Botany." *Journal of the History of Biology* 14 (1981): 43–81.

————. "Byzantine Commentaries on Dioscorides." *Dumbarton Oaks Papers* 38 (1984): 95–102.

————. *Quid pro Quo: Studies in the History of Drugs*. Collected Studies Series CS 367. Brookfield, VT: Ashgate, 1992.

Roberg, Francesco J.M. "Studium zum *Antidotarium Nicholai* anhand der ältesten Handschriften." *Würzburger medizin-historische Mitteilungen* 21 (2002): 73–129.

————. "Text- und redaktionskritische Probleme bei der Edition von Texten des Gebrauchsschrifttums am Beispiel des 'Antidotarium Nicolai' (12. Jahrhundert): Einige Beobachtungen, mit einem Editionsanhang." *Mittellateinisches Jahrbuch* 42 (2007): 1–19.

Sallares, Robert. *Malaria and Rome: A History of Malaria in Ancient Italy*. New York: Oxford University Press, 2002.

Snowden, Frank M. *The Conquest of Malaria: Italy, 1900–1962*. New Haven: Yale University Press, 2006.

Soren, David. "Can Archaeologists Excavate Evidence of Malaria?" *World Archaeology* 35.2 (2003): *Archaeology of Epidemic and Infectious Disease*, ed. Peter Mitchell, 193–209.

Staden, Heinrich von. "'A Woman Does Not become Ambidextrous': Galen and the Culture of Scientific Commentary." In Roy K. Gibson and Christina Shuttleworth Kraus (eds), *The Classical Commentary: Histories, Practices and Theory*, 109–39. Leiden: Brill, 2002.

Stannard, Jerry. "The Herbal as a Medical Document." *Bulletin of the History of Medicine* 43 (1969): 212–20.

————. "Medieval Herbals and Their Development." *Clio Medica* 9 (1974): 23–33.

————. "Botanical Data in Medieval Medical Recipes." *Studies in the History of Medicine* 1 (1977): 80–87.

Stork, Nancy Porter. *Through a Gloss Darkly: Aldhelm's Riddles in the British Library MS Royal 12. C. xxiii*. Toronto: Pontifical Institute of Mediaeval Studies, 1990.

Thomson, Rodney M., with Michael Gullick. *A Descriptive Catalogue of the Medieval Manuscripts in Worcester Cathedral Library*. Woodbridge, UK: D.S. Brewer, 2001.

Totelin, Laurence. "Mithridates' Antidote: A Pharmacological Ghost." *Early Science and Medicine* 9 (2004): 1–19.

Van Arsdall, Anne. "The Transmission of Knowledge in Early Medieval Medical Texts: An Exploration." In Glaze and Nance, *Between Text and Patient*, 201–16.

Ventura, Iolanda. "Per una storia del *Circa Instans*. I *Secreta Salernitana* ed il testo del manoscritto London, British Library, Egerton 747: note a margine di un'edizione." *Schola Salernitana: Annali* 7–8 (2002–03): 39–109.

———. "Salvatore De Renzi e la letteratura farmacologica salernitana." In Jacquart and Paravicini Bagliani, *La "Collectio Salernitana" di Salvatore De Renzi*, 89–126.

———. "Un manuale di farmacologia medievale ed i suoi lettori: il *Circa instans*, la sua diffusione, la sua ricezione dal XIII al XV secolo." In Jacquart and Paravicini Bagliani, *La scuola medica salernitana*, 465–533.

Vettori, Vincenzo. *Inventarium omnium codicum manuscriptorum graecorum et latinorum Bibliothecae Vallicellanae digestum anno Domini MDCCXLIX*. Unpublished. Digital facsimile at http://cataloghistorici.bdi.sbn.it/code/seq _elenco_gruppi.asp?ResetFilter=Y&FiltraCatalogo=171 (accessed February 19, 2012).

Wack, Mary. "'Alī ibn al-'Abbās al-Maǧūsī and Constantine on Love, and the Evolution of the *Practica Pantegni*." In Burnett and Jacquart, *Constantine the African*, 161–202.

Wallis, Faith. "Inventing Diagnosis: Theophilus' *De urinis* in the Classroom." *Dynamis* 20 (2000): *Medical Teaching and Classroom Practice in the Medieval Universities*, ed. Roger French and Cornelius O'Boyle, 31–73.

———. "The *Articella* Commentaries of Bartholomaeus of Salerno." In Jacquart and Paravicini Bagliani, *La scuola medica salernitana*, 125–64.

Wieland, Gernot R. "Interpreting the Interpretations: The Polysemy of the Latin Gloss." *Journal of Medieval Latin* 8 (1998): 59–71.

Wölfel, Hans. "Das Arzneidrogenbuch *Circa instans* in einer Fassung des XIII. Jahrhunderts aus der Universitätsbibliothek Erlangen: Text und Kommentar als Beitrag zur Pflanzen- und Drogenkunde des Mittelalters." Inaugural dissertation. Friedrich-Wilhelms-Universität Berlin, 1939.

Chapter 4

The Ghost in the *Articella*:
A Twelfth-century Commentary on the
Constantinian *Liber Graduum*[1]

Faith Wallis

1. Introduction: John Riddle and the Ghost in the *Articella*

During his career as a historian of medieval medicine, John Riddle's scholarly interests have turned around a question that is both deeply important and singularly difficult: how did premodern societies identify and understand the power of natural substances to alter the body's workings, and how did they put these powers to use? Riddle is persuaded that the physiological and medical effects of the substances these people used are objectively verifiable, and that historians need to take this reality into consideration when analyzing the textual record. This commitment to a certain pharmacological realism, exemplified by his work on contraceptives and abortifacients, was already announced in his article "Theory and Practice in Medieval Medicine."[2] In this essay, Riddle argued that early medieval medicine, overwhelmingly practical in character, was a seamless continuation of ancient medicine, and that it was clinically innovative and effective. The theoretical turn of the twelfth century, associated with the translations of Arabic medical works and the elaboration of a scholarly style of medical literature oriented toward the construction of abstract models of physiology, pathology, and therapy, was not the dawn of medical progress that historians commonly thought it was. To the contrary, in those branches of medical learning that impinged on practice, notably pharmacology and pharmacy, the effect of theory was at best negligible and at worst pernicious. Scholastic pharmacology's construction of a theory of staged "degrees" of the primal qualities of heat, cold, moisture, and dryness, especially when applied to compound remedies, was unworkable in its complexity. In fact, it was ignored by

[1]   I wish to express my thanks to Professor Michael R. McVaugh for his helpful comments on the draft of this essay.

[2]   John M. Riddle, "Theory and Practice in Medieval Medicine," *Viator* 5 (1974): 157–81.

most practitioners, even the most highly educated. Nonetheless, the ascendancy of "theory" had the negative effect of demoting the value of the empirical knowledge recorded in the older medical literature.

It may thus seem rather odd for me to honor John Riddle with an edition of a twelfth-century text about pharmacological degrees. I dare to do so, because John is also a perceptive student of how ancient and medieval writers tried to classify and explain the effect of drugs. His study of Dioscorides is valuable not only in uncovering the empirical basis of ancient pharmacy, but also in detecting the organizing principle of drug affinities that underlies *De materia medica*. These affinities of physiological effects were identified through observation and experience, and Dioscorides never presented any general theory of drug action. Yet he was not a pure empiricist either, for he drew a logical link between drug "properties" (*dynameis*) and medical usage—e.g., a "warming and astringent" plant like camel's thorn will be an effective treatment for suppurating wounds. Dioscorides' genius for abstracting generic drug actions, and correlating these to therapeutic situations, bridged theory and practice.

Though the challenge which he threw down to historians of medieval medicine remains a valid one, some details of Riddle's "Theory and Practice in Medieval Medicine" have been nuanced by recent scholarship. It can no longer be stated without qualification that scholastic pharmacology automatically allowed theory untrammeled dominion over experience. This has been demonstrated by Michael R. McVaugh in connection with the study of theriac at Montpellier in the late thirteenth and early fourteenth centuries, the theater of vigorous debates between Bernard of Gordon's *via pragmatica* and Arnau de Vilanova's *via intellectualis*.[3] Moreover, Arnau's project to rationalize pharmacy had as its goal the creation of a pharmaceutical theory that was actually workable. That the theoretical approach tended to prevail is less significant for my purposes here than the fact that, as late as 1300, the question of the epistemological status of knowledge about drugs was still open. We can expect, then, that positions were even more fluid in the twelfth century, when Western European pharmacy, still rooted in ancient empirical soil, first confronted the Galenic theory of complexions and degrees. The locus of this encounter was the *Liber graduum*— the *Book of Degrees*. The *Liber graduum* is commonly ascribed to Constantine the African, because it was incorporated (under the title *De gradibus*) into book 2 of Constantine's *Pantegni Practica*, an adaptation of the medical encyclopedia of ʿAlī ibn al-ʿAbbās al-Maǧūsī, known in the West as Haly Abbas. It is the earliest medieval Latin text to address Galen's theory of how medicinal simples

---

3   Michael McVaugh, "Theriac at Montpellier 1285–1328 (with an edition of the 'Quaestiones de tyriaca' of William of Brescia)," *Sudhoffs Archiv* 56 (1972): 113–43.

behave and, for over a century, almost the only one. Arnau and Bernard of Gordon's debates centered on the effects of compound medicine—in other words, on pharmacy rather than pharmacology; but they based their analysis on discussions that took place during the period of consolidation from 1100 to 1250, when the Latin West labored to grasp the implications of the *Liber graduum*'s Galenic paradigm. These preliminary efforts were not particularly original or influential, but they highlighted the questions that preoccupied people who thought about drug action.[4] In this essay, I introduce a hitherto unnoticed twelfth-century commentary on the *Liber graduum*. I argue that the commentary is the work of Bartholomaeus of Salerno, a man with a strong interest in the new medical theory, who was also deeply rooted in a traditional world of practice. Bartholomaeus may have intended to incorporate the *Liber graduum* into an anthology of texts for academic instruction in medicine, the *Articella*—in short, to bridge the domains of theory and practice. He did not prevail, but the spectral image of this ghost in the *Articella* still has much to reveal.

2. The *Liber graduum* and Its Affiliated Texts

The *Liber graduum* comprises a prologue (inc. "Quoniam simplicis medicine disputationem prout ratio postulauit expleuimus …")[5] followed by a catalogue of simples with annotations explaining their qualitative "degrees," e.g., whether the substance was hot in the first degree, wet in the third degree, and so on. When it appears as part of the *Pantegni Practica*, the *Liber graduum* arranges the simples by degree, and within each degree, in rough alphabetical order. There may have been two versions of this list, one beginning with *absinthium* and ending with *titimallus* or *thuthia*,[6] and another beginning with *rosa*. The text I present here follows the first arrangement, but alludes to the second. I have not to date been able to survey all the manuscripts of the *Liber graduum* so as to ascertain the number or distribution of different versions. My provisional impression is that when it appears as a self-

---

4   Michael R. McVaugh, "'Apud antiquos' and Mediaeval Pharmacology," *Medizinhistorisches Journal* 1 (1966): 16.

5   Lynn Thorndike and Pearl Kibre, *Incipits of Mediaeval Scientific Writings in Latin*, 2nd edn (Cambridge, MA: Medieval Academy of America, 1963), cols 1273–1303. Hereafter abbreviated TK.

6   This is the version found in the edition of the *Pantegni* in *Omnia opera Ysaac* (2 vols, Lyons: J. de Platea, 1515), 2: fols lxxviii^r–lxxxvi^r.

standing text,[7] the *Liber graduum* catalogue may be either in a single alphabetical sequence (*absinthium* to *zedoar* or *zizania*),[8] or in the rationalized alphabetical sequence of the *Pantegni*.[9]

Like most of the Constantinian *Pantegni Practica*, the *Liber graduum* was not by Haly Abbas. Constantine only translated what is now book 1 of the *Pantegni Practica*, plus the first section of the present book 2 (chs 1–34, *De probanda medicina*) and the beginning of book 10 on surgery: this is referred to as the *Ur-Practica*.[10] Neither Constantine nor his immediate successors possessed the remainder of Haly Abbas's encyclopedia, but they were aware of its structure and the character of its contents. Hence they recruited texts from elsewhere to fill out the program of their absent source.[11] The *Liber graduum* was one such recruit. Its catalogue of simples was adapted from the *Adminiculum* of Abū Ǧaʿfar Aḥmad ibn Ibrāhīm ibn Abī Khālid al-Ǧazzār (d. 979/1004),[12] whose work *Provisions for the Traveler and the Nourishment of the Settled*, translated and adapted by Constantine under the title *Viaticum*, furnished many other parts of the confected *Pantegni Practica*. The prologue, however, was original: it is commonly assumed to be by Constantine himself, particularly as Peter the Deacon's biobibliography of Constantine names him as the author of a *Liber*

---

7   As printed in the Basel 1536 *Constantini opera*, 342–87, with slightly variant incipit ("Cum disputationem simplicis medicine liber prout ratio ...").

8   Examples include: Cambridge, Corpus Christi College, MS 466 (s. xiii), fols 13–100 (*Absinthium ... zedoar*); Cambridge, St John's College, MS D. 24 (99) (s. xiii), fols 3v–10v (*Absinthium ... zizania*); Salzburg, Universitätsbibliothek, MS M. II. 152 (1467–72), fols 202va–217vb (*Absinthium ... zedoar*). Further examples are cited by Mary Wack, "'Alī ibn al-ʿAbbās al-Maǧūsī and Constantine on Love, and the Evolution of the *Practica Pantegni*," in Charles Burnett and Danielle Jacquart (eds), *Constantine the African and ʿAlī ibn al-ʿAbbās al-Maǧūsī: The "Pantegni" and Related Texts* (Leiden: Brill, 1994), 180 n. 38.

9   E.g., Cambridge, Trinity College, MS R. 14. 31 (904) (s. xii), fols 109–65. For manuscripts, see TK, col. 11, where the Constantinian text is sometimes confounded with pseudo-Mesue, *De gradibus*. An alphabetized *Liber graduum* appears in Basel, Öffentliche Bibliothek der Universität, MS D. III. 3, pt 1 (s. xiv), fols 49r–53r; however, both its prologue ("De gradibus primo quid sit secundo quot sint uideamus ...," TK 375) and its text differ from the *Pantegni Liber graduum*: see Wack, "'Alī ibn al-ʿAbbās," 182. It relates non-medical uses, does not discuss different species or parts of the herb, or include *quid pro quo*.

10   The phrase is Mary Wack's: "'Alī ibn al-ʿAbbās," 182.

11   On the process of constructing the *Pantegni Practica*, see Monica Green, "The Re-creation of *Pantegni, Practica*, Book VIII," in Burnett and Jacquart, *Constantine the African*, 121–60, and Raphaela Veit, "Al-Maǧūsī's *Kitāb al-Malakī* and Its Latin Translation Ascribed to Constantine the African: The Reconstruction of *Pantegni, Practica*, Liber III," *Arabic Sciences and Philosophy* 16 (2006): 133–68.

12   Moritz Steinschneider, "Constantin's *Liber de gradibus* und ibn al-Gezzar's *Adminiculum*," *Deutsches Archiv für Geschichte der Medizin* 2 (1879): 1–22.

graduum.[13] Eventually another recruit was enlisted in *Pantegni Practica* book 2: *De simplici medicina* (chs 35–75 in the Lyons 1515 edition) is a catalogue of medicinal simples organized by type (leaves, seeds, gums, etc.). In the later manuscripts and printed editions, *De simplici medicina* comes between *De probanda medicina* and the *Liber graduum*.

Constantine's unaugmented *Ur-Practica* is preserved in a handful of manuscripts,[14] but I wish to draw particular attention to its inclusion in the medical section of the *Codex Gigas* (Stockholm, Kungliga Biblioteket, MS A. 148, fols 243vb–248vb). In the *Codex Gigas* the *Ur-Practica* material is followed by the prologue only of the *Liber graduum* (fols 248vb–249ra),[15] but both are appended to a copy of the five-book *Articella*. The *Articella* is the conventional late medieval title of a stable anthology of medical texts used for academic instruction from the early twelfth century onward. By the 1120s, it contained Constantine the African's own translation of the *Isagoge*—an adaptation of the *Masā'il fi-tibb* (*Questions about Medicine*), a summary of Galen's *Art of Medicine* by Hunayn ibn Ishāq (809–87), known in the West as Johannitius—as well as translations of the *Aphorisms* and *Prognosis* of Hippocrates, and two Byzantine tracts on pulse and urine by Philaretus and Theophilus. It was this version of the anthology that first acquired integral suites of glosses—the anonymous Chartres and Digby glosses, and those by Bartholomaeus of Salerno (*fl. c.* 1150–80). Later in the twelfth century, the anthology was augmented by the *Ars medicinae* or *Tegni* of Galen, and the Hippocratic *Regimen in Acute Diseases*. Bartholomaeus of Salerno was probably responsible for the inclusion of the *Tegni*, as his *Articella*

---

[13]   Peter the Deacon, *De viris illustribus*, ch. 23, in Herbert Bloch, *Montecassino in the Middle Ages* (3 vols, Cambridge, MA: Harvard University Press, 1986), 1:126–9, at 128. When this section of book 2 of *Pantegni Practica* appears as a self-standing text, *Liber graduum* is its normal title; within the *Pantegni*, it is usually entitled *De gradibus*. However, the *Liber graduum* is by no means always ascribed to Constantine in the manuscripts or by medieval commentators.

[14]   Hildesheim, Dombibliothek, MS 748 (*ante* 1161), Durham, Dean and Chapter Library, MS C. IV. 4 (s. xiii), and London, British Library, MS Add. 22719 (s. xii). Book 1 and *De probanda medicina* alone are found in Bamberg, Staatsbibliothek, MS med. 6 (s. xii² or xiii¹), Paris, Bibliothèque nationale de France, MS lat. 6887 (s. xii¹, Italy), Rome, Biblioteca Vallicelliana, MS B. 48 (s. xiv), and in Basel, Öffentliche Bibliothek der Universität, MS D. III. 3, pt 1 (s. xiv), where it is followed by the *De gradibus* text described above. For descriptions of all of these manuscripts except the Codex Gigas, see "A Catalogue of Renaissance Editions and Manuscripts of the *Pantegni*," in Burnett and Jacquart, *Constantine the African*, 316–51, at 340–41 (Hildesheim), 333 (Durham), 342–3 (London), 329–30 (Bamberg), 347 (Paris), 349–50 (Rome), and 330–31 (Basel).

[15]   Constantine's *De oculis* follows on fols 249ra–252ra. For a detailed description of the manuscript, see www.kungligabiblioteket.se/codex-gigas/eng/Long/catalogue-description. This description accompanies a full electronic facsimile of the manuscript and valuable ancillary essays.

commentaries were the first to include this work. In sum, the *Articella* in the twelfth century was "canonized" to a large degree, and yet was still in a state of evolution.[16] The *Articella* played a crucial role in the formation of a new academic style of medical discourse and instruction in the twelfth century, and will figure prominently in the argument this essay sets out.

The *Liber graduum* presented the basics of Galenic teaching on the four primal qualities of hot, cold, wet, and dry in relation to simple substances used as medicines. In particular, it explained Galen's concept of a scale of intensity, as laid out in books 3–4 of *De simplici medicina*. The theory can be summarized as follows. Everything in nature will exhibit the dominance of one of the four primal qualities of hot, cold, wet, and dry, or else the dominance of a pair of

---

[16]   On the origin and evolution of the *Articella*, the pioneering studies of Paul Oskar Kristeller remain indispensable: "The School of Salerno: Its Development and Its Contribution to the History of Learning," *Bulletin of the History of Medicine* 17 (1945): 138–94; "Nuove fonti per la medicina salernitana del secolo XII," *Rassegna storica salernitana* 18 (1957): 61–75, trans. by Christine Porzer and reprinted as "Neue Quellen zur salernitaner Medizin des 12. Jahrhunderts," in Gerhard Baader and Gundolf Keil (eds), *Medizin im mittelalterliche Abendland*, Wege der Forschung 363 (Darmstadt: Wissenschaftliche Buchgesellschaft, 1982), 191–208; "Beitrag der Schule von Salerno zur Entwicklung der scholastichen Wissenschaft im 12. Jahrhundert: Kurze Mitteilung über handschriftliche Funde," in Josef Koch (ed.), *Artes Liberales von der antiken Bildung zur Wissenschaft des Mittelalters*, Studien und Texte zur Geistesgeschichte des Mittelalters 5 (Leiden: Brill, 1959), 84–90; *La scuola medica di Salerno secondo ricerche e scoperti recenti*, Quaderni Centro di Studi e Documentazione della Scuola Medica Salernitana 5 (Salerno: Mutalipassi, 1980); "Bartholomaeus, Musandinus and Maurus of Salerno and Other Early Commentators of the *Articella*, with a Tentative List of Texts and Manuscripts," *Italia medioevale e umanistica* 29 (1976): 57–87, translated, with additions and corrections, as "Bartolomeo, Musandino, Mauro di Salerno e altri antichi commentatori dell'*Articella*, con un elenco di testi e di manoscritti," in Paul Oskar Kristeller, *Studi sulla scuola medica salernitana* (Naples: Istituto Italiano per gli Studi Filosofici, 1986), 97–151. For more recent perspectives, see Giles E.M. Gaspar and Faith Wallis, "Anselm and the *Articella*," *Traditio* 59 (2004): 129–74, and the literature cited therein. On the early commentaries, see Mark D. Jordan, "Medicine as Science in the Early Commentaries on 'Johannitius,'" *Traditio* 43 (1987): 121–45, and "The Construction of a Philosophical Medicine: Exegesis and Argument in Salernitan Teaching on the Soul," *Osiris*, 2nd ser., 6 (1990): 42–61; Pietro Morpurgo, "I commenti salernitani all'*Articella*," in Monika Asztalos, John E. Murdoch, and Ilkka Niiniluoto (eds), *Knowledge and the Sciences in Medieval Philosophy: Proceedings of the Eighth International Congress of Medieval Philosophy, Helsinki, 24–29 August 1987* (3 vols, Helsinki: Yliopistopaino, 1990), 2:97–105; Faith Wallis, "The Medical Commentaries of Master Bartholomaeus," in Danielle Jacquart and Agostino Paravicini Bagliani (eds), *La scuola medica salernitana: gli autori e i testi*, Edizione Nazionale "La Scuola Medica Salernitana" 1 (Florence: SISMEL, Edizioni del Galluzzo, 2007), 125–64; and Faith Wallis, "Twelfth-century Commentaries on the *Tegni*: Bartholomaeus of Salerno and Others," in Nicoletta Palmieri (ed.), *L'Ars medica (Tegni) de Galien: lectures antiques et médiévales*, Mémoires du Centre Jean Palerne 32 (Saint-Étienne: Publications de l'Université de Saint-Étienne, 2008), 127–68.

these qualities (hot and wet, hot and dry, cold and wet, cold and dry). This is its "complexion." The exception would be something that is perfectly tempered. A substance acts as a medicine when its complexion changes the complexion of the body into which it is introduced. These changes are detectable to the senses. Furthermore, the extent of this change varies in intensity from virtually imperceptible to destructive in its extremity. This can be plotted on a scale of four degrees, each of which can be subdivided into initial, medial, and final stages.[17]

The prologue of the *Liber graduum* introduces the text as a logical continuation of a preceding discussion, apparently *De probanda medicina*. The ancients established that the complexion of every medicinal simple consists of a dominant quality or qualities that can be measured on a scale of four degrees. Each degree was divided into three sections, called the beginning, the middle, and the end. All ancient authors agree with Galen that there are nine complexions, one equal and eight unequal. Four of the unequal ones are simple (with one quality dominating) and four composite (with a pair of qualities dominating). Therefore every body constructed from the four elements exhibits one of these complexions; it is either hot or cold, wet or dry, or hot and dry, or cold and dry, or hot and wet, or cold and wet, or equal, so that no quality dominates another. This applies to the human body as well. But although complexion cannot be discovered by the senses, nonetheless it is to be known intellectually. Physicians, however, focus on maintaining bodies in health and curing the sick, and they do so through foods and medicines, all of which are made from the four elements. Hence it behooves us first to know the nature of foods and medicine, so that individual bodies that exceed the bounds of temperament may be cured with medicines of contrary quality.

When we say that some medicines are hot in a certain degree, we understand this to be in comparison to the human complexion. The comparison can be either simple or composite. It is composite when something is compared to the equal complexion, and simple when something is compared to the equal complexion with respect to a quality of any kind. For example, what is hot in the first degree is hotter than the equal complexion, but less hot than the heat of that equal complexion; hence it neither warms it, nor increases its warmth. (In short, there are two scales: an absolute one, beginning at zero, and a scale relative to the ability of the equal complexion to sense the quality.)[18]

---

[17]   Michael McVaugh, "The Medieval Theory of Compound Medicine" (unpublished Ph.D. diss., Princeton University, 1965), 8–11. McVaugh argues that Galen's *De simplici medicina* may have been available in Latin translation as early as 1100.

[18]   "There are consequently two parallel non-interchangeable meanings of the temperate, the *equa complexio*: in the absolute sense, this refers to the absence of qualities; in the relative sense, to the equality of the members of an opposite-pair at whatever absolute level. While Constantine

Therefore the ancients and especially Galen said that the equal complexion is poised between the two extremes, that is, between the first and fourth degree. Since every surface is contained by two lines and these lines may not be joined without an intermediary, there are of necessity four degrees.[19] Therefore what is hot in the first degree is less hot than natural heat, i.e., in an equal complexion; in the second degree, it is as hot as natural heat itself; in the third degree, it is hotter than natural heat; in the fourth, it exceeds it. The same is the case for cold, moist, and dry.

If we want to test out anything with our senses, it behooves us to taste it. If the sense "dominates" the substance with respect to a certain quality, the substance possesses that quality in the first degree. If the substance matches the sense, so that one does not dominate the other, it possesses the quality in the second degree. If the sense is altered by the substance, but nonetheless tolerates it, the substance is said to be in the third degree. But if the sense is altered by the substance to an unbearable extent, the substance possesses the quality in the fourth degree.

3. The Commentary on the *Liber graduum*: Manuscripts and the Text

Constantine's text bristles with logical paradoxes and problems, to which at least three twelfth-century readers composed responses: the anonymous author of a short tract with the incipit "Apud antiquos,"[20] Urso of Calabria,[21] and the author of our commentary on the *Liber graduum* (hereafter *LGC*). The *LGC* stands

---

manages to preserve this distinction, with the example that 'what is hot in the first degree is hotter than the *equa complexio*, but less hot than the heat of that *equa complexio* ...,' he draws from it the mistaken conclusion that if administered medicinally 'it neither heats nor increases it [the *equa complexio*].' ... The distinction between absolute and relative *gradus* proves to be the most consistently difficult element of pharmacological theory for Constantine to grasp." McVaugh, "Medieval Theory," 15–16.

[19]   On the possible sources of this intriguing argument in the *Timaeus* of Plato, see McVaugh, "Medieval Theory," 17.

[20]   Edited by McVaugh in "'Apud antiquos'" (note 3 above), 18–23. References hereafter are to the line numbers in McVaugh's edition. This edition replaces the less satisfactory text in Lynn Thorndike's "Three Texts of Degrees of Medicines (*De gradibus*)," *Bulletin of the History of Medicine* 38 (1964): 533–7. Note that TK 115 identifies "Apud antiquos artis nostre tractatores ..." as Constantine, *Liber graduum*, even though Thorndike's article says that it is a commentary (and a critical one as well) on this text.

[21]   *De gradibus*, ed. Karl Sudhoff, "Die Salernitaner Handschrift in Breslau, ein *Corpus medicinae Salerni*," *Archiv für Geschichte der Medizin* 12 (1920): 135–8. References hereafter are to the line numbers in this edition.

out as being the only true commentary on the *Liber graduum*, analyzing the text lemma by lemma. By contrast, "Apud antiquos" claims that it will supplement the *Liber graduum* by supplying detail and (implicitly) correcting errors,[22] and Urso's *De gradibus* does not refer explicitly to the *Liber graduum* at all. Urso points to a number of deficiencies in the *Liber graduum*, but dilates only on one: the question of why there are four and no more than four degrees. "Apud antiquos" by contrast is exercised by the problem of the double scale: how can something hot in the first degree be both hotter and less hot than the equal temperament? As we shall see, the *LGC* is closely related in terms of content to "Apud antiquos": both critique the idea of a double scale of degrees, although "Apud antiquos" presents a much more detailed and profound argument.

The *LGC* begins "Liber iste graduum tercia pars est illius Pantegni que practica appellatur,"[23] and is found in four manuscripts. Two contain the complete text: Munich, Bayerische Staatsbibliothek, Clm 28219 (s. xiii[2]), fols 116ra–118v,[24] and Berlin, Staatsbibliothek Preussischer Kulturbesitz, MS lat. q. 255, pt 1 (s. xii[ex]–xiii[in]), fols 122ra–124ra.[25] Partial versions survive in Brussels, Bibliothèque royale, MS II. 1399 (s. xii), fols 68vb–69ra, and Basel, Öffentliche Bibliothek der Universität, MS D. III. 3, pt 2 (s. xiii), fols 75r–76r. The edition of the *LGC* presented below collates all four manuscripts but uses the Munich manuscript as a base text. While Brussels is the oldest manuscript, it is disqualified as a base text because it is incomplete. Munich generally agrees with the oldest complete witness, Berlin. Basel often reads against the consensus of Munich, Brussels, and Berlin, and though its readings rarely affect the sense of the argument, they are occasionally superior. The Basel text is also shorter than Munich's, though unlike the Brussels manuscript, it ends deliberately and with an *explicit*. This suggests a majority and minority tradition of the *LGC* text—a pattern that is characteristic of Bartholomaeus of Salerno's writings.

The *LGC* explicitly identifies the *Liber graduum* as part of the enlarged ten-book *Pantegni*; indeed, the position of the *Liber graduum* as a component of the *Pantegni* is underscored by the author when he explains that he will provide an *accessus* to the *Liber graduum*, despite the fact that an *accessus* already exists for the work as a whole (i.e., *Pantegni Theorica* book 1, ch. 2). This indicates that the

---

22   "Apud antiquos," lines 10–13.

23   This incipit is not listed in TK or in the Voigts-Kurtz eTK database: http://cctr1.umkc.edu/cgi-bin/search.pl.

24   Hermann Hauke, *Katalog der lateinischen Handschriften der Bayerischen Staatsbibliothek München: Clm 28111–28254*, Catalogus codicum manu scriptorum bibliothecae Monacensis 4.7 (Wiesbaden: Harrassowitz, 1986): 184–6.

25   This manuscript is not included in Joseph van den Gheyn, *Catalogue des manuscrits de la Bibliothèque royale de Belgique* (Brussels: Henri Lamartin, 1901).

author was not working from a freestanding version of the text, but it may not mean that he actually was working from the fully elaborated ten-book text of the *Pantegni Practica*. No manuscript of the full *Pantegni Practica* exists from before the early thirteenth century, yet it is plain that twelfth-century authors knew that the *Pantegni Practica* ought to have ten books. Hence the author of the *LGC* might have been working from a version of the *Pantegni Practica* 2 that was still under construction. This suggestion is reinforced by clues that the author envisions the *Liber graduum* following directly upon *De probanda medicina*, without the intervention of *De simplici medicina*. He says:

> For [Constantine] says above that he has treated simple medicine in a global way by
> showing from the complexion what makes a medicine aperitive—that is, from heat
> and dryness, and from subtilty of substance—and what makes one constrictive, namely
> from coldness and dryness. There he did not get down to particulars, designating them
> by their particular names. This is what he will do here by showing what the complexion
> of wormwood is, and southernwood, and so forth. (Edition, lines 51–7)

The passage "above" is the closing words of *De probanda medicina* (*Pantegni Practica*, 2.34): "Hic autem finitur nostra disputatio de uniuersali virtute simplicis medicine. Est autem incipienda simplicium medicinarum diuisio de naturis et disputatio deo adiuuante" (Lyons 1515 edn, vol. 2, fol. lxvii^v). Again, at lines 27–30 of our edition, the author paraphrases a passage from *De probanda medicina*, but his specific comments on wormwood and vinegar do not match those found in *De simplici medicina*.[26] His reference copy of the *Pantegni* may therefore have represented a transitional stage between the *Ur-Practica* and the "vulgate" version, one where book 2 was not yet consolidated into its "vulgate" form.

The author also notes that there are two versions of the catalogue of simples: one organized by degree, beginning with *rosa*, and an alphabetical version beginning with *absinthium*. He is working with an *absinthium* catalogue. He does not seem to recognize the option actually found in the vulgate *Pantegni*, namely a catalogue in rational order by degree, but beginning with *absinthium*.[27] To complicate matters, in the analysis of wormwood that ends the commentary, neither the lemmata nor the contents match those in the standard text of the *Liber graduum*, as represented by the 1515 Lyons edition.

Being a commentary, the *LGC*, like the commentaries on the *Articella* texts, begins with an *accessus ad librum*, or formal introduction to the work's purpose, utility, and design. The *LGC accessus* explains that the author's purpose is to

---

[26]   See "*Liber graduum commentary* Sources and Notes," below.

[27]   Note that in the Lyons 1515 edition, the *Liber graduum* catalogue begins with *aurum*, *argentum*, and *agaricum* but then moves to *absinthium*.

assign complexions, degrees, virtues, and operations to commonly used medical simples. The usefulness of the text lies in the knowledge it conveys that will permit an appropriate administration of a medicine. Though entitled *Book of Degrees*, the text also deals with complexions: the two are interconnected topics. A degree is then defined as a departure from the equal complexion which can be detected by the senses.

There are nine complexions: one equal and eight unequal. An equal complexion is one in which the qualities of the elements are contained in equal measure; hence in an equal complexion, there are no degrees. But if there is a "dominion" (*dominium*) of one or more qualities within the substance, this is expressed as a degree. The four degrees are then explained in terms of how the body experiences them. The first is when bodily sensation perceives the dominance of one or more qualities; the second is when this level of departure from the equal complexion puts the medicine on a par with the sense itself; the third is when this distemper harms the sense; the fourth is when it destroys it. There follows a detailed explanation of how the equal complexion, unlike the unequal ones, cannot be detected by sensory means, but only conceptually. This is because complexions are declared by signs (such as the color of the skin) that vary from person to person, and can be influenced by environment and behavior (the "non-naturals"). In the absence of such signs, a perfectly tempered complexion cannot be discovered by the senses. Therefore it has to be perceived by the intellect, since otherwise there would be no awareness of unequal complexions which are called "distempered" in relation to the temperate.

Much of the *LGC* is devoted to the problem of the relationship between a drug's efficacy and its detection by physical sensation. The underlying issue is the double scale of intensity referred to above; this was the principal concern of the "Apud antiquos" text as well, though its analysis differs in substance from that of the *LGC*.[28] The *LGC*'s solution is to distinguish the effect of the drug from the body's ability to perceive that effect. The action of a medicine is judged in relation to the corresponding capacity of the body to experience it (the body's *passio*) and not in relation to the quality of the body itself. The latter would seem to be what the author of the *Liber graduum* implies, but it leads to the absurd conclusion that the heat of a medicine which is hot in the first degree is less than the heat of the equal complexion and cannot therefore alter it by making it hotter. In fact, it would diminish rather than increase its heat. The corollary is that something hot in the first degree would also have no degree since it would effect no change in an equal complexion. In fact, the comparison is made between the action of the

---

28 See the parallels to "Apud antiquos" recorded in the "*Liber graduum commentary* Sources and Notes" below, at lines 219–21, 256–7, 274–84, 302 sqq.

quality of the medicine and the passion of the quality of the body. For medicine acts out of a given quality which it possesses, and the body suffers that action because of a certain quality which it possesses, which is distempered. The *Liber graduum* seems to posit two contrary things, saying that what is hot in the first degree is hotter than the equal complexion, and nevertheless has less heat than the heat of the equal complexion. The contradiction, however, is only apparent. For what is hot in the first degree is indeed hotter than the equal complexion, because it changes it. Nevertheless the heat of a medicine is less than the heat of the equal complexion in the sense that the action of a hot medicine is beneath the "passion" of the body. The *LGC* then attacks certain masters at Montpellier who argue for a double definition of temperament: one in which no quality exceeds any other, so that what is hot in the first degree is hotter than the equal complexion, and another which refers to an equal complexion which is in the second degree (or, as the "Apud antiquos" explains, on the cusp of the second and third degrees, exactly at the midpoint of the scale),[29] according to which the heat of something hot in the first degree is less than the heat of the equal complexion. The *LGC* refutes this theory of double temperament. When the ancients said that the equal human temperament was at the midpoint of the scale, they were not referring to the qualities of the body *per se* but to the judgment of the senses.

Urso of Calabria's *De gradibus*, on the other hand, is entirely focused on the question of why there are four and only four degrees. "Apud antiquos" is indifferent to this problem, and the *LGC* addresses it only to the extent that its author wishes to explain the *Liber graduum*'s analogy between the four degrees and the four lines bounding a geometric surface. The solution is ingeniously graphic, but not particularly profound or persuasive: two curved lines can enclose a space in this way: (); but if the lines are straight, they can only be joined by two additional lines, like this: □.

The *LGC* closes by providing a bridge to the first entry in the catalogue of simples, namely that for wormwood (*absinthium*). The author does not, apparently, intend to proceed through the entire catalogue, but he cannot resist delving into the properties of wormwood in order to digress on the action of purgative drugs. This digression includes a somewhat alarming story of a peasant who helped himself to some lime mixed with wine which he found in a doctor's house, and suffered a massive evacuation. The peasant cured himself, but by pure luck, and the author does not recommend this therapy.

---

[29] "Apud antiquos," lines 138–55.

4. The Ghost in the *Articella* and Bartholomaeus of Salerno

Though the author of the *LGC* is never identified in the manuscripts, there is sufficient evidence both external and internal to support the hypothesis that it is the work of Bartholomaeus of Salerno. Bartholomaeus, it will be recalled, is the first identified author of a full suite of commentaries on the *Articella*; he also wrote a popular *Practica*.[30]

It is remarkable that, in all the manuscripts, the *LGC* accompanies Bartholomaeus' *Articella* commentaries. In the Basel manuscript, the *LGC* is sandwiched between Bartholomaeus' commentary on the *Isagoge* of Johannitius (fols 54r–74r) and his glosses on Hippocrates' *Prognosis* (fols 77r–85v).[31] This pattern is replicated in the Brussels manuscript, where the *LGC* (fols. 68vb–69ra) is set between Batholomaeus' commentaries on Johannitius (fols 1va–46rb), *Prognosis* (fols 47ra–62vb), and Philaretus (fols 63ra–68vb) on the one side, and his commentary on Hippocrates' *Aphorisms* (fols 70ra–110va) on the other. In the Berlin codex, the *LGC* follows upon the full suite of Bartholomaeus' *Articella* glosses (*Isagoge*, fols 1ra–35v; *Aphorisms*, fols 36ra–85va; *Prognosis*, fols 85va–100vb; Philaretus, fols 100vb–105vb; Theophilus, fols 106ra–116ra) as part of a group of short works on digestion, fevers, foodstuffs and temperament, and special pathology.[32] Finally, in the Munich manuscript, the *LGC* is directly preceded by Bartholomaeus' *Aphorisms* commentary (fols 1ra–36vb), an anonymous commentary on Philaretus (fols 37ra–48vb), and Bartholomaeus' *Tegni* commentary (fols 49ra–116ra).

---

[30] Biographical information about Bartholomaeus is summarized in the two essays by Wallis (see n. 16 above); see also Faith Wallis, "Bartholomaeus of Salerno," in Steven Livesey, Thomas Glick, and Faith Wallis (eds), *Medieval Science, Technology and Medicine: An Encyclopedia* (London: Routledge, 2005), 77–8. For a list of Bartholomaeus' works and secondary bibliography, see Marco Tosti, "Bartholomaeus Salernitanus," in Michael Lapidge et al. (eds), *Compendium auctorum latinorum medii aevi (500–1500)*, vol. 2.1 (Florence: SISMEL, Edizioni del Galluzzo, 2004), 56–9.

[31] On fol. 74rv there is a fragment of another commentary on Johannitius, inc. "Desiderium sciendi mentibus humanis naturaliter insitum esse ...." Fol. 76v, between the *LGC* and the *Prognosis* commentary, is blank.

[32] Fols 116vb–118rb: inc. "<P>er urinam demonstratur in sanis qualis digestio sana sit ..." (not in TK). Fol. 118rb: "<C>um omnis febris sit aut mastica. epauemastica. aut omotona ..." (not in TK). Fols 118va–121rb: Johannes de Sancto Paulo, *Flores dietarum* (TK 269), inc. "<C>orpus hominis constat ex IIIIor humoribus ..." Fols 121va–122ra: "<P>hisici rerum naturalium inuestigantes. et qualiter distemperantiam ..." (not in TK). Fols 122ra–124rb: *LGC*. Fols 124va–125vb: A treatise on special pathology, inc. "De pleuresi[s] et peripleumonia. Fit pleuresis ex catarro humorum et ebrietate. multoque coitu ..." (not in TK).

In a letter of medical advice addressed to Peter the Venerable, abbot of Cluny, Bartholomaeus includes material explicitly taken from the *Liber graduum*.[33] Furthermore, in his commentary on the *Isagoge*, ch. 4, Bartholomaeus' remarks about the perfectly equal temperament refer twice to the "prologue of the *Liber graduum*,"[34] and at one point he explicitly reveals that he has written a commentary on this work.[35] There are a number of striking similarities of substance and wording between the *LGC* and Bartholomaeus' commentary on *Isagoge* 4. These are detailed in the "*Liber graduum commentary* Sources and Notes" below, particularly with reference to lines 69–71, 136–7, 137–8, 141–5, 149–51, 159–68, and 173–8. The *LGC*'s disparaging remarks on the opinion of "other masters at Montpellier" ("alii uero magistri apud Montepessulanum") that there could be two kinds of "temperament" (lines 251–7) find an echo in the sharply critical stance toward the medical teaching at Montpellier ("apud montem pessulanum") adopted by Bartholomaeus in his commentary on ch. 25 of the *Tegni*.[36]

Of course, it could be argued that Bartholomaeus need not be the author of the *LGC*; someone else could have exploited Bartholomaeus' *Articella* commentaries to expound the *Liber graduum*. Supporting this position is the fact that the *accessus* of the *LGC* differs from that found in Bartholomaeus' other commentaries. The *LGC*'s rubrics are: *auctoris intentio*, *utilitas*, *modus agendi uel ordo*, and *titulus*; but Bartholomaeus consistently uses a six-part *accessus*

---

[33]   "Quod auctoritate confirmatur, uerbi gratia: Mirra ut in libro graduum habetur sicca est, unde et putridos humores desiccat, sicut ibidem dicitur, lenit tamen asperitatem canalium pulmonis et palpebrarum. Quod facit ex glutinositate et gummositate." Giles Constable (ed.), *The Letters of Peter the Venerable* (Cambridge, MA: Harvard University Press, 1967), 383. The chapter on myrrh in the *Liber graduum* (Lyons 1515 edn, 2: fol. lxxxiᵛ) says that "putridos humores uulue dessicat," "asperitatem canalium pulmonis lenit," and "asperitatem palpebrarum lenit."

[34]   "Notandum est quod dicitur in pantegni. de perfecte temperata complexione quoniam intellectualiter non actualiter inueni potest. Actualiter accipiendum est hic pro sensualiter sicut in prologo primi libri graduum inuenitur ... In sequentibus autem. uel super prologum primi libri graduum rationabilior et euidentior sentencia ponetur. qua liquido patebit. quomodo equalis complexio non sensualiter. sed intellectualiter. inueniri possit." Commentary on *Isagoge* 4, Winchester, Winchester College, MS 24, fol. 26va.

[35]   "De equali uero complexione quomodo sit calida humida in IIᵒ gradu humana complexio. super primum prologum libri graduum ostendimus." Winchester 24, fol. 27rb. Bartholomaeus was in the habit of cross-referencing his own writings, and numerous examples can be found in his commentaries. The frequency of such cross-referencing in the twelfth-century anatomical text known as the *Second Salernitan Demonstration* (in conjunction with internal evidence) is an argument in favor of Bartholomaeus' authorship of this treatise: Morris H. Saffron, "Salernitan Anatomists," *Dictionary of Scientific Biography*, vol. 12 (New York: Scribner, 1975), 80–83.

[36]   See Wallis, "*Articella* Commentaries," 133 and n. 17.

that includes *causa, ad quem partem philosophie spectat*, and *quo genere doctrine utitur*, and never uses *modus agendi* as a synonym of *ordo* (he prefers *diuisio*). Also striking is the fact that Bartholomaeus, in his commentaries, uses both *commixtio* and *complexio* to denote "temperament"; the *LGC* prefers *complexio*.[37]

However, whether Bartholomaeus composed the *LGC* (and I incline to the view that he did) or served as a significant source of its substance, the fact remains that someone writing in the second half of the twelfth century wanted to present the *Liber graduum* as a companion to the other texts in the *Articella* anthology. The *LGC* was conceived along the same lines as Bartholomaeus' *Articella* commentaries, with a formal *accessus* and a lemma-by-lemma analysis, punctuated by questions. It refers to other texts in the *Articella* (*Isagoge, Aphorisms, Tegni*), just as Bartholomaeus cross-references his own *Articella* commentaries. Finally, the *LGC* was actually transmitted with Bartholomaeus' commentaries. It will be recalled that the admission of Galen's *Tegni* into the *Articella* is signaled by Bartholomaeus producing a commentary on that work. It is not inconceivable that he or a disciple also hoped to expand the *Articella* by including the *Liber graduum*. Indeed, Bartholomaeus' own *Practica* is an index of his lively interest in drug action, and its opening chapters both mirror and draw heavily on the *De probanda medicina* section of *Pantegni Practica*, book 2.[38]

The issue of "degrees" was the point where theory and practice intersected in the new medicine of the twelfth century. It was the bridge between the physiology of Johannitius on the one hand and the pharmacy conveyed by works like the *Circa instans* on the other. As the *LGC* (in company with Urso and the author of "Apud antiquos") points out, clinical choices depend not only on a proper grasp of the theory of degrees, but also on trained senses, particularly the sense of taste. Bartholomaeus opened his *Practica* with a disquisition on

---

[37]   *Commixtio* is the word for "temperament" used in the *Isagoge*; it was frequently glossed as *complexio*, which is the term used in the *Pantegni*: see Danielle Jacquart, "De *crasis* à *complexio*: note sur le vocabulaire du tempérament en latin médiéval," in Guy Sabbah (ed.), *Textes médicaux latins antiques*, Mémoires du Centre Jean Palerne 5 (Saint-Étienne: Publications de l'Université de Saint-Étienne, 1984), 71–6; and Danielle Jacquart, "À l'aube de la renaissance médicale des XIe–XIIe siècles: l'*Isagoge Johannitii* et son traducteur," *Bibliothèque de l'École des Chartes* 144 (1986): 226–7.

[38]   The *Practica* was edited from Venice, Biblioteca nazionale Marciana, MS VII. 17 by Salvatore De Renzi, *Collectio Salernitana*, vol. 4 (Naples: Sabezio, 1856), 321–406; and from an unidentified manuscript in San Gimignano containing a rather different version of the text by Francesco Puccinotti, *Storia della medicina*, vol. 2.1 (Livorno: Massimiliano Wagner, 1855), lxvi–lxxix. My own collation of seven manuscripts of the *Practica* suggests that there are at least three different recensions of the text, but they all contain the sections on the recognition of medicines by taste and odor, as well as the actions of medicine, based on *Pantegni Practica* 2.

the eight tastes.[39] But to grasp fully the dynamics of theory and practice in the twelfth century, we must understand the ambivalent and fluid identity of the *Articella*. This is an anthology of materials that addresses diagnosis and prognosis (*Aphorisms*, *Prognosis*, Philaretus, Theophilus) but that is equipped with a theoretical rationale (*Isagoge*, and later *Tegni*). Diagnosis and prognosis are grounded in a theory of semiotics, but point to therapeutic action; hence the *Articella* also absorbed Hippocrates' *Regimen in Acute Diseases*. So there was nothing inherently improbable about the prospect of incorporating pharmacy into the anthology, particularly because the *Articella* traveled in the company of texts that contained a considerable body of information on the properties of foods and medicinal simples like the *Viaticum* or Isaac Judaeus' *Diaetae universales*.

In the end, the *Liber graduum* never gained admission: it remains the "ghost" in the *Articella*. There are several reasons for this failure. All the texts that address the *Liber graduum* point to serious ambiguities and deficiencies in the way its prologue presents the theory of degrees. But the fact that the three texts on the *Liber graduum* seem to have been composed in isolation from each other points to the lack of any coherent approach to dealing with these contradictions.[40] In consequence, none of these texts exerted much influence "in the post-Constantinian, pre-scholastic clarification of the pharmacological paradigm."[41] The *Liber graduum* continued by default to be a mainstay of pharmacology,[42] but there was little incentive to go any further with it: in particular, it offered no guidance to the pressing problem—at once theoretical and practical—of how a drug's efficacy could be tested. Hence the literature of pharmacy in the crucial early decades of medical scholasticism tended to be resolutely empiricist in its approach. And when the discourse on pharmacology revives in the mid-thirteenth century, the focus will be on theories of quantification, for which the *Liber graduum* will offer scant assistance.[43] Meanwhile, the *Articella* was also undergoing structural changes that would transform it into a vehicle of

---

[39]   Ed. De Renzi, 323–5. On the high value placed on the sense of taste by medical writers of this period, see Charles Burnett, "The Superiority of Taste," *Journal of the Warburg and Courtauld Institutes* 54 (1991): 230–38, and "*Sapores sunt octo*: The Medieval Latin Terminology for the Eight Flavours," *Micrologus* 9 (2002): 99–112.

[40]   Eliza Glaze discusses a striking parallel case of multiple commentaries on a "Salernitan" text that ultimately did not achieve canonical academic status in ch. 3 of this volume.

[41]   McVaugh, "'Apud antiquos,'" 17; on the defects of the *Liber graduum*, see McVaugh, "Medieval Theory," 11–12.

[42]   Winston Black traces the long and successful career of the *Liber graduum/De gradibus* as a source for medieval drug lore in ch. 5 of this volume.

[43]   McVaugh, "Medieval Theory," ch. 3: "The Transition to a Theoretical Science."

medical theory, notably through the substitution of Galen's commentaries on Hippocrates for the Salernitan glosses, and the incorporation of Haly Ridwan's commentary on the Tegni.[44] There was considerably less room for a text like the *Liber graduum* in the new *Ars commentata* version of the *Articella*.

***

Liber graduum commentary Edition

Sigla

Ba   Basel, Öffentliche Bibliothek der Universität, MS D. III. 3, pt 2 (s. xiii), fols 75r–76r. Text ends at line 295 of edition, with "Explicit."

Be   Berlin, Staatsbibliothek Preussischer Kulturbesitz, MS lat. q. 255 (s. xii^ex–xiii^in), fols 122ra–124ra.

Br   Brussels, Bibliothèque royale, MS II. 1399 (s. xii), fols 68vb–69ra. Text incomplete: breaks off at line 71 of edition.

M   Munich, Bayerische Staatsbibliothek, Clm 28219 (s. xiii²), fols 116ra–118v.

This edition collates the four manuscripts above, but uses the text found in the Munich manuscript as a base text. The Munich text is reproduced except when a reading from one or more of the other manuscripts is evidently superior. Punctuation and capitalization are editorial. Insignificant orthographical anomalies (e.g., *transsitu* instead of *transitu*) have been silently corrected. The *apparatus lectionum* does not record insignificant variations in word order; orthography (e.g. *Be*'s *actor* and *Ba*'s *autor* as opposed to *auctor* in *M Br*); or corrections made by the original scribe of errors made in the course of copying (e.g., adding a missing word above the line). Sources are recorded at the end of the edition.

---

[44]   Cornelius O'Boyle, *The Art of Medicine: Medical Teaching at the University of Paris, 1250–1400* (Leiden: Brill, 1998), 129–57; Per-Gunnar Ottosson, *Scholastic Medicine and Philosophy: A Study of Commentaries on Galen's Tegni, ca. 1300–1450* (Naples: Bibliopolis, 1984).

Liber iste graduum tertia pars est illius partis Pantegni que practica appellatur. Liber autem ille[1] quia[2] ex eo tocius artis comprehensio habetur[3] in duas partes[4] diuiditur quarum prima theorice secunda practice attribuitur, et quelibet earum in X uolumina diuiditur. Quamuis[5]
5   autem in principio illius uoluminis hec ad totum opus communiter pertinentia sint ostensa scilicet que sit auctoris intentio et que[6] utilitas et cetera, tamen hic ad maiorem euidentiam sequentium particulariter[7] est ostendendum que sit auctoris[8] intentio et que[9] utilitas, quis modus agendi uel ordo,[10] et quis titulus.[11] Intentio[12] auctoris in hoc opere est
10   simplicium[13] medicinarum que ad usum humani corporis frequentius exiguntur particulariter complexiones cum gradibus uirtutes cum operationibus assignare. Simplices autem medicine dicuntur que sine alicuius compositionis artificio habent corpus alterare, tales existentes quales eas natura produxit, ut sunt herbe, metalla, grana. Composite
15   autem sunt que artificio quodam[14] ex his componuntur, ut sunt unguenta, electuaria, emplastra, de quibus auctor non agit hic. Et ideo dictum est simplicium medicinarum de quibus agit hic. Sequitur:[15] "que ad usum humani corporis exiguntur."[16] Non enim ostendit complexiones uel[17] uirtutes gradus uel operationes omnium medicinarum quia nec omnium
20   nouerat complexiones[18] uel gradus[19] uirtutes uel operationes, cum hec[20] omnia sint occulta in quibusdam, nec omnium complexiones assignare

---

1   ille] iste *Be*
2   quia] eo quod *Br*
3   habetur] *sic M² Ba Be;* dicitur *M¹;* appellatur *Br*
4   in duas partes] qui in duas partes *M Ba;* que in duas partes *Be*
5   Quamuis] Quam uix *Br*
6   que] que libri *Br*
7   particulariter] particularum *Ba*
8   sit auctoris] *om. Br*
9   et que] que *Ba;* que libri *Br*
10   quis modus agendi uel ordo] *om. Ba Br;* et cetera *Be*
11   et quis titulus] quis ut deus *Br*
12   Intentio] Intentio igitur *Br*
13   simplicium] illarum simplicium *Br*
14   quodam] *om. Br*
15   Sequitur] Sed non de omnibus. nisi de his *Ba*
16   exiguntur] frequentius exiguntur *Br*
17   uel] *om. Ba*
18   nouerat complexiones] notat complexiones *Ba;* nouerat *Br*
19   uel gradus] uel sunt gradus *Br*
20   hec] *om. Be*

erat necessarium, sed earum tantum que frequentius in confectionibus occurrunt et ad usum humani corporis exiguntur.[21] Sequitur:[22] "complexiones cum gradibus" et cetera. Hec enim[23] IIIIor assignat circa

25 simplicia medicamina, complexiones dicendo aliquid esse calidum,[24] frigidum, humidum, siccum; gradum[25] etiam ostendit dicendo esse[26] calidum in primo gradu[27] siccum autem in tertio.[28] Virtutes etiam assignat dicendo medicamen quoddam[29] esse laxatiuum, quoddam aperitiuum, quoddam attractiuum.[30] Operationes etiam ostendit cum dicit acetum

30 appetitum irritat,[31] absinthium lapidem frangit, digestionem procurat.[32] Vtilitas uero[33] est predictorum cognitio et ex his curandis corporibus congrua medicine exibitio.[34] [Hoc autem ordine usus est Ali filius Tabernarii tractando de simplicibus medicinis; primum quidem tractauit de calidis, frigidis, humidis et siccis in primo gradu, deinde in secundum,

35 et sic de ceteris. In translatione autem apud latinos permutatus est ordo et tractatur de eis secundum ordinem literarum in alfabeto positarum.[35]] Titulus talis est:[36] Incipit liber graduum.[37] Sed queritur quare liber graduum appelletur[38] cum non de solis gradibus agat, sed etiam[39] de

---

21 exiguntur] frequentius exiguntur *Br*

22 Sequitur] Sequitur et *Be*

23 enim] *om. Be*

24 calidum] *om. Be*

25 gradum] gradus *Ba Br*

26 esse] *om. Be; fortasse exp. Br*

27 gradu] *om. Be*

28 siccum autem in tertio] siccum in tertio *Ba;* aut in secundo aut tercio gradu *Br*

29 medicamen quoddam] medicinam quandam *Ba*

30 laxatiuum quoddam aperitiuum quoddam attractiuum] laxatiuam quandam aperitiuam quandam attractiuam *Ba;* laxatiuum quoddam aperitiuum quoddam autem constrictiuum *Br*

31 irritat] minuat *Br*

32 absinthium ... procurat] *om. Ba*

33 uero] *om. Ba Be*

34 et ex his curandis corporibus congrua medicine exibitio] et his curandis ... exibitio *Ba;* et ex eorum cognitione in curandis corporibus simplicium medicinarum exibitio. et ex curandis corporibus congrua medicine exhibitio *Br*

35 Hoc autem ordine... positarum] *om. Ba Be Br* [see comment in "Sources and Notes," below]

36 est] *om. Br*

37 liber graduum] liber graduum constantini *Br*

38 appelletur] dicatur *Br*

39 etiam] *om. Be*

reliquis tribus predictis. De eis[40] tantum[41] tractare non posset; qui enim
40   gradum[42] demonstrat dicendo aliquid esse calidum uel frigidum in primo
gradu,[43] necessario complexionem demonstrat.[44] Ad quod dicendum
quod[45] a digniori librum inscripsit et[46] ab eo cuius noticia reliquorum
dat nobis scientiam.[47] Est[48] autem subtilior et obscurior scientia graduum
quam complexionum, et si quis nouerit aliquid[49] esse calidum in primo
45   gradu, necessario cognoscet et complexionem, sed non conuertitur.

Quoniam disputationem simplicis.[50] De predictis IIIIor tractaturus
premittit[51] proemium in quo precipue docilitatem captat; componendo[52]
graduum distinctionem, que difficillima erat, animos auditorum[53] ad
consequentia[54] preparat.[55] Utitur autem in prima parte proemii transitu[56]
50   continuando se ad predicta, demonstrando de quo in antecedentibus[57]
libris tractauerit[58] et quomodo. Dicit enim superius se [59] uniuersaliter
de[60] simplici medicina tractasse[61] ostendendo ex qua complexione
medicina est aperitiua scilicet ex caliditate et siccitate,[62] et subtilitate
substantie ex[63] qua est constrictiua scilicet ex frigiditate et siccitate.

---

40   De eis] ~~Quia~~ de eis *Ba;* De eis enim *Be Br*
41   tantum] tantum tantum *Ba*
42   gradum] gradus *Br*
43   uel frigidum in primo gradu] frigidum. humidum. siccum. in uno gradu *Ba*
44   demonstrat] ostendit *Ba*
45   dicendum quod] *om. Ba*
46   et] uel *Ba*
47   scientiam] notitiam *Ba Be*
48   Est] uel quia est *Ba*
49   nouerit aliquid] aliquid nouerit aliquid *Br*
50   simplicis] simplicis medicine *Be Br*
51   premittit] premitti *Be* promittit *Br*
52   componendo] et ponendo *Be*
53   auditorum] predictorum *Br*
54   ad consequentia] ad sequentia *Ba; om. Be*
55   preparat] preparet *Br*
56   transitu] *om. Br*
57   antecedentibus] precedentibus *Ba Br*
58   tractauerit] dixerit *Ba;* tractauit *Be*
59   superius se] se superius *Ba Be;* superius *M*
60   de] *om. Br*
61   tractasse] *om. Be*
62   et siccitate] siccitate *Ba; om. Br*
63   ex] et ex *Br*

55 Hoc[64] autem fecit non descendendo ad singulas[65] nec eas[66] specialibus nominibus designando, quod hic facit ostendendo cuius complexionis sit absinthium, abrotanum et cetera.[67] Et hoc est.

Quoniam compleuimus id est perfecte tractauimus **prout ratio** id est ordo competens. Per[68] hoc quod dicit "compleuimus" ostendit
60 hoc opus priori esse continuum. **ut ordo sequatur** id est ordinate post illum tractaturum[69] subiungatur. **de unaquaque specie singulariter** id est speciali uocabulo ipsas medicinas designando, ut est rosa, lilium. **Vnde dicimus quod antiqui** et cetera continua hoc modo. Tractandum est de simplici medicina specialiter,[70,71] et ideo ad huius rei euidentiam
65 est dicendum quot sint gradus. Videndum est autem in hoc loco quid sit gradus,[72] et quot sint, et quot[73] partes eorum.[74] Est autem gradus discessus ab equali[75] complexione manifeste sensu determinabilis. Sunt autem complexiones IX una equalis et VIII inequales, de quibus dicitur in libro *Ysagogarum*.[76] Est autem equalis complexio que qualitates
70 elementorum[77] equaliter continet. In complexione autem[78] equali nullus gradus attenditur. In rebus enim equalem partium positionem habentibus nullus gradus attenditur.[79] Ex quo uero fit discessus ab equali positione statim[80] gradus attenditur uel ante, uel retro, dextrorsum uel sinistrorsum.[81] Similiter cum nulla qualitas dominatur nec gradus

---

64 Hoc] *om. Br*

65 singulas] singula *M Ba Br*

66 eas] ea *Br*

67 et cetera] *om. Br*

68 Per] secundum *Br*

69 tractaturum] tractatum *Ba*

70 specialiter] singulariter gradus ipsius ostendendo. quod manifestatur ex titulo *Br*

71 *in marg. of Be* G<alieni> in libro graduum fine gradus est excessus qualitatis in quocumque sensu determinabilis

72 Videndum est autem in hoc loco quid sit gradus] *om. Be;* Videndum autem prius in hoc loco quid sit gradus *Br*

73 quot] que *Ba;* quod *Be*

74 eorum] eorumdem *Ba Br*

75 ab equali] *om. Br*

76 dicitur in libro *Ysagogarum*] in libro ysagogarum agitur *Br*

77 elementorum] duarum *Ba*

78 autem] enim *Be*

79 In rebus enim equalem ... attenditur] In rebus equalem ... attenditur *Ba; om. Br*

80 statim] ibi statim *Be*

81 uel sinistrorsum] sinistrorsum *Be*] uel sinistrum *M Ba Br*

75   attenditur, sed si dominium alicuius qualitatis uel plurium fit[82] in
      subiecto, dicitur gradus. Discessus ergo ab equali complexione manifeste
      sensu determinabilis gradus dicitur siue dominium unius qualitatis uel
      plurium.[83] "Manifeste uero sensu determinabilis" additur ad differentiam
      partium ipsorum graduum, inter quas non potest manifeste differentia
80   assignari. Hic autem discessus aut est paruus, aut maximus, aut medius. Et
      sunt IIII gradus: primus, secundus, tertius, quartus. Primus est cum sensus
      primum percipit dominium siue discessum qualitatis unius uel plurium.
      Secundus est[84] cum ipse discessus coequatur sensui. Tertius est[85] cum ipsa
      distemperantia ledit sensum; quartus cum destruit. Partes uero gradus
85   sunt tres, principium, medium et finis, de quibus dicetur in sequentibus.
      De equali ergo[86] complexione pretermittens ait **complexionem medicine
      diuidi**.[87] Non est autem absolute dictum complexionem diuidi, sed
      complexionem medicine id est discessum ab equali complexione diuidi[88]
      in IIII partes que gradus uocantur. In omni enim medicina est[89] discessus
90   ab equali complexione, cum omnis medicina sit distemperata.[90] Omnis
      enim[91] medicina habet corpus alterare; alterare autem[92] non potest nisi
      sit distemperata, et ita[93] omnia possunt dici[94] farmaca his exceptis[95] que
      humane complexioni[96] temperate conueniunt ut est panis galline que
      sui qualitate non alterant sed quantitate forsan possent alterare. Et ideo
95   artificiose[97] dictum est complexionem medicine diuidi in IIII partes.
      Complexio enim[98] non diuiditur in gradus, nec ut in partes uniuersales,

---

82   fit] *om. Ba*
83   plurium] plurimum *Br*
84   est] *om. Ba*
85   est] *om. Ba*
86   ergo] *om. Ba*
87   diuidi] posse diuidi *Ba*
88   sed complexionem ... complexione diuidi] sed complexionem ... complexione posse
diuidi *Ba; om. Be*
89   est] fit *Be*
90   ab equali ... distemperata] *om. Be*
91   enim] autem *Ba*
92   autem] uero *Ba*
93   et ita] *om. Ba*
94   dici] *om. Ba*
95   his exceptis] exceptis his *Ba;* His expletis *Be*
96   *Text in Br breaks off incomplete here*
97   artificiose] inartificiose *Ba*
98   enim] *om. Ba*

nec ut in integrales, sed ipsa quantitas distemperantie. **Nam**[99] **omnem**
medicinam. Vere complexio medicine diuiditur in hec IIII quia
omnis medicina distemperata est in aliquo gradu, et[100] unusquisque

100   habet tres partes. Et quamuis inter extremitates id est inter[101] finem et
principium possent[102] alie partes reperiri, tamen quia auctores non
potuerunt manifestas assignare differentias pretermiserunt. **Verum quia**
quantitatem. Non tamen[103] partes graduum non distinxerunt, uerum
etiam quantitatem gradus non assignauerunt, id est[104] non ostenderunt

105   quantum unusquisque gradus protenderetur, quia uel ignorauerunt
uel[105] scribere noluerunt. **Sed gloriosissimus Galienus**. Galienus dicitur
gloriosissimus id est famosus quia de singulis rebus speciales tractatus
instituit, unde famam assecutus est. **Quantitatem graduum** id est
quantum quisque[106] gradus protenderetur. **Quantitas difficultatem** id

110   est graduum[107] distinctionem que difficillima erat[108] non ostendit. **Sua**
tamen <uerba quantitatem graduum ostendunt, proinde tanti uiri
sermones bene enarrare> uolumus. Difficultatem istam non ostendit.
Tamen uolumus narrare sua uerba id est[109] ipsius Diascoridis qualiter
ipse tractat[110] uerba Galieni de gradibus uolumus inquam enucleare.

115   **proinde**. id est sicut[111] "sermones tanti uiri." Sed ad intelligenciam
uerborum Galieni que recitat Diascorides sunt quedam pretermittenda
[ad intelligentiam uerborum Galieni].[112]

Palam itaque et cetera. Positurus uerba Diascoridis recitantis uerba
Galieni de graduum distinctione[113] premittit quedam introductoria ad
120   euidentiam uerborum Galieni. Cum enim gradus circa complexionem

---

[99]   Nam] Non *Ba*

[100] et] *om. Ba*

[101] inter] *om. Ba*

[102] possent] possint *Ba*

[103] Non tamen] Verumtamen *Ba*

[104] id est] et *Ba*

[105] uel] uel quia *Be*

[106] quisque] unusquisque *Ba*

[107] graduum] *om. Be*

[108] erat] est *Ba*

[109] id est] scilicet *Ba;* sed *Be*

[110] tractat] recitat *Ba Be*

[111] id est sicut *Be*] sicut *Ba;* id est sic *M*

[112] ad intelligentiam uerborum Galieni] *om. Ba*

[113] de graduum distinctione] *om. Be*

attendatur[114] necessarium fuit ponere numerum complexionum,[115] quod facit auctor hic dicens antiquos Galieno consensisse[116] dicenti IX esse complexiones, unam equalem et VIII inequales. Commento. Ponenda sunt quedam introductoria; itaque[117] incipiam. Equalis autem
125   complexio est que equaliter continet qualitates elementorum; additur[118] a quibusdam et quantitates. Inequalis uero[119] est que non habet hec[120] que diuiditur in VIII species. De complexionibus uero suo loco dicetur. **Ideoque**[121] **necessarium** et cetera. Ad hoc ut ex precedentibus hic uere inferatur[122] oportet ut hoc extra intelligatur: omne corpus ex IIII
130   elementis compositum est alicuius complexionis, sed non sunt nisi IX, igitur omne corpus habet aliquam istarum IX. Et hoc est quod ait.

Nullum corpus indigere una complexione.[123] Tunc enim indigeret aliqua earum[124] si eam non haberet, sed cum aliquam habeat ex illis, nec ea indiget. Est autem notandum quod si forsan sit aliquod corpus quod non
135   constet ex IIII elementis[125] sed ex duabus tantum uel tribus particulis, nullius est complexionis. Est enim complexio IIII elementarum qualitatum coniunctio, sed ex unius uel duarum dominio nomen sortitur. Que autem sunt a lunari globo inferius sunt alicuius complexionis.[126] Celestia uero ut est sol, luna et cetera celestia corpora nec sunt ex IIII elementis
140   composita, nec sunt alicuius complexionis. **Verbi gratia aut est calidum.** Quasi diceret[127] omne corpus est alicuius complexionis, quia uel alicuius simplicis uel alicuius composite. Nec mireris si dicatur complexio[128] simplex. Cum complexio exigat pluralitatem simplicitas uero excludat.

---

114   attendatur] attenduntur *Be*
115   ponere numerum complexionum] positio complexionis *Ba*
116   consensisse] concessisse *Be*
117   itaque] et illud itaque *Be*
118   additur] additur autem *Ba*
119   uero] *om. Ba*
120   non habet hec] non habet *Ba;* hec non habet *Be; add.* hec *in marg. M*
121   Ideoque] Iam *Ba*
122   inferatur] inferat *Ba*
123   complexione] *om. Be*
124   aliqua earum] aliqua istarum *Be; om. Ba*
125   si forsan sit aliquod corpus quod non constet ex IIII elementis] sit aliquod corpus quod forsan ex IIII non constet elementis *Ba*
126   Est enim complexio IIII elementarum ... complexionis] est enim complexio IIII elementarum... complexionis *Be; om. Ba*
127   diceret] d<iceret> *M Be;* dicerer *Ba*
128   complexio] complexio et *M*

Est namque in coniunctione qualitatum pluralitas, sed intensione est[129]
145 simplicitas. **Humani ergo corporis** et cetera. Infert a toto hoc modo.
Omne corpus compositum ex IIII elementis est alicuius[130] complexionis;
ergo humanum corpus est alicuius complexionis. Ponit autem simplices
tantum in quibus etiam intelligit compositas[131] et equalem.

Sed quamuis equalitas et cetera. Commento. Omne corpus est
150 alicuius complexionis inequalis, uel equalis. Sed equalis non potest
inueniri sensualiter sed intellectualiter. Hoc loco fit questio utrum
equalis complexio sit, uel non sit;[132] sed siue sit siue non,[133] competenter
potest exponi[134] hoc modo hec litera. Temperata siquidem perfecte
complexio sensualiter[135] inueniri non[136] potest. Circa humanum enim
155 corpus nunquam concurrunt signa[137] equalem complexionem indicantia,
et ideo ipsa sensu comprehendi non potest, utpote permutata ab
extrinsecus[138] accidentibus corpus alterantibus scilicet ex <VI>[139] rebus
necessariis. Complexiones autem non nisi per signa declarari possunt.
Signa uero per incompetentem usum VI rerum non naturalium uariantur
160 in singulis. Sit enim positum aliquem habere temperatum colorem qui
est compositus ex albo et rubeo et mediocriter esse carnosum. Si uero
fuerit soli expositus, efficietur color niger uel rubeus. Si uero more
uirginis degat[140] in umbra efficietur color albus. Poterit etiam exercicio
extenuari. Color autem niger uel rubeus signum est[141] dominantis
165 caliditatis,[142] albus[143] uero frigiditatis, extenuatio uero[144] dominantis[145]
siccitatis. Et ita per incompetentem dietam perdit signa proprie
complexionis. His ergo signis remotis non poterit sensu reperiri perfecte

---

129 est] *om. Ba Be*

130 compositum ... est alicuius] est compositum ... quod est alicuius *Ba*

131 compositas] compositum *Be*

132 uel non sit] aut non sit *Ba;* uel non *Ba*

133 non] non sit *Ba Be*

134 exponi] exponere *Be*

135 sensualiter] *om. Ba*

136 non] *Ba Be; om. M*

137 nunquam concurrunt signa] Duo namque concurrunt signa *Be*

138 extrinsecus] extrinsecis *Ba*

139 alterantibus scilicet ex] alterantibus sed ex VI *Be;* scilicet ex VI *Ba*

140 degat] *corr. a* deget *Be*

141 signum est] signa sunt *Ba*

142 caliditatis] caloris *Be*

143 albus] album *Ba M*

144 uero] *om. Ba*

145 dominantis] dominium *M;* dominicium *Be*

temperata complexio. Verumtamen intellectus percipit ex quibusdam
aliis signis istam permutationem fieri extrinsecus[146] accidentibus, non[147]

170 ex complexione, et nisi alteraretur corpus ab extrinsecus[148] accidentibus,
perfecte concurrerent[149] signa equalem complexionem indicatiua. Quod
uero non indicatur,[150] non est ex complexione, sed ex permutatione que
est[151] ab extrinsecis. Habetur autem alia littera in *Pantegni*,[152] que est[153]
huiusmodi: non potest inueniri actualiter sed potentialiter. Cum enim

175 nunquam sit actu, ex[154] etate impediente, et humano corpore incessanter
fluente, nec[155] sensus eam[156] comprehendit utpote illam[157] que non est.
Verumtamen intellectus eam intelligit, quia ad eam referendum est
distemperamentum omnium inequalium complexionum. Vnde Galienus
in *Tegni*: "Spissum enim[158] ad hoc dicitur spissum et[159] rarum et tenue,"

180 scilicet respectu equalis complexionis. Ideo oportet ut intellectus eam
percipiat, cum aliter non haberetur noticia inequalium complexionum
que respectu temperate[160] dicuntur distemperate. **Vnde corpus**[161]
calidum aut frigidum. Dictum est quod[162] equalis complexio[163] sensu
non potest inueniri sed intellectualiter, ut expositum est. Vnde dicitur

185 ad similitudinem illius quod[164] aliquod corpus est calidum aut frigidum,
quia he qualitates manifeste sensu percipiuntur,[165] et earum effectus
circa subiecta. Verumtamen non indigent[166] aliis qualitatibus quia eas

---

146 extrinsecus] extrinsecis *Ba Be*
147 non] et non *Ba*
148 extrinsecus] extrinsecis *Be*
149 concurrerent] concurrunt *Be*
150 indicatur] indicantur *Be*
151 que est] *om. Ba*
152 Habetur … *Pantegni*] Aut altera littera in principio est *Ba*
153 que est] que est actu *Be*
154 ex] *om. Ba*
155 incessanter fluente nec] *om. Ba*
156 eam] eam non *Ba*
157 illam] eam *Ba*
158 enim] *om. Ba*
159 spissum et] spissum *Be; om. Ba*
160 temperate] temperate quidem *Be*
161 corpus] corpus est *Ba*
162 quod] quia *B*
163 equalis complexio] equale *Ba*
164 illius quod] quidem illius *Ba*
165 percipiuntur] reperiuntur *Ba*
166 indigent] indiget *Be*

habent ex elementis componentibus, sed eas sensus[167] non discernit, cum
earum effectus circa subiecta non percipiantur.[168] Intellectus tamen alias
190 inesse qualitates percipit, quia ex IIII elementis esse composita nouit,
ut[169] in pipere sensus discernit[170] caliditatem sed non frigiditatem que
tamen inest ex elementis ipsum componentibus. Sed cur non omnium
nomina recipiat cum omnes habeat declarat[171] dicens. **Nomen enim ab
ea que dominatur** attribuitur id est eius[172] recipit nomen[173] cuius habet
195 intensionem.

At quoniam intentio medicorum et cetera.[174] Omnis complexio est
calida et[175] frigida, humida et[176] sicca, et[177] corpora[178] alia sunt perfecte
sana, alia uicina perfecte temperantie, alia uero sunt plurimum
distemperata. Perfecte autem temperata uel uicina per usum[179] salubrium
200 cibariorum[180] sunt conseruanda in sanitate; egra uero[181] reducenda ad
temperantiam, quod non potest fieri nisi cum medicinis. Quoniam
inquam[182] hoc est, oportet inquirere naturam id est complexionem
medicinarum et cibariorum[183] dicentes aliam esse in primo gradu, aliam
in secundo et cetera. In plurimis locis natura pro complexione reperitur[184]
205 ut in libro *Afforismorum*, "naturarum he quidem bene nate sunt ad
estatem, he uero ad hiemem," pro[185] natura habentes ducere. **Intelligimus
hoc dici ad <comparationem humane> complexionis.** Dixerat[186]
medicinarum aliam esse calidam in primo gradu, aliam in secundo et

---

167 sensus] sensu *Be; om. Ba*
168 percipiantur] percipiantur sicut non inequali *Be*
169 ut] Vnde *Ba*
170 discernit] discernit qualitatem scilicet *Ba*
171 declarat] declarat ipse *Ba*
172 id est eius] ei *Ba*
173 nomen] numen *M*
174 medicorum et cetera] medici *Ba*
175 et] uel *Ba*
176 et] uel *Ba*
177 et] et quoniam *M Be*
178 corpora] corporum *Ba*
179 uicina per usum] uicina perfecte usu *Ba*
180 cibariorum] ciborum *Ba*
181 uero] *om. Ba*
182 inquam] inquit *Be*
183 cibariorum] ciborum *Ba*
184 reperitur] *om. M Be*
185 pro] et pro *Be*
186 Dixerat] Dixit enim *Ba*

cetera; nunc[187] ostendit quod hec[188] assignatio complexionum et graduum
210 ad humanam complexionem referenda est temperatam uel uicinam
perfecte temperate. Humanus uero[189] sensus inuentor est graduum et
complexionis[190] hoc modo. Quicquid enim accedens ad humanum corpus
et illum attingens[191] exterius uel receptum interius non immutat,[192]
iudicatur equalis siue temperate complexionis, ut est panis galline et
215 consimilia,[193] que sui quidem qualitate non immutant. Sui uero quantitate
forsan[194] possent immutare. Quicquid autem attingens[195] humanum
corpus exterius uel receptum interius immutat, dicitur distemperatum[196]
in illa qualitate in[197] qua immutat, ut si immutet in caliditatem[198] et
distemperet iudicatur[199] calide complexionis, et ita de aliis. Itaque
220 secundum qualitatem inuenitur complexio. Secundum quantitatem
autem distemperantie reperitur gradus[200] hoc modo. Si enim parum
aliquid humanum corpus immutet[201] calefaciendo, infrigdando,
humectando, desiccando et adeo[202] parum ut ipsam immutationem
tantum sensus percipiat nec ipsa distemperantia plenitudinem sensus
225 excedat, iudicatur calidum aut frigidum in primo gradu, cuius gradus
principium est cum primum[203] incipit sentiri immutatio,[204] finis uero cum
plene[205] sentitur. Inter hec duo attenditur medium. Si uero[206] tantum
immutet ut ipsa distemperantia sensui coequatur, dicitur calidum aut

---

187 nunc] nunc autem *Be*
188 hec] *om. Be*
189 uero] enim *Be*
190 complexionis] complexionum *Ba*
191 et illum attingens] et illud attingens *Be; om. Ba*
192 uel receptum interius non immutat] immutati uel receptum interius *Be*
193 consimilia] similia *Ba Be*
194 forsan] *om. Be*
195 autem attingens] contingens *Ba*
196 distemperatum] temperatum *Be*
197 in] *om. Ba*
198 caliditatem] caliditate *Ba*
199 iudicatur] dicitur *Ba*
200 gradus] *om. Ba*
201 aliquid humanum corpus immutet] humanum corpus *Ba;* aliquid corpus immutet *Be*
202 et adeo] *om. Be*
203 primum] *om. Ba*
204 immutatio] mutatio *Be*
205 plene] plenarie *Ba*
206 uero] autem *Be*

frigidum in secundo gradu, cum nec ipsa sensui nec sensus ei dominetur;[207]
230   cuius principium est cum ipsa immutatio incipit ultra plenitudinem
sensus protendi, finis uero cum coequatur, quando scilicet sensus fert[208]
ipsam immutationem sine ulla molestatione.[209] Sed si plus intenderetur
sensum infestaret, ac molestaret,[210] et hoc est ipsam[211] sensui coequari.
Inter hec autem[212] duo attenditur medium. Si uero aliqua qualitate[213]
235   tantum intendatur quod ex ipsa immutatione sensus molestetur relabitur
in gradum[214] tercium, cuius principium est cum primum sensus[215] incipit
molestari et ledi, finis uero est cum plenarie leditur. Inter hec duo
attenditur medium. Si uero adeo distemperet[216] quod[217] sensum corrumpat
relabitur in quartum gradum, cuius principium est cum primum[218] incipit
240   sensum destruere, finis uero cum ex toto sensum destruit, et inter hec duo
attenditur medium. Quod tali licet[219] demonstrare[220] exemplo. Ponatur
enim aquam esse temperatam remota frigiditate actuali, ita quod sensus
non percipiat alicuius qualitatis excessum. Si uero aliquantulum incipiat
calefieri discedit[221] a temperantia et relabitur in primum gradum, cuius
245   principium est cum primum incipit sensus percipere, et adeo parum quod
adhuc sit iudicium sensus ambiguum, ut[222] scilicet sit in dubio utrum
calidum[223] debeat iudicari[224] uel non. Finis uero est[225] cum sensus percipit
caliditatem plenarie ita quod si plus intenderetur, plenitudo[226] sensus

[207] dominetur] dominetur uel coequatur *Ba;* ordinetur *Be*
[208] fert] *om. Ba*
[209] molestatione] molestatione patitur *Ba*
[210] ac molestaret] *om. Be*
[211] est ipsam] ipsum est *Be*
[212] autem] *om. Ba*
[213] qualitate] qualitatum *Be*
[214] gradum] gradu *M Be*
[215] sensus] *om. Ba*
[216] distemperet] distemperat *M Be*
[217] quod] ut *Be*
[218] primum] primo *Be*
[219] licet] libet *Be*
[220] demonstrare] declarare *Ba*
[221] discedit] descendit *Ba*
[222] ut *M Be*] *om. Ba*
[223] calidum] frigidum an calidum *Ba*
[224] iudicari] iudicare *M*
[225] est] *om. Ba*
[226] plenitudo] *om. Be*

superaretur, cum minor ea[227] siue[228] remissior sensu posset[229] percipi.
250 Secundus uero est cum amplius non posset intendi sine sensus
molestatione. Tertius uero incipit a sensus lesione et finitur in eo, quod si
plus intenderetur et sensum inciperet destruere.[230] Quartus est[231] cum
sensus destruitur. Si quis enim[232] circumdaretur aqua feruente uel igne
quemadmodum aere circumdatur sincopizaret statim, et omnino sensus[233]
255 destrueretur. Patet ergo qualiter respectu humane complexionis temperate
assignetur complexio cibariorum et medicinarum. Si enim[234] attingens
exterius uel receptum interius non immutat temperatam complexionem,
iudicatur[235] equalis et consimilis complexionis. Si autem humanam
complexionem transcendat uel superet aliqua sui qualitate, dicitur
260 distemperata[236] in illa qualitate in quam[237] immutat. Et notandum quod
cum duplex ab auctore assignetur complexio[238] simplex et composita,
hec[239] est composita secundum quam assignatur complexio. Fit enim[240]
comparatio ad rem compositam id est ad humanam complexionem. Ad
hoc autem ut gradus inueniatur fit comparatio inter actionem medicine
265 et passionem corporis secundum sensum, et hec est simplex comparatio.
Fit enim ad rem simplicem id est ad passionem corporis. Si enim actio
medicine sit infra passionem[241] qualitatis corporis distemperate secundum
sensum, dicitur primus gradus. Si uero coequatur, est secundus.[242] Si uero
transcendat[243] et superet ita quod ledat, dicitur tertius gradus. Si uero
270 destruit, dicitur quartus.[244] Est autem notandum quod male quidam
intelligunt hanc comparationem fieri inter qualitatem medicine et

---

227 cum minor ea] et si minor esset eo *Ba*

228 siue] sui *Be*

229 posset] non posset plene *Ba*]

230 et sensum inciperet destruere] sensus pateretur et inciperet destrui *Ba*

231 est] *om. Ba*

232 enim] enim ita *Ba;* enim ista *Be*

233 omnino sensus] in sensu *Ba;* omnino *Be*

234 enim] autem *Be*

235 iudicatur] diiudicatur *Ba*

236 distemperata *Be*] distemperatum *Ba;* distemperate *M*

237 quam] qua *Be*

238 complexio] comparatio *Ba*

239 hec] et hec *Ba Be*

240 enim] *om. Be*

241 passionem] *corr. a* accionem *Be*

242 est secundus] in secundo *Ba*

243 transcendat] transeat *Ba*

244 dicitur quartus] quartus gradus *Be*

qualitatem corporis quod auctor uelle uidetur, et in ueritate non fit comparatio inter ipsas qualitates, sed inter actionem medicine et passionem corporis. Si quis enim eam dicat fieri inter qualitatem[245]

275 medicine et qualitatem corporis,[246] multa sequi inconuenientia manifestum est, sicut auctor uelle uidetur. Dicit enim minorem esse caliditatem medicine calide in primo gradu[247] caliditate equalis complexionis, quod sic intellectum omnino est falsum. Si enim est minor non poterit immutare in caliditatem[248] equalem complexionem. Minus

280 enim calida magis calidis adiuncta eorum[249] calorem pocius minuunt[250] quam augmentant.[251] Sequitur autem[252] aliud inconueniens: calida in primo gradu nullius gradus esse, cum circa equalem complexionem nullam faciant[253] immutationem, que tamen et primi et aliorum inuentrix est graduum. Aliter etiam probari potest hoc esse falsum. Sit enim

285 positum aliquid constans[254] ex IIII particulis[255] frigidis et totidem calidis esse equalis complexionis,[256] et ita in nullo esse gradu. Subtracta uero una parte frigida totum efficietur[257] calidius et statim inprimum gradum relabetur,[258] et ita erit maior calor medicine quam equalis complexionis, et ita apparet in frigidis et humidis et siccis[259] in omnibus gradibus. In

290 ueritate ergo fit comparatio inter actionem qualitatis medicine et passionem qualitatis corporis. Agit enim medicina ex[260] aliqua sui qualitate, patitur uero corpus propter aliquam sui qualitatem que[261] distemperatur. Hec uero aliquando est infra passionem sensus, aliquando

---

[245] qualitatem] qualitate *Be;* om. *Ba*

[246] quod auctor ... qualitatem corporis] om. *Ba*

[247] minorem ... primo] caliditatem medicine calide in primo gradu minorem *Ba*

[248] in caliditatem] om. *Ba;* in qualitatem *Be*

[249] eorum] earum *Be*

[250] minuunt] imminuit *Ba*

[251] augmentant] augmentet *Ba*

[252] Sequitur autem] Est etiam *Ba;* Sequitur etiam *Be*

[253] faciant] faciat *Ba*

[254] constans] constare *Ba*

[255] particulis] elementis *Be*

[256] esse equalis complexionis] om. *Ba*

[257] efficietur] erit *Ba*

[258] gradum relabetur] relabitur gradum *Ba*

[259] ih frigidis et humidis et siccis] in frigido et sicco et humido et sic *Ba;* in frigidis et humidis et sic *Be*

[260] ex] om. *Ba*

[261] que] qua *Ba*

coequatur,[262] aliquando superat.[263] **Minus calidum est equa complexione**.

295   Videtur ponere duo contraria, dicens quod in primo gradu calidum est
esse calidius equa complexione, et tamen habere calorem minorem calore
eque complexionis. Ad quod dicendum quod secundum predictam
expositionem nulla est contrarietas. Quod enim in primo gradu est
calidum reuera est calidius equa complexione quia eam immutat, sed

300   tamen calor medicine est minor calore eque complexionis, id est actio
caloris medicine est infra passionem corporis secundum sensum, ut
dictum est. Alii uero magistri apud Montepessulanum locum istum[264]
exposuerunt hoc modo. Est enim secundum eos duplex temperamentum.[265]
Vnum est in quo nulla qualitatum aliam[266] excedit, secundum quod dicit

305   auctor quod calidum est in primo gradu calidius[267] equa complexione.
Aliud uero temperamentum est complexionis existentis equalis in[268]
secundo gradu, iuxta quod dictum est calorem rei calide in primo gradu
esse minorem calore equalis complexionis. Sed littera sequens repugnat,
maxime cum in aliis gradibus hoc assignare non possint.[269] <Nam

310   secundum hoc complexio equalis ad proprium modum calida, humida,
frigida, sicca inuenietur in secundo gradu, quod esse non potest, quod
inuestigando gradus frigiditatis et aliarum qualitatum eodem modo
inuenies.>[270] **Vnde nec calefacit**. Et quia est actio medicine infra
passionem corporis, ideo calidum in primo gradu non[271] calefacit nec

315   augmentat calorem equalis complexionis ita scilicet quod ledat. **Nam
licet ut calor**. Dixerat non augmentari calorem equalis complexionis[272]
alio calore adiuncto. Hoc autem uidebatur absonum et rationi
contrarium.[273] Ideo his uerbis respondet,[274] dicens quia licet (id est licitum
est) ut calor non fiat calidior adiuncto alio calore, ut si aqua tepida

---

[262]   aliquando coequatur] *om. Ba*

[263]   superat] superatur *M*

[264]   Alii uero … istum] Alii *Ba;* Alii autem … istum *Be*

[265]   duplex temperamentum] hoc temperamentum duplex *Ba*

[266]   aliam] alias *Ba*

[267]   calidius] calidius est *Be*

[268]   in] *om. Ba*

[269]   possint] possunt *Be*

[270]   Nam secundum … inuenies] *om. Ba M*

[271]   non] nec *Ba*

[272]   ita scilicet … complexionis] *om. Be*

[273]   uidebatur … contrarium] absonum et rationi contrarium uidetur *Ba*

[274]   respondet] respondeo *M Be*

320 feruenti admisceatur quamuis[275] sit calida tamen infrigdat. **Eodem modo**
et cetera. Quasi diceret quemadmodum dictum est de calido intelligendum
est in[276] frigido. **Ideoque antiqui maxime**. Et quia humana complexio
duobus gradibus dominatur a[277] duobus superatur, ideo antiqui[278]
posuerunt eam inter primum gradum[279] et quartum, non[280] habitu

325 qualitatum, scilicet quod habeat qualitates[281] duos gradus transcendentes
infra uero[282] tertium et quartum existentes, sed iudicio sensus, qui cum[283]
sit inuentor et iudicatiuus graduum et complexionum duobus gradibus
dominatur et a duobus uincitur. **Nam cum omnis superficies**. Dixerat[284]
inter duos gradus extremos[285] secundum et tercium esse medios. Ad hoc

330 enim ut gradus continentur[286] extremi oportet duos medios interponi.
Hoc ostendit per similitudinem non expressam sed qualemcumque.
Dicit enim quod quemadmodum omnis superficies tetragona si fuerit
geometrica (id est directa) constat ex duabus lineis que non possint
coniungi nisi per alias duas ex transuerso positas, sic et duo gradus non

335 possunt continuari[287] nisi per medios duos secundum et tertium. Si autem
non fuerit directa sed obliqua poterunt partes coniungi sine aliis[288]
duabus lineis hoc modo ()[289] sed si linee in directum procedant oportet
alias duas lineas apponi ad hoc ut alie coniungantur hoc modo □;[290] ecce
enim he due linee directe claudunt superficiem, sed ipse nequaquam

340 iungi[291] possunt nisi per alias duas[292] lineas ut in proxima figura apparet.
Qua de re IIIIor. Quia non possunt coniungi nisi per medios, ideo
fuerunt IIII gradus. **Quod si aliquid sensualiter**. Ac si aliquis quereret

---

275 quamuis] Et quamuis *Be*

276 intelligendum est in] ita intelligendum est in *Ba;* intelligendum est ita de *Be*

277 a] aut *Ba*

278 antiqui] antiquiter *Ba;* antiquius *M*

279 posuerunt ... gradum] primum gradum posuerunt *Ba*

280 non] ut *Be*

281 habeat qualitates] habeant *Be*

282 uero] *om. Be*

283 cum] *om. Ba*

284 Dixerat] Dixerat autem *Ba*

285 extremos] extremos et *Be;* om. *Ba*

286 gradus continentur] duo gradus continet (? *ut vid.*) *Ba*

287 continuari *M Ba*] commutare *Be*

288 aliis] *om. Be*

289 ()] *om. Ba*

290 □] *om. Ba*

291 iungi] *om. Ba*

292 duas] *om. Ba*

quomodo sensus inuenerit gradus. Respondeo quia[293] gustando, et ita
gustu et tactu percipit graduum diuersitates. **Nam si sensus dominetur**
345   **uel coequetur attenditur**[294] **primus et secundus gradus.** Si uero superetur,
tertius et quartus,[295] et plane hic innuit illam superiorem expositionem de
simplici comparatione. In fine huius proemii fit questio in qua scilicet
quantitate ea que sunt in gradu tertio sensum ledant uel ea que in quarto
sensum destruant; ad quod dicimus quod[296] sumpta in ea quantitate in
350   qua cetera cibaria solent suscipi ista suscepta[297] sensum ledunt uel
destruunt, aliter uero minime.[298]

   Absinthium est calidum in primo gradu. Assignata graduum
distinctione siue discretione[299] in prohemio accedit ad propositum,
scilicet ad ostendendum singularum[300] medicinarum simplicium que
355   frequencius usui medicine[301] occurrunt complexiones cum gradibus,
uirtutes cum operationibus, ut in principio[302] dictum est. Mixtim autem et
simul gradus et complexionem designat, dicens esse calidum uel frigidum
in primo gradu. Tercio uero ostendit uirtutem medicine et supponit de
operatione, et hoc frequentius; quandoque tamen premittit de operatione
360   et supponit de uirtute, sed raro. In his uero ostendendis duplex ordo
attenditur. Vnus qui habetur in *Pantegni* secundum ordinem graduum,
secundum quem ordinem tractatur hoc modo de his primum de omnibus
calidis, frigidis, siccis, humidis in primo gradu, et eodem ordine in reliquis.
Est autem alius ordo secundum quem liber dispositus est[303] secundum
365   ordinem alfabeti ut quod queritur facilius inueniatur, secundum quem
ordinem agit primum de his que ab *a* incipiunt, deinde[304] de his que a
b et ita de aliis. Secundum priorem uero ordinem sumitur[305] exordium
a rosa, secundum alium ab absinthio,[306] cuius ostendit complexionem

---

293   quia] quod *Be*
294   attenditur] *om. Ba*
295   quartus] quartus sicut *(? ut vid.) Ba*
296   ad quod dicimus quod] ad quidem *M*
297   suscepta] recepta *Be*
298   minime] non *Ba*
299   discretione] descriptione *Be*
300   singularum] singulariter *Be*
301   usui medicine] *om. Ba*
302   principio] proemio *Ba*
303   quem liber dispositus est] quemlibet dispositus *Ba;* quem liber iste dispositus est *Be*
304   deinde] Secundo *Ba*
305   uero ordinem sumitur] fiunt *Ba*
306   ab absinthio] absinthium *Be*

370 esse calidam et gradum[307] dicens in primo gradu calidum, in secundo siccum. Deinde supponit operationem, dicens **Stomacum confortat.** Duobus modis dicuntur aliqua membrum confortare:[308] uel quia partes constringunt et consolidant,[309] uel quia operationem uirtutis[310] ipsius membri iuuant. Quemadmodum per contrarium illa dicuntur membrum debilitare uel que partes ipsius rarefaciunt ut diagridium substantiam

375 epatis debilitat quia[311] partes ipsius rarefacit, aut quia operationem uirtutis debilitant quemadmodum frigida et dura[312] operationem[313] uirtutis digestiue. Absinthium uero utroque modo confortat: et partes rarefactas[314] constringendo, et hoc terrestretate[315] substantie et ponticitate, et ex caliditate complexionis[316] iuuat uirtutem digestiuam.

380 **Coleram rubeam purgat.** Hoc loco dicendum est quot modis purget[317] medicina laxatiua. Omnis autem medicina[318] que purgat aliquo istorum modorum[319] purgat: aut comprimendo, aut leniendo,[320] aut dissoluendo, aut attrahendo. Purgant autem comprimendo et constringendo et in unum distancia reducendo[321] quemadmodum mirobalani omnes qui[322]

385 sunt frigidi et sicci et tamarindi. Sunt autem V genera mirobalanorum[323] qui hoc uersiculo enumerantur:[324] citrinus, kebulus, belliricus, emblicus, indus.[325] Hec autem omnia purgant comprimendo sed iuuant maxime ex lubricitate quam habent. Si enim aliquid lubricum contineatur quanto magis locus constringitur et illud quod continetur facilius elabitur, ut

---

307 gradum] gradus *Be*

308 dicuntur aliqua membrum confortare] dicitur aliquid membra confortare *Ba;* dicuntur aliqua membra confortari *Be*

309 constringunt et consolidant *M Be*] constringit et consolidat *Ba*

310 uirtutis *om. Ba*

311 quia] quod *M*

312 dura] humida *Ba*

313 operationem] et operationem *Be*

314 rarefactas] ipsius *Ba*

315 terrestretate *ut uid. M*] terrestritate *Ba;* terrestricetate *(? ut vid.) Be*

316 et ex caliditate complexionis] *om. Ba*

317 purget] purgat *Ba*

318 medicina] *om. Be*

319 istorum modorum] modo istorum *Ba*

320 leniendo] lenificando *Be*

321 reducendo] deducendo *Be*

322 qui] et qui *Ba*

323 genera mirobalanorum] mirobalani *Be*

324 qui ... enumerantur] *om. Ba*

325 indus] indus. Explicit *Ba*

390   si anguilla manu contineatur quanto plus constringitur tanto cicius[326]
        elabitur. Lenificando autem que reddunt lubricum stomachum et
        intestina, ut est mercurialis, malua, et quedam pinguedines. Sunt uero
        alia que purgant dissoluendo, sed hec dissolutio duplex est. Dicitur enim
        dissolutio liquefactio que fit ex nimia caliditatis[327] intentione que fit ex
395   calidis in quarto gradu, ut est euforbium, calx uiua, uiride eris, lepidos
        calcis, es ustum, tartarum[328]—illud scilicet durum quod dolio adheret,
        quod per se cum uino distemperatum purgat. Calx etiam purgat,[329] ut
        accidit cuidam rustico que calcem distemperatam in domo cuiusdam
        medici inuenit, et putans esse medicamen bibit, et statim uentris
400   solutionem habuit, et ita euasit. Sed quamuis illi ita casu[330] contulerit
        non tamen suadeo hoc esse faciendum scilicet calx[331] ita bibatur. Est
        etiam et[332] alia dissolutio que fit cum salsugine[333] et amaritudine. Habent
        enim affinitatem in operatione salsa et amara, sed amara habent maiorem
        uim ut aloes, absinthium, fel taurinum. Cum salsedine purgant ut caro
405   galli,[334] nitrum et similia. Altera[335] est que purgat attrahendo, de qua est
        questio utrum ipsa existente in stomacho uirtus eius diffundatur per
        totum corpus, an ipsa per totum corpus diffundatur,[336] et si diffunditur,[337]
        utrum membra pacientia attrahant an ipsa in fumositatem resoluta
        per totum corpus dispergatur quemadmodum fumositates aromatum
410   in aere disperguntur.[338] Habetur autem in libro de simplici medicina
        quod[339] non potest esse quod ipsa in stomacho existente uirtus eius
        diffundatur quia accidens subiectum non potest relinquere. Sed hec[340]
        ratio debilis est. Posset enim fumositas medicine inficere humores
        et spiritus et illi alios quemadmodum facit uenenum quod membra

---

[326] cicius] facilius *Be*
[327] caliditatis] caloris *Be*
[328] tartarum] cantarum *Be*
[329] Calx etiam purgat] *in marg. M; om. Be*
[330] casu] cals *Be*
[331] calx] ut cals uiua *Be*
[332] et] *om. Be*
[333] salsugine] salsugere *Be*
[334] galli] galline *Be*
[335] Altera] Alia *Be*
[336] per ... diffundatur] *om. Be*
[337] diffunditur] diffunditur ipsa *Be*
[338] disperguntur] dispergantur *Be*
[339] quod *Be*] quia *M*
[340] hec] *om. Be*

415   pacientia attrahant cum sint debilia; non uidetur, sed potest dici quia attrahunt[341] contraria, quemadmodum stomacus distemperatus appetit contraria. Quod si eius fumositas per totum corpus dispergitur tunc equaliter potest educere[342] et bonos et malos humores. Ad quod dicimus quod fumositas eius diffunditur per totum corpus et offendit corruptos

420   humores et ex habilitate quam habet ad illos, circa illos immoratur. Vnde illuc fit discursus medicine, et ita corrupti educuntur humores. Per poros enim illos per quos uirtus medicine penetrauit ingrediuntur et ad epar transducuntur, et ita secundum habilitatem[343] humorum superius aut inferius purgantur. **Coleram rubeam** et flegma purgat sed minimum de

425   colera rubea admixtum totum colorat. Nota quod extenuatis non confert absinthium. Explicit.[344]

Liber graduum commentary Sources and Notes

4–5 "Quamuis autem in principio illius uolumnis ...": i.e., *Pantegni Theorica*, 1.2 (Lyons 1515 edn, vol. 2, fol. i^rb).

27–30 "Virtutes etiam assignat ... digestionem procurat." This passage paraphrases *Pantegni Practica*, 2.2 (Lyons 1515 edn, vol. 2, fol. lxv^va): "Virtus itaque simplicis medicine tribus modis est: una est complexio et natura. Secunda est actio a prima procedens id est maturatiua: mollatiua: induratiua: dissolutiua: oris uenarum aperitiua: carnium minutiua: attenuatiua: dolorum mitigatiua. Tertia est lapides frangens: urinam et menstrua prouocans: pectus mundificans: lac generans." However, the chapter of *Pantegni Practica*, 2.3 (*De simplici medicina*) dealing with wormwood (ch. 36 in the Lyons 1515 edn) does not mention breaking up stone (though it does discuss wormwood's properties of strengthening the stomach), nor do the sections on vinegar (ch. 43) state that it provokes appetite. This suggests that the author of the *LGC* was working with a version of *Pantegni Practica* book 2 that had not yet incorporated *De simplici medicina*. But it should be noted that the chapter of *Liber graduum* on wormwood also does not mention the stone (see comment on lines 352 sqq. below), and the *Liber graduum* contains no chapter on vinegar.

---

[341] cum sint ... attrahunt] *om. Be*

[342] educere] ducere *M*

[343] habilitatem] aptitudinem *Be*

[344] Explicit] *om. Be*

32–6 "Hoc autem ordine ... positarum." This passage appears only in *M*, and it is unclear whether it forms part of the text or is a later intrusion. For this reason, it is placed within square brackets. From the context—a comparison of the Arabic original of the *Liber graduum* catalogue to its Latin translation—it would appear that "Ali filius Tabernarii" is a garbled rendition of the name of Abū Ǧaʿfar Aḥmad ibn Ibrāhīm ibn Abī Khālid al-Ǧazzār. How the author of the *LGC* (assuming he actually wrote this passage) knew that al-Ǧazzār composed the *Liber graduum* catalogue is not clear. However, "Ali filius Tabernarii" could also refer to ʿAli ibn Sahl Rabban al-Tabarī (*c.* 838–*c.* 870), scholar, teacher of Rhazes, and author of the earliest Islamic medical encyclopedia, *Firdaus al-hikma* (*Paradise of Wisdom*), of which Part 6, discourse 2, ch. 245 constitutes a catalogue of medicinal simples: see Max Meyerhof, "ʿAli at-Tabarîʾs 'Paradise of Wisdom', One of the Oldest Arabic Compendiums of Medicine," *Isis* 16 (1931): 6–54; David Thomas, "al-Tabari," in P.J. Bearman et al. (eds), *Encyclopedia of Islam*, 2nd edn (Leiden: Brill, 2010), accessed through Brill Online, McGill University, January 14, 2010: http://www.brillonline.nl/subscriber.entry?entry=islam _SIM-7248. I wish to thank my colleague Dr Keren Abbou for assistance in locating information on al-Tabarī. Al-Tabarī was an extraordinarily influential figure in the field of pharmacology and drug lore. However, there is no evidence that his work on medicinal simples was ever translated into Latin. The author of the *LGC* may have heard at second hand through another translated Arabic source about al-Tabarīʾs reputation, and concluded that he was the author of the original *Liber graduum*. To date, however, I have been unable to locate such a source.

51–4 "Dicit enim superius ... ex frigiditate et siccitate." This refers to the end of *De probanda medicina* (*Pantegni Practica*, 2.34): "Hic autem finitur nostra disputatio de uniuersali virtute simplicis medicine. Est autem incipienda simplicium medicinarum diuisio de naturis et disputatio deo adiuuante" (Lyons edn, vol. 2, fol. lxvii^{va}). See above, p. 116.

65–7 "Videndum est ... determinabilis." Cf. Urso, *De gradibus*, 29–35 (ed. Sudhoff, p. 136): "Vnde uidendum est, quid sit gradus et quot partes habeat et quare tot et non plures, et quot partes unusquisque habeat gradus, et quid sit esse in gradu, et cuius respectu aliquid dicitur esse in gradu et alia [h]utilia, que inquirenda sunt circa gradus. Gradus est excessus qualitatum uel qualitatis ab optima temperantia sensu determinabilis."

69–71 "in libro *Ysagogarum* ... attenditur." Johannitius, *Isagoge*, 4, ed. Gregor Maurach, *Sudhoffs Archiv* 62 (1978): 152. Note that where the *LGC* uses the term *complexiones* Johannitius prefers *commixtiones*. Bartholomaeus of Salerno's commentary on *Isagoge* 4 exhibits striking verbal similarities with this passage: "com<m>ixtio est elementorum prima in corporibus coniunctio. huius autem due sunt species. equalis. et inequalis. Equalis est. <u>qualitates</u> et quantitates <u>elementorum equaliter continens</u>. ex qualitate namque elementorum coequata qualitatum ipsarum coequacio procedit. ut nulla scilicet earum alii dominentur" (Winchester, Winchester College, MS 24, fol. 26rb).

123 "Commento" (cf. line 149 below). Bartholamaeus uses this distinctive first-person declaration to mark points in his commentaries where he assumes an assertive and magisterial "exegetical voice." Examples are particularly abundant in his *Tegni* commentary, e.g., "Nunc uero [Galienus] assignat differentiam inter neruos per anteriorem partem capitis et posteriorem. et etiam inter partem anteriorem et posteriorem per neruos. et hoc totum ad cognicionem cerebri. Commento. dixi quod occipicium uel spina participat neruis motum uoluntarium prebentibus ..." *Commentare* had become an acceptable substitute for the classical *commentari* by the thirteenth century at the latest: see R.E. Latham, ed., *Dictionary of Medieval Latin from British Sources*, vol. 1 (London: Oxford University Press for the British Academy, 1975), 393.

136–7 "Est enim complexio IIII elementarum qualitatum coniunctio." Cf. Bartholomaeus' commentary on *Isagoge* 4: "complexio est elementarum qualitatum in corporibus coniunctio" (Winchester 24, fol. 26rb).

137–8 "Que autem sunt a lunari globo inferius ... alicuius complexionis." Cf. Bartholomaeus' commentary on *Isagoge* 4: "Queritur utrum omnia corpora preter elementum. a lunari globo inferius ex IIIIor elementis conste\<n>t. et dicimus quod non omnia sunt enim quedam partes corporum. ex duabus tamen. uel tribus particularibus constantes. que licet corpora sint non tamen ex IIIIor elementis constant. Vtpote IIIIor partes non habencia. Verumtamen ille partes pro sui paruitate sensum effugiunt. Cum autem repereatur [*sic*] in auctoribus omnia corpora ex IIIIor elementis constare. de hiis que sensu subiacent intelligas ita tamen quod ipsa elementa excludas" (Winchester 24, fol. 26ra). Bartholomaeus uses the phrase "globo lunari inferius/superius" many times in the *Isagoge* commentary.

141–5 "Quasi diceret ... sed intensione est simplicitas." Note the particularly close parallel in Bartholomaeus' commentary on *Isagoge* 4: "Equalis autem subdiuidi non potest. Vnde ab inequali incipiamus. Huius due sunt species scilicet simplex et composita. Simplex est unius tantum qualitatis intensionem habens. <u>Composita uero plurium. nec te moueat quod dicitur commixtio. et complexio simplex. cum alterum pluralitatem exigat. alterum uero repudiet. Est namque in plurium coniunctione pluralitas. In intensione uero qualitatis simplicitas</u>" (Winchester 24, fol. 26rb).

149–51 "Omne corpus ... sensualiter sed intellectualiter." Cf. Bartholomaeus' commentary on *Isagoge* 4: "In sequentibus autem. uel super prologum primi libri graduum rationabilior et euidentior sentencia ponetur. qua liquido patebit.

quomodo equalis complexio non sensualiter. sed intellectualiter. inueniri possit" (Winchester 24, fol. 26va).

159–68 "Signa uero per incompetentem usum ... temperata complexio." Cf. Bartholomaeus' commentary on *Isagoge* 4: "Cum enim humanum corpus ex aere. cibo. potu. motu. requie. et cetera. rebus non naturalibus immutetur. licet in se perfecte sit temperatum. sensus tamen circa ipsum distemperancie. et inequalitatis percipit signa. Vnde Galienus in Tegni [14.4]. Si quis tempore messis. nudum se soli exposuerit. uel in umbra degens more uirginis fuerit permutabuntur signa complexionis. quidam tamen istud male exponunt intelligentes scilicet perfecte temperatam complexionem non actualiter sed intellectualiter consistere id est ut penitus non sit. sed ut esse intelligatur" (Winchester 24, fol. 26va).

173–8 "Habetur autem alia littera ... complexionum." Cf. Bartholomaeus' commentary on *Isagoge* 4: "Notandum est quod dicitur in Pantegni de perfecte temperata complexione quoniam intellectualiter non actualiter inueni potest. Actualiter accipiendum est hic pro sensualiter sicut in prologo primi libri graduum inuenitur. Cum enim humanum corpus ex aere. cibo. potu. motu. requie. et cetera. rebus non naturalibus immutetur. licet in se perfecte sit temperatum. sensus tamen circa ipsum distemperancie. et inequalitatis percipit signa" (Winchester 24, fol. 26va). The reference is to *Pantegni Theorica*, 1.7: "Complexionem dicimus intemperatam calidam. frigidam. humidam. siccam. que aut[em] intelliguntur qualitates sole: extra subiectum: aut in subiecto sunt. In subiecto actualiter uel potentialiter. siue accidentaliter. siue potestatiue. que cum sensu non apparent: tamen esse possunt: ut piper cum calide sit nature. non tamen sensualiter discernitur: nisi cum calefaciat corpus comedentis" (Lyons edn, vol. 2, fol. ii^{va}).

178–9 "Vnde Galienus ... tenue." *Tegni*, 14.6. Cf. Bartholomaeus' commentary on this passage: "**Vt dicantur** et intelligit. ad hoc autem respectu huius temperantie dicitur aliquid calidum. frigidum. quia excedit illam mediocritatem quantum enim sit lapsus corporum intelligitur ex collatione frigidi ad equalem complexionem. **etenim spissum.** Ostendit in parte quod dixerat omnia refer<r>i ad perfectum temperamentum" (Winchester 24, fol. 75ra).

205–6 "ut in libro *Afforismorum* ... hiemem." Hippocrates, *Aphorisms*, 3.2. In his commentary on this passage, Bartholomaeus also equates *natura* with *complexio* (Winchester 24, fol. 118vb), but this is also found in earlier glosses on the *Aphorisms*, e.g., the Digby Commentary (Oxford, Bodleian Library, MS Digby 108, fol. 39v).

219–21 "Itaque secundum qualitatem ... hoc modo." Cf. "Apud antiquos," lines 111–12: "complexionem quidem secundum proprietatem immutationis, gradum vero secundum quantitatem immutationis."

221–5 "Si enim parum ... primo gradu." Cf. Urso, *De gradibus*, 89–92 (ed. Sudhoff, p. 137): "Immutatio autem fit secundum magis et minus, unde si excessus parum distet ab optima temperantia, ita tamen quod sensum immutet et sensus maiorem potest pati sine lesione, dicitur esse in primo gradu, et ibi et meta primi gradus." Also 107–10 (p. 138): "unde quicquid inmutat instrumentum sensus, ita quod sensus maiorem potest pati sine lesione mutationem siue caliditatis, siue frigiditatis, siue siccitatis, siue humiditatis, dicitur esse in primo gradu." It should be noted, however, that Urso's definitions of the second, third, and fourth grade are differently expressed from, although not opposed to, those of the *LGC*.

227–33 "Si uero tantum ... coequari." Cf. Urso, *De gradibus*, 111–15 (ed. Sudhoff, p. 138): "Secundus gradus est ex qualitate uel qualitatibus ab optima temperantia, cui sensus humane complexionis adequatur. Adequari dicitur sensus excessui, quando excessus inadequatur sensui, quod si maior esset et posset percipi, ledere et sensus sine lesione sensibili pati non posset ..."

256–7 "Si enim attingens exterius ... immutat." Cf. "Apud antiquos," lines 112–16: "Cum enim aliquid temperato corpori adhibetur, sive exterius appositum sive intrinsecus receptum, ipsum necessario aut immutat aut non. Si immutat, corpori est dissimile et inequalis complexionis; si vero non immutat, ei simile est et equalis complexionis."

274–84 "Si quis ... est graduum." This is substantially the same criticism put forward in "Apud antiquos," lines 138–60, esp. lines 155–60: "Contrarium enim qualitatum hoc est natura, ut quantum una intenditur, tantum in sua contraria remittatur. Et ideo sicut predictum est temperati corporis intensa caliditas sit in tertio gradu, eiusdem frigiditas proportionaliter remissa erit in secundo: unde et idem corpus in secundo frigidum et in tertio calidum reperitur, quod opinari ridiculum est et absurdum."

302 sqq. The proponents of this "double temperament" argument have not been identified. Their theory can be compared to the opinion of "quidam" recorded in "Apud antiquos," lines 138 sqq., namely that the equal temperament in the human body is situated on the frontier of the second and third degrees.

352 sqq. "Absinthium est calidum in primo gradu." Neither the lemmata nor the contents of the *LGC* discussion of wormwood match those found in the text of the *Liber graduum* printed in the Lyons 1515 *Pantegni Practica*, vol. 2, fol. lxxviii[rb]: "Absinthium calidum in initio primi gradus siccum in secundo ponticum et amarum: aperit oppilationem epatis: ualet yctericis ex cholera rubea. succus fortior frondibus. ualet tertianis: humores de mery et stomacho et uenis purgat de eisdem humoribus: cuius apozima si datur ualet melancholicis

..." The lemmata **Stomachum confortat** and **Coleram rubeam purgat** seem closer to Galen, *De simplici medicina*, 6.71 (*Opera*, Venice 1490, fol. 61rb): "Absinthium: sapor absinthium habet stipicitatem et amaritudinem in simile: et acumen ipsum calefacit: et mundificat: et confortat desiccat: et ideo euacuat illud quod inuenit in stomacho de humore colerico: et purgat cum urina."

385–7 "Sunt autem V genera mirobalanorum ... indus." Cf. the chapter on myrobolans in the *Liber graduum*, fol. 89rb: "Myrobalanorum quinque sunt genera. citrini: indi: kebuli: emblici: bellirici." However, no source or analogue of this list as a mnemonic *versus* has been traced.

410–12 "Habetur autem in libro de simplici medicina quod non potest esse quod ipsa in stomacho existente uirtus eius diffundatur. quia accidens subiectum non potest relinquere." The author may be referring to Galen's *De simplici medicina*, but no cognate passage has been found in the two sections of the work devoted to the operation of "attractive" medicines, namely book 3, dist. 4, chs 4–5 (*Opera*, ed. Diomede Bonardi [2 vols, Venice: F. Pinzi, 1490], vol. 1, fol. 42rv), and book 5, dist. 4, ch. 4 (fol. 54rv).

Bibliography

Bloch, Herbert. *Monte Cassino in the Middle Ages*. 3 vols. Cambridge, MA: Harvard University Press, 1986.

Bonardi, Diomede (ed.). *Galieni opera*. 2 vols. Venice: F. Pinzi, 1490.

Burnett, Charles. "The Superiority of Taste." *Journal of the Warburg and Courtauld Institutes* 54 (1991): 230–38.

———. "*Sapores sunt octo*: The Medieval Latin Terminology for the Eight Flavours." *Micrologus* 9 (2002): 99–112.

——— and Danielle Jacquart (eds). *Constantine the African and ʿAlī ibn al-ʿAbbās al-Maǧūsī: The "Pantegni" and Related Texts*. Leiden: Brill, 1994.

Constable, Giles (ed.). *The Letters of Peter the Venerable*. Cambridge, MA: Harvard University Press, 1967.

Constantini africani post Hippocratem et Galenum ... posthabendi opera. Basel: Heinrich Petri, 1536.

Gaspar, Giles E.M., and Faith Wallis. "Anselm and the *Articella*." *Traditio* 59 (2004): 129–74.

Green, Monica H. "The Re-creation of *Pantegni, Practica*, Book VIII." In Burnett and Jacquart, *Constantine the African*, 121–60.

Hauke, Hermann. *Katalog der lateinischen Handschriften der Bayerischen Staatsbibliothek München: Clm 28111–28254*. Catalogus codicum manu scriptorum bibliothecae Monacensis 4.7. Wiesbaden: Harrassowitz, 1986.

Jacquart, Danielle. "De *crasis* à *complexio*: Note sur le vocabulaire du tempérament en latin médiéval." In Guy Sabbah (ed.), *Textes médicaux latins antiques*, 71–6. Mémoires du Centre Jean Palerne 5. Saint-Étienne: Publications de l'Université de Saint-Étienne, 1984.

———. "À l'aube de la renaissance médicale des XIe–XIIe siècles: l'*Isagoge Johannitii* et son traducteur." *Bibliothèque de l'École des Chartes* 144 (1986): 209–40.

——— and Agostino Paravicini Bagliani (eds). *La scuola medica salernitana: gli autori e i testi*. Edizione Nazionale "La Scuola Medica Salernitana" 1. Florence: SISMEL, Edizioni del Galluzzo, 2007.

Jordan, Mark D. "Medicine as Science in the Early Commentaries on 'Johannitius.'" *Traditio* 43 (1987): 121–45.

———. "The Construction of a Philosophical Medicine: Exegesis and Argument in Salernitan Teaching on the Soul." In Michael R. McVaugh and Nancy G. Siraisi (eds), *Renaissance Medical Learning: Evolution of a Tradition. Osiris*, 2nd ser., 6 (1990): 42–61.

Kristeller, Paul Oskar. "The School of Salerno: Its Development and Its Contribution to the History of Learning." *Bulletin of the History of Medicine* 17 (1945): 138–94.

———. "Beitrag der Schule von Salerno zur Entwicklung der scholastichen Wissenschaft im 12. Jahrhundert: Kurze Mitteilung über handschriftliche Funde." In Josef Koch (ed.), *Artes Liberales von der antiken Bildung zur Wissenschaft des Mittelalters*, 84–90. Studien und Texte zur Geistesgeschichte des Mittelalters 5. Leiden: Brill, 1959.

———. *La scuola medica di Salerno secondo ricerche e scoperti recenti*. Quaderni Centro di Studi e Documentazione della Scuola Medica Salernitana 5. Salerno: Mutalipassi, 1980.

———. "Nuove fonti per la medicina salernitana del secolo XII." *Rassegna storica salernitana* 18 (1957): 61–75. Trans. by Christine Porzer and reprinted as "Neue Quellen zur salernitaner Medizin des 12. Jahrhunderts." In Gerhard Baader and Gundolf Keil (eds), *Medizin im mittelalterliche Abendland*, 191–208. Wege der Forschung 363. Darmstadt: Wissenschaftliche Buchgesellschaft, 1982.

———. "Bartholomaeus, Musandinus and Maurus of Salerno and Other Early Commentators of the *Articella*, with a Tentative List of Texts and Manuscripts." *Italia medioevale e umanistica* 29 (1976): 57–87. Translated, with additions and corrections, as "Bartolomeo, Musandino, Mauro di Salerno e altri antichi commentatori dell'*Articella*, con un elenco di testi e di manoscritti." In Paul Oskar Kristeller, *Studi sulla scuola medica salernitana*, 97–151. Naples: Istituto Italiano per gli Studi Filosofici, 1986.

Lapidge, Michael, et al. (eds). *Compendium auctorum latinorum medii aevi (500–1500)*. Vol. 2.1. Florence: SISMEL, Edizioni del Galluzzo, 2004.

Maurach, Gregor. "Johannicius: *Isagoge ad Techne Galieni*." *Sudhoffs Archiv* 62 (1978): 148–74.

McVaugh, Michael R. "The Medieval Theory of Compound Medicine." Unpublished Ph.D. diss., Princeton University, 1965.

———. "'Apud antiquos' and Mediaeval Pharmacology." *Medizinhistorisches Journal* 1 (1966): 16.

———. "Theriac at Montpellier 1285–1328 (with an edition of the 'Quaestiones de tyriaca' of William of Brescia)." *Sudhoffs Archiv* 56 (1972): 113–43.

Meyerhof, Max. "'Ali at-Tabarî's 'Paradise of Wisdom', One of the Oldest Arabic Compendiums of Medicine." *Isis* 16 (1931): 6–54.

Morpurgo, Pietro. "I commenti salernitani all'*Articella*." In Monika Asztalos, John E. Murdoch, and Ilkka Niiniluoto (eds), *Knowledge and the Sciences in Medieval Philosophy: Proceedings of the Eighth International Congress of Medieval Philosophy, Helsinki, 24–29 August 1987*, 2:97–105. 3 vols. Helsinki: Yliopistopaino, 1990.

O'Boyle, Cornelius. *The Art of Medicine: Medical Teaching at the University of Paris, 1250–1400*. Leiden: Brill, 1998.

Omnia opera Ysaac. 2 vols. Lyons: J. de Platea, 1515.

Ottosson, Per-Gunnar. *Scholastic Medicine and Philosophy: A Study of Commentaries on Galen's Tegni, ca. 1300–1450*. Naples: Bibliopolis, 1984.

Puccinotti, Francesco. *Storia della medicina*. Vol. 2.1. Livorno: Massimiliano Wagner, 1855.

Renzi, Salvatore De. *Collectio salernitana*. Vol. 4. Naples: Sabezio, 1856.

Riddle, John M. "Theory and Practice in Medieval Medicine." *Viator* 5 (1974): 157–81.

———. "Dioscorides." In Ferdinand E. Cranz and Paul Oskar Kristeller (eds), *Catalogus Translationum et Commentariorum: Mediaeval and Renaissance Translations and Commentaries*, 4:1–143. Washington, D.C.: Catholic University of America Press, 1980.

Saffron, Morris H. "Salernitan Anatomists." In *Dictionary of Scientific Biography*, vol. 12, 80–83. New York: Scribner, 1975.

Steinmann, Martin. *Die Handschriften der Universitätsbibliothek Basel: Register zu den Abteilungen C I–C VI, D–F sowie zu weiteren mittelalterlichen Handschriften und Fragmenten*. Basel: Universitätsbibliothek, 1998.

Steinschneider, Moritz. "Constantin's *Liber de gradibus* und ibn al-Gezzar's *Adminiculum*." *Deutsches Archiv für Geschichte der Medizin* 2 (1879): 1–22.

Sudhoff, Karl. "Die Salernitaner Handschrift in Breslau, ein *Corpus medicinae Salerni*." *Archiv für Geschichte der Medizin* 12 (1920): 101–48.

Thomas, David. "al-Tabari." In P.J. Bearman et al. (eds), *Encyclopedia of Islam.* 2nd edn. Leiden: Brill, 2010. Available online through subscription at http://www.brillonline.nl (accessed February 19, 2012).

Thorndike, Lynn. "Three Texts of Degrees of Medicines (*De gradibus*)." *Bulletin of the History of Medicine* 38 (1964): 533–7.

———, and Pearl Kibre. *Incipits of Mediaeval Scientific Writings in Latin.* 2nd edn. Cambridge, MA: Medieval Academy of America, 1963.

Tosti, Marco. "Bartholomaeus Salernitanus." In Lapidge et al., *Compendium auctorum latinorum medii aevi (500–1500),* 56–9.

van den Gheyn, Joseph. *Catalogue des manuscrits de la Bibliothèque royale de Belgique.* Brussels: Henri Lamartin, 1901.

Veit, Raphaela. "Al-Maǧūsī's *Kitāb al-Malakī* and Its Latin Translation Ascribed to Constantine the African: The Reconstruction of *Pantegni, Practica,* Liber III." *Arabic Sciences and Philosophy* 16 (2006): 133–68.

Wack, Mary. "ʿAlī ibn al-ʿAbbās al-Maǧūsī and Constantine on Love, and the Evolution of the *Practica Pantegni.*" In Burnett and Jacquart, *Constantine the African,* 161–202.

Wallis, Faith. "Bartholomaeus of Salerno." In Steven Livesey, Thomas Glick, and Faith Wallis (eds), *Medieval Science, Technology and Medicine: An Encyclopedia,* 77–8. London: Routledge, 2005.

———. "The *Articella* Commentaries of Bartholomaeus of Salerno." In Jacquart and Paravicini Bagliani, *La scuola medica salernitana,* 125–64.

———. "Twelfth-century Commentaries on the *Tegni*: Bartholomaeus of Salerno and Others." In Nicoletta Palmieri (ed.), *L'Ars medica (Tegni) de Galien: lectures antiques et médiévales,* 127–68. Mémoires du Centre Jean Palerne 32. Saint-Étienne: Publications de l'Université de Saint-Étienne, 2008.

Chapter 5

"I will add what the Arab once taught": Constantine the African in Northern European Medical Verse

Winston Black

The importance of the eleventh-century monk Constantine the African to the history of European medicine can hardly be overstated. Thanks to his translations of Arabic and Greek medical works, compilations of those works, and original compositions, he can be credited (without excessive hyperbole) with bringing rationality back to medieval medicine. The concern of most scholars currently studying Constantine is with accurately reconstructing his texts, most importantly the *Pantegni* ("The Whole Art"), and tracing their critical reception in the later Middle Ages.[1] There is one area of medieval medicine, however, seemingly at odds with Constantine's rationality where he nonetheless had a significant influence: medical verse. Latin verse was composed in the Middle Ages not only for entertainment; it was also a popular medium for conveying technical information, particularly from the eleventh century. It is a testament to the fame and utility of Constantine's writings that several poets included medical information from his works in their own didactic verse compositions. In this essay, I will examine the influence of one of Constantine's most popular works, his book of simples[2] (individual herbs or minerals with known medicinal properties) usually known as the *Liber de gradibus* or *Liber graduum* ("The Book of Degrees"), originally part of the *Practica* section of his *Pantegni*, but copied separately from an early date in two recensions (one is alphabetized

---

[1]   In particular, see Charles Burnett and Danielle Jacquart (eds), *Constantine the African and ʿAlī ibn al-ʿAbbās al-Maǧūsī: The "Pantegni" and Related Texts* (Leiden: Brill, 1994).

[2]   Simples are defined in the commentary on the *Liber graduum* edited by Faith Wallis in ch. 4 of this volume (p. 124, lines 12–14): "Simple medicines are called thus because they are thought to alter the body without the process of any composition, and exist just as nature produced them, such as herbs, metals, and grains." (The translation is my own.)

within each degree).[3] Faith Wallis has provided a more complete history of the *Liber graduum* in Chapter 4 of this volume. Let it suffice here to say that Constantine first popularized the system of degrees in the Latin West through this work. It provided physicians and apothecaries with a tool for measuring the Galenic qualities (hot or cold and wet or dry) of an herb and its relative intensity, or degree (*gradus*), measured from the first to the fourth degree. The rational organization of his pharmacopoeia by degrees had a great appeal to scholars of the High Middle Ages, and Constantine's work quickly became the subject of poems, glosses, and commentaries,[4] placing him on a pedestal beside Dioscorides and Pliny in the halls of medieval pharmacology.

In this essay I have prepared a brief survey of authors who versified Constantine's *Liber graduum*, with some examples of their poems compared with their prose source. I have included as an appendix a catalogue of all the poems I have found so far which are based on the *Liber graduum*. I hope this will be of use both to scholars of Constantine the African in tracing his influence and to scholars of medieval verse when approached with that odd chimera of the times, the medical poem. As will become clear, these poet-physicians variously supplemented and glossed Constantine's text as they saw fit, as often as they confused, simplified, replaced, or removed some of his more technical descriptions of maladies and remedies. The final poems, while still in essence based on the *Liber graduum*, offered in some cases medical texts differing significantly from Constantine's original meaning, sometimes improving on the original and sometimes clearly failing in their attempt to improve on the master. Before I approach the individual poems directly, a few comments on the genre of medical verse are needed.

The tradition of medical treatises composed in Latin verse began in the Mediterranean sphere with works like Ovid's *Medicamina faciei femineae* (already

---

[3]   There is no critical edition of the *Pantegni*. A review of its difficulties and some advice toward a working edition are given by Mark Jordan, "The Fortune of Constantine's *Pantegni*," in Burnett and Jacquart, *Constantine the African*, 286–302. The *Liber graduum* can be found in two early modern editions of Constantine's collected works. It was first printed in the works of Isaac the Jew, *Omnia opera Ysaac* (2 vols, Lyons, 1515), 2: fols lxxviii^r–lxxxvi^r, and soon after with some changes in *Constantini africani post Hippocratem et Galenum ... posthabendi opera* (2 vols, Basel, 1536–59), 2:342–87. The Basel edition, while far from perfect, is usually accepted as superior to that of Lyons, and I will be using that version. See Eliza Glaze's contribution to this volume, ch. 3, for a discussion of the relationship of the *Liber graduum* to other contemporary pharmacological works associated with Salerno.

[4]   See Faith Wallis's important contribution to the field in this volume, ch. 4, where she has edited just such a commentary on the *Liber graduum*.

a parody of didactic poetry) and the *Liber medicinalis* of Quintus Serenus.[5] The Mediterranean tradition of medical verse would be continued primarily in the ever-expanding poem known as the *Regimen sanitatis salernitanum* or *Flos medicinae*, associated with physicians from Salerno in southern Italy but not necessarily produced there.[6] The most popular works of medical verse, judging from manuscript survivals, were not from the Mediterranean but from Northern Europe, such as the verse herbals of Walahfrid Strabo (early ninth century), Macer Floridus (a pseudonym for the Loire poet Odo de Meung, late eleventh century), and Henry of Huntingdon (*c.* 1135), as well as the verse lapidaries of Marbod of Rennes (late eleventh century).[7] Surviving in only one manuscript, but also relevant to this discussion of Constantine, is the verse lapidary of Henry of Huntingdon (*c.* 1135).[8] These collections of poems, while covering much of the same therapeutic and pharmacological information as their prose cousins, are often treated as footnotes to the supposedly more serious and legitimate prose works of scholar-physicians.[9] As will be clear from examples below, medical poems were not frivolous adaptations of prose works but can be

---

[5]   Ovid, *Amores, Medicamina faciei femineae, Ars amatoria, Remedia amoris*, ed. E.J. Kenney, rev. edn (Oxford: Oxford University Press, 1994); Quintus Serenus, *Liber Medicinalis*, ed. and trans. R. Pépin (Paris: Presses Universitaires de France, 1950).

[6]   The shortest and, most likely, oldest version of the poem in 364 lines is printed in Gustavo Barbensi (ed.), *Regimen sanitatis salernitanum* (Florence: L. Olschki, 1947). Much longer versions of the poem, of 2,130 and 3,520 lines, can be found in the *Collectio Salernitana* edited by Salvatore De Renzi (5 vols, Naples: Filiatre-Sebezio, 1852–59), 1:445–516 and 5:1–104.

[7]   Walahfrid Strabo, *Hortulus*, ed. Cataldo Roccaro (Palermo: Herbita, 1979); *Macer floridus de viribus herbarum*, ed. Ludwig Choulant (Leipzig: L. Voss, 1832), repr. in *Höhepunkte der Klostermedizin: der "Macer Floridus" und das Herbarium des Vitus Auslasser*, with introduction and German translation by Johannes Gottfried Mayer and Konrad Goehl (Holzminden: Reprint-Verlag Leipzig, 2001). The last herbal mentioned was discovered and partially edited by A.G. Rigg, "Henry of Huntingdon's Herbal," *Mediaeval Studies* 65 (2003): 213–92, and will be published in its entirety as Henry of Huntingdon, *Anglicanus ortus: A Verse Herbal of the Twelfth Century*, ed. and trans. Winston Black (Toronto: Pontifical Institute of Mediaeval Studies, 2012). Marbode's lapidary has been edited by John M. Riddle, *Marbode of Rennes' (1035–1123) "De lapidibus" Considered as a Medical Treatise with Text, Commentary and C.W. King's Translation, together with Text and Translation of Marbode's Minor Works on Stones* (Wiesbaden: Franz Steiner, 1977); and more recently by María Esthera Herrera, *Marbodo de Rennes Lapidario (Liber lapidum)* (Paris: Les Belles Lettres, 2005).

[8]   See Winston Black, "Henry of Huntingdon's Lapidary Rediscovered and His *Anglicanus ortus* Reassembled," *Mediaeval Studies* 68 (2006): 43–87.

[9]   Only one passing mention is given to Macer's herbal by Plinio Prioreschi in his otherwise encyclopedic *A History of Medicine*, vol. 5: *Medieval Medicine* (Omaha: Horatius Press, 2003), 573. Minta Collins, while she does focus on illustrated herbals, relegates Macer to one note in *Medieval Herbals: The Illustrative Traditions* (Toronto: University of Toronto Press, 2000), 284

seen as independent medical treatises with their own view and presentation of medicinal ingredients, their qualities and applications.

A few examples should suffice to demonstrate the vital role that medical verse played in the education and practice of the medieval cleric and physician. By far the most popular was *De viribus herbarum* (*On the Powers of Herbs*) of Macer Floridus, surviving in well over one hundred manuscripts, translated into most European vernaculars as well as Hebrew, and extant in at least 20 fifteenth- and sixteenth-century editions.[10] Writing in the 1180s, Alexander Neckam prescribed for the education of a well-formed priest the study of a significant number of medical texts, juxtaposing Macer with works of Galen, Constantine (the *Pantegni* is named specifically), Isaac the Jew, Dioscorides, and Alexander Tralles.[11] Neckam also based the seventh distinction of his encyclopedic poem *Laus sapientie divine* on Macer's herbal.[12] Bernat Serra, royal surgeon successively to kings Jaume and Alfons IV of Aragon in the 1320s and 1330s, still retained a copy of Macer together with the ancient masterworks of Galen and Hippocrates and newer technical literature on surgery.[13] Medical verse played a role in formal medical education at late medieval universities. Macer was a prime authority for Rufinus, teaching in Bologna in the 1290s and composing his monumental *De virtutibus herbarum*.[14] Verses frequently appear in copies of the scholastic

---

n. 9. John Riddle has been a happy exception to this trend, as witnessed by his edition and study of Marbode's lapidary, which he subtitled, "Considered as a Medical Treatise."

[10]   Discussed in the work of Bruce P. Flood, Jr.: "Macer Floridus: A Medieval Herbalism," unpublished Ph.D. dissertation (University of Colorado, 1968), and "The Medieval Tradition of 'Macer Floridus," *Pharmacy in History* 18 (1976): 62–6.

[11]   *Alexandri Neckam Sacerdos ad altare*, ed. Christopher J. McDonough, Corpus Christianorum Continuatio Mediaevalis 227 (Turnhout: Brepols, 2010), 200: "Studium medicine usibus filiorum Ade perutile subire quis desiderans audiat Iohannitium et tam aphorismos quam pronostica Ypocratis et Tegni Galieni et Pantegni. Huius operis auctor est Galienus, set translator Constantinus. Legat etiam tam particulares quam uniuersales dietas Ysaac et librum urinarum et uiaticum Constantini cum libro urinarum et libro pulsuum et Diascoriden et Macrum, in quibus de naturis herbarum agitur, et libros Alexandri." Cf. C.H. Haskins, *Studies in the History of Mediaeval Science* (Cambridge, MA: Harvard University Press, 1924), 356–76, with this passage found at 374–5; Cornelius O'Boyle, *The Art of Medicine: Medical Teaching at the University of Paris, 1250–1400* (Leiden: Brill, 1998), 12–13, 116–20.

[12]   *Alexandri Neckam De naturis rerum libri duo, with the Poem of the Same Author, De laudibus divinae sapientiae*, ed. Thomas Wright, Rolls Series 34 (London: Longman, Roberts, & Green, 1863), 472–81.

[13]   Michael R. McVaugh, "Royal Surgeons and the Value of Medical Learning: The Crown of Aragon, 1300–1350," in Luis García-Ballester et al. (eds), *Practical Medicine from Salerno to the Black Death* (Cambridge: Cambridge University Press, 1994), 211–36, at 232.

[14]   *The Herbal of Rufinus*, ed. Lynn Thorndike and F.S. Benjamin, Jr. (Chicago: University of Chicago Press, 1946), xxix, 2, 3, *et passim*.

medical compilation known as the *Ars medicine* or *Articella*. Most common were Giles of Corbeil's poems on *Urines* and *Pulses* with sets of glosses, the *De cognitione quarundam medicinarum* (possibly also by Giles), while the herbal of Macer continued to remain popular beyond the Middle Ages.[15] Also commonly included with copies of the *Ars medicine* were verses on phlebotomy, the humors and temperaments, and weights and measures necessary for the practicing physician or apothecary.[16]

There clearly was a market for poems on pharmacological and medical topics and a place for them in a physician's or medical student's library—but why? Few medieval medical poems, no matter how charming or artful their verse, can be credited with originality in terms of their content. Originality was not the goal of composing medical verse, but accessibility and memorability. Verse herbals, especially that of Macer Floridus, served as handy compilations and abbreviations of lengthier, more complicated prose works primarily from the Mediterranean, such as the *De materia medica* of Dioscorides, the *Natural History* of Pliny the Elder, the *Herbarius* of Pseudo-Apuleius, and the *Medicinae ex holeribus et pomis* of Gargilius Martialis, not to mention Constantine's *Liber graduum* by the late eleventh century. Yet verse herbals were not simply mnemonic repositories of ancient pharmacological knowledge. A poet, according to his own whim, the needs of his audience, and his personal knowledge or ignorance, modified, abbreviated, and added to his sources, sometimes drastically changing their original sense. More importantly, the demands of medieval Latin verse, which in the case of didactic poetry was almost always quantitative, in dactylic hexameters, required that the poet change or omit words as necessary to fit the meter.

A number of authors, active mostly during the "long twelfth century," included poems based on Constantine's *Liber graduum* in their verse herbals: Macer Floridus in his *De viribus herbarum*, Henry of Huntingdon in his *Anglicanus ortus* (containing his verse herbal and verse lapidary), and the authors of several anonymous herbals found in manuscript medical collections (three of which I will discuss). The anonymous poems are difficult to find and trace, not only because they were widely copied and inserted into medical miscellanies, and modified or added to as later copyists saw fit, but also because the overwhelming popularity of Macer's *De viribus herbarum* meant that any Latin poem on herbal simples, or even any herbal in prose, after the twelfth century could circulate under the name

---

[15]   O'Boyle, *The Art of Medicine*, 106–7, 112–13, 117–18.

[16]   Cornelius O'Boyle, *Thirteenth- and Fourteenth-century Copies of the "Ars Medicine": A Checklist and Contents Descriptions of the Manuscripts* (Cambridge: Wellcome Unit for the History of Medicine, 1998), 35, 62, 64, 74, 105.

of "Macer."[17] Two manuscripts of English provenance, for example, include verse adaptations of Constantine by one or more unknown poets, integrated with the poems of Macer and Henry.[18] By the end of the Middle Ages, many anonymous herbal poems had been accepted as part of the Macer tradition and printed alongside the original 77 poems generally accepted as genuine Macer. The *editio princeps* of Macer (Naples, 1477) includes nine extra poems, based primarily on Pseudo-Apuleius with one ("De ematite") cobbled together from three poems in Marbod of Rennes' *De lapidibus*.[19] Two later imprints of Macer (Frankfurt, 1540; Hamburg, 1590, copied in Leipzig, 1590) include a nearly identical set of poems (20 in the former, 19 in the latter), different from those in the *editio princeps*, and most likely written long after the real Macer.[20] These are based on the herbals of Pseudo-Apuleius and Dioscorides, among others, but not on Constantine's. Of greatest interest here is a fourth set of pseudonymous poems found in a late copy of Macer in Wolfenbüttel (Herzog-August-Bibliothek, MS Guelf. 58. 6. Aug. folio), dated 1508.[21] There are ten extra poems, seven of which are from Constantine the African.[22]

Despite the evident attraction of Constantine's works as a source for medical poems, he is rarely named by the poets. Neither Macer Floridus nor Henry of Huntingdon indicate that they know who wrote the *Liber graduum*, while they are both eager to drop the names of Hippocrates, Galen, Dioscorides, Pliny, Walahfrid Strabo, and others, whether or not they had read their actual works. Nonetheless, Henry is aware that, when he borrows from Constantine, his source is something special, even exotic. Book 6 of his *Anglicanus ortus* treats

---

[17]   One of the best-known examples is the Middle English herbal of John Lelamour in London, British Library, MS Sloane 5, fols 113–57, purporting to be a translation of "Macer the philizofur" (fol. 57r) when it is not. See David Moreno Olalla, "*The fautys to amende*: On the Interpretation of the *Explicit* of Sloane 5, ff. 13–57, and Related Matters," *English Studies* 88 (2007): 119–42.

[18]   Oxford, Bodleian Library, MS Digby 13, fols 89v–91r (s. xii), and Cambridge, Trinity College, MS O. 9. 10, fols 89r–108r (s. xv).

[19]   These nine poems were printed separately as "Floridi Macri de viribus herbarum capita," in Friedrich Anton Reuss (ed.), *Walafridi Strabi Hortulus: carmen ad cod. ms veterumque editionum fidem recensitum, lectionis varietate notisque instructum* (Würzburg: Stahel, 1834), 93–9.

[20]   Printed by Choulant in his edition, *Macer floridus de viribus herbarum*, 124–40.

[21]   Described by Choulant, ibid., 25.

[22]   The poems are "Quinquefolium," "Agaricus," "Gentiana," "Proserpinata," "Liquiritia," "Lupinus," "Solsequium," "Saliunca," "Sarcocolla," and "Sambucus." These 10 are printed by Reuss in "Floridi Macri de viribus herbarum capita" after his edition, *Walafridi Strabi Hortulus*, 100–105, hereafter cited as Reuss. Nine of the 10 poems (less "Saliunca") were reprinted in *Der deutsche "Macer": Vulgatfassung mit einem Abdruck des lateinischen Macer Floridus "De viribus herbarum"*, ed. Bernhard Schnell with William Crossgrove (Tübingen: Niemeyer, 2003), 476–9.

40 herbs, and is divided into two sections of 12 and 28 poems, separated by a verse interlude. The first section is based mostly on Macer with some Constantine, but the second is based almost entirely on Constantine's *Liber graduum*. The change is indicated in the interlude, which includes a conversation between the narrator and a wise old man, in which the narrator admits he knows about only the first 12 spices and passes the narration on to the old man:

> Then I replied: "Whether you are Socrates or of Chrysippus' race,
> O learned father, it is fitting that a people's poet fulfill
> The wishes of the people: they scarcely know these spices,
> And their names and virtues are known to me, but not of others."
> He replied to this: "I will add what the Arab once taught,
> And what the Chinese and Indian, traveling among them."[23]

Even though the *Liber graduum* gives no indication of where it was written and only rarely mentions where the simples come from, Henry clearly associated the work with foreign, even pagan, lands. As far as he (or rather, the character of the old man) knew, the information in his copy of the *Liber graduum* was penned by Arab, Chinese, and Indian philosophers. We may never know if Henry was intentionally covering up Constantine's identity or if he genuinely did not know it, but in either case he lends a feeling of novelty and exoticism to his work by attributing the material not to the usual ancients of the Mediterranean world but to knowledge of the Orient filtered through Greek intermediaries (as represented by the old man).

There was another medical poet, though, who not only knew that Constantine was the author of the *Liber graduum* and makes that clear in his herbal, but also made up for Macer's omission by pretending to be Macer (who was usually thought to be the ancient, not eleventh-century, author Aemilius Macer). This anonymous poet compiled a verse herbal of 90 poems, found in a fifteenth-century manuscript of English provenance (Cambridge, Trinity College, MS O. 9. 10, fols 89r–108r). Many of the poems are by Macer, Henry,

---

[23] Henry of Huntingdon, *Anglicanus ortus*, Book 6 Interlude, lines 8–13 (ed. Rigg, "Henry of Huntingdon's Herbal," 286–7; translation is my own):
> Tunc ego: "Seu Socrates sis uel de gente Crisippi,
> Docte pater, uulgo uulgarem ferre poetam
> Vota decet: uix has nouerunt, et michi note
> Sunt harum uires et nomina, non aliarum."
> Ille sub hec: "Quod Arabs quondam, quod Serus et Yndus
> Inter eos peregrinantes, docuere reponam."

and another, earlier anonymous poet,[24] but the compiler added lines and poems of his own based on information primarily from Constantine's *Liber graduum*. One poem in particular (called "Cuscute," fol. 93r) is based on two separate entries from Constantine (*Cuscute* and *Cacollae*, dodder and Guinea pepper or grains of paradise). The poet says of *cuscute*:

> It should be drunk with sugar-vinegar by the feverish
> (Since Constantine says it is particularly good for health),
> Especially if it is for boys suffering with a semi-tertian fever.[25]

The authority of Constantine must have been considered valuable, but the author, not one to hedge his bets, also pretends to be Macer himself. Apart from the obvious cachet of claiming to be a master herbalist who is citing another master, this claim may have been made in order to deal with Constantine's statement that "Guinea pepper is as beneficial as dodder" ("Cacollae ualet sicut cuscute," p. 347). This raises the question of the relation of these two herbs, a question "Macer" patently refuses to answer:

> Whatever dodder has they also say that Guinea pepper has,
> Which I, Macer, neither say nor deny is a variety of dodder.[26]

Constantine, the named authority for *cuscute*, is demoted to "they" and "Macer" takes his place, as if to say, if even the great Macer cannot explain the relationship of these two plants, no one can.

These examples provide an indication of how medieval medical poets viewed the *Liber graduum* when they used it as a source, if they thought about it all. But what exactly happened to Constantine's material when written as verse?

---

[24]   Verses by this other poet, who I believe is different from the compiler of the Trinity manuscript, are found in the twelfth-century manuscript mentioned above, Oxford, Bodleian Library, MS Digby 13, fols 89v–91r.

[25]   Anonymous, "Cuscute" (Cambridge, Trinity College, MS O. 9. 10, fol. 93r), lines 9–11:
Cum oxizacra bibitum sit febricitanti
(Ut Constantinus dicit speciale salutis),
Maxime si pueris laborantibus emitriteo [*ms* emitrites].
This is based on Constantine, *Cuscute*, p. 345: "Cum oxysaccharo bibitum conducit diu febricitantibus, maxime pueris, et haemitriteo ueteri laborantibus." All translations are my own unless otherwise indicated.

[26]   Anonymous, "Cuscute" (Cambridge, Trinity College O. 9. 10, fol. 93r), lines 12–13:
Cuscute quicquid habet dicunt et habere catalle,
Cuscute quam speciem nec dico, nec abnego Macer.

In the following survey, my focus will be on those poems of which significant portions are based on passages from the *Liber graduum*, but there also exist many poems in which the author has based only a line or two on Constantinian pharmacology. The most famous practitioner of this method was Macer Floridus. Over a century ago H. Stadler recognized that Macer based his herbal not only on Pliny, Gargilius Martialis, and the Latin Dioscorides, but also on Constantine's *Liber graduum*.[27] Nearly every entry in the *Liber graduum* begins with a statement of the herb, spice, or mineral's dominant Galenic qualities (hot or cold and wet or dry) and their respective strength measured from the first to fourth degree. This information helped the physician or apothecary prescribe herbs of the proper strength and quality according to the patient's condition. Several of Macer's poems contain similar passages on an herb's degrees, and the *Liber graduum* is the most likely possible source for such information in the later eleventh century. To give two brief examples:

Constantine, *Absinthium*, **344–5**	**Macer no. 3, "Absinthium," lines 52–3**
Wormwood [is] hot in the first degree, dry in the second. ("Absinthium calidum in primo gradu, siccum in secundo.")	The heat of Wormwood is said to be In the first degree, its dry power in the second. ("In primo calor esse gradu, vis sicca secundo Dicitur Absinthii.")
Constantine, *Apium*, **379**	**Macer no. 8, "Apium," lines 339–40**
Celery is hot at the beginning of the third degree, dry in the middle. ("Apium calidum est in initio tertii gradus, siccum in medio.")	It is also said to be of virtue hot and dry; The third degree is granted to it in each. ("Virtutis calidae siccae quoque dicitur esse; Tertius a medicis datus est gradus huic in utroque.")

Even when the poet is presented with the simple matter of repeating the degrees of an herb, there are differences in how he could rephrase his material. In the first example on wormwood (*absinthium*), Macer has copied Constantine's statement in its essentials, giving the degrees of each quality. The only change is a turn of phrase in which Macer indicates the degree of the "heat" and the "dry power" rather than of wormwood itself. In the second example, however, the poem shows a significant deviation from Constantine's original meaning. Constantine is usually satisfied with giving the degree as first through fourth, but in some instances he is more precise, specifying that the herb is in the beginning,

---

[27] H. Stadler, "Die Quellen des Macer Floridus," *Archiv für die Geschichte der Naturwissenschaften und der Technik* 1 (1908): 52–65.

middle, or end (*initium, medium, finis*) of a certain degree of a Galenic quality. Such is the case with celery (*apium*), which "is hot at the beginning of the third degree, dry in the middle [of the third]." Macer has entirely omitted this precision of degree, perhaps because he could not fit the phrase into his meter (the first three syllables of *initium* are all scanned short, which is impossible in dactylic hexameter), or simply because he did not understand or care about this finer qualification of degree.

The English archdeacon and historian Henry of Huntingdon similarly turned to Constantine's *Liber graduum* to supplement the poems in his verse herbal, about half of which is an imitation of Macer's *De viribus herbarum*. For example, Henry's poem 3.19 on centaury, "Centaurea," is based primarily on Macer's own "Centaurea" (no. 53, lines 1709–27). Macer does not describe centaury's Galenic qualities or degrees, apart from stating, "it is said to have a drying power."[28] Henry adds to Macer's material: "It is proven to dry and heat in the second degree, unless my books deceive."[29] Surely these books (*scripta*) are Constantine's *Liber graduum*, in which it is said of *centaurea*, "Some say that it is hot and dry in the second degree."[30] Henry must have felt that Macer's poem on centaury, while worth imitating, did not provide the most up-to-date information that he or his audience desired. Constantine's *Liber graduum* was the best source available in the first half of the twelfth century for new herbal information set in a rational framework.

For much of Macer's herbal (the first 65 poems), when he has borrowed from Constantine, it is usually only a description of the herb's degrees. Outside of a few lines (95–103, 1318–22), most of his material comes from much earlier herbalists, primarily Pliny and Gargilius Martialis. The case is different for the last 12 poems (nos 66–77), which he devotes explicitly to spices (*species*) rather than herbs.[31] Most of these spices, even if known to the ancient Mediterranean, came from the Indian subcontinent and southeast Asia, and a full description of their medicinal attributes was not available to Europeans until the appearance of Constantine's works and a newly enlarged and alphabetized

---

[28]   Macer, *De viribus herbarum*, line 1714 (ed. Choulant): "Desiccativae virtutis dicitur esse."

[29]   Henry of Huntingdon, *Anglicanus ortus*, 3.19, lines 3–4 (ed. and trans. Black): "Siccare secundo / Atque calere gradu (nisi fallunt scripta) probatur."

[30]   Constantine, *Liber graduum*, 362: "Quidam autem dicunt eam calidam et siccam esse in secundo gradu."

[31]   Macer Floridus, *De viribus herbarum*, lines 2056–8 (ed. Choulant):
Carmine iam dictis aliquot vulgaribus herbis
Nunc species illas, quas cunctis iam prope notas
Usus vendendi fecit, tentabo referre ...

version of the Latin Dioscorides, possibly also compiled by Constantine.[32] As should be expected, most of these poems (nos 67, 69–77) are based entirely on passages from Constantine.[33] Because of the significant differences between these 12 poems and Macer's poems nos 1–65 and because of the absence of poems 66–77 from several early manuscripts of *De viribus herbarum*, William Crossgrove has suggested that the herbal of "Macer" was actually composed in two parts, perhaps by two different authors.[34] Perhaps this is true, but whatever the case almost all copies of *De viribus herbarum* contain the poems of the late eleventh-century "Macer" who was dependent partly on Constantine's *Liber graduum*, and this was the version known to Henry of Huntingdon and most other readers of Macer.

When we have at hand a selection of poems, each based entirely on passages from the *Liber graduum*, it is easier to see where the author saw the need for changes, misunderstood his source, or omitted passages. Let us take a pair of short examples to examine closely, Macer's poems on galangal (*galanga*) and zedoary (*zedoar*), numbered 70 and 71 in Choulant's edition:

Constantine, *Galanga*, 372	**Macer no. 70, "Galanga," lines 2125–30**
Galangal is hot and dry in the third degree. It strengthens a phlegmatic stomach, aids the power of digestion, releases windiness, makes the mouth smell sweet, cures colic, heats the kidneys, and increases sexual drive. Cinnamon is beneficial in the same manner.[35]	Galangal, when taken, loosens phlegm in the stomach, And fortifies it if it should be phlegmatic. Taken, it chases off the enclosed wind of the inner parts, Helps the digestive power by this and

---

[32] On the new Dioscorides, see John M. Riddle, "Dioscorides," in Ferdinand E. Cranz and Paul Oskar Kristeller (eds), *Catalogus Translationum et Commentariorum: Mediaeval and Renaissance Latin Translations and Commentaries*, vol. 4 (Washington, D.C.: Catholic University of America Press, 1980), 1–143, at 20–27. A glossed version of the Latin Alphabetical Dioscorides is printed in Dioscorides, *De materia medica* (Colle: Johannes de Medemblick, 1478), reprinted in Lyons in 1512. I have used the twelfth-century manuscript copy in Cambridge, Jesus College, MS 44, which represents a tradition much closer to Macer than the later, glossed edition.

[33] Macer's "Pyrethrum," no. 67, is based on Constantine, 381; "Cyminum," no. 69 (374–5); "Galanga," no. 70 (372); "Zedoar," no. 71 (374); "Gariofilus," no. 72 (357); "Cinnama," no. 73 (368); "Costus," no. 74 (366–7); "Spica," no. 75 (348); "Thus," no. 76 (357); "Aloe," no. 77 (354–5).

[34] William C. Crossgrove, "Zur Datierung des 'Macer Floridus'," in Werner E. Gerabek et al. (eds), *Licht der Natur: Medizin in Fachliteratur und Dichtung. Festschrift für Gundolf Keil zum 60. Geburtstag* (Göppingen: Kümmerle, 1994), 55–63.

[35] "Galanga calida et sicca est in tertio gradu. Stomachum phlegmaticum corroborat, uim digestiuam adiuuat, uentositatem dissoluit, os odoriferum reddit, colicam curat, renes calefacit, et libidinem augmentat. Eodem modo ualet cinnamomum."

cures the colicky,

When eaten, it improves the mouth's odor not a little,

And taken, increases the heat of Venus and the kidneys.[36]

Constantine, *Zedoar*, 374

Zedoary [is] hot in the third degree, dry in the first. It is [useful] against poison and reptile bites. It releases swelling and heavy windiness, fortifies the stomach, provokes the appetite, [and] removes foulness of breath caused by garlic, if the zedoary is taken after the garlic. It similarly removes the smell of wine from the mouth.[37]

Macer no. 71, "Zedoar," lines 2131–40

They affirm that zedoary excellently counteracts

Swallowed poisons, and when drunk cures reptile bites.

It fortifies the stomach when taken and produces

Healthful belches, and represses distaste by frequent use;

They say it cures an old pain of the stomach

If the patient chews it on an empty stomach,

And thus slowly devours corrupt saliva in the mouth.

It is said when drunk to repel stomach worms;

It drives from the mouth the stench which garlic makes

And repels the odor of drinking too much wine.[38]

---

[36]   Flegmonem stomachi sumptum Galanga resolvit,
Et si flegmaticus fuerit corroborat illum,
Inclusum ventum sumptum fugat interiorum,
Vim digestivam iuvat hoc colicisque medetur,
Oris non modicum mansum commendat odorem,
Augmentat sumptum veneris renumque calorem.

[37]   "Zedoar calidum in tertio gradu, siccum in primo. Est contra uenenum et morsus reptilium. Inflationem et grossam uentositatem dissoluit, stomachum confortat, appetitum irritat, putorem oris propter allia amputat, si post allia zedoar accipiatur. Similiter et uini odorem ab ore aufert."

[38]   Adprime sumptis Zedoar obstare venenis
Affirmant, et reptilium morsus levat haustum.
Sumptum confortat stomachum ructusque salubres
Commovet, et crebro fastidia reprimit usu;
Antiquum stomachi dicunt curare dolorem,
Illud si patiens ieiuno masticet ore,
Et sic infectam sensim voret ore salivam.
Lumbricos ventris depellere dicitur haustum;
Allia quem faciunt foetorem pellit ab ore
Et nimium bibiti vini depellit odorem.

In terms of basic information, Macer has changed little by adapting these entries of the *Liber graduum* into verse, nor has he added anything significant. But if we treat the poems as medical documents which a student read or to which a physician referred, rather than merely as degraded imitations of Constantine, we can trace some vital differences. Most obviously, Macer has omitted the Galenic qualities from both of his poems. This is probably intentional, as he does give the qualities in most poems in the latter part of his herbal. Also omitted is the comparison to cinnamon at the end of Constantine's *Galanga*. In most cases, Macer's herbal poems stand alone as simples and do not make reference to other herbs, and Macer may have wanted to continue that pattern.

Macer's "Galanga" provides several variations on how Constantine's *Liber graduum* could be adapted into verse without changing the meaning too much. In lines 2125–6 Macer expands on Constantine's statement that galangal "strengthens a phlegmatic stomach" by saying that "Galangal, when taken, loosens phlegm in the stomach, and fortifies it if it should be phlegmatic." There are two ways to understand this change: Macer is confused about the meaning of *phlegmaticus* or is helpfully explaining what it means. In either case, the reader of the poem is now led to believe that galangal can perform two separate actions with regard to excess phlegm where Constantine described only one. The following two lines of Macer (2127–8) do not change Constantine's meaning, though Macer replaces "windiness" with "the enclosed wind of the interior parts," making clearer to the novice what is meant by the technical term *ventositas*. He has also missed or removed the statement that galangal "heats the kidneys" (*renes calefacit*), perhaps simply because he did not want to devote an entirely new line of verse to it. In the last line (2130), galangal does not "increase sexual drive," as found in Constantine's sterile language, but it "increases the heat of Venus." This is the sort of poetic turn, clothing technical language in a classical and mythological veil, that could make didactic verse more enjoyable, yet perhaps less immediately practical.

The second example, "Zedoar," shows how Macer could more thoroughly change the sense of a passage in Constantine by glossing statements and bringing in extra material to supplement his poem. Both versions emphasize zedoary's ability to help stomach problems and bad breath, yet Macer explains and expands on Constantine's terse indications of the herb's abilities using the new Alphabetical Latin Dioscorides (ALD) available in the eleventh century, which includes exotic spices like zedoary not found in the older Latin Dioscorides. For the stomach, Constantine simply says that zedoary "releases swelling and heavy windiness, fortifies the stomach, [and] provokes the appetite." His readers are left to their own devices to understand exactly how zedoary accomplishes these cures. Macer, however, explains: zedoary removes gas ("it produces healthful belches") and creates appetite ("it represses distaste [*fastidia*] by frequent use"). The first gloss comes by way of the ALD, which says that zedoary "causes belching and is suitable for the stomach,"[39] yet the second seems to be Macer's own invention. These details are not in *Liber graduum*, but it was the sort of material Macer must have felt his readers desired, that is, what exactly should a physician do to handle the problems indicated, generally without comment, by Constantine.

The rest of the poem provides contrasting examples of Macer on the one hand closely imitating his source and, on the other, finding it in need of clarification and expansion. In Macer's last two lines, we can see that he was satisfied with the model provided by Constantine or could find nothing to add; both works state, with only small differences in vocabulary, that zedoary removes bad breath caused by garlic and wine. Lines 2135–8 of the poem are not in the *Liber graduum* and probably should be seen as an elaborate gloss on Constantine's *stomachum confortat* ("fortifies the stomach"), a statement which begs explanation. How does it comfort the stomach? Macer adds three specific ways in which zedoary accomplishes this: it cures a lingering pain in the stomach, removes tainted saliva, and forces out stomach worms. The first and third cures come from the same passage of the ALD (see note 39), yet I have found no source for the *infecta saliva*, which could be understood as an expansion of Constantine's statements on bad breath, the source of which he does not name. Macer's poem on zedoary shows how in only ten lines of verse, material from Constantine's *Liber graduum* could be clarified, supplemented, and defined to make it more useful and more memorable for a physician or scholar seeking medical information.

Now that we have taken a close look at Macer's methods of adapting Constantine, let us turn briefly to another author, an anonymous poet whose work I have found in two manuscripts (Oxford, Bodleian Library, MS Digby 13; Cambridge, Trinity College, MS O. 9. 10). The Digby manuscript has been dated to the later twelfth century, which provides a *terminus ante quem* for this poet. The example below, comparing the anonymous poem "Luvestica" (lovage) with its source, Constantine's *Ligusticum*, shows that Macer was not alone in revising, glossing, and rewording entries in the *Liber graduum* for the poetic medium.

---

[39]   "Zedoary," Alphabetical Latin Dioscorides, Cambridge, Jesus College, MS 44, fol. 145r: "Zedoaria [zedoar *ante corr.*] calide uirtutis est et uiscide, unde et lumbricos occidit, ructum facit, et stomacho aptum est, cuius dolorem antiquum ieiunis sumptum masticatione tollit."

Constantine, *Ligusticum*, 379–80	**Anonymous, "Luvestica" (ed. Black, from MS Digby 13, fol. 90v, and Trinity MS O. 9. 10, fol. 98v)**
Lovage [is] hot and dry in the third degree. It digests food, opens blockages of the liver from the cold humor, relieves a pain of the stomach. It releases windiness and swelling, rumbling and spasming. It provokes urine and menstruation.[40]	Lovage is said [to be] of a dry and hot nature. Its degree is third. Hence the juice digests food well, Provokes urine and menstruation, and thus clears Hoarseness and cures a swollen and hard belly. If it is ingested when cooked with wine or beer It cures the liver; mixed with wine, it relieves the stomach. Spasming and rumbling of the stomach are cured by it And the wind which harms, if drunk often with soda.[41]

The simplicity of Constantine's entry suggests that the reader of the *Liber graduum* is expected to know how to use the herb. Its qualities and virtues are described, but no recipes are provided. The poet provides a more practical and didactic document for a physician despite the artifice of his medium: the simple addition of "hence" (*hinc*) in line 2 establishes the connection between lovage's hot and dry nature and its ability to accomplish the cures that follow. Such a connection could be assumed from Constantine's passage, but is not stated explicitly. The poet adds specific recipes for the cures listed by Constantine: the juice of the plant is used to aid digestion and bring out urine and menstrual blood (lines 2–3), lovage cooked with wine or beer cures the liver (lines 5–6), or lovage with soda (*nitro*) helps stomach problems (twisting, rumbling, and gas, lines 7–8). We are also told that lovage clears up hoarseness (*rauclum*), an addition not found in Constantine's passage nor in the poems on lovage in the herbals of Macer and Henry of Huntingdon. While the poet provides more detail in terms of practical recipes, he nonetheless strips away important details of a more theoretical nature, demonstrating the tension between *theorica* and *practica* explicit in Constantine's *Pantegni*. The poet simply says that lovage cures the liver (*curat epar*), where Constantine is more specific: lovage cures the

---

[40] "Ligusticum calidum et siccum in tertio gradu. Cibum digerit, oppilationem epatis de frigido humore aperit, dolorem stomachi mitigat. Ventositatem et inflationem, rugitum et torsionem dissoluit. Vrinam et menstrua prouocat."

[41] Nature sicce calideque luuestica fertur.
    Tercius est gradus. Hinc succus bene digerit escam,
    Prouocat urinas et menstrua sic quoque rauclum
    Sanat et inflato uentri duroque medetur.
    Cum uino uel ceruisia si cocta uoretur
    Curat epar; mitigat stomachum uino sociata.
    Tortio curatur per eam uentrisque rugitus
    Quique nocet uentus nitro si sepe bibatur.

liver because it opens up blockages (*oppilationes*) in it caused by the cold humor (or by "cold moisture"). A physician using only the poem to help a patient would be led to believe that lovage is a cure-all for the liver, or perhaps to draw the conclusion that its hot and dry powers at the relatively high third degree are effective in countering excessive coolness in any part of the body.

The type and variety of changes possible in a verse adaptation of Constantine become more apparent when we possess two different poems based on the same entry. Such is the case with Constantine's passage on the field mushroom (*agaricus* or *agaricum*), which was versified by both Henry of Huntingdon and yet another anonymous poet whose work is found in a late medieval manuscript (Wolfenbüttel, Herzog-August-Bibliothek, MS Guelf. 58. 6. Aug. folio), probably a different author from those in the Digby and Trinity manuscripts.

Constantine, *Agaricus*, 346	Anonymous, "Agaricus" (ed. Reuss, 101)
Agaric is twofold, namely male and female, yet the female is more praiseworthy. Its shape is recognized like this: little bits are found within it, one placed on top of another. The male, however, is round within and smooth. Both of these are hot in the first degree and dry in the second. It thins out heavy and viscous humors, and dissolves and purges phlegm. It is also [useful] against poison. One measure of it, drunk, is good against liver pain, swelling, strangury, and pain of the kidneys, jaundice, and pains of the womb and its suffocation, and it cures bruising of the skin. Given with new wine it is beneficial for a wounded lung. With sugar-water, it	There are two species of agaric, [as] this fact proves: One, of course, is of the male, and the other of the female, Yet the species of the female is said to be better. But if you desire to recognize the forms of these: [The female has] fruit placed, yet one on top of another, [5] The masculine is soft and round inside, And they are hot in the first degree and dry In the second, but they purge the chest through phlegm, Dissolve, thin out heavy, viscous humors, And this when taken restrains deadly poison. [10] When drunk, it is good against kidney and liver pains, They benefit the lung, and dissolve swellings of the spleen. Likewise they heal those with strangury, jaundice, and pains, They assist fevers, and when taken benefit epileptics, And thus call down a period and fan a wind outside, [15] Thus it heals penises if it is drunk when ground. It is no trouble to say, it is beneficial at any time.[42]

---

[42]   Agarici species geminae sunt; ipsa probat res:
   Altera nempe maris, ac altera sit mulieris,
   Esse tamen melior species fertur mulieris.
   Harum sed formas cognoscere si cupis ipsas,

dissolves swelling of the
spleen. Galen said that it is
purifying, and able to open
a blockage of the inner parts.
Therefore it is [useful] against
jaundice and blockage.
It is also beneficial for
epileptics, and it assists those
who are feverish with stiffness.
It assists those with sciatica and
arthritic pain, provokes
menstruation, [and] releases a
heavy windiness of the womb. It
also cures every pain which is inside
the body.[43]

Impositum fructum super hoc aliud tamen unum,   [5]
Masculus interius est levis atque rotundus,
Inque gradu primo calidi sunt atque secundo
Sicci, sed purgant pectus per flegmata, solvunt,
Grosos [*sic*] viscosos humores extenuantur, [*sic*]
Haec et mortiferum restringit sumpta venenum.   [10]
Hausta valet contra renis iecorisque dolores,
Prosunt pulmoni, splenis solvuntque tumores.
Stranguricos simul ictericos sanantque dolores,
Febribus occurrunt, prosunt et sumpta [*sic*] caducis,
Menstrua sicque vocat et ventum ventilat extra,   [15]
Glandes sic sanat haec si contrita bibatur.
Dicere non opus est: haec omni tempore prodest.

[43] "Agaricus duplex est, masculus uidelicet et foemina. Laudabilior tamen est foemina. Cuius forma sic dignoscitur. Intus in ea frustra [*sic, frustula* in edn Lyons (1515), fol. 78r] inueniuntur, unum super aliud positum. Masculus uero est rotundus intrinsecus et lenis. Qui utrique in primo gradu calidus est et siccus in secundo. Grossos et uiscosos humores attenuat, et dissoluit et phlegma purgat. Est etiam contra uenenum. De quo exagium unum potatum ualet contra dolorem epatis, inflationem et stranguiriam et renum dolorem, et icteritiam, et matricis dolores eiusque suffocationem, et cutis liuorem curat. Cum sapa datus prodest uulnerato pulmoni. Cum oxysaccharo, splenis tumorem dissoluit. Gal<ienus> mundificatiuum esse dixit, et oppilationis uiscerum aperitiuum. Ideo est contra ictericiam de oppilatione. Valet etiam epilepticis, et febricitantibus cum rigore occurrit. Ischiaticis et artetico dolori occurrit, menstrua prouocat, grossam uentositatem uuluae dissoluit. Curat etiam omnem dolorem qui est intra corpus."

Henry of Huntingdon, "Agaricum," *Anglicanus ortus* 6.2.2 (ed. and trans. Black)
The Mushroom, which Galen says is a diuretic, becomes
A pleasing gift for those with nephritis and pleurisy.
Dioscorides and Oribasius say that this,
When drunk, restrains thick humors and phlegm.
It soothes a swollen liver, strangury will depart   [5]
As does kidney pain. It is beneficial for wombs and for
The jaundiced; with wine must, it cleans wounds of the lungs.
Great Galen, praising the Mushroom, said it makes
The insides clean and at the same time loosens blockages.
One with jaundice profits by it and an epileptic improves.   [10]
It causes menstruation, chases off arthritis, sciatica, and fever,
And, so that the Philosopher might conclude all things, he alone did add:
It purges every hidden thing that bodies may conceal.
This Mushroom is called male, and that one is said to be female;
The one which is masculine is whole, light, and round.   [15]
That female, heavy with small pieces, is more valuable than the male;
It heats in the first degree and in the second dries.[44]

    Constantine, after describing the differences between the male and female varieties of *agaricus* and noting its Galenic degrees, addresses its ability to aid many conditions, including various imbalances of humors, poisoning, pains in the liver, kidneys, and womb, jaundice, and so on. He invokes the authority of Galen concerning mushroom's ability to clean blockages (*oppilationes*) throughout the body and their related conditions.

---

[44]   Agaricum, quod diureticum perhibet Galienus,
      Neffreticis et pleureticis fit amabile munus.
      Hoc Dyaschorides, hoc Oribasius aiunt
      Grossos humores et flecmata stringere potum.
      Inflatum tranquillat epar, strangiria cedet   [5]
      Atque dolor renum. Matricibus yctericisque
      Prodest; cum sapa pulmonis uulnera sanat.
      Agaricum laudans, inquit magnus Galienus:
      Viscera munda facit, simul opilata resoluit.
      Proficit yctericus, ualet epilenticus illo.   [10]
      Menstrua dat, fugat arteticam sciasimque febremque
      Et, quo philosophus concluderet omnia, solus
      Addidit: omne latens quod celant corpora purgat.
      Agaricum dicitur hic mas, hec femina fertur;
      Integer est qui masculus est leuis atque rotundus.   [15]
      Illa fit, ex frustis grauis, prestancius illo,
      Inque gradu primo feruet siccatque secundo.

A poet adapting this material had much, indeed too much, material to work with. If we examine the Wolfenbüttel poet's attempt, several trends appear. In the first place, the poet is a poor Latinist who misunderstood or misread his source at several points (note the ungrammatical *extenuantur*, and the confusion of *fructum* and *frustum*, although the latter is incorrect in the printed versions of Constantine as well). Second, the poet versified the description and remedies in the same order as Constantine, passing by cures that were difficult to put into verse, confusing, or perhaps offensive (all of the feminine problems are omitted apart from *menstrua*). Yet the farther we read in Constantine, the less material appears in the poem: the reference to Galen is omitted, and there is no mention of *oppilationes* (a defining feature of the original) or of sciatica and arthritis (*ischiaticis et artetico*). Why would the poet make these changes? Barring the possibility of a corrupt exemplar, the best explanations would be lack of interest or ignorance of the conditions described, and I am inclined to believe the latter. We must also take into account exhaustion: the versification of technical material replete with words that the poet may never have seen before and did not necessarily know how to scan had to be a difficult undertaking. What we are left with in this case is a poor imitation of Constantine which has little to recommend it apart from the mnemonic value of the meter.

Henry of Huntingdon, on the other hand, was a far superior poet and did not hold himself strictly to the order set down by Constantine. He took many more liberties with his source, while still covering essentially the same topics, and provided a reference in which the key points could be used and recalled far more easily by a physician or student than those in the *Liber graduum*. An important issue for Henry was stressing the authority of his sources (though he does not mention Constantine himself, as noted above). He has taken Constantine's attribution of one statement to Galen and applied it to the entire poem, also bringing in Dioscorides and Oribasius (a Greek medical writer and physician to Julian the Apostate, *c.* 320–400) to agree with Galen. While it is possible that Henry's copy of the *Liber graduum* was attributed to Galen or these other authors, it is just as likely that Henry made up these names to lend greater validity to his information. Not only has Henry assured his readers of the pedigree of his remedies, but he also makes his poem more immediately useful than the anonymous poet's by moving the explanation of mushroom's varieties and virtues to the end and beginning by summing up in only two lines what he sees as the most important curative properties of *agaricus*: it is diuretic and a "lovely gift" for those with nephritis and pleurisy.

At first glance, these descriptions appear to have been taken from some other source than Constantine, but what Henry is doing is providing his poem with an even loftier air of authority by using advanced medical terminology where

Constantine was relatively straightforward and providing specific instances of Constantine's more general claims. Henry came to the logical conclusion that *agaricus* is diuretic from Constantine's statements that "Galen said that [mushroom] is purifying" (*mundificatiuum*) and that it cures *strangiria* (strangury, or difficulty urinating). According to medieval Galenic medicine, a diuretic is used to purify a body of excess humors by purging them through urine, so *mundificatiuus* could be construed as *diureticus*. Following this sort of logic, Henry seems to have interpreted Constantine's claims that *agaricus* cures kidney pain (*renum dolorem*) as referring to *nephritis* (a kidney disease) and that it cures liver pain (*dolorem epatis*) or wounded lungs (*uulnerato pulmoni*) as manifestations of pleurisy. For the rest of his poem, Henry follows his source quite closely, versifying almost every one of Constantine's statements and not leaving out the remedies for the womb, blockages, sciatica, and arthritis which the anonymous Wolfenbüttel poet passed over.

Henry wrote 27 poems in his herbal and one in his lapidary based on the *Liber graduum*.[45] I refer the reader to the Appendix for a list of all of them. In most of these poems, he follows similar patterns of adaptation, summing up the herb or spice's primary virtues at the start, often rearranging the order of material, yet still providing most of Constantine's remedies in a condensed and memorable fashion. One of these poems, though, is different, in that he masterfully combined two different entries from the *Liber graduum* to compose it. The compiler of the Trinity herbal did the same, and I will conclude this survey of Constantinian verse by comparing the two.

The anonymous poem "Cuscute" in the Trinity manuscript was briefly discussed above. As noted there, the poet built this poem from two separate entries in the *Liber graduum*, *Cuscute* (dodder) and *Cacollae* (Guinea pepper, also called *acole*). There is no reason the poet would have attempted such a composite poem if Constantine had not noted their similarity ("Cacollae ualet sicut cuscute"), which provides a new focus for his poem in which *catalle* (for *cacollae*) can be defined in terms of *cuscute* (lines 12–14). Yet this poet has exaggerated their similarity, stating that *catalle* can do whatever *cuscute* can, essentially making them interchangeable. This ability to exchange ingredients was very popular in medieval medical literature, as attested by a wide range of extant *quid pro quo*, or substitution, lists.[46]

---

45   The one poem in the lapidary based on the *Liber graduum* is "Corallus," poem no. 18 in Black, "Henry of Huntingdon's Lapidary Rediscovered." The first six lines of the 12-line poem are based on Constantine's *Corallus* (354), while the rest comes from the lapidary of Marbod of Rennes. I discuss Henry's use of Constantine in the aforementioned article, pp. 66–7.

46   See Alain Touwaide's contribution to this volume, ch. 2, on the *quid pro quo* tradition.

Constantine, *Cuscute* (346) and *Cacollae* (347)

Dodder has diverse virtues, for it has bitterness and brininess, and is hot in the first degree, dry in the second. For this reason, by means of its bitterness and brininess, it is a thinner of humors, especially of red bile. It opens a blockage of liver, spleen, and gall bladder, fortifies the stomach with its bitterness and brininess. It purges veins and cavities of putrid humors. Drunk with sugar-vinegar it is fitting for the feverish, especially boys, and those suffering with an old semi-tertian fever.[47]

Guinea pepper is as beneficial as dodder. It is hot and dry in the first degree. It cures yellow water and *hyposarca* [a kind of dropsy]. It fortifies the liver and produces a sweet-smelling belch. Its juice is suitable for those having dropsy without yellow bile, yet it is changed in the stomach because it is a little viscous.[48]

Anonymous, "Cuscute" (Cambridge, Trinity College, MS O. 9. 10, fol. 93r

Dodder, which many have called *podagra lini*,
Is hot in the first and dry in the second of
   degrees.
It is a thinner of very acidic humors;
It especially restrains the sharpness of red
   bile.
It breaks up blockages of liver, spleen, and
   gall bladder.   [5]
By its brininess it fortifies the stomach and it
Is useful for the veins and cavities of the
   inner parts,
From which it purges heavy and putrid
   humors.
Let it be drunk with sugar-vinegar by the
   feverish
(For Constantine says it's particularly good
   for health),   [10]
Especially if it is for boys suffering with a
   semi-tertian fever.
Whatever dodder has they also say that
   Guinea pepper has,
Which I, Macer, neither say nor deny is a
   variety of dodder.
They call it hot and dry in the first [degree]
   like dodder,
It cures yellow water, as well as *hyposarca*,   [15]

---

[47] "Cuscute diuersarum uirtutum est. Habet enim amaritudinem et ponticitatem, et est calidum in primo gradu, siccum in secundo. Vnde cum sua amaritudine, suaque ponticitate, est humorum attenuatiuum, maxime cholerae rubeae. Oppilationem epatis et splenis et fellis aperit, stomachum cum sua amaritudine et ponticitate confortat. Venas et uasa a putridis humoribus purgat. Cum oxysaccharo bibitum conducit diu febricitantibus, maxime pueris, et haemitriteo ueteri laborantibus."

[48] "Cacollae ualet sicut cuscute, calidum est et siccum in primo gradu. Citrinam aquam atque hyposarcam curat. Epar confortat, et odoriferum ructum generat. Succus eius hydropicis choleram non habentibus, conuenit. In stomacho tamen quia aliquantulum est uiscosum mutatur."

> Fortifies the liver, creates a sweet-smelling
> belch.
> Let its juice when drunk aid those with a cold
> dropsy;
> Eaten, it affects the mood of the stomach by
> its heavy fatness.[49]

This poet made a variety of other changes to his source. Like Henry in his poem "Agaricus," the Trinity compiler has added references to other herbalists (lines 10 and 13) to provide further authority, going so far as to claim to be Macer himself. The poet has supplied a synonym not found in the *Liber graduum*, that is, *cuscute* is known as *podagra lini* (literally, "gout of linen"), a synonym given in the late thirteenth century by the herbalists Rufinus of Bologna and Simon of Genoa.[50] The names used by Constantine came primarily from Greek or Arabic sources, and he rarely supplies synonyms, but the poet, by providing a presumably more common name, has made his herbal accessible to a wider audience. Yet the poet has also removed material, most notably any reference to the *amaritudo* ("bitterness") of *cuscute*. What we have here, however, is probably not a matter of ignoring an unknown word, but rather a problem specific to

---

49   Cuscute, quam multi lini dixere podagram,
　　In graduum primo calida et sicca secundo.
　　Extenuancium [*sic*] est humorum ualde acidorum;
　　Maxime hoc colere rubee restringit acumen.
　　Epatis et splenis, fellis opilata [*ms* epilata] repandit.　　　　　　[5]
　　Ponticitate sua stomacum confortat et ipsa
　　Vtilis est uenis et uasis interiorum,
　　A quibus humores grossos purgat putridosque.
　　Cum oxizacra bibitum sit febricitanti
　　(Vt Constantinus dicit speciale salutis),　　　　　　　　　　　[10]
　　Maxime si pueris laborantibus emitriteo. [*ms* emitrites]
　　Cuscute quicquid habet dicunt et habere catalle,
　　Cuscute quam speciem nec dico nec abnego Macer.
　　In primo calidam dicuntque ut cuscute siccam,
　　Lympham citrinam curat, uero yposarcam,　　　　　　　　　[15]
　　Epar confortat, ructum generat redolentem.
　　Ydropicis gelidis eius ius subueniat haustum;
　　Mansa morum [*sic*] facit stomacho pinguedine crassa.
The final line is seriously confused, and my translation is only a guess at what this poet may have meant.
50   *The Herbal of Rufinus*, 107: "Cuscute, id est, podagra lini, et dicitur etiam gringus." The name is defined by Simon of Genoa (Simon Januensis) in his *Synonyma medicinae, sive Clavis sanationis* (Milan: Antonius Zirotus, 1473), fol. 49vb: "Podagra lini vocatur cuscuta eo quod serpendo linum necat."

quantitative verse: the first four syllables of *amaritudo* scan short-long-short-long, and therefore it cannot scan in the dactylic hexameters used by all of these poets. While he could simply have used the adjective *amarus*, it seems likely that he decided to focus on the herb's *ponticitas* ("brininess"), a word that does scan properly. Further changes could be charted, but the conclusions would be the same: this poet, while ignoring or misunderstanding some of Constantine's entry, had several tools apart from verse itself for making this material more accessible and apparently more authoritative than a prose work, combining similar ingredients, listing authorities, providing synonyms, and more.

In conclusion, if we turn to Henry of Huntingdon's own attempt at combining multiple entries from the *Liber graduum* in one poem, we can see just how extensively a poet could rework entries from the *Liber graduum* into a new medium, providing a commentary on those entries by the very structure of his poem. Constantine composed separate entries on the fruit (*fistula*) and bark (*lignea*) of the cassia tree. In reading the *Liber graduum*, Henry surely saw that these two entries could be more profitably presented as a single poem for easier comparison, just as the anonymous Trinity poet joined *cuscute* and *catalle* because of their similar powers:

Constantine, *Cassia fistula* (346–7) and *Cassia lignea* (369)	Henry of Huntingdon, "Cassia," *Anglicanus ortus* 6.1.6 (ed. Black)
Cassia fruit is midway between hot and cold. Concerning which Galen [says]: a medicine made temperate by a balanced compostion or similar in complexion can be judged as neither hor not cold, wct nor dry. It characteristically purges red bile, destroys the sharpness of blood, and dissolves an abscess which develops from [the blood]. In a gargle it cures abscesses of the throat and pharynx, especially if it is mixed with the juice of nightshade.[51] Cassia bark [is] hot and dry in the third degree. It fortifies the	Cassia bark does not provide the same things as Cassia fruit, For Cassia bark heats and dries in the second degree, But Galen says that Cassia fruit stands between Both degrees. He does not judge it hot, Nor cooling, nor moistening, nor dry— [5] Nature grants that it is effective by such modration. Cassia bark, eaten, strengthens the liver, [*lacuna*] and womb, And all parts retaining primacy in the body, But Cassia fruit purges red bile well. Cassia bark powerfully strengthens feminine parts [10]

---

[51] "Cassia fistula mediocris est inter calidum et frigidum. Vnde Galenus: medicina temperata aequali compositioni uel complexioni similis neque in calidum, neque in frigidum et humidum et siccum potest iudicari. Proprie choleram rubeam purgat, acumen sanguinis extinguit, et apostema ex eo genitum dissoluit. Gargarizata apostemata gulae et faucium curat, praecipue si misceatur cum succo stringni."

stomach, liver, wounds, and all principal body parts, opens blockages, dissolves heavy humors and windiness, and provokes urine and menstruation. When a woman sits on a salve of it, the womb is soon soothed. A wound of the womb is improved, and its blockage is opened, by a fumigation of this. But if it is mixed with a laxative medicine, it helps in the evacuation of heavy humors. When combined with honey and placed on top of hard and moist abscesses, it dissolves and cures them. Cleopatra used purple cinnamon in place of cassia bark, and cassia bark in place of cinnamon. Dioscorides ordered twice the weight of cinnamon to be used for one of cassia.[52]

If they should be washed with a warming
    salve of it;
Cassia fruit destroys the harmful power of
    blood.
Cassia bark properly dissolves windy problems;
Thus Cassia fruit dissolves the hard abscess
That blood itself creates, and nothing
    dissolves like it.   [15]
Purifying Cassia bark stops fatty humors;
Cassia fruit breaks up cheek ulcers well.
If Cassia bark arrives, a blockage of the womb
    departs;
If Cassia fruit is gargled it equally cures
Swollen gums and throats and uvulas,   [20]
And even better if Nightshade juice is
    added to it.
So you can scarcely see which one of these
    excels
The powers of the other with such lofty
    powers.
If Cleopatra is missing Cassia, she uses
    Cinnamon;
Dioscorides does otherwise; he doubles the
    Cinnamon;   [25]
If Cinnamon is lacking, Cassia, she uses you.
Choose whom you would rather follow, for
    either is the best.[53]

---

[52]   "Cassia lignea calida et sicca in tertio gradu. Stomachum, epar, uulnera, et omnia principalia membra confortat, oppilationem aperit, et grossos humores et uentositatem dissoluit, urinam et menstrua prouocat. Muliere in eius apozemate sedente, mox uulua confortatur. Suffumigata ex ea, dolor uuluae placatur, et eius oppilatio aperitur. Si uero cum medicina laxatiua misceatur, ad eijciendos grossos humores, iuuat. Cum melle temperata et super dura et humida apostemata imposita ea dissoluit et curat. Cleopatra cinnamomum alithinum pro cassia lignea, et cassiam ligneam pro cinnamomo posuit. Dioscorides duplum pondus cinnamomo pro uno cassiae poni iussit."

[53]   Cassia non eadem que cassia fistula confert,
    Cassia namque gradu feruet siccatque secundo
    Sed Galienus ait quod cassia fistula prestet
    Inter utrosque gradus. Calidam nec iudicat ipsam,
    Nec frigescentem, nec humentem, neque siccam—   [5]
    Tanta temperie dedit hanc Natura uigere.
    Cassia sumpta iecur confortat, [*lacuna*] sterasque
    Cunctaque primatum retinencia corpore membra
    At rubeam coleram bene cassia fistula purgat.

As was the case in his poem "Agaricum," Henry believes, or is pretending, that the passages from Constantine are by Galen, whom Constantine does cite. Instead of relating the attributes of one part of cassia followed by the other in the order found in the *Liber graduum*, Henry takes the dramatic step of blending the two, moving between *cassia fistula* and *cassia* (short for *cassia lignea*), comparing them in all their aspects: *cassia fistula* is discussed in lines 3–6, 9, 12, 14–15, 17, and 19–21, and *cassia lignea* in the intervening lines 2, 7–8, 10–11, 13, 16, and 18. The poem has become truly didactic, not merely listing a herb's abilities, but guiding the reader back and forth between the bark and fruit of the tree so that he may understand each of them better. The physician or apothecary in possession of cassia would more readily understand what part of the plant he possessed and how to use it if he were reading Henry's poem than if searching through the *Liber graduum*.

By comparing the two types of cassia in the framework of one poem, Henry can more easily provide important conclusions. In the first place, the reader is made aware immediately of the two kinds of cassia: "Cassia bark does not provide the same things as Cassia fruit" (line 1). This conclusion could be drawn easily enough by someone who had read all of the *Liber graduum*, but that is not necessary with this poem on hand. In the second place, he provides a commentary on the qualities of *cassia fistula*. While Constantine describes the most important aspect of *fistula*—its "balanced composition" (*aequali compositioni*), whereby it cannot be judged hot, cold, wet, or dry—he does not explain why this has happened or its significance. Henry explains that "Nature

---

Cassia confortat ualide muliebria membra   [10]
Eius si tepido sint apozimate fota;
Sanguinis extinguit uim cassia fistula diram.
Cassia uentosas dissoluit rite querelas;
Soluit apostema sic cassia fistula durum
Quod cruor ipse creat, nec quicquid soluit ut ipsa.   [15]
Cassia purificans grossis humoribus obstat;
Rumpit apostema bene cassia fistula bucce.
Cassia si ueniat, fugit opilacio uulue;
Gargarizetur si cassia fistula curat
Eque gingiuas, fauces uuasque tumentes   [20]
Et melius stringni succus si iungitur illi.
Vix igitur uideas quenam precellit earum
Viribus excelsis eque uires utriusque.
Cinnama Cleopatra, si desit cassia, ponit
At Dyascorides aliter (nam cinnama duplat);   [25]
Cinnama si desint eadem, te, cassia, ponit.
Elige quem pocius (nam summus uterque) sequaris.

ordained that [*cassia fistula*] is effective by such moderation" (line 6). The reader is given the reassurance that the idiosyncratic *moderatio* or *temperies* of *fistula* is part of a larger, even cosmological, plan, and it was designed that way specifically so that it could "be effective" (*uigere*). Finally, though the two parts of cassia do not accomplish the same thing, Henry concludes that "you can scarcely see which one of these excels the powers of the other with such lofty powers" (lines 22–3). All of these changes are combined most successfully in this poem, establishing it not only as a more enjoyable and memorable form of the *Liber graduum*, but as a commentary and gloss on its less clear passages.

I have reviewed in this essay only a small number of the 50 poems I have identified which are based on Constantine's *Liber graduum*. At least five authors appear to have written these poems: Macer Floridus, Henry of Huntingdon (in his herbal and lapidary), and the poets represented in the Trinity, Digby, and Wolfenbüttel herbals. This is only a preliminary survey and there are surely more authors and more poems to be found. While it is unlikely that we can know the specific intention of these authors in versifying the *Liber graduum*, it is certain that some of them expected to have an audience for their work, and that Macer in particular was read very widely for the next five hundred years, so there was a steady demand for such verse herbals. Some of the reasons for their composition can be found within the poems themselves. The Galenic qualities of herbs, first made widely known in Western Europe through Constantine, were quickly incorporated into the already existing tradition of verse herbals. Material that was deemed unnecessary or simply too difficult by the poet (or according to the demands of his audience) was removed and probably not missed in the new verse format. Other difficult terms and phrases could be reworded or made memorable within the hexameter verse, still popular after centuries of use as a didactic and mnemonic device by the time of Constantine. The poets and their readers expected the full support of ancient authority to accompany their medical information. Constantine provided some of that with apparently genuine references to Galen and Dioscorides, but the poets had few qualms about adding more authorities or even claiming to be one of them. The close relationship between certain items of materia medica encouraged some poets to combine multiple entries from the *Liber graduum* into one discreet package. Finally, the more creative and ambitious poets could use their verse as a vehicle both for a slightly modified version of Constantine's *Liber graduum* and for a commentary on his work, artfully blending in one medium the authority and the gloss.

Appendix 5.1:
Constantine the African in Medieval Latin Verse: A Preliminary Catalogue

The following is a preliminary catalogue listing medieval Latin herbal poems that are based primarily on information taken from the works of Constantine the African. It is by no means comprehensive and I expect many more such poems to be found. For example, it does not include poems with only a small portion taken from Constantine's works, such as the poems by Macer which borrow only the Galenic qualities from Constantine. I have also not included those poems on herbs by Alexander Neckam in his *Suppletio defectuum* that may be based on the *Liber graduum*, but that I have not been able to verify.[54] The list is arranged alphabetically according to the name given to the poem, if any, or by the spelling used by the poet for the herb. Each item is followed by the author, if known, the manuscript or printed source I have used in parentheses, the poem's incipit and number of lines, and finally in parentheses the name and page of the entry used in Constantine's *Liber graduum*. The following abbreviations are used in the catalogue:

AO: Henry of Huntingdon, *Anglicanus ortus: A Verse Herbal of the Twelfth Century*, ed. and trans. Winston Black (Toronto: Pontifical Institute of Mediaeval Studies, 2012)

Choulant: *Macer floridus de viribus herbarum*, ed. Ludwig Choulant (Leipzig, 1832)

Constantine: *Liber graduum*, as printed in *Constantini Africani ... opera* (2 vols, Basel, 1536–39), 2:344–87

D: Oxford, Bodleian Library, MS Digby 13, fols 89v–91r (s. xii)

Lapidary: Winston Black, "Henry of Huntingdon's Lapidary Rediscovered and His *Anglicanus ortus* Reassembled," *Mediaeval Studies* 68 (2006): 43–87.

Reuss: "Floridi Macri de viribus herbarum capita," in Friedrich Anton Reuss (ed.), *Walafridi Strabi Hortulus: carmen ad cod. ms veterumque editionum fidem recensitum, lectionis varietate notisque instructum* (Würzburg, 1834), 93–9

T: Cambridge, Trinity College, MS O. 9. 10, fols 89r–108r (s. xv)

---

[54] Cf. *Alexandri Neckam Suppletio defectuum; Carmina minora*, ed. Peter Hochgürtel, Corpus Christianorum Continuatio Mediaevalis 221 (Turnhout: Brepols, 2008); *Suppletio defectuum, Book I: Alexaander Neckam on Plants, Birds, and Animals. A Supplement to the Laus sapientie divine*, ed. Christopher J. McDonough (Florence: SISMEL, Edizioni del Galluzzo, 1999); and R.W. Hunt, *The Schools and the Cloister: The Life and Writings of Alexander Nequam (1157–1217)*, ed. and rev. Margaret Gibson (Oxford: Clarendon Press, 1984), 78–80, 139–40.

1. **Acorus**, Henry of Huntingdon (*AO*, 6.2.22), "Est acorus feruens gradu siccansque secundo," 6 lines (*Acorus*, 355)
2. **Agaricum**, Henry of Huntingdon (*AO*, 6.2.2), "Agaricum quod diureticum perhibet Galienus," 17 lines (*Agaricus*, 346)
3. **Agaricus**, anonymous (Reuss, 101), "Agarici species geminae sunt, ipsa probat res," 17 lines (*Agaricus*, 346)
4. **Aloë**, Macer no. 77 (Choulant, lines 2233–69), "Sunt Aloë species geminae, quae subrubet estque," 37 lines (*Aloes*, 354–5)
5. **Amomum**, Henry of Huntingdon (*AO*, 6.2.3), "Dulce Dei donum, mirabile fraglat amomum," 11 lines (*Amomum*, 376)
6. **Amoniacum**, Henry of Huntingdon (*AO*, 6.2.20), "Tercius in calido gradus, in siccando secundus," 6 lines (*Amoniacum*, 375)
7. **Anacardus**, Henry of Huntingdon (*AO*, 6.2.27), "Quarto uero gradu siccans, feruens anacardus," 7 lines (*Anacardi*, 382)
8. **Anisum**, Henry of Huntingdon (*AO*, 6.2.6), "Fit medicamentis anisi gratissima multis," 11 lines (*Anisum*, 376)
9. **Balsamum**, Henry of Huntingdon (*AO*, 6.2.1), "Sunt summi precii prestancia balsama mire," 31 lines (*Balsamus*, 356–7)
10. **Bdellium**, Henry of Huntingdon (*AO*, 6.2.21), "Sunt humecta gradu primo feruentque secundo," 7 lines (*Bdellium*, 359)
11. **Calamus aromaticus**, Henry of Huntingdon (*AO*, 6.2.28), "Cum calamus sit aromaticus uirtute coruscus," 15 lines (*Calamus aromaticus*, 357)
12. **Camphora**, Henry of Huntingdon (*AO*, 6.2.23), "Arboris est gumma quam profert India diues," 9 lines (*Camphora*, 370)
13. **Cardamomum**, Henry of Huntingdon (*AO*, 6.2.10), "Nec cardamomi laudes taceantur odori," 12 lines (*Cardamomum*, 347)
14. **Cassia**, Henry of Huntingdon (*AO*, 6.1.6), "Cassia non eadem que cassia fistula confert," 27 lines (*Cassia fistula*, 346–7, and *Cassia lignea*, 369)
15. **Cinnama**, Macer no. 73 (Choulant, lines 2147–64), "Cinnama tres species dicuntur habere, sed harum," 18 lines (*Cinnamomum*, 368)
16. **Corallus**, Henry of Huntingdon (Lapidary, no. 18, lines 1–6), "Corallus mire prodest, nam lumina mundat," 6 lines (*Corallus*, 354)
17. **Costus**, Macer no. 74 (Choulant, lines 2165–81), "Costi sunt geminae species: gravis una rubensque," 17 lines (*Costus*, 366–7)
18. **Cuscute**, anonymous (*T* 93r), "Cuscute quam multi lini dixere podagram," 18 lines (*Cuscute*, 346, and *Cacollae*, 347)
19. **Cyminum**, Macer no. 69 (Choulant, lines 2111–24), "Esse putant medici calidum siccumque Cyminum," 14 lines (*Cyminum*, 374–5)

20. **Dyagridium**, Henry of Huntingdon (*AO*, 6.2.19), "Ecce diagridium quantum eminet antidotorum," 5 lines (*Diagridium*, 369)

21. **Dragagantus**, Henry of Huntingdon (*AO*, 6.2.18), "Ponitur antidotis dragagantus sepe probatis," 6 lines (*Dragagantum*, 360–361)

22. **Euforbium**, Henry of Huntingdon (*AO*, 6.2.8), "Feruida, sicca gradu prestant euforbia quarto," 14 lines (*Euphorbium*, 381)

23. **Folium**, Henry of Huntingdon (*AO*, 6.2.9), "Et folium feruetque gradu siccatque secundo," 6 lines (*Lolium* [*sic*], 361)

24. **Galanga**, Macer no. 70 (Choulant, lines 2125–30), "Flegmonem stomachi sumptum Galanga resolvit," 6 lines (*Galanga*, 372)

25. **Gariofilus**, Macer no. 72 (Choulant, lines 2141–6), "Gariofilum dicunt calidum siccumque haustum," 6 lines (*Gariophyllum*, 357)

26. **Genciana**, Henry of Huntingdon (*AO*, 6.2.7), "Da ueniam, lector, quod genciana locatur," 11 lines (*Gentiana*, 367)

27. **Gentiana**, anonymous (Reuss, 101–2), "Herbae Gentianae vis est et sicca calensque," 8 lines (*Gentiana*, 367)

28. **Iacinctus**, anonymous (*T* 97r), "Iacinctus sequitur cuius species triplicatur," 23 lines (*Hyacinthi*, 352)

29. **Liquiricia**, Henry of Huntingdon (*AO*, 6.1.11), "Vis liquiricie non parua potest reputari," 20 lines (*Liquiritia*, 347)

30. **Lupinus**, anonymous (Reuss, 103), "Fervida lupini vis siccaque dicitur esse," 14 lines (*Lupinus*, 352)

31. **Luvestica**, anonymous (*D* 90v, *T* 98v), "Nature sicce calideque luvestica fertur," 8 lines (*Ligusticum*, 379–80)

32. **Mastix**, Henry of Huntingdon (*AO*, 6.2.5), "Est mastix species quam quidam mastica dicunt," 19 lines (*Mastix*, 354)

33. **Mirtus**, anonymous (*T* 100r), "Mirtus tam pulcra Veneri quam laurea Phebo," 28 lines (*Myrtus*, 350–51)

34. **Mirra**, Henry of Huntingdon (*AO*, 6.1.2), "Mirra, datum puero munus mirabile Christo," 23 lines (*Myrrha*, 359)

35. **Nitrum**, Henry of Huntingdon (*AO*, 6.2.25), "Dicit Aristotiles quod mundet flegmata nitrum," 7 lines (*Nitrum*, 384)

36. **Nux muscata**, Henry of Huntingdon (*AO*, 6.2.24), "Nux muscata gradu calet exsiccatque secundo," 5 lines (*Nux muscata*, 355)

37. **Pyrethrum**, Macer no. 67 (Choulant, lines 2086–2108), "Est Pyrethrum calidum siccumque, quartus in istis," 23 lines (*Pyrethrum*, 381)

38. **Reu**, Henry of Huntingdon (*AO*, 6.2.11), "Reu aliud Pontus, aliud parit India; primum," 9 lines (*Rheum*, 354)

39. **Sagapinum**, Henry of Huntingdon (*AO*, 6.2.13), "Carmine condignum non transierim sagapinum," 11 lines (*Sagapinum*, 373)

40. **Saliunca**, anonymous (Reuss, 104), "In primis siccae gradibus nam sunt saliuncae," 11 lines (error for *Salices*, 358)
41. **Sambucus**, anonymous (Reuss, 104–5), "Sunt gradibus primis sicci calidique secundis," 9 lines (*Sambucus*, 361)
42. **Sarcocolla**, anonymous (Reuss, 104), "Sarcocolla calet etiam fit sicca probata," 7 lines (*Sarcocolla*, 350)
43. **Siler**, Henry of Huntingdon (*AO*, 6.2.17), "Si sileri re nos celebremus carmine uires," 6 lines (*Seseleon*, 364)
44. **Solsequium**, anonymous (Reuss, 103–4), "Solis sponsa gradu primo cum frigore sicca," 4 lines (*Sponsa solis*, 353)
45. **Spica**, Macer no. 75 (Choulant, lines 2182–2203), "Esse gradu primo calidam siccamque periti," 22 lines (*Spica nardi*, 348)
46. **Squilla**, Henry of Huntingdon (*AO*, 6.2.16), "Squilla gradu quo thus manet humida spargit et aret," 6 lines (*Scilla*, 362)
47. **Squinantum**, Henry of Huntingdon (*AO*, 6.2.14), "Grata salutiferi recitemus dona squinanti," 8 lines (*Squinantum*, 372)
48. **Storax**, Henry of Huntingdon (*AO*, 6.2.4), "Primum storace que sit diuisio dicam," 10 lines (*Styrax*, 351)
49. **Thus**, Macer no. 76 (Choulant, lines 2204–32), "Thus calidum siccumque gradu dixere secundo," 29 lines (*Thus*, 357)
50. **Zedoar**, Macer no. 71 (Choulant, lines 2131–40), "Adprime sumptis Zedoar obstare venenis," 10 lines (*Zedoar*, 374)

Bibliography

Alexander Neckam. *Alexandri Neckam De naturis rerum libri duo, with the Poem of the Same Author, De laudibus divinae sapientiae*. Ed. Thomas Wright. Rolls Series 34. London: Longman, Roberts, & Green, 1863.

———. *Suppletio defectuum, Book I: Alexander Neckam on Plants, Birds, and Animals. A Supplement to the Laus sapientie divine*. Ed. Christopher J. McDonough. Florence: SISMEL, Edizioni del Galluzzo, 1999.

———. *Alexandri Neckam Suppletio defectuum; Carmina minora*. Ed. Peter Hochgürtel. Corpus Christianorum Continuatio Mediaevalis 221. Turnhout: Brepols, 2008.

———. *Alexandri Neckam Sacerdos ad altare*. Ed. Christopher J. McDonough. Corpus Christianorum Continuatio Mediaevalis 227. Turnhout: Brepols, 2010.

Barbensi, Gustavo (ed.). *Regimen sanitatis salernitanum*. Florence: L. Olschki, 1947.

Black, Winston. "Henry of Huntingdon's Lapidary Rediscovered and His *Anglicanus ortus* Reassembled." *Mediaeval Studies* 68 (2006): 43–87.

Burnett, Charles, and Danielle Jacquart (eds). *Constantine the African and 'Alī ibn al-'Abbās al-Maǧūsī: The "Pantegni" and Related Texts.* Leiden: Brill, 1994.

Collins, Minta. *Medieval Herbals: The Illustrative Traditions.* Toronto: University of Toronto Press, 2000.

Constantini africani post Hippocratem et Galenum ... posthabendi opera. 2 vols. Basel: Heinrich Petri, 1536–59.

Crossgrove, William C. "Zur Datierung des 'Macer Floridus.'" In Werner E. Gerabek et al. (eds), *Licht der Natur: Medizin in Fachliteratur und Dichtung. Festschrift für Gundolf Keil zum 60. Geburtstag*, 55–63. Göppingen: Kümmerle, 1994.

Dioscorides. *De materia medica.* Colle: Johannes de Medemblick, 1478.

Flood, Bruce P., Jr. "Macer Floridus: A Medieval Herbalism." Unpublished Ph.D. dissertation, University of Colorado, 1968.

———. "The Medieval Tradition of 'Macer Floridus.'" *Pharmacy in History* 18 (1976): 62–6.

Haskins, C.H. *Studies in the History of Mediaeval Science.* Cambridge, MA: Harvard University Press, 1924.

Henry of Huntingdon. *Anglicanus Ortus: A Verse Herbal of the Twelfth Century.* Ed. and trans. Winston Black. Toronto: Pontifical Institute of Mediaeval Studies, 2012.

Hunt, R.W. *The Schools and the Cloister: The Life and Writings of Alexander Nequam (1157–1217).* Ed. and rev. Margaret Gibson. Oxford: Clarendon Press, 1984.

Jordan, Mark. "The Fortune of Constantine's *Pantegni.*" In Burnett and Jacquart, *Constantine the African*, 286–302.

Macer floridus de viribus herbarum. Ed. Ludwig Choulant. Leipzig: L. Voss, 1832. Repr. in *Höhepunkte der Klostermedizin: der "Macer Floridus" und das Herbarium des Vitus Auslasser*, with introduction and German translation by Johannes Gottfried Mayer and Konrad Goehl. Holzminden: Reprint-Verlag Leipzig, 2001.

Marbod of Rennes. *Lapidario (Liber lapidum).* Ed. María Esthera Herrera. Paris: Les Belles Lettres, 2005.

McVaugh, Michael R. "Royal Surgeons and the Value of Medical Learning: The Crown of Aragon, 1300–1350." In Luis García-Ballester et al. (eds), *Practical Medicine from Salerno to the Black Death*, 211–36. Cambridge: Cambridge University Press, 1994.

Moreno Olalla, David. "*The fautys to amende*: On the Interpretation of the *Explicit* of Sloane 5, ff. 13–57, and Related Matters." *English Studies* 88 (2007): 119–42.

O'Boyle, Cornelius. *The Art of Medicine: Medical Teaching at the University of Paris, 1250–1400*. Leiden: Brill, 1998.

———. *Thirteenth- and Fourteenth-century Copies of the "Ars Medicine": A Checklist and Contents Descriptions of the Manuscripts*. Cambridge: Wellcome Unit for the History of Medicine, 1998.

Omnia opera Ysaac. 2 vols. Lyons: J. de Platea, 1515.

Ovid. *Amores, Medicamina faciei femineae, Ars amatoria, Remedia amoris*. Ed. E.J. Kenney. Rev. edn. Oxford: Oxford University Press, 1994.

Prioreschi, Plinio. *A History of Medicine*, vol. 5: *Medieval Medicine*. Omaha: Horatius Press, 2003.

Quintus Serenus. *Liber Medicinalis*. Ed. and trans. R. Pépin. Paris: Presses Universitaires de France, 1950.

Renzi, Salvatore De. *Collectio Salernitana, ossia documenti inediti, e trattati di medicina appartenenti alla scuola medica salernitana*. 5 vols. Naples: Filiatre-Sebezio, 1852–59.

Reuss, Friedrich Anton (ed.). *Walafridi Strabi Hortulus: carmen ad cod. ms veterumque editionum fidem recensitum, lectionis varietate notisque instructum*. Würzburg: Stahel, 1834.

Riddle, John M. *Marbode of Rennes' (1035–1123) "De lapidibus" Considered as a Medical Treatise with Text, Commentary and C.W. King's Translation, together with Text and Translation of Marbode's Minor Works on Stones*. Wiesbaden: Franz Steiner, 1977.

———. "Dioscorides." In Ferdinand E. Cranz and Paul Oskar Kristeller (eds), *Catalogus Translationum et Commentariorum: Mediaeval and Renaissance Latin Translations and Commentaries*, vol. 4, 1–143. Washington, D.C.: Catholic University of America Press, 1980.

Rigg, A.G. "Henry of Huntingdon's Herbal." *Mediaeval Studies* 65 (2003): 213–92.

Schnell, Bernhard, with William Crossgrove (eds). *Der deutsche "Macer": Vulgatfassung mit einem Abdruck des lateinischen Macer Floridus "De viribus herbarum."* Tübingen: Niemeyer, 2003.

Simon of Genoa (Simon Januensis). *Synonyma medicinae, sive Clavis sanationis*. Milan: Antonius Zirotus, 1473.

Stadler, H. "Die Quellen des Macer Floridus." *Archiv für die Geschichte der Naturwissenschaften und der Technik* 1 (1908): 52–65.

Thorndike, Lynn, and F.S. Benjamin, Jr. (eds). *The Herbal of Rufinus*. Chicago: University of Chicago Press, 1946.

Walahfrid Strabo. *Hortulus*. Ed. Cataldo Roccaro. Palermo: Herbita, 1979.

Chapter 6

A Problematic Plant Name: *elehtre.*
A Reconsideration[1]

Maria Amalia D'Aronco

Glosses constituted a meeting-point between Latin culture and the Germanic world,
a moment when the two civilizations came face to face. The latter attempted to set up
a relationship with the former and build a bridge across to it.

These were the words with which Patrizia Lendinara began her study of the
glossary in Oxford, Bodleian Library, MS Bodley 163.[2] Her words, however,
could as well be used to describe the situation of the Anglo-Saxon glossators
and translators of medical and pharmaceutical Latin texts when coping with
Latin names of medicinal plants that were either not common in England,
being of Mediterranean origin, or were not, as yet, used in native medicine.
To this might be added problems that arose when the names were first met by
the glossators in lists of Latin words where plant names were entered without
the original contextualization that could have given the translator a better
understanding of the lemma. In spite of these difficulties, however, the Anglo-
Saxons did translate Latin (and Greek) medicinal plant names and used them
to such an extent that many of these names have come down to us through the
centuries.

Our knowledge of medical practice in Anglo-Saxon England is undeniably
sparse and patchy. All recent studies, however, have stressed that Anglo-Saxon
medical treatises are not a jumble of superstitious and magical practices, filled
with "generally worthless remedies, practices and theories."[3] On the contrary,
they had a rational basis and preserved and re-elaborated the great medical

---

[1] This study is part of the research project "Rethinking and Recontextualizing Glosses: New
Perspectives in the Study of Late Anglo-Saxon Glossography," supported by the Italian Ministry of
Education (MIUR/PRIN 2007: Universities of Palermo, Rome LUMSA, and Udine).

[2] Patrizia Lendinara, "The Glossary in Oxford, Bodleian Library, Bodley 163," in Patrizia
Lendinara, *Anglo-Saxon Glosses and Glossaries*, Variorum Collected Studies Series CS 622
(Aldershot, UK: Ashgate, 1999), 329–55, at 329.

[3] M.L. Cameron, *Anglo-Saxon Medicine*, Cambridge Studies in Anglo-Saxon England 7
(Cambridge: Cambridge University Press, 1993), 2.

tradition of classical antiquity.[4] The Anglo-Saxons reveal a vast amount of learning, a profound knowledge of what had been handed down through the medical tradition, and, at the same time, an extraordinary capacity to innovate and experiment, as the collections of remedies without direct Latin sources attest. It is, therefore, evident that the Anglo-Saxon medical practitioners were not amateur collectors nor, quoting John Riddle, would a collector be "a novice medical apprentice sent by his master to replenish the jars," and certainly not "a monk on his initial assignment to infirmary duty."[5]

The greatest and earliest achievements in Western vernacular medicine of the late ninth century are Bald's *Læceboc* and the so-called *Book III* of the *Læceboc*,[6] which belong to the literature of *dynamidia*[7] and contain a great deal of material from late classical medicine together with remedies of obscure origin (maybe both traditional lore and re-elaborations from personal experiences by the Anglo-Saxon physicians).[8] These texts, together with the so-called Omont

---

4   See Cameron, *Anglo-Saxon Medicine*; M.L. Cameron, "The Sources of Medical Knowledge in Anglo-Saxon England," *Anglo-Saxon England* 11 (1983): 135–55; Maria Amalia D'Aronco, "How 'English' is Anglo-Saxon Medicine? The Latin Sources for Anglo-Saxon Medical Texts," in Charles Burnett and Nicholas Mann (eds), *Britannia Latina: Latin in the Culture of Great Britain from the Middle Ages to the Twentieth Century*, Warburg Institute Colloquia 8 (London/Turin: The Warburg Institute/Nino Aragno Editore, 2005), 27–41.

5   John M. Riddle, "Pseudo-Dioscorides' *Ex herbis femininis* and Early Medieval Medical Botany," *Journal of the History of Biology* 14 (1981): 43–81, at 45. On the expertise of a medieval practitioner, see Peter Murray Jones, "Herbs and the Medieval Surgeon," in Peter Dendle and Alain Touwaide (eds), *Health and Healing from the Medieval Garden* (Rochester, NY: Boydell & Brewer, 2008), 162–79.

6   The two texts are preserved in one manuscript, London, British Library, MS Royal 12 D. xvii, from Winchester (?), s. x^med, cf. N.R. Ker, *Catalogue of Manuscripts Containing Anglo-Saxon* (Oxford: Clarendon Press, 1957, repr. 1990), no. 264, and Helmut Gneuss, *Handlist of Anglo-Saxon Manuscripts and Manuscript Fragments Written or Owned in England up to 1100* (Tempe, AZ: Medieval and Renaissance Texts and Studies, 2001), no. 479. The tracts were published by Oswald Cockayne (ed.), *Leechdoms, Wortcunning, and Starcraft of Early England, Being a Collection of Documents for the Most Part Never Before Printed, Illustrating the History of Science in this Country before the Norman Conquest*, Rolls Series 35 (3 vols, London: Longman, 1864–66; repr. Nendeln, Liechtenstein: Kraus, 1965), 2:2–364.

7   Loren C. MacKinney, "'Dynamidia' in Medieval Medical Literature," *Isis* 24 (1935–36): 400–414.

8   See, in particular, M.L. Cameron, "Bald's *Leechbook*: Its Sources and Their Use in Its Compilation," *Anglo-Saxon England* 12 (1983): 153–82; M.L. Cameron, "Bald's *Leechbook* and Cultural Interactions in Anglo-Saxon England," *Anglo-Saxon England* 19 (1990): 5–12; Richard Scott Nokes, "The Several Compilers of Bald's *Leechbook*," *Anglo-Saxon England* 33 (2004): 51–76.

fragment,[9] attest to a consistent number of plant names that are loanwords from the Latin or are new formations created on Latin models.[10] However, the most interesting work to give us a feeling of the problems the Anglo-Saxon medical community had to deal with when facing the task of translating Latin plant names is the translation of a number of late antique Latin pharmacopoeias (the Pseudo-Apuleius herbal and other late antique herbals)[11] that is now called the *Old English Herbarium* and that was carried out toward the end of the tenth century.[12] Following its Latin models, the treatise deals with the virtues of a

---

[9] Louvain, Bibliothèque centrale de l'Université, Section des manuscrits, Fragmenta H. Omont no. 3/1a; s. ix^ex or x^in, cf. Ker, *Catalogue*, no. 417, and Gneuss, *Handlist*, no. 848. Published by Bella Schauman and Angus Cameron, "A Newly-Found Leaf of Old English from Louvain," *Anglia* 95 (1977): 289–312, and more recently by Stephen Pollington, *Leechcraft: Early English Charms, Plantlore and Healing* (Hockwold-cum-Wilton, UK: Anglo-Saxon Books, 2000), 74–6. See also Audrey L. Meaney, "Variant Versions of Old English Medical Remedies and the Compilation of Bald's *Leechbook*," *Anglo-Saxon England* 13 (1984): 235–68, at 243–5.

[10] See Peter Bierbaumer, *Der botanische Wortschatz des Altenglischen*, vol. 1: *Das Læceboc* (Frankfurt am Main: Peter Lang, 1975). On the formation of the Old English botanical lexicon, see Maria Amalia D'Aronco, "The Botanical Lexicon of the *Old English Herbarium*," *Anglo-Saxon England* 17 (1988): 15–33; Hans Sauer, "Towards a Linguistic Description and Classification of the Old English Plant Names," in Michael Korhammer, Karl Reichl, and Hans Sauer (eds), *Words, Texts and Manuscripts: Studies in Anglo-Saxon Culture Presented to Helmut Gneuss on the Occasion of His Sixty-fifth Birthday* (Cambridge: D.S. Brewer, 1992), 381–408; Hans Sauer, "On the Analysis and Structure of Old and Middle English Plant Names," in B. Santano Moreno et al. (eds), *Papers from the VIII International Conference of the Spanish Society for Medieval English Language and Literature* (Cáceres: Universidad de Extremadura, 1995), 299–325; and Hans Sauer, "Old English Plant Names in the Épinal-Erfurt Glossary: Etymology, Word Formation and Semantics," in Wolfgang Falkner and Hans-Jörg Schmidt (eds), *Words, Lexemes, Concepts— Approaches to the Lexicon: Studies in Honour of Leonhard Lipka* (Tübingen: Gunter Narr Verlag, 1999), 23–38.

[11] The translation consists of two parts, the first dealing with remedies derived from herbs, the second with remedies derived from animals. Full discussion of the Latin sources in M.A. D'Aronco, "Introduction," in M.A. D'Aronco and M.L. Cameron (eds), *The Old English Illustrated Pharmacopoeia: British Library Cotton Vitellius C III*, Early English Manuscripts in Facsimile 27 (Copenhagen: Rosenkilde & Bagger, 1998), 13–60. See also Maria Amalia D'Aronco, "Anglo-Saxon Plant Pharmacy and the Latin Medical Tradition," in Carole P. Biggam (ed.), *From Earth to Art: The Many Aspects of the Plant-World in Anglo-Saxon England. Proceedings of the First ASPNS Symposium, University of Glasgow, 5–7 April 2000* (Amsterdam: Rodopi, 2003), 133–51. The two pharmacopoeias were first published by Cockayne, *Leechdoms*, vol. 1, then by Hubert Jan de Vriend (ed.), *The Old English Herbarium and Medicina de Quadrupedibus*, Early English Text Society, Original Series 286 (London: Oxford University Press, 1984). Quotations, by page and line, are from the latter edition.

[12] See Maria Amalia D'Aronco, "The Old English Pharmacopoeia," *AVISTA Forum Journal* 13/2 (2003): 9–18.

number of herbs and the remedies that can be made using them. The herbs are introduced first by their Latin name, followed, at times, by a Greek synonym, then by the Anglo-Saxon equivalent when there was one available. Some names, however, were left untranslated, not because the translator did not know which herb he was discussing, but only because he did not know the corresponding name in his own language. His sense of professional duty and thorough, serious attitude prevented him from coining new names ad hoc, exposing users of the herbal to the potentially very dangerous consequences of mistaken identification. The problem was real and involved considerable responsibility, as the failure to recognize a particular plant or, even worse, mistaking one species for another could have had life-threatening consequences for patients.

Today, identifying the plants used in medieval medicine may seem an indifferent or even an academic exercise, at least from the point of view of their use as remedies. However, in recent times the lore of the old herbals has been re-evaluated—and we must be grateful to scholars such as John Riddle for this. Consequently, the failure to recognize a particular plant or, even worse, mistaking one species for another, can still cause real and serious risk to modern patients. There are, however, other risks, luckily not so dramatic: a wrong or partial identification can produce different outcomes that can end in curious or not fully corroborated deductions.

Such is, in my opinion, the case of the medicinal plant called *elehtre* in Old English. Its traditional identification with the lupin (*Lupinus* L.) suggested to Peter Dendle, as stated in his thorough and well-documented essay, the hypothesis that the Anglo-Saxons discovered some anticonvulsive properties of this plant and that they used it to cure epilepsy and other kinds of seizures:

> The most frequently prescribed herb for *deofulseocnesse* ("devil-sickness") and *feondseocnesse* ("fiend-sickness") in Old English medical compilations is the flower lupine or lupin (Old English *elehtre*). Though devil-sickness presumably included a wide range of mental illnesses, one of the conditions to which it almost certainly referred was epilepsy.[13]

Dendle, however, observes that this use is exceptional, since lupins in classical and late antique medical sources are employed only as anthelmintic and emmenagogue agents or as a skin cleanser. Therefore he prudently concludes:

---

[13]   Peter Dendle, "Lupines, Manganese, and Devil-Sickness: An Anglo-Saxon Medical Response to Epilepsy," *Bulletin of the History of Medicine* 75 (2001): 91–101, at 92.

Such a dietetic response to seizures—a transient element of Anglo-Saxon medicine, which does not seem to have survived into later periods—is never explicitly articulated or developed in the sources. The prevalence of lupines in the native recipes is exceptional, however, and stands in need of explanation.[14]

Dendle's words have prompted me to reconsider the conventional interpretation of *elehtre*, long after my first tackling this puzzling plant name some 20 years ago.[15] Nowadays, scholars can make use of a very powerful tool, the Toronto *Dictionary of Old English* (*DOE*), which is thoroughly changing and vastly improving our knowledge of the Old English language. Its new release, which "defines words more elaborately and with finer subdivisions than its predecessors,"[16] isolates, although prudently, the following main senses for *elehtre*:

1. a plant, probably lupin.

1.a. glossing *electrum* 'amber' (CLat), probably because of the phonetic similarity between *electrum* and *elehtre*.

2. glossing various other Latin lemmas.

2.a. glossing *malum terrae*, any of various plants, among which are the Aristolochia and mandrake. 2.b. glossing *maura* (? for *maurella*) a plant of uncertain identification, perhaps figwort or hog's fennel. 2.c. glossing *walupia* (? for *herba lupina* or ? *faba lupina*).

The suggested etymology is from Lat. *electrum*.[17]

The generally accepted identification of *elehtre* with lupin is based on three one-to-one correspondences with a Latin source out of some 60 occurrences in Old English. Of these, two are recorded in the *Old English Herbarium* and one in a gloss that appears in a botanical glossary much indebted to this translation, the *Laud Glossary* of the twelfth century:[18]

---

[14] Ibid., 101.

[15] Maria Amalia D'Aronco, "Divergenze e convergenze lessicali in inglese antico: Il caso di *elehtre*," in Maria Amalia D'Aronco, Anna Maria Luiselli Fadda, and Maria Vittoria Molinari (eds), "Studi sulla cultura germanica dei secoli IV–XII in onore di Giulia Mazzuoli Porru," special issue, *Romanobarbarica* 10 (1988–89): 65–102.

[16] Roberta Frank, "*F*-Words in *Beowulf*," in Antonette diPaolo Healey and Kevin Kiernan (eds), *Making Sense: Constructing Meaning in Early English* (Toronto: Pontifical Institute of Mediaeval Studies, 2007), 1–22, at 3.

[17] Antonette diPaolo Healey (ed.), *Dictionary of Old English: A to G on CD-ROM*, Version 2 (Toronto: Pontifical Institute of Mediaeval Studies, 2008; hereafter cited as *DOE*), s.v.

[18] Oxford, Bodleian Library, MS Laud Misc. 567, fols 67–73; s. xii, cf. Ker, *Catalogue*, no. 345. Published (but not satisfactorily) by J. Richard Stracke (ed.), *The Laud Herbal Glossary* (Amsterdam: Rodopi, 1974). Philip Rusche is preparing a new edition; in the meantime, I shall

1. *OEHerbarium, Harehune*, ch. 46.3, ed. de Vriend, 92, lines 4–7: "Wið rengwyrmas abutan nafolan genim þas ylcan wyrte marubium 7 wermod 7 elehtran, ealra þyssa wyrta gelice fela be gewihte, seoð on geswetton wætere 7 mid wine twie oððe þriwa lege to þam nafolan, hit cweld þa wyrmas."[19]

Pseudo-Ap. Herbarius, Herba marrubium, ch. 45.3, ed. Howard and Sigerist, 94, lines 8–11: "Ad lumbricos. Herbae marrubii, absintii et lupinorum paria pondera in aqua mulsa cocta, cum uino bis aut ter super umbilicum positum necat lumbricos."

2. *OEHerbarium, Wermod*, ch. 102.2, ed. de Vriend, 148, lines 15–18: "Wið þæt rengwyrmas ymbe þone nafolan derigen genim þas ylcan wyrte absinthium 7 harehunan 7 elechtran, ealra gelice mycel, seoð on geswettum wætere oþþe on wine, lege tuwa oððe þriwa to þam nafolan, hyt cwelþ þa wyrmas."[20]

Pseudo-Ap. Herbarius, Herba absynthium, ch. 101.3, ed. Howard and Sigerist, 182, lines 8-10: "Ad lumbricos. Herbae absintii et marrubii et lupinorum paria pondera in aqua mulsa cocta uel uino austeri, positum in umbilico necat lumbricos."

3. *Laud Glossary*, 644: "electrum .i. lupinus sapo."

It is, however, puzzling that the translator(s) did not insert the vernacular name of the plant *Lupinum montanum* at ch. 112, an omission that is emphasized by the blank left for a later insertion of the Anglo-Saxon name

---

be quoting from Stracke's edition. See Philip G. Rusche, "The Source for Plant Names in Anglo-Saxon England and the Laud Herbal Glossary," in Dendle and Touwaide, *Health and Healing*, 128–45, esp. 130 and 135–44.

[19]   "For worms around the anus, take equal amounts by weight of the *marubium* plant, wormwood, and lupin, and simmer them two or three times in sweetened water and wine. Put this on the anus, and it will kill the worms." Translation from Anne Van Arsdall, *Medieval Herbal Remedies: The "Old English Herbarium" and Anglo-Saxon Medicine* (New York: Routledge, 2002), 171. For the translation of *nafolan/umbilicum* as "anus," see ibid., 114. On intestinal worms and the Old English translation, see also Annalisa Bracciotti, "L'apporto della tradizione indiretta per la costituzione di un testo critico delle *Curae herbarum*," *Rivista di cultura classica e medioevale* 42 (2000): 61–102, at 89–90.

[20]   "If worms are a bother around the [navel], take equal amounts of the same plant absinthium, horeund, and lupine. Simmer them in sweetened water or in wine. Put it on the [navel] two or three times, and it will kill the worms." Translation in Van Arsdall, *Medieval Herbal Remedies*, 195 (slightly modified). See also Marcellus Empiricus, *De medicamentis liber*, 28.11–12; ed. Georg Helmreich (Leipzig: Teubner, 1889), 294: "Marrubii et absenthii et lupinorum paria pondera in aqua mulsa cocta ieiuno bis aut ter potui data adversum tineas et lumbricos plurimum prosunt. Farina lupinorum decocta ex aqua et more cataplasmatis ventri inposita lumbricos vel tineas necat."

(which was, however, never filled in)[21] in the two luxury copies of the Old English pharmacopoeia, namely London, British Library, MS Cotton Vitellius C. iii, fol. 53r (which is illustrated), and Oxford, Bodleian Library, MS Hatton 76, fol. 105r (which was intended for illustration):[22]

OEHerbarium, ch. 112, ed. de Vriend, 154, lines 23–4: "Ðeos wyrt þe man lupinum montanum 7 oþrum naman ... nemneþ by cenned wiþ hegas 7 on sandigum stowum."[23]

Since I began working on the *Old English Herbarium,* the reason for this omission, at variance with the previous confident equivalence of *lupinorum* = *elehtran,* has been puzzling me, particularly in view of the fact that the ingredient *elehtre* was widely employed already from the end of the ninth century, as the oldest medical texts such as Bald's *Læceboc, Book III,* and the Omont fragment attest.[24] Therefore, given the considerable knowledge of medicinal plants and of

---

[21]   See Maria Amalia D'Aronco, "The Missing Plant Names in the *Old English Herbal*: When Were the Blanks Filled In?" in Margit Reitbauer, Nancy Campbell, Sarah Mercer, and Renate Vaupetitsch (eds), *Contexts of English in Use: Past and Present. A Festschrift for Peter Bierbaumer on the Occasion of the 40th Anniversary of His Career at the University of Graz* (Vienna: Wilhelm Braumüller Universitäts-Verlagsbuchhandlung, 2007), 39–49.

[22]   The two pharmacopoeias are preserved in four manuscripts: (1) London, British Library, MS Harley 585, s. x–xi, not illustrated, cf. Ker, *Catalogue,* no. 231; de Vriend, *Old English Herbarium,* xxiii–xxviii; Edward Pettit (ed.), *Anglo-Saxon Remedies, Charms, and Prayers from British Library Ms Harley 585: The Lacnunga* (2 vols, Lampeter, UK: Edwin Mellen, 2001), 1:134–5. (2) London, British Library, MS Cotton Vitellius C. iii, s. xi[in], illustrated, cf. Ker, *Catalogue,* no. 219; de Vriend, *Old English Herbarium,* xi–xx; facsimile in D'Aronco and Cameron, *The Old English Illustrated Pharmacopoeia.* (3) Oxford, Bodleian Library, MS Hatton 76, s. xi[med], prepared for illustration, cf. Ker, *Catalogue,* no. 328; de Vriend, *Old English Herbarium,* xx–xxiii. (4) London, British Library, MS Harley 6258B, s. xii[ex], with herbs arranged in alphabetical order according to their Latin names, cf. Ker, *Catalogue,* xix; de Vriend, *Old English Herbarium,* xxviii–xxxviii; Danielle Maion, "The Fortune of the So-called *Practica Petrocelli Salernitani* in England: New Evidence and Some Considerations," in Patrizia Lendinara, Loredana Lazzari, and Maria Amalia D'Aronco (eds), *Form and Content of Instruction in Anglo-Saxon England: Papers from the International Conference, Udine, April 6th–8th, 2006,* Fédération Internationale des Instituts d'Études Médiévales, Textes et Études du Moyen Âge 39 (Turnhout: Brepols, 2007), 479–96. For the manuscript tradition, see also Maria Amalia D'Aronco, "The Transmission of Medical Knowledge in Anglo-Saxon England: The Voices of Manuscripts," ibid., 35–58.

[23]   "This plant, which is called *lupinum montanum* or ..., grows along hedges and in sandy places." Van Arsdall, *Medieval Herbal Remedies,* 198. Of less significance is the use of the Latin name *lupinum* in the context of the two following cures since in this position the plants are generally mentioned by their Latin name or just referred to as "this herb."

[24]   The ingredient *elehtre* is documented in Bald's *Læceboc,* I.31, 32, 33, 41, 45, 62 (two recipes), 63 (four recipes), 64 (four recipes), 66 (two recipes), 67 (three recipes); II.34, 53 (three

their usage shown by the Anglo-Saxon translator and his prudence in dealing with plants not (or not yet) familiar to the Anglo-Saxons, the only reason I could conceive of was that the translator might not have been as familiar with the plant lupin—as Dendle, although cautiously, suggests[25]—as he was with its seeds or grains, which were commonly used in classical medicine.

The current interpretation of *elehtre* as "lupin" is based upon the similarity between the color of *electrum* "amber" and that of the lupin. It was first proposed by Förster in 1917 and later by von Lindheim in 1941.[26] "Could *electrum* itself have been a popular name for the flower?" as J.D. Pheifer put it when editing the Old English glosses in the *Épinal-Erfurt Glossaries*.[27] The identification with *Lupinus luteus* L. was first proposed by Cockayne (1:227) for *lupinus montanus*, the plant at ch. 112 of the *Old English Herbarium*,[28] an interpretation not accepted by H.J. de Vriend who proposes *Lupinus albus* L., which has the

---

recipes), 65; *Book III*, 14, 22, 39, 41 (two recipes), 54, 61, 62 (two recipes), 63, 64 (two recipes), 67, 68; *Lacnunga*, ed. Pettit, 31 (lines 123–48), 50 (lines 204–6), 63 (lines 235–44), 72 (lines 526–7), 79 (lines 613–14), 83 (lines 627–34), 134 (lines 809–11), 135 (lines 812–15), 136 (lines 816–19); and in a recipe in the Omont fragment, see Schauman and Cameron, "A Newly-Found Leaf," 291, lines 7–11.

[25]   "Lupines are not indigenous to England, but were apparently introduced and thoroughly integrated with native medicine at an early period, because they are especially prominent in the medical compilations least dependent on continental sources." Dendle, "Lupines," 93.

[26]   "Als pflanzenname begegnet *electrum* schon in den ältesten altenglischen glossaren (Erf. 386, Corp. E 116; ebenso Ælfric ed. Zupitza 310[11], WW 322[7], Durhamer gloss. Lchd. III 302, Laud —gl. Lchd. III 324: *electrum vel lupinus*), indem wohl die gelbe farbe des bernsteins auf die lupine (*Lupinus*) übertragen ist. So werden wir auch ae. *elehtre* (in Erfurter glossar verschrieben als *elothr* fur *elohtr*) als 'lupine' fassen dürfen"; Max Förster, "Die altenglische Glossenhandschrift Plantinus 32 (Antwerpen) und Additional 32246 (London)," *Anglia* 41 (1917): 94–161, at 136 n. 3. See also "Lies *electrum*: *electre*. Gemeint ist die 'Lupine', die wegen ihrer gelben Farbe nach dem Bernstein (gr. ἤλεχτρον) benannt ist. Parallelstellen bei Förster, S. 136, Anm. 3"; Bogislav von Lindheim (ed.), *Das Durhamer Pflanzenglossar: Lateinisch und Altenglisch*, Beiträge zur englischen Philologie 35 (Bochum-Langendreer: Heinrich Pöppinghaus, 1941), 47.

[27]   "386. *elothr* (-*htr*) = *elehtre* 'lupin' (BT 246), from L. *electrum* 'amber' (*AEW* 89) because of its yellow colour according to von Lindheim, 47: could *electrum* itself have been a popular name for the flower?" J.D. Pheifer (ed.), *Old English Glosses in the Épinal-Erfurt Glossary* (Oxford: Clarendon Press, 1974), 85. See also Karl Schneider, "Zur Etymologie von ae. *eolhsand* 'Bernstein' und *elehtre* 'Lupine' im Lichte bronzezeitlichen Handels," in Günter Heintz and Peter Schnitter (eds), *Collectanea Philologica: Festschrift für Helmut Gipper*, Saecula Spiritalia 14–15 (2 vols, Baden-Baden: V. Koerner, 1985), 2:669–81.

[28]   In his first volume, dedicated to the *Læceboc*, Peter Bierbaumer suggested *Lupinus luteus*, but in his other two volumes, he sticks to the genus *Lupinus* L.: see Peter Bierbaumer, *Der botanische Wortschatz des Altenglischen*, vol. 1: *Das Læceboc*, vol. 2: *Lacnunga, Herbarium Apulei, Peri Didaxeon* (Frankfurt am Main: Peter Lang, 1976), and vol. 3: *Der botanische Wortschatz in altenglischen Glossen* (Frankfurt am Main: Peter Lang, 1979), s.vv.

medical uses specified for the herb in the *Pseudo-Apuleius Herbarius* (ch. 111),[29] while *Lupinus luteus* L. was generally used as fodder or as fertilizer.[30]

Remedies made with lupins are very common indeed in classical and late antique medicine, not only as anthelmintic and emmenagogue agents or as skin cleanser, but also in the case of liver, kidney, bladder, and rheumatic complaints. Lupins are documented in the Greek and Latin plant-name glossaries that contain material deriving from classical and late antique herbals, from medical texts and lists of synonyms already known and used by Pliny, Dioscorides, and others. In particular, they are well documented in some alphabetically arranged Latin glossaries such as the *Asaru, Anesus,* and *Arsenic Glossaries* that circulated on the Continent in manuscripts from at least the ninth century.[31] Lupins are listed under the headings *lupinus* or *termos,* the Greek forms transliterated into the Latin alphabet:

---

[29] See de Vriend, *Old English Herbarium,* 314.

[30] See Heinrich Marzell (ed.), *Wörterbuch der deutschen Pflanzennamen* (5 vols, Leipzig: Hirzel, 1943–79), 2:1420, *Lupinus* L.

[31] I am quoting these glossaries according to the titles given them by Philip Rusche, "The Source for Plant Names," 134–5 and nn. 30 and 31. See also Rusche's observation (141): "It is likely that the contents of these glossaries were more fluid than I suggested by giving them separate names, and we should probably think instead of simply a large body of Greek–Latin plant names lists that has recensions but which also freely copy from each other each time they are copied anew."

Asaru Glossary (*CGL* 3)[32]	**Arsenic Glossary** (*CGL* 3)[33]	
Vat. Reg. lat. 1260, *First Glossary*	*Vat. Reg. lat. 1260,* *Second Glossary*	*Paris lat. 11218*
meruiro .i. lupinus (569.59) terimus .i. lupinus (577.44) termosor .i. lupinus agrestis (577.57) termusorinus .i. lupino mundano (578.42) tarmus .i. lupinus (578.53)	ternus .i. lupinus (586.21)	termos lupinos (632.62)

	Anesus Glossary (*CGL* 3)[34]	
Vat. Reg. lat. 1260, *Third Glossary*	*Vat. lat. 4417*	*Sloane 475, pt 2* *(fols 143r–160r)*[35]
lupinus termus erinus (592.15) termus lupinus (596.11)	lupinus idest stremus eremis (625.61) termus idest lupinus (630.13)	lupinus .i. stermus eremis (fol. 154r1) termus .i. lupinus (fol. 159r10)

If we now take into consideration the situation documented by the Anglo-Saxon glossaries, it appears that the oldest ones, that is, the *Leiden, Épinal-Erfurt,* and *Corpus Glossaries,*[36] preserve no entries under any of the headwords *lupinus*

---

[32]   For the *Asaru Glossary*, cf. Rusche, "The Source for Plant Names," 134 and n. 30. The glossary is printed by Georg Goetz (ed.), *Corpus glossariorum latinorum* (7 vols, Leipzig: Teubner, 1888–1923), 3:549–79 (hereafter cited as *CGL* and quoted by volume, page, and line) from the first glossary in Vatican City, Biblioteca Apostolica, MS Reg. lat. 1260, fols 165ra–172vb (s. ix). Cf. Augusto Beccaria, *I codici di medicina del periodo presalernitano (secoli IX, X, e XI)* (Rome: Edizioni di Storia e Letteratura, 1956), no. 107.

[33]   I am quoting from the second glossary of Reg. lat. 1260, fols 172vb–174rb, and the glossary in Paris, Bibliothèque nationale de France, MS lat. 11218, fols 39v–41v (s. ix); Beccaria, *I codici*, no. 34. Printed in *CGL* 3:579–89 and 631–3, respectively.

[34]   I am quoting from the third glossary of Reg. lat. 1260, fols 175ra–177ra, and from a glossary in Vatican City, Biblioteca Apostolica Vaticana, MS Vat. lat. 4417, fols 119r–127v, s. xi/xii, Beccaria, *I codici*, no. 100. Printed in *CGL* 3:586–96 and 616–30, respectively.

[35]   Another copy of the *Anesus Glossary* is preserved in London, British Library, MS Sloane 475, Part 2, fols 143r–160r, s. xii[in], of English origin. Cf. Beccaria, *I codici*, no. 78; Gneuss, *Handlist*, no. 498.1; Rusche, "The Source for Plant Names," 137 and n. 36. The glossary is unpublished; I am quoting from the manuscript.

[36]   *Leiden Glossary*: Leiden, Bibliotheek der Rijksuniversiteit, MS Voss. lat. Q. 69, fols 20r–36r, St. Gallen, s. ix[in]. Edited by John Henry Hessels, *A Late Eighth-century Latin–Anglo-*

or *termus.* Lupins are also ignored by the later ones, more or less contemporary with the Old English translation of the herbal, that is, by the Anglo-Saxon glossaries in the Cleopatra,[37] Brussels,[38] and Antwerp-London manuscripts.[39] Only the late, twelfth-century, plant-name glossary in the Laud manuscript (*Laud Glossary*)[40] fills this gap:

Saxon Glossary Preserved in the Library of the Leiden University (Ms. Voss. Q° Lat. No. 69) (Cambridge: Cambridge University Press, 1906).

Épinal-Erfurt Glossaries: Épinal, Bibliothèque Municipale, MS 72, fols 94r–107v (England, s. viii^ex), and Erfurt, Wissenschaftliche Bibliothek, MS Amplonianus 2° 42, fols 1r–14v (Cologne, s. viii/ix). Edited by Goetz, *CGL* 5:337–401; the Old English entries alone in Pheifer, *Old English Glosses*. I quote from *CGL*. On the connection of these glossaries with seventh-century Canterbury, see Michael Lapidge, "The School of Theodore and Hadrian," *Anglo-Saxon England* 15 (1986): 45–72, and Rusche, "The Source for Plant Names," 131.

Corpus Glossary: Cambridge, Corpus Christi College, MS 144 (Canterbury, St. Augustine's, s. ix^in). See Bernhard Bischoff, Mildred Budny, M.B. Parkes, and J.D. Pheifer (eds), *The Épinal, Erfurt, Werden, and Corpus Glossaries*, Early English Manuscripts in Facsimile 22 (Copenhagen: Rosenkilde & Bagger, 1988), 25; Gneuss, *Handlist*, no. 45. Edited by W.M. Lindsay, *The Corpus Glossary* (Cambridge: Cambridge University Press, 1921).

[37] London, British Library, MS Cotton Cleopatra A. iii, fols 5–95 (St. Augustine's, Canterbury, s. x^med). Cf. Ker, *Catalogue*, no. 143. Three glossaries from this manuscript were recently edited by Philip G. Rusche, "The Cleopatra Glossaries" (Ph.D. diss., Yale University, 1996). In this paper, however, I am quoting from Thomas Wright, *Anglo-Saxon and Old English Vocabularies*, ed. and collated by Richard Paul Wülcker (2 vols, Darmstadt: Wissenschaftliche Buchgesellschaft, 1968), vol. 1, nos XI, 338–473, VIII, 258–83, XII, 474–553; hereafter referred to as WW. See also Patrizia Lendinara, "The Glossaries in London, BL, Cotton Cleopatra A. iii," in Rolf Bergmann, Elvira Glaser, and Claudine Moulin-Fankhänel (eds), *Mittelalterliche volkssprachige Glossen: Internationale Fachkonferenz des Zentrum für Mittelalterstudien der Otto-Friedrich-Universität Bamberg, 2. bis 4. August 1999* (Heidelberg: Carl Winter, 2001), 189–215.

[38] Brussels, Bibliothèque Royale, MS 1820–30, fols 36–109 (Canterbury, s. xi^in). Cf. Ker, *Catalogue*, no. 9; Gneuss, *Handlist*, no. 807. According to Rusche ("The Source for Plant Names," 132 n. 18), s. x, from Canterbury. Printed in WW, no. I, 284–303 (from where I am quoting), and by Rusche, "Cleopatra Glossaries." Cf. Rusche, "The Source for Plant Names," 132–5.

[39] Antwerp, Plantin-Moretus Museum, MS M.16.2 (47) + London, British Library, MS Additional 32246 (Abingdon, s. xi^1). Cf. Ker, *Catalogue*, no. 2; Gneuss, *Handlist*, no. 775. See also the recent paper (with supporting documentation) by Loredana Lazzari, "The Scholarly Achievements of Aethelwold and His Circle," in Lendinara, Lazzari, and D'Aronco, *Form and Content of Instruction*, 309–47, esp. 327–41. The glossaries have been printed by WW (from the Junius copy), nos IV and V, 104–67 and 168–219; by Förster, "Die altenglische Glossenhandschrift Plantinus 32 (Antwerpen) und Additional 32246 (London);" and by Lowell Kindschi (ed.), "The Latin–Old English Glossaries in Plantin-Moretus MS 32 and British Museum MS Additional 32,246" (Ph.D. diss., Stanford University, 1955).

[40] Reference numbers are from Stracke's edition.

Electrum .i. lupinus sapo (644)

Lupinum .i. montanum (904)

Termos .i. lupinus (1474)

Termos erinos .i. lupinus agrestis (1475)

The closest sources for entries 904, 1474, and 1475 can be found in the *Asaru Glossary* (578.42, 577.44, 577.57, see above) which, according to Rusche, could have been imported from the Continent during the tenth-century Benedictine Reform period together with the closely related *Anesus* and *Arsenic Glossaries*.[41] The first entry (644) is more problematic. The lemma, *electrum*, is followed by the definition *lupinus sapo*. This double interpretamentum is not easy to explain. In my opinion it is not a single gloss, *lupinus sapo*, but consists of two separate definitions, *lupinus* and *sapo*. The former interpretamentum, *lupinus* (the first documented in the Anglo-Saxon glossaries, by the way), could be derived from the two already-mentioned passages in the *Old English Herbarium* (see above) since the compiler of the *Laud Glossary* made extensive use of this translation.[42] The latter, *sapo*, could be an emendation by the copyist of Laud who might not have understood the connection between *electrum* and *sap* of the gloss "electrum .i. lupinus sap" (maybe the result of two originally separated entries) he found in his exemplar.[43] He might, therefore, have presumed that *lupinus sapo* was the name of some sort of plant—such as, for example, some kind of soapwort—since in the *Hermeneumata Pseudo-Dositheana* (in the section *De odoribus*, *CGL* 3:185.32 and 273.65), *radix lupini* glosses *strut(h)ium*, the usual name for soapwort (*Saponaria officinalis* L.). However, OE *sap* "sap, juice" could indeed gloss *electrum* in its meaning of amber/resin, as we can deduce from two glosses preserved in the eleventh-century subject glossary of the Antwerp-London manuscript, a glossary connected with the Canterbury glossary production.[44] The glosses are entered respectively in the *Nomina arborum* section and in a list of stone names:

Electrum, smylting, uel glær (WW 141.33)

Succinum, uel electrum, sap, smelting (WW 148.8)

---

[41]   See Rusche, "The Source for Plant Names," 134.

[42]   See ibid., 139–40.

[43]   As noted also by Philip Rusche in a private communication. I would like to thank Dr. Rusche for his kind help.

[44]   Cf. Rusche, "The Source for Plant Names," 141.

The two entries contain the standard interpretation of *electrum* as denoting both the alloy of gold and silver, and amber in the Latin glossary tradition[45] that draws upon Isidore's descriptions:

> De electro. Electrum vocatum quod ad radium solis clarius auro argentoque reluceat ... Defaecatius est enim hoc metallum omnibus metallis. Huius tria genera: unum, quod ex pini arboribus fluit, quod sucinum dicitur; alterum metallum, quod naturaliter invenitur et in pretio habetur; tertium, quod fit de tribus partibus auri et argenti una. Quas partes, etiam si naturale solvas, invenies (*Etym., De lapidibus et metallis,* 16.24.1–2).[46]
>
> Sucinus, quem appellant Graeci ἤλεκτρον, fulvi cereique coloris, fertur arboris sucus esse et ob id sucinum appellari ... Nascitur autem in insulis Oceani septentrionalis sicut gummis, densaturque ut crystallum rigore vel tempore. Ex ea fiunt decoris gratia agrestium feminarum monilia (*Etym., De rubris gemmis,* 16.8.6–7).[47]

On the whole, OE *smylting* translates *electrum* when denoting the alloy,[48] while OE *glær* is the Germanic vernacular word for amber, resin (cf. *DOE,* s.vv.).

---

[45] Cf. *Electrum:* "Sucinum, genus resinae pretiosae in lapidem duratae" and "genus metalli ex auro et argento conflati," *Thesaurus linguae latinae* (Leipzig: Teubner, 1900– [in progress]), vol. 5, s.v.

[46] W.M. Lindsay (ed.), *Isidori Hispalensis episcopi Etymologiarum sive originum libri XX* (2 vols, Oxford: Clarendon Press, 1911). "Electrum (*electrum*) is so named because it reflects in the sun's ray more clearly than silver or gold ... This metal is more refined than all the other metals. There are three kinds. The first kind, which flows from pine branches (i.e. amber, the primary meaning of *electrum*), is called 'liquid electrum.' The second, which is found naturally and held in esteem, is 'metallic electrum.' The third kind is made from three parts gold and one part silver. You will find these same proportions if you melt natural electrum." Translated by Stephen A. Barney, W.J. Lewis, J.A. Beach, and Oliver Berghof, *The "Etymologies" of Isidore of Seville* (Cambridge: Cambridge University Press, 2006), 332.

[47] "Amber (*sucinus*), which the Greeks call ἤλεκτρον, has the color of tawny wax, and is said to be the sap (*sucus*) of trees, and for this reason is called 'amber' ... It is formed in the islands of the northern Ocean as pine gum, and is solidified like crystal by the cold or by the passage of time. It is used to make beautiful necklaces that are popular with rural women." Translated by Barney et al., *"Etymologies" of Isidore of Seville,* 323–4.

[48] See Hans Schabram, "Ae. smylting 'electrum': Polysemie lat. Wörter als Problem der ae. Lexikographie," in Alfred Bammesberger (ed.), *Problems of Old English Lexicography: Studies in Memory of Angus Cameron* (Regensburg: Friedrich Pustet, 1985), 317–30; Hans Schabram, "The Latin and Old English Glosses to *electrum* in the Harley Glossary," in Kinshiro Oshitari et al. (eds), *Philologia Anglica: Essays Presented to Professor Yoshio Terasawa on the Occasion of His Sixtieth Birthday* (Tokyo: Kenkyusha, 1988), 29–34; Hans Schabram, "Ae. eolhsand 'electrum': Über den Umgang mit Glossenbelegen," in Andreas Fischer (ed.), *The History and the Dialects of Old English: Festschrift for Edward Kolb,* Anglistische Forschungen 203 (Heidelberg: Carl Winter,

As for OE *sap* "sap, juice," it can be considered a synonym of *glær*, on the strength of Isidore's *Etymologiae*:

> Pinus arbor picea ab acumine foliorum vocata ... In Germaniae autem insulis huius arboris lacrima electrum gignit. Gutta enim defluens rigore vel tepore in soliditatem durescit et gemmam facit, de qualitate sua et nomen accipiens, id est sucinum, eo quod sucus sit arboris (*Etym.*, *De propriis nominibus arborum*, 17.7.31).[49]

But how did *electrum* come to denote the lupin?

In the continental Latin glossaries, *electrum* can mean both the alloy (generally gold and silver, but also other metals) and amber, the resin. As alloy, it is documented in the *Abstrusa*, *Affatim*, *Abavus*, and *"AA" Glossaries*;[50] as amber it is preserved in the *Hermeneumata Pseudo-Dositheana*, in the sections *De aureis* (*Herm. Einsidlensia*) and *De diuitibus* (*Herm. Monacensia*),[51] as well as in the *Asaru* and *Asphaltum Glossaries*, where the glosses were rearranged in alphabetical order.

1989), 115–30; Hans Schabram, "Electre und A(u)mber zu den Bezeichnungen für Hellgold und Bernstein im mittel- und frühneuenglischen," *Anglia* 108 (1990): 1–18; K. Ostberg, "Zum Komplex der althochdeutschen Deutung von *electrum*," *Beiträge zur Erforschung der deutschen Sprache* 3 (1983): 269–77. Cf. also *eolhsand* in *DOE*, s.v.

[49]   "The pine (*pinus*), a resinous tree, is named from the sharpness of its needles ... on the islands of Germania the 'tears' of this tree produce amber (*electrum*), for the flowing sap hardens, from cold or warmth, into solidity and makes a gem taking its name from its character, namely amber (*sucinum*), because it consists of the sap (*sucus*) of the tree." Translated by Barney et al., *"Etymologies" of Isidore of Seville*, 345. See also Hans Schabram, "Altenglisch *sap*: Ein altes germanisches Wort für 'Bernstein'?" in Rolf Bergmann et al. (eds), *Althochdeutsch*, vol. 2: *Wörter und Namen: Forschungsgeschichte* (Heidelberg: Carl Winter, 1987), 1210–15.

[50]   Editions: *Abstrusa Glossary* in *CGL* 4:3–198; *Affatim Glossary* in *CGL* 4:471–581; *Abavus Glossary* in *CGL* 4:301–403; *"AA" Glossaries* in *CGL* 5:435–90.

[51]   *Hermeneumata Einsidlensia*, *CGL* 3:223–79; *Hermeneumata Monacensia*, *CGL* 3:119–220.

1. *electrum*, the alloy

Abstrusa Glossary (*CGL* 4)	*Affatim Glossary* (*CGL* 4)	*Abavus Glossary* (*CGL* 4)	*"AA" Glossaries* (*CGL* 5)
Electrum id est argentum et aurum mixtum (61.39, note)	Electrum aurum argentum incoctum (510.9) Electrum aurum et argentum qui in unum commiscitur (510.10)	Electrum aurum mixtum (335.20)	Elictorum aurum argentum plumbumque permixtum mixtaque materia (453.5)

2. *electrum*, amber

Herm. Ps.-Dositheana (*CGL* 3)	*Asaru Glossary* (*CGL* 3)	*Asphaltum Glossary* (*CGL* 3)
ilectron sucinum (202.59) τὰ ἠλέκτρινα sucina (274.28)	eltron .i. sucinum (560.74) electron sucinus hoc est classe (562.35)	eltrocucino (538.56)

The Anglo-Saxon glossaries document both *electrum* and *sucinum*:

Leiden Glossary (Hessels 1906)	*II Erfurt* (*CGL* 5)	*I Erfurt* (*CGL* 5)	*Corpus Glossary* (Lindsay)
Electrum: de auro et argento et ęrę (XV.37, p. 16)	Electrum aurum et argentum incoctum uel ignis aeraqua terra (288.71)	Electrum aurum et argentum mixtum (359.9) electirum elothr (359.20) sucinus lapis qui ferrum thrahit (390.8)	ii Electrum: aurum et argentum mixtum (E 118) electrum: elotr (E 116) sucinus: lapis qui ferrum trahit (S 633)

First Cleopatra	*Second Cleopatra*	*Third Cleopatra*
Electri eolhsandes (WW 395.2)	Succinum, glaer (WW 272.24; *De metallis* section)	Electri eolhsandes (WW 491.13) Sucine glæres (WW 491.14)

Antwerp-London	Ælfric Gl.[52]	Durham[53]	Harley 3376[54]
Electrum elehtre (WW 134.31; *Nomina herbarum* section)	Electrum, electre (310.11; *Nomina herbarum* section)	Eleotrum eleotre (147)	Electrum, .i. sucus arboris, cwicseolfer, uel mæstling[55] (WW 227.9)
Succinum, uel electrum, sap, smelting (WW 148.8; in a batch of names of precious stones)	Electrum smelting (319.3; in a batch of names of metals)		
Electrum, smylting, uel glær (WW 141.33; *Nomina arborum* section)			

These glosses can be divided into those with Latin interpretamenta and those with Old English translations. The Latin–Latin entries—documented only in the earliest glossaries—come from different sources: the Leiden gloss, according to Hessels, derives from Ezekiel;[56] as for the entries in the *First Erfurt* and *Corpus Glossaries*, "Electrum aurum et argentum mixtum" (*CGL* 5:359.9; E 118), they correspond to a gloss in the *Abstrusa Glossary* (*CGL* 4:61.39) inserted in the margin of the text in an eleventh-century manuscript from Montecassino,[57] which is rather interesting in the light of the contacts between the continental Benedictine monasteries and Anglo-Saxon England.[58] Also the entry in *Second Erfurt*, "Electrum aurum et argentum incoctum uel ignis aeraqua terra"

---

[52]   Julius Zupitza (ed.), *Ælfrics Grammatik und Glossar: Text und Varianten*, 2nd edn, with foreword by Helmut Gneuss (Berlin: Weidmann, 1966).

[53]   *Durham Glossary*: Durham, Cathedral Library, MS Hunter 100, from Durham, s. xii^in; Ker, *Catalogue*, no. 110. Printed by von Lindheim, *Das Durhamer Pflanzenglossar*.

[54]   *Harley Glossary*: London, British Library, MS Harley 3376, England (Worcester?), s. x/ xi; Ker, *Catalogue*, no. 240; Gneuss, *Handlist*, no. 436.

[55]   For *mæstling*, cf. Schabram, "The Latin and Old English Glosses to *electrum* in the Harley Glossary."

[56]   Hessels, *A Late Eighth-century Latin–Anglo-Saxon Glossary*, 102: "Ezech. i. 4 species electri, 27 vidi speciem *electri*; viii. 2 visio *electri*." The editor remarks (in the Introduction, p. viii) that the glossator has, most unusually, "turned the gen. *electri* of Ezech. i. 4 into *electrum*."

[57]   Montecassino, Archivio della Badia, MS 439.

[58]   See Maria Amalia D'Aronco, "The Benedictine Rule and the Care of the Sick: The Case of Anglo-Saxon England," in Barbara S. Bowers (ed.), *The Medieval Hospital and Medical Practice*, AVISTA Studies in the History of Medieval Technology, Science and Art 3 (Aldershot, UK: Ashgate, 2007), 235–51.

(*CGL* 5:288.71), seems to draw from a similar source combined with another entry in the same Montecassino manuscript: "Elementa ut aqua ignis aer terra" (*CGL* 4:61.18). On the other hand, the gloss to Lat. *sucinus* in the *First Erfurt* and *Corpus Glossaries*[59] depends on Isidore's *Etymologiae*, where *electrum* is described for its property of causing static electricity:

> Vocari autem a quibusdam harpaga, eo quod adtritu digitorum accepta caloris anima folia paleasque et vestium fimbrias rapiat, sicut magnes ferrum (*Etym.*, *De rubris gemmis*, 16.8.7).[60]

As for the entries that have undergone the typical Anglo-Saxon re-elaboration, that is, preserving the Latin headword and translating the Latin interpretamentum into its Old English equivalent, the late glossaries are quite consistent in the use of *smylting* and *eolhsand* to translate *electrum* when denoting the alloy, and of *glær/sap* to denote amber.[61] More complex is the interpretation of the entry "electrum elehtre" which is documented as early as in the *First Erfurt* and *Corpus Glossaries*, since the context of these glosses does not help. The term, however, seems to have denoted some sort of herb since it appears in the section of plant names in the eleventh-century *Antwerp-London* and *Ælfric Glossaries*, while the Durham plant-name glossary preserves a gloss that is clearly derived from the same source as *First Erfurt* and *Corpus*.

As I have already pointed out, the interpretation of *elehtre* as lupin has been built on the one-to-one correspondences in the *Old English Herbarium* and the gloss in Laud. There is, moreover, another gloss that had a crucial role in the lexicographical history of *elehtre*. A recension of the Salernitan plant-name glossary *Alphita*, preserved in a manuscript copied in England in the late

---

[59] See also the gloss to Aldhelm (AldV 1.1127, *DOE* numeration): "sucini glæres sucinus lapis qui ferrum trahit"; Louis Goossens (ed.), *The Old English Glosses of Ms. Brussels, Royal Library, 1650 (Aldhelm's "De Laudibus Virginitatis")*, Verhandelingen van de Koninklijke Academie voor Wetenschappen, Letteren en Schone Kunsten, Klasse der Letteren 36 (Brussels: Koninklijke Academie van België, 1974), no. 74.

[60] "But some people call it *harpaga* (lit. 'hook') because, once it has received the spirit of heat from being rubbed with the fingers, it attracts leaves and chaff and the fringes of clothing just as a magnet attracts iron." Translated by Barney et al., *"Etymologies" of Isidore of Seville*, 324.

[61] It has been argued that *smylting* and *glær* could be synonyms since they both gloss *electrum* in the *Antwerp-London Glossary* (WW 141.33). According to Schabram, however, multiple glossing can "reflect the polysemy of the lemma concerned"—something of which, in the case of *electrum*, the Anglo-Saxon glossators were well aware, as it appears in the other gloss in the same glossary: "Succinum, uel electrum, sap, smelting" (WW 148.8). Cf. Schabram, "Ae. smylting 'electrum,'" 317 and nn. 3–8.

fourteenth century (London, British Library, MS Sloane 284),[62] with strong connections with the *Durham* and *Laud Glossaries*, has the following gloss:

> **Electrum** multos habet stipites, folia uiridia, et flores croceos.[63]

Electrum is here described as a plant with many twigs and shoots, green leaves, and yellow flowers. Mowat, on the authority of Ælfric or, perhaps, on John Earle's,[64] identifies it with lupin,[65] thus giving a firm basis throughout the centuries to the interpretation *elehtre* = lupin.

On this evidence, previous scholarship assumed Lat. *electrum* as the model of the loanword *elehtre*. However, early on Pogatscher found it difficult to satisfactorily explain all the variants of this term;[66] in particular, the oldest Anglo-Saxon attestations—*elothr* and *elotr* (*First Erfurt* and *Corpus Glossaries* respectively)—consist of such unusual forms that Pheifer emended the manuscript form *elothr* to *elohtr*,[67] while Hessels suggested that:

> In *elotr* the *c* is dropped; in *eloþr* not only is the *c* dropped, but the *t* has become *þ* by "Lautverschiebung" which proves a *very early* borrowing.[68]

---

[62]   The manuscript is described in Alejandro García González (ed.), *Alphita*, Edizione Nazionale "La Scuola Medica Salernitana" 2 (Florence: SISMEL, Edizioni del Galluzzo, 2007), 99–100. *Alphita* is entered on fols 1r–48v. The same recension is preserved in another manuscript of English origin, Oxford, Bodleian Library, MS Arch. Selden B. 35, *c.* 1465; described ibid., 100–101. Fols 53r–82v contain an incomplete version of *Alphita* (letters *a–s*). The two witnesses seem to derive from a common ancestor; cf. García González, *Alphita*, 116–17.

[63]   J.L.G. Mowat (ed.), *Alphita: A Medico-Botanical Glossary, from the Bodleian Manuscript Selden B. 35*, Anecdota Oxoniensia, Mediaeval and Modern Series 1, Part 2 (Oxford: Clarendon Press, 1887), 54, lines 3–4. Mowat based his edition on MS Arch. Selden B. 35 with interpolations from MS Sloane 284.

[64]   Cf. John Earle, *English Plant Names from the Tenth to the Fifteenth Century* (Oxford: Clarendon Press, 1880), 13, "*Electrum*, elehtre"; Mowat, *Alphita*, 54 n. 2.

[65]   Lupin is mentioned in another gloss: "*Lupinus* faba egiptiaca idem, cuius ferina (*sic!*) cum melle comesta aut cum aceto bibita lumbricos excludit"; Mowat, *Alphita*, 106, lines 7–10.

[66]   Cf. Alois Pogatscher, *Zur Lautlehre der griechischen, lateinischen und romanischen Lehnworte im Altenglischen* (Strassburg: Trübner, 1888), 88–9. For the variants cf. *DOE*, s.v. *elehtre*: "Elehtre; lehtre (ÆGl MS C); elechtre (DurGl), electre | ealhtre (Med 3) | eluhtre (Lch II) | eleotre (DurGl) | elothr (ErfGl), elotr (CorpGl) || elehtran, elechtran (Lch I) | ealhtran (Med 3), ealehtran (Lch II) | eolectran (Med 5.10) | eluhtran (Lch II)."

[67]   Cf. Pheifer, *Old English Glosses*, 85 and note to line 386, and §§68 and 67.

[68]   Hessels, *A Late Eighth-century Latin–Anglo-Saxon Glossary*, 226.

Of course, when dealing with graphic variants, especially when attested in glossaries, caution is required before drawing any conclusions. There is nonetheless another aspect of the Anglo-Saxon term that has not yet drawn scholarly attention. From a morphological point of view, *elehtre*, which is the most recent form, is a weak feminine in *-e*, the usual grammatical category for plant names.[69] Conversely, *elothr* and *elotr* show an *a*-declension, a masculine or neuter ending, as did many early Latin loanwords of the Latin second declension.[70] It was evidently something unusual for a plant name, since the compiler (copyist?) of the *Durham Glossary* rectified it to *eleotre* (with a feminine ending) in the entry "eleotrum eleotre" that seems to draw from the same source as the *First Erfurt Glossary*, that "glossary of plant names related to Dioscorides' *De materia medica* brought to Canterbury in the seventh century."[71]

In the light of these considerations, I would advance the suggestion that the entry of *First Erfurt*, "electirum elothr," is not the result of a copyist's misinterpretation (although this remains a possibility).[72] Moreover, since the entries of the *First Erfurt* and *Durham Glossaries* are closely connected, what, then, if *electirum* and *eleotrum* were not graphic variants of *electrum*, but represented another word?

The medical corpus contains something that could answer this question: an element used as a strong purgative, *elaterium* (*-ius*),[73] the juice of the fruit of *cucumis agrestis* or *silvestris* (*Ecballus elaterium* Rich.), squirting cucumber, common in warm Mediterranean regions, near the sea; the term is also used for the plant itself.[74] *Elaterium* is well known in classical and late antique medicine[75] and extensively represented in all medico-botanical glossaries, i.e., the *Anesus*, *Asaru*, *Arsenic*, and *Asphaltum Glossaries*.[76]

---

69 Cf. Pogatscher, *Zur Lautlehre*, 160.

70 Alistair Campbell, *Old English Grammar* (Oxford: Oxford University Press, 1959), §519.

71 Rusche, "The Source for Plant Names," 140.

72 Similar OE forms, *eluhtre, -an* and *eolehtran*, are found in the oldest medical texts (ninth to tenth centuries), respectively in Bald's *Læceboc* and in the Omont fragment. Later texts, such as *Lacnunga*, preserve *ealhtre, -an* etc.

73 This interpretation was first advanced by Giulia Mazzuoli Porru, "Ambra 'lucida gemma': storia di una parola," *AION: Filologia Germanica* 28–9 (1985–86): 421–70.

74 Cf. Jacques André, *Les noms des plantes dans la Rome antique* (Paris: Les Belles Lettres, 1985), 93; see also Maud Grieve, *A Modern Herbal* (2 vols, New York: Dover, 1982), 1:241.

75 See Carmélia Opsomer, *Index de la pharmacopée du Ier au Xe siècle* (2 vols, Hildesheim: Olms-Weidmann, 1989), 1:232–4 and 262–3, s.vv. *cucumis* and *elaterium*.

76 Cf. "elictario .i. sucus [cu]cumeris agrestis," *Anesus Glossary* (*CGL* 3, Third Reg., 589.57; Herm. Bern., 610.67; Vat. lat. 4417, 623.20; and Sloane 475, fol. 149v7); "elaterium sucus cucumeris agrestis," *Asaru Glossary* (*CGL* 3:562.68); "elatirio siue sicis agrios cocummere agreste,"

If we assume *elaterium* as the model for the loanword *elothr*, at least some of these perplexities find an answer. In fact, since the *First Erfurt Glossary* is itself a copy by a German scribe, the Old English loanword must belong to a very early stratum of the language; consequently both the phonetic aspect of the loanword and its grammatical ending can appear more plausible. As for the lemma in *Corpus*, it is possible that the scribe, not understanding the unfamiliar form in his model, emended it into the more familiar *electrum*, thus establishing the correspondence *electrum—elotr*. And in the course of time, *elothr/elotr*, through its association with *electrum*, became *elehtre*.

In the light of these considerations, *elehtre* glossing various other plants, such as *malum terrae*, *maura*, *maurella*, makes more sense. Among the synonyms of *maura* is *peucedanum*, which can signify *cucumis siluestris/agrestis* (*elaterium*);[77] on the other hand, *malum terrae* usually denotes a plant with tuberous roots or round fruits such as cyclamen, mandrake, and aristolochia (birthwort). And cucumbers have round fruits and long twigs as described in a gloss of the *Second Erfurt Glossary*:

Cucumerus genus herbae et pomas habet (*CGL* 5:283.1).[78]

Cucumbers are mentioned also in the *Leiden Glossary* in an entry that reappears in the *First Cleopatra* and *Antwerp-London Glossaries*:

Leiden Gl.: "Cucumerarium: hortus in quo cucum[er]is crescit; bona herba ad manducandum sive ad medicinam" (XIII.1, p. 13)
First Cleopatra: "In cucumerario, on wyrttune" (WW 427.19)
Antwerp-London: "Cucumerarium, wyrttun" (WW 133.16)

It seems, therefore, that cucumbers were known at a very early stage in Anglo-Saxon England; the plant is, however, ignored by the early botanical

---

Arsenic Glossary (*CGL* 3:632.11); "elaterion id est cucumere agreste," "elaterium id est sucus cucumeris agresti," *Asphaltum Glossary* (*CGL* 3:538.54, 539.2).

[77]   Cf. André, *Les noms des plantes*, 195, *peucedanum* 2.

[78]   See also the description of the herb *colocintis agria* (*Citrullus colocynthis* Schrad.), bitter cucumber, in ch. 185 of the *Old English Herbarium*: "Just like other gourds it expands its branches over the ground. It has divided leaves like a cucumber and round and bitter fruit"; translation from Van Arsdall, *Medieval Herbal Remedies*, 230. The Old English text translates Pseudo-Dioscorides, *De herbis femininis*, ch. 47: "haec similiter ut cucumis vel cucurbita per terram flagella tendit, folia habens cucumeris similia et scissa, fructum habet rotundum." See H.F. Kästner (ed.), "Pseudo-Dioscoridis *De herbis femininis*," *Hermes* 31 (1896): 578–636, at 621–2.

glossaries.[79] In fact, only after the translation of the *Old English Herbarium* does *cucumis silvaticus*, OE *hwerhwette*, find its way into the Anglo-Saxon medical and botanical lexicon:

> *OEHerbarium*, ch. 114, ed. de Vriend, 156, lines 22–3: "Ðeos wyrt þe man cucumerem siluaticum ⁊ oþrum naman hwerhwette nemneþ"
> *Brussels Glossary* (*Nomina herbarum*): "Cucumeris, hwærhwætte" (WW 296.12)
> *Antwerp-London Glossary* (*Nomina herbarum*): "Cucumer, hwerhwette" (WW 134.10)
> *Durham Glossary*: "Cucumeris hservehete [*sic*] uel verhvete" (137)

The *Brussels Glossary* contains also a copy of the *Asaru Glossary* (fols 36r–46v) which mentions cucumber in connection with *elaterium*:

> elaterium de cucumere agresti fit (*CGL* 3:560.72)
> elaterium sucus cucumeris agrestis (*CGL* 3:562.68)

Similar entries can be found in the *Anesus Glossary*, of which there is an exemplar copied in England in the late eleventh century (London, British Library, MS Sloane 475),[80] and in the *Arsenic* and *Asphaltum Glossaries*.[81] The *Laud Glossary*, which draws upon a number of sources,[82] reflects this situation:

> elacterius seu siciatron .i. cucumeris agresti succus (590)
> eleaterium .i. succus cucumeris siluatici (612)[83]

To conclude, the connection between *elehtre* and lupins stands on a basis that seems to be more lexicographic than documentary. The only certainty is that *elehtre* denotes some sort of plant (lupins only from the end of the tenth century)

---

[79] It might have been mentioned in Bald's *Leechbook*; see Bierbaumer, *Der botanische Wortschatz des Altenglischen*, vol. 1: *Das Læceboc*, s.vv. *hwerhwette*, *hwerwe*.

[80] "Elaterio id est sucus de cucumeri agresti" (Sloane 475, fol. 149v7), and "elictario .i. sucus [cu]cumeris agrestis" (*CGL* 3, Third Reg., 589.57; *Herm. Bern.* 610.67; Vat. lat. 4417 623.20).

[81] The *Arsenic Glossary* states: "elatirio siue sicis agrios cocummere agreste" (*CGL* 3:632.11). The *Asphaltum Glossary* (Montecassino 69) has "elaterion idest cucumere agreste," "elaterium idest sucus cucumeris agresti" (*CGL* 3:538.54, 539.2, respectively).

[82] Rusche, "The Source for Plant Names," 135.

[83] See also the entry "ligridos .i. cucumeris amarus" (*Laud Glossary*, 910), which can be compared to the entries "litridos cucumer amarus," "latridus .i. cucumer amarus" of the *Asaru Glossary* (*CGL* 3:567.6, 567.15, respectively) and "litridos idest cucumere amaro," "latridos idest cucumeris amari" of the *Asphaltum Glossary* (in Montecassino 69: *CGL* 3:540.25, 540.34, respectively).

and that the herb *electrum* mentioned in the *Alphita Glossary* is known only to England, since the continental manuscript tradition ignores it.[84] No better explanation can be found in the Anglo-Saxon medical remedies, where *elehtre* is usually prescribed in numerous recipes that have only one trait in common, the lack of direct Latin sources and, perhaps, the absence of cures against intestinal worms, which is noteworthy since lupins were the "golden therapy" throughout antiquity against these parasites. In fact, the first textual mention of the use of lupins against intestinal worms is in the already-mentioned passages of the *Old English Herbarium*. In Anglo-Saxon medicine *elehtre* is employed together with other elements to cure a number of ailments that run from lung diseases to swellings of feet and shins, gout, rheumatism, arthritis, joint pains, paralysis and shingles, dropsy, jaundice, kidney complaints, heart problems, all kind of fevers, and so on. *Elehtre* also cures problems of the skin, such as black spots, pimples, boils, eruptions, abscesses, wounds, scars, scrofula, even elephantiasis. And, finally, *elehtre* helps in the event of consumption of bad food or drink, even of poison; it is an emetic and a strong purgative, and cures nervous diseases, insomnia, madness, and black magic.

For most of these remedies either lupins or *elaterium* could have been employed. There is perhaps one occurrence that lets us infer that the element prescribed is *elaterium*. In one remedy of *Book III*, *Wiþ deofle*, against devil possession/madness, the practitioner is advised to use the root of *elehtre* (*elehtran moran*):

> Book III, 64.1: "Wiþ deofle liþe drenc & ungemynde, do on ealu cassuc, elehtran moran, finul, ontre, betonice, hindheoloþe, merce, rude, wermod, nefte, elene, ælfþone, wulfescomb, gesing xii mæssan ofer þam drence & drince, him biþ sona wel."[85]

Not only is madness never cured with lupins in late antique and medieval medicine, but the roots of lupins are never mentioned in remedies, while the roots of *elaterium* are commonly used in a number of prescriptions. Madness, however, can be cured by purging the body; and lupins and *elehtre* are both purgative. Moreover, both ingredients are not indigenous to England, but were imported from the Continent; lupins, according to classical Mediterranean

---

[84]   Cf. García González, *Alphita*, 202–12.

[85]   "A light drink against devils and madness. Do in ale hassock, roots of *elehtre*, fennel, radish, betony, waterhemp (*or* wood germander), celery, rue, wormwood, catmint, elecampane, woody nightshade, wild teasel. Sing twelve masses over the drink, give it to drink, he will soon be well." My translation. Plant names according to *DOE* and Bierbaumer, *Der botanische Wortschatz des Altenglischen*, vol. 1: *Das Læceboc*.

medicine, were traded in grains, *elaterium* in dried pills (*eletuarium*) or even in seeds.[86]

In my opinion, these traits in common may have helped in confusing the two elements; there are other examples in the ancient botanical tradition where identical names denote different plants, and where different names are attributed to the same plant. The process is so complicated that there is no way to simplify it; however, we must consider that names of plants are less significant than their medicinal use, which tends to remain substantially unchanged. For practitioners, usage is determinant in the identification of the element.[87] Examples are numerous; one in particular is worth mentioning in this context. The plant name *peucedanum* denotes two very different plants. The first is *Peucedanum officinale* L., hog's fennel, sulphurwort; the second is *Ecballium elaterium* Rich., squirting cucumber. According to André, the explication could be found in the fact that the two plants have some uses in common.[88] Something similar seems to have been at work in Anglo-Saxon England. Little by little the element *elehtre*, connected to Lat. *electrum* by the more scholarly glossaries, became polysemic, denoting both *elaterium* and lupins. Its life, however, was not long. According to Tony Hunt, by the end of the thirteenth century *elehtre* has disappeared as interpretamentum for the entries *electarus, electra, electrum nigrum/elostrum nigrum* that gloss various (and doubtful) plants such as *regedewort* "ragwort (?)," *crousope, anglice tesel* "soapwort, teasel," or *scabgras, scabbewort, scabbegras* "lupin (?), elecampane (?)," while the loanword *lupin* made its first appearance glossing *lupinus* (cf. "gallice lupins," "lupins," "lupyn," "lasse lupyn," "anglice lupyns").[89]

The history of the lexicographic interpretation of *elehtre* adds another caveat to longstanding studies on the identification of medieval plant names. An incomplete identification has caused the assumption that the Anglo-

---

[86] Pliny, *Natural History*, 20.2.3–20.5.10; ed. and trans. H. Rackham, W.H.S. Jones, and D.E. Eichholz, Loeb Classical Library (10 vols, Cambridge, MA: Harvard University Press, 1938–63), 6:4–8.

[87] "Whereas names of herbs are usually quite labile through time, medicinal uses tend to remain constant for millennia, and one can find in a modern herbal the same uses for a herb that were given by Dioscorides and Pliny. Contrary to much of what one hears about the uselessness of much herbal medicine, it is a fact that a majority of the herbs used in earlier times did have some beneficial effect on the patient, and some still supply drugs to modern medicine for the same ailments for which the ancients prescribed them. It follows that modern medical use can be a criterion for identification." M.L. Cameron, "What Plant Was *attorlothe* (*atorlaþe*)?" *Parergon* 10/2 (1992): 27–34, at 31.

[88] "Les deux plantes homonymes sont très différentes d'aspect, mais ont quelques emplois communs." André, *Les noms des plantes*, 195, *peucedanum* 2.

[89] Tony Hunt, *Plant Names of Medieval England* (Cambridge: D.S. Brewer, 1989), 104–5 and 164.

Saxons discovered the extraordinary properties of lupins to cure epilepsy and convulsions since they are rich in manganese.[90] My issue with this assumption is that the Old English term might have denoted some other ingredient, such as the juice of the squirting cucumber, the use of which could be more appropriate, according to medieval medicine, for treating convulsions and mental disorders since it can purge the melancholic humors responsible for the complaints.

Intriguingly, a support for this suggestion comes from the English redaction of *Alphita* itself.[91] Here, the gloss regarding the plant *electrum* was entered immediately under the definition of *elacterium* by a copyist who might have connected *elacterium* with the plant *electrum* he knew from the *Nomina herbarum* sections of the vernacular glossaries. The copyist might have interpreted *elacterium* and *electrum* as being etymologically connected, the former being the name of the product, the latter the name of the plant from which *elacterium* is produced. Thus, he simply described the plant *Ecballium elaterium* that has many traits in common with common cucumber: a tuft from which rise numerous thick, fleshy stems, thick, fleshy leaves, and pale yellow flowers with a brighter yellow center.[92] The long journey of *elaterium*, from glossary to glossary through the centuries, seems to have gone back to its origin, the squirting cucumber.

Therefore, in a continuing dialogue with the *DOE*—the dictionary that, as Joyce Hill has pointed out, "has dialogue at the heart of its *modus operandi* and also at the heart of its lexicographical output"[93]—I would suggest adding the meaning "squirting cucumber" (*Ecballium elaterium* Rich.) and the etymology Lat. *elaterium* to the plant name *elehtre*. Thus lexicographers could help scholars to better understand the Anglo-Saxon medical sources' intelligent reworking of classical material based on first-hand experience enhanced with the everyday conduct of medical practice.

---

[90]   Or that the Anglo-Saxons grew lupins in their gardens. Cf. David Porter's translation of Ælfric Bata's *Colloquy* 25, "Crescit quoque ibi libestica, sandix ... feniculum, electrum, malua crispa ...": "Also growing there are lovage, woad ... fennel, lupine, violet ..."; Scott Gwara (ed.), *Anglo-Saxon Conversations: The Colloquies of Ælfric Bata*, trans. with an introduction by David W. Porter (Woodbridge, UK: Boydell, 1997), 104–5 and 164.

[91]   Cf. n. 61 above.

[92]   Cf. Grieve, *A Modern Herbal*, 241.

[93]   "Dictionary making requires great attention to detail and, in the systematic presentation of word-forms, meanings, and usages, it may seem to be an exact science. But questions remain, and a dialogue is maintained with the *DOE* even after entries are published"; Joyce Hill, "Dialogues with the Dictionary: Five Case Studies," in Healey and Kiernan, *Making Sense*, 23–39, at 38–9.

Bibliography

André, Jacques. *Les noms des plantes dans la Rome antique.* Paris: Les Belles Lettres, 1985.

Barney, Stephen A., W.J. Lewis, J.A. Beach, and Oliver Berghof (trans.). *The "Etymologies" of Isidore of Seville.* Cambridge: Cambridge University Press, 2006.

Beccaria, Augusto. *I codici di medicina del periodo presalernitano (secoli IX, X, e XI).* Rome: Edizioni di Storia e Letteratura, 1956.

Bierbaumer, Peter. *Der botanische Wortschatz des Altenglischen.* 3 vols. Frankfurt am Main: Peter Lang, 1975–79.

Bischoff, Bernhard, Mildred Budny, M.B. Parkes, and J.D. Pheifer (eds). *The Épinal, Erfurt, Werden, and Corpus Glossaries.* Early English Manuscripts in Facsimile 22. Copenhagen: Rosenkilde & Bagger, 1988.

Bracciotti, Annalisa. "L'apporto della tradizione indiretta per la costituzione di un testo critico delle *Curae herbarum.*" *Rivista di cultura classica e medioevale* 42 (2000): 61–102.

Cameron, M.L. "The Sources of Medical Knowledge in Anglo-Saxon England." *Anglo-Saxon England* 11 (1983): 135–55.

———. "Bald's *Leechbook*: Its Sources and Their Use in Its Compilation." *Anglo-Saxon England* 12 (1983): 153–82.

———. "Bald's *Leechbook* and Cultural Interactions in Anglo-Saxon England." *Anglo-Saxon England* 19 (1990): 5–12.

———. "What Plant Was *attorlothe* (*atorlape*)?" *Parergon* 10/2 (1992): 27–34.

———. *Anglo-Saxon Medicine.* Cambridge Studies in Anglo-Saxon England 7. Cambridge: Cambridge University Press, 1993.

Campbell, Alistair. *Old English Grammar.* Oxford: Oxford University Press, 1959.

Cockayne, Oswald (ed.). *Leechdoms, Wortcunning, and Starcraft of Early England, Being a Collection of Documents for the Most Part Never Before Printed, Illustrating the History of Science in This Country before the Norman Conquest.* Rolls Series 35. 3 vols. London: Longman, 1864–66. Repr. Nendeln, Liechtenstein: Kraus, 1965.

D'Aronco, Maria Amalia. "The Botanical Lexicon of the *Old English Herbarium.*" *Anglo-Saxon England* 17 (1988): 15–33.

———. "Divergenze e convergenze lessicali in inglese antico: Il caso di *elehtre.*" In Maria Amalia D'Aronco, Anna Maria Luiselli Fadda, and Maria Vittoria Molinari (eds), "Studi sulla cultura germanica dei secoli IV–XII in onore di Giulia Mazzuoli Porru." Special issue, *Romanobarbarica* 10 (1988–89): 65–102.

————. "Anglo-Saxon Plant Pharmacy and the Latin Medical Tradition." In Carole P. Biggam (ed.), *From Earth to Art: The Many Aspects of the Plant-World in Anglo-Saxon England. Proceedings of the First ASPNS Symposium, University of Glasgow, 5–7 April 2000*, 133–51. Amsterdam: Rodopi, 2003.

————. "The Old English Pharmacopoeia." *AVISTA Forum Journal* 13/2 (2003): 9–18.

————. "How 'English' is Anglo-Saxon Medicine? The Latin Sources for Anglo-Saxon Medical Texts." In Charles Burnett and Nicholas Mann (eds), *Britannia Latina: Latin in the Culture of Great Britain from the Middle Ages to the Twentieth Century*, 27–41. Warburg Institute Colloquia 8. London/Turin: The Warburg Institute/Nino Aragno Editore, 2005.

————. "The Benedictine Rule and the Care of the Sick: The Case of Anglo-Saxon England." In Barbara S. Bowers (ed.), *The Medieval Hospital and Medical Practice*, 235–51. AVISTA Studies in the History of Medieval Technology, Science and Art 3. Aldershot, UK: Ashgate, 2007.

————. "The Missing Plant Names in the *Old English Herbal*: When Were the Blanks Filled In?" In Margit Reitbauer, Nancy Campbell, Sarah Mercer, and Renate Vaupetitsch (eds), *Contexts of English in Use: Past and Present. A Festschrift for Peter Bierbaumer on the Occasion of the 40th Anniversary of His Career at the University of Graz*, 39–49. Vienna: Wilhelm Braumüller Universitäts-Verlagsbuchhandlung, 2007.

————. "The Transmission of Medical Knowledge in Anglo-Saxon England: The Voices of Manuscripts." In Lendinara, Lazzari, and D'Aronco, *Form and Content of Instruction in Anglo-Saxon England*, 35–58.

———— and M.L. Cameron (eds). *The Old English Illustrated Pharmacopoeia: British Library Cotton Vitellius C III*. Early English Manuscripts in Facsimile 27. Copenhagen: Rosenkilde & Bagger, 1998.

Dendle, Peter. "Lupines, Manganese, and Devil-Sickness: An Anglo-Saxon Medical Response to Epilepsy." *Bulletin of the History of Medicine* 75 (2001): 91–101.

de Vriend, Hubert Jan (ed.). *The Old English Herbarium and Medicina de Quadrupedibus*. Early English Text Society, Original Series 286. London: Oxford University Press, 1984.

Earle, John. *English Plant Names from the Tenth to the Fifteenth Century*. Oxford: Clarendon Press, 1880.

Förster, Max. "Die altenglische Glossenhandschrift Plantinus 32 (Antwerpen) und Additional 32246 (London)." *Anglia* 41 (1917): 94–161.

Frank, Roberta. "*F*-Words in *Beowulf*." In Antonette diPaolo Healey and Kevin Kiernan (eds), *Making Sense: Constructing Meaning in Early English*, 1–22. Toronto: Pontifical Institute of Mediaeval Studies, 2007.

García González, Alejandro (ed.). *Alphita.* Edizione Nazionale "La Scuola Medica Salernitana" 2. Florence: SISMEL, Edizioni del Galluzzo, 2007.

Gneuss, Helmut. *Handlist of Anglo-Saxon Manuscripts and Manuscript Fragments Written or Owned in England up to 1100.* Tempe, AZ: Medieval and Renaissance Texts and Studies, 2001.

Goetz, Georg (ed.). *Corpus glossariorum latinorum.* 7 vols in 8. Leipzig: Teubner, 1888–1923.

Goossens, Louis (ed.). *The Old English Glosses of Ms. Brussels, Royal Library, 1650 (Aldhelm's "De Laudibus Virginitatis").* Verhandelingen van de Koninklijke Academie voor Wetenschappen, Letteren en Schone Kunsten, Klasse der Letteren 36. Brussels: Koninklijke Academie van België, 1974.

Grieve, Maud. *A Modern Herbal.* 2 vols. New York: Dover, 1982.

Gwara, Scott (ed.). *Anglo-Saxon Conversations: The Colloquies of Ælfric Bata.* Trans. with an introduction by David W. Porter. Woodbridge, UK: Boydell, 1997.

Healey, Antonette diPaolo (ed.). *Dictionary of Old English: A to G on CD-ROM.* Version 2. Toronto: Pontifical Institute of Mediaeval Studies, 2008.

Hessels, John Henry (ed.). *A Late Eighth-century Latin–Anglo-Saxon Glossary Preserved in the Library of the Leiden University (Ms. Voss. Q° Lat. No. 69).* Cambridge: Cambridge University Press, 1906.

Hill, Joyce. "Dialogues with the Dictionary: Five Case Studies." In Antonette diPaolo Healey and Kevin Kiernan (eds), *Making Sense: Constructing Meaning in Early English,* 23–39. Toronto: Pontifical Institute of Mediaeval Studies, 2007.

Hunt, Tony. *Plant Names of Medieval England.* Cambridge: D.S. Brewer, 1989.

Jones, Peter Murray. "Herbs and the Medieval Surgeon." In Peter Dendle and Alain Touwaide (eds), *Health and Healing from the Medieval Garden,* 162–79. Rochester, NY: Boydell & Brewer, 2008.

Kästner, H.F. (ed.). "Pseudo-Dioscoridis *De herbis femininis.*" *Hermes* 31 (1896): 578–636.

Ker, N.R. *Catalogue of Manuscripts Containing Anglo-Saxon.* Oxford: Clarendon Press, 1957. Repr. 1990.

Kindschi, Lowell (ed.). "The Latin–Old English Glossaries in Plantin-Moretus MS 32 and British Museum MS Additional 32,246." Ph.D. diss., Stanford University, 1955.

Lapidge, Michael. "The School of Theodore and Hadrian." *Anglo-Saxon England* 15 (1986): 45–72.

Lazzari, Loredana. "The Scholarly Achievements of Aethelwold and His Circle." In Lendinara, Lazzari, and D'Aronco, *Form and Content of Instruction in Anglo-Saxon England,* 309–47.

Lendinara, Patrizia. "The Glossary in Oxford, Bodleian Library, Bodley 163." In Patrizia Lendinara, *Anglo-Saxon Glosses and Glossaries*, 329–55. Variorum Collected Studies Series CS 622. Aldershot, UK: Ashgate, 1999.

——. "The Glossaries in London, BL, Cotton Cleopatra A. iii." In Rolf Bergmann, Elvira Glaser, and Claudine Moulin-Fankhänel (eds), *Mittelalterliche volkssprachige Glossen: Internationale Fachkonferenz des Zentrum für Mittelalterstudien der Otto-Friedrich-Universität Bamberg, 2. bis 4. August 1999*, 189–215. Heidelberg: Carl Winter, 2001.

——, Loredana Lazzari, and Maria Amalia D'Aronco (eds). *Form and Content of Instruction in Anglo-Saxon England: Papers from the International Conference, Udine, April 6th–8th, 2006*. Fédération Internationale des Instituts d'Études Médiévales, Textes et Études du Moyen Âge 39. Turnhout: Brepols, 2007.

Lindheim, Bogislav von (ed.). *Das Durhamer Pflanzenglossar: Lateinisch und Altenglisch*. Beiträge zur englischen Philologie 35. Bochum-Langendreer: Heinrich Pöppinghaus, 1941.

Lindsay, W.M. (ed.). *Isidori Hispalensis episcopi Etymologiarum sive originum libri XX*. 2 vols. Oxford: Clarendon Press, 1911.

——. *The Corpus Glossary*. Cambridge: Cambridge University Press, 1921.

MacKinney, Loren C. "'Dynamidia' in Medieval Medical Literature." *Isis* 24 (1935–36): 400–414.

Maion, Danielle. "The Fortune of the So-called *Practica Petrocelli Salernitani* in England: New Evidence and Some Considerations." In Lendinara, Lazzari, and D'Aronco, *Form and Content of Instruction in Anglo-Saxon England*, 479–96.

Marcellus Empiricus. *De medicamentis liber*. Ed. Georg Helmreich. Leipzig: Teubner, 1889.

Marzell, Heinrich (ed.). *Wörterbuch der deutschen Pflanzennamen*. 5 vols. Leipzig: Hirzel, 1943–79.

Mazzuoli Porru, Giulia. "Ambra 'lucida gemma': storia di una parola." *AION: Filologia Germanica* 28–9 (1985–86): 421–70.

Meaney, Audrey L. "Variant Versions of Old English Medical Remedies and the Compilation of Bald's *Leechbook*." *Anglo-Saxon England* 13 (1984): 235–68.

Mowat, J.L.G. (ed.). *Alphita: A Medico-Botanical Glossary, from the Bodleian Manuscript Selden B. 35*. Anecdota Oxoniensia, Mediaeval and Modern Series 1, Part 2. Oxford: Clarendon Press, 1887.

Nokes, Richard Scott. "The Several Compilers of Bald's *Leechbook*." *Anglo-Saxon England* 33 (2004): 51–76.

Opsomer, Carmélia. *Index de la pharmacopée du Ier au Xe siècle*. 2 vols. Hildesheim: Olms-Weidmann, 1989.

Ostberg, K. "Zum Komplex der althochdeutschen Deutung von *electrum*." *Beiträge zur Erforschung der deutschen Sprache* 3 (1983): 269–77.

Pettit, Edward (ed.). *Anglo-Saxon Remedies, Charms, and Prayers from British Library Ms Harley 585: The Lacnunga.* 2 vols. Lampeter, UK: Edwin Mellen, 2001.

Pheifer, J.D. (ed.). *Old English Glosses in the Épinal-Erfurt Glossary.* Oxford: Clarendon Press, 1974.

Pliny. *Natural History.* Ed. and trans. H. Rackham, W.H.S. Jones, and D.E. Eichholz. 10 vols. Loeb Classical Library. Cambridge, MA: Harvard University Press, 1938–63.

Pogatscher, Alois. *Zur Lautlehre der griechischen, lateinischen und romanischen Lehnworte im Altenglischen.* Strassburg: Trübner, 1888.

Pollington, Stephen. *Leechcraft: Early English Charms, Plantlore and Healing.* Hockwold-cum-Wilton, UK: Anglo-Saxon Books, 2000.

Riddle, John M. "Pseudo-Dioscorides' *Ex herbis femininis* and the Early Medieval Medical Botany." *Journal of the History of Biology* 14 (1981): 43–81.

Rusche, Philip G. "The Cleopatra Glossaries." Ph.D. diss., Yale University, 1996.

———. "The Source for Plant Names in Anglo-Saxon England and the Laud Herbal Glossary." In Peter Dendle and Alain Touwaide (eds), *Health and Healing from the Medieval Garden*, 128–45. Rochester, NY: Boydell & Brewer, 2008.

Sauer, Hans. "Towards a Linguistic Description and Classification of the Old English Plant Names." In Michael Korhammer, Karl Reichl, and Hans Sauer (eds), *Words, Texts and Manuscripts: Studies in Anglo-Saxon Culture Presented to Helmut Gneuss on the Occasion of His Sixty-fifth Birthday*, 381–408. Cambridge: D.S. Brewer, 1992.

———. "On the Analysis and Structure of Old and Middle English Plant Names." In B. Santano Moreno et al. (eds), *Papers from the VIII International Conference of the Spanish Society for Medieval English Language and Literature*, 299–325. Cáceres, Spain: Universidad de Extremadura, 1995.

———. "Old English Plant Names in the Épinal-Erfurt Glossary: Etymology, Word Formation and Semantics." In Wolfgang Falkner and Hans-Jörg Schmidt (eds), *Words, Lexemes, Concepts—Approaches to the Lexicon: Studies in Honour of Leonhard Lipka*, 23–38. Tübingen: Gunter Narr Verlag, 1999.

Schabram, Hans. "Ae. smylting 'electrum': Polysemie lat. Wörter als Problem der ae. Lexikographie." In Alfred Bammesberger (ed.), *Problems of Old English Lexicography: Studies in Memory of Angus Cameron*, 317–30. Regensburg: Friedrich Pustet, 1985.

————. "Altenglisch *sap*: Ein altes germanisches Wort für 'Bernstein'?" In Rolf Bergmann et al. (eds), *Althochdeutsch*, vol. 2: *Wörter und Namen: Forschungsgeschichte*, 1210–15. Heidelberg: Carl Winter, 1987.

————. "The Latin and Old English Glosses to *electrum* in the Harley Glossary." In Kinshiro Oshitari et al. (eds), *Philologia Anglica: Essays Presented to Prof. Yoshio Terasawa on the Occasion of His Sixtieth Birthday*, 29–34. Tokyo: Kenkyusha, 1988.

————. "Ae. *eolhsand* 'electrum': Über den Umgang mit Glossenbelegen." In Andreas Fischer (ed.), *The History and the Dialects of Old English: Festschrift for Edward Kolb*, 115–30. Anglistische Forschungen 203. Heidelberg: Carl Winter, 1989.

————. "Electre und A(u)mber zu den Bezeichnungen für Hellgold und Bernstein im mittel- und frühneuenglischen." *Anglia* 108 (1990): 1–18.

Schauman, Bella, and Angus Cameron. "A Newly-Found Leaf of Old English from Louvain." *Anglia* 95 (1977): 289–312.

Schneider, Karl. "Zur Etymologie von ae. *eolhsand* 'Bernstein' und *elehtre* 'Lupine' im Lichte bronzezeitlichen Handels." In Günter Heintz and Peter Schnitter (eds), *Collectanea Philologica: Festschrift für Helmut Gipper*, 2:669–81. 2 vols. Saecula Spiritalia 14–15. Baden-Baden: V. Koerner, 1985.

Stracke, J. Richard (ed.). *The Laud Herbal Glossary*. Amsterdam: Rodopi, 1974.

Thesaurus linguae latinae. Leipzig: Teubner, 1900– (in progress).

Van Arsdall, Anne. *Medieval Herbal Remedies: The "Old English Herbarium" and Anglo-Saxon Medicine*. New York: Routledge, 2002.

Wright, Thomas. *Anglo-Saxon and Old English Vocabularies*. Edited and collated by Richard Paul Wülcker. 2 vols. Darmstadt: Wissenschaftliche Buchgesellschaft, 1968.

Zupitza, Julius (ed.). *Ælfrics Grammatik und Glossar: Text und Varianten*. 2nd edn, with foreword by Helmut Gneuss. Berlin: Weidmann, 1966.

Chapter 7
Herbs and Herbal Healing Satirized in Middle English Texts

Linda Ehrsam Voigts

Satire of a cultural practice is one measure of it as a popular and widely known phenomenon. Among the surviving vernacular writings of late medieval England are texts satirizing the use of herbs, primarily in medicines, often by quack doctors and would-be healers. Three texts from the fourteenth and fifteenth centuries witness to the entertainment value for medieval English audiences of parodies of the practice of herbal medicine. The best-known examples of such comic treatment come from the *Canterbury Tales* of Geoffrey Chaucer (c. 1343–1400), written for literate Londoners, but such entertainment was not restricted to elite readers like Chaucer's audience. Other less sophisticated instances can be identified from a rural area in the West Midlands, c. 1465–70, and in a comic scene of a doctor and his servant interpolated in the late fifteenth-century East Anglian miracle drama *The Play of the Sacrament*.

West Midlands Popular Satire

A short Middle English text from the West Midlands, c. 1465–70, satirizes both the epistolary genre and the herbal therapy of inept doctors. This work, which has been edited with a modern English version by Nancy Pope,[1] deals with a physician (*wesysyoun*) to whom the urine of a man, "a leper and a cripple ... half blind and lame," is sent. The physician "bade them go fare down into a great meadow to gather an herb, he wist never where, and make a plaster, he wist not whereof, and he should be whole, he wist never when, upon warranties (*warranttys*)." The letter, claiming to have been sent by "Nameless Deacon Pie-Baker Breechless," obviously makes sport of the expertise and truth claims of a rural healer.

---

[1] "A Middle English Satirical Letter in Brogyntyn MS II.1," *American Notes & Queries* 18 (2005): 35–9. The concluding truth claim is conventional in medical texts.

East Anglian Comic Dramatic Interlude

Lengthier and more complex satire is found in an inserted scene in the late fifteenth-century East Anglian *Play of the Sacrament*.[2] The play itself is a conversion play which employs anti-Semitic vilification, in this case, Jews abusing a consecrated host. At one point, the character Jonathas attempts to drive nails into the consecrated bread, and—when his comrades try to pull him away—his hand breaks off, remaining attached to the sacrament. When this happens, these characters withdraw, and the only comic scene in the play—an exchange between "þe lechys man" and his employer, a self-described physician and surgeon—begins (line 525).

Editors of this play agree that language and verse form indicate that this comic scene is a late addition to the play. Especially significant is the extensive metrical variety found in the scene but not in the rest of the play.[3] The dramatic connection between this scene and the rest of the play is loose at best. The scene ends when the physician offers to help the handless Jonathas, and his assistant Colle advises Jonathas that if he undertakes "in a pott ... to pyss, / He [the

---

[2]   I am grateful to David Klausner for calling my attention to this scene. *The Play of the Sacrament* is introduced, pp. 754–6, and edited, pp. 756–88, by David M. Bevington, *Medieval Drama* (Boston: Houghton Mifflin, 1974). The standard edition, edited by Norman Davis for the Early English Text Society, Supplementary Text 1, is *Non-Cycle Plays and Fragments* (London: Oxford University Press, 1970): "Introduction," lxx–lxxxv; play text, 58–89. Quotations from the play are cited from the Davis edition. I discuss this comic scene in relation to the legitimate banns for an East Anglian physician that survive in London, British Library, MS Harley 2390, "Fifteenth-century English Banns Advertising the Services of an Itinerant Doctor," in Florence Eliza Glaze and Brian Nance (eds), *Between Text and Patient: The Medical Enterprise in Medieval and Early Modern Europe*, Micrologus' Library 39 (Florence: SISMEL, Edizioni del Galluzzo, 2011), 245–77, especially Appendix II, "Contemporary Satirical Treatment of an Itinerant Doctor and His Banns," 267–74. There are significant parallels between the legitimate banns and the satirical treatment of the proclamation in *The Play of the Sacrament*. In both cases the doctor is described as a practitioner of both physic and surgery, and there is considerable emphasis in both the Harley banns and the dramatic scene on the importance of uroscopy for diagnosis and for prognosis. Both leeches are itinerant, in temporary lodgings—the satirized doctor in a coal shed—and there is no claim for miraculous cures by either doctor.

This scene has also been modernized by Faith Wallis in Section 107, "The Doctor as Comic Relief in the *Croxton Play of the Sacrament*," of her *Medieval Medicine: A Reader* (Toronto: University of Toronto Press, 2010), 537–42. Wallis describes the doctor satire in terms of the tradition of mummers' plays, whereas I argue in Appendix II of "Fifteenth-century English Banns" that what we have in the Croxton play is estates satire rather than a mummers' play episode.

[3]   Davis, *Non-Cycle Plays*, lxxv–lxxvi; Bevington, *Medieval Drama*, 755–6.

doctor] can tell yf yow be curable." Jonathas and his comrades then "bett [beat] away þe leche and hys man" (lines 648–9), and the main plot resumes.

The Play of the Sacrament survives as a discrete section of Trinity College, Dublin, MS F. 4. 20 (652), fols 338–56.[4] The play was probably composed not long after the date 1461 found in the colophon, although the manuscript was copied out a number of years later.[5] The comic scene of the doctor and his man was almost certainly inserted after the play had been written, as the stanza forms found in it differ from those in the rest of the play,[6] but the date of the manuscript suggests that it had been added before the sixteenth century.

The setting of this comic scene can be localized in East Anglia. Although the scribal dialect of the text is Anglo-Irish, beneath it a layer of dialect can be identified with Norfolk, both on the basis of orthography and on place names in the scene. The banns for this conversion play announce a performance at Croxton,[7] and in the episode of the doctor we are told that he is lodging in a coal shed "a lytyll besyde Babwell Myll" (line 621). Babwell Priory was between Bury Saint Edmunds and Thetford in Norfolk, and one of several Croxtons is close to Thetford.[8]

The satirical scene begins when the injured Jonathas and his comrades withdraw, and the stage direction reads: "Here shall þe lechys man come into þe place sayng" (following line 524). Colle then enters addressing the audience, telling them he wishes his master had a disease called "þe pyppe"[9] (lines 525–7). He confides to the audience that his master is a man of all science, but when it comes to profitable occupation, the doctor is sitting with a barmaid (*tapstere*) in a public house and is willing to sell his hood (lines 528–32).

---

4   Davis, *Non-Cycle Plays*, lxx–lxxii.

5   Ibid., lxxxv.

6   Ibid., lxxvi.

7   Ibid., lxxix and lxxxiv.

8   Ibid., lxxxiv–lxxxv.

9   An unidentified pathological condition; *MED* s.v. *pip(pe*. All citations to the *Middle English Dictionary* are cited as *MED*. The Dictionary is part of the online Middle English Compendium: http://quod.lib.umich.edu/m/med.

Colle then names his employer, "Mayster Brendyche of Braban,"[10] and tells the audience that he is "[c]alled þe most famous phesy[cy]an þat euer sawe vryne" (lines 533–6). Continuing his pattern of both praising the leech and ridiculing him, Colle says his master can diagnose from urine inspection as well as someone with no eyes (lines 537–40). He goes on to say that Master Brendyche is also a bone-setter with debts in every tavern (lines 541–4) and wonders why the doctor's appearance is delayed, mentioning that he "had a lady late in cure" who may have perished (lines 549–52). Colle also associates his master's "cunyng insyght" with good ale (lines 555–6).

Professing concern as to the doctor's whereabouts, Colle suggests "we mak a crye" (line 561) requiring anyone who sees the leech to apprehend him and lead him to the pillory. Colle repeats this "proclamacion" twice, invoking the "hue and cry" of English common law requiring anyone seeing a felon to apprehend him.[11] In the course of the proclamation he describes the physician as having a cut beard and flat nose, wearing a threadbare gown and torn hose (lines 569–70).

At this point Master Brendyche or Brundyche himself enters, inquiring as to what Colle has been telling the audience about him. Colle replies that he has been speaking to the doctor's credit, then adds as an aside that he has told some lies too (lines 574–80). Changing the subject, he asks the leech how his last patient fared. The doctor replies that she feels no pain. Colle concludes that she has died (lines 581–4), but the doctor says,

> I haue gyven hyr a drynke made full well
> With scamoly and with oxennell,
> Letwyce, sawge and pympernelle. (lines 585–7)

10   The name is also spelled "Brundyche" subsequently in the play, and "Brentberecly" once in the banns quoted below. Possible reasons for the identification with the Duchy of Brabant are discussed in Voigts, "Fifteenth-century English Banns," 271–3. Wallis in *Medieval Medicine: A Reader*, 537, translates the name as "Brownditch" and argues that it is an allusion to excrement.

11   *Oxford English Dictionary*, s.v. *hue and cry*.

In administering a drink of scammony,[12] oxymel,[13] lettuce,[14] sage,[15] and pimpernel,[16] the healer has provided the patient with a "broad-spectrum" medicine that at the least was a strong laxative. Colle's retort, almost certainly ironic, is "than she ys full saue" (line 588).

The physician subsequently brags that with cunning and with practice he has saved many a man's life. To this observation, Colle replies that the leech has spent his cunning on widows, maids, and wives (lines 593–6). The doctor then takes a flask from his wallet and gulps the contents (lines 597–600). Fortified with drink he concludes that there may be prospective patients in the audience and orders Colle to stand up and make what he calls "certyfycacyon," "proclamacion," and "declaracion" (lines 603–7). The stage directions indicate that Colle begins the banns: "Hic interim proclamacionem faciet."

In this proclamation the servant observes, in one of many double entendres, that the physician will be so attentive that

> What dysease or syknesse þat euer ye haue,
> He wyll neuer leue yow tyll ye be in yow[r] graue.
> Who hat þe canker, þe collyke, or þe laxe,[17]
> The tercyan, þe quartan, or þe brynny[n]g axs[18]—

---

[12]   The root of scammony (*Convolvulus scammonia*) was commonly recommended as a purgative. See the many citations from contemporary medical writings, *MED*, s.v. *Scamoni(e*.

[13]   Oximel, a compound medicine which added herbs or "laxing roots" to vinegar and honey, was recommended as both a laxative and a diuretic. See MED, s.v. *oximel*.

[14]   Lettuce (*Lactuca sativa*), also called sleepwort, was a common ingredient in soporifics, including the anesthetic dwale. See *MED*, s.vv. *lactuce* and *letuse (n.(1))*, and Linda Ehrsam Voigts and Robert P. Hudson, "'A drynke that men callen dwale to make a man to slepe whyle men kerven him': A Surgical Anesthetic from Late Medieval England," in Sheila D. Campbell, Bert S. Hall, and David N. Klausner (eds), *Health, Disease, and Healing in Medieval Culture* (New York: St. Martin's Press, 1992), 34–56.

[15]   Sage is a high-frequency Middle English word, apparently used to identify *Salvia officinalis*, *Salvia officinalis minor*, and *Teucrium scorodonia*. Medical recipes as well as culinary recipes that call for it are ubiquitous in surviving writings. It was utilized to treat a broad array of human and animal disorders, as a simple, in ointments, in cakes sopped in ale, combined with ale or wine or urine as a drink, and in distillation. See *MED*, s.v. *sauge*.

[16]   Pimpernell is difficult to identify. The *MED* identifies *pimpernel(e* as *Sanguisorba officinalis*, *Paterium sanguisorba*, *Pimpinella saxifraga*, and *Anagallis arvensis*. Middle English citations in the *MED* prescribe it for madness, as a remedy for ailments of the eyes, skin, and heart, and as a vermifuge.

[17]   Flux from the bowels; Juhani Norri, *Names of Sicknesses in English, 1400–1550: An Exploration of the Lexical Field* (Helsinki: Suomalainen Tiedeakatemia, 1992), s.v. *lax(e*.

[18]   Access, attack, or onset of fever; Norri, *Sicknesses*, s.v. *acces(se*. Tertian and quartan refer to intermittent fevers.

> For wormys, for gnawyng, gryndy[n]g in þe wombe or in þe boldyro[19]—
> All maner red eyn, bleryd eyn, and þe myegrym also,
> For hedache, bonache, and therto þe tothache—
> The colt-euyll[20], and þe brostyn[21] men he wyll undertak,
> All tho þat [haue] þe poose, þe sneke[22], or þe tyseke[23]—
> Thowh a man w[e]re ryght heyle, he cowd soone make hym sek. (lines 610–19)

At this point the physician and his servant quarrel over who will read the proclamation. The doctor then asks his man if he knows any there who need his help, and Colle offers to take him to Jonathas, who has lost his right hand (lines 622–9). Colle leads the doctor through a door to see Jonathas, and Master Brendyche/Brundyche says to Jonathas, "Syr, yf yow nede ony surgeon or physycyan, / Off yow[r] dyse[se] help yow welle I cane, / What hurtys or hermes so-euer they be" (lines 635–7). Jonathas orders him out, but Colle tells Jonathas that his master has saved the lives of many. When Jonathas remains unconvinced, Colle says, "Syr, ye know well yt can nott mysse; / Men that be masters of scyens be profytable. / In a pott yf yt please yow to pysse, / He can tell yf yow be curable." Jonathas then calls his fellows, and the stage direction reads "Here shall þe iiij Jewys bett [beat] away þe leche and hys man" (lines 646–52 and stage directions following).

Given the contemporary evidence of the banns and related texts for an actual itinerant physician in London, British Library, MS Harley 2390,[24] from the same time and place as the *Play of the Sacrament*, we have in the figure of Master Brendyche of Brabant and his man the conventions of medieval estates satire, which hold up·for humorous entertainment the foibles of actual doctors like the one advertised by the banns. Medieval estates satire addresses not only social and political classes, but also the role played by a person's work as "determining the estate to which he belongs."[25] In the case of the dramatic scene, an essential

---

[19]   Unidentified body part; not found in Juhani Norri, *Names of Body Parts in English, 1400–1550* (Helsinki: Academia Scientiarum Fennica, 1998); treated in *MED* as a synonym of *womb(e*.

[20]   Not found in *MED* or Norri, *Sicknesses*; *OED* provides citations from 1523 referring to a swelling of the penis in horses, and by transference to priapism.

[21]   Ruptured; *MED*, s.v. *bresten*.

[22]   Both "poose" and "sneke" refer to head cold; Norri, *Sicknesses*, s.v. *pose* and *snike*.

[23]   Phthisis, disease of the lungs, possibly pulmonary tuberculosis; Norri, *Sicknesses*, s.v. *tisik(e*.

[24]   See Voigts, "Fifteenth-century English Banns."

[25]   Jill Mann, *Chaucer and Medieval Estates Satire: The Literature of Social Classes and the General Prologue to the Canterbury Tales* (Cambridge: Cambridge University Press, 1973), 3. See also "The Role of Work," 10–16; and "The Doctor of Physic," 91–9, which deals with Chaucer's

aspect of his work involves administering powerful herbal medicine. Parodies provide information on the objects of the parody. The reciprocal relationship of the doctor scene in the *Play of the Sacrament* and evidence of an actual physician addressed in the Harley banns enables us to understand better both texts, as well as medieval English medical practice.

London Satire:
Chaucer's Many References to Herbs in the *Canterbury Tales*

Geoffrey Chaucer also employed estates satire in his portrait of the learned physician in the General Prologue of the *Canterbury Tales*.[26] In this depiction we are told the doctor is expert in physic and surgery and knowledgeable in astronomy and humoral physiology. He is described, with characteristic Chaucerian irony, as "a verray, parfit praktisour" (line 422) who has apothecaries to provide him with "drogges" and "letuaries." He is familiar with 15 ancient, Arabic, and medieval *auctores*, including "Deyscorides" (lines 429–34), although "his studie was but litel on the Bible" (line 438). Following comments on his expensive dress and his wealth is a single reference to a specific remedy in this depiction, which in this case is not herbal, but "gold in phisik is a cordial, / Therefore he lovede gold in special" (lines 443–4).[27]

Although there is no mention of therapeutic herbs in this physician's portrait, one need not look far in the *Canterbury Tales* for specific reference to herbs and spices. The description of alchemical processes in the Canon's Yeoman's Tale lists mineral and animal ingredients in his processes, but also "herbes koude I telle eek many oon, / As egremoyne,[28] valerian,[29] and lunarie"[30] (lines 799–800).

---

physician as an example of estates satire along with such satire in the French Renart tradition and the *Miroir de l'Omme* by John Gower (1330–1408).

[26]   Mann, "The Doctor of Physic." Still-useful discussions of Chaucer's portrait of the physician in the General Prologue are Walter Clyde Curry, *Chaucer and the Mediaeval Sciences* (New York: Oxford University Press, 1926), 3–36, and Huling E. Ussery, *Chaucer's Physician: Medicine and Literature in Fourteenth-century England* (New Orleans: Dept of English, Tulane University, 1971).

[27]   This and all subsequent citations are to Larry D. Benson (ed.), *The Riverside Chaucer*, 3rd edn (Boston: Houghton Mifflin, 1987).

[28]   Agrimony (*Agrimonia eupatoria*) was a herb frequently used for cleansing wounds. See *MED*, s.v. *egremoine*.

[29]   Valerian (*Valeriana officinalis*) was both prescribed as a simple and utilized in compound medicines, for both internal and external use. *MED*, s.v. *valerian(e*.

[30]   Lunary or moonwort was thought to derive its power from the moon. Although it had some medicinal uses, it was more typically associated with magical properties and uses. *MED*, s.v.

Another instance of a plant, in this case an exotic one well known to Chaucer's audience, occurs in the Prioress's Tale, an anti-Semitic Marian story, where a young choirboy, slain by Jews, is through the intercession of Mary preserved singing a hymn. He later says the Virgin had laid "a greyn upon my tonge" (line 662). When an abbot "took awey the greyn" (line 671), the child "yaf up the goost ful softely" (line 672). In this citation, and in the use of "grain" in the Miller's Tale (discussed below), we surely have a reference to the exotic spice, the seed of *Amomum meleguetta*, called in Middle English simply "grain," or "grain de Paris" or "grain of paradise," a hot and moist spice believed to have restorative powers.[31] According to Paul Freedman, this expensive and exotic spice, imported from West Africa, was marketed for its association with the spices of the earthly paradise, and enjoyed a "tremendous vogue in the fourteenth and early fifteenth centuries."[32]

In the dueling tales by the Miller and the Reeve, we find in the latter's account that two Cambridge students, John and Aleyn, who are temporary guests of the Trumpington miller Symkyn, have no difficulty sleeping after their evening spent drinking strong ale:

> To bedde goth Aleyn and also John;
> Ther nas na moore—hem nedede no dwale. (lines 4160–61)

This quite specific reference to a common herbal compound prescribed for use as an anesthetic in surgery or cautery makes it clear that Aleyn and John slept soundly.[33]

---

lunari(e, and Linda Ehrsam Voigts, "Plants and Planets: Linking the Vegetable with the Celestial in Late Medieval Texts," in Peter Dendle and Alain Touwaide (eds), *Health and Healing from the Medieval Garden* (Woodbridge, UK: Boydell, 2008), 29–46, esp. "Treatise on Individual Planet and Plant: Lunary," pp. 40–44.

[31]   *MED*, s.v. *grain (n.)* 5. See also the extensive discussion in Benson, *Riverside Chaucer*, 916, note on Prioress's Tale, line 662.

[32]   Paul H. Freedman, *Out of the East: Spices and the Medieval Imagination* (New Haven: Yale University Press, 2008), 12, and his discussion of the association of specific plants with Paradise, 89–91. See also the important study identifying this spice with the "greyn" in the Prioress's Tale by Paul E. Beichner, "The Grain of Paradise," *Speculum* 36 (1961): 302–7.

[33]   Voigts and Hudson, "'A drynke that men callen dwale.'" See also Linda Ehrsam Voigts and Patricia Deery Kurtz, *Scientific and Medical Writings in Old and Middle English: An Electronic Reference*, CD (Ann Arbor: University of Michigan Press, 2000), and the second edition, hereafter cited as eVK2, accessible through an online link at http://www.medievalacademy.org. The ubiquity of this recipe is witnessed by the 65 records in eVK2 for texts containing the recipe for dwale.

It is, however, in the preceding tale, that of the Miller, that we find more extensive references to the use of specific herbs. The tale begins with the description of Nicholas, a poor but learned Oxford student who lodges with a carpenter. His chamber is

> Ful fetisly ydight with herbes swoote;
> And he hymself as sweete as is the roote
> Of lycorys or any cetewale. (lines 3205–7)

Although it is not clear what sweet herbs this "poure scoler" (line 3190) uses to adorn his room, he is himself described in terms of exotic spices: licorice[34] and setewal or zedoary. The latter aromatic spice was an expensive import from southern Asia, and is particularly appropriate for Nicholas, with his designs on the carpenter's wife. It figures, along with licorice and grain of Paris/Paradise, in the garden of love described in the influential long French poem, the *Romance of the Rose*.[35] In Chaucer's translation of that work from the French, the Garden is described as

> ... wexyng many a spice,
> As clowe-gelofre and lycorice,
> Gyngevre and greyn de parys,
> Canell and setewale of prys,
> And many a spice delitable ... (lines 1367–71)[36]

Nicholas is not, however, the only young man in the Miller's Tale with designs on Alisoun, the attractive 18-year-old wife of the carpenter. The parish clerk, Absolon, also pursues her, with less success but more comedy. Absolon, however, like Nicholas is identified with two of the lover's spices that are found in Chaucer's version of the *Romaunt of the Rose*, and with the herb paris or "true-love":[37]

> Up rist this joly lovere Absolon,
> And hym arraieth gay, at poynt-devys.

---

[34]　Root of *Glycyrrhiz glabra* or *Abrus precatorius*; *MED*, s.v. *licoris*.

[35]　Root of *Curcuma zedoaria*, related to turmeric; *MED*, s.v. *setewal(e*. Freedman, *Out of the East*, 8 and 12.

[36]　*The Romaunt of the Rose*, in Benson, *Riverside Chaucer*, 701.

[37]　*MED*, s.v. *treu-love 4 (a)*, "a plant whose leaves and flowers are arranged symmetrically in whorls of four, herb paris (*Paris quadrifolia*)." The plant was thought to resemble the so-called truelove knot.

> But first he cheweth greyn and lycorys,
> To smellen sweete, er he hadde kembd his heer.
> Under his tonge a trewe-love he beer ... (lines 3688–92)

Whether these expensive exotics were actually affordable for a parish clerk is beside the point. Chaucer's well-off audience would have been aware of their significance, and of their pretension, for imported spices were markers of the social status and income of those for whom Chaucer wrote.[38]

Of the many tales told by Chaucer's Canterbury-bound pilgrims, the one with extensive satire of herbal medicines is the comic beast fable, the Nun's Priest's Tale. This tale, which has lent itself to a range of allegorical interpretations, revolves around a rooster, Chauntecleer, and the hen he loves, Pertelote. In the tale Chauntecleer dreams of a fox, who later appears, and tells Pertelote of his fear. She chides him for being a coward and insists that dreams have no significance, attributing them to a humoral imbalance:

> Swevenes engendren of replecciouns,
> And ofte of fume and of complecciouns,
> Whan humours been to habundant in a wight.
> Certes this dreem, which ye han met to-nyght,
> Cometh of the greete superfluytee
> Of youre rede colera, pardee,
> Which causeth folk to dreden in hir dremes
> Of arwes, and of fyr with rede lemes,
> Of rede beestes, that they wol hem byte ... (lines 2923–31)

Pertelote then lists the kinds of dreams caused by a superfluity of melancholy, citing Cato on the meaninglessness of dreams, and then offers a herbal remedy for Chauntecleer's frightening dreams:

> For Goddes love, as taak som laxatyf.
> Up peril of my soule and of my lyf,
> I conseille yow the beste—I wol nat lye—
> That bothe of colere and of malencolye
> Ye purge yow; and for ye shal nat tarie,
> Though in this toun is noon apothecarie,
> I shal myself to herbes techen yow
> That shul been for youre hele and for youre prow;

---

[38]　See Freedman, *Out of the East*, 1–7 and passim.

And in oure yeerd tho herbes shal I fynde
The whiche han of hire propretee by kynde
To purge yow bynethe and eek above.
Foryet nat this, for Goddes owene love!
Ye been ful coleryk of compleccioun;
Ware the sone in his ascencioun
Ne fynde yow nat repleet of humours hoote.
And if it do, I dar wel leye a grote,
That ye shul have a fevere terciane,
Or an agu that may be youre bane.
A day or two ye shul have digestyves
Of wormes,[39] er ye take youre laxatyves
Of lawriol,[40] centaure,[41] and fumetere,[42]
Or elles of ellebor,[43] that groweth there,
Of katapuce,[44] or of gaitrys beryis,[45]
Of herbe yve,[46] growyng in oure yeerd, ther mery is;
Pekke hem up right as they growe and ete hem yn.
Be myrie, housbonde, for youre fader kyn!
Dredeth no dreem; I kan sey yow namoore. (lines 2943–69)

---

[39] The worms frequently cited in Middle English recipes are *angeltwacches*, used mostly for topical medicines, but also in stale ale as a remedy for black jaundice. See *MED*, s.v. *angel-twacche*. Five records of incipits beginning a recipe or recipe collections that call for *angeltwacches* as an ingredient can be located in eVK2.

[40] Almost certainly the spurge laurel (*Daphne laureola*), an ingredient frequently found in purgatives and emetics. See *MED*, s.v. *laurel 2*.

[41] Whether Chaucer intends the common centaury (*Centaureum umbellatum*) or yellow centaury (*Chlora perfoliata*) is unclear. Both occur frequently in medical recipes. *MED*, s.v. *centorie (n.) 1*.

[42] Fumitory (*Fumaria officinalis*) was widely used in medicines, both internal and external. See eVK2 and *MED*, s.v. *fumetere*.

[43] Whether white or black hellebore (*Helleborus albus* or *helleborus niger*) is intended is unclear. The white is identified with emetics, the black with laxatives. The white was thought to purge phlegm, the black, melancholy. See *MED*, s.v. *ellebre*.

[44] Caper spurge (*Tithymalus lathyris*), recommended as both an emetic and a laxative. *MED*, s.v. *catapuce*.

[45] An unclear reference, possibly honeysuckle berries (*Lonicera periclymenum* or *Lonicera caprifolium*), buckthorn berries (*Rhamnus catharticus*), or dogwood berries (*Cornus sanguinea*).

[46] Possibly a variety of plantain (*Plantago coronopus*), ground pine (*Ajuga chamaepitys*), or ground ivy (*Nepeta glechoma*). *MED*, s.v. *herbe-ive*.

In response, Chauntecleer cites a long list of authorities to support his argument that his dream should be understood as prophetic. Convincing himself, he rejects Pertelote's herbal laxatives:

> Shortly I seye, as for conclusioun,
> That I shal han of this avisioun
> Adversitee; and I seye forthermoor
> That I ne telle of laxatyves no stoor,
> For they been venymes, I woot it weel;
> I hem diffye, I love hem never a deel! (lines 3151–6)

The rooster is, however, so smitten by Pertelote that he chooses to go against his superior knowledge, deciding to "diffye bothe sweven and dreem" (line 3171), but he does not ingest Pertelote's remedy. He is indeed captured by a fox, although Chauntecleer ultimately outwits the fox and escapes, and the Nun's Priest ends his tale by urging his listeners to take the "moralite" of the tale to heart.

This tale, a favorite of many readers, has attracted an extensive body of scholarship, some of which relates Pertelote's advice to larger philosophical and theological concerns in the later Middle Ages.[47] Another study, by Corinne Kauffman, attempts to relate herbal lore to the poem in some detail.[48] This study, published in 1969, did not have access to the *Middle English Dictionary* or to the considerable scholarship on medieval herbal medicine of the last 40 years, so it should not be faulted for relying on sixteenth-century sources.[49] It can be argued, however, that the four conclusions in the article concerning this passage miss the point of Chaucer's humor. Kauffman concludes that Chaucer's audience would have been aware (1) that not all the herbs Pertelote cites could be harvested in May; (2) that the herbs named could be dangerous; (3) that the compound is not appropriate to Chauntecleer;[50] and (4) that the remedy could

---

[47]   See especially John Block Friedman, "The 'Nun's Priest's Tale': The Preacher and the Mermaid's Song," *Chaucer Review* 7 (1973): 250–66; and Patrick Gallacher, "Food, Laxatives, and Catharsis in Chaucer's Nun's Priest's Tale," *Speculum* 51 (1976): 49–68.

[48]   Corinne E. Kauffman, "Dame Pertelote's Parlous Parle," *Chaucer Review* 4 (1969): 41–8.

[49]   Kauffman did cite, apparently unconsciously, a medieval source. She refers to "Batman's translation of Bartholomew" (p. 45), perhaps not realizing that what Stephen Batman published in 1582 was John Trevisa's fourteenth-century English translation of *De proprietatibus rerum* of Bartholomaeus Anglicus.

[50]   I have also suggested that, when one consults the translation of Bartholomaeus' *De proprietatibus rerum* by Chaucer's contemporary John Trevisa, one finds that the "rede colera" named by Pertelote in fact is a healthy state, needing no medicine: Linda Ehrsam Voigts, "Bodies," in Peter Brown (ed.), *A Companion to Chaucer* (Oxford: Blackwell, 2000), 40–57, at 51. See

have killed the rooster. Without rejecting the points Kauffman makes, it might be more appropriate to say Chaucer entertains his readers with a joke about a hen who thinks she is knowledgeable on the subjects of humoral physiology and herbal therapy.

When we look at the Nun's Priest's Tale, we should see it in the context of Chaucer's non-satirical use of herbs in his Canon's Yeoman's, Prioress's, Reeve's, and Miller's Tales. It should also be understood in the context of the West Midlands mock-epistle of "Nameless Deacon Pie-Baker Breechless" and the satirical scene of the doctor and his servant interpolated in the *Play of the Sacrament.* All three writers wrote to entertain, and "sending up" the behavior of herbal healers was entertaining on both a popular and a learned level.

Bibliography

Beichner, Paul E. "The Grain of Paradise." *Speculum* 36 (1961): 302–7.

Benson, Larry D. (ed.). *The Riverside Chaucer*. 3rd edn. Boston: Houghton Mifflin, 1987.

Bevington, David M. *Medieval Drama*. Boston: Houghton Mifflin, 1974.

Curry, Walter Clyde. *Chaucer and the Mediaeval Sciences*. New York: Oxford University Press, 1926.

Davis, Norman (ed.). *Non-Cycle Plays and Fragments*. Early English Text Society, Supplementary Text 1. London: Oxford University Press, 1970.

Freedman, Paul H. *Out of the East: Spices and the Medieval Imagination*. New Haven: Yale University Press, 2008.

Friedman, John Block. "The 'Nun's Priest's Tale': The Preacher and the Mermaid's Song." *Chaucer Review* 7 (1973): 250–66.

Gallacher, Patrick. "Food, Laxatives, and Catharsis in Chaucer's Nun's Priest's Tale." *Speculum* 51 (1976): 49–68.

Kauffman, Corinne E. "Dame Pertelote's Parlous Parle." *Chaucer Review* 4 (1969): 41–8.

Mann, Jill. *Chaucer and Medieval Estates Satire: The Literature of Social Classes and the General Prologue to the Canterbury Tales*. Cambridge: Cambridge University Press, 1973.

Middle English Dictionary. Ed. Hans Kurath et al. Ann Arbor: University of Michigan Press, 1952–2001. Available online at http://quod.lib.umich.edu/m/med (accessed February 20, 2012).

M.C. Seymour, G.M. Liegey, et al. (eds), *On the Properties of Things: John Trevisa's Translation of Bartholomaeus Anglicus, De proprietatibus rerum* (3 vols, Oxford: Clarendon Press, 1975–88), 1:157–62.

Norri, Juhani. *Names of Sicknesses in English, 1400–1550: An Exploration of the Lexical Field*. Helsinki: Suomalainen Tiedeakatemia, 1992.

———. *Names of Body Parts in English, 1400–1550*. Helsinki: Academia Scientiarum Fennica, 1998.

Pope, Nancy P. "A Middle English Satirical Letter in Brogyntyn MS II.1." *American Notes & Queries* 18 (2005): 35–9.

Seymour, M.C., G.M. Liegey, et al. (eds). *On the Properties of Things: John Trevisa's Translation of Bartholomaeus Anglicus, De proprietatibus rerum*. 3 vols. Oxford: Clarendon Press, 1975–88.

Ussery, Huling E. *Chaucer's Physician: Medicine and Literature in Fourteenth-century England*. New Orleans: Dept of English, Tulane University, 1971.

Voigts, Linda Ehrsam. "Bodies." In Peter Brown (ed.), *A Companion to Chaucer*, 40–57. Oxford: Blackwell, 2000.

———. "Plants and Planets: Linking the Vegetable with the Celestial in Late Medieval Texts." In Peter Dendle and Alain Touwaide (eds), *Health and Healing from the Medieval Garden*, 29–46. Woodbridge, UK: Boydell, 2008.

———. "Fifteenth-century English Banns Advertising the Services of an Itinerant Doctor." In Florence Eliza Glaze and Brian Nance (eds), *Between Text and Patient: The Medical Enterprise in Medieval and Early Modern Europe*, 245–77. Micrologus' Library 39. Florence: SISMEL, Edizioni del Galluzzo, 2011.

——— and Robert P. Hudson. "'A drynke that men callen dwale to make a man to slepe whyle men kerven him': A Surgical Anesthetic from Late Medieval England." In Sheila D. Campbell, Bert S. Hall, and David N. Klausner (eds), *Health, Disease, and Healing in Medieval Culture*, 34–56. New York: St. Martin's Press, 1992.

——— and Patricia Deery Kurtz. *Scientific and Medical Writings in Old and Middle English: An Electronic Reference*. CD-ROM. Ann Arbor: University of Michigan Press, 2000. Second edition available online through a link at http://www.medievalacademy.org (accessed February 20, 2012).

Wallis, Faith. *Medieval Medicine: A Reader*. Toronto: University of Toronto Press, 2010.

Chapter 8
"Kurze versuochte dinge."
Ein mährisch-schlesisches wundärztliches Rezeptar des 15. Jahrhunderts

Gundolf Keil

Abstract

Preparation of the second edition of *Die deutsche Literatur des Mittelalters: Verfasserlexikon* produced a great expansion of scholarship on older German technical treatises, including works on medicine. New texts were discovered and studied, among them three manuals on field surgery from Moravian Silesia dating from the twelfth to the fifteenth century (the *Prag-Olmützer Wundarznei*, *Notversorgung im Felde*, and the *Oberschlesische Roger-Aphorismen*). In fact, the total number of old Silesian texts has grown from six to more than 40 because of the extensive work on the new edition of the *Verfasserlexikon*.

The *Oberschlesische Roger-Aphorismen*, or *Upper Silesian Aphorisms of Roger*, are based on a surgical treatise, the *Practica chirurgiae*, by Roger of Salerno (*fl.* 1170), which was often excerpted and circulated in many forms throughout the Middle Ages. The Silesian *Aphorisms* constitute an unusual genre, one not found in other older German technical treatises. They are somewhere between a catalog of questions for an examination and mnemonic writings, in that they recall a text that had been memorized word for word. Addressed to a field surgeon who knew Roger's *Surgery* (which from *c.* 1250 was translated into German several times), the *Aphorisms* cite a surgical topic and then provide details of treatment using targeted aphorisms. In fact, another title for the work is *Merksätze von mancherlei Wunden*, or *Notes on Many Kinds of Wounds*. The original author of the *Aphorisms* excerpted topics from Roger's *Surgery*, arranged them with the goal of treating wounds in the field, gave each a short call-out title, entered the aphorisms as an aid to memory, and in this way created a work that would serve a surgeon in the battlefield, reminding him of treatment options. The original text has not been found but is thought to have been written around 1400. In solving a problem of interpreting a troublesome, hard-to-decipher segment of one paragraph (§18g), yet another surgical work was identified.

Two versions of the *Aphorisms* are known: O, believed to be the older, and K. O is found in Codex CO 352 in the Olmütz branch of the Troppauer Landesarchiv and was copied during the first third of the fifteenth century by a scribe who worked in Silesia. K is found in Codex Farfensis 200, now in the Biblioteca nazionale in Rome. K was written down in 1462 at the German-speaking monastery of Farfa, Italy, by a scribe who was from the mountainous region of Silesia. There are modern editions of both versions. The K scribe wrote as a kind of title at the beginning, "Nw sal man mercken von manicherley wunden" ("Now we shall take note of many kinds of wounds"); this section of the Farfa manuscript had early been identified as a stand-alone wound manual. O does not have a title, nor the same first paragraph as K.

K has 39 paragraphs on specific topics, recalling the original number of chapters in Roger's *Surgery*. O, in addition to omitting the introductory paragraph, also leaves out some of the text contained in K, most notably paragraphs 30–39. Inserted into the remaining text of O are bits and pieces of 31 instructions from a surgical materia medica, the *Wundärztliches Rezeptar*, or *Field Manual for the Surgeon*.

Despite critical editions, the meaning of paragraph 18g, on how to extract a projectile and then deal with build-up of pus in a wound, remained unclear for years, notwithstanding comparisons of O and K and various emendations to get at the correct meaning. The key to the problem lay close at hand in the Farfa manuscript itself and near the K version of the *Aphorisms*. Within the Farfa manuscript, the aphorism section (K) is appended to a surgical pharmacopoeia containing about 100 prescriptions (called the *Römische Chirurgie*, or *Roman Surgery*). This pharmacopoeia is connected to another part of the text, which is organized according to different principles and has its own section of materia medica. Remarkably, this section was found to contain excerpts from the same *Wundärztliches Rezeptar* that the O scribe had used to fill out his version of the *Aphorisms*. Luckily, paragraph 18, sections f and g are part of this *Rezeptar* and together have a title ("How to extract an arrow") indicating that 18f and g belong together. The surviving paragraphs of this *Rezeptar* show that it was a technically advanced surgical text from Silesia dealing with a number of complex topics. Among the paragraphs in this section is one on gunshot wounds—unfortunately, it cannot be proven whether this one paragraph was indeed an original part of the *Rezeptar*. It is a very early reference to the effects of gunshot wounds.

If our text were isolated from the other parts of the manuscript and a title assigned, it might be *"Kurze versuochte dinge"*: *Mährisch-schlesisches wundärztliches Rezeptar*, or *"Short, Proven Things": A Moravian-Silesian Surgical Field Manual*. Possibly, more sections from the manual may yet be found in other manuscripts. Together, the four Silesian manuals offer comprehensive, practical treatment of battlefield wounds, especially from projectiles, and also cover the related topic of handling abscesses. In addition, one of the oldest references in German—perhaps even the oldest—to wounds from gunfire is found here. All of the manuals reflect the turbulent conditions in Silesia around the time of the Hussite Wars (1420–34).

***

Selbstverständlich hat die Marbod von Rennes-Ausgabe unseres Jubilars mit zum Gelingen der Zweitauflage des *Verfasserlexikons*[1] beigetragen.[2] Dieses literaturwissenschaftliche Nachschlagewerk hat der germanistischen Mediävistik auf jeden Fall auf zahlreichen Gebieten wesentliche Impulse gegeben und neue Wissensräume erschlossen, was vor allem für das Gebiet der Fachprosaforschung gilt, die sich mit der Literatur der Eigenkünste (*artes mechanicae*) befaßt und darin auch das medizinistische Fachschrifttum und das Schriftgut der Verbotenen Künste (*artes incertae*) einbegreift; quadriviale Texte sind nur vereinzelt unter gebrauchsfunktionalen Gesichtspunkten einbezogen. Vergleichbaren Auswahlkriterien ist auch Ria Jansen-Sieben in ihrem berühmten *Repertorium van de Middelnederlandse artes-literatuur* gefolgt.[3]

Einen exemplarischen Einblick in den durch das *Verfasserlexikon* bedingten Wissenszuwachs geben die vier—jeweils maßgebenden—Fachprosa-Monographien, deren erste von Gerhard Eis[4] noch ohne Kontakt mit der Würzburger[5] lexikographischen Herausgebergruppe verfaßt wurde, deren

---

[1]   *Die deutsche Literatur des Mittelalters. Verfasserlexikon*, 2., völlig neu bearbeitete Aufl. hrsg. von Gundolf Keil, Kurt Ruh (federführend bis Bd. VIII [1992]), Werner Schröder, Burghart Wachinger (federführend ab Bd. IX [1995]) und Franz Josef Worstbrock, I–XIV (Berlin und New York, [1977–]1978–2008) [im Folgenden abgekürzt als *VL*].

[2]   Sie wird mehrere Male zitiert; vgl. die Nachweise im *VL* XIV (2008), S. 212[b].

[3]   Ria Jansen-Sieben, *Repertorium van de Middelnederlandse artes-literatuur* (Utrecht, 1989), mit mehreren Nachträgen, zuletzt Aanvulling VII*, Werkgroep Middelnederlandse Artesliteratuur 10 (2009), 1, S. 4–9.

[4]   Gerhard Eis, *Mittelalterliche Fachliteratur*, 2. Aufl., Sammlung Metzler, Abt. D, M 14 (Stuttgart, 1967).

[5]   Sitz des—zunächst von der Deutschen Forschungsgemeinschaft, dann von der Bayerischen Akademie der Wissenschaften, zuletzt vom de Gruyter-Verlag Berlin getragenen—*Verfasserlexikons*-Projektes war die Universität Würzburg.

zweite (von Peter Assion[6]) einen entsprechenden Kontakt[7] bereits erkennen läßt und deren dritte, von Bill Crossgrove[8] vorgelegte dann schon ganz im Banne des neuen Nachschlagewerks steht. Die vierte, die von mehreren Autoren[9] veröffentlicht wurde, ist schließlich zur Gänze aufs *Verfasserlexikon* abgestellt und konnte bereits auf dessen vollständiges Alphabet einschließlich des Nachtragsbandes zurückgreifen; sie ist parallel zu einem enzyklopädischen Lexikon der Medizingeschichte[10] erarbeitet worden und bietet sich für den Fachliteratur-Sektor geradezu als systematisches Register an—und dies umso mehr, weil ein Sachregister-Band für das *Verfasserlexikon* bisher ausgeblieben ist.[11]

    [6]   Peter Assion, *Altdeutsche Fachliteratur*, Grundlagen der Germanistik 13 (Berlin, 1973); vgl. auch *Deutsche Fachprosa des Mittelalters. Ausgewählte Texte*, hrsg. von Wolfram Schmitt, Kleine Texte für Vorlesungen und Übungen 190 (Berlin und New York, 1972), und *Fachprosaforschung. Acht Vorträge zur mittelalterlichen Artesliteratur*, hrsg. von Gundolf Keil und Peter Assion (Berlin, 1974), hier S. 24–69 der richtungweisende Beitrag von Ria Jansen-Sieben: "Middelnederlandse vakliteratuur."

    [7]   Er wird—zusätzlich zum "Fachprosaforschungs"-Vorträge-Band—greifbar in der zweiten Festschrift für Gerhard Eis: *Fachprosa-Studien. Beiträge zur mittelalterlichen Wissenschafts- und Geistesgeschichte*, hrsg. von Gundolf Keil zusammen mit Peter Assion, Willem Frans Daems und Heinz-Ulrich Roehl (Berlin, 1982).

    [8]   William [C.] Crossgrove, *Die deutsche Sachliteratur des Mittelalters*, Germanistische Lehrbuchsammlung 63 (Bern, Frankfurt am Main, und New York, 1994), hier S. 23f.: "Die Forschungssituation für mittelalterliche Sachliteratur änderte sich in den letzten Jahren grundlegend durch die laufende Erscheinung [lies: "das laufende Erscheinen"] der Bände des neubearbeiteten *Verfasserlexikons* (... 1978ff.) ...; grade für ... die Sachliteratur wird die Neubearbeitung des *Verfasserlexikons* in den kommenden Jahren zum Ausgangspunkt aller Forschung."

    [9]   Bernhard Dietrich Haage und Wolfgang Wegner zusammen mit Gundolf Keil und Helga Haage-Naber, *Deutsche Fachliteratur der Artes in Mittelalter und Früher Neuzeit*, Grundlagen der Germanistik 43 (Berlin, 2007).—Der Band ist zweigeteilt und bietet als zweiten Teil (S. 351–468) ein kommentiertes Lesebuch zur altdeutschen Fachprosa aller einschlägiger Artes.— Vorausgegangen war die umfassende Studie von Michael Horchler zur altdeutschen Fachprosa der (Al)Chemie: *Die Alchemie in der deutschen Literatur des Mittelalters. Ein Forschungsbericht über die deutsche alchemistische Fachliteratur des ausgehenden Mittelalters*, DWV-Schriften zur Medizingeschichte 2 (Baden-Baden, 2005).

    [10]   *Enzyklopädie Medizingeschichte*, hrsg. von Werner Erich Gerabek, Bernhard Dietrich Haage, Gundolf Keil und Wolfgang Wegner, I–III (Berlin und New York, 2005; 2. Aufl. ebd. 2007).

    [11]   Wie er hätte aussehen können, zeigen die beiden überaus hilfreichen Sacherschließungs-Bände zu: *Reallexikon der Germanischen Altertumskunde*, 2., völlig neu bearbeitete Aufl. begründet von Heinrich Beck, Herbert Jankuhn, Hans Kuhn, Kurt Ranke und Reinhard Wenskus, hrsg. von Heinrich Beck, Dieter Geuenich und Heiko Steuer, I–XXXV (Berlin und New York, [1968–] 1973–2007), dazu: *Register* I–II (ebd. 2008).

Vor gerade einem Jahr fertiggestellt, ist das *Verfasserlexikon* durch die laufende Forschung bereits eingeholt und überholt worden. Der beeindruckende Wissenszuwachs zeigt sich in einem halben Hundert an Fachprosa-Denkmälern, die neu über den Nachtragsband[12] ins *Verfasserlexikon* aufgenommen wurden, und er kommt in einer Vielzahl von mährisch-schlesischen Fachprosa-Texten[13] zum Ausdruck, deren Erfassung und Identifizierung sich zu einem nicht geringen Teil der Förderung durch die Tschechische Forschungsgemeinschaft verdankt.[14]

Zu den neuentdeckten altdeutschen Fachprosa-Texten gehören die *Oberschlesischen Roger-Aphorismen*, die gegen 1400 in Mährisch Schlesien verfaßt wurden und in zwei Abschriften erhalten sind. Beide Kopien wurden um 1450/60 gefertigt, beide Kopisten bieten Merkmale des mährisch-schlesischen Schreibdialekts, und in beiden Fällen zeigen Lese- und Verständnisfehler, daß eine vermutlich mehrgliedrige Überlieferungs-Kette zwischen Urschrift und Abschrift anzusetzen ist.[15]

Der möglicherweise ältere Textzeuge **O** ist auf Bl. 192^r–206^v im Kodex CO 352 der Olmützer Zweigstelle des Troppauer Landesarchivs überliefert;

---

[12]   *VL* XI (2004).

[13]   Die Anzahl altschlesischer Fachprosatexte des 12.–15. Jhs. ist dank der Arbeiten am *Verfasserlexikon* von 6 auf über 40 angewachsen; die Etappen des Wissenszuwachses lassen sich verfolgen an folgenden drei Publikationen: (1.) Arno Lubos, *Geschichte der Literatur Schlesiens*, I (Würzburg, 1960), 2. Aufl., I, 1: *Von den Anfängen bis ca. 1800*, ebd. 1995, S. 53–6: sechs Denkmäler; (2.) Gundolf Keil, "Technisches und wissenschaftliches Schrifttum im mittelalterlichen Schlesien," in *Anfänge und Entwicklung der deutschen Sprache im mittelalterlichen Schlesien. Verhandlungen des VIII. Symposions … in Würzburg, 1989*, hrsg. von Gundolf Keil und Josef Joachim Menzel, Veröffentlichungen des Gerhard-Möbus-Instituts für Schlesienforschung an der Universität Würzburg, Schlesische Forschungen 6 (Sigmaringen, 1995), S. 183–218: einundzwanzig Denkmäler; (3.) Gundolf Keil und Hilde-Marie Groß, "Die große Zeit schlesischer Fachliteratur—das 12. und 13. Jahrhundert. Mit einem Ausblick bis 1500," in *K periodizaci dějin slezska. Sborník z pracovniho zasedání v Opavě 11.–12. prosince 2007*, im Auftrage des Historischen Instituts an der Naturwissenschaftlich-philosophischen Fakultät der Schlesischen Universität zu Troppau hrsg. von Dan Gawrecki (Troppau/Opava, 2008), S. 75–102: vierzig Denkmäler altschlesischer Fachprosa.

[14]   Vgl. beispielsweise: *Mesuë a jeho "Grabadin"/Mesuë und sein "Grabadin." Standardní dílo středověké farmacie/Ein Standardwerk der mittelalterlichen Pharmazie. Edition—Übersetzung—Kommentar*, von Lenka Vaňková und Gundolf Keil (Mährisch Ostrau/Ostrava, 2005): Ausgabe des "Kunewalder Mesuë"; sieh *VL* XI (2004), Sp. 994f.

[15]   Lenka Vaňková, *Medizinische Fachprosa aus Mähren. Sprache—Struktur—Edition*, Wissensliteratur im Mittelalter. Schriften des Sonderforschungsbereichs 226 Würzburg/Eichstätt 41 (Wiesbaden, 2004), S. 61f.; Gundolf Keil, "Das 'Wässerbüchlein' Gabriels von Lebenstein und die 'Oberschlesischen Roger-Aphorismen': Beobachtungen zu Wirkungsgeschichte und Provenienz," *Fachprosaforschung—Grenzüberschreitungen* 1 (2005), S. 105–54, hier S. 137f.

Lenka Vaňková hat den Text 2004 untersucht[16] und herausgegeben.[17] Der deutsch schreibende mährisch-schlesische Kopist war anscheinend auch mit dem Tschechischen und Lateinischen vertraut und arbeitete nach Ausweis schreibdialektaler Merkmale in Österreichisch bzw. Mährisch Schlesien.

Der möglicherweise jüngere Textzeuge K ist auf Bl. 157ʳ–160ᵛ (alt 149ʳ–152ᵛ) des Codex Farfensis 200 überliefert, den heute die Biblioteca nazionale Vittorio Emanuele zu Rom aufbewahrt. Er wurde 1462 von einem Mönch oder Laienbruder des—damals deutschsprachigen—Benediktinerklosters Farfa in Latium aufgezeichnet. Der Kopist war Gebirgsschlesier aus dem Gebiet der Oderpforte oder des Gesenkes[18] und beherrschte außer dem Deutschen auch das Italienische; Anzeichen für Tschechischkenntnisse haben sich bei ihm bisher nicht nachweisen lassen.

Was die Gattungszugehörigkeit betrifft, so handelt es sich bei den *Oberschlesischen Roger-Aphorismen* um eine seltene, in der altdeutschen Fachprosa bisher nicht belegte Textsorte. Die *Aphorismen* lassen sich zwischen Prüfungsfragen-Katalog[19] und mnemotechnischem Schrifttum[20] einordnen— mit dem Unterschied freilich, daß sie keine Erinnerungswörter bereitstellen und keine Prüfung hinsichtlich vorhandenen Wissens vornehmen, sondern daß sie von einem memorierten, auswendig gelernten Fachtext ausgehen, aus dem sie einschlägige Kapitel jeweils durch ein kennzeichnendes Zitat aufrufen und anschließend durch prägnante Aphorismen ergänzen. Wäre der memorierte Text als Ganzes mitaufgezeichnet worden, würde es sich bei den ergänzenden Aphorismen um eine Art Glossen-Kommentar[21] handeln, und die exzerpierten Textstellen entsprächen den ausgehobenen Lemma-Zitaten. Der Autor ließe

---

16   Vaňková (2004) [wie Anm. 15], S. 61–70, 96–106, 145–56.

17   Vaňková (2004) [wie Anm. 15], S. 67˙–73˙(–86˙).

18   Keil (2005) [wie Anm. 15], S. 137, in Ergänzung zu Keil/Groß (2005) [wie Anm. 39], S. 161–8.

19   Die bisher erfaßten wundärztlichen Prüfungsfragen-Kataloge gehen von der "Großen Chirurgie" Lanfranks aus; sieh Gundolf Keil, "Lanfrank von Mailand," in *VL* V (1985), Sp. 560–72, hier Sp. 570.

20   Helmut Zedelmaier, "Mnemotechnik," in *Lexikon des Mittelalters*, I–X (München und Zürich, [1977–]1980–99 [VIII und IX: nur München; X: Lachen am Zürichsee; Neudruck gekürzt in 9 Bänden, Stuttgart und Weimar, 1999) [im Folgenden abgekürzt als *LexMA*], hier VI (1993), Sp. 698f.

21   Benedikt Konrad Vollmann, "Kommentar, I. Mittellatein," in *LexMA* V (1991), Sp. 1279f.

sich dann bei den Glossatoren[22] einreihen, und den *Aphorismen*-Text würde man als *Apparatus glossarum*[23] beschreiben können.

Trotz allen strukturellen Entsprechungen wollte der Autor der *Aphorismen* jedoch keinen Glossenkommentar erstellen, sondern er ging davon aus, daß der Wundarzt-Meister—und an den wendet er sich—in der Lage sein sollte, zusätzlich zum bereits memorierten deutschen *Roger-Urtext*[24] auch noch die prägnanten *Aphorismen* mnemotechnisch zu bewältigen. In diese Richtung weist die als Alternativ-Titel für die *Aphorismen* angebotene[25] Werkbezeichnung *Merksätze von mancherlei wunden*.

"Nw sal man mercken von manicherley wunden" hat der Kopist von K die *Roger-Aphorismen* überschrieben.[26] Er bringt durch diese Formulierung nicht nur den Merksatzcharakter zum Ausdruck, sondern weist über die mnemotechnische Intention des Textes hinaus auf die inhaltliche Zielsetzung. Der *Aphorismen*-Verfasser hat seine ergänzenden Merksätze unter traumatologischen Gesichtspunkten zusammengestellt, wobei es ihm nicht nur um ein gediegenes Wundmanagement, sondern auch um die medikamentöse Versorgung und die diätetische Führung des Verletzten ging. Zwei ohne Glosse gebliebene Lemma-Zitate[27] lassen erkennen, daß der Verfasser den Roger-Urtext zuerst exzerpierte und dann erst zu den kapitelkennzeichnenden Zitaten die ergänzenden Aphorismen hinzugefügt hat.

39 Lemmazitate sind in der Abfolge des Referenztextes geordnet und rufen ebensoviele Kapitel der Roger-*Chirurgie* auf. Daß es gerade 39 Paragraphen sind

---

[22] Peter Weimar, "Apparatus glossarum, Glossenapparat," in *LexMA* I ([1977–]1980), Sp. 1802f.

[23] Rosmarie Bitterli, "Glossatoren, I. Römisches Recht," in *LexMA* IV (1989), Sp. 1504–6.

[24] Roger Frugardi/Rüdiger Frutgard hat seine Parmäner Chirurgie-Vorlesungen in den 1170er Jahren gehalten; aufgrund von Hörermitschriften wurde der *Roger-Urtext* 1180 durch Guido d'Arezzo den Jüngeren redigiert; die deutschen Übertragungen setzen in Ostdeutschland (Schlesien, [Posen]) vor 1250 ein; auf welche der deutschen Übersetzungen der *Aphorismen*-Verfasser seine Ergänzungen bezogen hat, wurde noch nicht untersucht; vgl. Gundolf Keil und Werner Erich Gerabek, "Roger Frugardi und die Tradition langobardischer Chirurgie," *Sudhoffs Archiv* 86 (2002), S. 1–26; Wolfgang Wegner, "Guido von Arezzo der Jüngere," in *Enzyklopädie Medizingeschichte*, hrsg. von Werner Erich Gerabek, Bernhard Dietrich Haage, Gundolf Keil und Wolfgang Wegner, I–III (Berlin und New York, 2005), 2. Aufl. ebd. 2007 [im Folgenden abgekürzt als **EnzMedGesch**], I, S. 516[b]; Bernhard D. Haage und Wolfgang Wegner, "Roger Frugardi," in *EnzMedGesch* III, S. 1261[b]f.; Gundolf Keil, "'Rogerglosse,'" in *EnzMedGesch* III, S. 1262[ab]. Sieh auch unten Anm. 106.

[25] Keil (2005) [wie Anm. 15], S. 132.

[26] Im Textzeugen O fehlen der erste Paragraph und mit ihm der Texteingang.

[27] §§32 und 39.

und nicht 38 oder 40, könnte dem Bestreben des Verfassers entsprechen, die in ihrer Bedeutung ungünstigen Nachbarzahlen 38 und 40 zu vermeiden.[28]

Die *Oberschlesischen Roger-Aphorismen* haben früh Aufmerksamkeit auf sich gezogen. Nachdem Gerhard Eis die Farfenser Handschrift ins Blickfeld der Fachprosaforschung gerückt[29] und sein Schüler Volker Zimmermann[30] die *Aphorismen* als kleine "Wundarznei" definiert sowie als eigenständigen Text gegenüber den anrainenden Schriften abgegrenzt hatte, widmete Claus Ohm unter der Leitung Zimmermanns seine medizinische Dissertation[31] dem gedrungenen Text aus dem Benediktinerkloster Farfa und stellte ihn in einer faksimile-gestützten Edition vor (K). Da die Doktorarbeit von Ohm ungedruckt blieb, bot es sich an, den kleinen Text in einer Druckversion bereitzustellen, und zwar dort, wohin bezüglich seiner Entstehung die schreibdialektalen und lexikalischen Merkmale wiesen: in Mährisch Schlesien.[32] Die Lokalisierung des

---

[28]   Heinz Meyer und Rudolf Suntrup, *Lexikon der mittelalterlichen Zahlenbedeutungen*, Münstersche Mittelalter-Schriften 56 (München, 1987), S. 709–11; sieh auch Johannes Gottfried Mayer, "Text und Zahl—Zahl und Textstrukturen—Zahlenphänomene in der mittelalterlichen Literatur," in *Aspekte der Textgestaltung. Referate der Internationalen Germanistischen Konferenz, Ostrava ... 2001*, hrsg. von Lenka Vaňková und Pavla Zajícová (Mährisch Ostrau/Ostrava, 2001), S. 69–86. —Besonders beliebt war die 36, die als *quadratus senarius* die *perfectio perfecti* darstellte; sie wurde als zahlenspekulative Strukturvorgabe dem Aufbau von Meister Albrants *Roßarzneibuch* zugrunde gelegt, in der Gliederung des *Erlauer Frauenbüchleins* nachgestaltet und in der Anlage einer feldärztlichen Notversorgung verwirklicht; vgl. Groß/Keil (2006/07) [wie Anm. 43], S. 122f.; Jörg Siegfried Kotsch und Gundolf Keil, "Das 'Erlauer Frauenbüchlein'. Untersuchungen zu einem gynäkologischen Rezeptar aus dem spätmittelalterlichen Oberungarn. Text und Kommentar," *Fachprosaforschung—Grenzüberschreitungen* 4/5 (2008/09 [2010]), S. 47–112.

[29]   Gerhard Eis, "Nachricht über eine altdeutsche Sammelhandschrift aus dem italienischen Kloster Farfa," *Medizinische Monatsschrift* 13 (1959), S. 514ᵃ–516ᵇ, auch in G. Eis, *Medizinische Fachprosa des späten Mittelalters und der frühen Neuzeit*, Amsterdamer Publikationen zur Sprache und Literatur 48 (Amsterdam, 1982), S. 10–15.

[30]   Volker Zimmermann, *Rezeption und Rolle der Heilkunde in landessprachigen handschriftlichen Kompendien des Spätmittelalters*, Ars medica. Texte und Untersuchungen zur Quellenkunde der Alten Medizin, IV. Abteilung: Landessprachige und mittelalterliche Medizin 2 (Stuttgart, 1986), S. 14–16, 34f., 42–5, 52f., 63–9, 96, 102–5, 138–40, 144, 148f., 152f. u.ö., hier S. 15: "eine 'Wundarznei'"; vgl. auch V. Zimmermann, "Fleischbuch," in *VL* XI (2004), Sp. 447.

[31]   Claus Ohm, "Die 'Wundarznei' des Codex 200 von 1463 aus dem Benediktinerkloster Farfa," med. Diss. [masch.schr.] (Göttingen, 1986); dazu: Keil/Groß (2005) [wie Anm. 39], S. 157f.

[32]   Hilde-Marie Groß und Gundolf Keil (Hrsgg.), "Die 'Kleine Wundarznei' des Codex Farfensis 200. Spätmittelalterliche chirurgische Aphorismen aus dem böhmisch-schlesischen Raum," *Acta historica et museologica Universitatis Silesianae Opaviensis* 5 (2000), S. 200–213. — Vgl. unten Anm. 39.

in den Sabiner Bergen aufgezeichneten Textes allein aufgrund mundartlicher und wortgeographischer Merkmale schien gewagt, wurde indessen unmittelbar nach Veröffentlichung durch den Olmützer Textzeugen (O) bestätigt, dessen Identifizierung in Würzburg gelang[33] und den Lenka Vaňková untersuchte und 2004 edierte.[34]

Wie Vaňková bei ihrem Textvergleich bereits feststellte,[35] unterscheiden sich die Versionen K und O nicht unerheblich. Während der Farfenser Schreiber (K) die 39er-Folge der traumatologischen Paragraphen wahrte, hat der mährisch-schlesische Redaktor von O die Reihe der Aphorismen ausgedünnt, indem er—beginnend mit dem Eingangs-Paragraphen[36]—mehrere Textteile ausließ und auf das letzte Drittel der Aphorismen (die Paragraphen 30–39) ganz verzichtete. Trotzdem erscheint seine Version O umfangreicher als die konzise K-Fassung, und das ist darauf zurückzuführen, daß der mährisch-schlesische O-Redaktor den reduzierten *Aphorismen*-Text durch chirurgische *Materia medica* auffüllte, indem er an Kompositionsfugen zwischen den Paragraphen sowie dann am Schluß insgesamt 31 Vorschriften eines "wundärztlichen Rezeptars" einschob beziehungsweise anhängte.[37] Dabei bemühte er sich um inhaltliche Kontingenz, indem er die interkalierten Anweisungen möglichst stimmig zur Indikation des vorausgehenden Aphorismus einfügte. Das glückte ihm freilich nur, wenn er sich bei seinen Einschüben auf ein bis zwei Vorschriften beschränkte. Wenn es sich indessen um größere Zusätze aus einem halben Dutzend und mehr Textteilen handelte, gelang ihm der stimmige Anschluß nur bei der ersten, allenfalls noch bei der zweiten Präskription; die übrigen Vorschriften der an- oder eingefügten Rezeptgruppe weichen dann vom Indikationsprofil des vorausgehenden *Aphorismus regens* ab.

Um einen solchen größeren Einschub handelt es sich beim Segment §18⁺a–g, das neun Textteile umfaßt und dem Aphorismus von der Verwundeten-Ernährung (§18) angehängt ist, bei dem es um die geeignete *chost* bei Darmverletzungen geht. Die ersten beiden Vorschriften des eingeschobenen Segments (§18⁺a und 18⁺b) greifen diese Thematik auf, indem sie Hinweise auf Aderlaß und Abführtränke geben und sich des weiteren mit Diätfehlern bei der Verwundeten-*chost* befassen. Die sich anschließenden sieben Vorschriften folgen dann aber völlig abweichenden

---

[33] Vaňková (2004) [wie Anm. 15], S. 63, Anm. 77, und vgl. auch Lenka Vaňková, "Die *Olmützer Chirurgie*. Ein Beitrag zur Erforschung der frühneuhochdeutschen medizinischen Fachprosa aus Mähren," *Germanistisches Jahrbuch Ostrava/Erfurt* 6 (2000), S. 41–52.

[34] Wie Anm. 15.

[35] Vaňková (2004) [wie Anm. 15], S. 62–4 und 105.

[36] Sieh oben Anm. 26.

[37] Was den zehnteiligen, astromedizinischen Aderlaß-Anhang bei O betrifft, sieh Keil (2005) [wie Anm. 15], S. 139–41.

Indikationen, indem sie die Blutstillung lehren (unter anderem durch arterielle Umstechung) und sich danach der Extraktion von Fremdkörpern zuwenden. Der Wortlaut ist vielfach zersetzt, und insbesondere der abschließende Paragraph des Einschubs—§18⁺g—bereitete dem Textverständnis erhebliche Schwierigkeiten. Die Lösung des Problems wurde konjektural anhand eines Textabdrucks sowie einer kritischen Edition angegangen.

Den Olmützer Textzeugen (O) hat Lenka Vaňková[38] 2004 in buchstabengetreuem Abdruck vorgestellt. Eine kritische Edition, die beide *Aphorismen*-Überlieferungen—O und K—zusammenführt, folgte wenige Jahre später.[39] In beiden Fällen haben die Herausgeber die *crux interpretum* auszuräumen versucht, was zu folgenden Ergebnissen führte:

Der buchstabengetreue Abdruck Vaňkovás von O bietet den Paragraphen 18⁺g in verkürzter Gestalt:[40]

> Ist eyn wonde vnden an dem leibe, nym verch, das der aiter neder wert. Da sol man vnden mit eyner fliten ader mit eynem eisen czu ravmen vnd eyn ploster von aies veys dar auf legen.

> aiter neder wert] neder wert das der aiter auf steyget [*sic!*] Hs.

In der kritischen Edition von Keil/Groß, die wenige Jahre später publiziert bzw. veröffentlicht wurde,[41] erscheint §18⁺g in folgendem Wortlaut:[42]

> Ist eyn vonde vnden an dem leibe, nym verch*, das der neder wert, das der aiter <nicht> auf steyget. Do sol man vnden mit eyner fliten adir mit eynem eisen czu ravmen vnd eyn ploster von aies veys dar** auf legen.

> *nym verch] *lies:* nym war
> **dar] das O

---

38   Wie Anm. 15.

39   "'Von manicherley wunden.' Die 'kleine Wundarznei' des Codex Farfensis 200: 'Oberschlesische Roger-Aphorismen' des 14. Jahrhunderts," eingeleitet und herausgegeben von Gundolf Keil und Hildemarie Groß, *Fachprosaforschung—Grenzüberschreitungen* 1 (2005), S. 155–88 [= Kritische Edition von KO unter Einbezug der Zusätze aus dem "wundärztlichen Rezeptar"]. —Vgl. den Erstabdruck von K (wie Anm. 32).

40   Vaňková (2004) [wie Anm. 15], S. 72*, Z. 3–5.

41   Band 1 (2005) der *Fachprosaforschung—Grenzüberschreitungen* wurde erst 2007 ausgeliefert.

42   Keil/Groß (2005) [wie Anm. 39], S. 180.

Beide konjekturalkritischen Eingriffe gingen von der Auffassung aus, daß im Schußkanal ein Aufsteigen des Eiters entgegen der Schwerkraft vermieden werden sollte. Vaňková hat entsprechend *verch* als *war* ('wahr') sowie *wert* als *vert* ('fährt') gedeutet und richtig erkannt, daß der Eingang des Paragraphen überschüssige Wörter bietet, was sie zu einer Umstellung und der Elision von drei Lexemen (*das, der, auf steyget*) veranlaßte.

Keil und Groß sind Vaňková in Bezug auf die Deutung von *verch* und *wert* gefolgt, versuchten dann aber, ohne Elision auszukommen, weshalb sie—um den Sinngehalt zu wahren—den überlieferten Text nicht verkürzten, sondern durch das Einfügen von *nicht* um die Negationspartikel erweiterten.

Beide Konjekturen sind wenig befriedigend, und beide sind vom ursprünglichen Wortlaut gleich weit entfernt: Das zeigt eine unerwartete Parallele, die das kontextuelle Umfeld der Farfenser Überlieferung bereithält.

Die im Farfensis 200 erhaltenen *Roger-Aphorismen* (K) wurden—wie auch die "feldärztliche Notversorgung 'Wiltu die wunde wol bewarn'"[43]— einer chirurgischen Arzneimittellehre[44] angehängt, die, wie noch andere Gattungsvertreter, zunächst als Textkern über hundert Vollrezepte (geordnet in absteigender Konsistenzreihe nach Arzneiformen) bringt, um dann eine gleichfalls umfangreiche Textschleppe anzuschließen, die nach abweichenden Gliederungsprinzipien zusammengestellt wurde und in ihrer *Materia medica*[45]

---

[43] Hildemarie Groß und Gundolf Keil (Hrsgg.), "'Wiltu die wunde wol bewarn'. Ein Leitfaden feldärztlicher Notversorgung aus dem spätmittelalterlichen Schlesien," *Fachprosaforschung— Grenzüberschreitungen* 2/3 (2006/07), S. 113–34. —Vgl. zum kleinen traumatologischen Text auch Keil/Wolf (2009) [wie Anm. 55].

[44] Der sogenannten *Römischen Chirurgie*; vgl. zu ihr Gundolf Keil, "Römische Chirurgie," in *VL* VIII (1985), Sp. 160–62; Haage/Wegner/Keil/Haage-Naber (2007) [wie Anm. 9], S. 239, 244; Gundolf Keil, "Die absteigende Konsistenzreihe als makrostrukturelles Gliederungsprinzip in wundärztlichen Arzneimittelhandbüchern des Spätmittelalters," in *Parerga—Beiträge zur Wissenschaftsgeschichte: in memoriam Horst Rudolf Abe*, hrsg. von Jürgen Kiefer, Akademie gemeinnütziger Wissenschaften zu Erfurt: Sonderschrift 37 (Erfurt, 2007), S. 9–22, hier S. 16– 18; Gundolf Keil und Christine Wolf, "Die 'Römische Chirurgie'. Anmerkungen zu einem schlesischen Arzneimittel-Handbuch aus dem spätmittelalterlichen Kloster Farfa in Latium," in *Textsortentypologien und Textallianzen des 13. und 14. Jahrhunderts* (Verhandlungen der Internationalen Tagung vom Juni 2007 in Erlangen), hrsg. von Mechthild Habermann, Berliner sprachwissenschaftliche Studien 22 (Berlin, 2011), S. 201–66.

[45] Es handelt sich überwiegend um Voll- bzw. Kurzrezepte, die teils nach Arzneiform und Anwendung, teils nach der Heilanzeige geordnet sind und aus unterschiedlichen Provenienzen stammen. Eine Quellenuntersuchung steht noch aus; schlesische und italienische Vorlagen konnten jedoch schon nachgewiesen werden. Sieh Keil/Wolf (2011) [wie Anm. 44], S. 231: "Die Pillule ... hot gemacht meister Scoto vnd hot sie gesant dem Herczog von Meilant"; S. 232: "Das ... sint recepta Meister girardi ader erhart Von Come yn walischen landen <unter anderen für> den Bobest

auch einige Exzerpte[46] aus jenem "wundärztlichen Rezeptar" bietet, aus dessen
Vorschriften der O-Redaktor seinen Bestand an *Roger-Aphorismen* auffüllte.[47]
Und unter diesen wenigen Exzerpten, die aus dem "wundärztlichen Rezeptar" in
die chirurgische Arzneimittellehre des Farfensis 200 Eingang fanden, begegnet
glücklicherweise auch §18⁺g, den der Farfenser Kompilator einer vergleichsweise
wenig verderbten Vorlage entnehmen konnte: Er exzerpierte ihn zusammen mit
dem vorausgehenden Paragraphen 18⁺f.

Der Farfenser Kompilator hat sich mit dem Paragraphen 18⁺g nicht begnügt.
Er exzerpierte zusätzlich den vorausgehenden Textabschnitt 18⁺f und übernahm
auch die für beide Abschnitte geltende Überschrift—wohl weil er erkannt hatte,
daß die beiden Paragraphen eine gebrauchsfunktionale Einheit bilden. Und in
der Tat gehören 18⁺f und 18⁺g zusammen. Daß sie textpragmatisch aufeinander
abgestimmt sind, zeigt sich schon, wenn man ihre beiden Überlieferungen zum
synoptischen Vergleich nebeneinanderstellt:

Rom, Cod. Farf. 200 (chirurgische Arzneimittellehre [R])[48]	*Oberschlesische Roger-Aphorismen* Zusatz-Paragraphen in **O** (Olmütz)[49]
Wye man eyn Pheil sal aus gewynne Jst der pheil obene · man czie in aus mit einer czangen Jst er aber durch geschossen · So rewme an der andern seiten dor czu Jst es denn verswoln · so stos ein kern von holunder dorin Vnd ye lenger ye groser · daz es sich also weite So tu denn daz plaster dor auff / Sunder wisse daz cheine wunde nicht heilen mag die weile beine ader eysen ader hor dorynne ist Jst eine wunde vndene an dem leibe nyderwert do daz eiter auf steiget / do sal man vndene mit eyner flitten ader mit einem such eisen czu rewmen Vnd ein plaster von eier clor dor auf legen	Ist der feyl huch vbene, zo czye yn aus mit eyner czangen; ist her durch geschossen, revme an der seyt dar czu; ist her denne vor svollen, so stos eynen chern von holunder dor yn vnd as gros das is sich zo veyte; so thu den das plaster dor obir. Wisset, das keyne vonde haylet, dye veyl beyne adir hore adir eisen dinne seynt. Ist eyn vonde vnden an dem leibe, nym verch, das der neder wert, das der aiter auf steyget. Do sol man vnden mit eyner fliten ader mit eynem eisen czu ravmen vnd eyn ploster von aies veys das auf legen.

   [46]   Auf Bl. 156ᵛ (alt: 148ᵛ) begegnet beispielsweise §29⁺e.

   [47]   Den entsprechenden Hinweis verdanke ich Kollegen Knut Richter aus Emmerich.

   [48]   Bl. 157ʳ (alt: 149ʳ).—Vgl. oben die Angaben zu K (S. 241–2).

   [49]   Bl. 195ʳ.—Textwiedergabe nach Keil/Groß (2005) [wie Anm. 39], S. 180 (bzw. nach
Vaňková [2004] [wie Anm. 15], S. 71*–72*).

Die Aussage des Doppel-Paragraphen ist klar: Es geht dem Verfasser um die Behandlung von Schußverletzungen, die durch Pfeile verursacht worden sind. Der vorausgehende §18⁺f gibt dazu drei Ratschläge und einen allgemeinen Warn-Hinweis:

- Der erste Ratschlag—eingeleitet mit "Jst der pheil obene"—bezieht sich auf *oben* steckende, nicht zu tief eingedrungene Projektile; sie werden durch eine Pfeil-*czange* gefaßt und in der Gegen-Schußrichtung extrahiert.
- Der zweite Ratschlag—eingeführt mit "Jst er aber durch geschossen"—betrifft tief eingedrungene Projektile, die penetriert sind und von der Austrittsstelle her gefaßt sowie in Schußrichtung herausgezogen werden sollen. Erforderlichenfalls muß der Wundarzt von der zu erwartenden Austrittsstelle aus sich operativ den Weg zur Projektilspitze bahnen—er muß "an der andern seiten dor czu rewmen."⁵⁰
- Der dritte Ratschlag—konditional eröffnet mit "Jst es denne verswollen"—befaßt sich mit Schußkanälen, bei denen Schwellung das Lumen verlegt hat. Sie werden geweitet mit einem Quellmeißel, der zunächst *als gros* wie das Restlumen in den Wundkanal eingeschoben wird und nach gelungener Quellung durch andere Quellmeißel zu ersetzen ist, deren Umfang ständig dem sich weitenden Schußkanal angepaßt wird, so daß sie *ye lenger ye groser* werden und schließlich das Lumen *also weiten*, daß die Extraktion des eingedrungenen Projektils gelingt.
- Der allgemeine Warn-Hinweis am Schluß des Paragraphen zielt auf die Wundtoilette und schärft dem Wundarzt-Kollegen ein, alles an Fremdkörpern und Detritus, was den Heilungsvorgang hemmen könnte, aus der Wunde zu entfernen. Exemplarisch genannt sind Knochensplitter und eiserne Pfeil- oder Lanzenspitzen; unter *hor* scheint Schreiber O 'Haare' (*hore*) verstanden zu haben; es könnte jedoch der Sammelbegriff 'Schmutz' (frühneuhochdeutsch *hor*)⁵¹ gemeint sein.

---

[50] *rewmen* bzw. *ravmen*] hier in der Bedeutung 'Raum schaffen', 'Hindernisse <die sich dem Extrahieren entgegenstellen> beseitigen', vgl. *Deutsches Wörterbuch* von Jacob und Wilhelm Grimm, I–XVI und Quellenverzeichnis² (Leipzig, 1854–1971; Neudruck München, 1984 [in 33 Volumina]) [im Folgenden **DWB**], hier VIII = 14, Sp. 285–90, besonders Sp. 288: "zu etwas räumen" 'sich operativ Zugang verschaffen zu'; vgl. unten Anm. 58.

[51] Matthias von Lexer, *Mittelhochdeutsches Handwörterbuch*, I–III und Nachträge (Leipzig, [1869–]1872–78; Neudruck Stuttgart 1992 mit einer Einleitung von Kurt Gärtner), hier I, Sp. 1337f.; *DWB* IV/II = 10, Sp. 1801.

Nach dem Warn-Hinweis zur Wundtoilette folgt der zweite Teil des Doppel-Paragraphen: Auch §18⁺g befaßt sich mit Schußverletzungen, nur daß es sich jetzt um den zweiten Schritt der Therapie handelt, bei dem es nicht mehr um das *aus czien* des Pfeils und das Reinigen des Schußkanals geht, sondern bei dem das günstige Beeinflussen des Heilungsprozesses im Vordergrund stand. Angestrebt war wie üblich eine eitrige Heilung *per secundam intentionem*,[52] die bei tiefen Wunden wie Schuß- und Stichkanälen jedoch auf Schwierigkeiten stieß. Um ein sicheres Abfließen von Eiter und Wundsekreten zu gewährleisten, hat man sich der Hilfe der Schwerkraft bedient und den Patienten so gelagert, daß die Wundöffnung abwärts (*nyderwert*) gerichtet war und der Eiter problemlos ausfließen konnte. Bei längeren Schnittwunden hat man entsprechend darauf geachtet, die Wundsekrete unter Einwirkung der Schwerkraft ausströmen zu lassen, indem man den oberen Abschnitt der Wunde als ersten zuheilte, während der abhängige[53] untere Abschnitt möglichst lange offengehalten wurde, um als Austrittsöffnung für den sich noch bildenden Eiter zu dienen.[54]

Eine solche Austrittsöffnung gegebenenfalls durch operatives Eingreifen herzustellen rät der Verfasser des "wundärztlichen Rezeptars". Im Paragraphen 18⁺g schildert er den Fall, daß am Unterleib (*vndene*) ein Schuß- oder Stichkanal blind endet und obendrein abwärts (*nyderwert*) verläuft, so daß der sich bildende Eiter nicht nach unten abfließen kann, sondern entgegen der Schwerkraft nach oben *auf-steigen* muß. Heilungsverzögerung wäre das mindeste an Folge; in der Regel verursachte der Sekretstau putride Infektionen wenn nicht gar eine Phlegmone, die zu Recht gefürchtet war und zum Tod des Patienten führen konnte; sie wurde mit traumatologisch aufwendigen Verfahren wie der Volkmannschen Stichelung[55] bekämpft, erwies sich trotzdem aber vielfach als infaust. —Wollte man also "den gewunten menschen wol bewarn, daz her

---

[52]   "Sekundäre Wundheilung," *sanatio per secundam intentionem*, vgl. [Willibald] Pschyrembel, *Klinisches Wörterbuch*, 261. Aufl. besorgt von Martina Bach (Berlin und New York, 2006), S. 2083ªf.

[53]   "illa pars que magis dependet."

[54]   "In omnibus autem (similibus [hier 'schußbedingt penetrierenden']) uulneribus hoc diligenter est attendendum, ut illa pars, que magis dependet, diligentius procuretur et postremo ad consolidandum relinquatur; que uero superius eminet, ... sanationi non inmerito festinetur"; Rüdiger Frutgard/Roger Frugardi, *Chirurgie*, II, 2, vgl. Karl Sudhoff, *Beiträge zur Geschichte der Chirurgie*, I–II, Studien zur Geschichte der Medizin 10–11/12 (Leipzig, 1914–18), hier II, S. 188, Z. 59–62. —Wenn längere Wunden waagerecht verliefen, wurden sie als erstes in der Mitte zugeheilt, und die beiden seitlichen Bereiche blieben bis auf weiteres offen, um den Abfluß der Sekrete zu gewährleisten: "die wunde ... sal man in der mitte heften, daz daz eiter czu beiden seiten aus rinne," "'Oberschlesische Roger-Aphorismen'," §9, Keil/Groß (2005) [wie Anm. 39], S. 173.

[55]   Gundolf Keil zusammen mit Christine Wolf, "Pathologie und Reihung: Der abnehmende Schweregrad als serielles Gliederungsprinzip in der Rezeptliteratur," in *Pharmazie in Geschichte*

\<der selben wunden\> nit sterbe,"[56] war nach Entfernen von Fremdkörpern und Detritus wichtigstes Gebot der Wundbehandlung, für ungehinderten Abfluß des Eiters zu sorgen und jeden Sekretstau zu vermeiden.

Der Verfasser des "wundärztlichen Rezeptars" vermeidet den Sekretstau durch Inzision: Er empfiehlt seinen Kollegen, das "abhängige" untere Ende des Wundkanals von außen zu punktieren. Statt eines Trokars verordnet er ein kleines Lanzett-Messer, wie es als *phlebotomus* (*Fliete*) beim Aderlaß zum Öffnen gestauter Venen gang und gäbe war.[57] Mit solch "eyner flieten ... sol man vnden ('am abwärts weisenden unteren Ende') czu rewmen,"[58] das heißt: 'sich zum blinden unteren Ende des Schußkanals operativ Zugang verschaffen.' Daß die so entstandene Ausflußöffnung durch eingelegte Speck- oder Quellmeißel[59] offengehalten bzw. in ihrer Weite reguliert werden sollte, war so geläufig, daß der Verfasser—schon im Hinblick auf den dritten Ratschlag des vorausgehenden Paragraphen[60]—darauf hinzuweisen für überflüssig hielt. Er begnügt sich entsprechend mit dem Hinweis, das Stoma des Punktionskanals durch ein entzündungswidriges Eiklar-Kataplasma von außen abzudecken ("plaster von eier clor dor auf legen"), was keineswegs einen Verschluß, sondern nur einen Schutz bedeutete, und erst bei der Zielvorgabe für das punktierende Lanzett-Messerchen wird er deutlicher: Indem der Autor das *such eisen* erwähnt, bringt er die Knopfsonde ins Spiel, die in den Wundkanal eingeführt und bis zu dessen blindem Ende (dem *grunt*[61]) vorgeschoben wurde:[62] Die knopfartig verdickte

---

und Gegenwart. Festschrift Wolf-Dieter Müller-Jahncke, hrsg. von Christoph Friedrich und Joachim Telle (Stuttgart, 2009), S. 229–45, hier S. 232–6.

[56] "Feldärztliche Notversorgung," §2; Groß/Keil (2006/07) [wie Anm. 43], S. 125.

[57] Gundolf Keil, "Aderlaß," in *LexMA* I (1980), Sp. 150f.; ders., "Phlebotomie (Aderlaß)," in *EnzMedGesch* III (2007), S. 1155[ab].

[58] *czu rewmen*] *zu-räumen*, 'sich Zugang verschaffen zu'; vgl. oben Anm. 50.

[59] Während Rüdiger Frutgard (wie Anm. 54) das Einführen von Speckmeißeln vorschreibt ("lardonem ... immittere consueuimus iuxta os uulneris") und anschließend, wenn der Eiter fließt, das Einlegen einer Leinen-Wieke verordnet ("Cum autem fecerit saniem, stuellum de panno immittimus"), begnügt sich die "feldärztliche Notversorgung" beim Abfluß-Sichern für Wundsekrete mit einem Quellmeißel aus Holundermark (§26; Groß/Keil [2006/07] [wie Anm. 43], S. 127): "Wiltu einer wunde mit meiczel wern, daz sie nicht czu schier czu heile: Nym von einem holder den chern, der durre sey, vnd stos den yn die wunde ...: so rinnet daz vnsawber gar ['zur Gänze'] heraus."

[60] Vgl. oben S. 243.

[61] (§17; Groß/Keil [2006/07] [wie Anm. 43], S. 126): "... czeuch den pheil vnd los das vnsawber blut gar her aus gen. Dornoch nym eyn \<such\>eisen vnd lawch ['sondiere'] di wunde ein wenig ['inwendig'] bis auf den grunt."

[62] Vgl. §3 der *Oberschlesischen Roger-Aphorismen*, Keil/Groß (2005) [wie Anm. 39], S. 170: "Wenne grose wunden sint, ... so suche ... mit einem sucheisen ... yn der wunden."

Spitze der Sonde ließ sich von außen palpieren und wies der punktierenden Fliete exakt den Weg zum abhängigen Ende des Schußkanals, von wo der Eiter ausgeleitet werden sollte.

Soweit die Interpretation des Doppel-Paragraphen. Sie stützt sich im wesentlichen auf den Farfenser Textzeugen R, gegenüber dem die Olmützer Überlieferung deutlich abfällt: §18+f ist in O derart stark verderbt, daß die textzersetzenden Zerschreibungen ohne größere Eingriffe nicht gebessert werden können. Ohne die erforderlichen Korrekturen sind die sinnstörenden Verschreibungen so gravierend, daß die ursprüngliche Aussage des Textes an mehreren Stellen verlorengeht.

Anders beim Paragraphen 18+g: Hier kann anhand weniger Eingriffe die Lesbarkeit wiederhergestellt werden. Neben kleineren Besserungen (wie *das* zu *do*, *das* zu *dar*) und der Einfügung des Bestimmungswortes *such* vor *eisen* ist es insbesondere das Verlesen von *nyder verth* zu *nym verch*, das erst nach dem Schreiben zweier zusätzlicher Wörter bemerkt und nicht durch Tilgung korrigiert wurde. Hier reicht es, die vier dittographierten Lexeme einfach auszulassen:

> [18+g] Ist eyne vonde vnden an dem leibe nyder wert, do der aiter auf steyget, do sol man vndene[63] mit eyner fliten adir mit eynem such eisen[64] czu ravmen vnd eyn ploster von aies veys dar auf legen.

So sind es ein halbes Dutzend an Eingriffen gewesen, die nötig waren, um den von O überlieferten Wortlaut durch das Kollationieren von R lesbar zu machen. In umgekehrter Richtung ergab sich für R anhand der Lesarten von O kein Anlaß, in den Wortlaut einzugreifen. Im Farfenser Kodex ist §18+g offensichtlich in einer autornahen Überlieferung erhalten, was auch für den vorausgehenden Schußwunden-Paragraphen 18+f gilt.

---

[63] Entspricht althochdeutsch *untana* 'von unten her'; vgl. Walter Henzen, *Deutsche Wortbildung*, 3. Aufl., Sammlung kurzer Grammatiken germanischer Dialekte, B, 5 (Tübingen, 1965), §156, S. 229f.

[64] In der Wortfolge "fliete oder îsen" konnotiert *îsen* als *lâz-îsen* bzw. 'bickelartiges Hämmerlein' zum Punktieren der aufgestauten Vene; vgl. Moriz Heyne, *Körperpflege und Kleidung bei den Deutschen von den ältesten geschichtlichen Zeiten bis zum 16. Jahrhundert*, Fünf Bücher deutscher Hausaltertümer 3 (Leipzig, 1903), S. 109. Vgl. auch Gundolf Keil zusammen mit Christoph Weißer und Friedrich Lenhardt (Hrsgg.), *Vom Einfluss der Gestirne auf die Gesundheit und den Charakter des Menschen. Das "Iatromathematische Hausbuch," dargestellt am Nürnberger Kodex Schürstab*, [I: Faksimile; II:] *Kommentar zur Faksimile-Ausgabe des Manuskriptes C 54 der Zentralbibliothek Zürich* (Luzern, 1983), I, Bl. 40r; II, S. 89 und 186bf.: Abbildung eines *lâz-îsens* in der Hand des zur Ader lassenden Wundarztes.

"Wye man eyn[65] Pheil sal aus gewynne":[66] Trotz schreibdialektal schlesischer Färbung[67] gilt auch beim Schußverletzungs-Paragraphen 18⁺f das, was beim Wundsekret-Paragraphen 18⁺g für die Überlieferung von R gesagt wurde: Der vom Farfensis gebotene Wortlaut zum Pfeil-Extrahieren wirkt autornah und scheint—ganz im Gegensatz zu O—durch das Kollationieren kaum zu gewinnen. Die einzige Lesart der Olmützer Überlieferung, die hinsichtlich Berücksichtigung für die Farfenser Version erörtert werden könnte, betrifft den dritten Ratschlag des Paragraphen, wo es um das Weiten des *verswolnen* Wundkanals geht. Die zum Bougieren eingeschobenen Holundermark-Quellmeißel werden in ihrer Kalibrierung dem jeweiligen Lumen des Wundkanals angepaßt; sie entsprechen im Laufe der Aufdehnung mit ihrem wachsenden Durchmesser der zunehmenden Weite der Wunde. R deutet die zeitliche Dimension des Bougierens mit *lang* und das Kaliber der Quellmeißel mit *gros* an; im Verlauf erscheint dann der Komparativ *lenger* ('länger') und im Hinblick auf den wachsenden Umfang der Bougier-Meißel *groser* ('größer'). Die Korrespondenz zwischen zeitlichem Ablauf und wachsendem Durchmesser wird durch die zweimal gesetzte Partikel *ye* angezeigt, die—in Verbindung mit korrelierenden Komparativen—"ein Wachsen ... nach einem bestimmten Verhältnis"[68] (hier im Verhältnis zum Fortgang der Zeit) zum Ausdruck bringt. Ein Positiv, wie O ihn bietet, ließe sich den Komparativen eventuell voranstellen; der dritte Ratschlag von §18⁺f würde in R dann lauten:

---

[65] *eyn*] mit zweigipfligem *n* (/*n*ⁿ/), dessen zweites Segment zur Nasalierung neigt; es handelt sich um eine Enklise der Endung *-en* an die Wurzel *ein-*; vgl. Wolfgang Jungandreas, *Zur Geschichte der schlesischen Mundart im Mittelalter. Untersuchungen zur Sprache und Siedlung in Ostmitteldeutschland*, Deutschkundliche Arbeiten. Veröffentlichungen aus dem Deutschen Institut der Universität Breslau, B: Schlesische Reihe 3 (Breslau, 1937; Neudruck Stuttgart, 1987 mit einem Vorwort von Wolfgang Kleiber), hier §315, S. 300; sieh auch *Grammatik des Frühneuhochdeutschen*, hrsg. von Hugo Moser und Hugo Stopp, I, 1: *Vokalismus der Nebensilben*, bearbeitet von Karl Otto Sauerbeck (Heidelberg, 1970), §20, S. 201: "Schlesisch: ... Im *-nen* tritt oft Ekthlipsis ein."

[66] *-n*-Abfall nach vorausgegangener Nasalierung; Jungandreas (1937) [wie Anm. 65], S. 296–300.

[67] In O ist der zentralschlesische Einfluß noch ausgeprägter, wie schon die Hebung von /o/ zu /u/ erkennen läßt; vgl. *huch ubene* gegen *obene* in R und sieh auch das zweimalige *vonde* gegen *wunde*; dazu Jungandreas (1937) [wie Anm. 65], §106–7, S. 108–11 (*o* zu *u*) und §143, S. 143–6 (*u* zu *o* vor allem gebirgsschlesisch).

[68] Lexer (wie Anm. 51), I, Sp. 1413; *DWB* IV/II = 10, Sp. 2281.

Jst es[69] denn verswoln · so stos ein[70] kern von holunder dorin[71] also gros und ye lenger
ye groser · daz es sich also weite So tu denn daz plaster[72] dor auff

Die Überlieferung von R zeigt Autornähe und ist dem in O tradierten Wortlaut
weit überlegen. Ich werde dies anhand einer textkritischen Bearbeitung der
Olmützer Version des Paragraphen 18+g zu zeigen versuchen. Und auch in
Bezug auf die *Oberschlesischen Roger-Aphorismen* fällt auf, daß die Olmützer
Überlieferung reich an sinnentstellenden Fehlern ist[73] und nicht allzuviel zur
Korrektur des Farfenser Textzeugen beiträgt.[74]

Es gibt aber auch Ausnahmen, wie sich das beispielsweise am Paragraphen
29+e des "wundärztlichen Rezeptars" zeigen läßt, der sowohl in Farfenser
(R, 150ᵛ [148ᵛ]) wie im Olmützer Textzeugen (O)[75] überliefert ist. Er befaßt
sich mit dem Reifen von Abszessen und bietet dazu zwei wundärztliche Rezepte,
denen noch zwei purgative Ratschläge angehängt sind: einer für revulsiven
Aderlaß,[76] der andere für eine internistische Purgaz.[77]

---

[69]   *es*] kollektiver Singular zur Bezeichnung des—den festsitzenden Pfeil umgebenden—
Gewebes bzw. Schußkanals.

[70]   *ein*] Vgl. Anm. 65.

[71]   *dorin*] entspricht mittelhochdeutsch *dar innen* und steht hier richtungsanzeigend in der
Bedeutung 'da hinein', umgangssprachlich *rin*, vgl. *DWB* II = 2, Sp. 776.

[72]   Gemeint ist ein bestimmtes "Attraktiv" oder "Ziehpflaster"; vgl. die "feldärztliche
Notversorgung," §17, Groß/Keil (2006/07) [wie Anm. 43], S. 126: "Wenn einer geschussen
wirt ... czeuch den pheil ... her aus ... vnd lege eyn czie plaster doruber" 'über das Stoma der
Schußwunde'.

[73]   Vaňková (2004) [wie Anm. 15], S. 63f., spricht geradezu von "Verstümmelungen im
Olmützer Text."

[74]   Vgl. den Apparat bei Keil/Groß (2005) [wie Anm. 39], S. 170–87.

[75]   Bl. 196ʳ; Text nach Keil/Groß (2005) [wie Anm. 39], S. 184; vgl. Vaňková (2004) [wie
Anm. 15], S. 73*, Z. 23–6.

[76]   Vgl. zur Sache Keil (2007) [wie Anm. 57].

[77]   Ralf Vollmuth, "Purgieren, Purgation," in *EnzMedGesch* III, S. 1203ᵃ, mit Bezug auf Peter
Dilg und Franz Josef Kuhlen, "Purgantia (Reinigungsmittel)," in *LexMA* VII (1995), Sp. 328f.

R

Eynen swern reiff machen
Wiltu ein swern reiff mache*n* So nym
semel mel[78] vnd smer d*a*z alt ist daz
stose mit[79] Ader menge pappeln vnd
cletten wurcz vnd ophel[81] gestosen
smalcz[82] vn*d* leges dorauf

O

<W>il thu svern reyf machen, zo
nym semel mel vnd alt smer: dy stos.
Adir nym papilon[80] vnd cletten vurcz
vnd eppe: gestosen mit smalcz vnd
dor auf geleget. Man sal ym an der
andir*n* seyten[83] lozen vnd den leyp
reynygen[84] mit vilden papelen adir
colagogys,[85] dy dem[86] gleich sein.

---

[78] *semel mel*] *semel* mit Einlaßzeichen am Rand nachgetragen R.

[79] *mit*] R, ergänze *eyn ander.*

[80] *papilon*] O, von Keil/Groß (2005) [wie Anm. 39], S. 184, Anm. 432, richtig als 'Käsepappel, *Malva neglecta* Wallr.' gedeutet. Eigentlich aber ist *papilon* Nebenform von *populeon*, und das steht für die 'Pappelsalbe', die aus den Knospen der Schwarz- (oder Silber)pappel, *Populus nigra* L. (bzw. *P. alba* L.) hergestellt wird; vgl. Jörg Mildenberger, *Anton Trutmanns "Arzneibuch."* Teil II: *Wörterbuch*, I–V, Würzburger medizinhistorische Forschungen 56/I–V (Würzburg, 1997), hier III, S. 1483f., vgl. auch ebd. S. 1401f. sowie unten Anm. 94.

[81] *ophel*] ist kaum noch als Nebenform von *ephe*, 'Eppich' (*Apium graveolens* L.) zu werten sondern eher zu 'Apfel' zu stellen; vgl. Heinrich Marzell, *Wörterbuch der deutschen Pflanzennamen*, I–V (Leipzig, [1937–]1943–79 [III und IV: Stuttgart]; Neudruck Köln, 2000), hier I, Sp. 355 (*Apium*), und III, Sp. 24 (*Malus communis* Lam.).

[82] *smalcz*] bezeichnet im Gegensatz zu *smer* nicht nur das ausgelassene Schweinefett, sondern auch das *milch-smalz*, die 'ausgelassene Butter als Salbengrundstoff'; vgl. Mildenberger (1997) [wie Anm. 80], III, S. 1216; *DWB* IX = 15, Sp. 926: "In älterer Sprache ... zerlassene und geläuterte Butter."

[83] *an der andirn seyten*] 'kontralateral' in Bezug auf den revulsiven Aderlaß, der die (im Abszeß sich anschoppende) Krankheitsmaterie—wie auch die Purgaz—vom *swer* wegziehen soll; vgl. Keil (1980/2007) [wie Anm. 57]; vgl. auch die Wendung *an der andern seiten* oben S. 242 mit Anm. 50.

[84] *lozen*] ist ostmitteldeutsche Variante zu *lâzen* und entspricht in Sparsamkeit des Ausdrucks der Wendung 'daz bluot ze der âder lâzen'. —*reynygen*] ist der landessprachige Fachausdruck für 'purgieren'; Aderlaß und Purgaz wurden unter dem Oberbegriff der *evacuatio* zusammengefaßt; vgl. Dilg/Kuhlen (1995) [wie Anm. 77].

[85] *vilde papelen*] bezieht sich hier nicht auf die Käsepappel, *Malva neglecta* Wallr. [oben Anm. 80], sondern auf die Roßpappel, *Malva sylvestris* L.; vgl. Marzell (1937–79) [wie Anm. 81], III, Sp. 34f.; Mildenberger (1997) [wie Anm. 80], III, S. 1401. —*cholagoga* sind galletreibende Arzneimittel, χολαγωγὰ φάρμακα, vgl. Henry George Liddell und Robert Scott, *A Greek–English Lexicon*, weitergeführt von Henry Stuart Jones und Roderick McKenzie, 9. Aufl. (Oxford, 1940; Neudruck ebd. 1973), S. 1996[b].

[86] *dem*] kollektives Neutrum oder bezogen auf das *reynygen mit vilden papelen*, die als humoralpathologisch feucht und kalt im zweiten Grade galten und entsprechend als Absud oder Klistier gegen Darmträgheit bei Fieberkranken eingesetzt wurden; dabei erweichten sie—so hoffte man—gleichzeitig die durch übermäßige Hitze bedingte *durities splenis et <h>epatis*—die

Der Autor des "wundärztlichen Rezeptars" ist von einem heißen Abszeß[87] ausgegangen. Insofern gründet er seine Therapie auf die kalt-feuchte Schleimdroge[88] "Roßpappel," bezieht indessen die *apostem*-gerichtete Indikation zweier anderer Heilkräuter mit ein und verordnet außer der Roß- beziehungsweise Käsepappel noch die Wurzel der Großen Klette[89] sowie die

---

alternativ empfohlenen Cholagoga sollten von ihren Primär- beziehungsweise Sekundärqualitäten (*virtutes*) her also ein gleichartiges Indikations-Profil zeigen; vgl. das entsprechende *Circainstans*-Kapitel, das der feucht-kalten Roßpappel eine besondere Wirkung gegen heiße Abszesse bescheinigt ("Malva ... domestica ... <valet> contra calida apostema in principio ...; mollificat et maturat ...; trita cum axungia ... et superposita maturat, duricies relaxat et mollificat"). Und diese Wirkung ist selbstverständlich im cholagogen Sinne auch hepato- bzw. splenotrop: "Hoc etiam valet contra duriciem splenis et epatis"; vgl. *The Herbal of Rufinus, edited from the unique manuscript by Lynn Thorndike, assisted by Francis S. Benjamin Jr.*, Corpus of Mediaeval Scientific Texts 1 (Chicago, 1945; anastatische Nachdrucke ebd. 1946 und 1949), Bl. 66ra, S. 177; Hans Wölfel, "Das Arzneidrogenbuch *Circa instans* in einer Fassung des XIII. Jahrhunderts aus der Universitätsbibliothek Erlangen. Text und Kommentar als Beitrag zur Pflanzen- und Drogenkunde des Mittelalters," math.-nat. Diss. (Berlin, 1939), S. 72f. —Entsprechend äußert sich auch Isaak Judäus in den *Diaetae particulares*: "Malva ... dissolvit flegmones et digerit sanguinem vel saniem apostematis ...; apostema dissolvit et maturat et ad sanitatem ... perducit" (Rufinus, Bl. 66rb, S. 178).

[87]　"Apostematum calidorum aliud simplex aliud <compositum> calidum; simplex: ut ex uno humore calido; compositum: ex pluribus"; Julius Leopold Pagel, *Die Concordanciae des Johannes de Sancto Amando nach einer Berliner und zwei Erfurter Handschriften zum ersten Male herausgegeben* (Berlin, 1894), S. 19, nach Konstantins von Afrika *Pantegni* ('Alī ibn al-'Abbās al-Maǧūsī, *Kitāb al-Malakī*, I, 8).

[88]　"habet humiditatem et substantiam viscosam"; *Circa instans* [wie Anm. 86].

[89]　*radix bardanae, klëtten-wurzel*, die Pfahlwurzel der "Großen Klette" (*lappa major, Arctium lappa* L.), vgl. Mildenberger (1997) [wie Anm. 80], II, S. 970: "vertript die boesen geswere und böse geswulst"; *Älterer deutscher Macer*, Kap. 22, nach dem *Breslauer Arzneibuch* (1270), Bl. 129[r]: "Lapatium, <groß clette ..., trucken vnd heiß> ... Di wurzele ... uertribit bi bose swulst. vnde di bosen druse," C[onstantin] Külz, E. Külz-Trosse [und Joseph Klapper], *Das Breslauer Arzneibuch. R[hedigeranus] 291 der Stadtbibliothek. I. Teil: Text* [mehr nicht erschienen] (Dresden, 1908), S. 159, ergänzt nach Kap. 118 des *Speyrer Kräuterbuchs*: Barbara Fehringer, *Das "Speyrer Kräuterbuch" mit den Heilpflanzen Hildegards von Bingen. Eine Studie zur mittelhochdeutschen "Physica"-Rezeption mit kritischer Ausgabe des Textes*, Würzburger medizinhistorische Forschungen, Beiheft 2 (Würzburg, 1994), S. 133.

Knollen-Wurzel des Eppichs.[90] Beim Weizen-Feinmehl (*semelmel*)[91] ist er den Empfehlungen von Isaak Judäus[92] gefolgt. Und hinsichtlich Purgierens und in bezug auf den Aderlaß hat der Autor sich der schulmedizinischen Praxis angeschlossen.[93] Daß er Hochschulwissen bei seinen wundärztlichen Lesern voraussetzt, zeigt er durch den pharmakologischen Terminus *cholagoga*.

Inwieweit die Leser des "wundärztlichen Rezeptars" jeweils den Erwartungen des Autors entsprechen konnten, sei dahingestellt. Die synoptische Gegenüberstellung von R und O macht jedenfalls deutlich, daß weder in der Farfenser (R) noch in der Olmützer Überlieferung (O) der Text ohne sinnstörende Fehler überliefert ist. Drogennamen sind sowohl in R wie in O entstellt worden. Aber während bei O das Vertauschen von Roßpappel und Pappelsalbe pharmakodynamisch noch vertretbar scheint—beide Arzneimittel wurden antiphlogistisch und hepatotrop verwendet[94]—, ist bei R der Wechsel

---

[90] *Apium graveolens* L., Sellerie; vgl. Mildenberger (1997) [wie Anm. 80], II, S. 554–6: *ephich, ephich-krût, ephich-sâme, ephich-wurzel*; als heiß und trocken im dritten Grade galt der Eppich als bestens geeignet, Hämorrhoidalknoten zum Verschwinden zu bringen: "Virtutem habet ... dissolutivam et extenuativam viscositates, emoroydas inflatas exsiccat ...; superpositus emoroydas exsiccat," Rufinus, Bl. 23vb–24ra, Thorndike/Benjamin (1945) [wie Anm. 86], S. 28f. Entsprechend wurde er gegen "Knollen in der Brust der Frauen" äußerlich angewandt, die er "verzehren" sollte; vgl. Christine Mayer-Nicolai, *Arzneipflanzenindikationen gestern und heute. Hildegard von Bingen, Leonhart Fuchs und Hagers Handbuch im Vergleich*, DWV-Schriften zur Medizingeschichte 9 (Baden-Baden, 2010), S. 391.

[91] Mittelhochdeutsch *sëmel-mël, simel-mël* bezeichnet 'sehr feines Weizenmehl' vom Saatweizen *Triticum aestivum* L. emend. Fiori *et* Paol.; Mildenberger (1997) [wie Anm. 80], IV, S. 1734.

[92] Isḥāq ben Sulaimān al-Isrāʾīlī, *De diaetis particularibus*, Kap. 1 "Vom Weizen": "triticum ... facit ... ad durum apostema," Rufinus, Bl. 56ra, Thorndike/Benjamin (1945) [wie Anm. 86], S. 140; vgl. auch Susanne Nägele[-Bader], *Valentin Schwendes "Buch von menicherhande geschlechtte kornnes und menicherley fruchtte": Der "Liber de diaetis particularibus" ('Kitāb al-Aġdiya') des Isaak Judäus in oberschwäbischer Übersetzung des 15. Jahrhunderts. Einleitung und kritische Textausgabe*, Würzburger medizinhistorische Forschungen 76 (Würzburg, 2001), S. 29: "Vnd der jn [nämlich den "weißen"] suitte mitt olley vnd leitt vff ein hertte gswëre, das zyttigett err."

[93] Es handelt sich um revulsiven Aderlaß, der kontralateral durchgeführt wurde und die im Abszeß angeschoppte (*stans ibi*) Krankheitsmaterie an eine andere Körperstelle ziehen sollte: "Materia collecta in membro <debili> ad locum alium ... attrahitur ... per flebotomiam factam ex latere diverso," Johann von St. Amand, *Konkordanzen*, Pagel (1894) [wie Anm. 87], S. 19. Vgl. oben Anm. 83 und sieh unten Anm. 96.

[94] Was die Malve (Käse- bzw. Roßpappel) betrifft, sieh oben Anm. 85 und 86; was die Pappelsalbe (*Papuleon*) angeht, sieh oben Anm. 80 und vgl.: "Unguentum populeon ... dicitur 'populeon', quia fit de oculis populi. Valet contra calorem ...: cum oleo rosaceo vel violaceo mixtum et super epar inunctum calorem mirabiliter tollit," Rufinus, Bl. 114rb, Thorndike/Benjamin (1945) [wie Anm. 86], S. 339; *Eene Middelnederlandsche vertaling van het Antidotarium Nicolaï (Ms. 15624–15641, Kon[inklijke] Bibl[iotheek] te Brussel) met den Latijnschen tekst der eerste gedrukte*

vom hochwirksamen Eppich zum pharmakologisch inerten[95] Apfel unverzeihlich: Er führt therapeutisch ins Abseits (und stellt obendrein den Anwender als Ignoranten bloß).

Was die Farfenser Abschrift betrifft, so hat sie—und das ist ihr auffälligstes Merkmal—den gesamten Schlußabschnitt verloren und bietet den Paragraphen 29⁺e ohne auch nur eine Spur der obligaten[96] purgativen Ratschläge. Und damit nicht genug! Der Schreiber von R hat sich obendrein am "sparsamen Ausdruck"[97] gestoßen und auflockernd in die prägnante Satzstruktur einzugreifen versucht. Beim ersten Rezept, das Weizenfeinmehl verordnet, hat er das Adjektiv *alt* in einen attributiven Relativsatz umgewandelt, was ihn beim anschließenden Demonstrativum (*die*) in Aporien führte und schließlich anakoluthisch abbrechen ließ. —Beim zweiten Rezept ging es dem Schreiber von R mit seinem Eingreifen nicht besser. Nachdem er im ersten Rezept sich beim pronominalen Anschluß verheddert hatte und mit dem Versuch, das Mischen von Droge und Salbengrundlage darzustellen, gescheitert war, tauscht er beim zweiten Rezept das Initiator-"Recipe" (*nym*)[98] durch das mischungsbezogene *menge* aus, was ihn in Konflikt mit der pharmazeutischen Technologie[99] bringt und für den Tausch der harten Sellerie-Knolle (*ephen*) gegen einen Apfel (*ophel*) empfänglich macht. Am Schluß des zweiten Rezepts hat dann der Schreiber von R noch einmal in die Syntax eingegriffen und die beiden

---

uitgave van het Antidotarium Nicolaï uitgegeven door W[outer] S. van den Berg, hrsg. von Sophie J. van den Berg (Leiden, 1917), S. 168f.: "Maer op bekerende ongemaken en sal mens niet smeren."

[95]   Mildenberger (1997) [wie Anm. 80], s.v. *apfel* und *pomum*; vgl. auch das *Circa instans*, Wölfel (1939) [wie Anm. 86], S. 77f.; Irmgard Müller und Harry Kühnel, "Apfel, Apfelbaum (Malus sylvestris Mill./Rosaceae)," in *LexMA* I, Sp. 746; Karl Hiller und Matthias F. Melzig, *Lexikon der Arzneipflanzen und Drogen in zwei Bänden* (Berlin, 2003), II, S. 44ᵇ: als Obst gegessen und verarbeitet.

[96]   Die internistisch-chirurgische *evacuatio* als Begleit-Behandlung beim Reifen eines Abszesses gehörte zum therapeutischen Standard; vgl. oben Anm. 83 zum "Wegziehen" jener *aggregatio materierum*, die das "apostema" entstehen läßt: "Attractio ista ['ein solches Wegziehen'] fit aut per ventrem ... per medicinas attractivas aut per flebotomiam factam ex latere diverso. Evacuare materiam a loco apostemoso per ipsum locum corpore existente repleto est malum," Johann von St. Amand, *Konkordanzen*, Pagel (1894) [wie Anm. 87], S. 19f.; vgl. Anm. 93 und 94.

[97]   Zur "Sparsamkeit des Ausdrucks" sieh Hermann Paul, *Mittelhochdeutsche Grammatik*, 20. Aufl. besorgt von Hugo Moser und Ingeborg Schröbler, Sammlung kurzer Grammatiken germanischer Dialekte, A: Hauptreihe, Nr. 2 (Tübingen, 1969), §379, S. 473–6, und öfter.

[98]   Vgl. zur Sache Liselotte Buchheim, "Geschichte der Rezepteinleitung: Horusauge—Jupiterzeichen—Recipe," med. Habil.schr. (Bonn, 1965).

[99]   Von der Galenik her ist das <*ver*>*mengen* eines Krautes mit einer Pfahlwurzel und einer Knollenwurzel (vgl. Anm. 89 und 90) schon zu Beginn des Herstellungsprozesses schwer möglich; die Mischung erfolgt erst beim Zerstampfen im Mörser unter Zugabe des Vehikels (Exzipiens bzw. Salbengrundlage ist Butterschmalz) und wird durch das Partizip *gestôzen* angezeigt.

Participia absoluta[100]—markante Repräsentanten "sparsamen Ausdrucks"—in das Satzgefüge einzugliedern versucht. Das ist ihm glücklicherweise nur beim zweiten der Partizipien gelungen.

Die Ergebnisse des textkritischen Vergleichs sind also verschieden. Während beim Paragraphen 29[+]e der in R tradierte Wortlaut sich ungünstig gegenüber O abhebt und es durch Verlesungen, Auslassungen sowie syntaktische Mutationen zu sinnentstellenden Zersetzungen und Zerschreibungen[101] gekommen ist, zeigt die Synopse des Doppel-Paragraphen 18[+]f/18[+]g das umgekehrte Bild: Bei den Ratschlägen zur Pfeilextraktion und Schußwundenbehandlung erweist sich die Farfenser Überlieferung als autornah und gegenüber dem bis zur Unkenntlichkeit zerstörten Wortlaut von O hochüberlegen.

So unterschiedlich und schwankend die Dignität der beiden Textzeugen auch sein mag: Als unveränderlich erweist sich die Qualität des Textes. Und diese Beobachtung führt zum "wundärztlichen Rezeptar" als solchem, das sich in den wenigen Paragraphen,[102] die sich ihm zuweisen lassen, als chirurgischer Fachtext hohen Anspruchsniveaus zu erkennen gibt: Er ist aus kurzen Textteilen aufgebaut, die thematisch in Gruppen aus wenigen Gliedern geordnet sind und sich mit Blutstillung, Extraktion von Projektilen, Versorgung von Schußverletzungen befassen, die Abszeßbehandlung einbeziehen und vor allem auf die Wund-Traumatologie abheben, die bis zur Verwundeten-Diätetik dargestellt wird und das Versorgen offener Frakturen einbegreift. Akute Geschehnisse dominieren; chronische Erscheinungen wie Geschwüre bleiben unerwähnt und werden am Beispiel der Fisteln ausdrücklich aus der Darstellung ausgeschlossen. Knappe Merksätze wechseln mit Kurzrezepten ab; Vollrezepte beschränken sich auf wenige magistrale Präparate; außer Sondierung, Punktion, Extraktion und hämostyptischer Umstechung[103] stark blutender arterieller Gefäße (*cloppendinge odir*[104]) sind keine operativen Verfahren genannt, so daß der Text sich ausschließlich im Bereich der Kleinen Chirurgie bewegen würde,

---

[100] Paul/Moser/Schröbler (1969) [wie Anm. 97], §315e; S. 381: "Absolute Partizipialkonstruktionen."

[101] Im Sinne von Adolf Spamers berühmter Gießener Dissertation von 1910.

[102] Insgesamt sind es 31, in der Edition von Keil/Groß (2005) [wie Anm. 39] durch Kursivdruck gekennzeichnete Paragraphen, die bei der Paragraphenzählung durch ein exponentiell postponiertes Plus-Zeichen markiert und außerdem durch nachgestellte (bei seriellen Folgen: fortlaufende) Buchstaben-Kennung ausgewiesen wurden. Vgl. oben S. 239–40 mit Anm. 37–9 und unten Anm. 115.

[103] §29[+]i; Keil/Groß (2005) [wie Anm. 39], S. 185. —Vgl. unten Anm. 108.

[104] Hier bezogen auf Hals- sowie Schläfenarterien ("an dem halse adir an dem slafe," *Arteria carotis (externa), A. temporalis superficialis*). —Der Übergang des *nd* zu *ng* ist thüringisch-schlesisch, bei *cloppendinge* statt *cloppende/cloppinge* handelt es sich um eine Hybridform; vgl. Jungandreas (1937) [wie Anm. 65], §363, S. 341–3; sieh auch Anm. 65–7.

wären da nicht die Darmwunden, zu denen der Verfasser zumindest ernährungs-diätetische Hinweise gibt.[105] Er äußert sich auf Hochschulniveau; als seine wesentlichen Quellen läßt sich die lombardische Chirurgie[106] ausmachen; in Zusammenhang mit einem Leitspruch zitiert er Johannes Damascenus, zu dem er vielleicht über die Sentenzenkommentare nach Petrus Lombardus[107] Zugang hatte. Seine Maxime lautet: "laset euch an kurczen vorsuchten dingen genugen." Den Gegenbegriff bietet eine hochkomplexe "arthe, dy nyemant gar vol gelernen mag,"[108] weil sie zu verwickelt und verwirrend ist, auf jeden Fall nicht erprobt (*vorsucht*) wurde.

Wenn man dem "wundärztlichen Rezeptar," das sich als individueller Text abzuzeichnen beginnt, einen Namen geben wollte, könnte man vielleicht als Titel vorschlagen: *"Kurze versuochte dinge": Mährisch-schlesisches wundärztliches Rezeptar*. Der Begriff eines *dinges* ist dabei weit gefaßt und reicht von "Arzneistoff" über "Arzneimittel" bis zum "Heilverfahren,"[109] was Ätiologie und Indikation mit einbegreift; *kurz* bezieht sich ausschließlich auf die klare, bündige Darstellung bei Sparsamkeit des Ausdrucks; *mährisch-schlesisch* weist auf das Entstehungsgebiet, das sich an den Textzeugen, am Schreibdialekt und der Mitüberlieferung ablesen läßt und obendrein an wortgeographischen Eigenheiten zum Ausdruck kommt: "des heyligen geystes wurcze" als Pflanzenname[110] weist beispielsweise auf Niederösterreich, das über die Mährische Brücke[111] in engem Austausch mit Mährisch Schlesien stand.

Der Textzeuge R ist 1462 niedergeschrieben worden; der Wortlaut von O wurde etwa zur gleichen Zeit aufs Papier gebracht,[112] so daß die Entstehung des "Rezeptars" für die Zeit vor 1450 anzusetzen ist: Wahrscheinlich wurden die "kurzen versuochten dinge" im ersten Drittel des 15. Jahrhunderts verfaßt; vielleicht kann der prägnante chirurgische Text aber auch schon auf die Jahre

---

[105]   Sieh oben S. 239 zu den Paragraphen 18⁺a und 18⁺b.

[106]   Entsprechend Keil/Gerabek (2002) [wie Anm. 24]; vgl. auch Gundolf Keil, "Roger Frugardi," in *VL* VIII (1992), Sp. 140–53.

[107]   Vgl. *LexMA* V, Sp. 568; VI, Sp. 1977; VII, Sp. 1766–9; *VL* VII (1989), Sp. 511–16.

[108]   §29⁺i [wie Anm. 103].

[109]   Vgl. Mildenberger (1997) [wie Anm. 80], I, S. 463f.

[110]   Marzell (1937–79) [wie Anm. 81], I, S. 310: Brustwurz, *Angelica sylvestris* L. Es handelt sich bei unserm Text um den Erstbeleg.

[111]   Sie verläuft doppelsträngig und verliert erst in den Hussitenkriegen ihre ethnisch-sprachliche Kontinuität; vgl. Zdeněk Masařík, "Zu einigen Triebkräften der Sprachmischung in den frühneuhochdeutschen Mundarten Mährens," *Acta Facultatis philosophicae Universitatis Ostraviensis: Studia germanistica* 3 (Mährisch Ostrau, 2008), S. 11–12.

[112]   Zur Datierung von R—im selben Kodex überliefert wie K—sieh Zimmermann (1986) [wie Anm. 30], S. 14, und vgl. auch oben Anm. 44 (R steht für *Römische Chirurgie*); zur zeitlichen Eingrenzung von O sieh oben S. 235–6 mit Anm. 15–17.

um 1400 datiert werden. Seine Mikrostruktur mit ihren gebrauchsfunktional zusammengestellten Paragraphen ist unverkennbar; welchem Textmuster[113] die Makrostruktur folgte, läßt sich indessen noch nicht ausmachen,[114] wie auch der Textumfang mit Sicherheit über die bisher nachgewiesenen 31 Paragraphen[115] hinausgegangen ist, obwohl er sich in genaueren Konturen noch nicht darstellt. Die Tatsache, daß einzelne Paragraphen (18[+]f, 18[+]g; 29[+]e) sich in Streuüberlieferung nachweisen lassen und in R der Textschleppe zu einem wundärztlichen Handbuch[116] eingefügt sind, läßt es sinnvoll erscheinen, die Textschleppe zu durchforsten und in deren chirurgischen Segmenten nach Paragraphen zu fahnden, die eventuell zum "wundärztlichen Rezeptar" passen könnten und sich als versprengte Versatzstücke aus den "kurzen versuochten dingen" ausweisen ließen. Und da winkt auch gleich—gar nicht weit[117] von den drei bereits aufgespürten Paragraphen—ein zusätzlicher Fund, bei dem es sich um eine Therapievorschrift für Büchsenschuß-Verletzungen handelt, die in der Frühzeit der Handfeuerwaffen[118] meist oberflächlich waren, da die Projektile noch wenig Durchschlagskraft besaßen. Die Behandlungsvorschrift mit ihrem vorausgehenden Ratschlag und dem nachfolgenden Ein-Komponenten-Kurzrezept[119] scheint sich so gut in die Paragraphen des "Mährisch-schlesischen Rezeptars" zu fügen, daß man es gleich mit der Ziffer "18[+]h" ausstatten und unter die "kurzen versuochten dinge" einreihen möchte. Der Text lautet:

---

[113] Am ehesten zu vermuten ist eine traumatologische oder eine anatomische Anordnung "vom Scheitel bis zur Sohle"; vgl. Keil/Wolf (2009) [wie Anm. 55] und sieh Gundolf Keil, "Organisationsformen medizinischen Wissens," in *Wissensorganisierende und wissensvermittelnde Literatur im Mittelalter. Perspektiven ihrer Erforschung. <Verhandlungen des> Kolloquium<s vom> 5.-7. Dezember 1985*, hrsg. von Norbert Richard Wolf, Wissensliteratur im Mittelalter. Schriften des Sonderforschungsbereichs 226 Würzburg/Eichstätt 1 (Wiesbaden, 1987), S. 221–45, hier S. 230–33: "a capite ad calcem."

[114] Die beiden mehrgliedrigen Versatzstücke in K [vgl. Anm. 102] zeigen funktionsbezogene Gruppierung der Paragraphen nach traumatologischen Gesichtspunkten.

[115] 4[+]a, 11[+]a, 14[+]a–14[+]b, 15[+]a–15[+]b, 18[+]a–18[+]g, 29[+]a–29[+]m.

[116] Der *Römischen Chirurgie* (R); vgl. oben Anm. 44.

[117] R, Bl. 156[r] (alt: 148[r]).

[118] Einer der frühest nachweisbaren deutschen Schützen ist Heinz Schaub vom Wallis, der im 14. Jahrhundert sein Pulver selber herstellte und 20 steinerne Projektile je Schuß aus dem Flintenlauf abfeuerte; vgl. Gundolf Keil, in *VL* VIII (1992), Sp. 608.

[119] Vgl. zur Sache Gundolf Keil, "Medizinisches Wissen und der gemeine Mann: Heilkundliche Katechese im 17. und 18. Jahrhundert," in *Wissenschaftskommunikation in Europa im 18. und 19. Jahrhundert. Beiträge der Tagung vom 5. und 6. Dezember 2008 an der Akademie gemeinnütziger Wissenschaften zu Erfurt*, hrsg. von Ingrid Kästner, Europäische Wissenschaftsbeziehungen 1 (Aachen, 2009), S. 325–76, hier S. 335–43, und sieh auch Keil/Wolf (2011) [wie Anm. 44], S. 201–8 und 247, Anm. 304.

Wenn du mit einer buchsen geschussen wirst

dy weile daz puluer in der wunde ist so heilet es mit ni nichte[120] vnd frist yn sich[121]

Nym weibes milch vnd tauche ein tuchelein doreyn vnd lege es uber die wunde · daz

czeucht yn einer[122] nacht daz puluer aller[123] her aus vnd[124] heilet dornoch schone[125]

Bei näherem Hinsehen schwindet jedoch die Begeisterung: Das Kurzrezept ist zu schlicht;[126] der therapeutische Optimismus zu ausgeprägt; und im Gegensatz zum "Mährisch-schlesischen Rezeptar" wird vom Verfasser des Büchsenschuß-Paragraphen nicht der wundärztliche Kollege angeredet, sondern der Verwundete angesprochen, den der Verfasser zur Selbstbehandlung auffordert und anleitet. Als Bestandteil der "kurzen versuochten dinge" kann der Büchsenschuß-Paragraph also nicht ausgewiesen werden; allerdings erweist er sich als eines der ältesten, wenn nicht als das älteste Zeugnis deutscher Fachliteratur für den heilkundlichen Umgang mit Verletzungen durch Feuerwaffen.[127]

---

[120] Verstärkte Verneinung, zu übersetzen mit "auf keinen Fall," entspricht mittelhochdeutsch *mit nichtes nichten*, vgl. Lexer (1869/78) [wie Anm. 51], Sp. 84. Der heutige Schlesier sagt, wenn er seine Mundart noch beherrscht, *ninischte*.

[121] *in sich fressen* deutet die nekrotisierende Wirkung des *puluers* an und wäre zu übersetzen mit: 'im Innern der Schußverletzung umschriebene Zellgebiete zerstören'; vgl. Mildenberger (1997) [wie Anm. 80], IV, S. 2123f.

[122] lies *in einer*, "in einer einzigen."

[123] *aller*] erstarrter Genitiv Plural in adverbieller Verwendung, zu übersetzen mit "alles," "zur Gänze," "ganz und gar," vgl. *Frühneuhochdeutsches Wörterbuch*, hrsg. von Ulrich Goebel und Oskar Reichmann, Iff. (Berlin und New York, [1986–]1989ff.), hier I, Sp. 789.

[124] *vnd*] ergänze *die wunde*.

[125] Mittelhochdeutsch *schône* in der Bedeutung "komplikationslos," "vollständig," "ohne verunstaltende Narbenbildung."

[126] Auch Heinrich von Pfalzpaint verordnet 1460 Muttermilch (*frawenmilch*), um "Büchssen puluer aus wunden tzw brengen," doch läßt er Ziegenmilch als gleichwertig zu und ergänzt durch komplexe Medikation sowie durch innerlich wie äußerlich aufwendige Applikationen (beispielsweise durch Injektion: "das sprütz in die wunden"). Außerdem rechnet er mit langwieriger Behandlung: "das treib sso lang, bis das puluer auss kompt"; vgl. Ralf Vollmuth, "'Von den geschosszenen wunden'. Die Behandlung von Schußwunden in deutschsprachigen chirurgischen Werken des 15. Jahrhunderts," *Orvostörténeti Közlemények. Communicationes de Historia Artis Medicinae* XL, 1–2 = 145–6 (1994), S. 1–28, hier S. 14.

[127] Vgl. zur Sache Vollmuth (1994) [wie Anm. 126] und sieh auch die weiterführenden Ergänzungen: Ralf Vollmuth, "Anmerkungen zur Behandlung von Schußwunden durch Feuerwaffen in deutschsprachigen chirurgischen Werken des 15. Jahrhunderts. Drei Nachträge," *Würzburger medizinhistorische Mitteilungen* 17 (1998), S. 205–14; ders., "'Wann einer mit einer puchssen/ geschossen wirt'. Eine Mehrschritt-Therapie für Schußwunden aus der zweiten Hälfte des 15. Jahrhunderts," *Sudhoffs Archiv* 82 (1998), S. 102–4; ders., "Verbrannt oder vergiftet? Zur

Damit genug! Die Emendationen zu §18⁺g der *Oberschlesischen Rogerglossen* haben sich mit einer Behandlung für Pfeilschuß-Verletzungen befaßt und konnten dabei bis in die Abszeßtherapie ausgreifen. Als Nebenergebnis ist es gelungen, einen der ältesten, wenn nicht den ältesten[128] deutschen Text über Büchsenschuß-Verletzungen aufzufinden, herauszugeben und zu kommentieren. Vor allem aber ist es geglückt, zu den drei bisher bekannten feldchirurgischen Texten des mährisch-schlesischen Raums noch einen vierten nachzuweisen, so daß neben die *Prag-Olmützer Wundarznei*,[129] neben die *Oberschlesischen Roger-Aphorismen* und neben das Wundmanagement der *Notversorgung im Felde*[130] nun auch noch das *Mährisch-schlesische wundärztliche Rezeptar* tritt mit seinen "kurzen versuochten dingen." Alle vier Texte zeigen hohes chirurgisches Niveau, alle vier Texte sind vom Wundarzt für den ausgebildeten Fachkollegen geschrieben und alle vier Texte suchen die feldärztliche Praxis effizient zu gestalten sowie zusätzlich zu optimieren, indem sie sie "evidenzbasiert" auf einen Kanon bewährter Verfahren und Arzneimittel gründen. Beim Verfasser des *Mährisch-schlesischen Rezeptars* tritt diese Tendenz durch das Akzentuieren gerade der "versuochten dinge" und "gemeinen" Rezepturen[131] am deutlichsten hervor. Alle vier feldchirurgischen Texte spiegeln die Kriegswirren der Hussitenunruhen und lassen die Bedrohung des ostmitteldeutschen Siedelraumes erahnen, der nicht zuletzt durch die Rachefeldzüge des Corvinen in weiten Landstrichen seine Bevölkerung verlor.[132]

Theorie von Schußverletzungen durch Feuerwaffen im 15. und 16. Jahrhundert," *Würzburger medizinhistorische Mitteilungen* 20 (2001), S. 36–42.

[128] Für das Alter des hier edierten Textes spricht, daß er mit seinem Konzept des "fressenden" Büchsenpulvers noch außerhalb der gegen 1500 einsetzenden Theorienbildung zur Pathogenität von Schußverletzungen steht; vgl. zu den beiden konkurrierenden Theoremen Vollmuth (2001) [wie Anm. 127], S. 37f.

[129] Vgl. zu ihr Keil (1995) [wie Anm. 13], S. 205f.; Vaňková (2004) [wie Anm. 15], S. 57–61, 113–23, 156–60, 111*–190*, 200f.

[130] Sieh oben S. 241 mit Anm. 43 und vgl. auch S. 244–5 mit Anm. 55 und 56.

[131] Vgl. die *gemeynen pillen* von §29⁺g und das *gemayn ploster czu vonden* von §29⁺m, Keil/Groß (2005) [wie Anm. 39], S. 185f. —*gemein* konnotiert hier positiv im Sinne von "gängig," "üblich," "zum therapeutischen Standard gehörend" entsprechend den *usuales medicinae* des "Antidotarium Nicolai" (*Sudhoffs Archiv* 55 [1971], S. 265f.: "praxisgerechte Auswahl").

[132] Vgl. zur Sache Elmar Seidel, "Die spätmittelalterliche Siedlungskrise im Troppauer Land und im angrenzenden Nordostmähren," *Jahrbuch der Schlesischen Friedrich-Wilhelms-Universität zu Breslau* 38/39 (1997/98), S. 67–160.

Bibliography

Assion, Peter. *Altdeutsche Fachliteratur*. Grundlagen der Germanistik 13. Berlin: Erich Schmidt, 1973.

Bitterli, Rosmarie. "Glossatoren, I: Römisches Recht." *Lexikon des Mittelalters*, vol. 4, 1504–6. Munich: Artemis, 1989.

Braekman, Willy, and Gundolf Keil. "Fünf mittelniederländische Übersetzungen des *Antidotarium Nicolai*: Untersuchungen zum pharmazeutischen Fachschrifttum der mittelalterlichen Niederlande." *Sudhoffs Archiv* 55 (1971): 257–320.

Buchheim, Liselotte. "Geschichte der Rezepteinleitung: Horusauge—Jupiterzeichen—Recipe." Habilationsschrift, Universität Bonn, 1965.

Crossgrove, William. *Die deutsche Sachliteratur des Mittelalters*. Germanistische Lehrbuchsammlung 63. Bern: Peter Lang, 1994.

Dilg, Peter, and Franz Josef Kuhlen. "Purgantia (Reinigungsmittel)." *Lexikon des Mittelalters*, vol. 7, 328–9. Munich: Artemis, 1995.

Eis, Gerhard. "Nachricht über eine altdeutsche Sammelhandschrift aus dem italienischen Kloster Farfa." *Medizinische Monatsschrift* 13 (1959): 514–16. Repr. in Gerhard Eis, *Medizinische Fachprosa des späten Mittelalters und der frühen Neuzeit*, 10–15. Amsterdamer Publikationen zur Sprache und Literatur 48. Amsterdam: Rodopi, 1982.

———. *Mittelalterliche Fachliteratur*. 2nd edn. Sammlung Metzler 14. Stuttgart: Metzler, 1977.

Fehringer, Barbara. *Das "Speyerer Kräuterbuch" mit den Heilpflanzen Hildegards von Bingen: Eine Studie zur mittelhochdeutschen "Physica"-Rezeption mit kritischer Ausgabe des Textes*. Würzburger medizinhistorische Forschungen, Beiheft 2. Würzburg: Königshausen & Neumann, 1994.

Gerabek, Werner E., Bernhard D. Haage, Gundolf Keil, and Wolfgang Wegner (eds). *Enzyklopädie Medizingeschichte*. 3 vols. Berlin and New York: De Gruyter, 2005. 2nd edn, 2007.

Goebel, Ulrich, and Oskar Reichmann (eds). *Frühneuhochdeutsches Wörterbuch*, vol. 1. Berlin and New York: De Gruyter, 1989.

Grimm, Jacob, and Wilhelm Grimm. *Deutsches Wörterbuch*. 17 vols. Leipzig: Salomon Hirzel, 1854–1971. Repr. in 33 vols, Munich: Deutscher Taschenbuch Verlag, 1984.

Groß, Hilde-Marie, and Gundolf Keil (eds). "Die 'Kleine Wundarznei' des Codex Farfensis 200: Spätmittelalterliche chirurgische Aphorismen aus dem böhmisch-schlesischen Raum." *Acta Historica et Museologica Universitatis Silesianae Opaviensis* 5 (2000): 200–213.

———— (eds). "'Wiltu die wunde wol bewarn': Ein Leitfaden feldärztlicher Notversorgung aus dem spätmittelalterlichen Schlesien." *Fachprosaforschung—Grenzüberschreitungen* 2/3 (2006/07): 113–34.

Haage, Bernhard D., and Wolfgang Wegner. "Roger Frugardi." In Gerabek et al., *Enzyklopädie Medizingeschichte*, 3:1261–2.

Haage, Bernhard D., Wolfgang Wegner, Gundolf Keil, and Helga Haage-Naber. *Deutsche Fachliteratur der Artes in Mittelalter und Früher Neuzeit.* Grundlagen der Germanistik 43. Berlin: Erich Schmidt, 2007.

Henzen, Walter. *Deutsche Wortbildung.* 3rd edn. Sammlung kurzer Grammatiken germanischer Dialekte, B (Ergänzungensreihe), 5. Tübingen: Max Niemeyer, 1965.

Heyne, Moriz. *Körperpflege und Kleidung bei den Deutschen von den ältesten geschichtlichen Zeiten bis zum 16. Jahrhundert.* Fünf Bücher deutscher Hausaltertümer 3. Leipzig: Salomon Hirzel, 1903.

Hiller, Karl, and Matthias F. Melzig. *Lexikon der Arzneipflanzen und Drogen.* 2 vols. Berlin: Spektrum, 2003.

Horchler, Michael. *Die Alchemie in der deutschen Literatur des Mittelalters: Ein Forschungsbericht über die deutsche alchemistische Fachliteratur des ausgehenden Mittelalters.* DWV-Schriften zur Medizingeschichte 2. Baden-Baden: Deutscher Wissenschaftsverlag, 2005.

Jansen-Sieben, Ria. "Middelnederlandse vakliteratuur." In Keil and Assion, *Fachprosaforschung*, 24–69.

————. *Repertorium van de Middelnederlandse artes-literatuur.* Utrecht: HES, 1989.

Jungandreas, Wolfgang. *Zur Geschichte der schlesischen Mundart im Mittelalter: Untersuchungen zur Sprache und Siedlung in Ostmitteldeutschland.* Deutschkundliche Arbeiten. Veröffentlichungen aus dem Deutschen Institut der Universität Breslau, B: Schlesische Reihe 3. Breslau: Maruschke & Berendt, 1937. Repr. with foreword and index of words by Wolfgang Kleiber, Stuttgart: Franz Steiner, 1987.

Keil, Gundolf. "Aderlaß." *Lexikon des Mittelalters*, vol. 1, 150–51. Munich: Artemis, 1980.

————. "Lanfrank von Mailand." In Ruh et al., *Verfasserlexikon*, 5:560–72.

————. "Organisationsformen medizinischen Wissens." In Norbert Richard Wolf (ed.), *Wissensorganisierende und wissensvermittelnde Literatur im Mittelalter: Perspektiven ihrer Erforschung. Kolloquium 5.–7. Dezember 1985*, 221–45. Wissensliteratur im Mittelalter: Schriften des Sonderforschungsbereichs 226 Würzburg/Eichstätt 1. Wiesbaden: Ludwig Reichert, 1987.

————. "Roger Frugardi." In Ruh et al., *Verfasserlexikon*, 8:140–53.

————. "Römische Chirurgie." In Ruh et al., *Verfasserlexikon*, 8:160–62.

————. "Technisches und wissenschaftliches Schrifttum im mittelalterlichen Schlesien." In Gundolf Keil and Josef Joachim Menzel (eds), *Anfänge und Entwicklung der deutschen Sprache im mittelalterlichen Schlesien: Verhandlungen des VIII. Symposions vom 2. bis 4. November in Würzburg, 1989*, 183–218. Schlesische Forschungen 6. Sigmaringen: Jan Thorbecke, 1995.

————. "Das 'Wässerbüchlein' Gabriels von Lebenstein und die 'Oberschlesischen Roger-Aphorismen': Beobachtungen zu Wirkungsgeschichte und Provenienz." *Fachprosaforschung—Grenzüberschreitungen* 1 (2005): 105–54.

————. "Phlebotomie (Aderlaß)." In Gerabek et al., *Enzyklopädie Medizingeschichte*, 3:1155.

————. "'Rogerglosse.'" In Gerabek et al., *Enzyklopädie Medizingeschichte*, 3:1262.

————. "Die absteigende Konsistenzreihe als makrostrukturelles Gliederungsprinzip in wundärztlichen Arzneimittelhandbüchern des Spätmittelalters." In Jürgen Kiefer (ed.), *Parerga—Beiträge zur Wissenschaftsgeschichte: In Memoriam Horst Rudolf Abe*, 9–22. Akademie gemeinnütziger Wissenschaften zu Erfurt, Sonderschrift 37. Erfurt: Verlag der Akademie gemeinnütziger Wissenschaften zu Erfurt, 2007.

————. "Medizinisches Wissen und der gemeine Mann: Heilkundliche Katechese im 17. und 18. Jahrhundert." In Ingrid Kästner (ed.), *Wissenschaftskommunikation in Europa im 18. und 19. Jahrhundert: Beiträge der Tagung vom 5. und 6. Dezember 2008 an der Akademie gemeinnütziger Wissenschaften zu Erfurt*, 325–76. Europäische Wissenschaftsbeziehungen 1. Aachen: Shaker, 2009.

————. "Die 'Römische Chirurgie': Anmerkungen zu einem schlesischen Arzneimittel-Handbuch aus dem spätmittelalterlichen Kloster Farfa in Latium." In Mechthild Habermann (ed.), *Textsortentypologien und Textallianzen des 13. und 14. Jahrhunderts*, 201–66. Berliner Sprachwissenschaftliche Studien 22. Berlin: Weidler Buchverlag, 2011.

———— and Peter Assion (eds). *Fachprosaforschung: Acht Vorträge zur mittelalterlichen Artesliteratur*. Berlin: Erich Schmidt, 1974.

————, Peter Assion, Willem Frans Daems, and Heinz-Ulrich Roehl (eds). *Fachprosa-Studien: Beiträge zur mittelalterlichen Wissenschafts- und Geisteschichte*. Berlin: Erich Schmidt, 1982.

———— and Werner Erich Gerabek. "Roger Frugardi und die Tradition langobardischer Chirurgie." *Sudhoffs Archiv* 86 (2002): 1–26.

———— and Hilde-Marie Groß (eds). "'Von manicherley wunden': Die 'kleine Wundarznei' des Codex Farfensis 200: 'Oberschlesische Roger-Aphorismen' des 14. Jahrhunderts." *Fachprosaforschung—Grenzüberschreitungen* 1 (2005): 155–88.

———— and Hilde-Marie Groß. "Die große Zeit schlesischer Fachliteratur—das 12. und 13. Jahrhundert. Mit einem Ausblick bis 1500." In Dan Gawrecki (ed.), *K periodizaci dějin slezska: Sborník z pracovniho zasedání v Opavě 11.–12. prosince 2007*, 75–102. Troppau/Opava: Historisches Institut an der Naturwissenschaftlich-philosophischen Fakultät der Schlesischen Universität zu Troppau, 2008.

————, Christoph Weißer, and Friedrich Lenhardt (eds). *Vom Einfluss der Gestirne auf die Gesundheit und den Charakter des Menschen: Das "Iatromathematische Hausbuch," dargestellt am Nürnberger Kodex Schürstab*, vol. 2: *Kommentar zur Faksimile-Ausgabe des Manuskriptes C 54 der Zentralbibliothek Zürich*. Luzern: Faksimile-Verlag, 1983.

———— and Christine Wolf. "Pathologie und Reihung: Der abnehmende Schweregrad als serielles Gliederungsprinzip in der Rezeptliteratur." In Christoph Friedrich and Joachim Telle (eds), *Pharmazie in Geschichte und Gegenwart: Festgabe für Wolf-Dieter Müller-Jahncke zum 65. Geburtstag*, 229–45. Stuttgart: Wissenschaftliche Verlagsgesellschaft, 2009.

Kotsch, Jörg Siegfried, and Gundolf Keil (eds). "Das 'Erlauer Frauenbüchlein': Untersuchungen zu einem gynäkologischen Rezeptar aus dem spätmittelalterlichen Oberungarn. Text und Kommentar." *Fachprosaforschung—Grenzüberschreitungen* 4/5 (2008/09 [2010]): 47–112.

Külz, Constantin, and E. Külz-Trosse (eds). *Das Breslauer Arzneibuch: R. 291 der Stadtbibliothek*, pt 1: *Text*. Dresden: Friedrich Marschner, 1908.

Lubos, Arno. *Geschichte der Literatur Schlesiens*. 2nd edn, vol. 1, pt 1: *Von den Anfängen bis ca. 1800*. Würzburg: Bergstadtverlag Wilhelm Gottlieb Korn, 1995.

Marzell, Heinrich. *Wörterbuch der deutschen Pflanzennamen*. 5 vols. Leipzig: Salomon Hirzel/Stuttgart: Franz Steiner, 1943–79. Repr. Cologne: Parkland-Verlag, 2000.

Masařík, Zdeněk. "Zu einigen Triebkräften der Sprachmischung in den frühneuhochdeutschen Mundarten Mährens." *Acta Facultatis Philosophicae Universitatis Ostraviensis: Studia Germanistica* 3 (2008): 11–22.

Mayer, Johannes Gottfried. "Text und Zahl—Zahl und Textstrukturen— Zahlenphänomene in der mittelalterlichen Literatur." In Lenka Vaňková and Pavla Zajícová (eds), *Aspekte der Textgestaltung: Referate der Internationalen Germanistischen Konferenz, Ostrava, 15.–16. Februar 2001*, 69–86. Ostrava: Universität Ostrava, Philosophische Fakultät, 2001.

Mayer-Nicolai, Christine. *Arzneipflanzenindikationen gestern und heute: Hildegard von Bingen, Leonhart Fuchs und Hagers Handbuch im Vergleich.* DWV-Schriften zur Medizingeschichte 9. Baden-Baden: Deutscher Wissenschafts-Verlag, 2010.

Meyer, Heinz, and Rudolf Suntrup. *Lexikon der mittelalterlichen Zahlenbedeutungen.* Münstersche Mittelalter-Schriften 56. Munich: Wilhelm Fink, 1987.

Mildenberger, Jörg. *Anton Trutmanns "Arzneibuch,"* pt 2: *Wörterbuch.* 5 vols. Würzburger medizinhistorische Forschungen 56. Würzburg: Königshausen & Neumann, 1997.

Moser, Hugo, and Hugo Stopp (eds). *Grammatik des Frühneuhochdeutschen.* Vol. 1, pt 1: *Vokalismus der Nebensilben.* Heidelberg: Carl Winter, 1970.

Müller, Irmgard, and Harry Kühnel. "Apfel, Apfelbaum (Malus sylvestris Mill./ Rosaceae)." *Lexikon des Mittelalters*, vol. 1, 746. Munich: Artemis, 1980.

Nägele, Susanne. *Valentin Schwendes "Buch von menicherhande geschlechtte kornnes und menicherley fruchtte": Der "Liber de diaetis particularibus" ('Kitāb al-Aġḏiya') des Isaak Judäus in oberschwäbischer Übersetzung des 15. Jahrhunderts: Einleitung und kritische Textausgabe.* Würzburger medizinhistorische Forschungen 76. Würzburg: Königshausen & Neumann, 2001.

Ohm, Claus. "Die 'Wundarznei' des Codex 200 von 1463 aus dem Benediktinerkloster Farfa." Doctoral dissertation, Universität Göttingen, 1986.

Pagel, Julius Leopold. *Die Concordanciae des Johannes de Sancto Amando nach einer Berliner und zwei Erfurter Handschriften zum ersten Male herausgegeben, nebst einem Nachtrage über die Concordanciae des Petrus de Sancto Floro.* Berlin: Georg Reimer, 1894.

Paul, Hermann. *Mittelhochdeutsche Grammatik.* 20th edn, under the direction of Hugo Moser and Ingeborg Schröbler. Sammlung kurzer Grammatiken germanischer Dialekte, A (Hauptreihe), 2. Tübingen: Max Niemeyer, 1969.

Pschyrembel, Willibald. *Klinisches Wörterbuch.* 261st edn, under the direction of Martina Bach. Berlin and New York: De Gruyter, 2006.

Ruh, Kurt, Gundolf Keil, Werner Schröder, Burghart Wachinger, and Franz Josef Worstbrock (eds). *Die deutsche Literatur des Mittelalters: Verfasserlexikon.* 2nd edn. 14 vols. Berlin and New York: De Gruyter, 1977–2008.

Schmitt, Wolfram (ed.). *Deutsche Fachprosa des Mittelalters: Ausgewählte Texte.* Kleine Texte für Vorlesungen und Übungen 190. Berlin and New York: De Gruyter, 1972.

Seidel, Elmar. "Die spätmittelalterliche Siedlungskrise im Troppauer Land und im angrenzenden Nordostmähren." *Jahrbuch der Schlesischen Friedrich-Wilhelms-Universität zu Breslau* 38/39 (1997/98): 67–160.

Spamer, Adolf. "Ueber die Zersetzung und Vererbung in den deutschen Mystiktexten." Inaugural dissertation, Universität Giessen, 1910.

Sudhoff, Karl. *Beiträge zur Geschichte der Chirurgie: Graphische und textliche Untersuchungen in mittelalterlichen Handschriften.* 2 vols. Studien zur Geschichte der Medizin 10–11/12. Leipzig: Johann Ambrosius Barth, 1914–18.

Thorndike, Lynn, and Francis S. Benjamin, Jr (eds). *The Herbal of Rufinus.* Corpus of Mediaeval Scientific Texts 1. Chicago: University of Chicago Press, 1945. Repr. 1946 and 1949.

van den Berg, Wouter S. (ed.). *Eene Middelnederlandsche vertaling van het Antidotarium Nicolaï (Ms. 15624–15641, Kon. Bibl. te Brussel) met den Latijnschen tekst der eerste gedrukte uitgave van het Antidotarium Nicolaï.* Leiden: E.J. Brill, 1917.

Vaňková, Lenka. "Die *Olmützer Chirurgie*: Ein Beitrag zur Erforschung der frühneuhochdeutschen medizinischen Fachprosa aus Mähren." *Germanistisches Jahrbuch Ostrava/Erfurt* 6 (2000): 41–52.

———. *Medizinische Fachprosa aus Mähren: Sprache—Struktur—Edition.* Wissensliteratur im Mittelalter: Schriften des Sonderforschungsbereichs 226 Würzburg/Eichstätt 41. Wiesbaden: Ludwig Reichert, 2004.

——— and Gundolf Keil (eds). *Mesuë a jeho "Grabadin"/Mesuë und sein "Grabadin": Standardní dílo středověké farmacie/Ein Standardwerk der mittelalterlichen Pharmazie. Edition—Übersetzung—Kommentar.* Ostrava: Nakl. Tilia, 2005.

Vollmann, Benedikt Konrad. "Kommentar, I: Mittellatein." *Lexikon des Mittelalters,* vol. 5, 1279–80. Munich: Artemis, 1991.

Vollmuth, Ralf. "'Von den geschosszenen wunden': Die Behandlung von Schußwunden in deutschsprachigen chirurgischen Werken des 15. Jahrhunderts." *Orvostörténeti Közlemények/Communicationes de Historia Artis Medicinae* 40 (1994): 1–28.

———. "Anmerkungen zur Behandlung von Schußwunden durch Feuerwaffen in deutschsprachigen chirurgischen Werken des 15. Jahrhunderts: Drei Nachträge." *Würzburger medizinhistorische Mitteilungen* 17 (1998): 205–14.

———. "'Wann einer mit einer puchssen/ geschossen wirt': Eine Mehrschritt-Therapie für Schußwunden aus der zweiten Hälfte des 15. Jahrhunderts." *Sudhoffs Archiv* 82 (1998): 102–4.

————. "Verbrannt oder vergiftet? Zur Theorie von Schußverletzungen durch Feuerwaffen im 15. und 16. Jahrhundert." *Würzburger medizinhistorische Mitteilungen* 20 (2001): 36–42.

————. "Purgieren, Purgation." In Gerabek et al., *Enzyklopädie Medizingeschichte*, 3:1203.

Wegner, Wolfgang. "Guido von Arezzo der Jüngere." In Gerabek et al., *Enzyklopädie Medizingeschichte*, 1:516.

Weimar, Peter. "Apparatus glossarum, Glossenapparat." *Lexikon des Mittelalters*, vol. 1, 1802–3. Munich: Artemis, 1980.

Wölfel, Hans. "Das Arzneidrogenbuch *Circa instans* in einer Fassung des XIII. Jahrhunderts aus der Universitätsbibliothek Erlangen: Text und Kommentar als Beitrag zur Pflanzen- und Drogenkunde des Mittelalters." Doctoral dissertation, Friedrich-Wilhelms-Universität Berlin, 1939.

Zedelmaier, Helmut. "Mnemotechnik." In *Lexikon des Mittelalters*, vol. 6, 698– 9. Munich: Artemis, 1993.

Zimmermann, Volker. *Rezeption und Rolle der Heilkunde in landessprachigen handschriftlichen Kompendien des Spätmittelalters*. Ars Medica: Texte und Untersuchungen zur Quellenkunde der Alten Medizin, Section 4: Landessprachige und mittelalterliche Medizin 2. Stuttgart: Franz Steiner, 1986.

————. "Fleischbuch." In Ruh et al., *Verfasserlexikon*, 11:447.

Der vorliegende Beitrag entstand dank der Förderung durch die Forschungsagentur der Akademie der Wissenschaften der Tschechischen Republik—GAAV ČR—im Rahmen des Projekts "Soupis a základní filologické vyhodnocení středověkých a raně novověkých rukopisů dochovaných v českých zemích" (IAA 901860901).

Chapter 9

Saint John's Wort
(*Hypericum perforatum* L.) in the
Age of Paracelsus and the Great Herbals:
Assessing the Historical Claims for a
Traditional Remedy

Karen Reeds

In 1996–97, the herb Saint John's wort (*Hypericum perforatum* L.) suddenly achieved celebrity status in America as an alternative treatment for depression.[1] Before that, to the extent that Americans knew the shrubby yellow-flowered plant at all, it had been regarded as a noxious weed that endangered cattle.[2]

---

[1]   Ayo Wahlberg, "Pathways to Plausibility: When Herbs Become Pills," *Biosocieties* 3 (2008): 37–56. Articles in *Time* magazine, http://www.time.com/time/magazine: "Move Over, Prozac: German and American Researchers Report the Herb Known as Saint-John's-Wort May Be Effective in Treating DEPRESSION—But Only in Mild to Moderate Cases," August 12, 1996; J. Madeleine Nash, Dan Cray, Alice Park, and Ursula Sautter, "St. John's Wort: Nature's Prozac?" Sept. 22, 1997; Daniel Kadlec, "How to Invest in Herbal-Remedy Boom" (Front cover/Business), Nov. 23, 1998. Also Sue Miller, "A Natural Mood Booster," *Newsweek* (Lifestyle/Health), May 5, 1997, reproduced at http://www.hypericum.com/hyp12.htm. The front cover of *Hypericum and Depression*, by Harold H. Bloomfield, M.D., Mikael Nordfors, M.D., and Peter McWilliams (Los Angeles: Prelude Press, 1996; Web publication, 1996, http://www.hypericum.com/toc.htm)— the first mass-market paperback on the subject—quoted Barbara Walters and Hugh Downs on *ABC News* (June 27, 1997): "Next, an absolutely amazing medical discovery ... Now, a truly startling medical discovery ..." All URLs cited in notes were active as of February 22, 2012. For locating digitized facsimiles and collections of Latin and vernacular texts, I am deeply indebted to Dana F. Sutton's invaluable database, "An Analytic Bibliography of On-Line Neo-Latin Texts," http://www.philological.bham.ac.uk/bibliography/.

[2]   White-skinned cattle, after eating hypericum, react badly to sunlight. The earliest account I know is the 1759 description by the Pennsylvanian naturalist John Bartram of the "english hipericum" as a "very noxious weed" that poisoned horses and sheep, especially those with white hair: Edmund Berkeley and Dorothy Smith Berkeley (eds), *The Correspondence of John Bartram, 1734–1777* (Gainesville: University Press of Florida, 1992), 451. In cattle, ingestion of Saint

Since classical antiquity *Hypericum perforatum* has been familiar to Europeans from the Mediterranean to Scandinavia; the voyages of discovery introduced the plant to many other areas of the world.[3] (Following the popular usage of the last decade, I will use *hypericum* and *Saint John's wort* as interchangeable, generic terms.)

Given the suffering that depression causes and its high incidence—5.4 percent of the United States population at any given moment, according to the National Center for Health Statistics—any simple treatment would be welcome news.[4] The excitement about Saint John's wort was enhanced by appeals to its long history as a natural herbal remedy that had been "used for thousands of years as a medicine."[5] Modern science had now proven, the claim went, that the traditional medicine was a safe and efficacious therapy for depression.[6] Even the

---

John's wort "also affects the central nervous system, causing depression ... [lowered] milk yield, abortions"; William Thomas Parsons and Eric George Cuthbertson, *Noxious Weeds of Australia* (2nd edn, Collingswood, Victoria, Australia: CSIRO Publishing, 2001), 389.

[3]   Richard N. Mack, "Plant Naturalizations and Invasions in the Eastern United States: 1634–1860," *Annals of the Missouri Botanical Garden* 90 (2003): 77–90. Global Invasive Species Database, International Union for Conservation of Nature: http://www.invasivespecies.net/.

[4]   Laura A. Pratt and Debra J. Brody, "Depression in the United States Household Population, 2005–2006," NCHS Data Brief, Number 7, September 2008, http://www.cdc.gov/nchs/products/databriefs.htm. I use "simple" here both in the ancient technical sense of a single-herb remedy and in the everyday sense of "uncomplicated."

[5]   For example: "St. John's wort ... has been used for centuries for health purposes, such as for depression and anxiety." National Institutes of Health, National Center for Complementary and Alternative Medicine, NCCAM Publication No. D005, updated December 2007: http://nccam.nih.gov/health/stjohnswort/sjw-and-depression.htm. Bloomfield et al., *Hypericum and Depression*: "Hypericum has been used for thousands of years as a medicine" (flyleaf); "... the extensive use of St. John's wort in 2,400 years of folk and herbal medicine ..." (64–5). Sue Miller, "A Natural Mood Booster": "People have been ingesting Saint Johnswort ... for some 2,000 years. Some believe it was initially used in ancient Greece to drive away evil spirits. It's been popular for about 15 years in Europe as a natural remedy for depression ..." James C. Overholser's historical survey does not mention hypericum (or any herbal remedy except opium and cannabis): "Treatments for Depression: Wisdom Imparted from Treatments Discarded," *International Journal of Psychiatry in Medicine* 32 (2002): 317–36.

[6]   The herbalist Christopher Hobbs may have been the first to draw the attention of the English-speaking world to the potential use of Saint John's wort for depression. See his "St. John's Wort: A Literature Review," *HerbalGram* 18/19 (1989): 24–33; "St. John's Wort (*Hypericum Perforatum* L.): A Review," excerpted from *HerbalGram*, 1998; and "St. John's Wort—Ancient Herbal Protector," *Pharmacy in History* 32 (1990): 166–9, where he writes (166): "From the time of the ancient Greeks down through the Middle Ages, [*Hypericum perforatum* L.] was considered to be imbued with magical powers and was used to ward off evil and protect against disease. As a practical folk-remedy, it has been used widely to heal wounds, remedy kidney troubles, and alleviate nervous disorders, even insanity, and recent research makes a provocative

medieval Latin name, *fuga demonum* or "Flee-devil" or "Devil's scourge," seemed to suggest that it could keep the blue devils of melancholy at bay.[7]

So dramatic a change in an herb's reputation invited the historian's attention, and John Riddle and I independently began looking into the earlier traditions of its use. Both of us found much that is problematic about the historical claims made for hypericum. This Festschrift in John's honor offers a welcome opportunity to revisit some questions raised by the revival of Saint John's wort as an herbal medicine.

John's interest in Saint John's wort was roused by his knowledge that the classical authorities, Paulus Aegineta and Dioscorides, had noted abortifacient uses for two related species of *Hypericum*.[8] At the First International Conference on Saint John's Wort in 1998 and at the symposium on flavonoids at the American Chemical Society in 2000, John cautioned that—judging by the

---

statement about the ancient uses of St. John's wort by showing that it is a modern protector against depression and virus infection—two modern demons in their own right." All three articles are available at http:www.christopherhobbs.com/. Karen Kraft, M.D., and Christopher Hobbs are more cautious in *Pocket Guide to Herbal Medicine* (New York: Thieme Medical Publishing, 2004; Eng. transl. of *Phytotherapie* [Stuttgart: Georg Thieme Verlag, 2000]), 129: "It has only recently become known as a remedy for psychological disorders." Larry Katzenstein, *Secrets of St. John's Wort* (New York: St. Martin's Books, 1998): "St. John's wort ... has been used for thousands of years throughout Europe, but Americans are just finding out about ... the amazing natural antidepressant" (back cover copy); "St. John's wort has been used for at least 2,500 years to treat a wide variety of ailments, ranging from snakebite to anxiety. Only in the past 20 years has the herb been rediscovered and scientifically evaluated ... The recent clinical studies ... have confirmed what herbal healers have known for centuries, long before the term 'depression' was coined: that St. John's wort helps improve the psyche by elevating mood, soothing anxiety, and helping people think more clearly" (4–5).

[7]   Alan H. Pressman, with Nancy Burke, *St. John's Wort: The Miracle Medicine* (New York: Dell Publishing, 1998), 10: "the ancient belief that St. John's wort offered protection against evil spirits and bad luck may have risen in part from its early use by traditional healers as a treatment for what was called 'melancholia' or troubled spirits."

[8]   John M. Riddle, *Contraception and Abortion from the Ancient World to the Renaissance* (Cambridge, MA: Harvard University Press, 1992), 102–3 and 197 n. 71; *Hypericum* species, p. 432. On the difficulties of determining how possible abortifacients and emmenagogues were used in medieval practice, see Monica H. Green, "Gendering the History of Women's Healthcare," *Gender and History* 20 (2008): 487–518.

herbal tradition—Saint John's wort should not be used by pregnant women.[9] His warning was published on the front page of the *Los Angeles Times*.[10]

A decade later, although recent online accounts of hypericum usually alert readers to avoid the herb in pregnancy and to expect possible interactions with birth control pills, the World Wide Web is full of persistent earlier postings that imply safety in pregnancy by citing no contraindications.[11] As recently as 2009,

---

[9]   John M. Riddle, "Research Procedures in Evaluating Medieval Medicine," in Barbara S. Bowers (ed.), *The Medieval Hospital and Medical Practice*, AVISTA Studies in the History of Medieval Technology, Science and Art 3 (Aldershot: Ashgate, 2007), 3–18; Eric J. Buenz, David J. Schnepple, Brent A. Bauer, Peter L. Elkin, John M. Riddle, and Timothy Motley, "Techniques: Bioprospecting Historical Herbal Texts by Hunting for New Leads in Old Tomes," *Trends in Pharmacological Sciences* 25 (2004): 494–8; John M. Riddle, "Historical Data as an Aid in Pharmaceutical Prospecting and Drug Safety Determination [Personal Commentary]," *Journal of Alternative and Complementary Medicine* 5 (1999): 195–201, esp. 197.

[10]   Terence Monmaney, "Remedy's U.S. Sales Zoom, but Quality Control Lags; St. John's Wort: Regulatory Vacuum Leaves Doubt about Potency, Effects of Herb Used for Depression," *Los Angeles Times*, August 31, 1998, p. 1; reproduced at http://www.biopsychiatry.com/hypericum .html. Greg Thomas, "'New' Drugs, Ancient Uses; What Chemists Can Learn from the Past," North Carolina State University, NC State Press Release (March 23, 2000): http://www.ncsu.edu/ univ_relations/news_services/press_releases/00_03/70.htm. John M. Riddle, "History as a Tool in Identifying 'New' Old Drugs," in Béla Buslig and John Manthey (eds), *Flavonoids in Cell Function* (New York: Kluwer Academic Publishers, 2002), 89–94. Buenz et al., "Techniques," 494–8.

[11]   See, e.g., Hobbs, "St. John's Wort (*Hypericum Perforatum* L.): A Review," table 2, citing the 1984 German Health Department's Monograph E on *Hypericum*, "Contraindications: 'None known.' Side effects: 'Photosensitization is possible, especially in light skinned people.' Interference with other drugs: 'None known.'" Kay Morgenstern, "Preparing for Pregnancy," *Herb Quarterly* 77 (Spring 1998): 43–51, recommended hypericum to relieve the stress of infertility, anxieties about miscarriage, and the misery of post-partum depression. In the early 1990s, the development of search engines and the World Wide Web amplified the publicity in other media; the Internet also enabled individual consumers of hypericum to share their experiences with a very large audience. James A. Duke gave the earliest warnings I have seen in American consumer health literature on avoiding hypericum in pregnancy: *The Green Pharmacy* (New York: Rodale, 1997; paperback editions, 1999, 2002), 4 and 159. Michael McIntyre noted but dismissed possible interactions with oral contraceptives and did not discuss use in pregnancy: "A Review of the Benefits, Adverse Events, Drug Interactions, and Safety of St. John's Wort (*Hypericum perforatum*): The Implications with Regard to the Regulation of Herbal Medicines" (guest editorial), *Journal of Alternative and Complementary Medicine* 8 (2000): 115–24. In *The Big Doctors Book of Home Remedies*, ed. "editors of *Prevention*" (New York: Rodale, 2009), Andrew Weil, M.D., suggested hypericum for depression, without warnings (177); Sota Omoigui, M.D., recommended it for shingles but noted that hypericum "should not be combined with any other medication. Lab studies found it boosts the power of a liver enzyme known as CYP3A4, which plays a role in dismantling more than half of all medicines" (541). (An earlier edition, *The Doctors Book of Home Remedies*, Rodale 1990, Bantam paperback 1991, did not discuss Saint John's wort.)

it was easy to buy Saint John's wort supplements labeled for "mood elevation" that had no warning.[12]

My own interest in Saint John's wort began as a lecturer's ploy in 1998–99. For talks about sixteenth-century herbals and their readers, I chose Saint John's wort as an example of a plant that my audiences would be sure to recognize by name, if not on sight. In the course of the research, I was surprised to see that the historical evidence for the use of hypericum for depression was by no means clear-cut.[13]

It *is* true that Saint John's wort has been part of Western materia medica for thousands of years. The herb shows up in the works of Dioscorides, Galen, Pliny, and Paulus Aegineta and in the medieval and Renaissance herbal literature stemming from those ancient authorities. They recommended it for a wide range of medical problems: internally, to provoke urination and menstruation, to quell tertian and quartan fevers, to ease the pain of sciatica, to expel bilious humors, and externally, to heal wounds and burns.[14]

---

[12]   On August 15, 2009, at my local Shop-Rite supermarket in New Jersey, I purchased the house brand (Wakefern Food Corporation) of "St. John's Wort Extract, standardized to contain .3% hypericin." Its label (copyright 2006) said that the "herbal supplement ... Supports a Positive Mood" and did not mention use in pregnancy. Following John Riddle's example, I urged Wakefern to relabel the product. Wakefern has since added a warning (copyright 2009) to consult a healthcare professional before use "if you are pregnant, may become pregnant, breastfeeding or taking any prescription drug."

[13]   Noga Arikha, *Passions and Tempers: A History of the Humours* (New York: HarperCollins, 2007), esp. 111–70, 269–305; Stanley W. Jackson, *Melancholia and Depression, from Hippocratic Times to Modern Times* (New Haven: Yale University Press, 1988), and "A History of Melancholia and Depression," in Edwin R. Wallace and John Gach (eds), *A History of Psychiatry and Medical Psychology* (New York: Springer, 2008), 443–60. Neither Arikha nor Jackson mentions Saint John's Wort.

[14]   For Dioscorides, I use *Pedanii Dioscuridis Anazarbei De materia medica libri quinque*, ed. Max Wellmann (3 vols, Berlin: Weidmann, 1906–14, repr. 1958), hypericum entries in vol. 2, bk 3, chs 154–7, pp. 161–4; Pedanius Dioscorides of Anazarbus, *De materia medica*, Engl. trans. Lily Y. Beck, Altertumswissenschaftliche Texte und Studien 38 (Hildesheim: Olms-Weidmann, 2005), hypericum entries in bk 3, chs 154–7, pp. 248–50; and the Latin translation in Kurt Sprengel's Greek edition, *Pedanii Dioscoridis Anazarbei De materia medica libri quinque* (2 vols, Leipzig: C. Cnobloch, 1829–30), hypericum entries in vol. 1, bk 3, chs 161–4, pp. 497–500. Galen, *De simplicium medicamentorum temperamentis ac facultatibus libri XII*, in *Galeni Opera omnia*, ed. C.G. Kühn (20 vols in 22, Leipzig: C. Cnobloch, 1821–33), 11:830 and 12:148, and *De succedaneis liber*, ibid., 19:745. Pliny, *Natural History*, 26.85, 86, 90, 117, 119, 129, 130, 158, 164, and 27.26, 37; ed. and trans. H. Rackham, W.H.S. Jones, and D.E. Eichholz, Loeb Classical Library (10 vols, Cambridge, MA: Harvard University Press, 1938–63), 7:326–8, 332, 352, 354, 362, 380, 384, 404, 410. *The Seven Books of Paulus Ægineta*, comm. and trans. Francis Adams (3 vols, London: Sydenham Society, 1846), 3:44–5 (bk 7, sec. 3). The most extensive historical

However, those uses of hypericum as a simple medicine did not, as a rule, include depression—or, more accurately, melancholy.[15] Today "depression" and "melancholy" (or "melancholia") are often taken to be synonymous (or at least closely overlapping) conditions even though treatments and explanations have changed radically since the Renaissance.[16]

To any physician trained in Galenic medicine, the reason for omitting melancholy would have been obvious. *Melancholia* was the epitome of a malady caused by an excess of black bile, the humor from which it took its name. (This was not to be confused with the ordinary bile mentioned by Dioscorides in his hypericum entry.)[17] Melancholy manifested a temperament that was excessively cold and dry. Accordingly, it had to be treated by simples that were predominantly hot and moist: black hellebore was the classic remedy. Since Galen had classified hypericum as hot and dry, it could not be an effective treatment for melancholy.[18]

If Galenic medicine did not treat melancholy with hypericum, where else can we look for this use of the herb? Rather than try to survey the entire history of Saint John's wort from classical antiquity to the present, I focus on the period

---

survey of uses of hypericum is Michael Brück, *Heilkraft und Aberglaube: Die historische Entwicklung der Therapie mit Johanniskraut ("Hypericum perforatum" L.)* (Essen: KVC Verlag, 2004), published under the auspices of the Karl und Veronica Carstens-Stiftung, a foundation for the integration of natural healing, homeopathy, and complementary medicine with academic medicine; see pp. 19–31 on ancient authors. (I am very grateful to Chana Ellman for a copy of this book.)

[15]   In an eighth-century medical manuscript, *ipperici* was one of 20-plus ingredients in "Gera Locadion" (i.e., Hiera Logodion), a Galenic compound medicine for melancholia, mania, and epilepsy. See Ulrich Stoll, *Das "Lorscher Arzneibuch": Ein medizinisches Kompendium des 8. Jahrhunderts (Codex Bambergensis Medicinalis 1). Text, Übersetzung und Fachglossar, Sudhoffs Archiv*, Beiheft 28 (Stuttgart: Franz Steiner, 1992), MS page 97 (fol. 49, recipe 49); however, hypericum did not figure among the Lorsch compendium's other remedies for melancholy. Riddle, "Historical Data as an Aid," 197.

[16]   See Arikha, *Passions and Tempers*, Jackson, *Melancholia and Depression*, and the "Bibliography on the History of Melancholy" (undated; most recent entry, 2006) prepared by Ann-Marie Hansen for the Research Collective for History of Medicine, University of Victoria: http://web.uvic.ca/~histmed/. See also the works in *BIUM Collection medica: Mélancolie*, Bibliothèque Interuniversitaire Santé, Paris, http://www.bium.univ-paris5.fr/histmed/debut.htm.

[17]   Dioscorides, *De materia medica*, 3.155; ed. Wellmann, 2:162: ἄγει δὲ χολώδη καὶ κόπρια πολλά. Cf. ed. Sprengel, 1:98: "De Ascyro ... Nam biliosa recrementa plurima alvo detrahit."

[18]   My special thanks to Edith Sylla (personal communication, 1998) for this key observation. Galen, *De simplicium medicamentorum temperamentis*, 8.20.5; ed. Kühn, 11:148: Περὶ ὑπερικοῦ/*De hyperico*. For the proper Galenic treatment of melancholy, see Timothy Bright, *A Treatise of Melancholy. Contayning the Causes Thereof, and Reasons of the Straunge Effects It Worketh in Our Minds and Bodies: With the Phisicke Cure* (London: John Windet, 1586); digital facsimile, Bibliothèque Interuniversitaire Santé (Paris): http://www.bium.univ-paris5.fr/histmed/medica.htm.

when the first landmark Renaissance herbals were published, and on the account of hypericum in one of them: the 1546 *Kreüter Buoch* by Hieronymus Bock (1498–1554; called Hieronymus Tragus in the Latin literature).[19]

This period, from 1525 to 1560, was effectively the first time that physicians, pharmacists, and literate laypeople could encounter and compare three different ways of using hypericum: (1) Galenic academic medicine, (2) popular medicine and folklore, and (3) Paracelsus's *magica scientia*. To gauge the historical claims for Saint John's wort as a therapy for depression, we have to look at all three of these traditions.

This essay does not try to assess the efficacy of *Hypericum perforatum* for any medical or psychological condition—I am not qualified to do that. Rather, it is an effort to look carefully at the historical evidence, from the herbals themselves, for the ways hypericum was used in sixteenth-century Europe *and* at the ways that evidence is being used five centuries later.

The Galenic Tradition:
Hypericum in Hieronymus Bock's *Kreüter Buoch* (1546)

The textual tradition of herbal medicine is very conservative—two-thousand-year-old treatises continue to be cited today as reliable authorities. But preserving the text about an herb is one thing; using the herb in practice is quite another. How can we be sure that readers of Renaissance herbals actually used Saint John's wort?[20]

---

[19]   The full title is: *Kreüter Buoch. Darin Vnderscheid, Würckung vnd Namen der Kreüter so in deutschen Landen wachsen, auch der selbigen eigentlicher vnd wolgegründter gebrauch inn der Artznei fleissig dargeben, Leibs gesundheit zuo behalten vnd zuo fürderen seer nutzlich vnd tröstlich, vorab dem gemeinen einfaltigen man. Durch H. Hieronymum Bock aus langwiriger vnd gewisser erfarung beschriben, vnd jetzund von newem fleissig übersehen, gebessert vnd gemehret, dazuo mit hüpschen artigen Figuren allenthalben gezieret* (Strassburg: Wendel Rihel, 1546), hereafter cited as Bock 1546; digital facsimile, Biodiversity Library: http://www.biodiversitylibrary.org. The most thorough guide to Bock's herbal and earlier literature is Brigitte Hoppe, *Das Kräuterbuch des Hieronymus Bock: Wissenschaftshistorische Untersuchung, mit einem Verzeichnis sämtlicher Pflanzen des Werkes, der literarischen Quellen der Heilanzeigen und der Anwendungen der Pflanzen* (Stuttgart: Anton Hiersemann, 1969). (I am very grateful to Melissa Rickman for a copy of Hoppe.) Hoppe does not analyze the text of the 1546 edition in detail; Brück, *Heilkraft und Aberglaube*, 41, only cites the 1565 and 1572 editions, which incorporate material not written by Bock.

[20]   For two late fourteenth-century records of growing and prescribing hypericum, see John H. Harvey, "Westminster Abbey: The Infirmarer's Garden," *Garden History* 20 (1992): 97–115, esp. 101 and appendix II, 111.

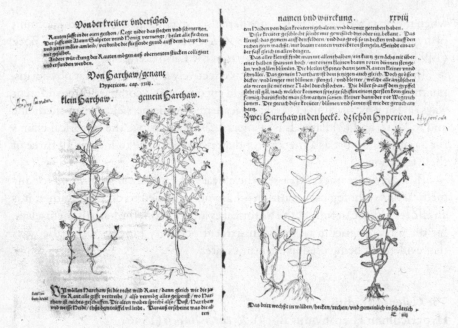

Figure 9.1   Saint John's wort in a Renaissance herbal, with hand-colored woodcut (far right), Latin manuscript annotations, and fragments of pressed plant

Source: Hieronymus Bock, *Kreüter Buoch* (Strassburg: Wendel Rihel, 1546), Part I, ch. 23, *Von Harthaw/ genant Hypericon*, fols xxvii[v]–xxviii[r]. New York, Columbia University, Rare Book and Manuscript Library, B581.62 B63.

For this question, a copy of Hieronymus Bock's *Kreüter Buoch* (Strassburg: Wendel Rihel, 1546; second edition/first illustrated edition), now in Columbia University Library, is an extraordinary artifact.[21] Its marks of ownership, Latin and German annotations, and unskilled hand-coloring of the woodcut illustrations offer strong evidence that at least two readers in the sixteenth and early seventeenth centuries were actively engaged with the herbal's content.[22] Even more telling are the remains of more than 30 plants saved inside this folio volume (Figure 9.1).

All three signs of readers' interest—annotations, hand-coloring, and pressed plants—converge in Bock's account of hypericum: Part I, chapter 23, *Von*

---

21   New York, Columbia University Library, Special Collections, shelfmark B581.62 B63 (Rare Book). The binding is contemporary with the book.

22   Signatures and bookplates show that the folio volume passed through the hands of at least five individual owners before Columbia University Library acquired it in 1922.

Harthaw/ genant Hypericon. Of the four woodcut illustrations on fols xxvii^v and xxviii^r, one (*das schön Hypericon*) has a yellow wash unskillfully applied to the flowers and stems, green to the leaves, and brown to the roots; two others (*gemein Harthaw*; *Zwei Harthaw in den hecken*) have yellow flowers.[23] In the margins next to two of the printed German plant names, an annotator has written Latin synonyms in a very legible italic hand: "Androsaemon" by *klein Harthaw,* and "Hypericúm" alongside *das schon Hypericon.*

Although most of the plants in the book have crumbled into unidentifiable scraps, a tiny sprig of two leaves tucked in the gutter of this chapter's opening pages is a striking exception.[24] Thanks to the distinctive translucent glandular dots still visible in the dried leaves, this plant can be identified with certainty as belonging to the genus *Hypericum* and almost certainly to the species *Hypericum perforatum* L., that is, Saint John's wort (Figure 9.2).[25]

---

[23] The four woodcuts show six flowering specimens, but none with the glandular dots. (1) *Klein Harthaw*: a tiny seedling and a taller, loosely branched plant with small flowers at the end of the topmost branches. (2) *Gemein Harthaw*: a single bushy stalk with many blossoms, each with many stamens, small, close-set, pointed leaves, and long branches. (3) *Zwei Harthaw in den hecken*: two specimens side by side, both with tightly packed heads of flowers at the top—on the left-hand plant, the buds in the leaf axils, the thickness of the stalk, and the strong leaf venation are emphasized, while on the right-hand plant, the stem is thin, the leaves smooth and larger than all the other specimens, and no buds or branches spring from the leaf axils. (4) *Das schon Hypericon*: a two-stalked plant with star-like blossoms whose petals alternate with stamens and with leaves whose tips are gently rounded and whose bases clasp the thin stems slightly. A fifth woodcut, *S. Johans kraut*, was added to the chapter in later editions; it was originally published in Bock 1546, but incorrectly placed in Part I, ch. 45, fol. liv^v, *S. Johans bluomen.*

[24] Although most of the pressed plants cannot be identified from the scraps, there is often enough left of, say, a leaf border, flower head, or petioles to rule out some of the plants described or pictured on the pages where the fragments are found. See also Karen Reeds, "Finding a Plant in an Early Herbal: *Hypericum*, Saint John's Wort, in Hieronymus Bock (Tragus), *Kreüter Buoch*, 1546," *AVISTA Forum Journal* 19 (2010): 70–72.

[25] *Hypericum perforatum* is a member of the plant family Clusiaceae (or Guttiferae, so called for the oil glands characteristic of Saint John's wort and many other members of the group); some botanists, however, regard the genus *Hypericum* and some closely related genera as a distinct family, the Hypericaceae. Wendy B. Zemlefer, *Guide to Flowering Plant Families* (Chapel Hill: University of North Carolina Press, 1994), 75–6. Following Jacques André, *Les noms des plantes dans la Rome antique* (Paris: Les Belles Lettres, 1985), Beck, *De materia medica*, 248–50, identifies Dioscorides' four kinds of Saint John's wort: 3.154, ὑπερικόν, *Hypericum crispum* L.; 3.155, ἄσκυρον, *Hypericum perforatum* L.; 3.156, ἀνδρόσαιμον, *Hypericum perfoliatum* L.; 3.157, κόρις, *Hypericum empetrifolium* L. or perhaps *Hypericum coris* L. The accepted name of *Hypericum crispum* L. is now *Hypericum triquetrifolium* Turra. The authoritative taxonomic study of the genus is N.K.B. Robson, "Studies in the Genus *Hypericum* L. (Guttiferae) 4(2). Section 9. *Hypericum* sensu lato (part 2): subsection 1. *Hypericum* series 1. *Hypericum*," *Bulletin of the Natural History Museum, Botany* 32 (2002): 61–123, at 84.

Figure 9.2   Translucent glandular "perforations" in leaves of *Hypericum* (probably *H. perforatum* L.), found pressed in Hieronymus Bock, *Kreüter Buoch*. The leaves are approximately one centimeter long
Source: (Strassburg: Wendel Rihel, 1546), Part I, ch. 23, *Von Harthaw/ genant Hypericon*, fols xxvii^v–xxviii^r. New York, Columbia University, Rare Book and Manuscript Library, B581.62 B63.

While it is impossible to date the coloring and the pressed plants with any certainty, the two marginal annotations in chapter 23 are unquestionably in a sixteenth-century humanist hand.[26]

In Bock's chapter on hypericum, that humanist annotator found an account that, in its general organization and scope, would have been familiar from the herbals of Otto Brunfels or Leonhart Fuchs, or indeed many manuscript herbals of the previous millennium. The text provided a description of the plant; its various kinds; its habitat; its names in Latin and other languages; its virtues and

---

[26]   I am still investigating the copy's provenance. A printed book label, "E bibliotheca C. Ph. F. Martii," pinpoints one owner as Carl Friedrich Philipp von Martius (1794–1868), eminent plant explorer of Brazil, professor of botany at the University of Munich, and superintendent of the Munich botanical garden. (I thank Sigrid von Moisy, Hajo Esser, Stephanie Witz, José Eugenio Borao, Chia-Ying Tsai, and Stephen Greenberg for their help in documenting Martius's inconsistent use of his middle initials on his book labels.)

operations ("Von der krafft und würckung"); and its specific medicinal uses. In this edition, woodcut illustrations of the plants accompanied the text.[27]

However, Bock departed from that standard format in several ways. First, he wrote in German, for Germans, about German plants. Second, he saw the "common, simple man" as his primary reader, not the educated physician.[28] While Bock provided a Latin index of plant names (and the text occasionally gave plant names in Greek), the *Register* of ailments was only in German. (The annotations in the Columbia copy testify that the book found readers well versed in Latin and Greek.) Unlike Brunfels and Fuchs, Bock rarely gave verbatim excerpts from the ancient sources or recent commentators and left out detailed commentary.[29] Third, although he strove to match up German plants with ancient names and descriptions as far as possible, Bock unapologetically included local plants that were not to be found in the classics of materia medica or had no known uses.[30] Fourth, from his first-hand observations, he crafted detailed descriptions that were, in Conrad Gessner's expert opinion, "so accurate and exquisite ... that no painter could represent them better."[31] Fifth, Bock rejected "the former old rule

---

[27] Bock's first edition of 1539 did not have illustrations. The printer, Wendel Rihel, commissioned David Kandel's illustrations for the second edition of 1546, and continued to add new ones in later editions. For Bock's justifications of both formats, see Karen Reeds, *Botany in Medieval and Renaissance Universities* (New York: Garland, 1991), 14, 32, and 145. Hoppe, *Das Kräuterbuch des Hieronymus Bock*, 15–26 and 44–6.

[28] The title of Bock 1546 used the phrase *nutzlich und tröstlich, vorab dem gemeinen einfaltigen man*; cf. *vorab gemein verstand* in the title of the first edition of 1539. See also Leonhart Fuchs, *New Kreüterbuch* (Basel: Michael Isingrin, 1543; reduced facsimile, *The New Herbal of 1543*, Cologne: Taschen, 2001), *Vorred*, fol. 2rv, on the utility of his own German herbal to unlearned apothecaries, layfolk, and the common man.

[29] Occasionally, Bock quoted Dioscorides in Latin and then provided a German translation. See, e.g., Part I, ch. 57, fol. lxvii[r], *Osterlucei* (aristolochia), which also gave the plant name in Greek.

[30] See, e.g., Bock 1546, Part I, ch. 45, fol. lv[r], *S. Johans bluomen*: "... Von der krafft vnd würckung/ Hab ich nichts gewiss/ wils einem andern befelhen [sic]"; Part I, ch. 97, fol. cix[v], *S. Jacobs bluom* (no classical synonyms); Part III, ch. 26, fol. xxvi[r], *Hartriegel*: "...Wo dieser baum im Winter seine bletter behielte/ wolte ich jnen ein Teutschen Celastrum nennen ... In der artznei weiss ich nichts von disem gewechs." Hoppe, *Das Kräuterbuch des Hieronymus Bock*, 135, 174, and 353. Bock's colleague, Otto Brunfels, was, by contrast, distressed at his printer's and artist's insistence on including local plants unknown to the ancients. See Edward Lee Greene, *Landmarks of Botanical History*, ed. Frank N. Egerton (2 vols, Stanford, CA: Stanford University Press, 1983), 1:484, n. 28. Leonhart Fuchs, *De historia stirpium* (Basel: Michael Isingrin, 1542), sigs α.5v–6r, criticized Bock for not recognizing that not all of the plants in Dioscorides grew in Northern Europe; see Sachiko Kusukawa, "Leonhart Fuchs on the Importance of Pictures," *Journal of the History of Ideas* 58 (1997): 403–27, at 413 n. 21.

[31] "Descriptiones singularum tam accuratas & exquisitas instituit ... ut nullus pictor repræsentare melius possit." Gessner's comment occurs on sig. c.v[v] of his preface to the Latin

or arrangement according to the A.B.C. which is seen in the old herbals. For the arrangement of plants by the A.B.C. occasions much disparity and error."[32] Instead, in language that echoed Dioscorides' preface to *De materia medica*, he asserted: "In describing things, I come as nearly as I can to keeping by themselves such plants as nature seems to have linked together."[33]

To illustrate the drawbacks of alphabetical herbals, Bock could have pointed to the extreme case of Saint John's wort in Fuchs's *De historia stirpium* (1542). Fuchs used the *Greek* alphabet as his ordering principle; as a result, *Hypericon* fell at the far end of the herbal, among plants beginning with Y, upsilon, while its cousins, *Androsaemon* and *Ascyron*, came at the beginning, under A, alpha.[34] To Fuchs's students and fellow humanist readers, that arrangement simplified

---

edition of Bock's herbal (hereafter Bock 1552): *Hieronymi Tragi De stirpium, maxime earum, quæ in Germania nostra nascuntur, usitatis nomenclaturis ... commentariorum libri tres ... His accesserunt ... præfationes duæ, altera D. Conradi Gesneri ... rei herbariæ scriptorum, qui in hunc usque diem scripserunt, catalogum complectens ... germanica primum lingua conscripti, nunc in latinam conversi, interprete David Kybero* (Strassburg: Wendel Rihel, 1552; Readex Landmarks of Science, II, microform edition of the British Museum copy). For analyses of Bock's phytography, see Hoppe, *Das Kräuterbuch des Hieronymus Bock*, 10–12; Agnes Arber, *Herbals, Their Origin and Evolution: A Chapter in the History of Botany*, intro. and annot. William T. Stearn, Cambridge Science Classics (3rd edn, Cambridge: Cambridge University Press, 1986), 55–63; and Agnes Arber, "From Medieval Herbalism to the Birth of Modern Botany," reprinted in Arber, *Herbals*, 319–38, esp. 327–9. Greene, *Landmarks of Botanical History*, 1:304–59, translates the Gessner passage. Fuchs, who did not know Bock personally, said of Bock's descriptions in the 1539 *New Kreütterbuoch*: "For the most part, they ... plainly show that he has examined with his own eyes the plants he depicts"; *The Great Herbal of Leonhart Fuchs: De historia stirpium commentarii insignes, 1542*, facsimile with comm. by Frederick G. Meyer, Emily Emmart Trueblood, and John L. Heller (2 vols, Stanford, CA: Stanford University Press, 1999), vol. 1, *Commentary*, 13 and 209.

32   Translated by Arber, *Herbals*, 166.

33   Translated by Greene, *Landmarks of Botanical History*, 1:327, from Bock 1552, *Præfatio*, ch. 14. To the frustration of later herbalists and botanists, Dioscorides did not explain his method. John Riddle elucidated Dioscorides' method of "drug affinities" in *Dioscorides on Pharmacy and Medicine* (Austin: University of Texas Press, 1985). Dioscorides' prefatory letter castigated the "modern" herbalist, Niger, for equating the "perfoliate St. John's wort" with the "crispate St. John's wort" (*De materia medica*, trans. Beck, 2, para. 3). Bock's organization was clearer: Part I, cultivated herbs of German kitchens and gardens; Part II, grasses, onions, wild herbs; Part III, woody plants, shrubs, and trees.

34   For Fuchs's justification, see Meyer et al., *Great Herbal*, vol. 1, *Commentary*, Appendix I, p. 212, para. 59. Meyer et al. identify the plants in Fuchs's woodcuts as: ch. 24, p. 73, *De Ascyro, Hypericum hirsutum* L. (= *Harthaw*, Fuchs 1543); ch. 25, p. 75, *De Androsaemo, Hypericum montanum* L. (= *Kunrath*, Fuchs 1543); ch. 321, p. 830, *De Hyperico, Hypericum perforatum* L. (= *S. Johanskraut*, Fuchs 1543). See also Reeds, "Finding a Plant," 72.

the task of looking up the plants in Galen's alphabetical list.[35] But to the readers of the German version of the herbal, which also followed the Greek alphabetical plan, the placement of *S. Johanskraut* must have been baffling.

In practice, for Bock, the aim of grouping similar plants together had two consequences. He put hypericum with all its close relatives into the single chapter on *Harthaw*; and he set that collective account into a series of chapters about domestic plants with common features.

As Edward Lee Greene pointed out in his invaluable analysis of Bock's botany, the first hundred pages of the herbal virtually all deal with plants with fibrous roots and simple opposite leaves on quadrangular stems.[36] Most of these were mints and related kitchen herbs. However, the series concluded with plants that Bock knew were not mints: rue, hypericum, chamaepitys (santolina), the cresses, and the mustards.

Given Bock's outstanding ability to notice and describe external details of plant form, there can be no doubt that he thought very carefully about how to use the visible characters of leaf, stalk, root, and flower in arranging the herbal. However, both intellectually and practically, he also had to take account of similarities of strong, distinctive smells, tastes, and saps that betokened inner medicinal properties—sweet and aromatic for the mints, but bitter, resinous, or sharp for rue, hypericum, and the herbs that followed. Hypericum's resinous tang was akin to the pungency of wild rue, so it made sense to place them side by side.

John Riddle has argued that such an understanding of internal "drug affinities" underlay the organizational plan of Dioscorides' *De materia medica*.[37] It may be that Bock was intuitively recognizing and applying aspects of that plan from Book III of *De materia medica* to the German plants he knew as gardener, naturalist, and "lover of medicine."[38]

---

[35] On the use of Galen's *De simplicium medicamentorum facultatibus* in humanist medical education *c.* 1530–50, see Karen Reeds, "Renaissance Humanism and Botany," *Annals of Science* 33 (1976): 519–42, reprinted in Reeds, *Botany*.

[36] Greene, *Landmarks*, 1:304–31, sampled the first 100 pages of the 1,200-page Latin edition of 1552 (74 species, 31 genera). Hoppe, *Das Kräuterbuch des Hieronymus Bock*, 31–43.

[37] Riddle, *Dioscorides*, especially chs 2, 3. Bock did not adopt Dioscorides' plan of "one plant, one chapter."

[38] Although the secondary literature often describes Bock as a physician, he himself never claimed the degree in his own books. Bock's publisher, Wendel Rihel, in his letter to the reader (Bock 1546, sig. b.i*ʳ*) referred to Bock as *Herr* rather than *doctor*. Bock's humanist-physician contemporaries used *Herr* as his title rather than *Arzt, physicus, medicus*, or *Doctor medicinae*. Bock's short treatise, *Hieronymi Tragi medici, Herbarum aliquot dissertationes & censuræ* (1531), in Otto Brunfels, *Noui herbarii tomus II* (Strassburg: Johann Schott, 1532), Appendix, p. 156, is the only place I have seen Bock called *medicus*. In the herbal's dedicatory letter to his patron (Bock 1546, sig. a.ii*ʳ*), Bock styled himself as "the lover of medicine" ("Hieronymus Bock der Artznei

These taxonomic innovations notwithstanding, Bock stayed close to Galen and Dioscorides when it came to describing the medicinal properties of hypericum. The section on the *Krafft und Würckung* followed—as it did throughout the *Kreüter Buoch*—Galen's assignment of temperament in *De simplicium medicamentorum temperamentis et facultatibus*:

> Hypericum warms and dries by the essence of the fine parts, to such an extent that it provokes the menses and urine, but for this the whole fruit is taken, not just the seed. The green fruit, smeared on with the leaves, brings both burns and other wounds to a scar. But if you sprinkle it on dry and crushed, you will heal both excessively soft and damp sores, and putrefying ones. There are also those who give it to drink to people with hip pains.[39]

Bock noted that the various kinds of *Harthaw* all had similar medicinal properties. For his list of internal and external uses, he merged Galen's and Dioscorides' overlapping recommendations for hypericum. Internally, hypericum, sodden in wine and drunk, would draw out poison in the urine and women's menses ("blödigkeit der weiber"); similarly, it was effective for tertian and quartan fevers, the sharp pain in the hip called *ischia*, and for blood spewed from internal injuries; as an infusion of the seeds, especially from plants growing in the woods, it was used to draw out bile (*cholera*). Externally, infusions of the plants and seeds would relieve and heal burns. Like wild rue, the leaves and seeds could be used as plasters to heal skin problems, swellings, and pains.[40]

---

liebhaber"). The title page of his pamphlet, *Kurtz Regiment für das grausam Haupt wehe vnd Breune, vor die Gemein vnd armes heuflin hin vnd wider im Wasgaw vnd Westereich* (Strassburg: Knobloch, 1544), called him "a lover and expert in medicine" ("der Artzney erfarnen vnd liebhabern"); digital facsimile, Bayerische Staatsbibliothek: urn:nbn:de:bvb:12-bsb00025828-4; http://www.digital-collections.de/.

[39]   I thank Timothy Graham and Vivian Nutton for their help with this translation of Kühn's Latin version of *De simplicium medicamentorum temperamentis et facultatibus*, 8.20.5; ed. Kühn, 12:148: "Hypericum calefacit et desiccat essentia tenuium partium, adeo ut et menses et urinas provocet, sed ad haec totus sumendus est fructus, non tantum semen. Porro cum foliis illitus viridis ad cicatricem ducit cum alia tum etiam ambusta. Caeterum si sicca contusa inspergas, sanabis et mollia nimis humidaque et putredinosa ulcerum. Sunt et qui ischiadicis bibendum exhibeant." See Jerry Stannard, review of Hoppe, *Das Kräuterbuch des Hieronymus Bock*, *Archives internationales d'histoire des sciences* 23 (1970): 228–32. Bock generally did not give degrees of the qualities of hot/cold and moist/dry.

[40]   Bock 1546, Part I, ch. 22, *Von Rauten*, fol. xxvi[v]; ch. 23, *Von Harthaw*, fol. xxix[r v].

Bock did recommend one internal use of hypericum that apparently did not stem from the ancient authorities: an alcoholic extract (*brennen wasser*) of hypericum, drunk for six days, would help stroke and falling sickness.[41]

Predictably, for a plant that Galen had described as hot and dry, Bock made no mention of melancholy.

Hypericum in Sixteenth-century Popular Medicine, Magic, and Folklore

Although Bock was not a professional physician, throughout his *Kreüter Buoch* he showed his primary allegiance to the medical humanism of the early sixteenth century and to the newly edited classics of ancient medicine.[42] However, as a Lutheran pastor and schoolmaster writing for the common man, he could not ignore the realm of magical beliefs and practices that he encountered in his flock and was bound to oppose.[43]

Two striking acknowledgements of popular medicine and magic bracketed Bock's account of Saint John's Wort. At the very beginning of the chapter, he writes:

> Many hold Harthaw to be the true wild rue because, as with the domestic rue, it expels
> all poison; and because wherever there is Harthaw, all specters are helpless. The old

---

[41]   Ibid., fol. xxix^r. This use of hypericum was not noted by an early user of the Columbia volume who marked its index entries for dropsy, stroke, and loss of speech and wrote "Schlag" or "sprachloss" in the margins of the rosemary and valerian chapters. Bock did not include peony seed in this remedy, unlike Brunfels, *Contrafayt Kreüterbuch* (Strassburg: Hans Schotten, 1532), fols ccli^r–cclii^v, *S. Johanns kraut oder Harthaw: oder Waldthopff*, and Hieronymus Brunschwig, *Liber de arte distillandi de compositis. Das buoch der waren kunst zu distillieren die Composita vnd simplicia* (Strassburg: [n.p.], 1512), bk III, ch. 21, fol. ccli^v; digital facsimile, Bayerische Staatsbibliothek: urn:nbn:de:bvb:12-bsb00005369-9, http://www.digital-collections.de/. (The pressed leaf at this opening is not hypericum.) In 2000, Health Canada warned that Saint John's wort may interact with anti-epilepsy drugs: http://www.hc-sc.gc.ca/. See also Steven C. Schachter, "Botanicals and Herbs: A Traditional Approach to Treating Epilepsy," *Neurotherapeutics* 6 (2009): 415–20.

[42]   See n. 38. See Hoppe, *Das Kräuterbuch des Hieronymus Bock*, 77–91, on Bock's sources.

[43]   Bock's pastoral duties almost certainly included informal doctoring. On the duty of Lutheran ministers to combat such "daily application of magic," see Jacqueline Van Gent, *Magic, Body and the Self in Eighteenth-century Sweden*, Studies in Medieval and Reform Traditions 135 (Leiden: Brill, 2009), 5. In a copy of Bock 1552 owned by a Jesuit house in 1644 (now in the University of Pennsylvania Library), this and several other passages bear marginal notes in a difficult sixteenth- or early seventeenth-century hand that express the annotator's intention to preach ("praedicam") on the subject of superstitions, magic, and sexually transmitted diseases.

wives say too: "Marjoram, Harthaw, heather white / Put the fiend in a proper fright." From this we see how the old heathens regarded and used these plants.[44]

And, at the end, among the external uses: "Many people carry these plants with them against evil spirits and thunderstorms, and (to speak according to nature) that is not completely a lie."[45] These comments were the closest Bock came to linking hypericum to anything resembling melancholy or mental disturbances.[46]

Popular magic surfaced as well in Bock's list of commonly used synonyms for hypericum: "In German lands one calls this plant: *Sant Johans kraut*, Saint John's wort; *Harthaw*, hard-hay; *Waldthoff*, forest-hops, [or] *vnser Frawen betstro*, our Lady's bedstraw. In Latin, *fuga demonum* [or] *perforata.*"[47]

The names *Sant Johans kraut* and *vnser Frawen betstro* smacked of the Catholic piety that Bock, as an early Lutheran convert, also regarded as superstition.[48] But it was *fuga demonum*—as much imprecation as plant name—that invoked a host of European magical beliefs. As Fuchs put it: "Some, led by a certain superstition, believed that it could make devils flee, [and] called it *Fuga daemonum.*"[49]

---

[44] Bock 1546, Part I, ch. 23, fols xxvii^v–xxviii^r: "Vil woellen Harthaw sei die recht wild Raut/ dann gleich wie die zame Raut alle gifft vertreibe/ also vermoeg alles gespenst/ wo Harthaw ist/ nichts geschaffen. Die alten weiber sprechen also/ Dost/ Harthaw vnd weisse Heidt/ thuot dem teüffel vil leidt. Darauss erscheint was die alten Heiden von disen Kreütern gehalte/ vnd darmit getriben haben." *Dost* (see fol. xiiii^r) is usually identified as oregano. Jacob Grimm, *Teutonic Mythology*, 4th edn, trans. James Steven Stallybrass (4 vols, London: W. Swan Sonnenschein & Allen, 1880–88; repr. London: Routledge/Thoemmes Press, 1999), 3:1214. Cf. Brunfels's explanation of the name *fuga demonum*, in *Contrafayt Kreüterbuch*, 1532, fol. ccli^r: where such a plant is kept, no devil comes and no spirits can stay ("wo solichs kraut behalten würt/ da komm der teuffel nicht hyn/ möge auch kein gespenst bleiben").

[45] Bock 1546, Part I, ch, xxiii, fol. xxix^r: "Vil menschen tragen dise kreüter bei sich/ für boese gespenst vnd vngewitter/ vnd ist (der natur nach zuoreden) nit gar erlogen." Cf. Bock 1552, 76: "Multi præterea homines Hypericum secum portant, aduersus præstigias dæmonum & tempestates. Et, si naturam ipsam consideres, forte non abs re ista de Hyperico prædicantur." (I thank Shelley Frisch, Peter Groner, Margaret Schleissner, Elaine Tennant, and Maaike van der Lugt for suggestions about rendering this passage.)

[46] Bock did not suggest that epilepsy or stroke had anything but physical causes.

[47] Bock 1546, Part I, ch. 23, fol. xxviii^v.

[48] In Bock 1546, Part I, ch. 45, fol. liv^v, *S. Johans bluomen*, Bock rationalized the name as a reference to its flowering around St John's Day (June 24).

[49] *De historia stirpium*, ch. 321, p. 830: "Fugam dæmonum aliqui, quod superstitione quadam inducti, fugare posse dæmones crediderint, appellauerunt." Fuchs omitted this point in his 1543 German edition.

Figure 9.3   Warding off a demon with *fuga demonum*

Source: Italian Herbal, Burlington, University of Vermont Library, Special Collections, TR F Herbal (disbound), fol. 27r, lower half: *Erba ypericon*.

Its effectiveness at warding off devils was dramatically illustrated in a number of late medieval alchemical herbals: a little winged devil was depicted turning away in alarm from the hypericum plant, schematically but recognizably shown with its opposite leaves and bright yellow little flowers at the ends of branches (Figure 9.3).[50]

---

[50] See: (1) Burlington, University of Vermont Library, Special Collections, Italian Herbal, TR F Herbal, http://cdi.uvm.edu/collections/item/mrmc002, fol. 27r: *Erba ypericon vel perforata vel fuga demonum communiter vel herba sancti johannis*. (2) Paris, Bibliothèque nationale de France, MS hébr. 1199, Italian label, *pericon*, with Hebrew transliteration; illustrated in Michel Garel, *D'une main forte: Manuscrits hébreux des collections françaises* (Paris: Bibliothèque nationale, 1991), 173, no. 132 (folio number not given). I thank Gerrit Bos for alerting me to this image and providing a copy. (3) Pavia, Biblioteca Universitaria, MS Aldini 211, fol. 74r, *Ypericon Alii fugademon*, illustrated in Vera Segre Rutz (ed.), *Il giardino magico degli alchimisti: un erbario illustrato trecentesco della Biblioteca universitaria di Pavia e la sua tradizione*, Testi e documenti 12 (Milan: Il Polifilo, 2000), lix, top left. (4) Florence, Biblioteca di Botanica dell'Università di Firenze, MS 106: *Upericon a. fugademon* (figure of demon apparently scraped off). See Stefania Ragazzini, *Un erbario del XV secolo: il ms. 106 della Biblioteca di Botanica dell'Università di Firenze* (Florence: Leo Olschki, 1983), pl. 131. Cf. the devil in Kandel's woodcut of the beech-tree (*Buxbaum*), Bock 1546, Part III, ch. 55, fol. I^r; Heinrich Marzell, "Das Buchsbaum-Bild im

From surveys of folklore, it is clear that these apotropaic uses required only the plant's presence. Growing it, carrying a branch on a journey, hiding it under a hat or in an armpit, tucking a sprig in bed (especially for women giving birth), putting it in a cattlefold, hanging the plant on doors and windows, or burning it on a Midsummer's Eve bonfire or fumigating a house—all were effective at warding off the devil and ghosts.[51] Moreover, these uses of *fuga demonum* presumed the actual existence of specters: these were not the sad fantasies associated with the melancholic's low spirits.

In short, while *fuga demonum* was a powerful herb in popular magic, simply displaying it was sufficient: there was no need to consume Saint John's wort to keep the demons away.

Hypericum in Alchemical and Paracelsan Medicine: *Magica Scientia*

In the midst of the media excitement about Saint John's wort in the 1990s, Norman Rosenthal, M.D., was the only American writer who looked seriously into the history of its use for depression. In his consumer health book, *St. John's Wort: The Herbal Way to Feeling Good*, Dr. Rosenthal, clinical professor of psychiatry at Georgetown University and a notable researcher on depression at the National Institute of Mental Health, pointed to the Paracelsan roots of the modern interest in hypericum and noted that Theophrastus Paracelsus von Hohenheim (1493–1541)

> wrote of using St. John's wort to treat three separate conditions: wounds, parasites, and what he called "phantasmata," which appear to be the equivalent of psychotic symptoms, or delusions and hallucinations. But he also recommended St. John's wort for curing the soul. Although he mentioned melancholia in his writings, he did not specifically recommend St. John's wort for this condition.

It was another scientist, about a century later, who in 1630 made the first detailed observations about the value of St. John's wort in the treatment of melancholia.

Kräuterbuch (1551) des Hieronymus Bock," *Sudhoffs Archiv für Geschichte der Medizin und der Naturwissenschaften* 38 (1954): 97–103.

[51]   A.R. Vickery, "Traditional Uses and Folklore for Hypericum in the British Isles," *Economic Botany* 35 (1981): 289–95. Frederick J. Simoons, *Plants of Life, Plants of Death* (Madison: University of Wisconsin Press, 1998), 256–7. Franz-C. Czygan, "Kulturgeschichte und Mystik des Johanniskrauts," *Zeitschrift für Phytotherapie* 14 (1993): 256–82 (my thanks to Gerhard Helmstaedter for a copy). Brück, *Heilkraft und Aberglaube*, 9–18.

The writer Angelo Sala credited Paracelsus as his major inspiration, but actually Sala's writings go far beyond those of his predecessor in this regard.[52]

This is true in broad outline, but the ways Paracelsus and Paracelsans employed hypericum—and understood melancholia—need a closer look.

Paracelsus and Hieronymus Bock were contemporaries; they explored some of the same terrain; and they shared a commitment to making native German remedies known to Germans in their own language. It is hard to imagine that Bock did not hear about Paracelsus and his iconoclastic medical and theological ideas from Conrad Gessner or colleagues in Strassburg and Basel, but Bock's silence about this controversial figure is one sign of the deep divide between Paracelsus and the herbal tradition of Dioscorides and Galen.[53]

Paracelsus's writings referred to hypericum more than 70 times under several names: *hypericon, Sanct Johans samen, perforata, consolida regalis* (or *aurea*).[54] His

---

[52] I am deeply grateful to Dr Rosenthal for alerting me, in a personal communication following my 1998 National Library of Medicine lecture, to the significance of Paracelsus and Angelo Sala; see his *St. John's Wort: The Herbal Way to Feeling Good* (New York: HarperCollins, 1998), 275–91, 311–12. See also Walter Pöldinger, "Paracelsus und das Johanniskraut," in Walter Pöldinger (ed.), *Johanniskraut—Angst—Depression: Zur Geschichte der Paracelsus-Gesellschaften. Vorträge 1999*, Salzburger Beiträge zur Paracelsusforschung, Folge 33 (Vienna: Österreichischer Kunst- und Kulturverlag, 2000), 9–15.

[53] Hoppe, *Das Kräuterbuch des Hieronymus Bock*, 61. Bock's recommendation of hypericum in alcohol for wounds may indirectly refer to Paracelsus, but more likely echoes Brunfels and Brunschwig (see n. 41 above). Bock's name appears at the end of an alchemical manuscript in Latin and German with pen-drawings of distillation equipment: Heidelberg, Universitätsbibliothek, Cod. Pal. germ. 294, Hieronymus Bock (?), "Alchemistisches Kunstbuch" (southwest Germany, *c.* 1550); digital facsimile, Universitätsbibliothek Heidelberg, http://digi.ub.uni-heidelberg .de/diglit/cpg294. The manuscript's content is late medieval rather than Paracelsan; I suspect Bock was the copyist, not the author. Gessner was particularly hostile toward Paracelsus; see Charles Webster, *Paracelsus: Medicine, Magic and Mission at the End of Time* (New Haven: Yale University Press, 2008), esp. 64–5, 170; and Charles Webster, "Conrad Gessner and the Infidelity of Paracelsus," in Sarah Hutton and John Henry (eds), *New Perspectives on Renaissance Thought: Essays in the History of Science, Education and Philosophy in Memory of Charles B. Schmitt* (London: Duckworth, 1990), 13–23. Gessner, *Bibliotheca universalis* (Zurich: Froschauer, 1545), 614. Gessner's fundamental biobibliography of botany in Bock 1552 omitted Paracelsus. Cf. Lynn Thorndike, *A History of Magic and Experimental Science* (8 vols, New York: Columbia University Press, 1923–58), vol. 5: *The Sixteenth Century*, 431–42. Arber, *Herbals*, 250, estimated that Paracelsus knew only a couple of dozen plants. I think Arber's count is too low, but the number is certainly much smaller than in any contemporary herbal or antidotarium. For Gessner's annotations in Paracelsan volumes, see Urs B. Leu, Raffael Keller, and Sandra Weidmann, *Conrad Gessner's Private Library* (Leiden: Brill, 2008), nos 272, 273, and his copy of Paracelsus's *Grosse Wundarznei*, now in the National Library of Medicine, Bethesda, Maryland (not in Leu et al.).

[54] Tallied from the *Registerband*, compiled by Martin Müller, Nova Acta Paracelsica: Supplementum (Einsiedeln: Jos. & Karl Eberle, 1960), to Karl Sudhoff's authoritative

obscurity of language and his predilection for revision, coupled with the complex publishing history of his manuscripts, make it pointless to expect consistency or a clear system in his names and uses for the plant.[55] Nonetheless, the combination of his scattered references and the new theoretical context he offered for them seems to have spurred his followers to try hypericum in new ways.

The audiences at Paracelsus's iconoclastic medical lectures at the University of Basel in the summer of 1527 might not have been surprised by his declaration that "oil of *hypericon* is the best cure for wounds": that was comparable to Galen's treatment of wounds and burns.[56] Paracelsus's recipe for a pessary of *hypericon* flowers and six other herbs to treat sores in the vulva, vagina, and anus could have followed from Dioscorides' recommendation of a hypericum pessary as an emmenagogue.[57] The internal treatment for constipation (*secessum*) also sounded like the classical hypericum purge of bilious excrements.[58] Some other external therapies for, e.g., swelling of the tongue (*ranula*) and oral abscesses (*brancae*) may have struck Paracelsus's hearers as novel uses of hypericum.[59] But Paracelsus's

---

edition, Theophrast von Hohenheim gen. Paracelsus, *Sämtliche Werke*, Pt I, *Medizinische, naturwissenschaftliche und philosophische Schriften* (15 vols, Munich: R. Oldenbourg, 1922–31), hereafter cited as Paracelsus, ed. Sudhoff. Entries for *Sant Johannes öl* probably refer to Saint John's wort; entries for *Sant Johannes blumen* may mean the daisy-like *Sanct Johans bluomen* (*Chrysanthemum segetum* L.), described in Bock 1546, Part I, ch. 45, fol. liv[v] (see n. 23 above).

[55] On the early publishing history of Paracelsus's works, see Webster, *Paracelsus*. On his manuscripts, see Debra L. Stoudt, "The Medical Manuscripts of the Bibliotheca Palatina," in Margaret R. Schleissner (ed.), *Manuscript Sources of Medieval Medicine: A Book of Essays* (New York: Garland, 1995), 159–81 (especially 170–72).

[56] Galen, *De simplicium medicamentorum temperamentis*, 8.20.5; ed. Kühn, 12:148. An auditor's note recorded Paracelsus as saying, "Oleum hypericonis cura vulnerum optima est"; Paracelsus, ed. Sudhoff, vol. 4, *De gradibus, de compositionibus et dosibus receptorum ac naturalium libri septem*, 112 (see also 30, 86, 114, 255, 257, 343–4). See also Paracelsus, ed. Sudhoff, vol. 2, *Liber de contractis membris*, 484–5: "Von den arcanen zu heilen die contracturen, Caput VIII." Brück, *Heilkraft und Aberglaube*, 35–40, 65.

[57] Dioscorides, *De materia medica*, 3.154; ed. Wellmann, 2:162. Paracelsus, ed. Sudhoff, vol. 4, *Von apostemen, geschweren, ofnen scheden und anderen gewechsen am leib*, auditor's notes: "Pessarium in ragadiis vulvae ... Recipe succi ... de floribus hypericonis ... Illa compositio optima est, mit tüchern hinein gestossen, so fern die ragadien gent ..." (313–14, 316); "Aliud perdonium [ein kreuterwein]. Rec. consolidae regalis [i.e., hypericum] lib. sem ... Alia descriptio sparallii [utuntur ut pessaria]. Rec. succi hypericonis ... fiat sparallium pro matrice" (346–7).

[58] Dioscorides, *De materia medica*, 3.155–6; ed. Wellmann, 2:162–3. Paracelsus, ed. Sudhoff, vol. 4, *De gradibus*, 119, auditor's notes: "Descriptio quae incarnat per secessum."

[59] Paracelsus, ed. Sudhoff, vol. 4, *Von apostemen, geschweren, ofnen scheden und anderen gewechsen am leib*, auditor's notes: "De ranula, vulgo der frosch ... Cura ... understreichs cum aqua brassatellae ... oder mit oleo hypericonis" (248–9); "Gargarismus contra brancam ... succi hypericonis ... hypericon scilicet facit" (296).

audience was certainly taken aback—and outraged—by his wholesale dismissal of the medical profession and of the Galenic humors as the basis of medical theory and therapy: "I do not wish you to know Melancholia, Choler, Phlegma, or Sanguis, for this is the mother of all lying surgeons and physicians."[60]

In the late 1520s—that is, before the publication of the first humanist herbals of Brunfels, Bock, and Fuchs—Paracelsus projected writing an herbal (*Herbarius*) of his own.[61] A related treatise from the same period, *Von den natürlichen Dingen* (*On Natural Things*), shows that he intended to address the full range of materia medica; the surviving chapters dealt with turpentine, salt (*Salz*), sulphur, the magnet, vitriol, arsenic, and a half-dozen herbs, including hypericum.[62] A briefer version, "On *hypericon* or *perforata*, also known as Saint John's wort," with similar accounts of coral and the herb *persicaria*, appeared posthumously as an appendix to his commentary on Hippocrates' *Aphorisms*.[63]

---

[60] Paracelsus, *Chirurgia minor quam alias Bertheoneam intitulauit ... ex versione Gerardi Dorn* (Basel: Petrus Perna, [n.d.]), 55; digital facsimile, DigitaleBibliothek, Memoria Medicinae, Medizinische Bibliothek Wien, http://www.memoriamedicinae.meduniwien .ac.at/: 'Ad vulnerum cognitionem intelligere nolo vos Melancholiam, Choleram, Phlegma, neque Sanguinem, quod fundamentum hoc mater sit mendosorum chirurgorum & medicorum omnium." An anonymous lampoon of Paracelsus, written in the voice of Galen's shade, prescribed the Galenic remedy, black hellebore, for the "mad alchemical vapourings [of Cacophrastus]": "novimus helleborum. / Helleborum cuius capiti male gramina sano / Mitto, simul totas imprecor anticyras. / Quid tua sint fateor spagyrica sompnia, Vappa, / Nescio." See Anna M. Stoddart, *The Life of Paracelsus: The Life of Theophrastus von Hohenheim* (London: John Murray, 1911), 133 and Appendix C, 299.

[61] See "The *Herbarius* of Paracelsus," trans. and intro. Bruce T. Moran, *Pharmacy in History* 35 (1993): 99–127. "The Herbarius of Theophrastus [Paracelsus], Concerning the Powers of the Herbs, Roots, Seeds, etc. of the Native Land and Realm of Germany" comprised a prologue and short tractates on black hellebore, *persicaria* (*Flohkraut*), salt, angelic thistle (English thistle), corals, and the magnet. Cf. Paracelsus, ed. Sudhoff, 2:1–57. Paracelsus's early works are difficult to date, but the consensus seems to be that they were at least begun before 1530: see Paracelsus, ed. Sudhoff, 2:v–x; Andrew Weeks, *Paracelsus: Speculative Theory and the Crisis of the Early Reformation*, SUNY Series in Western Esoteric Traditions (Albany: State University of New York Press, 1997), 39–41; Udo Benzenhöfer, *Studien zum Frühwerk des Paracelsus im Bereich Medizin und Naturkunde* (Münster: Klemm & Oelschager, 2005), 60–81, 171–90.

[62] Paracelsus, ed. Sudhoff, 2:111–21. The reference to "we in Switzerland" ("wir im schweiss"), 111, suggests his stay in Basel in 1527. The treatise's title invokes the alternative title of Konrad von Megenberg's *Buch der Natur*; see Webster, *Paracelsus*, 55, 111, 153, 274.

[63] *Ein ander tractat Doctoris Theophrasti Paracelsi, vom Hyperico oder Perforata, so auff teutsch Sant Johanns kraut genandt wirdt*, sigs J.iv^v–K.ii^v, in Paracelsus, *Aphorismorum aliquot Hippocratis genuinus sensus ... Neben dreyen hochnützlichen tractaten, von sonderlicher verborgner kraft und würckung Coraliorum, Hyperici, & Persicariae* (Augsburg: M. Franck for G. Willer, 1568); digital facsimile, Bayerische Staatsbibliothek, urn:nbn:de:bvb:12-bsb00015630-1; http:// www.digital-collections.de/. See also a very similar passage in another early work, *Archidoxorum*

These short discussions of hypericum in *Von den natürlichen Dingen* and the appendix to the *Aphorisms* were typical of Paracelsus's *magica scientia*.[64] His distinctive amalgam of pharmaceutical preparations, alchemy, astrology, natural philosophy, magic, cosmology, religion, German nationalism, and contempt for ancient and medieval authority insured that anything he wrote about medicinal plants would be very different in character from existing herbals of the late fifteenth and early sixteenth centuries.[65]

Paracelsus had nothing but disdain for the German authors who

> have described herbs and plants in books. But their work is like the coat of a beggar, patched together from all sorts of things ... and falls apart like a beggar's coat ... so there is nothing there when one most needs it. All these raving sorts, these seducers, false informers, and teachers of medicine should not concern me. They are really of use to no one except to the printers of books who get rich and very fat in their kitchens. The person who buys the books, however, finds very little in them.[66]

There was no point, Paracelsus asserted, to learning what Dioscorides, Serapion, and Pliny ("not to mention others it would be only annoying to name") had said about plants.[67] Their method was wrong from the start, because these authors

---

Aureoli Ph. Theophrasti Paracelsi de secretis naturæ mysteriis libri decem ... His accesserunt libri ... De præparationibus ... (Basel: Petrus Perna, 1570), 348: *Perforatæ cura contra phantasiam*; digital facsimile, Bayerische Staatsbibliothek, urn:nbn:de:bvb:12-bsb00034166-8; http://www.digital-collections.de/.

[64] Paracelsus, *Aphorismorum*, "Von der *Persicaria*, das ist vom Floechkraut oder Wasserpfeffer," sig. K.iiii[rv]: "Ich hab vil mal begert dz die natürlichen mayster nit sollen lernen in der natur als allein schwetzen. So nun in grundt sol gangen werden/ so muoss *magica scientia* der anfang sein und der grundt zu lernen. Sol ein Arzt werden/ und den krancken sagen/ das ist also in seiner natur/ und weiss *magicam scientiam* nit so saget er närrisch."

[65] Paracelsus, *Aphorismorum*, "Persicaria," sig. K.iv[v]: "Was soll das sein/ das einer redt nach hören sagen: Wöller jr lehrnen die Kreüter in jrer natur erkennen/ so volgt dem Capitel nach/ das ich jetzt angriffen hab/ und lasst *Dioscoridem Dioscoridem* sein/ *Macrum Macrum*, nicht nach hören sagen."

[66] Moran, "The *Herbarius* of Paracelsus," 105. Cf. Paracelsus, ed. Sudhoff, vol. 2, *Herbarius*, 5–6.

[67] Paracelsus's citations suggest he knew early printed editions of Dioscorides, Pliny, Macer, Serapion, *Gart der Gesundheit* and *Ortus sanitatis*, Konrad von Megenberg's *Buch der Natur*, Hieronymus Brunschwig's *Liber de arte distillandi*, the *Liber aggregationis seu liber secretorum* ascribed to Albertus Magnus, and the *Artzney Buchlein der kreutter* of Johannes Tollat. The manuscript herbal literature potentially available to him was of course much larger. Paracelsus, ed. Sudhoff, vol. 2, *Prologus in librum de herbis* (fragments on *Virtutes herbarum* and *Kräften anderer Naturdinge*), 208: "Wir achten das für das höchst in beschreibung natürlicher dingen, das erstlich erkent werd, was das sei, darvon man schreibt. nicht das ich woll sagen, sie kenten die form nicht.

were only interested in the plants' names and outer material forms, not their inner virtues and substance.[68] Since we can learn the virtue of wallflower by its taste, asafetida by its stench, gentian by its bitterness, and sugar by its sweetness, we have no need to read about them.[69]

In Paracelsus's cosmology, the only visible aspects of plants that mattered were the God-given signs that revealed those secret powers that the heavens had instilled in them for the benefit of humanity.[70] For hypericum, that special *signatum* was revealed in the pores in the leaves and flowers, veins in the leaves,

---

die form gibt das wissen der tugenden nicht, dorumb ich das nicht also mein. das mein ich, das kennen, das die tugent ist. dan ir wissen, das golt golt ist, aber noch wissent ir aus dem nicht, was sein tugent sei. dorumb mir nicht so gach ist, euch der unform unwissend zu heissen, aber der materia, der tugent, substanz und corpus. Ob sich nicht gebürte Theophrasto, anfenglich solche corpora zu beschreiben, ehe das er in die kreft natürlicher ding anfing einzutreten? und ob schon der herbarius, es wer Dioscorides, Serapio, Plinius &c (deren namen ich verdruss halben nicht sez) iren besonderen stilum gebrauchen und Theophrastus den seinen, des will er ein lob haben und dorzu den ersten pracht und pomp mit dem triumph under allen natürlichen scribenten, zu beschreiben das corpus eins ietlichen dings, und wird hie ein rum sein und ein êr uber die, so beschriben haben die transmutationes der natürlichen dingen." See also Paracelsus on the quintessence and degrees of the humors, ed. Sudhoff, vol. 4, *De gradibus*, 25: "In superioribus capitibus quicquid tractavi, in hoc solum tractavi, ut in sequentia graduum signa descenderem, atque adeo palam fieret, qua ratione gradus in elementis consisterent. non enim ignoro, quantum ab hoc loco dissentiant Platearius, Dioscorides, Serapio caeterique, qui hos sunt sequuti, qui non pauca de quinta essentia scripserunt, sed falso."

[68] Paracelsus, ed. Sudhoff, vol. 2, *Prologus in librum de herbis*, 208 (quoted in n. 67 above).

[69] Paracelsus, ed. Sudhoff, vol. 2, *Prologus in librum de herbis*, 209: "Solt mich aber nicht befrembden und etwas mich dorab entsezen in solchem rohen schreiben der scribenten, die do virtutes anzeigen so gar ungekocht. es legt doch kein maurer kein stein, er weist am ersten, wie er ist und was er im vertrauen mag. aber schreiben, so tut der cheiri schmecken, der aza stinken, gentiana ist bitter, zuccarum süss: solchs wissen die, so weder buchstaben noch lesen erkennen, solt dises physisch sein und gemess des lobs und des preis?"

[70] Paracelsus, *Aphorismorum*, "Persicaria," sig. K.vi[r]: "So sein das die zeichen durch die ich sie erfaren hab. Vnd nit allein dz ichs von disem kraut allein meine/ sondern von allen natürlichen dingen/ ein jegkliches in seiner art/ dermassen auch zuerkennen im Wasserbluot für rodte Bluots tropffen. Das ist nun *signatum*/ das es ein besondere arth vnnd natur in ihme hat/ vber andere Kreüter alle. Das ist nun *influentia carnalis*, die jhr *subiectum* auss den Elementen nimpt. Nun volgt auff dz/ dieweyl dise Bluotstropffen dz *sydereum signatum*/ das jetzt dieselbige influentz fürgenommen werde/ vnd derselbigen nach judicieret. Also muoss der *Medicus* zuvor ein *Astronomus* sein/ vnd auss der *Astronomia* die tugendt ausslegen. Weyter so hats ein ander *signatum*, das ist die form vnd gestalt/ vnd hat noch ein *signatum,* das ist der *Gustus*. Auss den dreyen *signatis* werden jetzt die tugendt erfaren/ was im kraut ist/ vnnd nicht allein in dem/ sondern in allen. Darumb soll ein jegklicher der da schreybt oder schreiben will/ von Kreütern oder andern natürlichen dingen/ auss dem *signato* schreiben/ so wirt der grundt gefunden/ vnd nichts wirt so heimlich sein in denselbigen/ das nit herfür bracht werde."

and the blood-like juice. These embodied the herb's power of expelling evil things—foulness in wounds, worms (unspecified parasites and vermin) both in the body and in cheese, and *phantasmata*:

> I declare to you that the holes that make the leaves so porous indicate that this plant is a help for all inward and outward openings in the skin—whatever should be driven out through the pores ... and the putrefaction of its flowers into the form of blood, that is a sign that it is good for wounds ... the veins in its leaves are a sign that *perforata* drives all phantasms out of people ... phantasms that cause the sicknesses that make people kill themselves, see and hear ghosts, fall into mania, craziness, and the like.[71]

For wounds, Paracelsus explained how to make a topical balm (*Balsam*) by boiling hypericum flowers in red wine, olive oil, or alcohol and then setting the liquid in the sun to digest for a month. The balsamic liquor was poured onto the wound and bound with a strip of linen to keep it moist.[72] For worms on the skin or in the navel, the smell by itself could do the trick.[73]

---

[71]   Paracelsus, ed. Sudhoff, vol. 2, *Von den natürlichen Dingen*, 111–21: "Von dem sanct Johanns kraut ... wil ich euch dise declaration geben, das die löcherung, so porosisch in seinen blettern sind, anzeigen, das dises kraut zu aller öffnung inwendig der haut, auch auswendigen ein hilf ist. auch was durch poros sol getriben werden ... auch sein blumen putrificiren sich in ein blutsform. das ist ein signatur, das zun wunden gut ist, und was von wunden komt ... weiter seine adern auf den blettern ist ein signatum, das perforata all phantasmata austreibt im menschen, auch ausserthalb. dan die phantasmata geben spectra, also das der mensch sicht geist, gespenst und hört solche fantasei und ist von natur. und sind die krankheiten, welche die leut zwingen sich selbs zu töten, ach von sinnen komen, und fallen in toubsucht, aberwiz und dergleichen" (p. 114). Cf. Paracelsus, *Vom* Hyperico *oder* Perforata, sig. J.iv^v: "*Perforata* ist ein hülff zu aller oeffnung/ innwendig vnd ausswendig der haeut/ auch was durch *poros* soll getryben werden/ ist guot zu wunden."

[72]   Paracelsus, *Vom* Hyperico *oder* Perforata, sigs J.vii^v–K.i^v. A similar preparation could be drunk for internal injuries.

[73]   Paracelsus, ed. Sudhoff, vol. 2, *Von den natürlichen Dingen*: "dozu auch ist sein sapor [of *perforata*] den würmen zu stark, dorumb sie fliehen von im, wo es ligt" (114); "... uber di haut legen oder auf den nabel, so rücken sie abstat" (118). Paracelsus (117–18) distinguished between worms generated by putrefaction (maggots?)—hypericum did not help against these— and worms that grew out of foulness within the body and lay in the navel ("solcher würm sind, die aus feule wachsen im leib, und auf den nabel gelegt"). Cf. Paracelsus, ed. Sudhoff, vol. 4, *De gradibus*, 108: "Primi gradus medicamina valent contra ascarides, lumbricos, vermes. Rec[ipe] herbae perforatae [i.e., *hypericum*], betonicae ana Manus 5"; and Paracelsus, *Vom* Hyperico *oder* Perforata, sig. J.vii^r. Melchior Sebizius, the editor of Bock 1577, added Paracelsan indications to the *Harthaw* chapter, fol. 29v: hypericum oil taken internally for "die würm im leib" and topically for fresh wounds and tremors.

For expelling the *phantasmata* most effectively, one had to gather the tallest plants, with the most and fullest blossoms. The influence of the heavens also had to be taken into account. The plant should not be picked at midday or when the moon was in opposition, but plucked at night or at dawn, under the signs of Mars, Jupiter, or Venus.[74]

The secret power (*arcanum*) in *perforata* did its work by being carried "under a cap, in the bosom, in a garland, or else in the hands where it could be smelled often. Or it could be tucked under a pillow in the night, or hung in a house, or over a window."[75] Its strength and power came completely from within itself, as a medicine compounded by God Himself, not from drugs or recipes compounded by "bungling apothecaries who only read *lumen apothecariorum* rather than *lumen naturae*" or recommended by the "ass-headed university physicians."[76]

---

[74] Paracelsus, *Vom* Hyperico *oder* Perforata, sigs J.v^v–J.vi^r: "Nun von disem allen insonderheit/ so man will *perforatam* brauchen zu den fantaseyen/ von den gemelt ist/ so soll sie nach dem Himlischen lauff genommen werden/ also das dieselbig influentz auch wider die gaister sey/ vnd nemlich am ersten im Marte/ im Joue/ vnd Venere/ und mit nichtem nach dem Mon/ sondern wider den Mon/ auch nit nach Mittag/ noch in der Nacht/ sonder im auffgang der Sonnen/ in *Aurora* oder *diluculo*/ zu morgens. Vnd die ist am besten/ die bey guoten andern Bluomen steht/ oder vnder jnen wechst vnnd je hoeher sie ist/ je besser/ je mehr mit bluomen am hoechsten sind." Cf. Paracelsus, ed. Sudhoff, vol. 2, *Von den natürlichen Dingen* (*Von dem sanct Johanns kraut*), 116–17.

[75] Paracelsus, *Vom* Hyperico *oder* Perforata, sig. J.vi^r: "Dises kraut wie es an jm selbs ist/ soll für vnd für getragen werden/ vndter dem paretlien/ im busen/ in krantz weiss/ oder sunst in henden/ offt daran schmecken/ zu nacht vnder das kuess thuon/ dz hauss darmit vmbstecken/ oder vmb die wendt hencken. Vnnd das soll ein jeder Artzet wissen/ das Gott ein gross *arcanum* in das kraut gelegt hat/ allein von wegen der Gayster vnd tollen fantaseyen/ die den menschen in verzweyflung bringen."

[76] Paracelsus, ed. Sudhoff, vol. 2, *Von den natürlichen Dingen*, 114–15: "nun ist zu diser krankheit [*phantasmata*] nicht vil arznei verordnet von got, di mir wissend sei, als in perforata und corallis. dan do sol ein arzt wissen, das solche fantasei nicht ein krankheit ist der melancholei oder der gleichen, wie die hohenschuler plerren, sonder ist nur ein geist, der nicht mit den dingen genomen wird, die melancholiam nemen, sonder alein mit der arznei, in der die sterki und kraft ist, mit gewalt hinzutun. nun ist solch kraft nicht in den recepten oder compositis, wie sie in der apoteken gefunden werden, sonder es ist ein arznei, die got selbs componirt hat on den arzt, und ist ein ganz volkomen compositum selbs von der natur componirt. dorumb so es gebraucht sol werden wider die fantasei, sol es on allen zusaz geben werden. dan do ist der recht compositor, von dem die hohen schulen wenig wissen, sondern allemal understont ir compositum zu erhalten in iren sudlerischen apoteken. und zeige solchs alein dorumb an, das ein arzt wissen sol, nicht alein in sein composition vertrauen, sondern das lumen naturae lesen, nicht apothecariorum. die got selbs componirt hat, die selbigen composita sollent fürgenomen werden, seind on betrug. aber die hohenschüler vermeinen, was ir dolle eselsköpfe nicht erfaren, sei weder der natur noch got müglich." Paracelsus was playing on the alchemical quest for the "light of nature" and the title of

Paracelsus rarely acknowledged any authority except God. So, it is not surprising that, although he certainly knew the alchemical work of both his older contemporary, the Strassburg surgeon Hieronymus Brunschwig (1450–*c.* 1512), and the fourteenth-century alchemist John of Rupescissa, he did not cite them on hypericum.[77] Paracelsus's *arcanum* is, however, very reminiscent of the demon-chasing quintessence (*quinta essentia*) that Rupescissa ascribed to gold, pearls, and "the seed of the herb which is called *hypericon* or *perforata*, *transcala* in the vernacular of Aquitaine, and *fuga daemonum* by the most trustworthy Philosophers."[78]

The apotropaic and astrological details in Paracelsus are similar to Rupescissa as well:

> Demons hate the glory and love of God and by extension, the clarity of the Sun ...
> They naturally prefer darkness, shadows, sadness, *melancholia*, and other things that
> resemble the complexion of hell ... It is often found that the seed alone [of *hypericon*]
> expels the infesting demons from dwellings. And in our time, it chased an incubus
> from a certain girl. And its operation is stronger if the seed is gathered with the plant,
> for then it bears the influx of the Sun and Jupiter and other planets whose influences
> the demons detest.[79]

Lumen apothecariorum ("Light of Apothecaries"), a section of *Lumen maius*, by Joannes Jacobus de Manliis, a standard work of late medieval pharmacy in print by 1492.

[77] See Walter Pagel, *Paracelsus: An Introduction to Philosophical Medicine in the Era of the Renaissance* (Basel: S. Karger, 1958), 69, 258, 263–6; and Pagel, "Paracelsus: Traditionalism and Medieval Sources," in Lloyd G. Stevenson and Robert P. Multhauf (eds), *Medicine, Science and Culture: Historical Essays in Honor of Owsei Temkin* (Baltimore: Johns Hopkins University Press, 1968), 50–75. Webster, *Paracelsus*, 180–84.

[78] John of Rupescissa, *De consideratione Quintae essentię rerum omnium, opus sane egregium ... nunc primum in lucem data* (Basel: n.p., [1561?]), 141; digital facsimile at Universidad Complutense Madrid, Biblioteca Digital Dioscórides, http://www.ucm.es/BUCM/atencion/24063.php: "Maxime autem hoc efficacius fiet cum quinta Essentia auri & perlarum, & semine herbæ quæ vocatur hypericon seu perforata, & in vulgari Aquitanico transcalam. Illud enim semen a Philosophis probatissimis vocatur fuga dæmonum."

[79] Ibid., 140–41: "Et Saturnus niger, & Luna maculosa, & nigra, & carceres nigri, præfigurant conditionem inferni: Et hinc est quod sicut dæmones sunt damnati ... habentes odio gloriam ... Dei realem, & figuralem ac participatiuam mundanam, ipsi habent odio Solem & claritatem eius ... Ideo ... naturaliter sibi complacent in tenebris & in vmbra, in ira, tristitia, melancholia, & in rebus alijs quæ prætendunt complexionem inferni ... Et est pluries expertum quod illud solum semen dæmones infestos expellit ab habitationibus domorum. Et tempore nostro incubum dæmonem a quadam puella fugauit. Et fortior operatio eius est, si solum semen colligatur cum herba: fert enim in se influxum Iouis & Solis & planetarum, quorum influentias dæmones detestantur, rationibus supradictis."

In Hieronymus Brunschwig's *Liber de arte distillandi*, the standard work on distillation in late fifteenth- and early sixteenth-century Germany, Paracelsus ignored "a water which is good for a devilish spirit, women in childbirth ... and for magic and for all evil melancholic fantasies."[80] Brunschwig's *Wasser* combined Saint John's wort, rue, fern, periwinkle, boxwood leaves, devils-bit, peony seeds, yellow amber, and red coral—all substances with apotropaic reputations.[81] The plants' powers were enhanced by being picked on St. Peter's Eve, June 28, shortly after St. John's Day. The drink could also "be carried and frequently smelled" or used to moisten the childbed curtains to keep away the specters.[82]

Three points are key here. First, as in the practices of folk magic (or the similar claims for "wonder drugs"), for Paracelsus, the mere presence of hypericum was all that was needed to dispel the *phantasmata*.[83] It was not taken internally. Second, to Paracelsus, these *phantasmata* were not actual demons or specters but lunatic fantasies that were like other illnesses: generated in the soul by natural processes, not by the devil.[84] Finally, as far as Paracelsus was concerned, because the humors were not real, this illness was not melancholy and remedies

---

[80] Brunschwig, *Liber de arte distillandi*, bk 3, ch. 21, fol. ccliᵛ: "Ein wasser das gut ist für ein teuffelisch gespenst/ so die frauwen in einer kintbet ligen/ des gleichen so man tuechlein darinnen netzt vnd die lassen wider trucken werden vnd das tuoch oder wasser so einer dz bey im treit das ist guot für zouberey vnd für alle böse melancolische fantasey das wasser also getruncken vnd bey im tragen vnnd offt daran geschmacket. Das wasser mach also Nym sant Johans krut mitt aller seiner substantz/ des bletter durchlöcheret seint des wassers. xxiiii. lot. Farn krut wasser iedes xviii lot Ingrien wasser daruss man schepel machet Teüffels biss wasser Ruten wasser Buchssboum bletter wasser iedes vi lot Rot Corallen gepüluert iiii lot Gelen Agstein gepüluert ii lot Beonyen körner i lot Also sol man dis wasser machen Nim die kruoter an sant Peters aben als vil dz man wol weisst das man dar vss brennen mag als vil wasser als obgeschscriben stont/ vnnd thuo darzuo die Corallen vnd Agstein/ Beonien körner vnd bestell das an sant Peters abent vnd weihen dz an sant Peters tag alles mit einander/ vnd foh an dem selbigen an die kreüter zuobrennen/ vnd nym iedes nach seinen gewichten die wasser wie vorstot vnd stoss dan die stück vnd thuo sie zuosamen vnd distillier vnd bruch es wie oben stot/ doch sol es kein kintbeterin in dem leib bruchen/ sunder das tuoch bruchen das darin genetzt sey/ wan es treibt Menstruum zuofast."

[81] For the magical properties of these plants (and a sixteenth-century Dutch pastor's use of them), see Siegfried Seligmann, *Die magischen Heil- und Schutzmittel aus der belebten Natur*, ed. Jürgen Zwernemann (3 vols, Berlin: Reimer, 1996–2001), vol. 1: *Das Pflanzenreich*, 27, 80–81, 87, 103–5, 120, 134, 138–42, 229, 238–41, 269.

[82] See passage quoted above, n. 80.

[83] Paracelsus, ed. Sudhoff, vol. 2, *Von den natürlichen Dingen*, 116–17. On apotropaic wonder drugs and charms, see Francis B. Brévart, "Between Medicine, Magic, and Religion: Wonder Drugs in German Medico-Pharmaceutical Treatises of the Thirteenth to the Sixteenth Centuries," *Speculum* 83 (2008): 1–57.

[84] Paracelsus, ed. Sudhoff, vol. 2, *Von den natürlichen Dingen*, 117: "und das sol ein ietlicher arzt wissen, das got ein gross arcanum in das kraut gelegt hat, alein von wegen der geisten und

for melancholy would not be effective: "such fantasies were not a sickness of *melancholia* or the like, as the academics prattle about, but rather only a spirit which could not be treated by the things that are taken for *melancholia*."[85]

Did Paracelsus's unorthodox uses of hypericum make any difference in the way later physicians prescribed the herb? The evidence from three seventeenth-century physicians suggests that it may have.

Angelo Sala (1576–1637), the Italian Protestant physician whom Rosenthal identified as "a pioneer in the pharmacological treatment of depression," devoted a chapter of his *Anatome essentiarum vegetabilium* (1630) to Saint John's wort.[86] In *De essentia hyperici*, Sala listed a very wide range of conditions that this home-grown remedy could treat: wounds, dislocations, broken bones, ruptures, kidney stones, dysuria, problems of the nerves and joints, worms generated by the corruption of food, and poisonings. Above all, he said, hypericum had the "remarkable faculty of correcting false imaginings, fears, melancholy, and corruption of the intellect—conditions that by day or night, like a thunderbolt, can suddenly beset even men endowed with a good temper and in whom there is no manifest excess of a melancholic humor."[87]

Sala referred approvingly to Paracelsus's account in *De rebus naturalibus* about *perforata*'s power against bewitchments (*veneficia*), but without explicitly invoking the plant's signature or *arcanum*.[88] At the same time, by intermingling

---

dollen fantaseien, die den menschen in verzweiflung bringen und nicht durch den teufel, sonder von natur."

[85]   Ibid., 114–15: "das solche fantasei nicht ein krankheit ist der melancholei oder der gleichen, wie die hohenschuler plerren, sonder ist nur ein geist, der nicht mit den dingen genomen wird, die melancholiam nemen." Cf. John of Rupescissa, *De consideratione Quintae essentię*, 135–40, on the theological *quaestio* whether demons proceeded from a melancholic humor or whether some other corporeal property prevented demons from fleeing.

[86]   Rosenthal, *St. John's Wort*, 280. Sala practiced mostly in Germany.

[87]   Angelo Sala, *Opera omnia medico-chymica hactenus separatim diversisque linguis excusa*, ed. Johannes Schröderus (Frankfurt: Hermannus à Sande and Johannes Andreae, 1682): *Anatome essentiarum vegetabilium*, sect. 2, ch. 4, p. 7; digital facsimile at Universidad Complutense Madrid, Biblioteca Digital Dioscórides, http://www.ucm.es/BUCM/atencion/24063.php: "Idcirco tamen reapse, virtuti ejus ne hilum quidem decedit, qua vulnera, luxationes, ossium fracturas, & rupturas sanandi pollet: Interne vero adhibita, contra renum calculum, dysuriam, nervorum & articulorum affectus, verminationes ex ciborum corruptione ortas, ac venena insignis est; nec infimum in potionibus vulnerariis locum obtinet. Præterea insignem facultatem, imaginationes falsas, terrores, melancholiam, & intellectus depravationem corrigendi sortita est; quæ accidentia etiam, homines proba temperie præditos, & in quibus nullus manifestus excessus, humoris melancholici, quandoque subito instar fulminis die vel nocte corripiunt."

[88]   Ibid., 7–8: "Nec si uspiam simplex aliquod reperire detur, quod ad veneficia abolenda valeat, ullo merito huic præferri potest; teste Theophrasto Paracelso, libro primo, de rebus naturalibus, capite quinto, de Perforata." In *Ternarius triplex hemeticorum, bezoardicorum et*

indications from Paracelsus and ancient authors (without naming them) and by using the humoral vocabulary, Sala implied that the two medical systems were not mutually exclusive: physicians did not have to choose between them. Moreover, he asserted, it was no crime to add to the uses discovered by the ancients: he himself had obtained and experimented with an aqueous and a resinous preparation from hypericum. The resinous gum served as a topical plaster for ruptures and dislocations; or it could be drunk in wine or broth "to treat dysuria, stones, worms, poisons, and mental aberrations."[89]

Sala's editor, Joannes Schröderus (1600–64), a Frankfurt physician and alchemist, continued the process of bringing classical and Paracelsan pharmacology together. The entry for hypericum in his massive *Pharmacopëia medico-chymica* juxtaposed the Galenic complexion and virtues with Paracelsus's use of it as an amulet, and cited Sala's tincture as well.[90] Following the recipe from Schröderus, a Nuremberg physician, Johannes Georgius Fabricius, administered oil of hypericum to a five-year-old girl who, under the influence of the evil eye, had been vomiting needles, sand, mud, excrement, and "many-legged, multicólored worms the size of earthworms."[91] In Fabricius's successful

---

laudanorum, Sala also recommended a *Conserva Hypericonis* for epilepsy (p. 567). Sala omitted hypericum's emmenagogic property. Rosenthal, *St. John's Wort*, 278–80, translates key passages from Sala's chapter; my readings are slightly different, perhaps because we are using different editions. I have not seen the original German edition: *Angeli Salæ Essentiarum vegetabilium anatome. Darinnen von den fürtrefflichsten Nutzbarkeiten der vegetabilischen Essentzen in der Artzney* (Rostock: Joh. Richels Erben and Johan Hallervord, 1630).

[89] Sala, *Anatome essentiarum vegetabilium*, 8: "Accedo ad præparationem hujus simplicis, in quo duas natura differentes partes reperio: Unam in aqua solubilem: Alteram dissimilem resinosam, & balsamicam ... nullius alterius gummi aut resinæ, utpote quæ tota balsamica est, additione indigeat: In rupturis vero, & luxationibus, admixtione aliarum rerum, ut in emplastri formam redigi possit, opus habet: Contra dysuriam, calculum, lumbricos, venena, & mentis aberrationem, in vino vel jusculo dissoluta, bis in die ... exhibenda ... nisi obstaret nescio quæ stoliditas, ac vana religio eorum, quæ veterum inventis addere criminis loco haberent; quod alioquin salva antiquorum authoritate, incrementum rei medicæ illustre adferre posset."

[90] Johannes Schröder, *Pharmacopëia medico-chymica: sive, Thesaurus pharmacologicus* (Lyons: Philippus Borde, Laurentius Arnaud, and Claudius Rigaud, 1656), bk 2, ch. 72, pp. 210–15; bk 4, ch. 170, p. 516; digital facsimile, Internet Archive: http://www.archive.org.

[91] Wolfgang Ambrosius Fabricius, *ΑΠΟΦΗΜΑ ΒΟΤΑΝΙΚΟΝ: De signaturis plantarum, quod Romae, mens. Jul., anno MDCLII., exercitii gratia, καὸ δύναμιν & per theses tractavit Wolfg. Ambros. Fabricius Norimbergensis, medicin. candidatus* (Nuremberg: Wolfgang Endterus, Senior, 1653; facsimile reprint, Lecce: Conte, 1997), 36–7, probably citing the Ulm, J. Gerlin, 1649 edition of Schröder (not seen): "... cum superiori biennio, mense Augusto, Norimbergæ in Patria, Acus, Arenam, Lutum & Vermiculos diversicolores ac multipedes, lumbricorum terrestrium magnitudinem referentes, cum copiosissimis alvi excrementis, per os freqventissime rejecisset [puella quinquennis], a Cl. Dn. Parente meo, Oleo Hyperici composito (cujus descriptionem

treatment of the bewitched child, the apotropaic use of hypericum, Paracelsus's topical remedy for worms, and Sala's drink for melancholy converged.

There is one last twist to these seventeenth-century reinterpretations of Saint John's wort. Wolfgang Ambrosius Fabricius had obtained the recipe from Schröderus for his father and then recounted the case in his own medical thesis in 1652.[92] The thesis itself was on the pros and cons of the doctrine of signatures in plants. It illustrated hypericum's signature with an engraving, after the Paracelsan Oswald Croll, that juxtaposed the plant, with dots on the leaves, next to "the pores of the skin"—memorably depicted on a flayed human skin, draped over a stick.[93] But, despite all his pride in his father's cure, the younger Fabricius came down on the side of Galenists.

Consequences

Historical claims for the efficacy of a traditional herbal remedy have to assume considerable continuity across centuries in: (1) the identification of the plant; (2) the medical conditions it has been used to treat; and (3) the methods of preparing and administering it.

With Saint John's wort, the identification is more certain than for a great many medicinal plants. The glandular dots in its leaves are of so distinctive a botanical character that any name, description, picture, or specimen that invokes those "perforations" can be reasonably assumed to indicate *Hypericum perforatum* L. or a closely related species that is apt to have similar properties.

But, on other grounds, the appeal to history for Saint John's wort's effectiveness against depression falters.

In the tradition stemming from Dioscorides and Galen and followed by Hieronymus Bock and his fellow early sixteenth-century humanist botanists, hypericum was prescribed in both topical and internal forms—but not for melancholy. The hot and dry humoral qualities attributed to it by Galen ruled it

---

Cl. Dn. Schröderus, Pharmacop. libr. 2. cap. 72. folio mihi .245., communicavit) ceu particulari remedio, post præmissa universalia demum exhibito, feliciter, per Dei gratiam, curata est." Mariangela Napoli, "The Plants, Rituals and Spells That 'Cured' Helminthiasis in Sicily," *Journal of Ethnobiology and Ethnomedicine* 4/21 (2008): 13, notes that Sicilian folk healers still use *pirico* (*Hypericum perforatum* L.) against parasitic worms.

[92]   Fabricius, *De signaturis plantarum*, 36–7; Fabricius (p. 35) had witnessed German peasants selling hypericum in the marketplace to protect cattle against witchcraft.

[93]   Fabricius, *De signaturis plantarum*, table 2 and p. 11: "Poros Cutis. *Hyperici folia.* adversus pororum obstructiones & ad pellendum sudorem." The image may allude to Juan Valverde, *Anatomia del corpo humano* (Rome: Ant. Salamanca and Antonio Lafreri, 1560), bk 2, table 1, 64.

out as an effective therapy for melancholy's characteristic excess of cold and dry humors.

In the tradition of popular magic, Saint John's wort was credited with remarkable protective powers against the devil, specters, and thunderstorms—but not against deep dejection. And, because hypericum was used as an amulet, its apotropaic properties cannot be equated to modern preparations for depression.

Paracelsus's characterization of the mental derangements that led to phantasmic visions, mania, and suicide perhaps comes closest to the Galenists' *melancholia* and by extension to modern notions of depression. However, because Paracelsus vehemently rejected the term *melancholia*, along with its accompanying Galenic explanation and remedies, we cannot be sure how well the constellation of symptoms he treated with hypericum matched those of either Galenic melancholy or depression today.[94]

In any case, Paracelsus, like the folk healers, was confident that simply holding or sniffing branches of Saint John's wort drove away the *phantasmata*. So, here too any physiological effect comparable to today's hypericum preparations must be ruled out.

While Paracelsus did not himself employ hypericum as an internal medicine for melancholy, he did offer alternatives to the Galenic humoral explanations and treatments of illness generally, and melancholy in particular. That made it possible for his followers to experiment with "off-label" uses and thus enlarge the realm of materia medica.

Can the lack of testimonials (before Angelo Sala) for the internal use of hypericum for melancholy be reconciled with the recent hopeful experience of its use as an antidepressant? Here are some possibilities that might warrant historical and biomedical exploration:

- Because, on theoretical grounds, a hot and dry remedy would not have been prescribed for melancholy, there was little opportunity for Galenic practitioners to accumulate much experience with *Hypericum* for that condition. However, Dioscorides' 40-day prescription of a hypericum-seed drink for "hip ailments" might have unintentionally relieved depression arising from the debilitating misery of sciatica.[95]

---

[94] For careful analyses of the problems in mapping early modern accounts of madness, demonic possession, and melancholy onto modern categories of mental illness and of Luther's and Paracelsus's religious interpretations of melancholic symptoms, see H.C. Erik Midelfort, *A History of Madness in Sixteenth-century Germany* (Stanford, CA: Stanford University Press, 1999), introduction and ch. 2. Midelfort does not mention Saint John's wort.

[95] Ronda Nelson conjectures along these lines, but with respect to the wound therapies, in "History of St. John's Wort," *Dr. [John R.] Christopher's Herbal Legacy*: http://www.herballegacy

- In Galenic compound medicines, hypericum's mood-elevating effects might not have been dramatic enough for healers and patients to spot it as a key ingredient. A quantitative pharmacological analysis of hypericum in early modern formulations could perhaps address that question.
- Out of professional disapproval of their Paracelsan competitors, sixteenth-century Galenic practitioners would have been even less likely to experiment with the drug for melancholic disorders.
- The physiologically active constituents of *Hypericum* species might vary with local conditions of climate, soil, cultivation, or pharmaceutical preparation, so that Dioscorides' and Galen's experience in the Mediterranean could have been quite different from that of sixteenth-century Germans.[96]
- The pungent resinous smell of Saint John's wort might have physiological effects in itself.

Does the weakness of the historical case for Saint John's wort as an antidepressant matter?

Varro E. Tyler has drawn attention to the "fictional histories" of proprietary medicines, where the eighteenth-, nineteenth-, and twentieth-century promoters ascribed the discovery of their drugs to an ancient time, distant place, or exotic culture (e.g., Chinese temple priests, Incan medicine men in Peru, Amazonian tribes, American Indians), or even, in the case of Hoxsey's Cancer Cure, to a sagacious horse.[97] The unabashed commercial purpose of such "prefabricated 'ancient' histories" distinguishes them from the invented traditions described by Eric Hobsbawm:

> "Invented tradition" is taken to mean a set of practices governed by overtly or tacitly accepted rules and of a ritual or symbolic nature, which seek to inculcate certain values and norms of behaviour by repetition, which automatically implies continuity with

---

.com/Nelson_History.html. Michael Adams, Caroline Berset, Michael Kessler, and Matthias Hamburger, "Medicinal Herbs for the Treatment of Rheumatic Disorders—A Survey of European Herbals from the 16th and 17th Century," *Journal of Ethnopharmacology* 121 (2009): 343–59.

[96] A similar question arises with the photosensitivity reaction of cattle (see n. 2). Did different skin colors among breeds, different patterns of herding, biogeographic variation in *Hypericum*, or even the presence of *Hypericum*'s natural predators affect the response?

[97] Varro E. Tyler, "Fictional Histories of Factual Herbal Remedies," in Wolf-Dieter Müller-Jahncke, Anna Maria Carmona-Cornet, and François Ledermann (eds), *Materialien zur Pharmaziegeschichte: Akten des 31. Kongresses für Geschichte der Pharmazie, Heidelberg, 3.–7. Mai 1993*, Heidelberger Schriften zur Pharmazie- und Naturwissenschaftsgeschichte, Beiheft 1 (Stuttgart: Wissenschaftliche Verlagsgesellschaft, 1995), 315–19, esp. 316.

the past. In fact, where possible, they normally attempt to establish continuity with a suitable historic past.[98]

In the twentieth century, I think we can see both kinds of traditions at work—most recently, in marketing Saint John's wort as a commercial pharmaceutical product, and earlier in the promotion of Paracelsus as a German national hero of science and medicine.[99]

If *Hypericum* is effective against depression, there is no need to claim a historical tradition for its use. But, whenever herbal traditions are the basis for new drugs from old remedies, then it is wise to examine what that tradition actually says.

By taking seriously the possibility that traditional herbal remedies worked, by underscoring the corollary that early sources also signaled potent side effects, by recognizing that the practices and materials of herbal medicine could change over time, and by speaking out when it was clear that ignorance of the historical record could harm modern users of botanical medicines, John Riddle has shown us how to do just that.

Bibliography

Adams, Michael, Caroline Berset, Michael Kessler, and Matthias Hamburger. "Medicinal Herbs for the Treatment of Rheumatic Disorders—A Survey of European Herbals from the 16th and 17th Century." *Journal of Ethnopharmacology* 121 (2009): 343–59.

André, Jacques. *Les noms des plantes dans la Rome antique.* Paris: Les Belles Lettres, 1985.

Arber, Agnes. *Herbals, Their Origin and Evolution: A Chapter in the History of Botany.* 3rd edn, introduced and annotated by William T. Stearn. Cambridge Science Classics. Cambridge: Cambridge University Press, 1986.

Arikha, Noga. *Passions and Tempers: A History of the Humours.* New York: HarperCollins, 2007.

Benzenhöfer, Udo. *Studien zum Frühwerk des Paracelsus im Bereich Medizin und Naturkunde.* Münster: Klemm & Oelschager, 2005.

---

[98] Hobsbawm, "Introduction," in Eric Hobsbawm and Terence Ranger (eds), *The Invention of Tradition* (Cambridge: Cambridge University Press, 1983), 1.

[99] On motives for German and Swiss interest in Paracelsus after World War I, see Midelfort, *History of Madness*, 109 n. 136; Mark Morrisson, *Modern Alchemy: Occultism and the Emergence of Atomic Theory* (Oxford: Oxford University Press, 2007), 4, 100, 129.

Berkeley, Edmund, and Dorothy Smith Berkeley (eds). *The Correspondence of John Bartram, 1734–1777.* Gainesville: University Press of Florida, 1992.

The Big Doctors Book of Home Remedies. New York: Rodale, 2009.

Bloomfield, Harold H., Mikael Nordfors, and Peter McWilliams. *Hypericum and Depression.* Los Angeles: Prelude Press, 1996. Web publication, 1996, http://www.hypericum.com/toc.htm (accessed February 22, 2012).

Bock, Hieronymus. *Kurtz Regiment für das grausam Haupt wehe vnd Breune, vor die Gemein vnd armes heuflin hin vnd wider im Wasgaw vnd Westereich.* Strassburg: Knobloch, 1544.

———. *Kreüter Buoch. Darin Vnderscheid, Würckung und Namen der Kreüter so in deutschen Landen wachsen, auch der selbigen eigentlicher und wolgegründter gebrauch inn der Artznei fleissig dargeben, Leibs gesundheit zuo behalten und zuo fürderen seer nutzlich und tröstlich, vorab dem gemeinen einfaltigen man. Durch H. Hieronymum Bock aus langwiriger und gewisser erfarung beschriben, und jetzund von newem fleissig übersehen, gebessert und gemehret, dazuo mit hüpschen artigen Figuren allenthalben gezieret.* 2nd edn. Strassburg: Wendel Rihel, 1546. Digital facsimile, Biodiversity Library: http://www.biodiversitylibrary.org (accessed February 22, 2012).

———. *De stirpium, maxime earum, quæ in Germania nostra nascuntur, usitatis nomenclaturis, propriisque differentiis, neque non temperaturis ac facultatibus, commentariorum libri tres, Germanica primum lingua conscripti, nunc in Latinam conversi.* Strassburg: Wendel Rihel, 1552.

Brévart, Francis B. "Between Medicine, Magic, and Religion: Wonder Drugs in German Medico-Pharmaceutical Treatises of the Thirteenth to the Sixteenth Centuries." *Speculum* 83 (2008): 1–57.

Bright, Timothy. *A Treatise of Melancholy. Contayning the Causes Thereof, and Reasons of the Straunge Effects It Worketh in Our Minds and Bodies: With the Phisicke Cure.* London: John Windet, 1586. Digital facsimile, Bibliothèque Interuniversitaire Santé (Paris): http://www.bium.univ-paris5.fr/histmed/medica.htm (accessed February 22, 2012).

Brück, Michael. *Heilkraft und Aberglaube: Die historische Entwicklung der Therapie mit Johanniskraut ("Hypericum perforatum" L.).* Essen: KVC Verlag, 2004.

Brunfels, Otto. *Contrafayt Kreüterbuch nach rechter vollkommener Art, vnnd Beschreibungen der alten, besstberümpten Ärtzt, vormals in teütscher Sprach, der massen nye gesehen, noch im Truck aussgangen.* Strassburg: Hans Schotten, 1532.

———. *Noui herbarii tomus II.* Strassburg: Johann Schott, 1532.

Brunschwig, Hieronymus. *Liber de arte distillandi de compositis. Das buoch der waren kunst zu distillieren die Composita vnd simplicia.* Strassburg: [n.p.], 1512.

Buenz, Eric J., David J. Schnepple, Brent A. Bauer, Peter L. Elkin, John M. Riddle, and Timothy Motley. "Techniques: Bioprospecting Historical Herbal Texts by Hunting for New Leads in Old Tomes." *Trends in Pharmacological Sciences* 25 (2004): 494–8.

Czygan, Franz-C. "Kulturgeschichte und Mystik des Johanniskrauts." *Zeitschrift für Phytotherapie* 14 (1993): 256–82.

Dioscorides. *De materia medica libri quinque.* Ed. Kurt Sprengel. 2 vols. Leipzig: C. Cnobloch, 1829–30.

———. *De materia medica libri quinque.* Ed. Max Wellmann. 3 vols. Berlin: Weidmann, 1906–14. Repr. Berlin: Weidmann, 1958.

———. *De materia medica.* Trans. Lily Y. Beck. Altertumswissenschaftliche Texte und Studien 38. Hildesheim: Olms-Weidmann, 2005.

The Doctors Book of Home Remedies. New York: Rodale, 1990.

Duke, James A. *The Green Pharmacy.* New York: Rodale, 1997.

Fabricius, Wolfgang Ambrosius. *ΑΠΟΡΗΜΑ ΒΟΤΑΝΙΚΟΝ: De signaturis plantarum, quod Romæ, mens. Jul., anno MDCLII., exercitii gratia, καθ᾽ δύναμιν & per theses tractavit Wolfg. Ambros. Fabricius Norimbergensis, medicin. candidatus.* Nuremberg: Wolfgang Endterus, Senior, 1653. Facsimile repr., Lecce: Conte, 1997.

Fuchs, Leonhart. *De historia stirpium commentarii insignes, maximis impensis et vigiliis elaborati, adiectis earundem vivis plusquam quingentis imaginibus nunquam antea, ad naturæ imitationem artificiosius effictis et expressis.* Basel: Michael Isingrin, 1542.

———. *The Great Herbal of Leonhart Fuchs: De historia stirpium commentarii insignes, 1542.* With commentary by Frederick G. Meyer, Emily Emmart Trueblood, and John L. Heller. 2 vols. Stanford, CA: Stanford University Press, 1999.

———. *New Kreüterbuch, in welchem nit allein die gantz histori, das ist, namen, gestalt, statt vnd zeit der wachsung, natur, krafft vnd würckung, des meysten theyls der Kreüter so in Teütschen vnnd andern Landen wachsen, mit dem besten vleiss beschriben, sonder auch alle derselben wurtzel, stengel, bletter, bluomen, samen, frücht, vnd in summa die gantze gestalt, allso artlich vnd kunstlich abgebildet vnd contrafayt ist, das dessgleichen vormals nie gesehen, noch an tag kommen.* Basel: Michael Isingrin, 1543. Facsimile repr., *The New Herbal of 1543.* Cologne: Taschen, 2001.

Galen. *Claudii Galeni Opera omnia.* Ed. C.G. Kühn. 20 vols in 22. Leipzig: C. Cnobloch, 1821–33. Repr. Hildesheim: Georg Olms, 1964–65.

Garel, Michel. *D'une main forte: Manuscrits hébreux des collections françaises.* Paris: Bibliothèque nationale, 1991.

Gessner, Conrad. *Bibliotheca universalis, siue catalogus omnium scriptorum locupletissimus, in tribus linguis, Latina, Græca, Hebraica, extantium et non extantium, veterum et recentiorum in hunc usque diem, doctorum et indoctorum, publicatorum et in bibliothecis latentium.* Zurich: Froschauer, 1545.

Green, Monica H. "Gendering the History of Women's Healthcare." *Gender and History* 20 (2008): 487–518.

Greene, Edward Lee. *Landmarks of Botanical History.* Ed. Frank N. Egerton. 2 vols. Stanford, CA: Stanford University Press, 1983.

Grimm, Jacob. *Teutonic Mythology.* Translated from the 4th edn by James Steven Stallybrass. 4 vols. London: W. Swan Sonnenschein & Allen, 1880–88. Repr. London: Routledge/Thoemmes Press, 1999.

Harvey, John H. "Westminster Abbey: The Infirmarer's Garden." *Garden History* 20 (1992): 97–115.

Hobbs, Christopher. "St. John's Wort: A Literature Review." *HerbalGram* 18/19 (1989): 24–33.

———. "St. John's Wort—Ancient Herbal Protector." *Pharmacy in History* 32 (1990): 166–9.

———. "St. John's Wort (*Hypericum Perforatum* L.): A Review." Electronic publication: http://www.christopherhobbs.com/website/library/articles/article_files/st_johnswort_01.html (accessed February 22, 2012).

Hobsbawm, Eric, and Terence Ranger (eds). *The Invention of Tradition.* Cambridge: Cambridge University Press, 1983.

Hoppe, Brigitte. *Das Kräuterbuch des Hieronymus Bock: Wissenschaftshistorische Untersuchung, mit einem Verzeichnis sämtlicher Pflanzen des Werkes, der literarischen Quellen der Heilanzeigen und der Anwendungen der Pflanzen.* Stuttgart: Anton Hiersemann, 1969.

Jackson, Stanley W. *Melancholia and Depression, from Hippocratic Times to Modern Times.* New Haven: Yale University Press, 1988.

———. "A History of Melancholia and Depression." In Edwin R. Wallace and John Gach (eds), *A History of Psychiatry and Medical Psychology,* 443–60. New York: Springer, 2008.

John of Rupescissa. *De consideratione Quintae essentię rerum omnium, opus sane egregium. Arnaldi de Villanova Epistola de sanguine humano distillato. Raymundi Lullii Ars operativa: et alia quædam. Omnia ad selectissimam materiam medicam, et morborum curationem, vitæque conservationem mirabilia facientia; nunc primum in lucem data.* Basel: n.p., [1561?]. Digital facsimile, Universidad Complutense Madrid, Biblioteca Digital Dioscórides: http://www.ucm.es/BUCM/atencion/24063.php (accessed February 22, 2012).

Katzenstein, Larry. *Secrets of St. John's Wort.* New York: St. Martin's Books, 1998.

Kraft, Karen, and Christopher Hobbs. *Pocket Guide to Herbal Medicine.* New York: Thieme Medical Publishing, 2004.

Kusukawa, Sachiko. "Leonhart Fuchs on the Importance of Pictures." *Journal of the History of Ideas* 58 (1997): 403–27.

Leu, Urs B., Raffael Keller, and Sandra Weidmann. *Conrad Gessner's Private Library.* Leiden: Brill, 2008.

Mack, Richard N. "Plant Naturalizations and Invasions in the Eastern United States: 1634–1860." *Annals of the Missouri Botanical Garden* 90 (2003): 77–90.

Marzell, Heinrich. "Das Buchsbaum-Bild im Kräuterbuch (1551) des Hieronymus Bock." *Sudhoffs Archiv für Geschichte der Medizin und der Naturwissenschaften* 38 (1954): 97–103.

McIntyre, Michael. "A Review of the Benefits, Adverse Events, Drug Interactions, and Safety of St. John's Wort (*Hypericum perforatum*): The Implications with Regard to the Regulation of Herbal Medicines." *Journal of Alternative and Complementary Medicine* 8 (2000): 115–24.

Midelfort, H.C. Erik. *A History of Madness in Sixteenth-century Germany.* Stanford, CA: Stanford University Press, 1999.

Moran, Bruce T. "The *Herbarius* of Paracelsus." *Pharmacy in History* 35 (1993): 99–127.

Morgenstern, Kay. "Preparing for Pregnancy." *Herb Quarterly* 77 (Spring 1998): 43–51.

Morrisson, Mark. *Modern Alchemy: Occultism and the Emergence of Atomic Theory.* Oxford: Oxford University Press, 2007.

Müller, Martin. *Registerband* to Paracelsus, *Medizinische, naturwissenschaftliche und philosophische Schriften*, ed. Sudhoff. Nova Acta Paracelsica, Supplementum. Einsiedeln: Jos. & Karl Eberle, 1960.

Napoli, Mariangela. "The Plants, Rituals and Spells That 'Cured' Helminthiasis in Sicily." *Journal of Ethnobiology and Ethnomedicine* 4/21 (2008). Published electronically; doi: 10.1186/1746-4269-4-21.

Nelson, Ronda. "History of St. John's Wort." Published electronically: http://www.herballegacy.com/Nelson_History.html (accessed February 22, 2012).

Overholser, James C. "Treatments for Depression: Wisdom Imparted from Treatments Discarded." *International Journal of Psychiatry in Medicine* 32 (2002): 317–36.

Pagel, Walter. *Paracelsus: An Introduction to Philosophical Medicine in the Era of the Renaissance.* Basel: S. Karger, 1958.

———. "Paracelsus: Traditionalism and Medieval Sources." In Lloyd G. Stevenson and Robert P. Multhauf (eds), *Medicine, Science and Culture: Historical Essays in Honor of Owsei Temkin*, 50–75. Baltimore: Johns Hopkins University Press, 1968.

Paracelsus (Phillippus Aureolus Theophrastus Bombastus von Hohenheim). *Aphorismorum aliquot Hippocratis genuinus sensus & vera interpretatio. Das ist Eygendtlicher verstandt, vnd warhafftige gegründte erklerung, vber etliche kurtze haupt sprüch Hippocratis, als nemlich vber alle XXV. Aphorismos primæ sectionis, vnd vber die ersten VI. Aphorismos secundæ sectionis. Neben dreyen hochnützlichen tractaten, von sonderlicher verborgner kraft und würckung Coraliorum, Hyperici, & Persicariae.* Augsburg: M. Franck for G. Willer, 1568. Digital facsimile, Bayerische Staatsbibliothek: http://www.digital-collections.de/ (accessed February 22, 2012).

———. *Archidoxorum Aureoli Ph. Theophrasti Paracelsi de secretis naturae mysteriis libri decem, quorum tenorem versa pagella dabit. His accesserunt libri De tinctura physicorum, De præparationibus, De vexationibus alchimistarum, De cementis metallorum, et De gradationibus eorundem. Singula per Gerardum Dorn e Germanico sermone Latinitati nuperrime donata.* Basel: Petrus Perna, 1570. Digital facsimile, Bayerische Staatsbibliothek: http://www.digital-collections.de/ (accessed February 22, 2012).

———. *Chirurgia minor quam alias Bertheoneam intitulauit ... ex versione Gerardi Dorn.* Basel: Petrus Perna, n.d. Digital facsimile, DigitaleBibliothek, Memoria Medicinae, Medizinische Bibliothek Wien: http://www.memoriamedicinae.meduniwien.ac.at/ (accessed February 22, 2012).

———. *Sämtliche Werke*, Pt I: *Medizinische, naturwissenschaftliche und philosophische Schriften.* Ed. Karl Sudhoff. 15 vols. Munich: R. Oldenbourg, 1922–31.

Parsons, William Thomas, and Eric George Cuthbertson. *Noxious Weeds of Australia.* 2nd edn. Collingswood, Victoria, Australia: CSIRO Publishing, 2001.

Paul of Aegina. *The Seven Books of Paulus Ægineta.* Trans. with comm. by Francis Adams. 3 vols. London: Sydenham Society, 1846.

Pliny. *Natural History.* Ed. and trans. H. Rackham, W.H.S. Jones, and D.E. Eichholz. 10 vols. Loeb Classical Library. Cambridge, MA: Harvard University Press, 1938–63.

Pöldinger, Walter. "Paracelsus und das Johanniskraut." In Pöldinger, *Johanniskraut—Angst—Depression*, 9–15.

————— (ed.). *Johanniskraut—Angst—Depression: Zur Geschichte der Paracelsus-Gesellschaften. Vorträge 1999.* Salzburger Beiträge zur Paracelsusforschung, Folge 33. Vienna: Österreichischer Kunst- und Kulturverlag, 2000.

Pressman, Alan H., with Nancy Burke. *St. John's Wort: The Miracle Medicine.* New York: Dell Publishing, 1998.

Ragazzini, Stefania. *Un erbario del XV secolo: Il ms. 106 della Biblioteca di Botanica dell'Università di Firenze.* Florence: Leo Olschki, 1983.

Reeds, Karen. *Botany in Medieval and Renaissance Universities.* New York: Garland, 1991.

—————. "Finding a Plant in an Early Herbal: *Hypericum*, Saint John's Wort, in Hieronymus Bock (Tragus), *Kreüter Buoch*, 1546." *AVISTA Forum Journal* 19 (2010): 70–72.

Riddle, John M. *Dioscorides on Pharmacy and Medicine.* Austin: University of Texas Press, 1985.

—————. *Contraception and Abortion from the Ancient World to the Renaissance.* Cambridge, MA: Harvard University Press, 1992.

—————. "Historical Data as an Aid in Pharmaceutical Prospecting and Drug Safety Determination [Personal Commentary]." *Journal of Alternative and Complementary Medicine* 5 (1999): 195–201.

—————. "History as a Tool in Identifying 'New' Old Drugs." In Béla Buslig and John Manthey (eds), *Flavonoids in Cell Function*, 89–94. New York: Kluwer Academic Publishers, 2002.

—————. "Research Procedures in Evaluating Medieval Medicine." In Barbara S. Bowers (ed.), *The Medieval Hospital and Medical Practice*, 3–18. AVISTA Studies in the History of Medieval Technology, Science and Art 3. Aldershot, UK: Ashgate, 2007.

Robson, N.K.B. "Studies in the Genus *Hypericum* L. (Guttiferae) 4(2). Section 9. *Hypericum* sensu lato (part 2): subsection 1. *Hypericum* series 1. *Hypericum*." *Bulletin of the Natural History Museum, Botany* 32 (2002): 61–123.

Rosenthal, Norman. *St. John's Wort: The Herbal Way to Feeling Good.* New York: HarperCollins, 1998.

Sala, Angelo. *Essentiarum vegetabilium anatome. Darinnen von den fürtrefflichsten Nutzbarkeiten der vegetabilischen Essentzen in der Artzney.* Rostock: Joh. Richels Erben and Johan Hallervord, 1630.

————. *Opera omnia medico-chymica hactenus separatim diversisque linguis excusa*. Ed. Johannes Schröderus. Frankfurt: Hermannus à Sande and Johannes Andreae, 1682. Digital facsimile, Universidad Complutense Madrid, Biblioteca Digital Dioscórides: http://www.ucm.es/BUCM/ atencion/24063.php (accessed February 22, 2012).

Schachter, Steven C. "Botanicals and Herbs: A Traditional Approach to Treating Epilepsy." *Neurotherapeutics* 6 (2009): 415–20.

Schröder, Johannes. *Pharmacopëia medico-chymica. Siue, Thesaurus pharmacologicus. Quo composita quæque celebriora; hinc mineralia, vegetabilia et animalia chymico-medice describuntur, atque insuper principia physice Hermetico Hippocraticæ candide exhibentur. Opus non minus vtile physicis, quam medicis*. Lyons: Philippus Borde, Laurentius Arnaud, and Claudius Rigaud, 1656. Digital facsimile, Internet Archive: http://www .archive.org (accessed February 22, 2012).

Segre Rutz, Vera. *Il giardino magico degli alchimisti: Un erbario illustrato trecentesco della Biblioteca universitaria di Pavia e la sua tradizione*. Testi e documenti 12. Milan: Il Polifilo, 2000.

Seligmann, Siegfried. *Die magischen Heil- und Schutzmittel aus der belebten Natur*. Ed. Jürgen Zwernemann. 3 vols. Berlin: Reimer, 1996–2001.

Simoons, Frederick J. *Plants of Life, Plants of Death*. Madison: University of Wisconsin Press, 1998.

Stoddart, Anna M. *The Life of Paracelsus: The Life of Theophrastus von Hohenheim*. London: John Murray, 1911.

Stoll, Ulrich. *Das "Lorscher Arzneibuch": Ein medizinisches Kompendium des 8. Jahrhunderts (Codex Bambergensis Medicinalis 1). Text, Übersetzung und Fachglossar. Sudhoffs Archiv*, Beiheft 28. Stuttgart: Franz Steiner, 1992.

Stoudt, Debra L. "The Medical Manuscripts of the Bibliotheca Palatina." In Margaret R. Schleissner (ed.), *Manuscript Sources of Medieval Medicine: A Book of Essays*, 159–81. New York: Garland, 1995.

Thorndike, Lynn. *A History of Magic and Experimental Science*. 8 vols. New York: Columbia University Press, 1923–58.

Tyler, Varro E. "Fictional Histories of Factual Herbal Remedies." In Wolf-Dieter Müller-Jahncke, Anna Maria Carmona-Cornet, and François Ledermann (eds), *Materialien zur Pharmaziegeschichte: Akten des 31. Kongresses für Geschichte der Pharmazie, Heidelberg, 3.–7. Mai 1993*, 315–19. Heidelberger Schriften zur Pharmazie- und Naturwissenschaftsgeschichte, Beiheft 1. Stuttgart: Wissenschaftliche Verlagsgesellschaft, 1995.

Valverde, Juan. *Anatomia del corpo humano*. Rome: Ant. Salamanca and Antonio Lafreri, 1560.

Van Gent, Jacqueline. *Magic, Body and the Self in Eighteenth-century Sweden.* Studies in Medieval and Reform Traditions 135. Leiden: Brill, 2009.

Vickery, A.R. "Traditional Uses and Folklore for Hypericum in the British Isles." *Economic Botany* 35 (1981): 289–95.

Wahlberg, Ayo. "Pathways to Plausibility: When Herbs Become Pills." *Biosocieties* 3 (2008): 37–56.

Webster, Charles. "Conrad Gessner and the Infidelity of Paracelsus." In Sarah Hutton and John Henry (eds), *New Perspectives on Renaissance Thought: Essays in the History of Science, Education and Philosophy in Memory of Charles B. Schmitt*, 13–23. London: Duckworth, 1990.

———. *Paracelsus: Medicine, Magic and Mission at the End of Time.* New Haven: Yale University Press, 2008.

Weeks, Andrew. *Paracelsus: Speculative Theory and the Crisis of the Early Reformation.* SUNY Series in Western Esoteric Traditions. Albany: State University of New York Press, 1997.

Zemlefer, Wendy B. *Guide to Flowering Plant Families.* Chapel Hill: University of North Carolina Press, 1994.

Chapter 10

Revisiting Eve's Herbs:
Reflections on Therapeutic Uncertainties

John K. Crellin

In entering relatively uncharted areas of scholarship, John Riddle's two books, *Contraception and Abortion from the Ancient World to the Renaissance* (1992) and *Eve's Herbs: A History of Contraception and Abortion in the West* (1997), prompted polarized responses.[1] Some reviews and commentaries have been highly skeptical, while others accepted Riddle's general argument that widespread popular knowledge of effective contraceptive/abortifacient herbs, which existed prior to early modern times, was subsequently forgotten aside from lingering remnants in folklore. The diverse views (Box 10.1) about Riddle's interpretation of data encouraged the discussion that follows; it is intended to prompt general reflections on therapeutics by considering (1) the differing opinions expressed in a nineteenth-century abortion trial—one considered by Riddle—about two alleged emmenagogues/abortifacients, and (2) the uncertainty of therapeutic outcomes.

---

[1]   John M. Riddle, *Contraception and Abortion from the Ancient World to the Renaissance* (Cambridge, MA: Harvard University Press, 1992) and *Eve's Herbs: A History of Contraception and Abortion in the West* (Cambridge, MA: Harvard University Press, 1997). For further comments, see John M. Riddle, *Goddesses, Elixirs, and Witches: Plants and Sexuality throughout Human History* (New York: Palgrave Macmillan, 2010).

Box 10.1   Some excerpts from book reviews of and later commentaries
on John Riddle's *Eve's Herbs: A History of Contraception and
Abortion in the West* (1997)

"Eve's herbs worked better than physicians were long willing to admit, better than anything science had to offer for thousands of years." Burkhard Bilger, book review, *HerbalGram* 45 (1999): 70.

"Yes there are interesting continuities of traditions concerning certain plants' effects, and remarkable evidence of the fragmentary persistence of knowledge over centuries, tantalising, evocative, suggestive. It is dubious, however, that these support the edifice here erected upon them." Lesley A. Hall, book review, *American Historical Review* 103 (1998): 1211–12.

"*Eve's Herbs* is a revisionist study that is certain to provoke debate. While Riddle has left no stone unturned in his effort to demonstrate that premodern women were able to limit conception on a wide scale, one must conclude that his thesis remains unproved and unlikely." Gary B. Ferngren, book review, *New England Journal of Medicine* 337 (1997): 1398.

"Readers unconvinced by Riddle's original arguments will find little to change their minds here. One key weakness in particular becomes more rather than less apparent as the story progresses. Riddle never clearly demonstrates the validity of his suggestion that the historical medical literature on which he focuses can serve as a bridge between the findings of modern science and the everyday practices of the past." Rebecca Flemming, book review, *Isis* 90 (1999): 102–3.

"Claims have recently been made ... for the historical efficacy of a great variety of herbal contraceptives and abortifacients (Riddle 1992, 1997). But there are serious problems with the evidence." Gigi Santow, "Emmenagogues and Abortifacients in the Twentieth Century: An Issue of Ambiguity," in Étienne van der Walle and Elisha P. Renne (eds), *Regulating Menstruation: Beliefs, Practices, Interpretations* (Chicago: University of Chicago Press, 2001), 64–92, at 82.

My discussion may well seem out of place in a volume focused principally on ancient and medieval medicine. However, while critiques of Riddle's work on contraception and abortion have spotlighted differing interpretations of texts and contexts, the matter of therapeutic uncertainty receives less consideration. This is despite its being a constant issue for clinicians and their patients over time, and hence one for all historians of health care to be constantly mindful of.[2]

---

2   For a sense that uncertainty was a constant issue, see, most recently, Stephen Pender, "Examples and Experience: On the Uncertainty of Medicine," *British Journal of the History of Science* 39 (2006): 1–28. The issue of uncertainty has been raised by other authors. Of relevance to the present account is John H. Warner, *The Therapeutic Perspective: Medical Practice, Knowledge, and Identity in America, 1820–1885* (Princeton: Princeton University Press, 1997). The chapter,

Moreover, for historians who assiduously comb modern science to understand better therapies of the past—Riddle is a pioneer in this—relatively recent examples of ways to cope with uncertainty of therapeutic outcomes can be salutary.

Different Opinions about the Effectiveness of Emmenagogues/Abortifacients

In reviewing a report on the 1871 British trial in which Wallis, a solicitor, was charged with supplying alleged abortifacients to a "lady pregnant by him," Riddle indicated that certain aspects indicated "just how much physicians had forgotten." The aspects were (1) the conflict of medical opinion on the properties (notably abortifacient action) of Griffith's mixture and pennyroyal;[3] and (2) the failure of defense witnesses, whom Riddle labeled as "poor historians," to accept abortifacient properties. Riddle also supported his view on physician forgetfulness through noting a reversal of opinion between two editions (1865 and 1905) of Taylor's *Principles and Practice of Medical Jurisprudence*. In commenting on a negative 1905 statement (apparently contradicting the 1865 view), Riddle states: "This is a case of unwitting ignorance; medical professionals came to view all non-prescription drugs—patent medicines, women's remedies, anything available from a traveling salesman—as superstitious nonsense."[4]

Whether Riddle's comments on "forgetfulness" or "unwitting ignorance" are apt raises the question: Just why did differences of opinion exist? In considering

---

"Physiological Therapeutics and the Dissipation of Therapeutic Gloom," provides background to the time of the Wallis trial, even though focused on the other side of the Atlantic. Among other recent discussions spotlighting a diversity of views: James Bradley and Marguerite Dupree, "A Shadow of Orthodoxy? An Epistemology of British Homeopathy, 1840–1858," *Medical History* 47 (2003): 173–94. My discussion, in providing an overview of opinion over emmenagogues/abortifacients, adds to other accounts.

[3] Riddle, *Eve's Herbs*, 241–2; see also Riddle, *Contraception*, 158–9. Riddle's account is taken from A. Swaine Taylor, *Principles and Practice of Medical Jurisprudence*, ed. F.J. Smith (2 vols, London: Churchill, 1905), 2:168–9.

[4] Riddle, *Eve's Herbs*, 243. However, A. Swaine Taylor and T. Stevenson, *The Principles and Practice of Medical Jurisprudence* (2 vols, London: Churchill, 1883), 2:185, added more detail in stating that the first edition of the book had been misquoted; what had been written, the authors stated, was that pennyroyal had "acquired 'popular repute' for procuring abortion."

Riddle did make clear that there were few villains in his story, which, he says, reflects how "changing attitudes toward human life both influenced and were influenced by the complexities of human society." He added (p. 9): "At times I found both fault and folly, but those times are few."

this, I will suggest that, in large measure, it relates to different physician efforts to cope with therapeutic uncertainty. Such responses are, of course, not easy to explore, except in general terms, since the written record reveals little of an individual physician's reasoning and competence; this resulted from such imponderable factors as the quality of their medical education, clinical experiences, and diagnostic acumen, as well as whether they were conservative in treatment, and, perhaps, recognized that society and the medical profession created fashions in treatments. Even so, there are good reasons to suggest that differences of opinion were, to some degree, a reflection of a relatively high level of conscientiousness among physicians in keeping up to date. While some historians have tended to view clinical practice of the past somewhat negatively (a "cup half empty" interpretation), the discussion that follows might be seen more as a "cup half full" because it presupposes that physicians, amid conflicting opinions, felt they had good reasons for the views they held. After all, physicians needed a good reputation with patients and fellow practitioners for successful practice. Appropriate bedside manners only went so far, and it was helpful to be relatively up to date with an ability to rationalize clinical decisions.

Griffith's Mixture: Iron and Myrrh

The story of Griffith's mixture is especially intriguing because of different views as to whether the key active ingredient was an iron salt or myrrh—an issue relevant to whether the mixture could be classed as an emmenagogue with potential abortifacient activity. The uncertainty persisted even after Griffith's formula—it was first publicized by Moses Griffith in 1776—achieved pharmacopoeial status (first in 1809) as "Compound Mixture of Iron."[5] In 1837, for instance, the pharmacopoeial formula was noted to be "an excellent tonic," similar to "Griffith's *myrrh* mixture."[6] It was compounded from powdered myrrh, carbonate of potash, rose water, sulfate of iron, spirit of nutmeg, and

---

5   For the original publication, Moses Griffith, *Practical Observations on the Cure of Hectic and Slow Fevers, and the Pulmonary Consumption* (London: Benjamin Wright, 1776). (Later editions, actually reprints, appeared in 1795 and 1799.) For some general information, John Cule, "The Iron Mixture of Dr. Griffith," *Pharmaceutical Journal* 198 (1967): 399–401.

6   James Rennie, *A New Supplement to the Latest Pharmacopoeias of London, Edinburgh, Dublin and Paris* (London: Baldwin & Cradock, 1837), 255 (emphasis added). Earlier, Anthony T. Thomson, *The London Dispensatory* (London: Longman, 1811), 618, also noted it was "nearly the same as the celebrated antihectic mixture of Dr. Griffith [and] is a useful tonic in all cases in which preparations of iron are indicated."

sugar, although in America, following the lead of the 1820 *Pharmacopoeia of the United States of America*, spirit of lavender was substituted for spirit of nutmeg.[7]

By the time of the Wallis trial, Griffith's mixture had become popular among many iron preparations widely listed for numerous conditions. Those relevant to the present topic were, according to one author, to "*promote the uterine functions*, as in chlorosis, amenorrhoea, dysmenorrhoea, and menorrhagia"; the author added, "and often with success."[8] Iron had already gained acceptance by the early eighteenth century for an emmenagogue action to relieve amenorrhoea when this was associated with chlorosis. The latter was also known as green sickness, so named for a yellow-greenish pallor diagnosed in some sufferers who, typically, tended to be young, languid, and tired females with non-specific symptoms.[9] This is not the place to notice the many issues surrounding the history of chlorosis, which has had a central place in the story of emmenagogues, except to mention (1) a diversity of treatment regimens, and (2) confusion over the precise nature of the condition and the extent to which a diagnosis reflected a physician's social attitudes towards and stereotyping of patients.[10] (In 1836, it was said that "there is by no means an agreement of professional opinion as to [its] nature."[11])

Amid such issues, iron's reputation as an emmenagogue was somewhat mixed. Although medical textbooks throughout the 1800s continued to note a role for iron (sometimes specifically citing Griffith's mixture) for treating chlorosis and for "simple" amenorrhoea, it was generally recognized to be only one aspect

---

[7]　*Pharmacopoeia of the United States of America* (Boston: Wells & Lilly, 1820), 167. It should be added that the issue of chlorosis was of concern on both sides of the Atlantic. Textbook information readily crossed the Atlantic, hence the use of both British and American texts in this discussion.

[8]　Jonathan Pereira, *The Elements of Materia Medica and Therapeutics* (2 vols, London: Longman, 1842), 1:833 (italics in original).

[9]　For indication of early eighteenth-century reputation, John Quincy, *A Complete English Dispensatory* (London: Bell, 1719), 245 and 249, where steel wine is noted as being "given in chlorosis, i.e., a Green-Sickness with good success." The widely reported symptoms of chlorosis are taken from Robert Hooper, *Lexicon-Medicum or Medical Dictionary* (New York: Harper, 1826), 252.

[10]　For general issues, especially on social issues framing the disease, see Robert P. Hudson, "The Biography of Disease: Lessons from Chlorosis," *Bulletin of the History of Medicine* 51 (1977): 448–63, who considers that more than one disease entity (as understood today) came together under the label of chlorosis; and Joan J. Brumberg, "Chlorotic Girls, 1870–1920: A Historical Perspective on Female Adolescence," *Child Development* 53 (1982): 1468–77.

[11]　For the quotation, Hudson, "Biography of Disease," 449.

of regimens that provided individualized care.[12] As one textbook indicated in 1864: "It is certain that in [the treatment of 'menstrual derangements'] an almost essential adjunct to iron consists of the use of aloetic laxatives and other uterine stimulants, and such general hygienic measures that tend to stimulate and strengthen all the functions of the economy."[13] Aside from iron, other mineral treatments listed for chlorosis and menstrual problems included arsenic (albeit often with iron), manganese, and hydrochloric acid, as well as vigorous purgatives alone.[14] Uncertainties over appropriate regimens were somewhat diminished as chlorosis became more generally viewed, during the last years of the 1800s, as essentially iron-deficient anaemia. One medical authority, William Osler, who influenced the practice of countless physicians, seemingly pushed uncertainty aside. In his celebrated textbook, *The Principles and Practice of Medicine* (1892), he wrote that the use of iron for chlorosis "affords one of the most brilliant instances ... of the specific action of a remedy." On the other hand, he still found it necessary to write that iron only "*usually* restored" amenorrhoea or dysmenorrhoea in chlorosis.[15] Inconsistencies in outcomes were well recognized and, with regard to Griffith's mixture, were sometimes linked to different ways it was prepared from slightly different formulae, and failure to follow the directive that only fresh preparations be used.[16]

The uncertainty over iron as an effective emmenagogue spilled over into whether it could be classed as an abortifacient (an ecbolic). After all, as noted, iron was commonly administered along with a laxative such as aloes, which was recognized in its own right as a potential abortifacient. Yet, for the general public, it seemed logical that *any* reputed emmenagogue could possess abortifacient action if taken in sufficiently large dosage, despite what seems to have been a general awareness of many failures. Direct testimony for this is sparse, but in the

---

[12]   For simple amenorrhoea, Fleetwood Churchill, *Outlines of the Principal Diseases of Females* (Dublin: Martin Keene & Son, 1838), 67–73.

[13]   Alfred Stillé, *Therapeutics and Materia Medica* (2 vols, Philadelphia: Blanchard & Lea, 1864), 1:398.

[14]   For a discussion on these treatments at a time when a key role for iron was being recognized: Ralph Stockman, "The Treatment of Chlorosis by Iron and Some Other Drugs," *British Medical Journal* (1893): 1/881–5 and 942–4. See also Frank P. Foster (ed.), *Reference-Book of Practical Therapeutics* (2 vols, New York: Appleton, 1899), 1:374–5.

[15]   William Osler, *The Principles and Practice of Medicine* (New York: Appleton, 1892), 695 (emphasis added). Undoubtedly some physicians persisted in agreeing with another authority whose 1881 textbook on materia medica and therapeutics stated: "In chlorosis the good effects of iron are not so conspicuous [as in anaemia], although they are allied states." (Roberts Bartholow, *A Practical Treatise on Materia Medica and Therapeutics* [New York: Appleton, 1881], 121.)

[16]   For use of fresh preparations, Pereira, *Elements*, 1:862. This work is quoted a number of times in this discussion, since it and a later edition became a well-recognized standard work.

early twentieth century one woman wrote: "I confess without shame that when well-meaning friends said: 'You cannot afford another baby; take this drug,' I took their strong concoctions to purge me of the little life that might be mine. *They failed, as such things generally do*, and the third baby came."[17]

Physicians interpreted failures, in part, as due to misunderstandings over the actions of true emmenagogues. Although the term was evidently treated by some of the witnesses at the Wallis trial as synonymous with "ecbolic or abortive" action, many medical writers at the time distinguished between emmenagogues and abortifacients.[18] Most of the former were considered to act, like iron, "indirectly," that is, aiding menstrual disturbances by improving the "general systems" of the body, or the general state of health (akin to tonic action). In contrast, some emmenagogues, more likely to be considered as potential abortifacients, were believed to have a "direct" action on the uterus (sometimes referred to as oxytocics) or on nearby pelvic organs. A key example of a natural substance having a direct action on the uterus was ergot, which by the mid-1800s had become commonly used in medical practice to assist slow labor. Not surprisingly, ergot became very much part of the "criminal" abortion scene, even though it soon became recognized that the effect of ergot extracts on early pregnancies (for abortion purposes) was inconsistent.[19]

The uncertain reputation of iron was compounded by the fact that, in improving the state of health, it was also considered to ease menorrhagia, the opposite of amenorrhoea; in consequence, one authority stated in 1842 that "We cannot, therefore, regard the preparations of this metal as having any direct emmenagogue effect, as some have supposed."[20] Given the diversity of medical

---

[17] [Women's Co-operative Guild,] *Maternity Letters from Working-Women collected by the Women's Co-operative Guild* (London: Bell, 1915), 45 (emphasis added). Some home medicine books probably left readers with uncertainty. For instance, physician John King, *The American Family Physician; or Domestic Guide to Health* (Indianapolis: Robert Douglas, 1878), 233, after listing 22 botanical emmenagogues, added a noncommittal statement: "These medicines are supposed to influence the sexual organs as to bring on and regulate the menstrual function."

[18] For comment on witnesses, Taylor, *Principles and Practice* (1905), 2:169.

[19] For one mid-century discussion as a "special parturifacient," Robley Dunglison, *General Therapeutics and Materia Medica* (2 vols, Philadelphia: Lea & Blanchard, 1850), 1:425–30. For comment on its being part of the abortion scene, Taylor and Stevenson, *The Principles and Practice* (1883), 2:191.

[20] Pereira, *Elements*, 1:831. At the time, another British authority reinforced this opinion in writing that there is "no proof of any of the substances styled emmenagogues producing their effects by any specific influence on the uterine system." (J.A. Paris, *Pharmacologia, being an Extended Inquiry into the Operations of Medicinal Bodies* [London: Highley, 1843], 212.) And, in the U.S., Dunglison (*General Therapeutics*, 1:413) strongly expressed the view that amenorrhoea is most commonly "connected with a state of atony of the general system."

opinions, even physicians who had little confidence in iron as having consistent emmenagogue activity, but who recognized that women often tried it as an abortifacient, were probably reassured to hear in 1870—a year before the Wallis trial—about the clinical experiences of a Dr Woodman, who had constantly prescribed iron for the anaemia of pregnant women "for the last nine years without the fear of ill result."[21]

Leaving aside the adversarial nature of a criminal trial and how circumstantial and scientific evidence can be woven together and shaped by social attitudes, the above comments suggest that the prosecutors in the Wallis trial had difficulty in responding to defense experts who "agreed that Griffiths's [*sic*] mixture was a good iron tonic, that it was not an abortive, and in the small quantity taken by the prosecutrix could have had no effect in producing abortion."[22] However, the prosecution had another opening, namely that Griffith's mixture, as already noted, also contained myrrh that some viewed as the principal ingredient. Myrrh, a gum resin, classified as an aromatic bitter, entered the nineteenth century with a long history (invariably in compound preparations); its effects were commonly rationalized as associated with aromatic/bitter substances, namely to "warm and strengthen the viscera" and to "stimulate languid conditions" that included "suppression of the uterine discharges that proceed from a cold."[23] Griffith himself had made clear that myrrh was a significant ingredient in his mixture, although for treating "hectic and slow fevers." (As an aromatic bitter, it could be assumed to enhance diaphoresis, as well as improve the palatability of a medicinal preparation.[24]) He had no concern with its long, albeit inconsistent, history as an emmenagogue/abortifacient, although he did note its value for the "slow fever, which often attends chlorosis."[25] Robley Dunglison in 1850 misleadingly stated that the myrrh had been added on account of reputed emmenagogue virtues.[26] He said the same with regard to spirits of lavender used in American formulae.

---

21   "Obstetrical Society Report," *British Medical Journal* (1870): 1/141.

22   See Taylor and Stevenson, *Principles and Practice* (1883), 2:186.

23   William Lewis, *Edinburgh New Dispensatory* (London: Wingrave, 1799), 186. Various theories had rationalized sensory properties to suggest emmenagogue activity. For instance, John Friend referred to the astringent taste of "Cortex of Peru." He wrote that although "as yet, it obtains no place among the Emmenagogues; [it] ought however to be ranked with them upon the account of its remarkable effect on attenuating the Blood." (See John Friend, *Emmenologia* [London: T. Cox, 1729, English translation], 179.)

24   For Griffith's reference to its use "merely as a bitter" (in a modified formula), *Practical Observations*, 62. He acknowledged his formula was not wholly original (pp. iv–v).

25   Ibid., 6.

26   Dunglison, *General Therapeutics*, 2:62.

Although myrrh for treating menstrual irregularities continued to be mentioned in textbooks on materia medica for many years, nothing emerged to change the minds of those who doubted its efficacy as an abortifacient.[27] Indeed, influential Jonathan Pereira expounded (1842): "Myrrh has been supposed to have a specific stimulant operation on the uterus, and has, in consequence, been termed emmenagogue but it does not appear to have title to this appellation."[28] However, he did allow that a general stimulant action (associated with the "tonic-balsamic" property) lay behind use for a "disordered state of menstrual function characterized by a lax debilitated state of the system as in many cases of amenorrhoea and chlorosis."

At the time, the role of myrrh in Griffith's mixture was being indirectly challenged by Blaud's pills. Introduced in 1832 by Frenchman Pierre Blaud, their popularity for treating chlorosis soon spread to the English-speaking world. Also known as "chlorotic pills," they had the same basic iron compound, ferrous carbonate, as did Griffith's mixture (and Griffith's pills), but no myrrh. In fact, some doubts over the effectiveness of myrrh in Griffith's mixture also related to whether it was available for absorption from what was a complex mixture, as hinted at in the following note on its preparation:

> Double decomposition takes place ... The quantity of carbonate of potash directed to
> be used is almost twice as much as required to decompose the quantity of sulphate of
> iron ordered to be employed. The excess combines with the myrrh, and forms a kind
> of saponaceous compound, which assists in suspending the carbonate of iron in the
> liquid.[29]

Additional questions were raised about the quality of different varieties of myrrh on the market, as well as the best form of administration, maybe chewing the myrrh.[30]

It is not surprising that statements appeared expressing both uncertainty and skeptical views. George Wood mused: "Though I confess that I cannot bear a strong personal testimony to the emmenagogue properties of [myrrh]; yet the general medical opinion, which has so long maintained it among the

---

[27] Foster, *Reference-Book of Practical Therapeutics*, 1:651, stated, although not wholeheartedly, "Myrrh has slight stimulating properties that have been considered to influence especially the lungs and the uterus ... Internally myrrh has been used as a tonic in catarrhal gastritis, in gastralgia, in bronchorrhoea, in amenorrhoea, and in leucorrhoea."

[28] Pereira, *Elements*, 2:1631–2.

[29] Pereira, *Elements*, 1:862.

[30] For a sense of quality issues, Friedrich A. Flückiger and Daniel Hanbury, *Pharmacographia: A History of the Principal Drugs of Vegetable Origin* (London: Macmillan, 1879), 140–46.

standard remedies of amenorrhoea, can scarcely have been quite mistaken."[31] On the other hand, it was said in 1882: "Tradition and the habit of prescribers have ... invested [myrrh] with some supposed influence over the uterus; but no trustworthy evidence has ever been brought forward on this point, and it is more than probable that its emmenagogue influence is quite secondary to the other drugs in combination with which it is prescribed."[32]

One further wrinkle in the Griffith's mixture history is whether the combined action of iron and myrrh was more effective than anticipated from the independent effects of each substance alone. Although no hint of the possibility of synergistic action has been found, it is quite possible that some physicians felt this was the case.[33]

Pennyroyal

Conceivably, the prosecutors at the Wallis trial may have felt that the core of their case rested on pennyroyal, at least until it was said that it had not actually been taken. Even if it had, leaves were provided, presumably to make a tea (infusion). Although this herb had reputed emmenagogue properties, it was the pennyroyal oil (or "spirit of pennyroyal," a mix of oil and alcohol) that had a principal reputation as an emmenagogue/abortifacient.[34] The possibility exists, despite the absence of supporting evidence, that Wallis's defense was ready to argue that an infusion of the leaves was intended as a carminative (the plant belongs to the mint family) to settle the stomach if discomfort followed a dose of Griffith's mixture.

Given the various issues raised so far on the differences of opinion surrounding iron and myrrh, there is little need to detail the analogous situation that existed over pennyroyal, although it is useful to note the consequent ambivalence in the minds of many. British physician Charles Tidy, for example, would not commit himself in 1884; in noting the testimony of defense witnesses at the Wallis trial, and of "any author of repute" that pennyroyal was not an abortifacient, Tidy wrote, perhaps from his own experiences: "It is, however, frequently given for

---

[31]   George B. Wood, *A Treatise on Therapeutics and Pharmacology or Materia Medica* (2 vols, Philadelphia: Lippincott, 1868), 2:707.

[32]   Robert Farquharson, *A Guide to Therapeutics and Materia Medica*, 3rd American edition enlarged and adapted to U.S. Pharmacopoeia by Frank Woodbury (Philadelphia: Henry C. Lea's Son, 1882), 333–4.

[33]   For a sense of the issue of synergistic properties, Paris, *Pharmacologia*, 387–9.

[34]   For use of leaves, see, e.g., Lewis, *Edinburgh New Dispensatory*, 212–13.

this object, and certain facts known to the author make him hesitate in joining in this opinion of its absolute innocence."[35]

Certainly pennyroyal remained well known as part of women's public stock of knowledge about abortifacients. In 1907 a physician, when writing about "Emmenagogues in the Newspapers," covered pennyroyal oil in his general comments: "There is no known abortifacient which is certain, or anything like certain, in its action, but there can be no doubt that the unchecked administration to pregnant women of aloes, iron sulphate, and oil of pennyroyal, which with purgatives and carminatives, are the ingredients of nearly all these [female] nostrums—cannot fail to produce harmful and even possibly fatal results."[36] Such an opinion came at a time when the medical profession was expressing increasing concern over the availability of abortifacients. Some might see this as efforts to impose morality from a male-dominated profession, but the concern over potential toxic effects of the oil on the mother (and the baby if it survived) was supported by case histories.[37]

---

[35] Charles M. Tidy, *Legal Medicine* (New York: Wood, 1884), 105.

[36] Anonymous, "Emmenagogues in the Newspapers," *British Medical Journal* (1907): 2/1672–3.

[37] Concerns over toxicity were part of general worries over accidental and criminal poisonings increasingly viewed, in Britain at least, as a public health issue. It was also a time when, as many historians have noted, deliberate abortions were seemingly on the rise. It is noteworthy that one author has argued that the notion of iron preparations as abortifacients only became widespread in the late nineteenth and early twentieth centuries, linked to the "messages" of relieving obstructions and irregularities behind the marketing of secret "female remedies." (P.S. Brown, "Female Pills and the Reputation of Iron as an Abortifacient," *Medical History* 21 (1977): 291–304 (esp. 300).

As an example of one of various reports of cases of poisoning from pennyroyal: J. Girling, "Poisoning by Pennyroyal," *British Medical Journal* (1887): 1/1214. Although, in a later anonymous article "The Traffic in Abortifacients" (*British Medical Journal* [1899]: 1/110–11), there is some moralizing about criminal abortion, there is no reason to see that it biased the following opinion: "The [commercial female] pills generally given for the purpose are those containing iron or aloes, or both; and it is probable that in a few cases the irritation of the lower bowel so produced may bring about the expulsion of an early ovum." The article also stated: "Is it not time for medical witnesses to recognize and make known that there are no drugs which have any appreciable effect?"

Approaching Therapeutic Uncertainties: Differing Views

Around the time of the Wallis trial various shades of information found in medical textbooks and journals or heard at medical society meetings challenged many existing treatments and promoted new ones. Physicians found themselves in quandaries over numerous treatment regimens. Nevertheless, at the same time, nineteenth-century trends in medicine offered new ways to approach therapeutic uncertainty, which, as already said, had long frustrated physicians and patients alike.

Although the trends can only be noted here briefly, my comments should make clear that any lack of interest or forgetfulness on the part of physicians over many emmenagogues/abortifacients rested on more than moral concerns over improper or criminal usage. Additional to continuing "reform" of the materia medica that had been well under way in the eighteenth century—namely simplifying formulae and expunging from pharmacopoeias medicines that were little used or of inconsistent activity—new trends included: (1) a growing emphasis on the "numerical method," or "medical statistics" as it was called by 1850;[38] (2) increasing numbers of clinical trials, albeit relatively unsophisticated in dealing with potential biases; (3) studies on actions of drugs and poisons on animals, all of which accelerated longstanding interest in finding specific medicines for specific diseases;[39] (4) changing theories of diseases and modes of drug action, in part from advances in pathology brought about by improved microscope lenses and chemical tests; (5) developments to improve the standardization of medicines; and (6) new diagnostic tools that, if not always adding precision to a diagnosis, might offer guidance in, for example, responding to a woman's complaint of a single missed menstrual period. Was it a sign of pregnancy, an indication of developing chlorosis, or some other condition? In turn, the guidance could help with a decision on, say, whether Griffith's mixture should be prescribed, or whether pennyroyal was safe as a carminative (iron preparations could always upset the stomach).[40]

Despite difficulties for physicians in sifting "the results of true from false observations" in the rapidly expanding medical literature recording the

---

[38]   Dunglison, *General Therapeutics*, 1:37–8.

[39]   The search for specific medicines has attracted much attention; for some relevant commentary pertaining to the nineteenth century, Warner, *The Therapeutic Perspective*, various pages, but especially 250–57.

[40]   It seems that, by the mid-1800s, pennyroyal was rarely prescribed. See Pereira, *Elements*, 2:1200. Despite lack of popularity, preparations were still included in pharmacopoeias.

trends, new approaches to evaluating therapeutic outcomes emerged.[41] These approaches aimed to standardize and thus reduce variability in a physician's personal observations and experiences as well as provide greater confidence in establishing what was average or normal in clinical practice. Thus, together, the new approaches can be viewed as a new chapter in a longstanding debate on the roles of theory and experience in trying to determine therapeutic effectiveness.

To appreciate better the nature of this change, it is appropriate to recognize that the debate had already been heightened in the eighteenth century with new treatments and emphasis on the value of case histories, albeit supplemented by growing interest in clinical trials and experimentation. In 1776 Moses Griffith made an indirect reference to the debate when describing experiences with his mixture: "It is generally acknowledged, that, in matters of this kind, experience is a surer guide than theory and speculative reasoning" so that a "fair trial of the medicines may effectively remove any prejudices against them."[42] The remark on speculative reasoning was an obvious reference to the many new theories that had emerged in previous decades.

Like other physicians, Griffith's advocacy of "experience" did not rely on his alone. To a greater or lesser extent, personal experiences were compared with and monitored by those reported in textbooks, journals, and by colleagues.[43] Nevertheless, it was still easy to overlook the pitfalls and limitations of experience, as was made clear by William Cullen, the eighteenth-century medical authority who influenced the practice of many physicians until well into the next century. He critiqued the observations of medical authorities of the past and listed general reasons for errors in a physician's reliance on personal experiences. For instance, of his own clinical practice Cullen wrote: "In all cases, therefore, where medicines show active parts, I advise farther trials to be made, as I may not have emphasised large enough doses, nor have adapted them properly in the circumstances of disease."[44] His remarks made clear that "an attachment to particular theories" could account for general usage of what he felt to be an

---

[41]   For sifting, Robley Dunglison, *New Remedies: Pharmaceutically and Therapeutically Considered* (Philadelphia: Lea & Blanchard, 1843), 9.

[42]   Griffith, *Practical Observations*, vii.

[43]   Although Griffith did not cite other authors, he made clear that he often consulted with other physicians over patients. For some consideration of how experience was used in one eighteenth-century practice, see John K. Crellin, "Mentors and Formulae: Continuity and Change in Eighteenth-century Therapeutics," in Jürgen Helm and Renate Wilson (eds), *Medical Theory and Therapeutic Practice in the Eighteenth Century: A Transatlantic Perspective* (Stuttgart: Steiner, 2008), 176–96.

[44]   William Cullen, *A Treatise of the Materia Medica* (2 vols, Dublin: Luke White, 1789), 1:xii. For his discussion on mistakes, see the section "Of acquiring the Knowledge of the Virtues of Medicines by Experience," 1:114–24.

ineffective remedy, and that fallibilities existed in collective experience perhaps from overreliance on authorities when a physician's own experiences were limited. Moreover, finding comparable cases could be problematic at a time when much attention was given to evaluating the constitution and personal habits of a patient when making a diagnosis (of disease *plus* patient) in order to decide on an individualized treatment regimen.

Cullen, too, commented specifically on emmenagogues, and hinted that, since many claims were false, abortifacient action was even less likely; he underscored a critical tone that helped to set the scene for nineteenth-century writers on therapeutics to incorporate the already mentioned new trends as they tried to synthesize experience and theory.[45] Robley Dunglison, for one, admonished readers in 1850 to remember that the treatment of disease "requires—contrary to what has been confirmed by the empirics—not simply observation, but the constant use of reason to rectify the erroneous impressions, which imperfect observation—imperfect that is without it—so often occasions."[46]

Although the nineteenth-century trends inexorably changed clinical practice, many reasons accounted for the uneven initial reception of many aspects among physicians. Practitioners who promoted the trends as part of a sense of "progress" in medicine were in the vanguard of questioning many existing medicines, including emmenagogues. They supported such questioning on grounds already noted such as few emmenagogues having a direct effect on the uterus (unlike the well-known ergot), and also the inconsistency of action recognized by physicians and women. The thinking of such practitioners may also have been shaped by professional biases against the longstanding herbal emmenagogues; after all, the nineteenth century witnessed intense confrontations between orthodox medicine and those, in belonging to various medical sects, who promoted herbs and other "natural" practices as alternatives to conventional treatments.

In contrast, there were always physicians who were more cautious about change and less likely to dismiss remedies that, seemingly, had withstood the test of time. Certainly, the ambivalence some authors expressed over myrrh and pennyroyal as emmenagogues is an indication of the unevenness of changing practice. Indeed, an historian has suggested strongly that one of the characteristics of nineteenth-century change was the relatively static nature of

---

[45]   For Cullen's comment on emmenagogues, ibid., 1:118.

[46]   Dunglison, *General Therapeutics*, 1:38. He added (p. 43): "It behooves the student to observe well for himself—carefully, repeatedly; yet not to discard the observations of others; to reject not all at once as apocryphal, or to hold as no binding authority, all the traditions of the fathers, unless they are sustained and sanctioned by his own experience."

therapy, despite many new additions to the physician's armamentarium.[47] The persistence of remedies increasingly viewed by contemporaries as ineffective is an important feature of therapeutic uncertainty that cannot be elaborated here except that it is useful to note one aspect illustrated by George Bernard Shaw's thoughts on patients' therapeutics; he reminded physicians in the preface (1911) to his play *The Doctor's Dilemma* that, when a patient has a prejudice, the doctor must either "keep it in countenance or lose his patient ... If he gets ahead of the superstitions of his patients he is a ruined man."[48]

Among other reasons for a slow embrace of changes, Dunglison noted that the new "number medicine" was more "applicable to the phenomenon presented by the healthy or diseased economy than to the therapeutics or the treatment of disease."[49] The new statistical approach certainly discouraged attention to anecdotal information with the greater likelihood of dismissal of popular stories of emmenagogues acting as abortifacients, especially since natural abortions of unknown cause were known to be commonplace. Older physicians in particular might feel that the trends were taking the focus away from clinical skills that assessed the constitution and temperaments of the patient. Nowadays this is likely to be viewed as a loss of individualized therapy, although not so much loss of "holistic care" as understood today when it refers to attending to the mind and spirit, but the loss of attention to regimens suited to improving the general state of health to facilitate natural healing of a specific ailment.[50]

Undoubtedly, it was easy for physicians to be overwhelmed by the mass of information from new trends that focused on the disease, and specific action of new remedies. This allowed physician William Osler, with his inestimable influence on medicine in the late nineteenth century and beyond, to complain

---

[47] M.A. Flannery, "What Did Doctors Really Do? In Search of a Therapeutic Perspective of American Medicine," *Journal of Clinical Pharmacy and Therapeutics* 24 (1999): 151–6. The persistence of remedies is also noted by Charles E. Rosenberg, "The Therapeutic Revolution: Medicine, Meaning, and Social Change in Nineteenth-century America," in his *Explaining Epidemics and Other Studies in the History of Medicine* (Cambridge: Cambridge University Press, 1992), 9–31.

[48] George Bernard Shaw, *The Doctor's Dilemma, Getting Married, & The Shewing-Up of Blanco Posnet* (London: Constable, 1924), lxxiv.

[49] Dunglison, *General Therapeutics*, 1:38.

[50] To reinforce the emphasis on individual therapeutics, it is noteworthy how Dunglison, in discussing amenorrhoea as an aspect of the general "body systems," focused on the needs of the individual: "the plan of medication must, in all cases, vary according to the state of the general health." (*General Therapeutics*, 1:414; see also 2:55.) Yet it can be argued that concern with, say, individual constitutions gradually became associated more with the rise of various alternative (sectarian) medical reform movements in the nineteenth century such as phrenology and hydropathy.

of physicians who did not appreciate the difference between giving medicines and treating a disease, in other words caring more for the disease than for the patient.[51]

Some Summary Comments

By the time of the Wallis trial, medicine had changed considerably since 1771 when physician Henry Manning—at a time when therapeutic uncertainty was clearly in the minds of practitioner and patient alike—stated: "There is no disease in which the indications of cure are more various, or where greater precision is necessary in forming a judgment of the cause, than in menstrual obstructions. For medicines which are proper in one case may prove ineffectual or even harmful in another."[52] Thereafter, a gradual shift occurred from individualized regimens towards tendencies to accept a "one medicine fits all" approach.

Coping with therapeutic uncertainty was also changing through the trends already noted, often described today as reductionist. This shift could only accentuate polarized views and encourage a sharpening of differences of opinion such as those expressed at the Wallis trial. For physicians who followed the new trends (and new "good practices"), many longstanding emmenagogues failed to reach the new criteria of collective "professional" wisdom, namely observations controlled by widespread experiences, consistent action, and compatibility with new physiological/pharmacological knowledge. On the other hand, other physicians, who remained ambivalent and were less committed to a mindset that a remedy either does or does not "work," continued to see the need to find an appropriate remedy and regimen for the individual patient, perhaps taking into account the latter's wishes.

Given the shifts in attitudes and practices, it is appropriate to add an additional thought, namely whether any effective remedies were pushed aside by

---

[51]   For giving medicines and treating disease, see William Osler, "The Treatment of Disease," reprinted in John P. McGovern and Charles G. Roland (eds), *The Collected Essays of Sir William Osler* (3 vols, Birmingham: Classics of Medicine Library, 1985), 2:357–76, at 365. For emphasis on the disease rather than the patient, see the quotation in Mark E. Silverman, T. Jock Murray, and Charles S. Bryan (eds), *The Quotable Osler* (Philadelphia: American College of Physicians, 2003), 43.

[52]   For a sense of the uncertainty at the time, M. Stolberg, "Therapeutic Pluralism and Conflicting Medical Opinions in the Eighteenth Century," in Helm and Wilson, *Medical Theory and Practice in the Eighteenth Century*, 95–111. For the quotation: Henry Manning, *A Treatise on Female Diseases: In which are also comprehended those most incident to Pregnant and Child-Bed Women* (London: Baldwin, 1771), 74.

the eighteenth- and nineteenth-century efforts to limit therapeutic uncertainty. Such a question is prompted by Riddle and others who stress the importance of herbal histories as a way to uncover evidence of effectiveness.[53] Of course, the resources of history always need critical evaluation amid a multiplicity of pitfalls, a number of which are discussed in recent publications.[54] At the very least, it should be determined whether a need exists to demonstrate that a usage was relatively mainstream over a lengthy period of time and to examine closely the reasons for the inconsistent information in texts. It is always important to appreciate that multiple uses are commonly listed for remedies; many of these fit today's designation of "off-label" or non-recommended, sometimes idiosyncratic, uses not generally accepted. Evaluation must assess whether a reputation continues to draw on additional and comparable clinical experience over time (even if this does not discount placebo action), rather than merely slavish copying from earlier texts as has often been the case.

A lasting legacy of Riddle's work is the challenge to historians to study therapies, a challenge sometimes overlooked amid polarized opinions such as those noted in Box 10.1. Hopefully, my discussion fits with others who see the importance of the challenge, while offering a reminder that the nature of therapeutics is complex. I end with another quotation from William Osler (1886): "In therapeutics we do not so much need new remedies as a fuller knowledge of when and how to use the old ones."[55] Although directed to physicians in 1886, I suggest that nowadays the quotation can be seen as a call for historians to examine a remedy in the context of the difficulties a clinician has always faced in coping with uncertainty amid medical and social disagreements and changes.

---

[53] The question of effectiveness must also consider why "new" examples were suddenly listed in some textbooks, for example, alcohol (as an "indirect emmenagogue") and cod-liver oil (a "direct emmenagogue"); see S.O.L. Potter, *Therapeutics, Materia Medica and Pharmacy*, ed. Elmer H. Funk (Philadelphia: Blakiston's Son, 1917), 32.

[54] For a recent discussion, John K. Crellin, "'Traditional Use' Claims for Herbs: The Need for Competent Historical Research," *Pharmaceutical Historian* 38 (2008): 34–40. Many accounts also consider why ineffective uses continued; for instance, Janet F. Brodie, "Menstrual Interventions in the Nineteenth-century United States," in Étienne Van de Walle and Elisha P. Renne (eds), *Regulating Menstruation: Beliefs, Practices, Interpretations* (Chicago: University of Chicago Press, 2001), 39–63 (esp. 51–4). Also Santow, "Emmenagogues and Abortifacients in the Twentieth Century," ibid., 64–92 (esp. 81–4).

[55] Silverman, Murray, and Bryan, *The Quotable Osler*, 167.

Bibliography

Anonymous. "The Traffic in Abortifacients." *British Medical Journal* (1899): 1/110–111.

Anonymous. "Emmenagogues in the Newspapers." *British Medical Journal* (1907): 2/1672–3.

Bartholow, Roberts. *A Practical Treatise on Materia Medica and Therapeutics.* New York: Appleton, 1881.

Bilger, Burkhard. Review of John M. Riddle, *Eve's Herbs: A History of Contraception and Abortion in the West. HerbalGram* 45 (1999): 70.

Bradley, James, and Marguerite Dupree. "A Shadow of Orthodoxy? An Epistemology of British Homeopathy, 1840–1858." *Medical History* 47 (2003): 173–94.

Brodie, Janet F. "Menstrual Interventions in the Nineteenth-century United States." In Étienne Van de Walle and Elisha P. Renne (eds), *Regulating Menstruation: Beliefs, Practices, Interpretations*, 39–63. Chicago: University of Chicago Press, 2001.

Brown, P.S. "Female Pills and the Reputation of Iron as an Abortifacient." *Medical History* 21 (1977): 291–304.

Brumberg, Joan J. "Chlorotic Girls, 1870–1920: A Historical Perspective on Female Adolescence." *Child Development* 53 (1982): 1468–77.

Churchill, Fleetwood. *Outlines of the Principal Diseases of Females.* Dublin: Martin Keene & Son, 1838.

Crellin, John K. "Mentors and Formulae: Continuity and Change in Eighteenth-century Therapeutics." In Jürgen Helm and Renate Wilson (eds), *Medical Theory and Therapeutic Practice in the Eighteenth Century: A Transatlantic Perspective*, 176–96. Stuttgart: Steiner, 2008.

———. "'Traditional Use' Claims for Herbs: The Need for Competent Historical Research." *Pharmaceutical Historian* 38 (2008): 34–40.

Cule, John. "The Iron Mixture of Dr. Griffith." *Pharmaceutical Journal* 198 (1967): 399–401.

Cullen, William. *A Treatise of the Materia Medica.* 2 vols. Dublin: Luke White, 1789.

Dunglison, Robley. *New Remedies: Pharmaceutically and Therapeutically Considered.* Philadelphia: Lea & Blanchard, 1843.

———. *General Therapeutics and Materia Medica.* 2 vols. Philadelphia: Lea & Blanchard, 1850.

Farquharson, Robert. *A Guide to Therapeutics and Materia Medica.* 3rd American edition enlarged and adapted to U.S. Pharmacopoeia by Frank Woodbury. Philadelphia: Henry C. Lea's Son, 1882.

Ferngren, Gary B. Review of John M. Riddle, *Eve's Herbs: A History of Contraception and Abortion in the West*. *New England Journal of Medicine* 337 (1997): 1398.

Flannery, M.A. "What Did Doctors Really Do? In Search of a Therapeutic Perspective of American Medicine." *Journal of Clinical Pharmacy and Therapeutics* 24 (1999): 151–6.

Flemming, Rebecca. Review of John M. Riddle, *Eve's Herbs: A History of Contraception and Abortion in the West*. *Isis* 90 (1999): 102–3.

Flückiger, Friedrich A., and Daniel Hanbury. *Pharmacographia: A History of the Principal Drugs of Vegetable Origin*. London: Macmillan, 1879.

Foster, Frank P. (ed.). *Reference-Book of Practical Therapeutics*. 2 vols. New York: Appleton, 1899.

Friend, John. *Emmenologia*. London: T. Cox, 1729.

Girling, J. "Poisoning by Pennyroyal." *British Medical Journal* (1887): 1/1214.

Griffith, Moses. *Practical Observations on the Cure of Hectic and Slow Fevers, and the Pulmonary Consumption*. London: Benjamin Wright, 1776.

Hall, Lesley A. Review of John M. Riddle, *Eve's Herbs: A History of Contraception and Abortion in the West*. *American Historical Review* 103 (1998): 1211–12.

Hooper, Robert. *Lexicon-Medicum or Medical Dictionary*. New York: Harper, 1826.

Hudson, Robert P. "The Biography of Disease: Lessons from Chlorosis." *Bulletin of the History of Medicine* 51 (1977): 448–63.

King, John. *The American Family Physician; or Domestic Guide to Health*. Indianapolis: Robert Douglas, 1878.

Lewis, William. *Edinburgh New Dispensatory*. London: Wingrave, 1799.

Manning, Henry. *A Treatise on Female Diseases: In which are also comprehended those most incident to Pregnant and Child-Bed Women*. London: Baldwin, 1771.

"Obstetrical Society Report." *British Medical Journal* (1870): 1/141.

Osler, William. *The Principles and Practice of Medicine*. New York: Appleton, 1892.

———. "The Treatment of Disease." Reprinted in John P. McGovern and Charles G. Roland (eds), *The Collected Essays of Sir William Osler*, 2:357–76. 3 vols. Birmingham: Classics of Medicine Library, 1985.

Paris, J.A. *Pharmacologia, being an Extended Inquiry into the Operations of Medicinal Bodies*. London: Highley, 1843.

Pender, Stephen. "Examples and Experience: On the Uncertainty of Medicine." *British Journal of the History of Science* 39 (2006): 1–28.

Pereira, Jonathan. *The Elements of Materia Medica and Therapeutics*. 2 vols. London: Longman, 1842.

Pharmacopoeia of the United States of America. Boston: Wells and Lilly, 1820.

Potter, S.O.L. *Therapeutics, Materia Medica and Pharmacy.* Ed. Elmer H. Funk. Philadelphia: Blakiston's Son, 1917.

Quincy, John. *A Complete English Dispensatory.* London: Bell, 1719.

Rennie, James. *A New Supplement to the Latest Pharmacopoeias of London, Edinburgh, Dublin and Paris.* London: Baldwin & Cradock, 1837.

Riddle, John M. *Contraception and Abortion from the Ancient World to the Renaissance.* Cambridge, MA: Harvard University Press, 1992.

———. *Eve's Herbs: A History of Contraception and Abortion in the West.* Cambridge, MA: Harvard University Press, 1997.

———. *Goddesses, Elixirs, and Witches: Plants and Sexuality throughout Human History.* New York: Palgrave Macmillan, 2010.

Rosenberg, Charles E. "The Therapeutic Revolution: Medicine, Meaning, and Social Change in Nineteenth-century America." In Charles E. Rosenberg, *Explaining Epidemics and Other Studies in the History of Medicine,* 9–31. Cambridge: Cambridge University Press, 1992.

Santow, Gigi. "Emmenagogues and Abortifacients in the Twentieth Century: An Issue of Ambiguity." In Étienne van der Walle and Elisha P. Renne (eds), *Regulating Menstruation: Beliefs, Practices, Interpretations,* 64–92. Chicago: University of Chicago Press, 2001.

Shaw, George Bernard. *The Doctor's Dilemma, Getting Married, & The Shewing-Up of Blanco Posnet.* London: Constable, 1924.

Silverman, Mark E., T. Jock Murray, and Charles S. Bryan (eds). *The Quotable Osler.* Philadelphia: American College of Physicians, 2003.

Stillé, Alfred. *Therapeutics and Materia Medica.* 2 vols. Philadelphia: Blanchard & Lea, 1864.

Stockman, Ralph. "The Treatment of Chlorosis by Iron and Some Other Drugs." *British Medical Journal* (1893): 1/881–5 and 942–4.

Stolberg, M. "Therapeutic Pluralism and Conflicting Medical Opinions in the Eighteenth Century." In Jürgen Helm and Renate Wilson (eds), *Medical Theory and Therapeutic Practice in the Eighteenth Century: A Transatlantic Perspective,* 95–111. Stuttgart: Steiner, 2008.

Taylor, A. Swaine, and T. Stevenson. *The Principles and Practice of Medical Jurisprudence.* 2 vols. London: Churchill, 1883.

Taylor, A. Swaine. *Principles and Practice of Medical Jurisprudence.* Ed. F.J. Smith. 2 vols. London: Churchill, 1905.

Thomson, Anthony T. *The London Dispensatory.* London: Longman, 1811.

Tidy, Charles M. *Legal Medicine.* New York: Wood, 1884.

Warner, John H. *The Therapeutic Perspective: Medical Practice, Knowledge, and Identity in America, 1820–1885.* Princeton: Princeton University Press, 1997.

[Women's Co-operative Guild.] *Maternity Letters from Working-Women collected by the Women's Co-operative Guild.* London: Bell, 1915.

Wood, George B. *A Treatise on Therapeutics and Pharmacology or Materia Medica.* 2 vols. Philadelphia: Lippincott, 1868.

Chapter 11

Modding Medievalists: Designing a Web-based Portal for the Medieval Plant Survey/ Portal der Pflanzen des Mittelalters (MPS/PPM)

Helmut W. Klug and Roman Weinberger[1]

> "Modding" is a slang expression that is derived from the verb "to modify." The term can refer to the act of modifying a piece of hardware or software or anything else for that matter ...[2]

In recent decades, scholars have increasingly asserted the value of ancient and medieval medical lore, among them John M. Riddle, who early championed its importance and value. During his long career, Riddle has demonstrated that the medicine practiced by our distant ancestors is greatly undervalued and that a key to this medical knowledge is an understanding of the people relying on it. In his studies of Dioscorides, in his research on the use of contraceptives, and in his approach toward a myriad topics, astounding results have emerged, all of which provide valuable data for modern pharmacognosy—it is here that Riddle most effectively combines traditional knowledge with contemporary research.[3] Encouraged by these pioneering efforts, today many scholars from

---

[1]   Research was divided according to competence; the collective "we" throughout the article indicates that Helmut Klug mainly contributed on medieval matters, Roman Weinberger on psychological and technical topics.

[2]   Wikipedia, "Modding," http://en.wikipedia.org/wiki/Modding. All URLs cited in notes were active as of February 20, 2012.

[3]   See John M. Riddle, *Dioscorides on Pharmacy and Medicine* (Austin: University of Texas Press, 1985); John M. Riddle, *Eve's Herbs: A History of Contraception and Abortion in the West* (Cambridge: Cambridge University Press, 1997); John M. Riddle, "Historical Data as an Aid in Pharmaceutical Prospecting and Drug Safety Determination," *Journal of Alternative and Complementary Medicine* 5 (1999): 195–201; and John M. Riddle, "History as a Tool in

various disciplines work on historical medicine, pharmacy, and botany, with the result that a need has arisen to unite these efforts. Our portal, the Medieval Plant Survey/Portal der Pflanzen des Mittelalters (MPS/PPM),[4] aims at filling this need. It can also serve as a prototype for other collaborative ventures using Internet resources, especially as we intend to make the necessary software available on an open source basis.

The Internet is a rich source for information and is the primary modern means of communication; it can be used as a publicly available storage space or as a presentation platform. In recent years, it has gained a good reputation within the academic community as a source for electronically readable texts, online dictionaries, or Web-accessible databases. The central concept of Web 2.0[5]—to give the user a means to create the content of a Web site—has not yet been fully accepted for academic research. Moreover, the content of Web sites that rely on the collaboration of their users (for example, Wikipedia) is regarded skeptically by the academic community—an attitude we fully support.[6] Nevertheless, "modding" contemporary medieval research strategies and adapting them to modern technologies will help design the research strategies of the future, when collaboration of specialists could be the primary means to achieve significant, universally acceptable results. Thus, this paper outlines a way to bring together experts in a wide variety of disciplines from all over the world to contribute to and work on a central topic, the plants of the Middle Ages—a topic as differentiated as it can get. As noted earlier, our project can serve as a model for similar research projects.

Before we studied possible technical solutions for the MPS/PPM online platform, we assessed the current status of electronic and online aids for researching medieval plants. Considerable effort was directed at collecting and evaluating resources that (a) are suitable for academic research, (b) deal with plants of the Middle Ages, and (c) are available on the Internet.[7] Our search was focused on Web sites with general scholarly content, electronic texts, and/

Identifying 'New' Old Drugs," in Bóla S. Buslig and John A. Manthey (eds), *Flavonoids in Cell Function* (New York: Kluwer Academic Publishers, 2002), 89–94.

   4   http://medieval-plants.org.

   5   Cf. Tim O'Reilly, "What is Web 2.0?" at http://www.oreillynet.com/pub/a/oreilly/tim/news/2005/09/30/what-is-Web-20.html, September 30, 2005.

   6   The main point of criticism is that the qualifications of the authors cannot be verified and consequently the information available cannot be assessed adequately. Therefore, many think it is not safe to use sources such as Wikipedia for scholarly work.

   7   Here we mainly concentrate on resources for Old English and Old High German/Middle High German concerning linguistic, literary, and cultural studies, these being the fields of our current research. "Resources" include both tools for conducting research and also published research results. We here describe the situation as of 2009. Since then the Humanities have

or collections of medical plant illustrations. Surprisingly and sadly, there is very, very little to report.

For both German and English medieval studies, there are online "umbrella organizations" that are meant to channel and support scholarly research. The Medieval Academy of America states its goal as "the support of research, publication, and teaching in medieval art, archeology, history, law, literature, music, philosophy, religion, science, social and economic institutions, and all other aspects of the Middle Ages."[8] The organization's Web site offers information on its own journal and book series, meetings and conferences, and fellows and graduate students. The organization seems to be well structured and its Web site a good source for general information on organizational matters. The plant researcher might profit from the link to the Voigts-Kurz Search Program, a database on scientific and medical texts of the Middle Ages at the University of Missouri-Kansas City.[9] The overall site search provided two links, one dealing with the development of Penn State University's medieval garden, the other referring only to the homonymous "plant = factory." Mediaevum.de is a European online portal for German and Latin medieval studies (a comparable English-language site is The Labyrinth: Resources for Medieval Studies).[10] The European Web site is privately organized by several scholars and concentrates on collecting relevant and reliable scholarly resources and tools. The links presented range from information on organizations, research tools, bibliographies, and collections of electronically available texts to manuscripts and manuscript databases. Several sub-pages are dedicated to presenting valuable resources for students. The site search generated ten suitable hits, all of which are from the various available bibliographies or the journal database. There are no references to resources directly dealing with plant studies.

Attributing these rather poor results to our highly specialized topic, we resorted to Google and tried its unfailing databases. But regardless of which search engine and what search terms we used the results were less and less satisfactory, especially when analyzing the hits for academic relevance.[11] In the

---

become considerably more digital but the overall situation for medieval plant research has not changed much.

8   Medieval Academy of America, "About Us," http://www.medievalacademy.org/about/about.htm.

9   http://cctr1.umkc.edu/cgi-bin/search.

10   http://www.mediaevum.de; http://labyrinth.georgetown.edu/. Apparently the latter Web site is no longer maintained.

11   For English-language resources we used http://www.google.com and the search terms "medieval," "Middle Ages," "plants," "herb," "herbal medicine," etc., in various combinations; for searching the German-language database Google Österreich (http://www.google.at) we used

end only a few, already well-known resources remained. Old English plants, or more specifically their names, are comprehensively represented by the Anglo-Saxon Plant-Names Survey (ASPNS)[12] and the Dictionary of Old English Plant Names (DOEPN).[13] The ASPNS is a decentralized organization, and the Web site has only general information, such as plant lists, select bibliography, and annual reports. Its interdisciplinary research is conducted by "ASPNS-authors" who are aided by specialized "ASPNS-advisers." Currently the DOEPN Web site, which is based on the work of Peter Bierbaumer,[14] offers interlinked Old English, Latin, Modern English, and German plant-name indices; all entries have been brought up to date to reflect more current research results. We found no other relevant scholarly English-language sources dealing with plants of the Middle Ages. Concerning German-language sources, the Web site of the Forschergruppe Klostermedizin, a collaboration between the Institute for Medical History at the University of Würzburg and the pharmaceutical company Abtei, reports most promising research and even offers some plant portraits with a diachronic perspective, but overall the Web site holds little content for academic use.[15] There are no other relevant scholarly resources to be found. Summing up on these resources, we conclude that the Internet has not been accepted as a means for publishing academic research; the majority is handled by publishing companies, and consequently distribution is limited, especially when compared to the possibilities the Internet has to offer.[16]

---

the key words "Kräuter," "Kräutermedizin," "Medizin," "Mittelalter," "Pflanze," etc. We looked at only the first 50 hits displayed. Most were either Web sites from universities advertising medieval studies or pages presented by historical reenactment societies. We are, of course, aware that these databases map only the so-called "surface Web"; there may be more resources available in the "deep Web," but as they are intentionally or unintentionally hidden from inquirers, they are of no use for this study—or to anyone else, for that matter.

[12]   http://www.gla.ac.uk/departments/englishlanguage/research/researchprojects/anglo-saxonplant-namessurvey/. The ASPNS was a great source of inspiration; we want to thank Dr Carole Biggam, the director of ASPNS, for her critical but always helpful advice on planning MPS/PPM.

[13]   http://oldenglish-plantnames.uni-graz.at.

[14]   Peter Bierbaumer, *Der botanische Wortschatz des Altenglischen* (3 vols, Frankfurt am Main: Lang, 1975–79).

[15]   http://www.klostermedizin.de.

[16]   A striking example is the pricing policy of publishers and "online libraries" like SpringerLink (http://www.springerlink.com); on this topic, see Helmut W. Klug, "Grundsätzliche Überlegungen rund um ein künftiges mediävistisches Text-Portal," in Wernfried Hofmeister and Andrea Hofmeister-Winter (eds), *Wege zum Text: Beiträge des Grazer Kolloquiums über die Verfügbarkeit mediävistischer Editionen im 21. Jahrhundert (17.–19. September 2008)* (Tübingen: Niemeyer, 2009), 121–31, at 125–6 and esp. n. 23.

Another problematic aspect is the availability of source texts, in either Greek, Latin, or the vernacular.[17] In short, there is a wide range of sources that provide e-texts to choose from, but in reality the number of documents available is rather small. For example, a search for *De materia medica* of Dioscorides on the Internet did not result in the expected mass of sources at all.[18] One of the first hits was one volume of the 1830 edition by Sprengel, which is available on Google Books. Scrolling down the hit list provided by Google, the next full-text source was the translation by Osbaldeston (2007), which is available on the Web site of an online magazine.[19] However, there is a third edition of Dioscorides' work available, too: the 1902 German translation by Berendes is on the Web as electronically enhanced scan-text.[20] Unfortunately, this version is not indexed well enough to be present in the hit list provided by Google. Besides looking for e-texts with the help of search engines, the researcher can fall back on various Web sites (privately as well as officially operated) for source texts. The most useful source for scientific historical e-texts is the Web site of Thomas Gloning of the German Faculty at the University of Giessen, who offers digital copies of a variety of herbals, cookbooks, and other historical texts.[21] There are of course other initiatives for digitizing historical texts; best known are the University of Virginia Digital Collection (i.e., the former "E-Text Center") and the Digital Middle High German Text Archive, both of which focus on poetic texts.[22] As more general sources, Google Books and Wikisource should be mentioned, the latter offering a variety of Greek and Latin texts.[23] The major obstacles all these Web sites face are the prevailing copyright laws, and for this reason a great number of the editions are outdated.

Copyright and other applicable laws are even more restrictive when dealing with images on the Internet. Besides the historical texts, depictions of plants are an important source of information. We are aware that opinions on this matter differ considerably; various scholars argue for and against the value of medieval

---

[17] The exception is Old English, which is available as a finalized corpus in the Corpus of Old English, published online and as a CD-Rom by the Toronto *Dictionary of Old English* project.

[18] We used the same method as described in n. 11. The search terms were "De materia medica," "Dioscorides," "full text," "e-text," and "De materia medica," "Dioskurides," "Volltext," "e-text." In Google Books we searched only for "full view only."

[19] *Cancerlynx: An Online Zine for Cancer Patients and Professionals*, http://www .cancerlynx.com/.

[20] http://buecher.heilpflanzen-welt.de/Dioskurides-Arzneimittellehre/.

[21] http://www.uni-giessen.de/gloning/.

[22] http://search.lib.virginia.edu/catalog?f[source_facet][]=Digital+Library; http://mhgta .uni-trier.de.

[23] http://wikisource.org.

plant images, but one should keep in mind that this is still the only means to link contemporary plants to their historical counterparts via visual evidence.[24] Since pictures as means of artistic decoration make manuscripts even more desirable for libraries and reproduction more costly, electronic sources are sparse. We differentiate between image collections based on different contributors and material provided on the basis of manuscript ownership by single libraries. Of the former there are two renowned projects; one is the Index of Medieval Medical Images and the other is the MacKinney Collection of Medieval Medical Illustrations.[25] Both offer *c.* 250 well-annotated images showing plant drawings derived from various manuscripts.[26] Looking for images provided by libraries is tedious work, and the researcher is well advised to know exactly what he is looking for and where to search. The outcome is respectable but hardly worth the effort. With its Catalogue of Illuminated Manuscripts, the British Library has a well-structured Web site and offers sample images from many manuscripts.[27] Other possible resources are available at the Pierpont Morgan Library, the Bodleian Library, and the Biblioteca Nazionale di Napoli.[28]

When attempting any interdisciplinary approach toward plants of the Middle Ages, problems start multiplying. Bernhard Schnell pointedly sums up the situation for the study of herbals and predicts a rather dark future:[29]

---

[24]   Constructive approaches toward this topic have been made by, for example, Minta Collins, *Medieval Herbals: The Illustrative Traditions* (Toronto: University of Toronto Press, 2000); Wolfgang Schiedermaier, "Pflanzenmalereien in drei unterfränkischen Kirchen: Ikonographie, Kunstgeschichte und aktuelle Bedeutung in Bezug auf die Entwicklung von Medizin und Pharmazie" (Ph.D. diss., Universität Würzburg, 2003); Ülle Sillasoo, "Medieval Plant Depictions as a Source for Archeobotanical Research," *Vegetation History and Archeobotany* 16 (2006): 61–70; Eva Wagner, "Untersuchungen zu Lesbarkeit und Aussagekraft von Pflanzendarstellungen in mittelalterlichen Kräuterbuchhandschriften am Beispiel des *Codex latinus monacensis* 28531" (Ph.D. diss., Universität Freiburg, 2006); and various publications of Maria Amalia D'Aronco, including "Gardens on Vellum: Plants and Herbs in Anglo-Saxon Manuscripts," in Peter Dendle and Alain Touwaide (eds), *Health and Healing from the Medieval Garden* (Rochester, NY: Boydell & Brewer, 2008), 101–27.

[25]   http://unitproj.library.ucla.edu/biomed/his/immi/; http://www.lib.unc.edu/dc/mackinney/.

[26]   Both Web sites seem to have the permissions to display the images; when other copyright-related matters are concerned both refer the user to the libraries holding the various manuscripts.

[27]   http://www.bl.uk/catalogues/illuminatedmanuscripts/.

[28]   Respectively http://www.themorgan.org/collections/collectionsMedRen.asp; http://image.ox.ac.uk/; and http://www.bnnonline.it/biblvir/dioscoride/index.htm.

[29]   Bernhard Schnell, "Pflanzen in Bild und Text: Zum Naturverständnis in den deutschsprachigen illustrierten Kräuterbüchern des Spätmittelalters," in Peter Dilg (ed.), *Natur im Mittelalter: Konzeptionen—Erfahrungen—Wirkungen. Akten des 9. Symposiums des Mediävistenverbandes, Marburg, 14.–17. März 2001* (Berlin: Akademie Verlag, 2003), 442–59, at 442–3.

Trotz der großen Bedeutung, welche die Kräuterbücher im Alltag des Mittelalters besaßen, ist die Erforschung dieser Texte—vor allem derjenigen, die vor dem Zeitalter des Buchdrucks liegen—immer noch in einem unwegsamen und verlassenen Niemandsland zwischen den angrenzenden Fächern Geschichte der Medizin, Pharmaziegeschichte, Botanik, Philologie und Kunstgeschichte angesiedelt, das zu betreten aus keiner Richtung einladend zu sein scheint, da es das Vertrautsein des Bearbeiters mit den Methoden und Erkenntnissen aller beteiligter Wissensgebiete erfordert. Angesichts der fortschreitenden Spezialisierung und Wissensvermehrung in den einschlägigen Einzeldisziplinen kann dies nur Utopie bleiben.

[In spite of the great importance herbals had for everyday life during the Middle Ages, research on these texts—especially those dating from before the age of print—is even now confined to a pathless and forsaken no-man's-land between the neighboring disciplines of history of medicine, history of pharmacy, botany, philology, and history of art. This no-man's-land appears to invite entry from no direction, because it demands the researcher's intimacy with the methods and findings of all the participating fields. Given the advancing specialization in researchers' training and the steady gain of knowledge in the relevant disciplines, this can only remain a utopia.]

To get to know medieval plants (or just a single plant) fully, it is mandatory to apply a holistic approach toward the topic. Using Schnell's list as a basis, expertise in the following fields of research (sorted alphabetically) is pertinent to studies of historical plant use: archeology, art history, botany, classical philology, folklore studies, history, linguistics, literary studies, medical and pharmaceutical history, pharmacy, and theology. It is equally necessary to make diachronic use of poetic, scientific, and theological texts in different languages, at least those of insular and continental Europe. Besides that, it would be helpful to know Hebrew and Arabic sources. Considering these needs, it is not surprising that the few existing attempts at interdisciplinary work can only scratch the surface of this inexhaustible topic and only focus on a few aspects.[30] This is where the planned MPS/PPM seeks to intervene: the Web-based platform can be a tool

---

[30] For example, the plant studies in Carole P. Biggam, _"Blue" in Old English: An Interdisciplinary Semantic Study_ (Amsterdam: Rodopi, 1997); Carole P. Biggam, _"Grey" in Old English: An Interdisciplinary Semantic Study_ (London: Runetree, 1998); Christine Becela-Deller, _Ruta graveolens L.: Eine Heilpflanze in kunst- und kulturhistorischer Bedeutung_ (Würzburg: Königshausen & Neumann, 1998); Thomas Richter, _Melissa officinalis L.: Ein Leitmotiv für 2000 Jahre Wissenschaftsgeschichte_ (Würzburg: Königshausen & Neumann, 1998); Dorit Wittlin, _Mandragora: Eine Arzneipflanze in Antike, Mittelalter und Neuzeit_ (Basel: Deitikon, 1999); and Anne Van Arsdall, Helmut W. Klug, and Paul Blanz, "The Mandrake Plant and Its Legend: A New Perspective," in Peter Bierbaumer and Helmut W. Klug (eds), _Old Names—New Growth:_

for collecting information as well as for cooperation; experts in the various disciplines conducting historical plant research can easily share knowledge and communicate ideas and problems. Interdisciplinary research and collaborative papers with international colleagues can be easily arranged, while individual scholars can place emphasis on their own fields of study.

The initial idea for this online portal came through the various projects the authors are working on. Developing the Dictionary of Old English Plant Names was an introduction to modern database design, content management, and online presentation as well as to the ideas and workings of the ASPNS.[31] Helmut Klug's dissertation was incipiently (and rather naively) conceived as a complementary approach toward plants in German medieval literature and has since been adapted several times. Finally it boiled down to collecting, structuring, and analyzing plants in Middle High German cooking recipes; the data and findings will be fed into the MPS/PPM database and will provide a sound basis for further work on medieval plants.[32] Working on a joint paper about the mandrake legend with Anne Van Arsdall and Paul Blanz confirmed Klug's belief in international and interdisciplinary collaboration.[33] His talk at the 2008 conference "Wege zum Text" finally connected all these facts with the idea of making this data available online to an academic community.[34] This thought was expressed earlier by other scholars, for example Minta Collins, who during her work with plant illustrations realized: "I do not consider that a proper study of these books can be made until far more work has been done on the text of the individual manuscripts—a vast undertaking that would involve several scholars working in different languages over a long period."[35] Carole Biggam of the ASPNS summarizes the merits of joint effort:[36]

Proceedings of the 2nd ASPNS Conference, University of Graz, Austria, 6–10 June 2007, and Related Essays (Frankfurt am Main: Lang, 2009), 285–346.

[31]   Helmut W. Klug and Roman Weinberger, "Old English Plant Names Go Cyber: The Technical Aspects of the Dictionary of Old English Plant Names Project," in Bierbaumer and Klug, *Old Names—New Growth*, 181–209.

[32]   The working title of the dissertation is "Plants in German Literature of the Middle Ages: A Data-base Supported Stocktaking with an Analysis of Literary, Linguistic and Cultural Contexts"; the anticipated completion date is the end of 2012.

[33]   Van Arsdall, Klug, and Blanz, "Mandrake Plant."

[34]   A podcast is available at the conference Web site: Wernfried Hofmeister, *Wege zum Text: Grazer germanistisches Kolloquium über die Verfügbarkeit mediävistischer Editionen im 21. Jahrhundert*, October 5, 2008, http://www.uni-graz.at/wernfried.hofmeister/wegezumtext/.

[35]   Collins, *Medieval Herbals*, 14.

[36]   Carole Biggam, "Anglo-Saxon Plant-Names Survey"; cf. n. 12 above.

It is expected that the value of the Survey [i.e., the ASPNS] will become even more apparent as the information accumulates, since it will provide data for further research into topics which are linguistic (e.g., dialect studies), geographic (e.g., land use studies), economic (e.g., food studies), scientific (e.g., medicine), and social (e.g., clothing). It is hoped that the work of the Survey will be of interest to historians, botanists, archaeologists, art historians, linguists, geographers, gardeners, herbalists, and many others.

What initially sounded like an unusual idea could soon become reality, and research confirms that this approach has already been used in other areas as well. The Institut für Realienkunde des Mittelalters und der frühen Neuzeit of the Austrian Academy of Sciences (Krems, Austria), for example, is currently working on a Medieval Animal Data-Network that fundamentally uses the same ideas as the MPS/PPM but attempts a different approach in organizational and technical matters.[37]

Before outlining the basic design of our online portal, we can describe some fundamental concepts on which we based our project. When developing and effectively using tools and platforms for knowledge management, the most important factor—the human one—is the most neglected. The central issues here are the motivation that drives authors to contribute to these platforms, and how social interaction and other forms of social dynamics influence author contribution. Such questions have great influence on the quality and quantity of articles that might be submitted. While designing our online research platform, we tried to take into consideration research findings on these topics. To describe activities on social platforms, psychologists today use the so-called "Activity Theory" that was introduced by Kuutti in 1995 and was originally developed by the Russian scholar Voytsky as early as the nineteenth century.[38] The core of this theory is that together with the monitored elements of an action (i.e., subject, object, tool), the systemic elements (rules, community, division of labor), which significantly influence the final outcome, are considered, too.

---

[37] See Ingrid Matschinegg, "(M)edieval (A)nimal (D)atabase: A Project in Progress," in Gerhard Jaritz and Alice Mathea Choyke (eds), *Animal Diversities* (Krems: Medium Aevum Quotidianum, 2005), 167–73; and the project's Web site at http://www.imareal.oeaw.ac.at/mad/. Compare also the Animaliter project at the University of Mainz: http://www.encyclopaedia-animalium.germanistik.uni-mainz.de/.

[38] Kari Kuutti, "Activity Theory as a Potential Framework for Human-Computer Interaction Research," in Bonnie A. Nardi (ed.), *Context and Consciousness: Activity Theory and Human-Computer Interaction* (Cambridge, MA: MIT, 1996), 17–44.

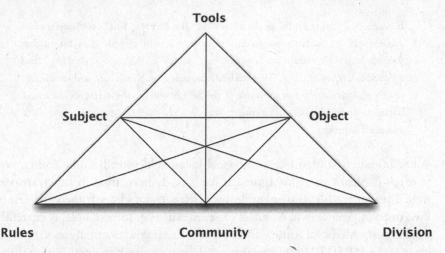

Figure 11.1   Activity Triangle[39]

These interrelations can best be illustrated by an Activity Triangle (Figure 11.1), a model that describes the socio-technological system within which users work as a sum of six interacting factors. The activity, together with its source and its outcome, is called "object." The user is labeled "subject"; he is more or less integrated into the "community," the social context of the system. The "division" of labor between subjects within a system is as important as the "tools" the subject needs to fulfill a task. The final element is a fixed set of "rules" that influence and interact with all other factors. Illustrating these interactions with the help of a triangle, of course, tends to simplify the whole action, because the importance of the single factors changes not only their valence but also their adjacency to each other. Therefore, changing one factor ultimately indicates a change in user behavior. The activity triangle and the social and technical interrelations it conveys describe the main constituents on which we based the development of the MPS/PPM.

Most major changes to user behavior and how users regard, for example, an online platform are based on their experience within a social network. Viégas et al. presented a study on how working with knowledge-management tools

    [39]   Based on S.L. Bryant, A. Forte, and A. Bruckman, "Becoming Wikipedian: Transformations of Participation in a Collaborative Online Encyclopedia," in Kjeld Schmidt, Mark Pendergast, Mark S. Ackerman, and Gloria Mark (eds), *GROUP '05: Proceedings of the 2005 International ACM SIGGROUP Conference on Supporting Group Work* (New York: Association for Computing Machinery, 2005), 1–10, at p. 3.

like Wikipedia influences consensus building.[40] One of the main advantages is that these kinds of tools aid in solving conflicts and oppositional positions in a subliminal way. If we contrast classical publishing—where scholarly discussion mainly works through reviews and other papers over a rather long period of time—with discussions in online forums leading to the development of articles, in the latter disagreements more easily reach a consensus. In the former, opinions harden and soon fronts are irreversibly set. By analyzing the development history of articles in the online encyclopedia Wikipedia, Viégas et al. demonstrated that the advantage of online collaboration and the use of versioning for article development lies in all the little changes that occur. In the long run those ease the process of finding common ground.

One of the known problems of knowledge-management tools is the disproportionate ratio between active authors and passive readers, which in some cases is estimated to be 1:9.[41] According to Korsgaard Sorensen, the main reason for this disparity is the lack of social interaction.[42] Several studies analyzing the success of Wikipedia conclude that the barrier-free handling[43] and the rather low barrier to entry[44] are the most important factors for this Web site. Another problem and a known phenomenon in workgroup settings, which has been proven again and again in various studies, is that members of collaborative projects work less enthusiastically and contribute less working time because negative group dynamics can lower the esteem of one's own work and equally the expected personal benefits.[45] Karau and Williams describe this

---

[40] Cf. Fernanda B. Viégas, Martin Wattenberg, and Kushal Dave, "Studying Cooperation and Conflict between Authors with History Flow Visualizations," in *CHI 2004: Proceedings of the 2004 Conference on Human Factors in Computing Systems* (New York: Association for Computing Machinery, 2004), 575–82.

[41] Cf. Jenny Preece, Blair Nonnecke, and Dorine Andrews, "The Top Five Reasons for Lurking: Improving Community Experiences for Everyone," *Computers in Human Behavior* 2 (2004): 201–23, at 205.

[42] Cf. E.K. Sorensen, "Networked eLearning and Collaborative Knowledge Building: Design and Facilitation," *Contemporary Issues in Technology and Teacher Education* 4 (2005): 446–55, at 447.

[43] Cf. William Emigh and Susan C. Herring, "Collaborative Authoring on the Web: A Genre Analysis of Online Encyclopedias," in *Proceedings of the 38th Hawaii International Conference on System Sciences, 2005*, http://ieeexplore.ieee.org/xpls/abs_all.jsp?arnumber=1385436.

[44] Cf. Bryant, Forte, and Bruckman, "Becoming Wikipedian," 1.

[45] Cf. B. Latane, K. Williams, and S. Harkins, "Many Hands Make Light the Work: The Causes and Consequences of Social Loafing," *Journal of Personality and Social Psychology* 37 (1979): 822–32; S.J. Karau and K.D. Williams, "Social Loafing: A Meta-Analytic Review and Theoretical Integration," *Journal of Personality and Social Psychology* 65 (1993): 681–706; and E. van Leeuwen and D. van Knippenberg, "How a Group Goal May Reduce Social Matching in

problem, which is also known as "social loafing," through the Collective Effort Model (Figure 11.2).[46] The initial stage is defined by the "effort" of a person or a group. This effort results in "performance," which in the one scenario is assessed by the person him- or herself, and in the other through a workgroup. In both scenarios the "value" attached to the performance causes a certain amount of "motivation." The amount of motivation again influences the effort a person or member of a workgroup puts into a new assignment.

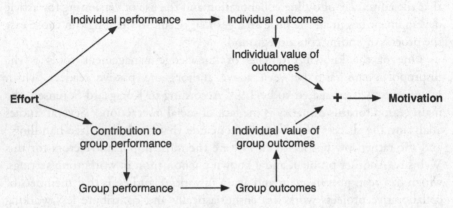

Figure 11.2   Collective Effort Model[47]

Beenen et al. deduce the following ground rules for online collaboration from this model.[48] User participation will increase if

- users feel that their efforts have significant impact on the overall results;
- users feel that their contributions remain individually recognizable;
- users feel that they receive personal gain through their contributions.

An important additional factor is general "liking," because the parameter "group comfort" greatly influences all factors listed above. All these elements can very easily be used to increase online collaboration. There are, of course,

Group Performance: Shifts in Standards for Determining a Fair Contribution of Effort," *Journal of Social Psychology* 142 (2002): 73–86.

[46]   Cf. Karau and Williams, "Social Loafing."

[47]   As presented in Karau and Williams, "Social Loafing," 683.

[48]   Cf. G. Beenen et al., "Using Social Psychology to Motivate Contributions to Online Communities," in *CSCW '04: Proceedings of the 2004 ACM Conference on Computer Supported Cooperative Work* (New York: ACM Press, 2004), 212–21, at 214ff.

other simple means to increase contribution:[49] Short but precise informational mailings, periodic user contact and, equally, setting clear goals—e.g., deadlines for certain contributions—do boost user commitment. Another means is the distinct parceling out of different tasks, which causes users to assume responsibility for their work. All these little devices go hand in hand with the Collective Effort Model. The special situation of the MPS/PPM platform—here the user group consists solely of experts in their different fields—only supports our problem-solving strategies.

When structuring and designing a project of this size, the main proposition is simplicity. The groundwork has to be set by defining the main goals, which for the MPS/PPM are:

- Collecting relevant source and research data in different languages, such as plant names, references, and quotations from academic historical and contemporary texts, references and quotations from poetic historical texts, and plant pictures. This data will be available through an online workspace with restricted access for registered users only.
- Providing a summary of the project data available and displaying this information publicly on the project's homepage.
- Having experts available to interpret data from their own fields of research and willing to lend their expertise to fellow researchers from other disciplines. Facilitating cross-disciplinary study carried out collaboratively.
- Making research findings available to the online community on the basis of a Creative Commons License[50] and assessing them by peer reviews, comments, and discussions. News of additions and changes are communicated through a thorough information management system, based on e-mail and RSS (that is, Really Simple Syndication) technology.
- The results of international and interdisciplinary collaboration are opened out into publicly available, diachronic plant portraits/monographs.

These goals are firmly grounded on a few basic rules:

- The language for the academic work will be English to provide an international basis.

---

49 Cf. Preece, Nonnecke, and Andrews, "Top Five Reasons."

50 http://creativecommons.org/.

- The online interface will be available in different languages. (We will provide German and English interfaces; additional translations are welcome.)
- The organization is decentralized; collaboration should function on a freelance basis with independent funding, including private contributions as well as publicly funded research. Only additional database design and programming has to be coordinated through us to guarantee a consistent online presence. Major research partners will get fully functioning copies of the online software as well as periodic database dumps.
- Database and workspace access is restricted to researchers and students only. Users willing to participate will have to provide real and verifiable identification data.
- The timeframe of interest is *c.* AD 500 to AD 1500. Including older texts to outline diachronic development is perfectly acceptable (and will be absolutely necessary) but references should not be later than humanist and Renaissance sources.
- The geographical area of research is—and here we can conveniently refer to the title of this Festschrift—"the Ancient Mediterranean [and] the Medieval West."
- Source texts have to be recorded in their original languages (accompanying English translations are welcome) and thoroughly documented.
- Citations of reference texts have to be recorded and filed in an online reference management software; the information on the availability of quotable digital copies of (contributors' own) books and articles would be an additional bonus.

Our approach to developing an online platform that is up to a high academic standard and equally encourages and motivates users to contribute is based on easily accessible and inviting implementation. Contrary to the general custom of knowledge-management systems, the MPS/PPM online platform is designed partly as a publicly accessible Web site and partly as a protected research environment. This structure on the one hand helps to avoid problems with copyright matters and on the other minimizes moderation efforts. The public part of the portal is intended to hold the final plant portraits, but also general information on the content and goals of the platform as well as on the contributing scholars (cf. Figure 11.3). Public content can be accessed by browsing the available categories (for example, languages, fields of research) and via a search engine. To liven up the online presence, we plan to add RSS-feeds and a blog to announce news and changes, as well as the opportunity to add comments and to invite other experts to cooperate. When displaying user-generated content, we attach great importance to naming all contributors and to providing means for easy printing or downloading as well as the correct citation of the content displayed.

The protected area of the Web site is the online workspace of the authors (cf. Figures 11.4 and 11.5). After registering once (see requirements above), the user's pages are easily accessible by providing the correct username and password. When accessing the Web site for the first time the user is invited to provide some personal information (for example, name and photo, contact information, fields of expertise, list of publications, curriculum vitae, etc.) so that other users can easily identify their coworkers. This information is also displayed publicly for the purpose of advertising the platform to other scholars. The online workspace is the main feature for the contributing authors: here they can combine, comment on, and tag data (see below) as well as comment (or ask questions, or offer advice) on the work of their fellow researchers. To boost collaborative knowledge generation, any user is allowed to modify any other entry; the newly changed entries are saved as a new version and the original author is informed by e-mail. Different versions can be interlinked, recovered, and compared to earlier versions. On the one hand this ensures that no work of any author is lost, on the other it is the solid basis for an open scholarly discourse, as we do not plan to implement means for direct, hidden communication (e.g., internal mails, etc.).

The ultimate aim of the platform is to fuse together all these bits and pieces that make up a plant's characteristic features into one publicly accessible monograph. Any user can initiate a plant monograph and is ultimately responsible for the development of that particular project. The groundwork for a plant monograph is the interlinking of all available data associated with a plant (provided there is already some data available), an activity that is supported by automatically set intelligent links while feeding information into the database. In a next step the user can invite scholars from different fields to advise and/or contribute; the user is also able to set deadlines or open discussions. When preliminary preparations are done, the process of writing the monograph in a joint online document can start, and all arguments can be based on and linked to the data and expertise available.

Figure 11.3 MPS/PPM public Web site for data presentation

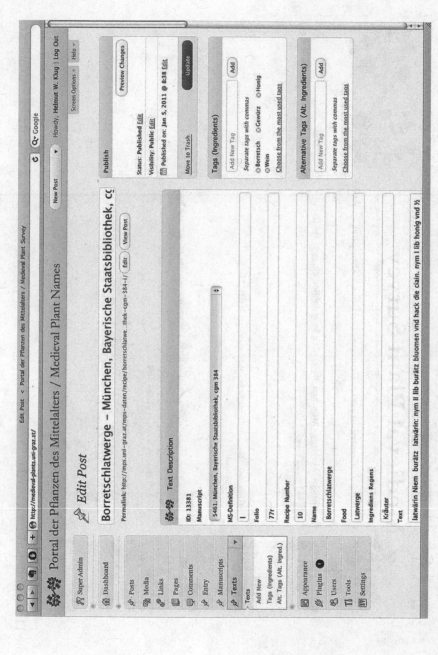

Figure 11.4 WordPress backend: workspace for main data input

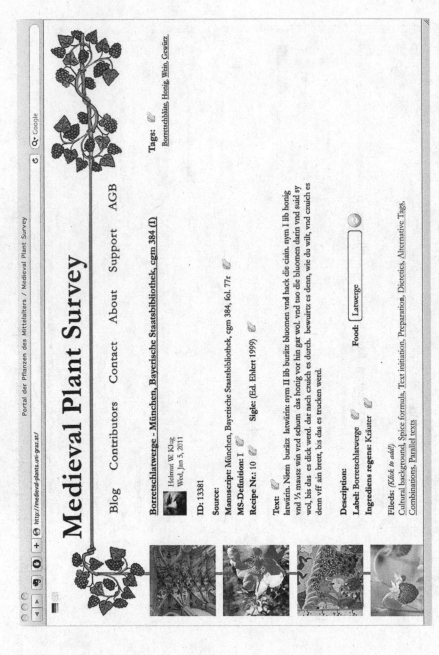

Figure 11.5   Workspace for researching as well as adding or changing data

To sum up, basic elements of the workspace are its simple handling, various structured possibilities for academic discourse, a low barrier to entering any means of input or editing data, and integrated versioning. In our opinion, this is the best approach toward a collaborative production of highly structured and scientific content, while at the same time maintaining incentives for authors.

But long before there is a possibility of analyzing texts and images and all interrelations, working with MPS/PPM requires adding data to the pool. These pieces of information (source and reference texts, images, etc.) are meant to provide a long-term data pool out of which all contributing researchers can extract information without having to go back to all the source material again and again. Provided there are no pieces of information on the preferred subject available, a characteristic workflow might look as described below. The single steps first describe the data needed in theoretical terms, then detailed examples from previous research are given. All data and references cited here were collected while working on the mandrake legend.[51] The data provided serves only as an example and is not aimed at completeness.

Collecting plant names: As a means to denote the problem researchers are working on, the plant names form the core of the data structure and are the basis for several interconnected and equal indices. Through these, additional data can be accessed and organized. Each plant-name index is associated with one language, either contemporary or historical. At the moment we plan to add the following languages:[52] Classical Latin, Medieval Latin,[53] Old English, Modern English, Old High German, Middle High German, Modern German, and botanical plant names. This would boil down to the following set of plant names for the study of the mandrake (possibly erroneous associations have been neither deleted nor labeled): Greek: *mandragoras, panakes*; Classical Latin: *antiminion, apollinaris, bulboquilon, circaeon, hippophlomos, mandragoras, malum, morion, orci beta, periculosa, thridacias*;[54] Medieval Latin (from British sources): *mandragora, terre malum, cyclaminos*;[55] Medieval Latin (from German

---

[51] See Van Arsdall, Klug, and Blanz, "Mandrake Plant."

[52] There has been no cunning selection process; the current data is just easily available, partly from other projects, partly through private study. It is to be desired that at some point the languages and plant-name indices will cover all historical (and contemporary) European languages. Generating Old and Middle High German indices is a part of Klug's dissertation.

[53] Since Medieval Latin is a very heterogeneous form of language closely linked with the mother-tongue of the speaker/writer, we will provide the possibility of tagging the entries accordingly.

[54] Based on Jacques André, *Les noms des plantes dans la Rome antique* (Paris: Les Belles Lettres, 1985).

[55] Based on the DOEPN.

sources): *abollena, bulaquilon, mandragora, niacullon, pomum macianum*;[56] Old English: *eorþæppel*;[57] Modern English: †*mandragon, mandragora, mandrake*;[58] Old High German: *alrûn/alrûne, ârzatwurz, dilwurz, friudilwurz, maltzappel, mandragora, twalm*;[59] Middle High German: *alrûne, mandragôre*;[60] Modern German: *Alraune, Mandragora*; and botanical plant names: *Mandragora autumnalis* Bertol., *Mandragora officinarum* L.[61]

Collecting historical texts: The occurrences of plants in historical scientific and literary texts of all featured languages have to be collected and documented in order to make it possible to ascertain a diachronic development of a plant's use, distribution, or reputation. At the moment we plan to file each entry associated with one or more plant names (i.e., consequently associated with the correct language) and the respective fields of research it may affect: entries in herbals, for example, might be associated with "biology,"[62] "pharmacy," "medicine." According to the user's needs, quotations could even be tagged with much more detail: entries from herbals or recipes could, for example, be labeled with the preferred habitat of a plant or the different medical indications with which a plant is associated.

For example, for the study of the mandrake legend, the first relevant historical text is *Enquiry into Plants* by Theophrastus, where a digging ritual is first mentioned.[63] With the help of our intelligent linking system, Theophrastus' passage 9.8.8 would automatically be associated with the language "Greek" because the plant name, *mandragoras*, with which the quotation has to be associated in the database, first hand, is part of the Greek plant-name index.

---

56   Different sources, collected and cited at the MPS/PPM.

57   Based on the DOEPN.

58   *Oxford English Dictionary*, Draft revisions June 2008, Mar. 2009, Dec. 2008, http://www.oed.com/.

59   Based on Jörg Riecke, *Die Frühgeschichte der mittelalterlichen medizinischen Fachsprache im Deutschen*, vol. 2: *Wörterbuch* (Berlin: De Gruyter, 2004), and various other sources, collected and cited at the MPS/PPM.

60   Based on the *Mittelhochdeutsches Handwörterbuch von Matthias Lexer* (3 vols, Stuttgart: S. Hirzel, 1992).

61   Robert Zander, *Handwörterbuch der Pflanzennamen*, 18th edn, ed. Walter Erhardt (Stuttgart: Ulmer, 2008).

62   This term is used (quite loosely) to summarize descriptions of habitat and habitus as provided by herbals.

63   Theophrastus, *Enquiry into Plants*, ed. and trans. Sir Arthur Hort, Loeb Classical Library (2 vols, London: Heinemann, 1916; repr. Cambridge, MA: Harvard University Press, 1980), 2:238–9; Van Arsdall, Klug, and Blanz, "Mandrake Plant," 296. If we wanted to thoroughly analyze the mandrake from a medical point of view, too, recording would have to start much earlier, of course. On the detailed medical history of the mandrake, see Wittlin, *Mandragora*.

In addition, the text can be tagged "gathering." Passage 9.8.1, when correctly interlinked, is equally automatically labeled "Greek," and could have the tags "medical" and possibly "leaf," "wound," "root," "erysipelas," "gout," "sleeplessness," "love potion," "storage." Subsequently, the tags can be used to work out parallels between different plants: if starting from scratch, the tag "gathering" will soon become more refined and with the addition of other plant descriptions, perhaps be additionally labeled with "gathering + iron" and "gathering + wood," thus marking groups of plants with similar features concerning their harvesting. Provided enough data is available, the tags can also easily be used to structure data according to which indication is given, e.g., displaying all plants that can be used as a cure for sleeplessness.

Going back to the notes on the mandrake legend, available electronic resources provide more than 60 entries from Greek, Latin, and German herbals, and likewise about 40 entries for German literary texts and quotations from ecclesiastical works, as well as select entries from French and English texts. Nevertheless, this considerable collection still leaves a number of questions open, particularly concerning the development of the legend in the period from the thirteenth to the fifteenth century. When adding more source texts and texts from other European languages—the goal has to be completeness of records—the final corpus of texts, hopefully, will provide a solid basis for writing a complete and detailed portrait of the mandrake in medieval times.

Annotated bibliography: Historical and current research on single plants and plants in general will have to be documented to provide a sound basis for further work. Data on relevant research literature should be fed into the online reference management application. Again, the entries are tagged with a plant name and additionally with the respective discipline to which the text belongs: for example, an etymological treatise on an Old English plant name would then be automatically labeled with "Old English" (through the plant name with which the text is associated), and manually with the tags "linguistics," "etymology," etc.

Research on the mandrake generated an impressive list of reference literature. When feeding information from Dorit Wittlin's work into the database, the citation (or excerpt, or digital copy) could be linked to the botanical name of the plant and, if previously all names have also been interlinked, they would automatically be associated with Greek, Latin, Old and Middle High German, and Modern German plant names, too. Because Wittlin conducts a diachronic search of the plant in a medical context, this would be perfectly suitable. The tags describing the database entry of this book should contain at least the following keywords: "medicine," "botany," "pharmacy," "plant names," and "etymology."

Collecting plant images: There is no doubt about the usefulness of medieval images, especially in a culture in which the ability to read was not widespread and images were the major means to reach a wide audience; in addition, the images almost always convey more meaning than the simple depiction of a healing herb. Plant images in single herbals or certain image traditions have been analyzed to some extent for their function, but research on plant illustrations still holds an enormous potential. The foremost aim of the MPS/PPM is to make images more easily available to researchers from different disciplines and to attract notice to them. At the moment, medieval plant images can, if at all, only be accessed through the sources available in print and online. If there is no copy of a manuscript available, the researcher has to consult the respective libraries, but due to the fragility of original manuscript sources, exhaustive studies are hardly encouraged.

To ease this problem, the MPS/PPM is designed to include a Corpus of Medieval Plant Images. Concerning the plant illustrations of herbals we again aim at achieving completeness of records. From the beginning, all images will be tagged with the name of the plant as noted in the manuscripts (provided this information is available), the name of the library holding the manuscript, its shelf mark, and the respective folio. We want to concentrate primarily on herbals as sources for our collection but plants do occur in other contexts, too: as part of (ornamental) illuminations, in paintings, and in frescoes and sculptures. Sooner or later these latter sources of plant imagery should also be completely recorded, as they add information to the topic. Currently we hold around four thousand digital copies of plant illustrations from assorted manuscripts and early printed books (either from online sources or privately digitized), photographs of plant frescoes in Styrian churches, and idealized plant drawings, which provide the best basis for comparison.[64] For describing the evolution of the mandrake legend,

---

[64] *Manuscripts and early printed books:* Basel, Universitätsbibliothek, MS K.II.11; Berleburg, Fürstlich Sayn-Wittgenstein'sche Bibliothek, MS RT2/6; Burlington, University of Vermont Library, MS 2; Linz, Oberösterreichische Landesmuseum, MS 4; London, British Library, MSS Egerton 2020, Harley 1585, Harley 3736, Harley 4986, Harley 5294, Sloane 56, Sloane 335, Sloane 795, Sloane 1975, Sloane 4016; Munich, Bayerische Staatsbibliothek, Clm 337; Naples, Biblioteca Nazionale, MS ex Vind. gr. 1; New Haven, Yale Medical Library, MS 18; New York, Pierpont Morgan Library, MS M.652; Oxford, Bodleian Library, MSS Ashmole 1413, Ashmole 1462, Bodley 130; Schloss Anholt, Fürstlich Salm-Salm'sche Bibliothek, MS 46; Vienna, Österreichische Nationalbibliothek, MSS med. gr. 1, Vind. 93, Vind. S.N. 2644; *Herbarius Maguntie impressus* (Mainz: Peter Schöffer, 1484); Wonnecke von Cube, *Hortus sanitatis deutsch* (Mainz: Peter Schöffer, 1485).

Churches: Allerheiligen im Mürztal, parish church; Kammern im Liesingtal, parish church; Kathal, subsidiary church; Leoben, Waasenkirche; Mariahof, parish church; Neuberg an der Mürz, former collegiate church; Neumarkt in der Steiermark, ossuary; St. Katharein an der Laming, subsidiary church; St. Marein bei Knittelfeld, parish church; Weisskirchen in der Steiermark, parish church.

referring to and citing images was inevitable. Van Arsdall, for example, bases her argument about the role of the dog partly on a series of illustrations and their date of origin, to outline the diachronic development of the animal's role in the legend.[65] Another example of the use of images to prove a point is the illustration in the elephant chapter in the Millstatt *Physiologus*, which provides proof of the enormous influence Honorius Augustodunensis' description of the mandrake in his *Expositio in Cantica canticorum* had on his contemporaries in Europe.[66]

Planning the MPS/PPM on a theoretical basis is fairly easy, but when considering the portal in a productive environment, three major problems arise: How can we motivate scholars to become users of the MPS/PPM? How can we motivate them to contribute over a long period of time and use the portal as a central research platform? How do we deal with problems that arise from presenting copyright-protected material (text and images) online? The first problem might be solved by the theme of the portal itself—in medieval studies, plants and plant-related matters do cover a great variety of branches of science, which increases the number of potentially interested scholars. When the design of the database and programming of the Web site are finished and the final version of the portal is launched, we will send out an initial letter of invitation to join efforts on plant research via different channels, relying on the snowball effect to reach as many addressees as possible.[67] In addition, we trust that the idea of open access for academic knowledge and electronic and online publishing will soon become more trusted and their value thus increased.[68] A development like this will certainly help scholars to overcome their inhibitions concerning "virtual knowledge presentation." But in the long run—and this must also be part of the solution for the second problem—the interest in the topic covered and the drive of the individual users have to keep the MPS/PPM maintained, just as Wikipedia thrives on the energy of its users.

Finally, the problems arising from copyright and associated laws are the most restrictive factor and might cause some parts of MPS/PPM to collapse. If, for example, the libraries holding the manuscripts refuse usage of the digitized plant illustrations, we will be instantly missing a large part of the prerequisites for our research. Unfortunately, there are no definitive findings on this topic as yet and

---

[65] Van Arsdall, Klug, and Blanz, "Mandrake Plant," 295–309.

[66] Van Arsdall, Klug, and Blanz, "Mandrake Plant," 314–15; the illustration is from Klagenfurt, Kärntner Landesarchiv, MS 6/19, fol. 90r.

[67] As means of active advertising we intend to use different mailing lists (e.g., Liste Mediävistik at the University of Regensburg, or the MEDMED-L list at Arizona State University), private mail contacts, and filing the project with adequate link lists (e.g., Mediaevum.de). Equally, this paper can also be regarded as active advertising of MPS/PPM.

[68] Klug, "Grundsätzliche Überlegungen," 124–7.

we are currently seeking legal assistance to base our portal on as firm legal ground as possible. One step to solve this dilemma will be strict user management, which can be seen as a means to define the portal as an independent e-research platform, so that legal findings based on online e-learning tools can be applied here, too.

All in all, the platform is being developed to accommodate a wide variety of academic disciplines; moreover, it provides an online location for knowledge storage as well as handy tools for online research and collaboration. Its generally open design provides the potential for continuous consolidation but also for future expansion of the topic. The general use of open-source software and program code would even make it possible to use it for other platforms dealing with topics that can be analyzed in a manner analogous to medieval plants.[69]

Update

In early 2011, the MPS/PPM Web site, which until then consisted only of a blog containing references to plant research-related essays, saw a major upgrade in terms of software and data additions. As outlined in this paper, it now provides a fully functional showcase to illustrate the potential of the project for the scholarly community as well as the general public. The data was derived from Klug's dissertation project[70] and the software update was influenced by recent research, which we presented at the Ninth Brno International Conference of English, American, and Canadian Studies, held in Brno, February 4–6, 2010.[71]

The newly added work-platform of the MPS/PPM project is based on a WordPress multisite installation, which is an open-source weblog platform and software framework. This very popular software package is regularly serviced through periodic updates and security fixes, and the active user- and developer-community continuously produces add-ons and plug-ins, which permanently increase its applicability. WordPress allows for very rigid user, rule, and capability management according to the standards we have introduced above. Therefore users can be categorized according to their different administrational rights or

---

[69]   A similar approach is already used for the study of animals (see Medieval Animal Data-Network and the Mainz Animaliter project, both mentioned above). One could envisage it in particular for the study of stones and gems, and probably also of monsters and grotesques of the Middle Ages. With few alterations it could in practice be used to manage any kind of data-generated research in the Humanities.

[70]   See n. 32 above for details.

[71]   Helmut W. Klug and Roman Weinberger, "Exploiting Social Media Techniques for the Dictionary of Old English Plant Names and the Medieval Plant Survey."

they can be assigned to/banned from different projects. This capability on the one hand simplifies working with the platform for inexperienced users and, on the other, might be advantageous in future projects that do not want to offer the high level of open access that we do now. This software also allows an equally strict level of data management, for which we utilized the already implemented tasks: these are the base functions for data acquisition and similarly basic means for publishing data. We expanded the base implementation in order to meet our requirements concerning data diversification by providing our own database and database structure for maintaining data detachment between software-side database and research-database, but combined them with customized WordPress templates for data input and data output. Besides that, we implemented several levels of data interconnection to provide means for multifaceted research activities.

The data fed into the MPS/PPM research database includes several plant-name indices (Old English, Old High German, Medieval Latin from British sources, Middle High German, Modern English, Modern German, and botanical, which add up to *c.* 9,400 plant names),[72] bibliographical information on the 57 manuscripts containing Middle High German cooking recipes,[73] 2,725 historical texts which were compiled from those recipe collections already edited as of 2010, and a tag collection detailing the *c.* 1,300 different ingredients (350 of which are plants or plant products) mentioned in the cooking recipes. All this information is recorded in separate categories (plant names, manuscripts, texts) as well as individual entries. The latter are interconnected either through direct means (an individual recipe is linked to a certain manuscript) or through indirect relations (an individual recipe is described by a certain tag), which can be individually adjusted for each entry. This high flexibility is the basis for various possibilities for data retrieval: recipes can, for example, be listed according to source manuscript, or by ingredient, or by any other defining information recorded for a text.

This way of data management is also the basis for novel research approaches, such as a corpus-based evaluation of plants used in Middle High German upper-class cooking, as in Klug's dissertation project, or as in a comprehensive analysis of parallel transmission of recipes throughout the different recipe collections, which was the central subject of a seminar at the Department of German Studies

---

[72] The respective sources are discussed above.

[73] Based on Constance B. Hieatt, Carole Lambert, Bruno Laurioux, and Alix Prentki, "Répertoire des manuscrits médiévaux contenant des recettes culinaires," in Carole Lambert (ed.), *Du manuscrit à la table: Essais sur la cuisine au Moyen Âge et répertoire des manuscrits médiévaux contenant des recettes culinaires* (Montreal: Les Presses de l'Université de Montréal, 1992), 315–62, and the further work of Trude Ehlert, Karin Kranich-Hofbauer, and Helmut Klug.

at the University of Graz in the summer term of 2011. Besides that, the clear display of the recorded data quite naturally results in the revelation of such desiderata as an edition of as yet unedited recipe collections.

Bibliography

Printed Sources

André, Jacques. *Les noms des plantes dans la Rome antique*. Paris: Les Belles Lettres, 1985.

Becela-Deller, Christine. *Ruta graveolens L.: Eine Heilpflanze in kunst- und kulturhistorischer Bedeutung*. Würzburg: Königshausen & Neumann, 1998.

Beenen, G., K. Ling, X. Wang, K. Chang, D. Frankowski, P. Resnick, and R.E. Kraut. "Using Social Psychology to Motivate Contributions to Online Communities." In *CSCW '04: Proceedings of the 2004 ACM Conference on Computer Supported Cooperative Work*, 212–21. New York: ACM Press, 2004.

Bierbaumer, Peter. *Der botanische Wortschatz des Altenglischen*. 3 vols. Frankfurt am Main: Lang, 1975–79.

———— and Helmut W. Klug (eds). *Old Names—New Growth: Proceedings of the 2nd ASPNS Conference, University of Graz, Austria, 6–10 June 2007, and Related Essays*. Frankfurt am Main: Lang, 2009.

Biggam, Carole P. *"Blue" in Old English: An Interdisciplinary Semantic Study*. Amsterdam: Rodopi, 1997.

————. *"Grey" in Old English: An Interdisciplinary Semantic Study*. London: Runetree, 1998.

Bryant, S.L., A. Forte, and A. Bruckman. "Becoming Wikipedian: Transformations of Participation in a Collaborative Online Encyclopedia." In Kjeld Schmidt, Mark Pendergast, Mark S. Ackerman, and Gloria Mark (eds), *GROUP '05: Proceedings of the 2005 International ACM SIGGROUP Conference on Supporting Group Work*, 1–10. New York: Association for Computing Machinery, 2005.

Collins, Minta. *Medieval Herbals: The Illustrative Traditions*. Toronto: University of Toronto Press, 2000.

Cube, Wonnecke von. *Hortus sanitatis deutsch*. Mainz: Peter Schöffer, 1485.

D'Aronco, Maria Amalia. "Gardens on Vellum: Plants and Herbs in Anglo-Saxon Manuscripts." In Peter Dendle and Alain Touwaide (eds), *Health and Healing from the Medieval Garden*, 101–27. Rochester, NY: Boydell & Brewer, 2008.

Herbarius Maguntie impressus. Mainz: Peter Schöffer, 1484.

Hieatt, Constance B., Carole Lambert, Bruno Laurioux, and Alix Prentki. "Répertoire des manuscrits médiévaux contenant des recettes culinaires." In Carole Lambert (ed.), *Du manuscrit à la table: Essais sur la cuisine au Moyen Âge et répertoire des manuscrits médiévaux contenant des recettes culinaires*, 315–62. Montreal: Les Presses de l'Université de Montréal, 1992.

Karau, S.J., and K.D. Williams. "Social Loafing: A Meta-Analytic Review and Theoretical Integration." *Journal of Personality and Social Psychology* 65 (1993): 681–706.

Klug, Helmut W. "Grundsätzliche Überlegungen rund um ein künftiges mediävistisches Text-Portal." In Wernfried Hofmeister and Andrea Hofmeister-Winter (eds), *Wege zum Text: Beiträge des Grazer Kolloquiums über die Verfügbarkeit mediävistischer Editionen im 21. Jahrhundert (17.–19. September 2008)*, 121–31. Tübingen: Niemeyer, 2009.

———. "Plants in German Literature of the Middle Ages: A Data-base Supported Stocktaking with an Analysis of Literary, Linguistic and Cultural Contexts." Ph.D. diss., Universität Graz, in preparation.

——— and Roman Weinberger. "Old English Plant Names Go Cyber: The Technical Aspects of the Dictionary of Old English Plant Names Project." In Bierbaumer and Klug, *Old Names—New Growth*, 181–209.

Kuutti, Kari. "Activity Theory as a Potential Framework for Human–Computer Interaction Research." In Bonnie A. Nardi (ed.), *Context and Consciousness: Activity Theory and Human–Computer Interaction*, 17–44. Cambridge, MA: MIT, 1996.

Latane, B., K. Williams, and S. Harkins. "Many Hands Make Light the Work: The Causes and Consequences of Social Loafing." *Journal of Personality and Social Psychology* 37 (1979): 822–32.

Lexer, Matthias. *Mittelhochdeutsches Handwörterbuch.* 3 vols. Leipzig: S. Hirzel, 1872. Repr. Stuttgart: S. Hirzel, 1992.

Matschinegg, Ingrid. "(M)edieval (A)nimal (D)atabase: A Project in Progress." In Gerhard Jaritz and Alice Mathea Choyke (eds), *Animal Diversities*, 167–73. Krems: Medium Aevum Quotidianum, 2005.

Preece, Jenny, Blair Nonnecke, and Dorine Andrews. "The Top Five Reasons for Lurking: Improving Community Experiences for Everyone." *Computers in Human Behavior* 2 (2004): 201–23.

Richter, Thomas. *Melissa officinalis L.: Ein Leitmotiv für 2000 Jahre Wissenschaftsgeschichte.* Würzburg: Königshausen & Neumann, 1998.

Riddle, John M. *Dioscorides on Pharmacy and Medicine.* Austin: University of Texas Press, 1985.

————. *Eve's Herbs: A History of Contraception and Abortion in the West.* Cambridge: Cambridge University Press, 1997.

————. "Historical Data as an Aid in Pharmaceutical Prospecting and Drug Safety Determination." *Journal of Alternative and Complementary Medicine* 5 (1999): 195–201.

————. "History as a Tool in Identifying 'New' Old Drugs." In Béla S. Buslig and John A. Manthey (eds), *Flavonoids in Cell Function*, 89–94. New York: Kluwer Academic Publishers, 2002.

Riecke, Jörg. *Die Frühgeschichte der mittelalterlichen medizinischen Fachsprache im Deutschen.* Vol. 2: *Wörterbuch.* Berlin: De Gruyter, 2004.

Schiedermaier, Wolfgang. "Pflanzenmalereien in drei unterfränkischen Kirchen: Ikonographie, Kunstgeschichte und aktuelle Bedeutung in Bezug auf die Entwicklung von Medizin und Pharmazie." Ph.D. diss., Universität Würzburg, 2003.

Schnell, Bernhard. "Pflanzen in Bild und Text: Zum Naturverständnis in den deutschsprachigen illustrierten Kräuterbüchern des Spätmittelalters." In Peter Dilg (ed.), *Natur im Mittelalter: Konzeptionen—Erfahrungen— Wirkungen. Akten des 9. Symposiums des Mediävistenverbandes, Marburg, 14. 17. März 2001*, 442–59. Berlin: Akademie Verlag, 2003.

Sillasoo, Ülle. "Medieval Plant Depictions as a Source for Archeobotanical Research." *Vegetation History and Archeobotany* 16 (2006): 61–70.

Sorensen, E.K. "Networked eLearning and Collaborative Knowledge Building: Design and Facilitation." *Contemporary Issues in Technology and Teacher Education* 4 (2005): 446–55.

Theophrastus. *Enquiry into Plants.* Ed. and trans. Sir Arthur Hort. Loeb Classical Library. 2 vols. London: Heinemann, 1916. Repr. Cambridge, MA: Harvard University Press, 1980.

Thomé, Otto Wilhelm. *Flora von Deutschland, Österreich und der Schweiz.* 4 vols. Gera-Untermhaus: Köhler, 1885–1905.

Van Arsdall, Anne, Helmut W. Klug, and Paul Blanz. "The Mandrake Plant and Its Legend: A New Perspective." In Bierbaumer and Klug, *Old Names—New Growth*, 285–346.

van Leeuwen, E., and D. van Knippenberg. "How a Group Goal May Reduce Social Matching in Group Performance: Shifts in Standards for Determining a Fair Contribution of Effort." *Journal of Social Psychology* 142 (2002): 73–86.

Viégas, Fernanda B., Martin Wattenberg, and Kushal Dave. "Studying Cooperation and Conflict between Authors with History Flow Visualizations." In *CHI 2004: Proceedings of the 2004 Conference on Human Factors in Computing Systems*, 575–82. New York: Association for Computing Machinery, 2004.

Wagner, Eva. "Untersuchungen zu Lesbarkeit und Aussagekraft von Pflanzendarstellungen in mittelalterlichen Kräuterbuchhandschriften am Beispiel des *Codex latinus monacensis* 28531." Ph.D. diss., Universität Freiburg, 2006.

Wittlin, Dorit. *Mandragora: Eine Arzneipflanze in Antike, Mittelalter und Neuzeit.* Basel: Deitikon, 1999.

Zander, Robert. *Handwörterbuch der Pflanzennamen.* 18th edn. Ed. Walter Erhardt. Stuttgart: Ulmer, 2008.

Electronic Sources

Anglo-Saxon Plant-Name Survey. http://www.arts.gla.ac.uk/STELLA/ihsl/projects/plants.htm (accessed February 20, 2012).

Animaliter: Animalia in litteris medii aevi—Tiere in der Literatur des Mittelalters. http://www.encyclopaedia-animalium.germanistik.uni-mainz.de/ (accessed February 20, 2012).

Biblioteca Nazionale di Napoli, Dioscurides Neapolitanus. http://digitale.bnnonline.it/index.php?it/113/dioscurides-neapolitanus (accessed February 20, 2012).

Biggam, Carole. "ASPNS: About the Survey." http://www.arts.gla.ac.uk/STELLA/ihsl/projects/ASPNS/about.htm (accessed February 20, 2012).

British Library Catalogue of Illuminated Manuscripts. http://www.bl.uk/catalogues/illuminatedmanuscripts/ (accessed February 20, 2012).

CancerLynx: An Online Zine for Cancer Patients and Professionals. http://www.cancerlynx.com/ (accessed February 20, 2012).

Dictionary of Old English Plant Names. http://oldenglish-plantnames.uni-graz.at (accessed February 20, 2012).

Digitales Mittelhochdeutsches Textarchiv. http://mhgta.uni-trier.de (accessed February 20, 2012).

Early Manuscripts at Oxford University. http://image.ox.ac.uk/ (accessed February 20, 2012).

Emigh, William, and Susan C. Herring. "Collaborative Authoring on the Web: A Genre Analysis of Online Encyclopedias." In *Proceedings of the 38th Hawaii International Conference on System Sciences, 2005.* http://ieeexplore.ieee.org/xpls/abs_all.jsp?arnumber=1385436 (accessed February 20, 2012).

Forschergruppe Klostermedizin. http://www.klostermedizin.de (accessed February 20, 2012).

Gloning, Thomas. Personal Web site. http://www.uni-giessen.de/gloning/ (accessed February 20, 2012).

Heilpflanzen-Welt. http://www.heilpflanzen-welt.de/ (accessed February 20, 2012).

Hofmeister, Wernfried. *Wege zum Text: Grazer germanistisches Kolloquium über die Verfügbarkeit mediävistischer Editionen im 21. Jahrhundert.* Conference Web site. http://www.uni-graz.at/wernfried.hofmeister/wegezumtext/ (accessed February 20, 2012).

Index of Medieval Medical Images. http://unitproj.library.ucla.edu/biomed/ his/immi/ (accessed February 20, 2012).

The Labyrinth: Resources for Medieval Studies. http://labyrinth.georgetown .edu/ (accessed February 20, 2012).

The MacKinney Collection of Medieval Medical Illustrations. http://www.lib .unc.edu/dc/mackinney/ (accessed February 20, 2012).

Mediaevum.de. http://www.mediaevum.de (accessed February 20, 2012).

Medieval Academy of America. "About Us." http://www.medievalacademy.org/ about/about.htm (accessed February 20, 2012).

Medieval Animal Data-Network. http://www.imareal.oeaw.ac.at/mad/ (accessed February 20, 2012).

The Morgan Library and Museum Medieval and Renaissance Manuscripts. http://www.themorgan.org/collections/collectionsMedRen.asp (accessed February 20, 2012).

O'Reilly, Tim. "What is Web 2.0?" September 30, 2005. http://www.oreillynet .com/pub/a/oreilly/tim/news/2005/09/30/what-is-Web-20.html (accessed February 20, 2012).

Oxford English Dictionary. http://www.oed.com/ (accessed February 20, 2012).

Portal der Pflanzen des Mittelalters. http://medieval-plants.uni-graz.at (accessed February 20, 2012).

SpringerLink. http://www.springerlink.com (accessed February 20, 2012).

University of Virginia Digital Collections. http://search.lib.virginia.edu/ catalog?f[source_facet][]=Digital+Library (accessed February 20, 2012).

Voigts-Kurtz Search Program. http://cctr1.umkc.edu/cgi-bin/search (accessed February 20, 2012).

Wikisource. http://wikisource.org (accessed February 20, 2012).

The Publications of John M. Riddle, 1964–2010

Compiled by Anne Van Arsdall and Timothy Graham

Items marked with an asterisk are included in the Variorum Collected Studies Series collection of John Riddle's articles, *Quid pro Quo: Studies in the History of Drugs* (item 38 below).

1. "Amber: An Historical-Etymological Problem." In Mary Francis Gyles and Eugene Wood Davis (eds), *Laudatores Temporis Acti: Studies in Memory of Wallace Everett Caldwell, Professor of History at the University of North Carolina by His Friends and Students*, 110–20. James Sprunt Studies in History and Political Science 46. Chapel Hill: University of North Carolina Press, 1964.

*2. "Pomum Ambrae: Amber and Ambergris in Plague Remedies." *Sudhoffs Archiv für Geschichte der Medizin und Naturwissenschaften* 48 (1964): 111–22.

*3. "The Introduction and Use of Eastern Drugs in the Early Middle Ages." *Sudhoffs Archiv für Geschichte der Medizin und Naturwissenschaften* 49 (1965): 185–98.

*4. "Lithotherapy in the Middle Ages ... Lapidaries Considered as Medical Texts." *Pharmacy in History* 12 (1970): 39–50.

5. *Tiberius Gracchus: Destroyer or Reformer of the Republic?* Problems in European Civilization. Lexington, MA: D.C. Heath, 1970.

6. "Dioscorides." In Charles Coulston Gillispie (ed.), *Dictionary of Scientific Biography*, vol. 4, 119–23. New York: Charles Scribner's Sons, 1971.

7. Review of John Scarborough, *Roman Medicine* (Ithaca: Cornell University Press, 1969). *The Historian* 33 (1971): 283.

*8. "Amber in Ancient Pharmacy: The Transmission of Information about a Single Drug." *Pharmacy in History* 15 (1973): 3–17.

*9. "The Latin Alphabetical Dioscorides." *Proceedings of XIIIth International Congress of the History of Science*, vol. 5, section IV: *History of Science and Technology in the Middle Ages*, 204–9. Moscow: Nauka, 1974.

*10. "Theory and Practice in Medieval Medicine." *Viator* 5 (1974): 157–84.

11. *Marbode of Rennes' (1035–1123) "De Lapidibus" Considered as a Medical Treatise with Text, Commentary and C.W. King's Translation, Together with Text and Translation of Marbode's Minor Works on Stones.* Sudhoffs Archiv, Beiheft 20. Wiesbaden: Franz Steiner, 1977.

*12. "Book Reviews, Lectures, and Marginal Notes. Three Previously Unknown Sixteenth Century Contributors to Pharmacy, Medicine and Botany— Ioannes Manardus, Franciscus Frigimelica, and Melchior Guilandinus." *Pharmacy in History* 21 (1979): 143–55.

*13. (With James A. Mulholland.) "Albert on Stones and Minerals." In James A. Weisheipl (ed.), *Albertus Magnus and the Sciences: Commemorative Essays 1980*, 203–34. Studies and Texts 49. Toronto: Pontifical Institute of Mediaeval Studies, 1980. Translated into Italian as "Alberto, le pietre e i minerali." In James A. Weisheipl (ed.), *Alberto magno e le scienze*, 219–53. Bologna: Edizioni Studio Domenicano, 1994.

14. "Dioscorides." In F. Edward Cranz and Paul Oskar Kristeller (eds), *Catalogus Translationum et Commentariorum: Medieval and Renaissance Latin Translations and Commentaries. Annotated Lists and Guides*, vol. 4, 1–143. Washington, D.C.: Catholic University of America Press, 1980.

*15. "Pseudo-Dioscorides' *Ex herbis femininis* and Early Medieval Medical Botany." *Journal of the History of Botany* 14 (1981): 43–81.

16. Review of Fred Rosner (trans.), *Moses Maimonides' Glossary of Drug Names* (Philadelphia: American Philosophical Society, 1979). *Journal of the History of Medicine and Allied Sciences* 36 (1981): 352–4.

17. Review of Hedwig Schleiffer (ed.), *Narcotic Plants of the Old World Used in Rituals and Everyday Life: An Anthology of Texts from Ancient Times to the Present* (Monticello, NY: Lubrecht & Cramer, 1979). *Pharmacy in History* 23 (1981): 99–100.

*18. "Gargilius Martialis as a Medical Writer." *Journal of the History of Medicine and Allied Sciences* 39 (1984): 408–29.

*19. "Ancient and Medieval Chemotherapy for Cancer." *Isis* 76 (1985): 319–39.

*20. "Byzantine Commentaries on Dioscorides." In John Scarborough (ed.), *Symposium on Byzantine Medicine*, 95–102. Dumbarton Oaks Papers 38. Washington, D.C.: Dumbarton Oaks Research Library and Collection, 1985.

21. *Dioscorides on Pharmacy and Medicine.* Austin: University of Texas Press, 1985.

22. "Dioskurides im Mittelalter, I: Überlieferung." In *Lexikon des Mittelalters*, vol. 3, 1095–7. Munich: Artemis, 1985.

23. Review of G.E.R. Lloyd, *Science, Folklore, and Ideology: Studies in the Life Sciences in Ancient Greece* (Cambridge: Cambridge University Press, 1983). *Journal of the History of Medicine and Allied Sciences* 40 (1985): 220–21.

24. "The Herbal in History." Pamphlet accompanying the facsimile publication of Hans Biedermann, *Medicina Magica: Metaphysical Healing Methods in Late-Antique and Medieval Manuscripts, with Thirty Facsimile Plates*, trans. Rosemarie Werba. The Classics of Medicine Library, sub-series Notes from the Editors. Birmingham, AL: Gryphon Editions, 1986.

25. Review of P.V. Taberner, *Aphrodisiacs: The Science and the Myth* (Philadelphia: University of Pennsylvania Press, 1985). *Journal of the History of Medicine and Allied Sciences* 41 (1986): 367–8.

*26. "Folk Tradition and Folk Medicine: Recognition of Drugs in Classical Antiquity." In John Scarborough (ed.), *Folklore and Folk Medicines*, 33–61. Madison, WI: American Institute of the History of Pharmacy, 1987.

27. Editor, *Society for Ancient Medicine and Pharmacy Newsletter* 16 (1988).

28. Review of R.K. French and Frank Greenaway (eds), *Science in the Early Roman Empire: Pliny the Elder, His Sources and Influence* (Totowa, NJ: Barnes & Noble, 1986). *American Historical Review* 93 (1988): 398–402.

*29. "The Pseudo-Hippocratic Dynamidia." In Gerhard Baader and Rolf Winau (eds), *Die hippokratischen Epidemien: Theorie—Praxis—Tradition. Verhandlungen des Ve Colloque International Hippocratique veranstaltet von der Berliner Gesellschaft für Geschichte der Medizin in Verbindung mit dem Institut für Geschichte der Medizin der Freien Universität Berlin, 10.– 15.9.1984*, 283–311. *Sudhoffs Archiv*, Beiheft 27. Stuttgart: Franz Steiner, 1989.

30. Editor, *Society for Ancient Medicine and Pharmacy Newsletter* 17 (1989).

31. Co-editor, *Society for Ancient Medicine and Pharmacy Newsletter* 18 (1990).

32. "Oral Contraceptives and Early-Term Abortifacients during Classical Antiquity and the Middle Ages." *Past and Present* 132 (1991): 1–32.

33. Review of Albert Dietrich (ed.), *Dioscurides triumphans: Ein anonymer arabischer Kommentar (Ende 12 Jahrh. n. Chr.) zur Materia medica. Arabischer Text nebst kommentierter deutscher Übersetzung* (Göttingen: Vandenhoeck & Ruprecht, 1988). *Medical History* 34 (1991): 120–21.

34. Review of Mirko D. Grmek, *Diseases in the Ancient Greek World* (Baltimore: Johns Hopkins University Press, 1989). *American Historical Review* 96 (1991): 143–4.

35. Review of José Luis Valverde and José A. Pérez Romero, *Drogas americanas en fuentes de escritores franciscanos y dominicos* (Granada: Universidad de Granada, 1988). *Isis* 82 (1991): 746–7.

36. (With J. Worth Estes.) "Oral Contraceptives in Ancient and Medieval Times." *American Scientist* 80 (May–June 1992): 226–33.

37. *Contraception and Abortion from the Ancient World to the Renaissance.* Cambridge, MA: Harvard University Press, 1992.

38. *Quid pro Quo: Studies in the History of Drugs.* Collected Studies Series CS 367. Aldershot, UK: Variorum, 1992.

*39. "Methodology of Historical Drug Research." In John M. Riddle, *Quid pro Quo: Studies in the History of Drugs*, item 15.

40. "Spices." In Silvio A. Bedini (ed.), *The Christopher Columbus Encyclopedia*, vol. 2, 648–50. New York: Simon & Schuster, 1992.

41. "High Medicine and Low Medicine in the Roman Empire." In Wolfgang Haase (ed.), *Aufstieg und Niedergang der römischen Welt: Geschichte und Kultur Roms im Spiegel der neueren Forschung*, pt II, vol. 37.1: *Wissenschaften: Medizin und Biologie*, 102–20. Berlin: De Gruyter, 1993.

42. "Introduction." In Irene Jacob and Walter Jacob (eds), *The Healing Past: Pharmaceuticals in the Biblical and Rabbinic World*, xi–xv. Leiden: Brill, 1993.

43. Review of Albert Dietrich (ed.), *Die Dioskurides-Erklärung des Ibn al-Baitar: Ein Beitrag zur arabischen Pflanzensynonymik des Mittelalters. Arabischer Text nebst kommentierter deutscher Übersetzung* (Göttingen: Vandenhoeck & Ruprecht, 1991). *Medical History* 37 (1993): 108–9.

44. Review of J. Worth Estes, *Dictionary of Protopharmocology: Therapeutic Practices, 1700–1850* (Canton, MA: Science History Publications, 1990). *Isis* 83 (1993): 705–6.

45. Review of Mott T. Greene, *Natural Knowledge in Preclassical Antiquity* (Baltimore: Johns Hopkins University Press, 1992). *American Historical Review* 98 (1993): 1213–14.

46. Review of Theophrastus, *De causis plantarum*, ed. and trans. Benedict Einarson and George K.K. Link, 3 vols (Cambridge, MA: Harvard University Press, 1976–90). *Isis* 84 (1993): 557–8.

47. (With J. Worth Estes and Josiah C. Russell.) "Ever Since Eve ... Birth Control in the Ancient World." *Archaeology* 47, no. 2 (1994): 29–35.

48. "Everybody, the Historian, and the Scientist." President's Address, American Institute of the History of Pharmacy. *Pharmacy in History* 37 (1995): 159–64.

49. "Historical Role of Herbs in Contraception." In David L. Gustine and Hector E. Flores (eds), *Phytochemicals and Health: Proceedings, Tenth Annual Penn State Symposium in Plant Physiology, May 18–20, 1995*, 105–11. *Current Topics in Plant Physiology* 15. Rockville, MD: American Society of Plant Physiologists, 1995.

50. "Manuscript Sources for Birth Control." In Margaret R. Schleissner (ed.), *Manuscript Sources of Medieval Medicine: A Book of Essays*, 145–58. New York: Garland, 1995.

51. (With Judith Wilcox.) "Qustā ibn Lūqā's Physical Ligatures and the Recognition of the Placebo Effect, with an Edition and Translation." *Medieval Encounters* 1 (1995): 1–48.

52. Review of Hellmut Baumann, *The Greek Plant World in Myth, Art, and Literature*, trans. and augmented by William T. Stearn and Eldwyth Ruth Stearn (Portland, OR: Timber Press, 1993). *American Scientist* 83 (1995): 669–70.

53. Review of Mary Beagon, *Roman Nature: The Thought of Pliny the Elder* (New York: Oxford University Press, 1992). *American Journal of Philology* 116 (1995): 669–70.

54. "Contraception and Early Abortion in the Middle Ages." In Vern L. Bullough and James A. Brundage (eds), *Handbook of Medieval Sexuality*, 261–77. New York: Garland, 1996.

55. "Dioscorides." In Simon Hornblower and Antony Spawforth (eds), *The Oxford Classical Dictionary*, 483–4. 3rd edn. Oxford: Oxford University Press, 1996.

56. "Geology." In F.A.C. Mantello and A.G. Rigg (eds), *Medieval Latin: An Introduction and Bibliographical Guide*, 406–10. Washington, D.C.: Catholic University of America Press, 1996.

57. "The Medicines of Greco-Roman Antiquity as a Source of Medicines for Today." In Bart Holland (ed.), *Prospecting for Drugs in Ancient and Medieval European Texts: A Scientific Approach*, 7–17. Amsterdam: Harwood Academic Publishers, 1996.

58. Review of Albertus Magnus, *De vegetabilibus, Buch VI, Traktat 2: Lateinish-deutsch*, ed. and trans. Klaus Biewer (Stuttgart: Wissenschaftliche Buchverlagsgesellschaft, 1992). *Isis* 87 (1996): 720–24.

59. "Medieval Latin Medicine." Review article. *Society for Ancient Medicine Review* 24 (1996–97): 214–16.

60. Consulting editor, sections on Mesopotamian medicine, Egyptian medicine, Greek and Roman medicine. *Ancient Healing: Unlocking the Mysteries of Health and Healing through the Ages*. Lincolnwood, IL: Publications International, 1997.

61. *Eve's Herbs: A History of Contraception and Abortion in the West*. Cambridge, MA: Harvard University Press, 1997.

62. "Old Drugs, Old and New History." In Gregory J. Higby and Elaine C. Stroud (eds), *The Inside Story of Medicines: A Symposium*, 15–30. Madison, WI: American Institute of the History of Pharmacy, 1997.

63. Review of M.L. Cameron, *Anglo-Saxon Medicine* (Cambridge: Cambridge University Press, 1993). *Speculum* 72 (1997): 121–2.

64. "Classical, Medieval and Modern Uses of St. John's Wort." *First International Conference on St. John's Wort, March 16-17, 1998, Anaheim Marriott, Anaheim, California,* 1–14. Silver Spring, MD: American Herbal Products Association, 1998.

65. Review of Joan Cadden, *Meanings of Sex Difference in the Middle Ages: Medicine, Science, and Culture* (Cambridge: Cambridge University Press, 1993). *Bulletin of the History of Medicine* 72 (1998), 107–8.

66. Review of Clara Pinto Correia, *The Ovary of Eve: Egg and Sperm and Preformation* (Chicago: University of Chicago Press, 1997). *Journal of the American Medical Association* 280 (1998): 1961–2.

67. "Introduction." In Jerry Stannard, *Pristina Medicamenta: Ancient and Medieval Medical Botany*, ed. Katherine E. Stannard and Richard Kay, ix–xiv. Variorum Collected Studies Series CS 646. Aldershot, UK: Ashgate, 1999.

68. "Introduction." In Jerry Stannard, *Herbs and Herbalism in the Middle Ages and Renaissance*, ed. Katherine E. Stannard and Richard Kay, ix–xiv. Variorum Collected Studies Series CS 650. Aldershot, UK: Ashgate, 1999.

69. "Contraception and Abortion." In G.W. Bowersock, Peter Brown, and Oleg Grabar (eds), *Late Antiquity: A Guide to the Postclassical World*, 392–3. Cambridge, MA: Belknap Press, 1999.

70. "Fees and Feces: Laxatives in Ancient Medicine with Particular Emphasis on Pseudo-Mesue." In John A.C. Greppin, Emilie Savage-Smith, and John L. Gueriguian (eds), *The Diffusion of Greco-Roman Medicine into the Middle East and the Caucasus*, 7–26. Anatolian and Caucasian Studies. Delmar, NY: Caravan Books, 1999.

71. "Historical Data as an Aid in Pharmaceutical Prospecting and Drug Safety Determination." *Journal of Alternative and Complementary Medicine* 5 (1999): 195–201.

72. "Abortion," "Contraception," and "Theophrastus." In Graham Speake (ed.), *Encyclopedia of Greece and the Hellenic Tradition*, vol. 1, 1–2, 390–91; vol. 2, 1633–4. Chicago: Fitzroy Dearborn, 2000.

73. Review of Anonymus Medicus, *De morbis acutis at chroniis*, ed. Ivan Garofalo, trans. Brian Fuchs (Leiden: Brill, 1997). *Bulletin of the History of Medicine* 74 (2000): 352–4.

74. Review of Annette Müller, *Krankheitsbilder im Liber de plantis der Hildegard von Bingen (1098–1179) und im Speyerer Kräuterbuch (1456): Ein Beitrag zur medizinisch-pharmazeutischen Terminologie im Mittelalter* (Hürtgenwald: Pressler, 1997). *Bulletin of the History of Medicine* 74 (2000): 148–9.

75. "Birth, Contraception, and Abortion." In Peter N. Stearns (ed.), *Encyclopedia of European Social History from 1350 to 2000*, vol. 2, 181–91. New York: Charles Scribner's Sons, 2001.

76. "Science, Technology, and Health." In John T. Kirby (ed.), *World Eras*, vol. 3: *Roman Republic and Empire, 264 B.C.E.–476 C.E.*, 375–414. Detroit: Gale Group, 2001.

77. Review of James Longrigg, *Greek Medicine: From the Heroic to the Hellenistic Age. A Source Book* (New York: Routledge, 1998). *Isis* 92 (2001): 152–3.

78. "History as a Tool in Identifying 'New' Old Drugs." In Béla S. Buslig and John A. Manthey (eds), *Flavonoids in Cell Function*, 89–94. New York: Kluwer Academic Publishers, 2002.

79. Review of Wilhelmina F. Jashemski, *A Pompeian Herbal: Ancient and Modern Medicinal Plants* (Austin: University of Texas Press, 1999). *International Journal of the Classical Tradition* 8 (2002): 470.

80. Review of Peter Biller, *The Measure of Multitude: Population in Medieval Thought* (New York: Oxford University Press, 2000). *Journal of Social History* 37 (2003): 555–6.

81. Review of Mark Grant, *Galen on Food and Diet* (New York: Routledge, 2000). *Isis* 94 (2003): 518.

82. Review of Michael J. O'Dowd, *The History of Medications for Women: Materia Medica Woman* (New York: Parthenon, 2001). *Bulletin of the History of Medicine* 77 (2003): 422–4.

83. "Kidney and Urinary Therapeutics in Early Medieval Monastic Medicine." *Journal of Nephrology* 17 (2004): 324–8.

84. (With Eric J. Buenz, David J. Schnepple, Brent A. Bauer, Peter L. Elkin, and Timothy J. Motley.) "Techniques: Bioprospecting Historical Herbal Texts by Hunting for New Leads in Old Tomes." Review article. *Trends in Pharmacological Science* 25 (2004): 494–8.

85. "The Great Witch-Hunt and the Suppression of Birth Control: Heinsohn and Steiger's Theory from the Perspective of an Historian." Appendix to Gunnar Heinsohn and Otto Steiger, *Witchcraft, Population Catastrophe and Economic Crisis in Renaissance Europe: An Alternative Macroeconomic Explanation*, 29–31. 2nd edn. IKSF Discussion Paper 31. Bremen: Institut für Konjunktur- und Strukturforschung, 2004. Translated into German as "Die Grosse Hexenverfolgung und die Unterdrückung der

Geburtenkontrolle: Die Theorie von Heinsohn und Steiger aus der Sicht eines Geschichtswissenschaftlers." Appendix to Gunnar Heinsohn and Otto Steiger, *Die Vernichtung der weisen Frauen: Beiträge zur Theorie und Geschichte von Bevölkerung und Kindheit*, 471–3. 4th edn. Erftstadt: Area Verlag, 2005.

86. Review of Helen King, *Greek and Roman Medicine* (London: Bristol Classical Press, 2001). *Bulletin of the History of Medicine* 78 (2004): 465–6.

87. Review of Jole Shackelford, *A Philosophical Path for Paracelsian Medicine: The Ideas, Intellectual Context, and Influence of Petrus Severinus (1540–1602)* (Copenhagen: Museum Tusculanum Press, 2004). *Pharmacy in History* 47 (2005): 75–7.

88. Review of Pedanius Dioscorides of Anazarbos, *De materia medica*, trans. Lily Y. Beck (Hildesheim: Olms-Weidmann, 2005). *Medical History* 50 (2006): 553–4.

89. "Research Procedures in Evaluating Medieval Medicine." In Barbara S. Bowers (ed.), *The Medieval Hospital and Medical Practice*, 3–17. AVISTA Studies in the History of Medieval Technology, Science and Art 3. Aldershot, UK: Ashgate, 2007.

90. "Women's Medicines in Ancient Jewish Sources: Fertility Enhancers and Inhibiters." In I.L. Finkel and M.J. Geller (eds), *Disease in Babylonia*, 200–214. Cuneiform Monographs 36. Leiden: Brill, 2007.

91. "Early History and Leadership of the Padua Botanical Garden." *HerbalGram* 77 (2008): 38–9.

92. *A History of the Middle Ages, 300–1500*. Lanham, MD: Rowman & Littlefield, 2008.

93. Review of Lester K. Little (ed.), *Plague and the End of Antiquity: The Pandemic of 541–750* (New York: Cambridge University Press, 2007). *Journal of the History of Medicine and Allied Sciences* 64 (2009): 250–52.

94. *Goddesses, Elixirs, and Witches: Plants and Sexuality throughout Human History*. New York: Palgrave Macmillan, 2010.

95. Review of Gary B. Ferngren, *Medicine and Health Care in Early Christianity* (Baltimore: Johns Hopkins University Press, 2009). *Journal of the History of Medicine and Allied Sciences* 65 (2010): 253–5.

Index of Manuscripts

General Index

Printed in the United States
by Baker & Taylor Publisher Services